G000134959

Italian
Pocket Dictionary

Italian – English
Inglese – Italiano

Berlitz Publishing
New York · Munich · Singapore

Original edition edited by the
Langenscheidt editorial staff

Compiled by LEXUS

Book in cover photo: © Punchstock/Medioimages

© 2017 Langenscheidt GmbH & Co. KG, Munich

Printed in Germany
ISBN 978-178-004-484-2

Contents
Indice

Abbreviations / Abbreviazioni

vedi	☞	see
marchio registrato	®	registered trademark
aggettivo	*adj*	adjective
avverbio	*adv*	adverb
aggettivo	*agg*	adjective
agricoltura	AGR	agriculture
inglese americano	*Am*	American English
anatomia	ANAT	anatomy
architettura	ARCHI	architecture
articolo	*art*	article
astronomia	AST	astronomy
astrologia	ASTR	astrology
uso attributivo	*attr*	attributive usage
automobilismo	AUTO	motoring
aviazione	AVIA	civil aviation
avverbio	*avv*	adverb
biologia	BIO	biology
botanica	BOT	botany
inglese britannico	*Br*	British English
chimica	CHEM	chemistry
chimica	CHIM	chemistry
commercio	COM	commerce, business
informatica	COMPUT	computers, IT term
congiunzione	*cong*	conjunction
congiunzione	*conj*	conjunction
diritto	DIR	law
eccetera	*ecc*	et cetera
educazione	EDU	education

elettricità, elettronica	EL	electricity, electronics
elettricità, elettronica	ELEC	electricity, electronics
specialmente	*esp*	especially
eccetera	*etc*	et cetera
eufemismo	*euph*	euphemistic
familiare	F	familiar, colloquial
femminile	*f*	feminine
sostantivo femminile e aggettivo	*flagg*	feminine noun and adjective
ferrovia	FERR	railways
figurato	*fig*	figurative
finanze	FIN	financial
fisica	FIS	physics
uso formale	*fml*	formal usage
fotografia	FOT	photography
femminile plurale	*fpl*	feminine plural
femminile singolare	*fsg*	feminine singular
gastronomia	GASTR	cooking
generalmente	*gen*	generally
geografia	GEOG	geography
geologia	GEOL	geology
grammatica	GRAM	grammatical
informatica	INFOR	IT term
interiezione	*int*	interjection
invariabile	*inv*	invariable
diritto	LAW	law
maschile	*m*	masculine
sostantivo maschile e aggettivo	*m/agg*	masculine noun and adjective
marineria, navigazione	MAR	nautical

matematica	MAT	mathematics
matematica	MATH	mathematics
medicina	MED	medicine
maschile e femminile	*m/f*	masculine and feminine
militare	MIL	military
mineralogia	MIN	mineralogy
automobilismo	MOT	motoring
maschile plurale	*mpl*	masculine plural
maschile singolare	*msg*	masculine singular
musica	MUS	music
sostantivo	*n*	noun
marineria, navigazione	NAUT	nautical
sostantivo plurale	*npl*	plural noun
sostantivo singolare	*nsg*	singular noun
sé, se stesso	o.s.	oneself
popolare	P	popular, slang
spregiativo	*pej*	pejorative
fotografia	PHOT	photography
fisica	PHYS	physics
pittura	PITT	painting
plurale	*pl*	plural
politica	POL	politics
participio passato	*pp*	past participle
preposizione	*prep*	preposition
pronome	*pron*	pronoun
preposizione	*prp*	preposition
psicologia	PSI	psychology
psicologia	PSYCH	psychology
qualcosa	qc	something

qualcuno	qu	someone
radio	RAD	radio
ferrovia	RAIL	railways
religione	REL	religion
sci	SCI	skiing
singolare	*sg*	singular
qualcuno	s.o.	someone
sport	SP	sports
uso spiritoso	*spir*	humorous
uso spregiativo	*spreg*	pejorative
qualcosa	sth	something
congiuntivo	*subj*	subjunctive
teatro	TEA	theatre
tecnica	TEC	technology
tecnica	TECH	technology
telecomunicazioni	TELEC	telecommunications
teatro	THEA	theatre
tipografia	TIP	typography, typesetting
televisione	TV	television
università	UNIV	university
volgare	V	vulgar
verbo ausiliario	*v/aus*	auxiliary verb
verbo ausiliario	*v/aux*	auxiliary verb
verbo intransitivo	*v/i*	intransitive verb
verbo transitivo	*v/t*	transitive verb
zoologia	ZO	zoology

Pronuncia delle parole inglesi

Vocali e dittonghi

[ɑ:]   *a* molto lunga, più che in *mare*: *far* [fɑː(r)]

[ʌ]   simile alla seconda *a* in *mamma* non accentata:
        mother ['mʌðə(r)]

[æ]   simile alla prima *a* in *mamma*: *man* [mæn]

[ɛə]   dittongo composto da una *e* molto aperta e
        lunga e da [ə]: *care* [kɛə(r)]

[aɪ]   dittongo composto da [a] e [ɪ]: *time* [taɪm]

[aʊ]   dittongo composto da [a] e [ʊ]: *cloud* [klaʊd]

[e]   *e* aperta e breve, più che in *bello*: *get* [ɡet]

[eɪ]   dittongo composto da una *e* lunga, seguita da
        un leggero suono di *i*: *name* [neɪm]

[ə]   suono atono simile alla *e* nell'articolo francese
        le: *about* [ə'baʊt]

[ɜ:]   forma più prolungata del suono anteriore:
        bird [bɜːd]

[ɪ]   suono molto breve tra la *i* di *fitto* e la *e* di *fetta*:
        city ['sɪtɪ]

[i:]   *i* molto lunga, più che in *vino*: *tea* [tiː]

[ɪə]   dittongo composto da [ɪ] e [ə]: *here* [hɪə(r)]

[ɒ]   simile alla *o* di *lotta*: *not* [nɒt]

[ɔ:]   *o* aperta e lunga, più che in *noto*: *ball* [bɔːl]

[ɔɪ]   dittongo composto da [ɔ] e [ɪ]: *boy* [bɔɪ]

[əʊ]   dittongo composto da una *o* lunga, seguita da
        un leggero suono di *u*: *boat* [bəʊt]

[ʊ]   suono molto breve tra la *u* di *tutto* e la *o* di *rotto*:
        book [bʊk]

[uː]   *u* lunga, più che in *fiume*: *fruit* [fruːt]

[ʊə]   dittongo composto da [ʊ] e [ə]: *sure* [ʃʊə(r)]

Consonanti

Le consonanti si pronunciano nella maggior parte dei casi quasi come in italiano. Le doppie si pronunciano come se fossero semplici.

[b]   come la *b* in *burro*: *bag* [bæg]

[d]   come la *d* in *dare*: *dear* [dɪə(r)]

[f]   come la *f* in *forte*: *coffee* ['kɒfɪ]

[g]   come la *g* in *gatto*: *give* [gɪv]

[h]   suono aspirato simile a quello della *c* di *casa* dei fiorentini: *head* [hed]

[j]   come la *i* in *ieri*: *yes* [jes], *use* [juːz]

[k]   ome la *c* in *casa*: *come* [kʌm]

[l]   come la *l* in *lungo*: *land* [lænd]

[m]   come la *m* i *madre*: *summer* ['sʌmə(r)]

[n]   come la *n* in *no*: *night* [naɪt]

[p]   come la *p* in *pane*: *top* [tɒp]

[r]   una *r* gutturale che si pronuncia soltanto quando precede una vocale: *right* [raɪt], *carol* ['kærəl]

[s]   *s* aspra come in *sono*: *cycle* ['saɪkl], *sun* [sʌn]

[t]   come la *t* in *torre*: *take* [teɪk]

[v]   come la *v* in *valore*: *vain* [veɪn]

[w]   come la *u* in *uomo*: *wait* [weɪt], *quaint* [kweɪnt]

[z]   *s* dolce come in *rosa*: *rose* [rəʊz]

[ŋ]   come la *n* in *banca*: *bring* [brɪŋ]

[ʃ]	come *sce* in *scena*: *she* [ʃiː]
[tʃ]	come *ce* in *cento*: *chair* [tʃeə(r)], *rich* [rɪtʃ]
[dʒ]	come *ge* in *gente*: *join* [dʒɔɪn], *range* [reɪndʒ]
[ʒ]	non esiste in italiano, simile alla *j* francese in *je*: *leisure* [ˈleʒə(r)], *usual* [ˈjuːʒʊəl]
[θ]	lingua tra i denti: *think* [θɪŋk]
[ð]	lingua dietro l'arcata superiore dei denti: *the* [ðə], *lather* [ˈlɑːðə(r)]
'	il segno dell'accento viene sempre collocato prima della sillaba accentata, es. *ability* [əˈbɪlətɪ]

Italian pronunciation

Vowels

a	mare	as in father but shorter
e	bello	as in bed
	neve	like the *e* sound in they
i	vino	as in machine
o	lotta	as in pot
	nome	like the *o* sound in blow
u	fiume	as *oo* in cool but shorter

Consonants

b, d, f, l, m, n, p, t and **v** are pronounced as in English.
When a word has double consonants, each consonant is
pronounced separately: contat-to.

c	certo	before *e* and *i* as *ch* in **ch**urch
	canto	before *a, o, u* (almost) as in **c**ake
ch	chiamare	before *e* and *i* to make *c* hard as in **c**at
g	gelo	before *e* and *i* as in **g**eneral
	gatto	before *a, o, u* as in **g**ate
gh	laghi	before *e* and *i* to make *g* hard as in **g**ot
gl	biglietto	like English *lli* in mi**lli**on
gn	ogni	like English *ni* in o**ni**on
h	hanno	not pronounced
r	rotto	with the tongue against the upper teeth
s	sole	unvoiced as in ca**s**e
	rosa	voiced as in chee**s**e
sc	uscire	before *e* and *i* like *sh* in **sh**ip
z	prezzo	unvoiced as *ts* in ha**ts**
	mezzo	voiced as *ds* in mai**ds**
j, k, w,		these letters do not belong to the
x, y		Italian alphabet and are found only in
		foreign words

Italian-English
Italiano-Inglese

A

A (= *autostrada*) M (= motorway), *Am* I (= interstate)

a ◇ *stato in luogo* at; **~ Roma** in Rome; **~ casa** at home ◇ *moto a luogo* to; **andare ~ Roma** go to Rome ◇ *tempo*: **alle quattro** at four o'clock; **~ Natale** at Christmas; **~ maggio** in May; **~ vent'anni** at the age of twenty; **~ due ~ due** two at a time ◇ *modo*: **~ piedi** on foot ◇ *mezzo*: **ricamato ~ mano** embroidered by hand ◇ *prezzo, misura*: **~ che prezzo** at what price; **al metro** by the metre; **100 km all'ora** 100 km an hour

abate *m* abbot

abbacchio *m* GASTR young lamb

abbagliante 1 *agg* dazzling **2** *m gen pl* **-i** AUTO full beam; **abbagliare** dazzle

abbaiare bark

abbandonare abandon; **abbandono** *m* abandon; (*rinuncia*) abandonment

abbassare lower; *radio* turn down; **abbassarsi** (*chinarsi*) bend down; *di prezzo* come down; *fig* **~ a** stoop to; ab-

basso: **~ la scuola!** down with school!

abbastanza enough; (*alquanto*) quite

abbattere knock down; *casa* demolish; *albero* cut down; *aereo* shoot down; *fig* dishearten; **abbattersi** fall; *fig* become disheartened; **abbattuto** *fig* disheartened

abbazia *f* abbey

abbellire embellish

abbi, abbia ☞ **avere**

abbigliamento *m* clothing; **~ sportivo** sportswear

abbinare match; (*combinare*) combine

abboccare *di pesce* bite; *fig* swallow the bait

abbonamento *m a giornale*, TEA subscription; *a treno*, *bus* season ticket; **abbonare** take out a subscription for; (*condonare*) deduct; **abbonarsi** subscribe; **abbonato** *m* subscriber; TELEC **elenco *m degli* -i** telephone directory, phone book

abbondante abundant; *porzione* generous; *vestito* loose; *nevicata* heavy

abbordabile *persona* approachable; *prezzo* reasonable; **abbordare 1** *v/t persona* approach; F *persona dell'altro sesso* chat up F, *Am* come on to; *argomento* tackle **2** *v/t* MAR board

abbottonare button up

abbozzo *m* sketch

abbracciare embrace, hug; *fig* take up; **abbracciarsi** embrace, hug; **abbraccio** *m* embrace, hug; **un ~** *a fine lettera* love

abbreviare abbreviate; **abbreviazione** *f* abbreviation

abbronzante *m* sun-tan lotion; **lettino** *m* sunbed; **abbronzare** *pelle* tan; **abbronzarsi** get a tan; **abbronzatura** *f* tan

abbrustolire roast

abbuffarsi stuff o.s. (*di* with)

abdicare abdicate

abete *m* fir

abile good (*in* at); fit (*a* for); **abilità** *f inv* ability

abilitazione *f* qualification

abisso *m* abyss

abitacolo *m* AUTO passenger compartment

abitante *m/f* inhabitant; **abitare 1** *v/t* live in **2** *v/i* live; **abitato 1** *agg* inhabited **2** *m* built-up area; **abitazione** *f* house

abiti *mpl* clothes; **abito** *m* dress; *da uomo* suit; **~ da sera** evening dress

abituale usual; **abituarsi: ~ a**

get used to; **abitudinario 1** *agg* of fixed habits **2** *m* creature of habit; **abitudine** *f* habit

abolire abolish; **abolizione** *f* abolition

abominevole abominable

aborigeno *m/agg* aboriginal

abortire MED miscarry; *volontariamente* have an abortion; *fig* fail; **aborto** *m* MED miscarriage; *provocato* abortion

abrogare repeal

abusare: ~ di abuse; (*approfittare*) take advantage of; **~ nel bere** drink to excess; **abusivo** illegal; **abuso** *m* abuse

a.C. (= *avanti Cristo*) BC (= before Christ)

accademia *f* academy; **~ di belle arti** art college; **accademico** academic

accadere happen; **accaduto** *m*: **raccontami l'~** tell me what happened

accaldato overheated

accampamento *m* camp; **accampare 1** *v/t*: **~ scuse** come up with excuses **2** *v/i* e **accamparsi** camp

accanimento *m* (*tenacia*) tenacity; (*furia*) rage; **accanirsi** (*ostinarsi*) persist; **~ contro qu** rage against s.o.; **accanito** *odio* fierce; *fumatore* inveterate

accanto 1 *prp* **~ a** next to **2** *avv* near, nearby; *abitare* next door

accantonare put aside

accappatoio *m* bathrobe; *da mare* beachrobe

accarezzare caress; *speranza* cherish; *animale* stroke

accasciarsi flop down

accattone *m* beggar

accavallare cross; **accavallarsi** *fig* overlap

accecare 1 *v/t* blind **2** *v/i* be blinding

accedere: **~ a** enter

accelerare speed up; AUTO accelerate; **acceleratore** *m* AUTO accelerator, *Am* gas pedal; **accelerazione** *f* acceleration

accendere light; RAD, TV turn on; **accendersi** light up; *apparecchio* come on; **accendino** *m* (cigarette) lighter; **accendisigari** *m inv* (cigarette) lighter

accennare indicate; *con parole* mention; **~ a fare qc** show signs of doing sth; **accenno** *m* (*cenno*) gesture; (*indizio*) sign; (*allusione*) hint

accensione *f* ignition

accento *m* accent; **accentuare** accentuate

accertare check; **accertarsi**: **~ di qc** check sth

acceso *colore* bright; *motore* running; TV, *luce* on

accessibile accessible; *prezzo* reasonable; **accesso** *m* access; *fig e* MED fit; **divieto d' ~** no entry

accessori *mpl* accessories; **accessoriato** AUTO complete with accessories

accetta *f* axe, *Am* ax

accettabile acceptable; **accettare** accept; **accettazione** *f* acceptance; *di albergo* reception; **~ bagagli** check-in

acchiappare catch

acciaio *m* steel; **~ inossidabile** stainless steel

accidentale accidental

accidentato terreno rough

accidenti F damn! F; *di sorpresa* wow!

accigliato frowning

accingersi: **~ a fare qc** be about to do sth

acciottolato *m* cobbles

acciuffare grab

acciuga *f* anchovy

acclimatarsi get acclimatized

accludere enclose; **accluso** enclosed; **qui ~** enclosed

accogliente welcoming; *richiesta* grant

accollarsi take on

accollato *abito* high-necked

accoltellare knife

accolto *pp* **▶ accogliere**

accomodante accommodating; **accomodare** (*riparare*) mend; *lite* resolve; **accomodarsi** make o.s. at home; **si accomodi!** come in!; (*sedersi*) have a seat!

accompagnare accompany; **accompagnatore** *m*, **-trice** *f* escort; MUS accompanist

acconciatura *f* hairdo

acconsentire consent (**a** to)

accontentare satisfy; **accontentarsi** be happy (**di** with)

acconto m deposit

accorciare shorten; **accorciarsi** get shorter

accordare grant; MUS tune; (*armonizzare*) harmonize; **accordarsi** agree; **di colori** match; **accordo** m agreement; (*armonia*) harmony; MUS chord; **essere d'~** agree; **mettersi d'~** reach an agreement; **d'~**! OK!

accorgersi: **~ di** notice

accorrere hurry; **~ in aiuto di qu** rush to help s.o.

accortezza f forethought

accorto 1 pp ☞ **accorgersi** 2 agg shrewd

accostare approach; *porta* leave ajar; **accostarsi** get close

accreditare confirm; FIN credit; **accredito** m credit

accrescere increase; **accrescersi** grow bigger

accudire 1 v/t look after 2 v/i: **~ a qc** attend to sth

accumulare accumulate; **accumulatore** m battery

accuratezza f care; **accurato** careful

accusa f accusation; DIR charge; **accusare** accuse; DIR charge; **accusato** m, **-a** f accused

acerbo unripe

acero m maple

aceto m vinegar

acetone m nail varnish remover

ACI m (= **Automobile Club d'Italia**) Automobile Club of Italy

acidità f acidity; **~ di stomaco** heartburn; **acido** 1 agg acid; *fig* sour 2 m acid

acne f acne

acqua f water; **~ minerale** mineral water; **~ potabile** drinking water; **~ di rubinetto** tap water; **~ ossigenata** hydrogen peroxide; **-e pl territoriali** territorial waters; *fig* **in cattive -e** in deep water

acquaforte f etching

acquaio m sink

acquario m aquarium; ASTR **Acquario** Aquarius

acquascivolo m water slide

acquatico aquatic

acquavite f brandy

acquazzone m downpour

acquedotto m aqueduct

acqueo: **vapore ~** water vapour o Am vapor

acquerello m watercolour, Am watercolor

acquirente m/f purchaser; **acquisizione** f acquisition; **acquistare** 1 v/t buy; *fig* gain 2 v/i improve; **acquisto** m purchase

acquolina f: **mi viene l'~ in bocca** my mouth's watering

acre sour; *voce* harsh

acrilico acrylic

acrobata m/f acrobat

adrenalina

acustica f acoustics; **acustico** acoustic

acuto 1 agg intense; nota, dolore sharp; suono, voce shrill; MED acute **2** m MUS high note

ad ☞ **a** (before vowels)

adagiarsi lie down; **adagio 1** avv slowly; con cautela cautiously **2** m MUS adagio

adattamento m adaptation; (rielaborazione) reworking; **adattare** adapt; **adattarsi** (adeguarsi) adapt (**a** to); (addirsi) be suitable (**a** for); **adattatore** m adaptor; **adatto** right (**a** for)

addebitare FIN ~ **qc a qu** debit s.o. with sth; fig ascribe sth to s.o.; **addebito** m FIN debit; **nota f di** ~ debit note

addensarsi thicken

addestramento m training; **addestrare** train

addetto 1 agg assigned (**a** to) **2** m, -**a** f person responsible; **vietato l'ingresso ai non -i** authorized personnel only

addio 1 int goodbye **2** m goodbye, farewell

addirittura (assolutamente) absolutely; (perfino) even

additivo m additive; **addizionare** add; **addizione** f addition

addobbare decorate; **addobbo** m decoration

addolcire sweeten; fig soften

addolorare grieve

addome m abdomen

addomesticare tame

addominale abdominal

addormentarsi fall asleep; **addormentato** asleep; (assonnato) sleepy

addossare (appoggiare) lean (**a** on); fig colpa put, lay (**a** on); **addossarsi** lean (**a** on); fig shoulder; **addosso 1** prp on; vicino next to **2** avv: **avere** ~ vestiti have on; **avere** ~ **qu** have s.o. breathing down one's neck

adeguarsi conform; **adeguato** adequate

adempiere: ~ **a dovere** carry out, do

aderente 1 agg vestito tight **2** m/f follower; **aderire**: ~ **a** adhere to; partito support; richiesta agree to; **adesione** f adhesion; (consenso) agreement; **adesivo 1** agg adhesive **2** m sticker

adesso now; **da** ~ **in poi** from now on; **fino a** ~ up to now; **per** ~ for the moment

adiacente adjacent; ~ **a** next to, adjacent to

adirato angry

adolescente m/f adolescent, teenager; **adolescenza** f adolescence, teens

adoperare use

adorare adore

adottare adopt; **adottivo** genitori adoptive; figlio adopted; **adozione** f adoption

adrenalina f adrenalin

adriatico Adriatic; *mare m* **Adriatico** Adriatic Sea

adulare flatter

adulterio *m* adultery; **adulto 1** *agg* adult **2** *m*, *-a f* adult

adunare assemble

aerare air; **aereo 1** *agg* air *attr*, *fotografia* aerial; **compagnia** *f* *-a* airline; **posta** *f* *-a* airmail **2** *m* plane

aerobica *f* aerobics *sg*

aerodinamico aerodynamic

aeronautica *f*: ~ **militare** Air Force

aeroplano *m* plane, aeroplane, *Am* airplane

aeroporto *m* airport

aerosol *m inv contenitore* aerosol; MED inhaler

aerostazione *f* air terminal

afa *f* closeness, mugginess

affabile affable

affaccendarsi busy o.s. (*in* with); **affaccendato** busy

affacciarsi appear

affamato starving

affannato breathless; **affanno** *m* breathlessness; *fig* anxiety

affare *m* matter, business; FIN transaction; *-i pl* business; **non sono -i tuoi** it's none of your business; **uomo** *m* **d'-i** businessman

affascinante fascinating; **affascinare** fascinate

affaticarsi tire o.s. out

affatto completely; **non ... ~** not ... at all

affermare state; **affermarsi** become established; **affermazione** *f* assertion; (*successo*) achievement

afferrare seize, grab; (*comprendere*) grasp; **afferrarsi** cling (*a* to)

affettare (*tagliare*) slice

affettato[1] *m* sliced meat

affettato[2] *agg* affected

affetto *m* affection; **affettuoso** affectionate; **affezionarsi**: ~ *a qu* become fond of s.o.; **affezionato**: ~ *a qu* fond of s.o.

affibbiare: ~ *qc a qu* saddle s.o. with sth

affidabilità *f* dependability; **affidamento** *m* trust; **fare** ~ **su** rely on; **affidare** entrust; **affidarsi**: ~ *a* rely on

affiggere *avviso* put up

affilare sharpen; *fig* make thinner; **affilato** sharp; *naso* thin

affiliato *m*, *-a f* member

affinché so that

affine similar

affinità *f inv* affinity

affiorare *dall'acqua* emerge; *fig* (*mostrarsi*) appear

affissione *f* bill-posting; **affisso 1** *pp* ☞ **affiggere 2** *m* bill

affittacamere *m/f* landlord; *donna* landlady; **affittare** rent; **affittasi** for rent; **affitto** *m* rent; **dare in** ~ rent (out); **prendere in** ~ rent

affliggere distress; *di malattia* trouble, plague; **afflitto** distressed

affluente *m* tributary; **affluenza** *f fig* influx

affogare drown

affollare, affollarsi crowd; **affollato** crowded

affondare sink

affrancare free; *posta* frank; **affrancatura** *f* franking; (*tassa di spedizione*) postage

affresco *m* fresco

affrettarsi hurry

affrontare face, confront; *spese* meet

affumicare *stanza* fill with smoke; *alimenti* smoke; **affumicato** smoked

afoso sultry

Africa *f* Africa; **africano 1** *agg* African **2** *m*, **-a** *f* African

afroamericano 1 *agg* African-American **2** *m*, **-a** *f* African-American

afrodisiaco *m/agg* aphrodisiac

agenda *f* diary

agente *m/f* agent; **~ immobiliare** estate agent, *Am* realtor; **~ di pubblica sicurezza** police officer

agenzia *f* agency; **~ di cambio** bureau de change; **~ immobiliare** estate agency, *Am* real estate office,; **~ di viaggi** travel agency

agevolare make easier; **agevolazione** *f FIN* special term

agganciare hook; *cintura, collana* fasten

aggeggio *m* gadget

aggettivo *m* adjective

agghiacciante spine-chilling

aggiornamento *m* updating; (*rinvio*) postponement; **corso** *m* **d'~** refresher course; **aggiornare** (*mettere al corrente*) update; (*rinviare*) postpone; **aggiornarsi** keep up to date

aggirare surround; *fig ostacolo* get around

aggirarsi hang around; FIN be in the region of

aggiudicare award; **all'asta** knock down

aggiungere add; **aggiunta** *f* addition

aggiustare (*riparare*) repair; (*sistemare*) settle

agglomerato *m*: **~ urbano** built-up area

aggrapparsi cling, hold on (**a** to)

aggravare *punizione* increase; (*peggiorare*) make worse; **aggravarsi** worsen, deteriorate

aggraziato graceful

aggredire attack; **aggressione** *f* aggression; (*attacco*) attack; **aggressività** *f* aggressiveness; **aggressivo** aggressive; **aggressore** *m* attacker; MIL aggressor

agguato *m* ambush

agguerrito hardened

agiato comfortable, well-off; (*comodo*) comfortable

agibile fit for human habitation

agile

agile agile; **agilità** f agility; fig liveliness

agio m ease; **sentirsi a proprio ~** feel at ease

agire act; *di medicina* take effect

agitare shake; *fazzoletto* wave; fig (*turbare*) upset, agitate; **agitato** agitated; *mare* rough; **agitazione** f agitation

agli = **a** and *art* **gli**

aglio m garlic

agnello m lamb

agnolotti mpl type of ravioli

ago m needle

agonia f agony

agonistico competitive

agopuntura f acupuncture

agorafobia f agoraphobia

agosto m August

agricolo agricultural; **agricoltore** m farmer; **agricoltura** f agriculture

agrifoglio m holly

agriturismo m farm holidays

agrodolce bittersweet; GASTR sweet and sour

agrumi mpl citrus fruit

aguzzare sharpen; **~ la vista** keep one's eyes peeled; **aguzzo** pointed

ahi! ouch!

ai = **a** and *art* **i**

Aids m o f Aids

airbag m inv airbag

airone m heron

aiuola f flower bed

aiutante m/f assistant; **aiutare** help; **aiuto** m help, assist-

ance; *persona* assistant

aizzare incite

al = **a** and *art* **il**

ala f wing

alabastro m alabaster

alano m Great Dane

alba f dawn; **all'~** at dawn

albanese agg, m/f Albanian; **Albania** f Albania

alberato tree-lined

alberghiero hotel attr; **albergo** m hotel

albero m tree; MAR mast; AUTO shaft; **~ genealogico** family tree; **~ di Natale** Christmas tree

albicocca f apricot; **albicocco** m apricot (tree)

albo m notice board, Am bulletin board; (*registro*) register; **radiare dall'~** strike off

album m inv album

alcol m alcohol; **alcolico 1** agg alcoholic **2** m alcoholic drink; **alcolismo** m alcoholism; **alcolizzato** m, **-a** f alcoholic; **alcoltest** m inv Breathalyzer®

alcuno 1 agg any; **non ~** no, not any **2** pron any; **-i** pl some, a few

aldilà m: **l'~** the next world

aletta f fin

alfabetico alphabetical; **alfabeto** m alphabet

alfiere m scacchi bishop

alga f seaweed

algebra f algebra

Algeria f Algeria; **algerino 1** agg Algerian **2** m, **-a** f Alge-

alloro

rian
aliante m glider
alice f anchovy
alienato 1 agg alienated **2** m, -a f madman; donna ~ madwoman; **alienazione** f alienation; ~ **mentale** madness
alimentare 1 v/t feed **2** agg food attr, **generi** mpl -i foodstuffs; **alimentazione** f feeding; **alimento** m food; -i pl DIR alimony
aliquota f share; ~ **d'imposta** rate of taxation
aliscafo m hydrofoil
alito m breath
all. (= **allegato**) enc(l). (= enclosed)
all', alla = **a** and art **l'**, **la**
allacciamento m TEC connection; **allacciare** fasten; TEC connect
allagamento m flooding; **allagare** flood
allargare widen; vestito let out; braccia open; **allargarsi** widen
allarmare alarm; **allarmarsi** become alarmed; **allarme** m alarm; **dare l'~** raise the alarm
allattare bambino feed
alle = **a** and art **le**
alleanza f alliance; **allearsi** ally o.s.; **alleato 1** agg allied **2** m, -a f ally
allegare documento enclose; INFOR attach; **allegato** m enclosure; INFOR attachment; **qui ~** enclosed

alleggerire lighten; fig: dolore ease
allegria f cheerfulness; **allegro 1** agg cheerful; colore bright **2** m MUS allegro
allenamento m training; **allenare, allenarsi** train (per for; **a** in); **allenatore** m, -trice f trainer
allentare 1 v/t loosen **2** v/i e **allentarsi** loosen
allergia f allergy; **allergico** allergic (**a** to)
allertare f alert
allestimento m preparation; MAR fitting out; TEA ~ **scenico** sets, scenery; **allestire** prepare; MAR fit out
allevamento m BOT, ZO breeding; **allevare** BOT, ZO breed; bambini bring up, raise; **allevatore** m, -trice f breeder
alleviare alleviate
allievo m, -a f pupil, student
alligatore m alligator
allineare line up; FIN adjust; TIP align
allo = **a** and art **lo**
allodola f skylark
alloggiare 1 v/t put up **2** v/i stay, put up; **alloggio** m accommodation, Am accommodations; **vitto e ~** bed and board
allontanarsi go away; fig grow apart
allora then; **da ~ in poi** from then on; **fin d'~** since then
alloro m laurel; GASTR bay

alluce *m* big toe

allucinante F incredible, mind-blowing F; **allucinazione** *f* hallucination

alludere allude (**a** to)

alluminio *m* aluminium, *Am* aluminum

allungare lengthen; (*diluire*) dilute; *mano* put out; **allungarsi** *di giorni* get longer; *di persona* stretch out, lie down

allusione *f* allusion

alluvione *f* flood

almeno at least

alogena *f* halogen

Alpi *fpl* Alps; **alpinismo** *m* mountaineering; **alpinista** *m/f* mountain climber; **alpino** Alpine

alquanto 1 *agg* some **2** *avv* a little, somewhat

alt stop

altalena *f* swing

altare *m* altar

alterare alter; **alterarsi** (*guastarsi*) go bad o off; (*irritarsi*) get angry

alternare, alternarsi alternate; **alternativa** *f* alternative; **alternativo** alternative; **alternato**: **corrente** *f* **-a** alternating current; **alterno**: **a giorni** *pl* **-i** on alternate days

altezza *f* height; *titolo* Highness

alticcio tipsy

altitudine *f* altitude

alto 1 *agg* high; *persona* tall; **a voce -a** in a loud voice; *leg-*

gere aloud; **in ~** at the top; *moto u* **2** *m* top

altoatesino 1 *agg* South Tyrolean **2** *m*, **-a** *f* South Tyrolean

altoparlante *m* loudspeaker

altopiano *m* plateau

altrettanto as much; **-i** *pl* as many

altrimenti (*in modo diverso*) differently; (*in caso contrario*) otherwise

altro 1 *agg* other; **un ~** another; **l'altr'anno** last year; **l'~ ieri** the day before yesterday **2** *pron* other; **l'un l'~** one another; **gli altri** other people; **tra l'~** what's more, moreover; **desidera ~?** anything else?; **tutt'~ che** anything but; **qualcun'~** someone o somebody else

altronde: **d'~** on the other hand

altrove elsewhere

altruismo *m* altruism

altura *f* hill

alunno *m*, **-a** *f* pupil, student

alzacristallo *m inv* AUTO window winder

alzare raise; **alzarsi** stand up, rise; *da letto* get up; *di sole* rise

amaca *f* hammock

amalgamare amalgamate

amante *m/f* lover; **amare** love; *amico* be fond of

amareggiato embittered

amarena *f* sour black cherry

amarezza *f* bitterness; **amaro**

1 *agg* bitter **2** *m liquore* bitters

ambasciata *f* embassy; **ambasciatore** *m*, **-trice** *f* ambassador

ambedue both

ambientale environmental; **ambientalista 1** *agg* environmental **2** *m/f* environmentalist; **ambientarsi** become acclimatized; **ambiente** *m* environment

ambiguità *f inv* ambiguity; **ambiguo** ambiguous

ambito *m* sphere

ambizione *f* ambition; **ambizioso** ambitious

ambo 1 *agg* both **2** *m lotteria* double

ambulante 1 *agg* travelling, *Am* traveling **2** *m/f* pedlar; **ambulanza** *f* ambulance; **ambulatorio** *m* MED outpatients

America *f* America; **americano 1** *agg* American **2** *m*, **-a** *f* American **3** *m* American English

ametista *f* amethyst

amianto *m* asbestos

amichevole friendly; **amicizia** *f* friendship; **amico 1** *agg* friendly **2** *m*, **-a** *f* friend

amido *m* starch

ammaccare dent; *frutta* bruise; **ammaccatura** *f* dent; *su frutta* bruise

ammaestrare teach; *animali* train

ammalarsi fall sick; **ammala**-

to 1 *agg* sick **2** *m*, **-a** *f* sick person

ammarare *di aereo* put down in the water; *di navetta spaziale* splash down

ammassare, ammassarsi mass; **ammasso** *m* pile; GEOL mass

ammazzare kill; *animali* slaughter; **ammazzarsi** (*suicidarsi*) kill o.s.

ammenda *f* (*multa*) fine

ammesso *pp* ☞ **ammettere**; **ammettere** admit; (*supporre*) suppose; (*riconoscere*) acknowledge; **ammesso che** ... supposing (that) ...

amministrare administer; *azienda* manage, run; **amministrativo** administrative; **amministratore** *m*, **-trice** *f* administrator; *di azienda* manager; **amministrazione** *f* administration

ammirare admire; **ammiratore** *m*, **-trice** *f* admirer; **ammirazione** *f* admiration; **ammirevole** admirable

ammobiliare furnish; **ammobiliato** furnished

ammollo: **in ~** soaking

ammonimento *m* reprimand, admonishment; (*consiglio*) warning; **ammonire** reprimand, admonish; (*avvertire*) warn; DIR caution; **ammonizione** *f* reprimand, admonishment; SP warning; DIR caution

ammontare: **~ a** amount to

ammorbidire soften

ammortizzare FIN pay off; **ammortizzatore** *m* AUTO shock absorber

ammucchiare pile up

ammuffire go mouldy, *Am* go moldy; *fig* moulder away, *Am* molder away

ammutolire be struck dumb

amnesia *f* amnesia

amnistia *f* amnesty

amo *m* hook; *fig* bait

amore *m* love; *fare l'~ con qu* make love to s.o.; *amoroso* loving; *sguardo* amorous; *lettera, poesia* love *attr*

ampiezza *f* *di stanza* spaciousness; *di gonna* fullness; *fig di cultura* breadth; *fig ~ di vedute* broadmindedness; **ampio** *stanza* spacious, large; *abito* roomy; *gonna* full

ampliamento *m* broadening, widening; *di edificio* extension; **ampliare** broaden, widen; *edificio* extend

amplificare TEC *suono* amplify; **amplificatore** *m* amplifier

amputare amputate

amuleto *m* amulet

anabbagliante dipped, *Am* low-beam

anacronistico anachronistic

anagrafe *f ufficio* registry office

analcolico 1 *agg* non-alcoholic 2 *m* non-alcoholic drink

anale anal

analfabeta *m/f* illiterate person, person who cannot read or write; **analfabetismo** *m* illiteracy

analgesico *m/agg* analgesic

analisi *f inv* analysis; *~ del sangue* blood test; **analista** *m/f* analyst; *~ programmatore* systems analyst

analizzare analyse, *Am* analyze

analogia *f* analogy; **analogo** analogous

ananas *m inv* pineapple

anarchia *f* anarchy; **anarchico** 1 *agg* anarchic 2 *m*, *-a f* anarchist

anatomia *f* anatomy; **anatomico** anatomical

anatra *f* duck

anca *f* hip

anche too, also; *(perfino)* even; *~ se* even if

ancora[1] *avv* still; *di nuovo* again; *di più* (some) more; *non ~* not yet; *~ una volta* once more; *dammene ~ un po'* give me a bit more

ancora[2] *f* anchor

andamento *m di vendite* performance

andare 1 *v/i* go; *(funzionare)* work; *~ via (partire)* leave; *di macchia* come out; *~ bene* suit; *taglia* fit; *~ a male* go off; *come va?* how are you?; *non mi va di vestito* it doesn't fit me; *non mi va di venire* I don't feel like coming **2** *m*: *a lungo ~* in the long run; *andarsene* go away; *andata* f outward journey; (*biglietto m di*) ~ single (ticket), *Am* oneway ticket, (*biglietto m di*) ~ *e ritorno* return (ticket), *Am* round-trip ticket; *andatura* f walk; SP pace

androne *m* hallway

aneddoto *m* anecdote

anello *m* ring

anemia f anaemia, *Am* anemia; **anemico** anaemic, *Am* anemic

anestesia f *sostanza* anaesthetic, *Am* anesthetic; **anestetico** *m* anaesthetic, *Am* anesthetic

anfibio 1 *agg* amphibious **2** *m* ZO amphibian; MIL amphibious vehicle

anfiteatro *m* amphitheatre, *Am* amphitheater

anfora f amphora

angelo *m* angel

anglicano 1 *agg* Anglican **2** *m*, **-a** f Anglican

angolo *m* corner; MAT angle; ~ *cottura* kitchenette; MAT ~ *retto* right angle

angoscia f anguish; **angoscioso** anguished; *che da angoscia* heart-rending

anguilla f eel

anguria f water melon

angusto narrow

anice *m* aniseed

anidride f: ~ *carbonica* carbon dioxide

anima f soul

animale *m* animal; ~ *domestico* pet

animare give life to; *conversazione* liven up; (*promuovere*) promote; **animato** *strada* busy; *conversazione, persona* animated; **animatore** *m*, **-trice** f *di gruppo* leader; **animazione** f animation; INFOR ~ *al computer* computer animation

animo *m* nature; (*coraggio*) heart; *perdersi d'~* lose heart

anitra f duck

annaffiare water; **annaffiatoio** *m* watering can

annata f *vintage*; (*anno*) year; *importo* annual amount

annegare 1 *v/t* drown **2** *v/i e* **annegarsi** drown

annerire, annerirsi turn black, blacken

annessione f POL annexation

annidarsi nest

anniversario *m* anniversary

anno *m* year; *buon ~!* Happy New Year!; *quanti -i hai?* how old are you?; *ho 33 -i* I'm 33 (years old)

annodare tie (together); *cravatta* tie, knot

annoiare bore; (*dare fastidio a*) annoy; **annoiarsi** get bored; **annoiato** bored

annotare make a note of; *testo* annotate; **annotazione** f note; *in testo* annotation

annuale annual, yearly; *di un*

anno year-long

annuire (*assentire*) assent (*a* to)

annullamento *m* cancellation; *di matrimonio* annulment; **annullare** cancel; *matrimonio* annul; *gol* disallow; (*vanificare*) cancel out

annunciare announce; **annunciatore** *m*, **-trice** *f* RAD, TV announcer; **Annunciazione** *f* REL Annunciation; **annuncio** *m* announcement; *in giornale* advertisement; **-i** *pl economici* classifieds

annuo annual, yearly

annusare sniff; *fig* smell

anomalo anomalous

anonimo anonymous

anoressia *f* anorexia; **anoressico** anorexic

anormale abnormal

ansia *f* anxiety

ansimare wheeze

ansioso anxious

antagonismo *m* antagonism; **antagonista** *m/f* antagonist

antartico Antarctic *attr*

antecedente 1 *agg* preceding **2** *m* precedent

antenato *m*, **-a** *f* ancestor

antenna *f* RAD, TV aerial, *Am* antenna; ZO antenna; *~ parabolica* satellite dish

anteprima *f* preview

anteriore front; *precedente* previous

anti ... anti ...

antibiotico *m/agg* antibiotic

anticamente in ancient times; **antichità** *f inv* antiquity

anticiclone *m* anticyclone

anticipato: *pagamento* *m* ~ advance payment; **anticipare** anticipate; *denaro* pay in advance; *partenza, riunione ecc* bring forward; **anticipo** *m* advance; (*caparra*) deposit; *in* ~ ahead of time, early

antico ancient; *mobile* antique

anticoncezionale *m/agg* contraceptive

anticonformista *m/f* nonconformist

anticostituzionale unconstitutional

antidoto *m* antidote

antifurto 1 *agg* antitheft **2** *m* anti-theft device

antigas *inv* gas *attr*

antincendio *inv* fire *attr*

antinebbia *m inv* foglamp

antiorario: *in senso* ~ anticlockwise, *Am* counterclockwise

antipasto *m* starter

antipatia *f* antipathy; **antipatico** disagreeable

antiquariato *m* antique business; *negozio m di* ~ antique shop; **antiquario** *m*, **-a** *f* antique dealer; **antiquato** antiquated

antiriflesso *inv* anti-glare

antiruggine *m* rust inhibitor

antisemitismo *m* anti-Semitism

antisettico m/agg antiseptic

antisismico earthquake-proof

antologia f anthology

anulare m ring finger

anzi in fact; (o meglio) (or) better still

anzianità f old age; ~ **di servizio** seniority; anziano 1 agg elderly; per servizio (most) senior 2 m, -a f old man; donna old woman; **gli -i** pl the elderly

anziché rather than

anzitutto first of all

aorta f aorta

apatia f apathy; apatico apathetic

ape f bee

aperitivo m aperitif

aperto 1 pp ☞ **aprire** 2 agg open; **all'** ~ piscina open-air; **mangiare all'~** eat in the open air, eat outside; apertura f opening; FOT aperture

apice m apex; fig height

apicoltura f bee-keeping

apnea f SP free diving

apostolo m apostle

apostrofo m apostrophe

app f INFOR app

appagare satisfy

appalto m (contratto) contract; **dare in** ~ contract out; **prendere in** ~ win the contract for

appannarsi di vetro mist up; di vista grow dim

apparato m apparatus; ~ **di-**

gerente digestive system

apparecchiare tavola set; (preparare) prepare; apparecchio m TEC device; AVIA F plane; per denti brace

apparenza f appearance; apparire appear; appariscente striking

appartamento m flat, Am apartment

appartarsi withdraw

appartenere belong

appassionare excite; (commuovere) move; appassionarsi become excited (**a** by); appassionato passionate

appassire wither

appellarsi appeal (**a** to; **contro** against); appello m appeal; **fare** ~ **a qu** appeal to s.o

appena 1 avv just 2 cong as soon as

appendere hang

appendiabiti m hatstand

appendice f appendix; appendicite f appendicitis

Appennini mpl Apennines

appesantire make heavier

appeso pp ☞ **appendere**

appetito m appetite; **buon** ~! enjoy (your meal)!; appetitoso appetizing

appiattire flatten

appiccicare stick; appiccicarsi stick; appiccicoso sticky; fig clingy

appiglio m per mani fingerhold; per piedi toehold; fig

excuse

applaudire applaud; **applauso** *m* applause

applicare *etichetta* attach; *regolamento* apply; **applicazione** *f* application

appoggiare lean (**a** against); (*posare*) put; *fig* support, back; **appoggiarsi ~ a** lean on; *fig* rely on; **appoggiatesta** *m inv* headrest; **appoggio** *m* support

apporre put; **~ la firma su qc** put one's signature to sth

apportare bring; *fig* (*causare*) cause

apposito appropriate

apposta deliberately, on purpose; (*specialmente*) specifically

apprendere learn; *notizia* hear

apprendistato *m* apprenticeship

apprensione *f* apprehension; **apprensivo** apprehensive

appreso *pp* ☞ **apprendere**

appresso 1 *prp* close, near; (*dietro*) behind. **2** *avv* near, close by; **portarsi qc ~** bring sth (with one)

apprezzare appreciate

approccio *m* approach

approdare land; *di barca* moor

approdo *m* landing; *luogo* landing stage

approfittare: ~ di qc take advantage of sth

approfondire deepen; *fig* study in depth

appropriarsi ~ di qc appropriate sth; **appropriato** appropriate

approvare approve of; *legge* approve; **approvazione** *f* approval

appuntamento *m* appointment

appuntito pointed; *matita* sharp

appunto 1 *m* note; **prendere -i** take notes **2** *avv*: (**per l'**) **~** exactly

apribottiglie *m inv* bottle opener

aprile *m* April

aprire open; *rubinetto* turn on; **aprirsi** open; **apriscatole** *m inv* can-opener, *Br anche* tin-opener

aquila *f* eagle

aquilone *m* kite

arabesco *m* arabesque; *spir* scrawl, scribble

Arabia Saudita *f* Saudi (Arabia)

arabo 1 *agg* Arab **2** *m*, **-a** *f* Arab **3** *m* Arabic

arachide *f* peanut

aragosta *f* lobster

arancia *f* orange; **aranciata** *f* orangeade

arancio 1 *agg inv* orange **2** *m albero* orange tree; *colore* orange; **arancione** *m/agg* orange

arare plough, *Am* plow; **aratro** *m* plough, *Am* plow

arazzo *m* tapestry

arbitrario arbitrary

arbitro *m* arbiter; SP referee

arbusto *m* shrub

arcaico archaic

arcata *f* arch

archeologia *f* archaeology, Am archeology; **archeologo** *m*, **-a** *f* archaeologist, Am archeologist

archetto *m* MUS bow

architetto *m* architect; **architettonico** architectural

archiviare file; **archivio** *m* archives

arcipelago *m* archipelago

arcivescovo *m* archbishop

arco *m* bow; ARCHI arch; **~ di tempo** period of time; **arcobaleno** *m* rainbow

ardere burn

area *f* surface; *zona* area; **~ di servizio** service area

arena *f* arena

arenarsi run aground; *fig* come to a halt

areo ... *☞* **aereo** ...

argano *m* winch

argentato silver-plated; **argenteria** *f* silver(ware)

Argentina *f* Argentina; **argentino 1** *agg* Argentinian **2** *m*, **-a** *f* Argentinian

argento *m* silver

argilla *f* clay; **argilloso** clayey

arginare embank; **argine** *m* embankment

argomento *m* argument; *(contenuto)* subject

arguto witty; *(perspicace)* shrewd

aria *f* air; *(aspetto)* appearance; MUS tune; *di opera* aria; **~ condizionata** air conditioning; **all'~ aperta** in the fresh air; **mandare all'~ qc** ruin sth; **aver l'~ stanca** look tired; **darsi delle -e** give o.s. airs

arido dry, arid

arieggiare *stanza* air

ariete *m* ZO ram; ASTR **Ariete** Aries

aringa *f* herring

arista *f* GASTR chine of pork

aristocratico 1 *agg* aristocratic **2** *m*, **-a** *f* aristocrat

aritmetica *f* arithmetic

arma *f* weapon; **~ da fuoco** firearm; **chiamare alle -i** call up; *fig* **essere alle prime -i** be a beginner

armadio *m* cupboard; **~ a muro** fitted cupboard

armamento *m* armament; **armarsi** arm o.s. *(di* with); **armato** armed

armatura *f* armour, Am armor; *(struttura)* framework

armistizio *m* armistice

armonia *f* harmony

armonica *f* harmonica; **~ a bocca** mouth organ, harmonica

armonioso harmonious

arnese *m* tool

arnia *f* beehive

aroma *m* aroma; **aromaterapia** *f* aromatherapy; **aromatico** aromatic

aromatizzare flavour, Am

flavor

arpa f harp

arpione m harpoon

arrabattarsi do everything one can

arrabbiarsi get angry; **arrabbiato** angry; (*idrofobo*) rabid

arrampicarsi climb; **arrampicata** f climb

arrangiarsi (*accordarsi*) agree (**su** on); (*destreggiarsi*) manage

arrecare bring; *fig* cause

arredamento m décor; *mobili* furniture; *arte* interior design; **arredare** furnish; **arredatore** m, **-trice** f interior designer

arrendersi surrender; *fig* give up; **arrendevole** soft, yielding

arrestare stop; DIR arrest; **arrestarsi** stop; **arresto** m coming to a stop; DIR arrest

arretrato 1 *agg* in arrears; *paese* underdeveloped **2** **-i** *mpl* arrears

arricchire *fig* enrich; **arricchirsi** get rich

arricciare *capelli* curl; **~ il naso** turn up one's nose

arringa f DIR closing speech for the defence *o Am* defense

arrivare arrive, come; **~ a** reach, get to; **~ a fare qc** manage to do sth

arrivederci, **arrivederla** goodbye

arrivista m/f social climber

arrivo m arrival; SP finish line

arrogante arrogant; **arroganza** f arrogance

arrossire blush

arrosto m roast

arrotolare roll up

arrotondare round off; *stipendio* supplement

arroventato red-hot

arruffato ruffled

arrugginire 1 *v/t* rust **2** *v/i* e **arrugginirsi** rust; *fig* get rusty

arruolarsi enlist

arsenale m arsenal; MAR dockyard

arso 1 *pp* ☞ **ardere 2** *agg* burnt; (*secco*) dried-up

arte f art; (*abilità*) gift

artefice m/f *fig* author, architect

arteria f artery; **arterioso** arterial

artico Arctic

articolazione f ANAT joint

articolo m item, article; GRAM **~ determinativo** definite article; GRAM **~ indeterminativo** indefinite article

artificiale artificial; **artificio** m artifice; **artificioso** *maniere* artificial

artigianale handmade; **artigianato** m craftsmanship; **artigiano** m, **-a** f craftsman; *donna* craftswoman

artiglieria f artillery

artiglio m claw

artista m/f artist; **artistico** artistic

arto *m* limb

artrite *f* arthritis

artrosi *f* rheumatism

ascella *f* armpit

ascendente 1 *agg* ascending;
strada sloping upwards; *movimento* upwards **2** *m* ASTR
ascendant; *fig* influence;

ascensione *f* ascent; REL
Ascension; **ascensore** *m*
lift, *Am* elevator; **ascesa** *f*
ascent

ascesso *m* abscess

ascia *f* axe, *Am* ax

asciugacapelli *m* hairdryer;
asciugamano *m* towel;
asciugare dry; **asciugarsi**
dry o.s.; **~ i capelli** dry one's
hair; **asciugatrice** *f* tumble
dryer; **asciutto** dry

ascoltare listen to; **ascoltatore** *m*, **-trice** *f* listener;
ascolto *m* listening; **dare ~**
listen (**a** to)

asettico aseptic

asfaltare asphalt; **asfalto** *m*
asphalt

asfissiare asphyxiate

Asia *f* Asia; **asiatico 1** *agg*
Asian **2** *m*, **-a** *f* Asian

asilo *m* shelter; **~ politico** political asylum; **~ nido** day
nursery, *Am* day care center

asimmetrico asymmetrical

asino *m* ass (*anche fig*)

asma *f* asthma

asociale antisocial

asola *f* buttonhole

asparago *m* spear of aspara-

gus; **-gi** asparagus

aspettare wait for; **~ un bambino** be expecting a baby;
aspettarsi expect; **aspettativa** *f* expectation; *da lavoro*
unpaid leave

aspetto[1] *m* look, appearance;
di problema aspect

aspetto[2]: **sala** *f* **d'~** waiting
room

aspirapolvere *m* vacuum
cleaner

aspirare 1 *v/t* inhale; TEC suck
up **2** *v/i*: **~ a qc** aspire to sth

aspirina *f* aspirin

asportare take away

aspro sour; (*duro*) harsh; *litigio* bitter

assaggiare taste; **assaggio**
m taste, sample

assai 1 *agg* a lot of **2** *avv* con
verbo a lot; *con aggettivo*
very; (*abbastanza*) enough

assalire attack

assaltare attack; **assalto** *m*
attack; *fig* **prendere d'~**
storm

assassinare murder; POL assassinate; **assassinio** *m*
murder; POL assassination;
assassino 1 *agg* murderous
2 *m*, **-a** *f* murderer; POL assassin

asse[1] *m* board; **~ da stiro** ironing board

asse[2] *m* TEC axle; MAT axis

assecondare support; (*esaudire*) satisfy

assediare besiege; **assedio**
m siege

assegnare *premio* award; (*destinare*) assign; **assegno** *m* cheque, *Am* check; **~ in bianco** blank cheque; **~ turistico** traveller's cheque, *Am* traveler's check; **contro ~** cash on delivery, *Am* collect on delivery; **-i familiari** child benefit; **emettere un ~** write a cheque

assemblea *f* meeting

assentarsi go away, leave; **assente** absent, away; *fig* absent-minded; **assenza** *f* absence; **~ di qc** lack of sth

assessore *m* councillor, *Am* councilor; **~ comunale** local councillor

assicurare insure; (*legare*) secure; *lettera, pacco* register; **assicurarsi** make sure, ensure; **assicurata** *f* registered letter; **assicurato 1** *agg* insured; *lettera, pacco* registered **2** *m*, **-a** *f* person with insurance, insured party; **assicurazione** *f* insurance

assideramento *m* exposure

assieme together

assillante nagging; **assillare** pester; **assillo** *m* fig: *persona* pest F, nuisance; (*preoccupazione*) nagging thought

assistente *m/f* assistant; **~ sociale** social worker; **~ di volo** flight attendant; **assistenza** *f* assistance; **~ medica** medical care; **assistere 1** *v/t* assist, help; (*curare*) nurse **2** *v/i* (*essere presente*) be pre-

sent (**a** at)

asso *m* ace

associare take into partnership; *fig* **~ qu a qc** associate s.o. with sth; **associarsi** enter into partnership (**a** with); (*unirsi*) join forces; (*iscriversi*) subscribe (**a** to); (*prendere parte*) join (**a** sth); **associazione** *f* association

assolo *m inv* MUS solo

assolto *pp* **~ assolvere**

assolutamente absolutely; **assoluto** absolute; **assoluzione** *f* DIR acquittal; REL absolution; **assolvere** DIR acquit; *da un obbligo* release; *compito* carry out; REL absolve, give absolution to

assomigliare: **~ a qu** be like s.o., resemble s.o.; **assomigliarsi** be like *o* resemble each other

assonnato sleepy

assorbente 1 *agg* absorbent **2** *m*: **~ igienico** sanitary towel, *Am* sanitary napkin; **assorbire** absorb

assordante deafening; **assordare 1** *v/t* deafen **2** *v/i* go deaf

assortimento *m* assortment

assorto engrossed

assuefatto *pp* **~ assuefare**; **assuefazione** *f* resistance, tolerance; *agli alcolici, alla droga* addiction

assumere *impiegato, incarico* take on

assunzione f di impiegato employment; REL **Assunzione** Assumption

assurdità f inv absurdity; **assurdo** absurd

asta f pole; IN auction; **mettere all'~** sell at auction

astemio 1 agg abstemious **2** m, -a f abstemious person; **astenersi ~ da** abstain from

asterisco m asterisk

astigmatico astigmatic; **astigmatismo** m astigmatism

astinenza f abstinence

astio m rancour, Am rancor

astratto abstract

astringente m/agg MED astringent

astro m star; **astrologia** f astrology; **astronauta** m/f astronaut; **astronave** f spaceship; **astronomia** f astronomy; **astronomico** astronomical

astuccio m case

astuto astute

ateo m, -a f atheist

atlante m atlas

atlantico Atlantic; **Oceano m Atlantico** Atlantic Ocean

atleta m/f athlete; **atletica** f athletics; **~ leggera** track and field (events); **atletico** athletic

atmosfera f atmosphere; **atmosferico** atmospheric

atomico atomic; **atomo** m atom

atrio m foyer, Am lobby

atroce atrocious; **atrocità** f inv atrocity

attaccabrighe m o f inv F troublemaker; **attaccante** m SP forward; **attaccapanni** m inv clothes hook; a stelo clothes hanger; **attaccare 1** v/t attach; (incollare) stick; (appendere) hang; (assalire) attack **2** v/i stick; **attaccarsi** stick; (aggrapparsi) hold on (a to); **attacco** m attack; (punto di unione) junction; SCI binding; MED fit

attaccaiamento m attitude; **atteggiarsi ~ a** pose as

attendere 1 v/t wait for **2** v/i: ~ **a** attend to

attendibile reliable

attenersi stick (a to)

attentare ~ a attack; **~ alla vita di qu** make an attempt on s.o.'s life; **attentato** m attempted assassination

attento 1 agg attentive; **stare ~ a** be careful of **2** int ~! look out!, (be) careful!

attenuante f extenuating circumstance; **attenuare** reduce; (colpo) cushion; **attenuarsi** lessen

attenzione f attention; ~! look out!, (be) careful!; **far ~ a qc** mind o watch sth

atterraggio m landing; **atterrare 1** v/t avversario knock down **2** v/i land

attesa f waiting; (tempo d'attesa) wait; (aspettativa) expectation

atteso pp ☞ **attendere**

attestato m certificate

attico m attic

attimo m moment; **un ~!** just a moment!

attirare attract

attitudine f attitude; **avere ~ per qc** have an aptitude for sth

attivare activate; **attività** f inv activity; pl FIN assets; **attivo 1** agg active **2** m FIN assets; GRAM active (voice)

atto m act; (gesto) gesture; (documento) deed; **mettere in ~** carry out; **prendere ~ di** note

attorcigliare, **attorcigliarsi** twist

attore m, **-trice** f actor; donna anche actress

attorno: ~ **a qc** around sth; **qui ~** around here

attraccare MAR berth, dock

attraente attractive; **attrarre** attract; **attrattiva** f attraction; **attratto** pp ☞ **attrarre**

attraversare strada, confine cross; ~ **un momento difficile** be going through a bad patch; **attraverso** across

attrazione f attraction

attrezzare equip; **attrezzarsi** get o.s. kitted out; **attrezzato** equipped; **attrezzatura** f equipment, gear F; **attrezzo** m piece of equipment

attribuire attribute

attrice f actress

attuale current; **attualità** f inv

news sg; **d'~** topical; **attuare** put into effect; **attuazione** f putting into effect

audace audacious

audioleso 1 agg hearing-impaired **2** m, **-a** f person who is hearing-impaired

audiovisivo audiovisual

audizione f audition

augurare wish; **augurio** m wish; **tanti -ri!** all the best!

aula f di scuola class room; di università lecture room

aumentare increase; **aumento** m increase

aureola f halo

auricolare m earphone

aurora f dawn

ausiliare m/agg auxiliary

australe southern

Australia f Australia; **australiano 1** agg Australian **2** m, **-a** f Australian

Austria f Austria; **austriaco 1** agg Austrian **2** m, **-a** f Austrian

autenticare authenticate; **autentico** authentic

autista m/f driver

auto f inv ☞ **automobile**

autoadesivo 1 agg self-adhesive **2** m sticker

autoambulanza f ambulance

autobiografia f autobiography

autobomba f car bomb

autobus m bus; ~ **di linea** city bus

autocarro m truck, Br anche lorry

autocisterna *f* tanker

autocontrollo *m* self-control

autodidatta *m/f* self-taught person

autodifesa *f* self-defence, *Am* self-defense

autodromo *m* motor racing circuit

autogol *m inv* own goal

autografo *m* autograph

autogrill *m inv* roadside café

autolavaggio *m* car-wash

automa *m* robot

automatico 1 *agg* automatic **2** *m bottone* press-stud, *Am* snap fastener

automezzo *m* motor vehicle

automobile *f* car, *Am anche* automobile; **automobilismo** *m* driving; *SP* motor racing; **automobilista** *m/f* driver

autonoleggio *m* car rental; *azienda* car-rental firm

autonomia *f* autonomy; *TEC* battery life; **autonomo** autonomous

autoradio *f inv* car radio

autore *m*, **-trice** *f* author; *DIR* perpetrator; **autorevole** authoritative

autorimessa *f* garage

autorità *f inv* authority; **autoritario** authoritarian; **autorizzare** authorize; **autorizzazione** *f* authorization

autoscuola *f* driving school

autostop *m*: **fare l'~** hitch-hike; **autostoppista** *m/f* hitchhiker

autostrada *f* motorway, *Am* highway

autovettura *f* motor vehicle

autrice *f* ☞ **autore**

autunno *m* autumn, *Am* fall

avambraccio *m* forearm

avanguardia *f* avant-garde; *azienda* leading-edge

avanti 1 *avv* in front, ahead; **d'ora in ~** from now on; **andare ~** *di orologio* be fast; **essere ~ nel programma** be ahead of schedule **2** *int* **~!** come in!

avanzare 1 *v/i* advance; *fig* make progress; *(rimanere)* be left over **2** *v/t* put forward

avanzo *m* remainder; *FIN* surplus; **gli -i** *pl* the leftovers

avaria *f* failure; **avariato** damaged; *cibi* spoiled

avarizia *f* avarice; **avaro 1** *agg* miserly **2** *m*, **-a** *f* miser

avena *f* oats

avere 1 *v/t* have; **~ 20 anni** be 20 (years old); **~ fame** / **sonno** be hungry / sleepy; **~ caldo** / **freddo** be hot / cold; **avercela con qu** have it in for s.o **2** *v/aus* have; **hai visto Tony?** have you seen Tony?; **hai visto Tony ieri?** did you see Tony yesterday? **3** *m FIN* credit; **-i** *pl* wealth

avi *mpl* ancestors

aviazione *f* aviation; *MIL* Air Force

avidità *f* avidness; **avido** avid

avocado *m* avocado

avorio m ivory

avvalersi ~ di qc avail o.s. of sth

avvantaggiare favour, Am favor; **avvantaggiarsi ~ di qc** take advantage of sth

avveduto astute

avvelenamento m poisoning; **avvelenare** poison; **avvelenarsi** poison o.s.

avvenimento m event; **avvenire 1** v/i (accadere) happen **2** m future

Avvento m Advent

avventura f adventure; **avventurarsi** venture; **avventuriero** m, **-a** f adventurer; donna adventuress; **avventuroso** adventurous

avvenuto pp ☞ **avvenire**

avverarsi come true

avverbio m adverb

avversario 1 agg opposing **2** m, **-a** f opponent, adversary

avversione f aversion (**per** to)

avvertenza f (ammonimento) warning; (premessa) foreword; **-e** pl (istruzioni per l'uso) instructions

avvertimento m warning; **avvertire** warn; (percepire) catch

avviamento m introduction; TEC, AUTO start-up; **avviare** start; **avviarsi** set out, head off; **avviato** established

avvicendarsi alternate

avvicinare approach; **~ qc a**

qc move sth closer to sth; **avvicinarsi** approach, near (**a** sth)

avvilire depress; (mortificare) humiliate; **avvilirsi** demean o.s.; (scoraggiarsi) get depressed; **avvilito** (scoraggiato) depressed

avvio m: **dare l'~ a qc** get sth under way

avvisare inform, advise; (mettere in guardia) warn; **avviso** m notice; **a mio ~** in my opinion

avvitare screw in; fissare screw

avvocato m lawyer

avvolgere wrap; **avvolgibile** m roller blind; **avvolto** pp ☞ **avvolgere**

avvoltoio m vulture

azienda f business; **aziendale** company attr

azionare activate; allarme set off; **azionario** share attr, **azione** f action; (effetto) influence; FIN share; **azionista** m/f stockholder, shareholder

azoto m nitrogen

azzannare bite into

azzardarsi dare; **azzardo** m hazard; **gioco** m **d'~** game of chance

azzerare TEC reset

azzuffarsi come to blows

azzurro 1 agg blue **2** m blue; SP **gli -i** pl the Italian national team

B

babbo m F dad F, pop F; *Babbo Natale* Santa (Claus), Br anche Father Christmas

babordo m MAR port (side)

baby-sitter m/f inv baby-sitter

bacato wormeaten

bacca f berry

baccalà m inv dried salt cod

baccano m din

bacchetta f rod; MUS *del direttore d'orchestra* baton; *per suonare il tamburo* (drum) stick; *~ magica* magic wand

bacheca f notice board, Am bulletin board; *di museo* showcase

baciare kiss; **baciarsi** kiss (each other)

bacillo m bacillus

bacinella f basin; FOT tray

bacino m basin; ANAT pelvis; MAR port

bacio m kiss

baco m worm; *~ da seta* silkworm

bada: tenere a ~ qu keep s.o. at bay; **badare**: *~ a* look after; *(fare attenzione a)* look out for, mind

baffo m: *-i* pl moustache, Am mustache; *di animali* whiskers

bagagliaio m FERR luggage van, Am baggage car; AUTO boot, Am trunk; **bagaglio** m luggage, baggage; *fare i -i* pack

bagliore m glare; *di speranza* glimmer

bagnante m/f bather; **bagnare** wet; *(immergere)* dip; *(inzuppare)* soak; *(annaffiare)* water; *di fiume* flow through; **bagnarsi** get wet; **bagnato** wet; **bagnino** m, *-a* f lifeguard; **bagno** m bath, Am (bath)tub; *stanza* bathroom; *gabinetto* toilet; *fare il ~* have a bath; *mettere a ~* soak; **bagnomaria** m inv double boiler, bain marie

baia f bay

baita f mountain chalet, Am mountain lodge

balaustra f balustrade

balbettare stammer; *di bambino* babble; **balbettio** m stammering; *di bambino* babble, prattle

balbuzie f stutter; **balbuziente** m/f stutterer

balconata f TEA dress circle, Am balcony; **balcone** m balcony

baldoria f revelry; *fare ~* have a riotous time

balena f whale

balenare *fig gli è balenata un'idea* an idea flashed through his mind; **baleno** m lightning; *in un ~* in a flash

balia f: *in ~ di* at the mercy of

balla f bale; *fig* F (*frottola*) fib F

ballare dance

ballata f MUS ballad

ballerina f dancer; *di balletto* ballet dancer; *di rivista* chorus girl; *scarpa* ballet shoe; **ballerino** m dancer; *di balletto* ballet dancer

balletto m ballet

ballo m dance; (*il ballare*) dancing; (*festa*) ball; **essere in ~** *persona* be involved; (*essere in gioco*) be at stake; **tirare in ~** *qc* bring sth up

balneare *centro* seaside *attr*

balordo 1 *agg ragionamento* shaky; *idea* stupid; *tempo, consiglio* unreliable **2** m (*teppista*) lout

balsamico *aceto* balsamic; *aria* balmy; **balsamo** m *per i capelli* hair conditioner

balzare jump, leap; **balzo** m jump, leap; *fig* **cogliere la palla al ~** jump at the chance

bambinaia f nanny; **bambino** m, -a f child; *in fasce* baby

bambola f doll; **bambolotto** m baby boy doll

bambù m bamboo

banale banal; **banalità** f inv banality

banana f banana

banca f bank; INFOR **~ dati** data bank

bancarella f stall

bancario 1 *agg istituto, segreto*

banking *attr*; *deposito, estratto conto* bank *attr* **2** m, -a f bank employee

bancarotta f bankruptcy

banchetto m banquet

banchiere m banker

banchina f FERR platform; MAR quay; *di strada* verge

banchisa f ice floe

banco m FIN bank; *di scuola* desk; *di bar* bar; *di chiesa* pew; *di negozio* counter; **bancomat®** m inv (*distributore*) ATM; *carta* cash card, debit card

bancone m (work)bench

banconota f banknote, Am bill

banda f band; *di delinquenti* gang; **banda** f **larga** broadband

banderuola f weathercock (*anche fig*)

bandiera f flag

bandire proclaim; *concorso* announce; (*esiliare*) banish; *fig* (*abolire*) dispense with; **bandito** m bandit; **bando** m proclamation; (*esilio*) banishment

bar m inv bar

bara f coffin

baracca f hut; *spreg* hovel

baraccopoli f inv shanty town

barare cheat

baratro m abyss

barattare barter

barattolo m can, Br anche tin; *di vetro* jar

barba *f* beard; *farsi la ~* shave; *fig che ~!* what a pain! F

barbabietola *f* beetroot, *Am* red beet; *~ da zucchero* sugar beet

barbarico barbaric; **barbaro 1** *agg* barbarous **2** *m* barbarian

barbecue *m inv* barbecue

barbiere *m* barber

barboncino *m* (miniature) poodle

barbone[1] *m* cane poodle

barbone[2] *m*, *-a f* (*vagabondo*) tramp, *Am* hobo

barca *f* boat; *~ a remi* rowing boat, *Am* rowboat; *~ a vela* sailing boat, *Am* sail boat

barcaiolo *m* boatman

barcollare stagger

barcone *m* barge

barella *f* stretcher

barile *m* barrel

barista *m/f* barman; *donna* barmaid; *Am* bartender; *proprietario* bar owner

baritono *m* baritone

barocco *m/agg* Baroque

barometro *m* barometer

barone *m*, *-essa f* baron; *donna* baroness

barra *f* bar

barricata *f* barricade

barriera *f* barrier (*anche fig*)

barzelletta *f* joke

basare base; **basarsi** be based (*su* on)

basco *m* (*berretto*) beret

base *f* base; *fig* basis; *in ~ a* on the basis of

basette *fpl* sideburns

basilica *f* basilica

basilico *m* basil

basso 1 *agg* low; *di statura* short; *MUS* bass; *fig* despicable **2** *avv*: *in ~ stato* below; *da ~ in una casa* downstairs **3** *m* MUS bass; **bassopiano** *m* GEOG lowland; **bassorilievo** *m* bas-relief; **bassotto** *m* dachshund

basta ☞ *bastare*

bastardo *m*, *-a f* cane mongrel; *fig* bastard

bastare be enough; (*durare*) last; *basta!* that's enough; *basta che* (*purché*) as long as

bastonare beat; **bastone** *m* stick; *di pane* baguette, French stick

battaglia *f* battle (*anche fig*)

battello *m* boat

battente *m di porta* wing; *di finestra* shutter

battere 1 *v/i* (*bussare*, *dare colpi*) knock **2** *v/t* beat; *record* break; *~ le mani* clap (one's hands); *~ al computer* key

batteri *mpl* bacteria

batteria *f* battery; MUS drums; **batterista** *m/f* drummer

battersela run off; **battersi** fight

battesimo *m* christening, baptism; **battezzare** christen, baptize

battibecco *m* argument; **batticuore** *m* palpitations; *fig con un gran ~* with great anxiety; **battipanni** *m inv* carpet beater

battistero *m* baptistry

battistrada *m inv* AUTO tread

battito *m* beating, beat; **~ cardiaco** heartbeat

battuta *f* beat; *in dattilografia* keystroke; MUS bar; TEA cue; *nel tennis* service; **~ (di spirito)** wisecrack

baule *m* trunk; AUTO boot, *Am* trunk

bavaglino *m* bib

bavaglio *m* gag

bavero *m* collar

bazzecola *f* trifle

bazzicare **1** *v/t un posto* haunt; *persone* associate with **2** *v/i* hang about

beatificare beatify; **beato** happy; REL blessed; **~ te!** lucky you!

beauty-case *m inv* toilet bag

bebè *m inv* baby

beccare peck; F *fig (cogliere sul fatto)* nab F; F *fig: malattia* catch, pick up F; **beccarsi** F *malattia* catch, pick up F

becchino *m* grave digger

becco *m* beak; *di teiera ecc* spout

befana *f kind old witch who brings presents to children on Twelfth Night*; REL Twelfth Night; *fig* old witch

beffa *f* hoax; **farsi ~e di q.** make a fool of s.o.; **beffardo** scornful; **beffare** mock; **beffarsi: ~ di** mock

bega *f (litigio)* fight, argu-

ment; *(problema)* can of worms

begli ☞ **bello**

bei ☞ **bello**

belare bleat

belga *agg*, *m/f* Belgian; **Belgio** *m* Belgium

bellezza *f* beauty

bellico *(di guerra)* war *attr*; *(del tempo di guerra)* wartime *attr*

bello **1** *agg* beautiful; *uomo* handsome; *tempo* fine, nice, beautiful; **questa è ~a!** that's a good one!; **nel bel mezzo** right in the middle **2** *m* beauty; **sul più ~** at the worst possible moment

belva *f* wild beast

belvedere *m inv* viewpoint

bemolle *m inv* MUS flat

benché although

benda *f* bandage; *per occhi* blindfold; **bendare** MED bandage

bene **1** *avv* well; **~!** good!; *per* **~** properly; **stare ~ di salute** be well; *di vestito* suit; **ben ti sta!** serves you right!; **va ~!** OK!; **andare ~ a q** *di abito* fit s.o.; *di orario, appuntamento* suit s.o.; **sentirsi ~** feel well **2** *m* good; **fare ~ alla salute** be good for you; **per il tuo ~** for your own good; **voler ~ a q** love s.o.; *(amare)* love s.o.; **-i** *pl* assets, property; **-i immobili** real estate

benedetto **1** *pp* ☞ **benedire** **2** *agg* blessed; REL **acqua** *f* **-a**

holy water; **benedire** bless; **benedizione** f blessing

beneducato well-mannered

beneficenza f charity; **spettacolo** m **di ~** benefit (performance)

beneficio m benefit; **a ~ di** for the benefit of; **benefico** beneficial; *organizzazione, istituto* charitable; *spettacolo* charity attr

benessere m well-being; (*agiatezza*) affluence; **benestante 1** agg well-off **2** m/f person with money

benigno MED benign

beninteso of course; **~ che** provided that

benone splendid

benpensante m/f moderate; spreg conformist

bensì but rather

benvenuto 1 agg welcome **2** m welcome; **dare il ~ a qu** welcome s.o.

benvolere: farsi ~ da qu win s.o. over

benzina f petrol, Am gas; **fare ~** get petrol; **benzinaio** m, **-a** f petrol o Am gas station attendant

bere drink; fig swallow

berlina f AUTO saloon, Am sedan

bermuda mpl Bermuda shorts

bernoccolo m bump

berretto m cap

berrò ☞ **bere**

bersaglio m target; fig: di

scherzi butt

bestemmia f swear-word; **bestemmiare 1** v/i swear (**contro** at) **2** v/t curse

bestia f animal; fig **andare in ~** fly into a rage; **bestiale** bestial; F (*molto intenso*) terrible; **bestiame** m livestock

bettola f spreg dive

betulla f birch

bevanda f drink

beve ☞ **bere**

biancheria f linen; **~ intima** underwear

bianco 1 agg white; *foglio* blank **2** m white; **~ d'uovo** egg white; **mangiare in ~** avoid rich food; **in ~ e nero** film black and white

biasimare blame; **biasimo** m blame

bibbia f bible

biberon m inv baby's bottle

bibita f soft drink

bibliografia f bibliography

biblioteca f library; *mobile* book-case; **bibliotecario** m, **-a** f librarian

bicamerale POL two-chamber

bicarbonato m: **~ (di sodio)** bicarbonate of soda

bicchiere m glass

bicentenario m bicentenary, Am bicentennial

bici f inv F bike F; **~ elettrica** e-bike; **bicicletta** f bike, bicycle; **andare in ~** go by bike, Br anche cycle

bidè m inv bidet

bidone m drum; *della spazzatura* (dust)bin, *Am* garbage can; F (*imbroglio*) swindle

biennale biennial; (*che dura due anni*) two-year; **biennio** m two-year period

bietola f beet

biforcarsi fork; **biforcazione** f fork

bigamo m, -a f bigamist

bigiotteria f costume jewellery o *Am* jewelry; *negozio* jeweller's, *Am* jewelry store

bigliettaio m, -a f ticket seller; *sul treno, tram* conductor, *Am* guard; **biglietteria** f ticket office; *di cinema, teatro* box office; **biglietto** m ticket; **~ d'auguri** (greetings) card; **~ da visita** business card; **un ~ da 10 dollari** a ten-dollar bill; **fare il ~** buy the ticket

bigodino m roller

bigotto 1 agg bigoted **2** m, -a f bigot

bikini m inv bikini

bilancia f scales; ASTR **Bilancia** Libra; **bilanciare** balance; (*pareggiare*) equal; *fig* weigh up; FIN **~ un conto** balance an account; **bilanciarsi** balance; **bilancio** m balance; (*rendiconto*) balance sheet; **~ preventivo** budget; **fare il ~** draw up a balance sheet; *fig* take stock

bile f bile; *fig* rage

biliardo m billiards sg, *Am* pool

bilico m: **essere in ~** be precariously balanced; *fig* be undecided

bilingue bilingual

bilocale m two-room flat o *Am* apartment

bimbo m, -a f child

bimotore m twin-engine plane

binario 1 agg binary **2** m track; (*marciapiede*) platform

binocolo m binoculars

biochimica f biochemistry

biodegradabile biodegradable

biografia f biography; **biografico** biographical; **biografo** m, -a f biographer

biologia f biology; **biologico** biological; *alimento* organic; **biologo** m, -a f biologist

biondo blonde

biossido m dioxide

birbante m rascal

birichino 1 agg naughty **2** m, -a f little devil

birillo m skittle

biro® f inv ballpoint (pen), *Br* anche biro

birra f beer; **~ alla spina** draught o *Am* draft beer; **birreria** f pub that sells only beer; *fabbrica* brewery

bis m inv encore

bisbetico bad-tempered

bisbigliare whisper

bisca f gambling den

biscia f grass snake

biscotto m biscuit, *Am* cookie

bisessuale bisexual

bisestile: anno m ~ leap year

bisnonno m, **-a** f great-grandfather; **donna** great-grandmother

bisognare: bisogna farlo it must be done, it needs to be done; **non bisogna farlo** it doesn't have to be done, there's no need to do it; **bisogno** m need; **(mancanza)** lack; **(fabbisogno)** requirements; **avere ~ di qc** need sth; **bisognoso** needy

bisonte m ZO bison

bistecca f steak

bisticciare quarrel; **bisticcio** m quarrel

bisturi m inv MED scalpel

bitter m inv aperitif

bivio m junction; fig crossroads sg

bizantino Byzantine

bizzarro bizarre

bizzeffe: a ~ galore

blando mild, gentle

blatta f cockroach

blindato armoured, Am armored

blitz m inv blitz

bloccare block; MIL blockade; (isolare) cut off; prezzi, conto freeze; **bloccarsi di** ascensore, persona get stuck; di freni, porta jam; **blocca-ruota** m AUTO wheel clamp, Am Denver boot; **mettere il ~ a** clamp; **bloccasterzo** m AUTO steering lock

blocchetto m per appunti notebook

blocco m block; di carta pad; **~ stradale** road block

bloc-notes m inv writing pad

blu blue

blusa f blouse

boa¹ m inv ZO boa constrictor

boa² f MAR buoy

boato m rumble

bob m inv SP bobsleigh, bobsled; **bobbista** m/f bobsledder

bobina f spool

bocca f mouth; (apertura) opening; **in ~ al lupo!** good luck!; **boccaccia** f (smorfia) grimace; **boccaglio** m di maschera per il nuoto mouthpiece

boccale m jug; da birra tankard

boccetta f small bottle

boccheggiare gasp

bocchino m per sigarette cigarette holder; MUS, di pipa mouthpiece

boccia f (palla) bowl; **bocciare** (respingere) reject, vote down; EDU fail; **boccia** hit, strike; **bocciatura** f failure

bocciolo m bud

bocconcino m morsel; **boccone** m mouthful

bocconi face down

body m inv body(suit)

boia m inv executioner; F **fa un freddo ~** it's freezing

boicottaggio m boycott; **boicottare** boycott

bolide m meteor; *come un ~* like greased lightning

bolla[1] f bubble; MED blister

bolla[2] f *documento* note, docket; *~ di consegna* delivery note

bollare stamp; *fig* brand

bollente boiling hot

bolletta f bill; *~ della luce* electricity bill

bollettino m: *~ meteorologico* weather forecast

bollire boil; **bollito 1** *agg* boiled **2** m boiled meat; **bollitore** m kettle

bollo m stamp

bomba f bomb; **bombardamento** m shelling, bombardment; *(attacco aereo)* air raid; *fig* bombardment; **bombardare** bomb; *fig* bombard

bombola f cylinder

bomboniera f wedding keepsake

bonaccia f MAR calm

bonaccione m, **-a** f kindhearted person

bonario kind-hearted

bonificare FIN *(scontare)* discount; *(accreditare)* credit; AGR reclaim; *(prosciugare)* drain; **bonifico** m *(trasferimento)* (money) transfer

bontà f *inv* goodness; *(gentilezza)* kindness

bora f bora *(a cold north wind)*

borbottare mumble

bordello m brothel; *fig* F bedlam F; *(disordine)* mess

bordo m *(orlo)* edge; *a ~* on board

boreale northern; *aurora f ~* northern lights

borgata f village; *(rione popolare)* suburb

borghese middle-class; *in ~* in civilian clothes; **borghesia** f middle classes *pl*

borgo m village

borraccia f flask

borsa f bag; *(borsetta)* handbag, *Am* purse; *per documenti* briefcase; FIN Stock Market; *~ di studio* scholarship; **borsaiolo** m, *-a* f pickpocket; **borsellino** m purse, *Am* coin purse; **borsetta** f handbag, *Am* purse

borsista m/f *speculatore* speculator; *studente* scholarship holder

boscaiolo m woodcutter; **bosco** m wood

bossolo m *di proiettili* (shell) case

botanico 1 *agg* botanical **2** m, *-a* f botanist

botola f trapdoor

botta f *blow*; *(numore)* bang; *fare a -e* come to blows

botte f barrel

bottega f shop; *(laboratorio)* workshop; **bottegaio** m, *-a* f shopkeeper; **botteghino** m box office; *(del lotto)* sales outlet for lottery tickets

bottiglia f bottle

bottino m loot

botto *m* (*rumore*) bang

bottone *m* button; **~ automatico** press-stud, *Am* snap fastener

bovino 1 *agg* bovine **2** *m*: **-i** *pl* cattle *pl*

box *m inv per auto* lock-up (garage); *per bambini* playpen; *per cavalli* loose box

boxe *f* boxing

bozza *f* draft; TIP proof; **bozzetto** *m* sketch

bozzolo *m* cocoon

braccetto: a ~ arm in arm

bracciale *m* bracelet; (*fascia*) armband; *di orologio* watch strap; **braccialetto** *m* bracelet; **bracciante** *m/f* day labourer, *Am* day laborer

bracciata *f nel nuoto* stroke; **braccio** *m* arm; **portare in ~ qu** carry s.o.; **bracciolo** *m* arm(rest)

bracconiere *m* poacher

brace *f* embers; **alla ~** char-grilled, *Am* char-broiled

braciola *f* GASTR chop

branca *f* branch (*anche fig*)

branchia *f* gill

branco *m di cani, lupi* pack; *di pecore, uccelli* flock; *fig spreg* gang

brancolare grope

branda *f* camp-bed, *Am* cot

brandello *m* shred, scrap; **a -i** in shreds *o* tatters

brano *m di testo, musica* passage

brasato *m di manzo* braised beef

Brasile *m* Brazil; **brasiliano 1** *agg* Brazilian **2** *m*, **-a** *f* Brazilian

bravata *f* boasting; *azione* bravado

bravo good; (*abile*) clever, good; **~!** well done!; **bravura** *f* skill

bretella *f* (*raccordo*) slip road, *Am* ramp; **-e** *pl* braces, *Am* suspenders

breve short; **in ~** briefly, in short

brevettare patent; **brevetto** *m* patent; *di pilota* licence, *Am* license

brezza *f* breeze

bricco *m* jug, *Am* pitcher

briciola *f* crumb; **briciolo** *m fig* grain, scrap

bricolage *m* do-it-yourself, DIY, *Am* home improvement

briga *f*: **darsi la ~ di fare qc** take the trouble to do sth; **attaccar ~ con qu** pick a quarrel with s.o.

brigadiere *m* MIL sergeant

brigante *m* bandit

briglia *f* rein

brillante 1 *agg* sparkling; *colore* bright; *fig* brilliant **2** *m* diamond; **brillare** shine

brillo tipsy

brina *f* hoar-frost

brindare drink a toast (**a** to); **~ alla salute di qu** drink to s.o.'s health; **brindisi** *m inv* toast

brioche *f inv* brioche

britannico 1 *agg* British **2** *m*, -a *f* Briton, Brit F

brivido *m di freddo, spavento* shiver; *di emozione* thrill

brizzolato *capelli* greying, *Am* graying

brocca *f* jug, *Am* pitcher

broccato *m* brocade

broccoli *mpl* broccoli *sg*

brodo *m* (clear) soup; *di pollo, di manzo, di verdura* stock; **brodoso** watery, thin

bronchite *f* bronchitis

broncio *m:* **avere il ~** sulk

broncopolmonite *f* bronchial pneumonia

brontolare grumble; *di stomaco* rumble; **brontolio** *m* grumble; *di stomaco* rumble; **brontolone 1** *agg* grumbling **2** *m,* -a *f* grumbler

bronzo *m* bronze

bruciapelo: **a ~** point-blank; **bruciare 1** *v/t* burn; *(incendiare)* set fire to **2** *v/i* burn; *fig: di occhi* sting; **bruciarsi** burn o.s.; **bruciato** burnt; *dal sole* scorched, parched; **bruciatura** *f* burn; **bruciore** *m* burning sensation; **~ di stomaco** heartburn

bruco *m* grub; *(verme)* worm

brufolo *m* spot

brulicare swarm

brullo bare

bruno brown; *capelli* dark

bruschetta *f* GASTR bruschetta *(toasted bread with garlic and olive oil, Naples variant with chopped tomatoes)*

brusco sharp; *persona, modi* brusque, abrupt; *(improvviso)* sudden

brutale brutal; **brutalità** *f inv* brutality

brutta *f:* **(copia** *f)* **~** rough copy; **bruttezza** *f* ugliness; **brutto** ugly; *(cattivo)* bad; *tempo, tipo, affare* nasty

Bruxelles *f* Brussels

buca *f* hole; *(avvallamento)* hollow; *del biliardo* pocket; **~ delle lettere** letter-box, *Am* mailbox; **bucare** make a hole in; *(pungere)* prick; *biglietto* punch; **~ una gomma** have a flat (tyre)

bucato *m* washing, laundry; **fare il ~** do the washing

buccia *f* peel

bucherellare make holes in; **bucherellato dai tarli** riddled with woodworm

buco *m* hole

budello *m* gut; *(vicolo)* alley

budget *m inv* budget

budino *m* pudding

bue *m* ox; *carne* beef

bufalo *m* buffalo

bufera *f* storm

buffet *m inv* buffet; *mobile* sideboard, *Am* buffet

buffo funny; **buffone** *m,* -a *f* buffoon, fool; *di corte* fool, jester

bugia *f (menzogna)* lie; **bugiardo 1** *agg* lying **2** *m,* -a *f* liar

buio 1 *agg* dark **2** *m* darkness; **al ~** in the dark

bulbo *m* BOT bulb

Bulgaria *f* Bulgaria; **bulgaro 1** *agg* Bulgarian **2** *m*, **-a** *f* Bulgarian

bullone *m* bolt

buoi *☞* **bue**

buon *☞* **buono**

buonafede *f*: **in ~** in good faith

buonanotte good night

buonasera good evening

buongiorno good morning, hello

buongustaio *m*, **-a** *f* gourmet; **buongusto** *m* good taste; **di ~** in good taste

buono 1 *agg* good; *momento* right; *alla ~* informal, casual **2** *m* good; FIN bond; *(tagliando)* voucher; **~ regalo** gift voucher, *Am* gift certificate; **~ sconto** discount voucher

buonsenso *m* common sense

burattino *m* puppet

burbero gruff, surly

burla *f* practical joke, trick; **burlarsi**: **~ di qu** make fun

of s.o.; **burlone** *m*, **-a** *f* joker

burocratico bureaucratic; **burocrazia** *f* bureaucracy

burrasca *f* storm; **burrascoso** stormy

burro *m* butter

burrone *m* ravine

bussare knock

bussola *f* compass

busta *f* *per lettera* envelope; *per documenti* folder; *(astuccio)* case; **~ paga** pay packet

bustarella *f* bribe

bustina *f*: **~ di tè** tea bag

busto *m* ANAT torso; *scultura* bust; *(corsetto)* girdle

buttafuori *m inv* TEA callboy; *di locale notturno* bouncer; **buttare 1** *v/i* BOT sprout **2** *v/t* throw; **~ via** throw away; *fig* waste; **~ giù** knock down; *lettera* scribble down; *boccone* gulp down; F **~ la pasta** put the pasta on; **buttarsi** throw o.s.; *fig* have a go (**in** at)

by-pass *m inv* by-pass

byte *m inv* INFOR byte

C

ca (= *circa*) ca (= circa)

c.a. (= *corrente alternata*) AC (= alternating current)

cabina *f* *di nave, aereo* cabin; *di ascensore, funivia* cage; **~ telefonica** phone box, *Am* pay phone

cabriolè, cabriolet *m inv* con-

vertible

cacao *m* cocoa

caccia *f* hunting; **cacciagione** *f* GASTR game; **cacciare** hunt; *(scacciare)* drive out; *(ficcare)* shove; **~ (via)** chase away; **cacciarsi**: **dove ti eri cacciato?** where did you get to?; **cacciatora** f: **alla ~** stewed; **cacciatore** m, **-trice** f hunter; **cacciavite** m inv screwdriver

cachemire m inv cashmere

cactus m inv cactus

cadavere m corpse

cadente stella f ~ falling star; **cadere** fall; di edificio fall down; di capelli, denti fall out; di aereo crash; **caduta** f fall

caffè m inv coffee; locale café; **~ corretto** espresso with a shot of alcohol; **~ macchiato** espresso with a splash of milk; **caffeina** f caffeine; **senza ~** caffeine-free; **caffellatte** m inv latte (hot milk with a small amount of coffee); **caffettiera** f (bricco) coffee pot; (macchinetta) coffee maker

cafone m boor

cagna f bitch

calabrese agg, m/f Calabrian

calabrone m hornet

calamari mpl squid

calamità f inv calamity; **~ naturale** natural disaster

calamita f magnet

calante luna f ~ waning moon; **calare 1** v/t lower **2** v/i di vento drop; di prezzi, sipario fall; di sole set, go down

calca f throng

calcagno m heel

calcare[1] (pigiare) press down; con i piedi tread; parole emphasize

calcare[2] m limestone

calcareo chalky

calce f lime

calcestruzzo m concrete

calciatore m football o soccer player

calcina f (malta) mortar; **calcinaccio** m (intonaco) bit of plaster; di muro bit of rubble

calcio[1] m kick; attività football, soccer; MIL butt; **~ di rigore** penalty kick

calcio[2] m CHIM calcium

calco m mould, Am mould

calcolare calculate; (valutare) weigh up; **calcolatore** m calculator; fig calculating person; elettronico computer; **calcolatrice** f calculator; **calcolo** m calculation

caldaia f boiler

caldarrosta f roast chestnut

caldo 1 agg warm; (molto caldo) hot **2** m warmth; molto caldo heat; **ho ~** I'm warm; I'm hot

calendario m calendar

calibro m calibre, Am caliber; TEC callipers

calice m goblet; REL chalice

calle f a Venezia lane

calligrafia f calligraphy

callo m corn

calma f calm; **prendersela con ~** take it easy; **calmante** m sedative; **calmare** calm; dolore soothe; **calmarsi** di dolore ease (off); **calmo** calm

calo m di peso loss; dei prezzi

drop, fall

calore *m* warmth; *intenso* heat

caloria *f* calorie

caloroso *fig* warm

calpestare walk on; *fig* trample over

calunnia *f* slander

calvario *m* REL Calvary; *fig* ordeal

calvizie *f* baldness; **calvo** bald

calza *f da donna* stocking; *da uomo* sock; **calzamaglia** *f* tights, *Am* pantyhose; *da ginnastica* leotard; **calzare 1** *v/t scarpe* put on; *(indossare)* wear **2** *v/i fig* fit; **calzascarpe** *m* shoehorn; **calzatoio** *m* shoehorn; **calzature** *fpl* footwear; **calzettone** *m* knee sock; **calzino** *m* sock; **calzolaio** *m* shoemaker

calzoncini *mpl* shorts; **~ da bagno** (swimming) trunks

calzone *m* GASTR folded-over pizza

calzoni *mpl* trousers, *Am* pants

camaleonte *m* chameleon

cambiale *f* bill (of exchange)

cambiamento *m* change; **cambiare 1** *v/t* change; *(scambiare)* exchange **2** *v/i e* **cambiarsi** change; **cambio** *m* change; FIN, *(scambio)* exchange; AUTO, TEC gear; *in ~* in exchange (*di* for)

camera *f* room; **~ da letto** bedroom; **~ singola** single

room; **~ matrimoniale** double room; **Camera dei Deputati** House of Commons, *Am* House of Representatives; **~ d'aria** inner tube; **~ dell'industria e del commercio** chamber of commerce; **camerata** *f stanza* dormitory; *in ospedale* ward

cameriera *f* waitress; *(domestica)* maid; **cameriere** *m* waiter

camerino *m* dressing room

camice *m di medico* white coat; *di chirurgo* gown; **camicetta** *f* blouse; **camicia** *f* shirt; **~ da notte** nightdress

caminetto *m* fireplace; **camino** *m* chimney; *(focolare)* fireplace

camion *m inv* truck, *Br anche* lorry; **camioncino** *m* van; **camionista** *m* lorry driver, *Am* truck driver

cammello *m* camel; *stoffa* camel hair

camminare walk; *(funzionare)* work, go; **camminata** *f* walk; **cammino** *m*: **un'ora di ~** an hour's walk; **mettersi in ~** set out

camomilla *f* camomile; *(infuso)* camomile tea

camoscio *m* chamois; **scarpe fpl di ~** suede shoes

campagna *f* country; *fig*, POL campaign

campana *f* bell; **campanello** *m* bell; *della porta* doorbell; **campanile** *m* bell tower

campare live

campeggiatore *m* camper; **campeggio** *m* camping; *posto* camp site; **camper** *m inv* camper van; **camping** *m* camp site

campionario *m* samples

campionato *m* championship

campione *m* sample; (*esemplare*) specimen; SP champion

campo *m* field; **~ da golf** golf course; **~ da calcio** football *o* soccer pitch; **~ da tennis** tennis court; **~ profughi** refugee camp; **camposanto** *m* cemetery

Canada *m* Canada; **canadese 1** *agg* Canadian **2** *m/f* Canadian **3** *f half-litre bottle of beer*

canale *m* channel; *artificiale* canal

canapa *f* hemp

canarino *m* canary

cancellare cross out; *con gomma* erase; INFOR delete; *appuntamento* cancel

cancellata *f* railings

cancelleria *f*: *articoli mpl di* **~** stationery

cancelliere *m* chancellor; DIR clerk of the court

cancello *m* gate

cancerogeno carcinogenic

cancrena *f* gangrene

cancro *m* MED cancer; ASTR **Cancro** Cancer

candeggina *f* bleach

candela *f* candle; **candelabro** *m* candelabra; **candeliere** *m* candlestick

candidarsi stand (for election), *Am* run; **candidato** *m*, **-a** *f* candidate; **candidatura** *f* candidacy, candidature

candido pure white; (*sincero*) frank; (*innocente*) innocent, pure; (*ingenuo*) naive

canditi *mpl* candied fruit

cane *m* dog

canestro *m* basket

canguro *m* kangaroo

canile *m* (*casotto*) kennel; *luogo* kennels

canino 1 *agg* dog *attr* **2** *m* (*dente*) canine (tooth)

canna *f* reed; (*bastone*) stick; P joint P; **~ da pesca** fishing rod

cannella *f* GASTR cinnamon

cannelloni *mpl* cannelloni *sg*

cannibale *m* cannibal

cannocchiale *m* telescope

cannone *m* MIL gun, cannon; (*asso*) ace

cannuccia *f* straw

canoa *f* canoe

canone *m* FIN rental (fee); RAD, TV licence (fee); (*norma*) standard

canottaggio *m* *a pagaie* canoeing; *a remi* rowing

canottiera *f* vest, *Am* undershirt

canotto *m* rowing boat, *Am* rowboat; **~ pneumatico** rubber dinghy

cantante *m/f* singer; **cantare** sing; **cantautore** *m*, **-trice** *f* singer-songwriter

cantiere *m* building site; MAR shipyard

cantina *f* cellar; *locale* wineshop

canto¹ *m* song; *(il cantare)* singing

canto² *m*: **d'altro ~** on the other hand

cantone *m* POL canton

canzonare tease

canzone *f* song

caos *m* chaos; **caotico** chaotic

C.A.P. *m* (= *Codice di Avviamento Postale*) postcode, *Am* zip code

capace *(abile)* capable; *(ampio)* large; **~ di fare qc** capable of doing sth; **capacità** *f inv* ability; *(capienza)* capacity

capanna *f* hut; **capannone** *m* shed; AVIA hangar

caparra *f* FIN deposit

capello *m* hair; **-i** *pl* hair

capezzolo *m* nipple

capiente large, capacious; **capienza** *f* capacity

capigliatura *f* hair

capillare MED capillary

capire understand; *capisco* I see; *ho capito* I see

capitale 1 *agg* capital; *fig* major **2** *f città* capital **3** *m* FIN capital; **capitalismo** *m* capitalism; **capitalista** *agg*, *m/f* capitalist

capitaneria *f*: **~ di porto** port authorities

capitano *m* captain

capitare *di avvenimento* happen; *di persona* find o.s.; **~ a proposito** come along at the right time

capitolo *m* chapter

capo *m* head; *persona* head, chief, boss; GEOG cape; **~ di vestiario** item of clothing; **da ~** from the beginning; **andare a ~** start a new paragraph; **capodanno** *m* New Year's Day; **capofamiglia** *m/f* head of the family; **capofitto**: **a ~** headlong; **capogiro** *m* dizzy spell; **capogruppo** *m/f* group leader; POL leader; **capolavoro** *m* masterpiece; **capolinea** *m* terminus; **capoluogo** *m* principal town; **caporeparto** *m/f di fabbrica* foreman; *donna* forewoman; *di ufficio* superintendent; **caposala** *m/f in ospedale* ward sister; *uomo* charge nurse; **capostazione** *m/f* station master; **capostipite** *m/f* founder; **capotavola**: **a ~** at the head of the table; **capotreno** *m/f* guard, *Am* conductor; **capoufficio** *m/f* supervisor; **capoverso** *m* paragraph; TIP indent; **capovolgere** turn upside down; *piani* upset; *situazione* reverse; **capovolgersi** turn upside down; *di barca* capsize; **capovolgimento**

m complete change; **capovolto** *pp* ⊳ **capovolgere**

cappa *f* (*mantello*) cloak; *di cucina* hood; **~ del camino** cowl

cappella *f* chapel

cappelletti *mpl* pasta, shaped like little hats, with meat, cheese and egg filling; **cappello** *m* hat

cappero *m* caper

cappio *m* noose

cappone *m* capon

cappotto *m* coat

cappuccino *m* bevanda cappuccino

cappuccio *m* hood; *di penna* top, cap

capra *f* (*nanny*)goat; (*cavalletto*) trestle; **capretto** *m* kid

capriccio *m* whim; *di bambini* tantrum; **fare i ~i** have tantrums; **capriccioso** capricious; *bambino* naughty; *tempo* changeable

Capricorno ASTR Capricorn

capriola *f* somersault

capriolo *m* roe deer; GASTR venison; **capro** *m* billy goat; **~ espiatorio** scapegoat

capsula *f* capsule; *di dente* crown

captare RAD pick up

carabiniere *m* police officer

caraffa *f* carafe

caramella *f* sweet

caramello *m* caramel

carato *m* carat

carattere *m* character; (*caratteristica*) characteristic; **-i** *pl*

TIP font; **caratteristica** *f* characteristic; **caratteristico** characteristic; **caratterizzare** characterize

caravan *m inv* caravan

carboidrato *m* carbohydrate

carbone *m* coal; **carbonella** *f* charcoal

carburante *m* fuel

carburatore *m* carburettor, *Am* carburetor

carcassa *f* carcass; TEC (*intelaiatura*) frame; MAR wreck

carcerato *m*, **-a** *f* prisoner; **carcerazione** *f* imprisonment; **~ preventiva** preventive detention; **carcere** *m* jail, prison

carciofo *m* artichoke

cardiaco cardiac, heart *attr*

cardinale *m/agg* cardinal

cardiologo *m*, **-a** *f* heart specialist, cardiologist

cardo *m* thistle

carena *f* MAR keel

carenza *f* lack (**di** of)

carestia *f* shortage

carezza *f* caress; **carezzare** caress

cariato: **dente** *m* **~** decayed tooth

carica *f* (*incarico*) office; (*slancio, energia*) drive; TEC load; MIL (*attacco*) charge; SP tackle; **caricabatteria** *m* TEL charger

caricare load; MIL charge; *orologio* wind up; **caricarsi** overload o.s. (**di** with)

caricatura *f* caricature

carico 1 *agg* loaded; EL charged **2** *m* load; MAR cargo

carie *f inv* tooth decay

carino (*grazioso*) pretty; (*gentile*) nice

carisma *m* charisma

carità *f* charity

carnagione *f* complexion

carne *f* flesh; GASTR meat; ~ **di maiale** | **manzo** pork | beef; ~ **tritata** mince, *Am* ground beef; **carneficina** *f* slaughter

carnevale *m* carnival

carnivoro *m* carnivore

caro 1 *agg* dear; (*costoso*) dear, expensive **2** *avv* a lot; **costare** ~ be very expensive; *fig* have a high price

carogna *f* carrion; F swine

carota *f* carrot

carotide *f* carotid artery

carovana *f* caravan

carovita *m* high cost of living; **indennità** *f* **di** ~ cost of living allowance

carpa *f* carp

carpire: ~ *qc a qu* get sth out of s.o.

carponi on all fours

carrabile ☞ **carraio**

carraio: **passo** *m* ~ driveway

carreggiata *f* roadway

carrello *m* trolley, *Am* cart; AVIA undercarriage

carretto *m* cart

carriera *f* career

carriola *f* wheelbarrow

carro *m* cart; AST Bear; ~ **ar-mato** tank; ~ **attrezzi** tow truck, *Am* wrecker

carrozza *f* FERR carriage, *Am* car; ~ **con cuccette** sleeping car; ~ **ristorante** restaurant car

carrozzella *f* **per bambini** pram, *Am* baby carriage; **per invalidi** wheelchair

carrozzeria *f* bodywork, coachwork; **carrozziere** *m* AUTO (*progettista*) (car) designer; (*costruttore*) coachbuilder; **chi fa riparazioni** panel beater; **carrozzina** *f* pram, *Am* baby carriage

carta *f* paper; (*menù*) menu; ~ **geografica** map; ~ **da gioco** (playing) card; ~ **da parati** wallpaper ~ **di credito** credit card; ~ **d'identità** identity card; ~ **d'imbarco** boarding card; ~ **igienica** toilet paper; ~ **stagnola** silver paper; GASTR tinfoil; ~ **telefonica** phone card; **cartamodello** *m* pattern; **cartapesta** *f* papier-mâché; **cartastraccia** *f* waste paper

cartella *f* (*borsa*) briefcase; *di alunno* schoolbag; *per documenti* folder, file; **cartellino** *m* (*etichetta*) label; *con prezzo* price tag; (*scheda*) card

cartello *m* sign; *nelle dimostrazioni* placard; FIN cartel; ~ **stradale** road sign

cartellone *m* **pubblicitario** hoarding, *Am* billboard; TEA bill

cartiera f paper mill
cartilagine f cartilage
cartina f GEOG map; (*bustina*) packet; *per sigarette* cigarette paper
cartoccio m paper bag; *a cono* bag paper cone; GASTR **al ~** baked in tinfoil
cartoleria f stationer's, Am stationery store
cartolina f postcard
cartoncino m (thin) cardboard; (*biglietto*) card
cartone m cardboard; **-i pl animati** cartoons
cartuccia f cartridge
casa f edificio house; (*abitazione*) home; **~ di cura** nursing home; **~ editrice** publishing house; **cambiare ~** move (house); **fatto in ~** homemade; **andare a ~** go home; **essere a ~** be at home; SP **giocare in / fuori ~** play at home / away; **casalinga** f housewife; **casalingo** domestic; (*fatto in casa*) home-made; **persona** home-loving; **-ghi** mpl household goods
cascare fall (down); fig **cascarci** fall for it; **cascata** f waterfall
cascina f (*casa colonica*) farmhouse; (*caseificio*) dairy farm
casco m helmet; *dal parrucchiere* hair dryer
caseggiato m (*edificio*) block of flats, Am apartment

block
caseificio m dairy
casella f di schedario pigeonhole; (*quadratino*) square; **~ postale** post office box; **~ sellario** m pigeon holes; **~ giudiziario** criminal records (office); **casello** m autostradale toll booth, pay station
casereccio homemade
caserma f barracks
casinò m inv casino
casino m P brothel; (*rumore*) din, racket; (*disordine*) mess
caso m case; (*destino*) chance; (*occasione*) opportunity; **~ d'emergenza** emergency; **per ~** by chance; **a ~** at random; **in ~ contrario** should that not be the case; **in ogni ~** in any case, anyway; **in nessun ~** under no circumstances
casolare m farmhouse
caspita! good heavens!
cassa f case; *di legno* crate; *di negozio* till; *sportello* cash desk; (*banca*) bank; **~ toracica** ribcage; **cassaforte** f safe; **cassapanca** f chest
casseruola f (sauce)pan
cassetta f box; *per frutta, verdura* crate; (*musicassetta*) cassette; **~ delle lettere** (*buca*) post box, Am mailbox; (*casella*) letterbox, Am mailbox
cassetto m drawer; **cassettone** m chest of drawers
cassiere m, **-a** f cashier; *di*

banca teller; *di supermercato* checkout assistant

cassonetto *m* dustbin, *Am* garbage can

casta *f* caste

castagna *f* chestnut; **castagno** *m* chestnut (tree)

castano *capelli* chestnut; *occhi* brown

castello *m* castle

castigo *m* punishment

castità *f* chastity

castoro *m* beaver

castrare castrate; *gatto* neuter; *femmina di animale* spay

casual 1 *agg* casual **2** *m* casual clothes, casual wear; **casuale** chance *attr*, casual

cataclisma *m* disaster

catacomba *f* catacomb

catalizzatore *m* catalyst; AUTO catalytic converter

catalogare catalogue, *Am* catalog; **catalogo** *m* catalogue, *Am* catalog

catapecchia *f* shack

catarifrangente *m* reflector; *lungo la strada* cat's eye, *Am* reflector

catarro *m* catarrh

catasto *m* land register

catastrofe *f* catastrophe; **catastrofico** catastrophic

categoria *f* category; *di albergo* class; **categorico** categoric(al)

catena *f* chain; **-e** *pl* **da neve** snow chains; **~ montuosa** mountain range, chain of mountains

cateratta *f* sluice(gate); (*cascata*) falls

catino *m* basin

catrame *m* tar

cattedra *f* (*scrivania*) desk

cattedrale *f* cathedral

cattiveria *f* wickedness; *di bambini* naughtiness; *azione* nasty thing to do; *parole crudeli* nasty thing to say; **cattivo** bad; *bambino* naughty, bad

cattolicesimo *m* (Roman) Catholicism; **cattolico 1** *agg* (Roman) Catholic **2** *m*, **-a** *f* (Roman) Catholic

cattura *f* capture; (*arresto*) arrest; **catturare** capture; (*arrestare*) arrest

caucciù *m* rubber

causa *f* cause; (*motivo*) reason; DIR lawsuit; **a ~ di** because of; **causare** cause

cautela *f* caution; (*precauzione*) precaution; **cauto** cautious; **cauzione** *f* (*deposito*) security; *per la libertà provvisoria* bail

cava *f* quarry

cavalcare ride; **cavalcavia** *m inv* flyover, *Am* overpass; **cavalcioni: a ~** astride; **cavaliere** *m* rider; *accompagnatore* escort; *al ballo* partner

cavalla *f* mare; **cavalletta** *f* grasshopper; **cavalletto** *m* trestle; FOT tripod; *da pittore* easel; **cavallo** *m* horse; *scacchi* knight; *dei pantaloni* crotch; **andare a ~** go riding;

cavallone m breaker; **cavalluccio** m: ~ **marino** sea horse

cavare take out; **cavarsela** manage, get by; **cavarsi da un impiccio** get out of trouble; **cavatappi** m inv corkscrew

caverna f cave

cavia f guinea pig (anche fig)

caviale m caviar

caviglia f ANAT ankle

cavillo m quibble

cavità f inv cavity

cavo 1 agg hollow **2** m cable; (fune) rope

cavolfiore m cauliflower

cavolo m cabbage; ~ **di Bruxelles** Brussels sprout

cazzo m V prick V; ~! fuck! V

CC (= **Carabinieri**) Italian police force

cc (= **centimetri cubici**) cc (= cubic centimetres)

c.c. (= **corrente continua**) DC (= direct current)

c/c (= **conto corrente**) current account, Am checking account

CD m inv CD; **lettore** m ~ CD player; **CD-Rom** m inv CD-Rom; **drive** m **per** ~ CD-Rom drive

ce = **ci** (before lo, la, li, le, ne) **c'è there is**

cecchino m sniper

cece m chickpea

ceco 1 agg Czech **2** m, -a f Czech

cedere 1 v/t (dare) hand over,

give up; (vendere) sell; ~ **il posto** give up one's seat **2** v/i give in, surrender (**a** to); muro, terreno collapse, give way; **non** ~! don't give in!

cedola f coupon

cedro m **del Libano** cedar

ceffone m slap

celebrare celebrate; **celebrazione** f celebration; **celebre** famous; **celebrità** f inv fame; persona celebrity

celeste sky blue; (divino) heavenly (anche fig)

celibato m celibacy; **celibe 1** agg single, unmarried **2** m bachelor

cella f cell

cellula f cell; **cellulare 1** agg cell attr; **telefono** m ~ mobile (phone), Am cell(ular) phone **2** m prison van; telefono mobile, Am cell (phone); ~ **con fotocamera** camera phone

cellulite f cellulite

cemento m cement; ~ **armato** reinforced concrete

cena f supper, evening meal; importante, con ospiti dinner; **cenacolo** m PITT Last Supper; **cenare** have supper; formalmente dine

cencio m rag; per spolverare duster; **bianco come un** ~ white as a sheet

cenere f ash; **le Ceneri** fpl Ash Wednesday

cenno m sign; della mano

wave; *del capo* nod; *con gli occhi* wink; *(breve notizia)* mention; *(allusione)* hint

cenone *m* feast, banquet

censimento *m* census

censura *f* censorship; **censurare** censor

centenario 1 *agg* hundred-year-old **2** *m persona* centenarian; *anniversario* centenary, *Am* centennial; **centesimo 1** *agg* hundredth **2** *m* FIN cent

centigrado *m* centigrade; **centimetro** *m* centimetre, *Am* centimeter; **~ cubo** cubic centimetre; **~ quadrato** square centimetre; **centinaio** *m* hundred; **un ~ di** about a hundred; **cento** hundred; **per ~** per cent

centrale 1 *agg* central **2** *f* station, plant; **centralinista** *m/f* switchboard operator; **centralino** *m* switchboard; **centrare** centre, *Am* center; **il bersaglio** hit the bull's eye

centrifuga 1 *agg* centrifugal **2** *f* spin-dryer; *GASTR* centrifuge; **centrifugare** spin-dry; TEC centrifuge

centro *m* centre, *Am* center; *di bersaglio* bull's-eye; **~ commerciale** shopping centre, *Am* downtown; **~ storico** old (part of) town

ceppo *m*: **~ bloccaruota** wheel clamp, *Am* Denver boot

cera *f* wax; *per lucidare* polish

ceramica *f* ceramics *sg*; *oggetto* piece of pottery

cerata *f* oilskins

cerca *f*: **in ~ di ...** in search of ...; **cercare 1** *v/t* look for **2** *v/i*: **~ di fare** try to do

cerchio *m* circle; **cerchione** *m* TEC rim

cereale 1 *agg* grain *attr* **2** **-i** *mpl* grain, cereals

cerebrale: **commozione ~** concussion

cerimonia *f* ceremony; REL service; **-e** *pl (convenevoli)* pleasantries

cerino *m* (wax) match

cernia *f* grouper

cerniera *f* hinge; **~ lampo** zip (fastener), *Am* zipper

cernita *f* selection, choice

cero *m* (large) candle

cerotto *m* (sticking) plaster, *Am* Bandaid®

certezza *f* certainty

certificare certify; **certificato** *m* certificate

certo 1 *agg (sicuro)* certain, sure; **un ~ signor Federici** a (certain) Mr Federici; **ci vuole un ~ coraggio** it takes (some) courage; **di una -a età** of a certain age; **-i** some **2** *avv (certamente)* certainly; *(naturalmente)* of course; **~ che ...** surely ... **3** *pron*: **-i**, **-e** some, some people

certosa *f* Carthusian monastery

cervello *m* brain; GASTR brains

cervo m deer; *carne* venison

cesareo: taglio m ~ Caesarean, *Am* Cesarean

cesoie *fpl* shears

cespuglio m bush, shrub

cessare stop, cease; **cessate il fuoco** m ceasefire; **cessazione** f *di contratto* termination

cessione f transfer, handover

cesso m P bog P, *Am* john F

cesta f basket

cestinare throw away, bin F; **cestino** m little basket; *per la carta* wastepaper basket, *Am* waste basket; **cesto** m basket

ceto m (social) class; **~ medio** middle class

cetriolino m gherkin; **cetriolo** m cucumber

che 1 *agg* what; **a ~ cosa serve?** what is that for?; **~ brutta giornata!** what a filthy day! **2** *pron persona: soggetto* who; *persona: oggetto* who, that, *fml* whom; *cosa* that, which; **ciò ~** what; **non c'è di ~** don't mention it; you're welcome **3** *cong dopo il comparativo* than

check-in m *inv* check-in

chemioterapia f chemotherapy, chemo F

chi who; **di ~ è il libro?** whose book is this? **a ~ ha venduto la casa?** who did he sell the house to?; **c'è ~ dice che** some people say that; **~ ... ~** some ... others

chiacchiera f chat; (*maldicenza*) gossip; (*notizia infondata*) rumour, *Am* rumor; **chiacchierare** chat, chatter; *spreg* gossip; **chiacchierata** f chat; **chiacchierone 1** *agg* talkative, chatty; (*pettegolo*) gossipy **2** m, **-a** f chatterbox; (*pettegolo*) gossip

chiamare call; **andare a ~ qu** go and get s.o., fetch s.o.; **chiamarsi** be called; **come ti chiami?** what's your name?; **mi chiamo ...** my name is ...; **chiamata** f call; TELEC (telephone) call, (phone)call

chiara f egg white; **chiarezza** f clarity; **chiarimento** m clarification; **chiarire** clarify; **chiarirsi** become clear; **chiaro** clear; *colore* light, pale; (*luminoso*) bright; **~!** obviously!; **chiaroscuro** m chiaroscuro

chiasso m din, racket; **fare ~** make a din *o* racket; **chiassoso** noisy

chiatta f barge; **ponte m di -e** pontoon bridge

chiave 1 *agg inv* key **2** f key; MUS clef; **~ inglese** spanner, *Am* monkey wrench; **chiavistello** m bolt

chiazza f (*macchia*) stain; *sulla pelle, di colore* patch

chic *inv* chic, stylish

chicco m grain; *di caffè* bean; **~ d'uva** grape

chiedere *per sapere* ask (*di*

about); *per avere* ask for; (*esigere*) demand, require; **~** *qc a qu* ask s.o. sth; **~** *di qu* (*chiedere notizie di*) ask about s.o.; *per parlargli* ask for s.o.; **~** *un piacere a qu* ask s.o. a favour; **~** *scusa a qu* apologize to s.o.; **chiedersi** wonder (*se* whether)

chiesa *f* church

chiesto *pp* ☞ **chiedere**

chiglia *f* MAR keel

chilo *m* kilo; **chilogrammo** *m* kilogram; **chilometraggio** *m* AUTO mileage; **chilometro** *m* kilometre, *Am* kilometer; **-i** *pl* **all'ora** kilometres per hour

chilowatt *m inv* kilowatt

chimica *f* chemistry; **chimico 1** *agg* chemical **2** *m*, **-a** *f* chemist

chinare *testa* bend; *occhi* lower; **chinarsi** stoop, bend down

chincaglierie *fpl* knick-knacks

chioccia *f fig* mother hen

chiocciola *f* snail; *in indirizzo e-mail* at; **scala** *f* **a ~** spiral staircase

chiodato: SP **scarpe** *fpl* **~** spikes

chiodo *m* nail

chioma *f* mane; *di cometa* tail

chiosco *m* kiosk

chiostro *m* cloister

chiromante *m/f* palmist

chirurgia *f* surgery; **chirurgo** *m* surgeon

chissà who knows; (*forse*) maybe

chitarra *f* guitar; **chitarrista** *m/f* guitarist

chiudere close, shut; *a chiave* lock; *strada* close off; *gas, luce* turn off; *fabbrica, negozio per sempre* shut down; **chiudersi** *di porta, ombrello* close, shut; *di ferita* heal up

chiunque anyone; *relativo* whoever; **~** *lo vede* whoever sees it

chiuso 1 *pp* ☞ **chiudere 2** *agg* closed, shut; *a chiave* locked; *persona* reserved; **chiusura** *f* closing, shutting

choc *m inv* shock

ci 1 *pron* ◇ us; *non* **~** *ha parlato* he didn't speak to us; **~** *siamo divertiti molto* we had a great time; **~** *vogliamo bene* we love each other ◇: **~** *penso* I'm thinking about it **2** *avv* here; (*lì*) there; *c'è* **...** there is ...; **~** *sono* **...** there are ...

ciabatta *f* slipper

cialda *f* wafer

ciambella *f* GASTR type of cake, baked in a ring-shaped mould; (*salvagente*) lifebelt

cianfrusaglia *f* knick-knack

ciao! hi!; *nel congedarsi* bye!

ciarpame *m* junk

ciascuno ~ 1 *agg* each; (*ogni*) every **2** *pron* everyone

ciber..., **ciber-**

cibo *m* food; **-i** *pl* foodstuffs, foods; **~** *pronto* fast food

cicala f insetto cicada

cicalino m buzzer, bleeper

cicatrice f scar; **cicatrizzare, cicatrizzarsi** heal

cicca f (mozzicone) stub, butt; (gomma da masticare) (chewing) gum

ciccia f (grasso) flab; **ciccione** m, **-a** f fatty

ciclamino m cyclamen

ciclismo m cycling; **ciclista** m/f cyclist; **ciclistico** bike attr, cycle attr; **ciclo** m cycle; **ciclomotore** m moped

ciclone m cyclone

cicloturismo m cycling holidays

cicogna f stork

cicoria f chicory

cieco 1 agg blind; **vicolo** m ~ dead end, blind alley **2** m, **-a** f blind man; **donna** f blind woman

cielo m sky; REL heaven; **grazie al** ~ thank heavens

cifra f figure; (monogramma) monogram; (somma) amount, sum; (codice) cipher, code

ciglio m ANAT eyelash; (bordo) edge

cigno m swan

cigolare squeak; **cigolio** m squeak

Cile m Chile

cilecca: **far** ~ di arma da fuoco misfire

cileno 1 agg Chilean **2** m, **-a** f Chilean

ciliegia f cherry; **ciliegio** m cherry (tree)

cilindro m cylinder; cappello top hat

cima f top; **in** ~ **a** on top of; **da** ~ **a fondo** from top to bottom; fig from beginning to end

cimentarsi: ~ **in** embark on

ciminiera f smokestack

cimitero m cemetery

cin cin! F cheers!

Cina f China

cineforum m inv film followed by a discussion; club film club

cinema m inv cinema, luogo cinema, Am movie theater; **cinematografico** film attr, movie attr

cinepresa f cine-camera

cinese agg, m/f Chinese

cinghia f strap; (cintura) belt

cinghiale m wild boar

cinguettare twitter

cinico 1 agg cynical **2** m **-a** f cynic; **cinismo** m cynicism

cinquanta fifty; **cinquantenne** m/f 50-year-old; **cinquantesimo** fiftieth; **cinquantina** f: **una** ~ **di** about 50; **cinque** five; **cinquecento 1** agg five hundred **2** m: **il Cinquecento** the sixteenth century; **cinquemila** five thousand

cintura f belt; (vita) waist; ~ **di sicurezza** seatbelt; **cinturino** m strap

ciò (questo) this; (quello) that; ~ **che** what; ~ **nonostante**

nevertheless

ciocca f _di capelli_ lock

cioccolata f chocolate; **cioc-colatino** m chocolate; **cioc-colato** m chocolate

cioè that is, i.e.

ciondolo m pendant

ciotola f bowl

ciottolo m pebble

cipolla f onion; _di pianta_ bulb; **cipollina** f small onion

cipresso m cypress (tree)

cipria f (face) powder

circa about

circo m circus

circolare 1 v/i circulate; _di persone_ move along **2** agg circular **3** f _lettera_ circular; **circolazione** f traffic; MED circulation; **mettere in ~** _voci_ spread

circolo m circle; (_club_) club

circondare surround

circonferenza f circumference

circonvallazione f ring road, Am beltway

circoscrizione f area, district; **~ elettorale** constituency

circostante surrounding; **circostanza** f circumstance; (_occasione_) occasion

circuito m SP (_percorso_) track; EL circuit; EL **corto ~** short circuit

cisterna f cistern; (_serbatoio_) tank; **nave** f ~ tanker

cisti f cyst; **cistifellea** f gall bladder; **cistite** f cystitis

citare quote; _come esempio_ cite, quote; DIR _testimone_ summons; **citazione** f quotation, quote; DIR summons _sg_

citofono m entry phone; _in uffici_ intercom

città f inv town; _grande_ city; **Città del Vaticano** Vatican City; **cittadina** f (small) town; **cittadinanza** f citizenship; (_popolazione_) citizens; **cittadino 1** agg town attr, city attr **2** m, -a f citizen; (_abitante di città_) city dweller

ciuccio m F (_succhiotto_) dummy, Am pacifier

ciuffo m tuft

civetta f ZO (little) owl; fig **far la ~** flirt

civico _della città_ municipal, town attr, _delle persone_ civic

civile 1 agg civil; _civilizzato_ civilized; (_non militare_) civilian **2** m civilian; **civiltà** f inv civilization

clacson m inv horn

clamoroso fig sensational

clandestino 1 agg clandestine; (_illegale_) illegal **2** m, -a f stowaway

clarinetto m clarinet

classe f class; (_aula_) classroom

classico 1 agg classical; (_tipico_) classic **2** m classic

classifica f classification; (_elenco_) list; _sportiva_ league standings, league table; _musicale_ charts; **classificare**

classify; **classificatore** *m* (*cartella*) folder; *mobile* filing cabinet, *Am* file cabinet

classismo *m* class consciousness

clausola *f* clause; (*riserva*) proviso

claustrofobia *f* claustrophobia

clavicola *f* collar-bone

clero *m* clergy

clessidra *f* hourglass

cliccare INFOR click (**su** on); **~ due volte** double-click

cliché *m inv* fig cliché

cliente *m/f* customer; *di professionista* client; *di albergo* guest; MED patient; **clientela** *f* customers, clientele; *di professionista* clients; *di medico* patients

clima *m* climate; **climatico** climate *attr*, climatic; **stazione** *f* **climatica** health resort

clinica *f* (*ospedale*) clinic; (*casa di cura*) nursing home; **clinico 1** *agg* clinical **2** *m* clinician

clip *m inv* clip

clonare BIO clone; **clonazione** *f* cloning; **clone** *m* clone

cloro *m* chlorine

clorofilla *f* chlorophyll(l)

cloroformio *m* chloroform

club *m inv* club

coabitare share a flat *o Am* an apartment

coagularsi *di sangue* coagulate, clot; *di latte* curdle; **coalizione** *f* coalition; **governo** *m* **di ~** coalition government; **coalizzarsi** join forces; POL form a coalition

cobra *m inv* cobra

cocaina *f* cocaine

coccinella *f* ladybird, *Am* ladybug

coccio *m* earthenware; *frammento* fragment (of pottery); **cocciuto** stubborn, obstinate

cocco *m albero* coconut palm

coccodrillo *m* crocodile

coccolare F cuddle; (*viziare*) spoil

cocktail *m inv* cocktail; *festa* cocktail party

cocomero *m* water melon

coda *f tail*; (*fila*) queue, *Am* line; *di veicolo, treno* rear; MUS coda; **fare la ~** queue (up), *Am* stand in line

codardo 1 *agg* cowardly **2** *m*, **-a** *f* coward

codice *m* code; **~ di avviamento postale** postcode, *Am* zip code; **~ fiscale** tax code; **~ segreto** PIN; **codificare** *dati* encode; DIR codify

codino *m* pigtail, plait, *Am* braid

coerente coherent; *fig* consistent; **coerenza** *f* coherence; *fig* consistency

coetaneo 1 *agg* the same age (**di**) as **2** *m*, **-a** *f* contemporary

cofanetto *m* casket

cofano *m* AUTO bonnet, *Am* hood

cogliere pick; *(raccogliere)* gather; *(afferrare)* seize; *occasione* take, seize; *(capire)* grasp

cognac *m inv* cognac

cognato *m*, **-a** *f* brother-in-law; *donna* sister-in-law

cognizione *f* knowledge; *filosofia* cognition; **parla con ~ di causa** he knows what he's talking about

cognome *m* surname, family name

coi = **con** and *art* **i**

coincidenza *f* coincidence; FERR connection; **coincidere** coincide

coinquilino *m*, **-a** *f* in *condominio* fellow tenant; *in appartamento* flatmate, *Am* roommate

coinvolgere involve; **coinvolto** *pp* ☞ **coinvolgere**

col = **con** and *art* **il**

colapasta *m inv* colander

colare **1** *v/t* strain; *pasta* drain **2** *v/i* drip; *(perdere)* leak; *di naso* run; *di cera* melt; **~ a fondo** *o* **a picco** sink, go down; **colazione** *f* **prima** breakfast; *di mezzogiorno* lunch; **far ~** have breakfast

colei *pron f* the one; **~ che** the one that

colera *m* cholera

colesterolo *m* cholesterol

colica *f* colic

colino *m* strainer

colla *f* glue; *di farina* paste

collaborare co-operate, collaborate; *con giornale* contribute; **collaboratore** *m*, **-trice** *f* collaborator; *di giornale* contributor; **collaborazione** *f* co-operation, collaboration

collana *f* necklace; *di libri* series *sg*

collant *m inv* tights, *Am* pantyhose

collare *m* collar

collasso *m* collapse

collaudare test; *fig* put to the test; **collaudo** *m* test

colle *m* hill; *(valico)* pass

collega *m/f* colleague, co-worker

collegamento *m* connection; MIL liaison; RAD, TV link; **collegare** connect, link; **collegarsi** RAD, TV link up

collegio *m* boarding school

collera *f* anger; **essere in ~ con qu** be angry with s.o.

colletta *f* collection; **collettività** *f* community; **collettivo** *m/agg* collective

colletto *m* collar

collezionare collect; **collezione** *f* collection; **fare ~ di qc** collect sth; **collezionista** *m/f* collector; **~ di francobolli** stamp collector

collina *f* hill

collirio *m* eyewash

collisione *f* collision

collo *m* neck; *(bagaglio)* piece of luggage; *(pacco)* package

collocamento *m* placing; *(impiego)* employment;

agenzia f **di ~** employment agency; **collocare** place, put

colloquiale colloquial

colloquio m talk, conversation; *ufficiale* interview; (*esame*) oral (exam)

colluttazione f scuffle

colmare fill (*di* with); fig: *di gentilezze* overwhelm (*di* with); **colmo** full (*di* of)

colomba f ZO, fig dove

colombo m pigeon

colon m colon

colonia f colony; *per bambini* holiday camp; *Am* summer camp; **colonizzare** colonize

colonna f column; **~ vertebrale** spinal column; **colonnato** m colonnade

colonnello m colonel

colorante m dye; **senza -i** with no artificial colouring *o Am* coloring; **colorare** colour, *Am* color; *disegno* colour in; **colorato** coloured, *Am* colored; **colore** m colour, *Am* color; *carte* suit; **a -i** *film, televisione* colour *attr*; **colorito 1** *agg volto* rosy-cheeked; fig (*vivace*) colourful, *Am* colorful **2** m complexion

coloro *pron pl* the ones; **~ che** those who

colossale colossal

colpa f fault; REL sin; **dare a qu la ~ di qc** blame s.o. for sth; **per ~ tua** because of you; **colpevole 1** *agg* guilty **2** *m/f* culprit, guilty party

colpire hit, strike; fig impress; **colpo** m blow; *di pistola* shot; MED stroke; **~ di telefono** phonecall; **di ~** suddenly

coltellata f *ferita* stab wound; **coltello** m knife

coltivare AGR, fig cultivate; **coltivazione** f cultivation; *di prodotti agricoli e piante* growing; *campi coltivati* crops

colto[1] cultured, learned

colto[2] *pp* **~ cogliere**

coltura f growing; *piante* crop

colui *pron* **~ che** the one; **~ che** the one that

coma m coma

comandante m commander; AVIA, MAR captain; **comandare 1** *v/t* (*ordinare*) order, command; *esercito* command; *nave* captain, be captain of; TEC control **2** *v/i* be in charge; **comando** m order, command; TEC control

combaciare fit together; fig correspond

combattere fight; **combattimento** m fight

combinare combine; (*organizzare*) arrange; **~ un guaio** make a mess; **combinazione** f combination; (*coincidenza*) coincidence; **per ~** by chance

combustibile 1 *agg* combustible **2** m fuel

come 1 *avv* as; (*in modo simile o uguale*) like; *interrogativo, esclamativo* how; (*prego?*)

pardon?, *Am* pardon me?; *fa'* ~ *ti ho detto* do as I told you; ~ *me* like me; *un cappello* ~ *il mio* a hat like mine; ~ *sta?* how are you?; ~ *mai?* how come?, why?; ~ *se* as if 2 *cong* (*come se*) as if, as though; (*appena, quando,*) as (soon as)

cometa *f* comet

comfort *m inv* comfort; *dotato di tutti i* ~ *moderni* with all mod cons

comico 1 *agg* funny, comical; *genere comic* 2 *m, -a f* comedian; *donna* comedienne

comignolo *m* chimney pot

cominciare start, begin (*a* to)

comitato *m* committee; ~ *direttivo* steering committee; **comitiva** *f* group, party

comizio *m* meeting

commedia *f* comedy; *fig* playacting; **commediografo** *m, -a f* playwright

commemorare commemorate; **commemorazione** *f* commemoration

commentare comment on; **commento** *m* comment

commerciale commercial; *relazioni, trattative* trade *attr*; *lettera* business *attr*; **commercialista** *m/f* accountant; **commercializzare** market; **commerciante** *m/f* merchant; (*negoziante*) shopkeeper, *Am* storekeeper; **commercio** *m* trade, business; *di droga* traffic; *essere*

in ~ be available

commesso *m, -a f* shop assistant, *Am* sales clerk

commestibile 1 *agg* edible **2** *-i mpl* foodstuffs

commettere commit; *errore* make

commiserare feel sorry for

commissariato *m*: ~ (*di pubblica sicurezza*) police station; **commissario** *m di polizia* police superintendent, *Am* police chief; *membro di commissione* commissioner

commissione *f* commission; (*incarico*) errand; *-i pl* shopping

commosso 1 *pp* ← **commuovere 2** *agg fig* moved, touched

commovente moving, touching; **commozione** *f* emotion; ~ *cerebrale* concussion; **commuovere** move, touch; **commuoversi** be moved *o* touched

comò *m inv* chest of drawers; **comodino** *m* bedside table

comodità *f inv* comfort; (*vantaggio*) convenience

comodo 1 *agg* comfortable; (*facilmente raggiungibile*) easy to get to; (*utile*) useful, handy; F *persona* laidback F; *stia* ~! don't get up! **2** *m* comfort; *con* ~ at one's convenience; *far* ~ *di denaro* come in useful; *le fa* ~ *così* she finds it easier that way;

fare il propio ~ do as one pleases

compagnia *f* company; (*gruppo*) group; ~ *aerea* airline; *far* ~ *a qu* keep s.o. company

compagno *m*, -*a f* companion; (*convivente*) partner; POL comrade; ~ *di scuola* schoolfriend

comparativo *m*/*agg* comparative

comparire appear; (*far figura*) stand out; comparizione *f*: DIR *mandato m di* ~ summons *sg*; **comparsa** *f* appearance; TEA person with a walk-on part; *in film* extra; **comparso** *pp* ☞ *comparire*

compartimento *m* compartment

compassione *f* compassion, pity; *provare* ~ *per qu* feel sorry for s.o.

compasso *m* compass

compatibile compatible; **compatibilità** *f* compatibility

compatire: ~ *qu* feel sorry for s.o.

compatto compact; *folla* dense; *fig* united

compensare (*controbilanciare*) compensate for, make up for; (*ricompensare*) reward; (*risarcire*) pay compensation to; **compenso** *m* (*ricompensa*, *risarcimento*) compensation; (*retribuzione*)

fee; *in* ~ (*d'altra parte*) on the other hand

compera *f* purchase; *fare le* -*e* go shopping

competente competent; (*responsabile*) appropriate; **competenza** *f* (*esperienza*) competence; *essere di* ~ *di qu* be s.o.'s responsibility

competere (*gareggiare*) compete; **competitivo** competitive; **competizione** *f* competition

compiacere please; **compiacersi** (*provare piacere*) be pleased (*di* with); **compiaciuto** ☞ *compiacere*

compiangere pity; *per lutto* mourn; **compianto** *pp* ☞ *compiangere*

compiere (*finire*) complete, finish; (*eseguire*) carry out; ~ *gli anni* have one's birthday

compilare compile; *modulo* complete

compito *m* task; EDU *i* -*i pl* homework

compiuto *lavoro, opera* completed, finished; *ha 10 anni* -*i* he's 10

compleanno *m* birthday; *buon* ~! happy birthday!

complementare complementary; **complemento** *m* complement; GRAM object

complessato full of complexes, uptight F; **complessivo** all-in; **complesso 1** *agg* complex **2** *m* complex;

MUS group; *di circostanze* set, combination; **in** *o* **nel ~** on the whole

completare complete; **completo 1** *agg* complete; (*pieno*) full; TEA sold out **2** *m* set; (*vestito*) suit; **al ~** (*pieno*) full (up); TEA sold out

complicare complicate; **complicarsi** get complicated; **complicato** complicated; **complicazione** *f* complication

complice *m/f* DIR accomplice

complimentarsi: ~ con qu congratulate s.o. (**per** on); **complimento** *m* compliment; **-i!** congratulations!; **non fare -i!** help yourself!

componente 1 *m* component **2** *m/f* (*persona*) member; **componibile** modular; *cucina* fitted; **comporre** (*mettere in ordine*) arrange; MUS compose; **~ un numero** dial a number

comportamento *m* behaviour, *Am* behavior; **comportare** involve; **comportarsi** behave

compositore *m*, **-trice** *f* composer; **composizione** *f* composition; *di fiori* arrangement; DIR settlement

composto 1 *pp* ☞ **comporre 2** *agg* compound; *abiti, capelli* tidy, neat; **~ da** made up of **3** *m* compound

comprare buy, purchase; (*corrompere*) bribe, buy off;

compratore *m*, **-trice** *f* buyer, purchaser; **compravendita** *f* buying and selling

comprendere (*includere*) comprise, include; (*capire*) understand; **comprensibile** understandable, comprehensible; **comprensione** *f* understanding; **comprensivo** (*tollerante*) understanding; **~ di** inclusive of; **compreso 1** *pp* ☞ **comprendere 2** *agg* inclusive; (*capito*) understood; **tutto ~** all in; **~ te** including you

compressa *f* (*pastiglia*) tablet; *di garza* compress

compresso *pp* ☞ **comprimere**; **comprimere** press; (*reprimere*) repress; FIS compress

compromesso 1 *pp* ☞ **compromettere 2** *m* compromise; **compromettere** compromise; **compromettersi** compromise o.s.

computer *m inv* computer; **~ portatile** laptop

comunale *del comune* municipal, town *attr*; **comune 1** *agg* common; *amico* mutual; (*ordinario*) ordinary, common; **in ~** in common; **fuori del ~** out of the ordinary **2** *m* municipality; **comunemente** commonly

comunicare 1 *v/t notizia* pass on, communicate; *contagio* pass on; REL give Communion to **2** *v/i* (*esprimersi*) communicate; *di persone* keep in touch, communicate; **comunicato** *m* announcement; ~ **stampa** press release; **comunicazione** *f* communication; (*annuncio*) announcement; TELEC (*collegamento*) connection

comunione *f* REL communion; *di idee* sharing

comunismo *m* Communism; **comunista** *m/f* Communist

comunità *f inv* community; **comunitario** community *attr*, *dell'Ue* Community *attr*

comunque 1 *cong* however, no matter how **2** *avv* (*in ogni modo*) in any case, anyhow; (*in qualche modo*) somehow; (*tuttavia*) however

con with; (*mezzo*) by

conato *m*: ~ **di vomito** retching

concedere grant; *premio* award; **concedersi** ~ **qc** treat o.s. to sth

concentramento *m* concentration; **concentrare**, **concentrarsi** concentrate; **concentrazione** *f* concentration

concentrico concentric

concepibile conceivable; **concepimento** *m* conception; **concepimento** *m* conception; **concepire** conceive

concernere concern

concerto *m* concert; *composizione* concerto

concessionario *m* agent

concesso *pp* ☞ **concedere**

concetto *m* concept; (*giudizio*) opinion

conchiglia *f* shell

conciare *pelle* tan; (*sistemare*) arrange; **come ti sei conciato!** what a state you're in!; ~ **qu per le feste** tan s.o.'s hide

conciliare reconcile; *multa* pay, settle

concimare *pianta* feed; **concime** *m* manure

conciso concise

concittadino *m*, **-a** *f* fellow citizen

concludere conclude; (*portare a termine*) achieve, carry off; ~ **un affare** clinch a deal; **concludersi** end, close; **conclusione** *f* conclusion; **in** ~ in short; **conclusivo** conclusive; **concluso** *pp* ☞ **concludere**

concordare 1 *v/t* agree (on); GRAM make agree **2** *v/i* agree; (*coincidere*) tally; **concorde** in agreement; (*unanime*) unanimous

concorrente 1 *agg* (*rivale*) competing, rival *attr* **2** *m/f* *in una gara, gioco* competitor, contestant; FIN competitor; **concorrenza** *f* competition; **concorrere** (*contribuire*) concur; (*competere*) compete (**a** for); *di strade* converge; **concorso** *m* (*competizione*) competition, contest

concreto concrete; (*pratico*) practical

condanna *f* DIR sentence;

condannare condemn (**a** to); DIR sentence (**a** to)

condensare, condensarsi condense

condimento m seasoning; di insalata dressing; **condire** season; insalata dress; **condito** seasoned

condividere share; **condiviso** pp ☞ **condividere**

condizionale 1 m/agg conditional **2 f** suspended sentence; **condizionamento** m PSI conditioning; **~ dell'aria** air conditioning; **condizionare** PSI conditioning; **condizionato: con aria -a** air-conditioned; **condizionatore** m air conditioner; **condizione** f condition; **a ~ che** on condition that

condoglianze fpl condolences; **fare le ~ a qu** express one's condolences to s.o.

condominio m (comproprietà) joint ownership; edificio block of flats, Am condo(-minium); **condominio** m owner-occupier, Am condo owner

condono m remission; **~ fiscale** conditional amnesty for tax evaders

condotta f (comportamento) behaviour, Am behavior, conduct; (canale) piping; **condotto 1** pp ☞ **condurre 2** m pipe; ANAT duct

conducente m/f driver; **condurre** lead; (accompagnare)

take; veicolo drive; **conduttore** m, **-trice** f RAD, TV presenter; **conduttura** f (condotto) pipe

confederazione f confederation

conferenza f conference; **~ stampa** press conference; **conferire 1** v/t (dare) confer; premio award **2** v/i: **~ con qu** confer with s.o.

conferma f confirmation; **confermare** confirm

confessare, confessarsi confess; **confessione** f confession

confetto m GASTR sugared almond; MED pill

confettura f jam, Am jelly

confezione f wrapping, packaging; di abiti making; **~ regalo** gift wrap; **-i pl** (abiti) garments

conficcare hammer, drive

confidare 1 v/t confide **2** v/i: **~ in** trust in, rely on; **confidarsi: ~ con** confide in; **confidenza** f (familiarità) familiarity, trust; **avere ~ con qu** be familiar with s.o.; **prendere ~ con qc** familiarize o.s. with sth; **confidenziale** (riservato) confidential

configurazione f configuration

confinante neighbouring, Am neighboring

confinare border (**con** sth); fig confine; **confine** m border; fra terreni, fig boundary

confisca *f* seizure; **confiscare** confiscate

conflitto *m* conflict

confluire merge

confondere confuse, mix up; (*imbarazzare*) embarrass; **confondersi** get mixed up

conformarsi: ~ *a* conform to; (*adattarsi*) adapt to; **conforme** (*simile*) similar; ~ *a* in accordance with; **conformismo** *m* conformity; **conformista** *m/f* conformist; **conformità** *f* conformity; **in ~ a** in accordance with

confortare comfort; **confortevole** comfortable; **conforto** *m* comfort

confrontare compare; **confronto** *m* confrontation; (*comparazione*) comparison; **a ~ di**, **in ~ a** compared with; **nei -i di** towards

confusione *f* confusion; (*disordine*) muddle, mess; (*baccano*) noise; (*imbarazzo*) embarrassment; **confuso 1** *pp* ☞ **confondere 2** *agg* (*non chiaro*) confused, muddled; (*imbarazzato*) embarrassed

congedare dismiss; MIL discharge; **congedarsi** take leave (**da** of); **congedo** *m* (*permesso*) leave; MIL ~ **assoluto** discharge

congelare 1 *v/t* freeze **2** *v/i e* **congelarsi** freeze; **congelato** frozen; **congelatore** *m* freezer

congenito congenital

congestionato congested; *volto* flushed; **congestione** *f* congestion

congettura *f* conjecture

congiungere join; **congiungersi** join (up)

congiuntivite *f* conjunctivitis

congiuntivo *m* GRAM subjunctive; **congiunto 1** *pp* ☞ **congiungere 2** *m*, **-a** *f* relative, relation; **congiunzione** *f* GRAM conjunction

congiura *f* conspiracy, plot

congratularsi: ~ **con qu** congratulate s.o. (**per** on); **congratulazioni** *fpl*: **fare le proprie** ~ **a qu** congratulate s.o.; **-i!** congratulations!

congressista *m/f* convention participant; *Am* conventioneer; **congresso** *m* convention

conguaglio *m* balance

coniare mint; *fig* coin

coniglio *m* rabbit

coniugare conjugate; **coniugato** married; **coniugazione** *f* conjugation; **coniuge** *m/f* spouse; **-i** *pl* husband and wife; **i -i Rossi** Mr and Mrs Rossi

connazionale *m/f* compatriot

connessione *f* connection

connotati *mpl* features

cono *m* cone; ~ **gelato** ice-cream cone

conoscente *m/f* acquaintance; **conoscenza** *f* knowledge; *persona* acquaintance;

(*sensi*) consciousness; **perdere** ~ lose consciousness, faint; **conoscere** know; (*fare la conoscenza di*) meet; **conosciuto** well-known

conquista *f* conquest; **conquistare** conquer; *fig* win

consacrare consecrate; *sacerdote* ordain; (*dedicare*) dedicate

consanguineo *m*, **-a** *f* blood relative

consapevole: ~ **di** conscious of, aware of; **consapevolezza** *f* consciousness, awareness; **conscio** conscious, aware

consecutivo consecutive; **tre giorni -i** three consecutive days, three days in a row

consegna *f* di *lavoro, documento* handing in; *di prigioniero, ostaggio* handover; ~ **bagagli** left luggage, *Am* baggage checkroom; **consegnare** *lavoro, documento* hand in; *prigioniero, ostaggio* hand over; *merci, posta* deliver

conseguenza *f* consequence; **di** ~ consequently; **conseguire 1** *v/t* achieve; *laurea* obtain **2** *v/i* follow

consenso *m* (*permesso*) consent, permission; **consentire 1** *v/i* (*accondiscendere*) consent **2** *v/t* allow

conserva *f* preserve; ~ **di pomodoro** tomato purée; ~ **di frutta** jam, *Am* jelly; **conservante** *m* preservative; **conservare** keep; GASTR preserve; **conservarsi** keep; *in salute* keep well; **conservatore** *m*, **-trice** *f* conservative; **conservatorio** *m* music school, conservatoire

considerare consider; **considerazione** *f* consideration; (*osservazione*) remark, comment; **prendere in** ~ take into consideration; **considerevole** considerable

consigliare advise; (*raccomandare*) recommend; **consigliarsi** seek advice; **consigliere** *m* adviser; ~ **municipale** town councillor, *Am* councilman; **consiglio** *m* piece of advice; (*organo amministrativo*) council; ~ **d'amministrazione** board (of directors); ~ **dei ministri** Cabinet; **consigli** *pl* advice

consistente substantial; (*denso*) thick; **consistenza** *f* (*densità*) consistency, thickness; *di materiale* texture; *di argomento* basis; **consistere** consist (**in**, **di** of)

consolare[1] *v/t* console, comfort

consolare[2] *agg* consular

consolarsi console o.s.

consolato *m* consulate

consolazione *f* consolation

console *m* *diplomatico* consul

consolidare consolidate; **consolidarsi** stabilize

consonante f consonant

consorte m/f spouse; **principe** m ~ prince consort

consorzio m di imprese consortium

constatare ascertain, determine; (notare) note; **constatazione** f statement

consueto usual

consulente m/f consultant; ~ **legale** legal adviser; ~ **tributario** tax consultant; **consulenza** f consultancy; **consultare** consult; **consultarsi con qu** consult (with) s.o.; **consultazione** f consultation; **consultorio** m family planning clinic

consumare acqua, gas use, consume; (logorare) wear out; (mangiare) eat, consume; (bere) drink; **consumarsi** wear out; **consumatore** m, -**trice** f consumer; **consumazione** f food; (bevanda) drink; **consumismo** m consumerism; **consumo** m consumption; (usura) wear

contabile m/f book-keeper; **contabilità** f FIN disciplina accounting; ufficio accounts department; **tenere la ~** keep the books

contachilometri m inv milometer, Am odometer

contadino 1 agg rural, country attr **2** m, -**a** f farmer; (bracciante) farm labourer o Am laborer

contagiare infect; **contagio** m infection; per contatto diretto contagion; (epidemia) outbreak; **contagioso** infectious; per contatto contagious

contagiri m inv rev(olution) counter; **contagocce** m inv dropper

container m inv container

contaminare contaminate, pollute; **contaminazione** f contamination, pollution

contante m cash; **in -i** cash

contare 1 v/t count **2** v/i count; ~ **di fare qc** plan on doing sth; **contascatti** m inv time meter on phone; **contatore** m meter

contatto m contact

conte m count

contemplare contemplate

contemporaneamente at the same time; **contemporaneo 1** agg contemporary (di with); movimenti simultaneous **2** m, -**a** f contemporary

contendersi contend for, compete for

contenere contain, hold; (reprimere) repress; (limitare) limit; **contenersi** contain o.s.; **contenitore** m container

contentezza f happiness; **contento** pleased (di with); (lieto) glad, happy

contenuto m contents

contesa f dispute

conteso pp ☞ **contendere**

contessa f countess

contestare protest; DIR serve; **contestazione** f protest

contesto m context

contiene ☞ **contenere**

continentale continental; **continente** m continent

continuare 1 v/t continue **2** v/i continue, carry on (**a fare** doing); **continuazione** f continuation; di film sequel; **in** ~ over and over again; (ininterrottamente) non stop; **continuità** f continuity; **continuo** (ininterrotto) continuous; (molto frequente) continual; **di** ~ (ininterrottamente) continuously; (molto spesso) continually

conto m (calcolo) calculation; FIN account; in ristorante bill, Am check; ~ **corrente** current account, Am checking account; **rendere** ~ **di qc** account for sth; **rendersi** ~ **di qc** realize sth; **tenere** ~ **di qc** take sth into account; ~ **alla rovescia** countdown; **in fin dei** -**i** when all's said and done, after all

contorcersi: ~ **dal dolore / dalle risate** roll about in pain / laughing

contorno m outline, contour; GASTR accompaniment

contorto twisted

contrabbandare smuggle; **contrabbandiere** m smuggler; **contrabbando** m contraband

contrabbasso m MUS double bass

contraccambiare return

contraccettivo m contraceptive

contraccolpo m rebound; di arma da fuoco recoil

contraddire contradict; **contraddizione** f contradiction

contraffare (falsificare) forge; (imitare) imitate; **contraffatto** forged; **voce** imitated; **contraffazione** f (imitazione) imitation; (falsificazione) forgery

contralto m MUS contralto

contrappeso m counterbalance

contrapporre set against; **contrapposizione** f opposition; **mettere in** ~ contrast; **contrapposto** pp ☞ **contrapporre**

contrariamente: ~ **a** contrary to

contrariare piani thwart, oppose; persona irritate, annoy; **contrariato** irritated, annoyed

contrarietà fpl difficulties

contrario 1 agg contrary; direzione opposite; vento adverse; **essere** ~ be against (**a** sth) **2** m contrary, opposite; **al** ~ on the contrary

contrarre contract; **contrarsi** contract

contrassegnare mark;

contrassegno *m* mark; FIN *(in)* ~ cash on delivery, *Am* collect on delivery

contrastante contrasting; **contrasto** *m* contrast; *(litigio, discordia)* dispute

contrattacco *m* counter-attack

contrattare negotiate; *persona* hire

contrattempo *m* hitch

contratto 1 *pp* → **contrarre 2** *m* contract

contravvenire contravene; **contravvenzione** *f* contravention; *(multa)* fine

contrazione *f* contraction; *(riduzione)* reduction

contribuente *m/f* taxpayer; **contribuire** contribute; **contributo** *m* contribution

contro against

controbattere *(replicare)* answer back; *(confutare)* rebut

controcorrente 1 *agg* non-conformist **2** *avv* against the current; *in fiume* upstream

controffensiva counter-offensive

controfigura *f* in film stand-in

controindicazione *f* MED contraindication

controllare control; *(verificare)* check; **controllo** *m* control; *(verifica)* check; MED check-up; ~ *(dei)* **passaporti** passport control; **controllore** *m* controller; *di bus, treno* ticket inspector

controluce *f*: *in* ~ against the light

contromano: *andare a* ~ be going the wrong way

controproducente counter-productive

contrordine *m* counterorder

controsenso *m* contradiction in terms; *(assurdità)* nonsense

controversia *f* controversy, dispute; DIR litigation; **controverso** controversial

controvoglia unwillingly

contusione *f* bruise; **contuso** bruised

convalescente 1 *agg* convalescent **2** *m/f* person who is convalescent; **convalescenza** *f* convalescence; *essere in* ~ be convalescing

convalidare validate

convegno *m* convention; *luogo* meeting place

convenevoli *mpl* pleasantries

conveniente *(vantaggioso)* good; *(opportuno)* appropriate; **convenienza** *f* di prezzo, offerta good value; di gesto appropriateness; *fare qc per* ~ do sth out of self-interest

convenire 1 *v/i* gather, meet; *(concordare)* agree; *(essere opportuno)* be advisable, be better **2** *v/t* *(stabilire)* stipulate

convento *m* di monache convent; *di monaci* monastery

convenuto pp ☞ **convenire**

convenzionale conventional; **convenzione** f convention; *(accordo)* agreement, convention

convergere converge

conversare talk, make conversation; **conversazione** f conversation

conversione f conversion; AUTO U-turn; **convertirsi** be converted

convincere convince; convinto pp ☞ **convincere**; **convinzione** f conviction

convivente m/f common-law husband; *donna* common-law wife; **convivenza** f living together, cohabitation; **convivere** live together

convocare call, convene

convoglio m MIL, MAR convoy; FERR train

cooperare co-operate (*a* in); *(contribuire)* contribute (*a* to); **cooperativa** f: *(società* f): ∼ co-operative; **cooperazione** f cooperation

coordinamento m co-ordination; **coordinare** co-ordinate; **coordinatore** m, **-trice** f co-ordinator; **coordinazione** f co-ordination

coperchio m lid, top

coperta f blanket; MAR deck; **copertina** f cover; **coperto 1** pp ☞ **coprire 2** agg covered (*di* with); *cielo* overcast, cloudy **3** m cover, shelter;

piatti e posate place; *prezzo* cover charge; **essere al** ∼ be under cover, be sheltered

copertone m AUTO tyre, *Am* tire

copia f copy; **copiare** copy

copione m *per attore* script

copisteria f copy centre *o Am* center

coppa f cup; *(calice)* glass; ∼ **(di) gelato** dish of icecream; **coppetta** f *di gelato* tub

coppia f couple, pair

copricapo m inv head covering; **copricostume** m inv beachrobe; **coprifuoco** m curfew; **copriletto** m inv bedspread; **coprire** cover; *errore, suono* cover up; **coprirsi** *(vestirsi)* put something on; *(rannuvolarsi)* become overcast

coraggio m courage; *(sfacciataggine)* nerve; **coraggioso** brave, courageous

corallo m coral

Corano m Koran

corda f cord; *(fune)* rope; *(cordicella)* MUS string; **essere giù di** ∼ feel down; **tagliare la** ∼ cut and run

cordiale 1 agg cordial; **-i saluti** kind regards **2** m cordial

cordoglio m *(dolore)* grief; *(condoglianze)* condolences

cordone m cord; *di marciapiedi* kerb, *Am* curb; *(sbarramento)* cordon; ∼ **ombelica-**

le umbilical cord

coreografo *m*, -a *f* choreographer

coriandolo *m* BOT coriander; **-i** *mpl* confetti *sg*

coricarsi lie down

cornacchia F crow

cornamusa *f* bagpipes

cornea *f* cornea

cornetta *f del telefono* receiver

cornetto *m* (*brioche*) croissant; (*gelato*) cone, cornet

cornice *f* frame

cornicione *m* ARCHI cornice

corno *m* horn; *ramificate* antlers; *fig* **F fare le -a a qu** cheat on s.o.; **facciamo le -a!** touch wood!; **cornuto** F cheated, betrayed

coro *m* chorus; *cantori* choir; **in ~** (*insieme*) all together

corona *f* crown; (*rosario*) rosary

corpo *m* body; MIL corps; (*a*) **~ a ~** hand-to-hand; **corporatura** *f* build

corpulento stout, corpulent

corredo *m* equipment; *da sposa* trousseau; *da neonato* layette

correggere correct; **correggersi** correct o.s.

correlazione *f* correlation

corrente 1 *agg* current; *acqua* running; *lingua* fluent; **2** *m*: **essere al ~** know (*di* sth); **tenere qu al ~** keep s.o. up to date, keep s.o. informed **3** *f* current; *fig*: *di opinione*

trend; *fazione* faction; **~ d'aria** draught, *Am* draft

correre 1 *v/t* run; **~ il pericolo** run the risk **2** *v/i* run; (*affrettarsi*) hurry; *di veicolo* speed; *di tempo* fly; **lascia ~!** let it go!; **corre voce** it is rumoured *o Am* rumored

correttezza *f* correctness; (*onestà*) honesty; **corretto 1** *pp* ☞ **correggere 2** *agg* correct; **correzione** *f* correction

corridoio *m* corridor; *in aereo, teatro* aisle

corridore *m in auto* racing driver; *a piedi* runner

corriera *f* bus

corriere *m* courier

corrispondente 1 *agg* corresponding **2** *m/f* correspondent; **corrispondenza** *f* correspondence; (*posta*) mail; **corrispondere 1** *v/t* (*pagare*) pay; (*ricambiare*) reciprocate **2** *v/i* correspond; (*coincidere*) coincide; (*equivalere*) be equivalent; **corrisposto 1** *pp* ☞ **corrispondere 2** *agg* reciprocated

corrodere, corrodersi corrode, rust

corrompere corrupt; *con denaro* bribe; **corroso** *pp* ☞ **corrodere**; **corrotto 1** *pp* ☞ **corrompere 2** *agg* corrupt

corrugare wrinkle; **~ la fronte** frown

corruzione *f* corruption; *con denaro* bribery

corsa f run; *attività* running; *di autobus* trip, journey; *(gara)* race; *di* ~ at a run; *in fretta* in a rush; **fare una** ~ rush, dash; **-e** pl races

corsia f aisle; *di ospedale* ward; AUTO lane; ~ **di emergenza** emergency lane; ~ **di sorpasso** fast lane; **a tre -e** three-lane

Corsica f Corsica

corsivo m italics

corso[1] 1 *agg* Corsican 2 m, **-a** f Corsican

corso[2] 1 *pp* ☞ **correre** 2 m course; *(strada)* main street; FIN *di moneta* circulation; *di titoli* rate; ~ **d'acqua** watercourse; ~ **di lingue** language course; FIN **fuori** ~ out of circulation; **lavori mpl in** ~ work in progress

corte f court

corteccia f bark

corteggiare court

corteo m procession

cortese polite, courteous; **cortesia** f politeness, courtesy; **per ~!** please!

cortile m courtyard

corto short; **essere a** ~ **di** be short of; **cortocircuito** m short (circuit)

corvo m rook; ~ **imperiale** raven

cosa f thing; **(che)** ~ what; **qualche** ~ something; **dimmi una** ~ tell me something; **una** ~ **da nulla** a trifle

coscia f thigh; GASTR leg

cosciente conscious; **coscienza** f conscience; *(consapevolezza)* consciousness; **coscienzioso** conscientious

così so; *(in questo modo)* like this; ~ ~ so-so; **e** ~ **via** and so on; **per** ~ **dire** so to speak; **proprio** ~! exactly!; **basta** ~! that's enough!; **cosicché** and so; **cosiddetto** so-called

cosmetico m/agg cosmetic

cosmo m cosmos

cosmopolita cosmopolitan

coso m F what-d'you-call-it F

cospargere sprinkle; *(coprire)* cover *(di* with); **cosparso** *pp* ☞ **cospargere**

cospiratore, **-trice** f conspirator; **cospirazione** f conspiracy

costa f coast, coastline; *(pendio)* hillside; ANAT rib

costante constant, steady; **costanza** f perseverance

costare cost; ~ **caro** be expensive, cost a lot; *fig* cost dear; **quanto costa?** how much is it?

costata f rib steak; ~ **di agnello** lamb chop

costeggiare skirt, hug

costellazione f constellation

costiero coastal

costituire constitute; *società* form, create; **costituirsi** give o.s. up; **costituzionale** constitutional; **costituzione** f constitution

costo m cost; ~ **della vita** cost of living; **ad ogni** ~ at all costs

costola f rib; *di libro* spine; **costoletta** f GASTR cutlet

costoso expensive, costly

costretto pp ☞ **costringere**; **costringere** force, compel

costruire build, construct; **costruttivo** *fig* constructive; **costruttore** m, **-trice** f builder; *(fabbricante)* manufacturer; **costruzione** f building, construction; GRAM construction

costume m *(usanza)* custom; *(condotta)* morals; *(indumento)* costume; **~ da bagno** swimming costume, swimsuit; **da uomo** (swimming) trunks

cotechino m *kind of pork sausage*

cotoletta f cutlet; **~ alla milanese** *breaded cutlet fried in butter*

cotone m cotton; MED **~ idrofilo** cotton wool, *Am* absorbent cotton

cotta f F crush

cottimo m: **lavorare a ~** do piecework

cotto 1 pp ☞ **cuocere 2** agg done, cooked; F *fig* head over heels in love (**di** with); **cottura** f cooking

covare 1 v/t sit on, hatch; F *fig: malattia* sicken for; *rancore* harbour, *Am* harbor **2** v/i sit on eggs; **covo** m den; *(nido)* nest; *fig* hideout

covone m sheaf

cozza f mussel

C.P. (= **Casella Postale**) PO Box (= Post Office Box)

crampo m cramp

cranio m skull

cratere m crater

cravatta f tie, *Am anche* necktie

creare create; *fig (causare)* cause; **creatività** f creativity; **creativo 1** agg creative **2** m copywriter; **creatore 1** agg creative **2** m Creator **3** m, **-trice** f creator; **creatura** f creature; **creazione** f creation

credente m/f believer

credenza[1] f belief

credenza[2] f *mobile* dresser

credenziali fpl credentials

credere 1 v/t believe, think; *(pensare)* believe, think; **lo credo bene!** I should think so too!; **credersi** believe o think o.s. to be **2** v/i believe; **~ a qu** believe s.o.; **~ in qu** believe in s.o; **non ci credo** I don't believe it; **credibile** credible; **credibilità** f credibility

credito m credit; *fig* trust; *(attendibilità)* reliability; **creditore** m, **-trice** f creditor

crema f cream; *di latte e uova* custard; **~ da barba** shaving foam; **~ idratante** moisturizer, moisturizing cream; **~ solare** suntan lotion

cremare cremate; **cremazione** f cremation

cren *m* horseradish

crepa *f* crack; crepaccio *m* cleft; *di ghiacciaio* crevasse; crepare (*spaccarsi*) crack; F (*morire*) kick the bucket F

crêpe *f inv* pancake

crepitare crackle

crepuscolo *m* twilight

crescente growing; *luna* crescent; crescere 1 *v/t* bring up, raise 2 *v/i* grow

crescione *m* watercress

crescita *f* growth

cresima *f* confirmation

crespo *capelli* frizzy

cresta *f* crest; *di montagna* peak

creta *f* clay

cretino F 1 *agg* stupid, idiotic 2 *m*, -a *f* idiot, cretin

cric *m inv* AUTO jack

criminale *agg*, *m/f* criminal; criminalità *f* crime; crimine *m* crime

criniera *f* mane

cripta *f* crypt

crisantemo *m* chrysanthemum

crisi *f inv* crisis; MED fit

cristallizzare, cristallizzarsi crystallize; cristallo *m* crystal

cristianesimo *m* Christianity; cristiano 1 *agg* Christian 2 *m*, -a *f* Christian; Cristo *m* Christ

criterio *m* criterion; (*buon senso*) common sense

critica *f* criticism; criticare criticize; critico 1 *agg* critical 2 *m*, -a *f* critic

croato 1 *agg* Croatian 2 *m*, -a *f* Croat, Croatian; Croazia *f* Croatia

croccante 1 *agg* crisp, crunchy 2 *m* GASTR nut brittle

crocchetta *f* GASTR potato croquette

croce *f* cross; **Croce Rossa** Red Cross; crociata *f* crusade; crociera *f* cruise; crocifiggere crucify; crocifisso *m* crucifix

crollare collapse; crollo *m* collapse

cronaca *f* chronicle; *di partita* commentary; *fatto di ~* news item; **~ nera** crime news *sg*

cronico chronic

cronista *m/f* reporter; *di partita* commentator

cronologico chronological

cronometrare time; cronometro *m* chronometer; SP stopwatch

crosta *f* crust; MED scab; *di formaggio* rind

crostacei *mpl* shellfish *pl*

crostata *f* GASTR tart

crostino *m* GASTR crouton

cruciale crucial

cruciverba *m inv* crossword (puzzle)

crudele cruel; crudeltà *f* cruelty

crudo raw

crumiro *m*, -a *f* scab

crusca *f* bran

cruscotto *m* dashboard; *scomparto* glove compartment

Cuba f Cuba; **cubano 1** agg Cuban **2** m, **-a** f Cuban

cubetto m (small) cube; **~ di ghiaccio** ice cube; **cubo 1** agg cubic **2** m cube

cuccagna f: (**paese** m **della**) **~** land of plenty

cuccetta f FERR couchette; MAR berth

cucchiaiata f spoonful; **cucchiaino** m teaspoon; **cucchiaio** m spoon; **~ da tavola** tablespoon

cuccia f dog's basket; esterna kennel

cucciolo m cub; di cane puppy

cucina f kitchen; (cibi) food; (il cucinare) cooking; **~ a gas** gas cooker; **cucinare** cook; **cucinino** m kitchenette

cucire sew; **cucito 1** agg sewn **2** m sewing; **cucitura** f seam

cuffia f da piscina swimming cap; RAD, TV headphones; **~ da bagno** shower cap

cugino m, **-a** f cousin

cui persona who, whom; fml; cose which; **la casa in ~ abitano** the house they live in, the house in which they live; **il ~ nome** whose name; **per ~** so

culinario cookery attr, culinary; **arte** f **-a** culinary art, cookery

culla f cradle; **cullare** rock

culminante punto m **~** cli-

max; **culmine** m peak

culo V m arse V, Am ass V

culto m cult; religione religion

cultura f culture; **culturale** cultural; **culturismo** m body-building

cumulativo cumulative; **biglietto** m **~** group ticket; **cumulo** m heap, pile

cuneo m wedge

cunetta f fondo stradale bump

cuocere cook; pane bake; **cuoco** m, **-a** f cook

cuoio m leather; **~ capelluto** scalp

cuore m heart; carte **-i** pl hearts; **di ~** wholeheartedly; **stare a ~ a qu** be very important to s.o.

cupo gloomy; suono deep

cupola f dome

cura f care; MED treatment; **~ dimagrante** diet; **avere ~ di qc** take care of sth; **curabile** curable; **curare** take care of, MED treat; **curarsi** look after o.s.; **non curarti di loro** don't bother about them

curiosare have a look around; spreg pry (**in** into); **curiosità** f inv curiosity; **curioso** curious

cursore m INFOR cursor

curva f curve; **curvare** curve; schiena bend; **curvarsi** bend; **curvo** curved; persona bent

cuscinetto m TEC bearing; **~ a sfere** ball bearing; POL **stato** m **~** buffer state; **cuscino** m cushion; (guanciale) pillow

custode *m/f* caretaker; *di parco, museo* attendant; **custodia** *f* care; DIR custody; *(astuccio)* case; **custodire**

(conservare) keep

cute *f* skin

CV *m* (= **curriculum vitae**) CV (= curriculum vitae), *Am* résumé

D

da *stato in luogo* at; *moto in luogo* from; *moto a luogo* to; *tempo* since; *con verbo passivo* by; *viene ~ Roma* he comes from Rome; *sono ~ mio fratello* I'm at my brother's (place); *passo ~ Firenze* I'm going via Florence; *vado dal medico* I'm going to the doctor's *o Am* doctor; *~ ieri* since yesterday; *~ oggi in poi* from now on; *~ bambino* as a child; *l'ho fatto ~ me* I did it myself; *qualcosa ~ mangiare* something to eat; *la donna dai capelli grigi* the woman with grey hair

dà ☞ **dare**

daccapo ☞ **capo**

dado *m* dice; GASTR stock cube; TEC nut

dagli = *da* and *art* **gli**

dai[1] = *da* and *art* **i**

dai[2] ☞ **dare**

daino *m* deer; *(pelle)* buckskin

dal = *da* and *art* **il**

dall', **dalla**, **dalle**, **dallo** = *da* and *art* **l'**, **la**, **le**, **lo**

daltonico colour-blind, *Am* color-blind

dama *f* lady; *gioco* draughts *sg*, *Am* checkers *sg*

damigiana *f* demijohn

danese 1 *m/agg* Danish **2** *m/f* Dane; **Danimarca** *f* Denmark

danneggiare *(rovinare)* damage; *(nuocere)* harm; **danno** *m* damage; *(a persona)* harm; **dannoso** harmful

danza *f* dance; *~ classica* ballet; **danzare** dance

dappertutto everywhere

dappoco *agg inv* *(inetto)* worthless; *(irrilevante)* minor, unimportant

dapprima at first

dare 1 *v/t* give; *~ qc a qu* give s.o. sth, give sth to s.o.; *~ uno sguardo a qc* have a look at sth; *dammi del tu* call me 'tu' **2** *v/i di finestra* overlook *(su* sth); *di porta* lead into *(su* sth); *~ e avere* debit and credit

darsena *f* dock

darsi give each other; *(dedicarsi)* devote o.s. *(a* to); *~ al commercio* go into business; *può ~* perhaps

data *f* date; *~ di nascita* date

of birth; **~ di scadenza** expiry date, Am expiration date; **datare 1** v/t date **2** v/i: **a ~ da oggi** from today

dato 1 pp *☞* **dare 2** agg (certo) given, particular; (dedito) addicted (**a** to); **in -i casi** in certain cases; **~ che** given that **3** m piece of data; **-i pl** data sg

datore m, **-trice** f: **~ di lavoro** employer

dattero m date; (albero) date palm

dattilografo m, **-a** f typist

davanti 1 prp: **~ a** in front of **2** avv in front; (dirimpetto) opposite **3** m/agg inv front

davanzale m window sill

davanzo more than enough

davvero really

d.C. (= **dopo Cristo**) AD (= anno domini)

dea f goddess

debito 1 agg due, proper **2** m debt; (dovere) duty; **avere un ~ con qu** be in debt to s.o.; **debitore** m, **-trice** f debtor

debole 1 agg weak; (luce) dim **2** m weakness; **avere un ~ per qu** have a soft spot for s.o.; **debolezza** f weakness

debutto m début

decadente decadent

decaffeinato decaffeinated, decaff F

decalcomania f transfer, Am decal

decappottabile f/agg AUTO convertible

decennio m decade

decente decent

decentrare decentralize

decesso m death

decidere 1 v/t questione settle; **data** decide on, settle on; **~ di fare qc** decide to do sth **2** v/i decide; **decidersi** decide (**a** to), make up one's mind (**a** to)

decifrare decipher

decimale m/agg decimal

decimo tenth

decina f MAT ten; **una ~** about ten

decisione f decision; (risolutezza) decisiveness; **prendere una ~** make a decision;

decisivo decisive; **deciso 1** pp *☞* **decidere 2** agg (definito) definite; (risoluto) determined; (netto) clear; (spiccato) marked

declinare 1 v/t decline; responsabilità disclaim **2** v/i (tramontare) set; (diminuire) decline; **declinazione** f GRAM declension; **declino** m fig decline

decodificatore m decoder

decollare take off; **decollo** m take-off

decomposizione f decomposition; CHIM breaking down

decompressione f decompression

decorare decorate; **decoratore** m, **-trice** f decorator; **decorazione** f decoration

decorrenza f: *con immedia-ta* ~ with immediate effect; **decorrere** pass; *a ~ da oggi* with effect from today; **decorso 1** *pp* ☞ **decorrere 2** *m di malattia* course

decrepito decrepit

decreto *m* decree; ~-*legge m decree passed in exceptional circumstances that has the force of law*

dedica f dedication; **dedicare** dedicate; **dedicarsi** dedicate o.s.; **dedito** dedicated (*a* to); *a un vizio* addicted (*a* to); **dedizione** f dedication

dedurre deduce; FIN deduct; (*derivare*) derive; **deduzione** f deduction

deficiente 1 *agg* (*mancante*) deficient, lacking (*di* in) **2** *m/f* idiot, moron

deficit *m inv* deficit; ~ *del bilancio pubblico* public spending deficit

definire define; (*risolvere*) settle; **definitivo** definitive; **definizione** f definition

deflettore *m* AUTO quarterlight

deformare deform; *legno* warp; *metallo* buckle; fig distort; **deformarsi** *di legno* warp; *di metallo* buckle; *di scarpe* lose their shape; **deformazione** f deformation; *di legno* warping; *di metallo* buckling; *fisica* deformity; fig, *visuale* distortion; **defor-**

me deformed

defunto 1 *agg* dead; fig defunct **2** *m*, -a f DIR: *il* ~ the deceased

degenerare degenerate (*in* into)

degente *m/f* patient

degli = *di* and art **gli**

degnare *v/t*: ~ *qu di una parola* deign to speak to s.o. **2** *v/i e* **degnarsi**: ~ *di* deign to, condescend to

degno worthy; ~ *di nota* noteworthy

degradante degrading; **degradarsi** demean o.s., lower o.s.; CHIM degrade; *di ambiente, edifici* deteriorate; **degradazione** f degradation; **degrado** *m* deterioration; ~ **ambientale** damage to the environment

degustazione f tasting

dei¹ = *di* and art **i**

dei² (*pl di* **dio**): **gli** ~ *mpl* the Gods

del = *di* and art **il**

delega f delegation; (*procura*) proxy; **delegare** delegate; **delegato 1** *agg*: **amministratore** *m* ~ managing director **2** *m*, -a f delegate; ~ **sindacale** (trade) union delegate

delfino *m* dolphin

deliberare 1 *v/t* decide **2** *v/i* DIR deliberate (*su* on)

delicatezza f delicacy; **delicato** delicate

delimitare define

delineare outline

delinquente *m/f* criminal; *fig* scoundrel; **delinquenza** *f* crime; **~ minorile** juvenile delinquency; **~ organizzata** organized crime

delirare be in raptures; MED be delirious; **delirio** *m* delirium; *fig* frenzy

delitto *m* crime

delizioso delightful; *cibo* delicious

dell', della, delle, dello = **di** and *art* **l', la, le, lo**

delta *m* delta; **deltaplano** *m* hang-glider; *attività* hanggliding

deludere disappoint; **delusione** *f* disappointment; **deluso** disappointed

demanio *m* State property

demente *m/f* MED person with dementia; F lunatic F

democratico 1 *agg* democratic **2** *m*, -a *f* democrat; **democrazia** *f* democracy

demografico demographic

demolire demolish (*anche fig*); *macchine* crush; **demolizione** *f* demolition; *di macchine* crushing

demonio *m* devil

demoralizzarsi become demoralized, lose heart

demotivato demotivated

denaro *m* money; **~ contante** cash

denaturato CHIM: **alcol** *m* **~** methylated spirits *sg*

denominare name, call; de-

nominazione *f* name; **~ di origine controllata** term signifying that a wine is of a certain origin and quality

denotare denote, be indicative of

densità *f* density; *della nebbia* thickness, density; **denso** dense; *fumo, nebbia* thick, dense

dentario dental; **dente** *m* tooth; **~ del giudizio** wisdom tooth; **mal** *m* **di -i** toothache; GASTR **al ~** al dente, *still slightly firm*

dentice *m* fish native to the Mediterranean

dentiera *f* dentures; **dentifricio** *m* toothpaste; **dentista** *m/f* dentist

dentro 1 *prp* in, inside; (*entro*) within **2** *avv* in, inside; (*nell'intimo*) inwardly; **qui** / **lì ~** in here / there

denuclearizzato nuclear-free, denuclearized

denuncia *f* denunciation; *alla polizia, alla società di assicurazione* complaint, report; *di nascita, morte* registration; **~ dei redditi** income tax return; **denunciare** denounce; *alla polizia, alla società di assicurazione* report; *nascita* register

denutrito undernourished

deodorante *m* deodorant

depilare *con pinzette* pluck; *con rasoio* shave; *con ceretta* wax

depilatorio m/agg depilatory

dépliant m inv leaflet; (opuscolo) brochure

deplorevole deplorable

deporre v/t put down; uova lay; re, presidente depose; ~ **il falso** commit perjury **2** v/i DIR testify, give evidence (**a favore di** for, **a carico di** against)

deportare deport

depositare deposit; (posare) put down, deposit; (registrare) register; **depositato: marchio** m ~ registered trademark; **deposito** m deposit; (magazzino) warehouse; **rimessa** depot; FERR ~ **bagagli** left-luggage office, Am baggage checkroom

depravato m, -a f depraved person

depressione f depression; **depresso 1** pp ☞ **deprimere** **2** agg depressed; **deprimente** depressing; **deprimere** depress; **deprimersi** get depressed

depurare purify; **depuratore** m purifier

deputato m, -a f Member of Parliament, Am Representative

deragliare FERR go off the rails; **far** ~ derail

deridere deride; **derisione** f derision; **deriso** pp ☞ **deridere**

deriva f MAR drift; **andare al-**

la ~ drift

derivare 1 v/t derive **2** v/i: ~ **da** come from, derive from

dermatologo m, -a f dermatologist

derubare rob

descritto pp ☞ **descrivere**; **descrivere** describe; **descrizione** f description

deserto 1 agg deserted **2** m desert

desiderare (volere) want, wish; intensamente long for; sessualmente desire; **desidera?** can I help you?; **lascia** ~ it leaves a lot to be desired; **desiderio** m wish (**di** for); intenso longing (**di** for); sessuale desire (**di** for)

design m inv design

designare (nominare) appoint, name; (fissare) fix

desistere: ~ **da** desist from

desolato desolate; **sono** ~! I am so sorry

dessert m inv dessert

destinare destine; (assegnare) assign; con il pensiero mean, intend; dati fix; (indirizzare) address (**a** to); **destinatario** m, -a f di lettera addressee; **destinazione** f: (luogo m **di**) ~ destination

destino m destiny

destra f right; (mano) right hand; **a** ~ to the right

destreggiarsi manœuvre, Am maneuver

destrezza f skill, dexterity; **destro** right; (abile) skilful,

Am skillful, dexterous

detenere hold; **detenuto** *m*, **-a** *f* prisoner; **detenzione** *f* (*imprigionamento*) detention

detergente *m* detergent; *per cosmesi* cleanser

deteriorabile perishable; **deteriorarsi** deteriorate, get worse

determinare determine, establish; (*causare*) cause, lead to; **determinato** certain; (*specifico*) particular, specific; (*risoluto*) determined; **determinazione** *f* determination

detersivo *m* detergent; *per piatti* washing-up liquid, *Am* dishwashing liquid; *per biancheria* detergent, *Br anche* washing powder

detestare hate, detest

detonare detonate

detrarre deduct (**da** from); **detratto** *pp* ☞ **detrarre**; **detrazione** *f* deduction

detrito *m* debris; GEOL detritus

detta: a ~ di according to

dettaglio *m* detail; FIN **commercio m al ~** retail trade

dettare dictate; **dettato** *m* dictation

detto 1 *pp* ☞ **dire**, **~ fatto** no sooner said than done; **come non ~** let's forget it **2** *agg* said; (*soprannominato*) known as **3** *m* saying

devastare devastate

deve, devi ☞ **dovere**

deviare 1 *v/t* traffico, sospetti divert **2** *v/i* deviate; **deviazione** *f* deviation; *di traffico* diversion

devo ☞ **dovere**

devoto 1 *agg* devoted; REL devout **2** *m*, **-a** *f* devotee; REL **il devoto** *pl*

di 1 *prp* of; *con il comparativo* than; **~ ferro** (made of) iron; **io sono ~ Roma** I'm from Rome; **l'auto ~ mio padre** my father's car; **~ giorno** by day; **parlare ~ politica** talk about politics; **d'estate** in the summer; **di ~** on Sundays; **più bello ~** prettier than **2** *art* some; *interrogativo* any, some; *negativo* any; **del vino** some wine

di' ☞ **dire**

dia ☞ **dare**

diabete *m* diabetes *sg*; **diabetico 1** *agg* diabetic **2** *m*, **-a** *f* diabetic

diadema *m* diadem

diaframma *m* diaphragm

diagnosi *f inv* diagnosis; **diagnosticare** diagnose

diagonale *f*/*agg* diagonal

diagramma *m* diagram

dialetto *m* dialect

dialisi *f inv* dialysis

dialogo *m* dialogue, *Am* dialog

diamante *m* diamond

diametro *m* diameter

diapason *m inv* tuning fork

diapositiva *f* FOT slide

diario *m* diary

diarrea f diarrhoea, *Am* diarrhea

diavolo m devil; *mandare al ~* tell s.o. to get lost; F *ma che~ fai?* what the heck are you doing? F

dibattersi struggle; **dibattito** m debate

dicembre m December

diceria f rumour, *Am* rumor

dichiarare state; *ufficialmente* declare; **dichiararsi** declare o.s.; **dichiarazione** f declaration; *~ dei redditi* income tax statement; *~ doganale* customs declaration

diciannove nineteen; **diciannovesimo** nineteenth; **diciassette** seventeen; **diciassettesimo** seventeenth; **diciottenne** m/f eighteen-year-old; **diciottesimo** eighteenth; **diciotto** eighteen; **dieci** ten; *alle / verso le ~* at / about ten (o'clock)

diesel m diesel

dieta f diet; *essere a ~* be on a diet; **dietetico** diet

dietro 1 prp behind; *~ l'angolo* around the corner; *~ di me* behind me **2** avv behind; *in auto* in the back; *di ~ stanza,* porch; *zampe* hind; AUTO rear **3** m inv back

difatti in fact

difendere defend; (*proteggere*) protect; **difensiva** f defensive; *stare sulla ~* be on the defensive; **difensivo** defensive; **difensore** m de-

fender; *~ d'ufficio* legal aid lawyer, *Am* public defender; **difesa** f defence, *Am* defense; *~ dei consumatori* consumer protection; *legittima ~* self-defence; **difeso** pp ☞ **difendere**

difetto m (*imperfezione*) defect; *morale* fault, flaw; (*mancanza*) lack; **difettoso** defective

diffamare slander; *scrivendo* libel; **diffamazione** f defamation of character

differente different (*da* from); **differenza** f difference; *~ di prezzo* difference in price, price difference; *a ~ di* unlike; **differenziarsi** differ (*da* from)

difficile difficult; (*improbabile*) unlikely; **difficoltà** f inv difficulty; *senza ~* easily, without any difficulty

diffidare 1 v/t DIR issue an injunction against; *~ qu dal fare qc* warn s.o. not to do sth **2** v/i: *~ di qu* distrust s.o.; **diffidente** distrustful; **diffidenza** f distrust

diffondere diffuse; *fig* spread; **diffondersi** *fig* spread; (*dilungarsi*) enlarge; **diffusione** f *di luce, calore* diffusion; *di giornale* circulation; **diffuso 1** pp ☞ **diffondere 2** agg widespread; *luce* diffuse

diga f *fluviale* dam; *litoranea* dyke; *portuale* breakwater

digerire digest; F (*tollerare*)

stomach F; **digestione** f digestion; **digestivo 1** agg digestive **2** m after-dinner drink, digestif

digitale digital; **impronta** f ~ fingerprint

digitare INFOR key

digiunare fast; **digiuno 1** agg fasting **2** m fast; **a** ~ on an empty stomach

dignità f dignity

digrignare gnash

dilagare flood; fig spread rapidly

dilaniare tear apart

dilatare expand; occhi open wide; **dilatarsi** di materiali expand; di pupilla dilate

dilazionare defer, delay

dileguarsi vanish, disappear

dilemma m dilemma

dilettante m/f amateur; spreg dilettante; **dilettarsi:** ~ **di qc** dabble in sth, do sth as a hobby; ~ **a fare qc** take delight in doing sth

diligente diligent; (accurato) accurate

diluire dilute

dilungarsi fig dwell (su on)

diluviare pour down; **diluvio** m downpour; fig deluge

dimagrante: cura f ~ diet; dimagrire lose weight

dimenarsi throw o.s. about

dimensione f dimension; (grandezza) size; (misure) dimensions

dimenticanza f forgetfulness, absent-mindedness; (svista)

oversight; **dimenticare** forget; **dimenticarsi** forget (di sth; di fare qc to do sth)

dimestichezza f familiarity

dimettere dismiss (da from); da ospedali discharge (da from); da carceri release (da from); **dimettersi** resign (da from)

dimezzare halve

diminuire 1 v/t reduce **2** v/i decrease, di prezzi, valore fall, go down; di vento, rumore die down; **diminuzione** f decrease; di prezzi, valore fall, drop (di in)

dimissioni fpl resignation; **dare le** ~ hand in one's resignation

dimora f residence

dimostrare demonstrate; (interesse) show; (provare) prove, show; **dimostrarsi** prove to be; **dimostrazione** f demonstration; (prova) proof

dinamica f dynamics; **dinamico** dynamic

dinamite f dynamite

dinanzi: ~ **a** al cospetto di before

dinastia f dynasty

dinosauro m dinosaur

dintorno 1 avv around **2** m: -**i** pl neighbourhood, Am neighborhood

dio m god; **grazie a Dio!** thank God! **per l'amor di Dio** for God's sake

diocesi f inv diocese

diossina f dioxin

dipartimento m department

dipendente 1 agg dependent **2** m/f employee; **dipendenza** f dependence; (edificio) annexe, Am annex; **essere alle ~ di** work for; **dipendere: ~ da** (essere subordinato a) depend on; (essere mantenuto da) be dependent on; (essere causato da) be due to; **dipende** it depends; **questo dipende da te** it's up to you; **dipeso** pp **di dipendere**

dipingere paint; fig describe, depict; **dipinto 1** pp **di dipingere 2** m painting, picture

diploma m diploma, certificate; **~ di laurea** degree (certificate); **diplomarsi** obtain a diploma

diplomatico 1 agg diplomatic **2** m diplomat; **diplomato 1** agg qualified **2** m, -a f holder of a diploma; **diplomazia** f diplomacy

diporto: imbarcazione f **da ~** pleasure boat

diradare thin out; **diradarsi** thin out; (di nebbia) clear, lift

dire 1 v/t say; (raccontare) tell; **~ qc a qu** tell s.o. sth; **~ a qu di fare qc** tell s.o. to do sth; **vale a ~** that is, in other words; **a ~ il vero** to tell the truth; **come si dice ... in inglese?** what's the English for ... ?, how do you say ... in English?; **voler ~** mean

2 v/i **~ bene di qu** speak highly of s.o.; **dico sul serio** I'm serious

direttiva f directive; **direttivo 1** agg managerial; comitato, consiglio, POL executive attr **2** m di società board (of directors); POL leadership

diretto 1 pp **di dirigere 2** agg (immediato) direct; **~ a** aimed at; lettera addressed to; **essere ~ a casa** be heading for home; RAD, TV **in (ripresa) -a** live **3** m direct train; SP straight

direttore m, -trice f manager; più in alto nella gerarchia director; EDU headmaster; donna headmistress; Am principal; di giornale, rivista editor (in chief); **~ generale** CEO; **~ d'orchestra** conductor

direzione f direction; di società management; di partito leadership; ufficio office; **sede generale** head office

dirigente 1 agg classe, partito ruling; personale managerial **2** m/f executive; POL leader; **dirigere** direct; azienda run, manage; orchestra conduct; **dirigersi** head (**a**, **verso** for, toward)

dirigibile m airship, dirigible

diritto 1 agg, avv straight **2** m right; DIR law; **aver ~ a** be entitled to; **di ~** by rights; **diritura** f straight line; SP straight; fig rectitude; **in ~**

d'arrivo on the home straight

diroccato ramshackle

dirottare *traffico* divert; *aereo* reroute; *con intenzioni criminali* hijack; **dirottatore** *m*, **-trice** *f* hijacker

dirotto: piove a ~ it's pouring

dirupo *m* precipice

disabile 1 *agg* disabled **2** *m/f* disabled person

disabitato uninhabited

disaccordo *m* disagreement

disadattato 1 *agg* maladjusted **2** *m/f* (social) misfit

disagio *m* (*difficoltà*) hardship; (*scomodità*) discomfort; (*imbarazzo*) embarrassment; **essere a ~** be ill at ease

disapprovare disapprove of; **disapprovazione** *f* disapproval

disappunto *m* disappointment

disarmato unarmed; *fig* defenceless, *Am* defenseless; **disarmo** *m* POL disarmament

disastro *m* disaster; **disastroso** disastrous

disattento inattentive; **disattenzione** *f* inattention; *errore* careless mistake

disavanzo *m* deficit

disavventura *f* misadventure

disboscamento *m* deforestation

discapito *m*: **a ~ di qu** to the detriment *o* disadvantage of s.o.

discarica *f* dumping; *luogo* dump

discendente 1 *agg inv* descending **2** *m/f* descendant; **discendere** descend; (*trarre origine*) be descended (**da** from); *da veicoli, da cavallo* get off (**da qc** sth)

discepolo *m* disciple

discesa *f* descent; (*pendio*) slope; *di bus* exit; **strada in ~** street that slopes downward

dischetto *m* INFOR diskette, floppy

disciplina *f* discipline; **disciplinato** disciplined

disco *m* disc, *Am* disk; SP discus; MUS record; INFOR disk; INFOR **~ rigido** hard disk; AUTO **~ orario** parking disc; **~ volante** flying saucer; **discobolo** *m* discus thrower

discolpare clear

discontinuo intermittent; (*disuguale*) erratic

discorde not in agreement, clashing; **discordia** *f* discord; (*differenza di opinioni*) disagreement; (*litigio*) argument

discorrere talk (**di** about); **discorso** **1** *pp* ☞ **discorrere 2** *m pubblico, ufficiale* speech; (*conversazione*) conversation, talk

discoteca *f locale* disco; *raccolta* record library

discrepanza *f* discrepancy

discreto (*riservato*) discreet; (*abbastanza buono*) fairly good; (*moderato*) moderate, fair; **discrezione** f discretion; **a ~ di** at the discretion of

discriminare 1 v/i discriminate 2 v/t *stranieri, donne* discriminate against; **discriminazione** f discrimination

discussione f discussion; (*litigio*) argument; **discusso** pp ☞ **discutere**; **discutere** 1 v/t discuss, talk about; *questione* debate; (*mettere in dubbio*) question; (*contestare*) dispute 2 v/i talk; (*litigare*) argue; (*negoziare*) negotiate; **discutibile** debatable

disdegnare disdain

disdetto pp ☞ **disdire**; **disdire** *impegno* cancel; *contratto* terminate

disegnare draw; (*progettare*) design; **disegno** m drawing; (*progetto*) design; **~ di legge** bill

diserbante m weed-killer

diseredare disinherit; **diseredato** underprivileged, disadvantaged

disertare desert; **disertore** m deserter; **diserzione** f desertion

disfare undo; *letto* strip; (*distruggere*) destroy; **~ la valigia** unpack; **disfarsi di** *ghiaccio* melt; **~ di** get rid of; **disfatta** f defeat; **disfatto** pp ☞ **disfare**

disgelo m thaw

disgrazia f misfortune; (*incidente*) accident; (*sfavore*) disgrace; **per ~** unfortunately; **disgraziato** 1 agg (*sfortunato*) unlucky 2 m, -a f poor soul; m (*farabutto*) bastard

disgregare break up; **disgregarsi** break up, disintegrate

disguido m hiccup, hitch

disgustare disgust; **disgusto** m disgust; **disgustoso** disgusting

disidratato dehydrated

disillusione f disillusionment; **disilluso** disillusioned

disinfettante m disinfectant; **disinfettare** disinfect

disinibito uninhibited

disinnescare *bomba* defuse

disinserire disconnect

disinteressarsi take no interest (**di** in); **disinteressato** disinterested; **disinteresse** m lack of interest; (*generosità*) unselfishness

disintossicare detoxify; **disintossicazione** f treatment for drug / alcohol addiction, detox F

disinvolto confident; **disinvoltura** f confidence

dislessia f dyslexia; **dislessico** dyslexic

dislivello m difference in height, height difference; *fig* difference

disobbedire ☞ **disubbidire**

disoccupato 1 agg unemployed, jobless 2 m, -a f unemployed person; i -i the unemployed pl, the jobless pl; **disoccupazione** f unemployment

disonestà f dishonesty; **disonesto** dishonest

disonore m dishonour, Am dishonor

disopra 1 avv above; **al ~ di** above 2 agg upper 3 m inv top

disordinato untidy, messy; **disordine** m untidiness, mess; **in ~** untidy, in a mess; **-i** pl riots, public disorder

disorganizzazione f disorganization

disorientamento m disorientation; **disorientare** disorientate, Am disorient; **disorientato** disorientated, Am disoriented

disotto 1 avv below; **al ~ di** beneath 2 agg lower 3 m underside

dispari inv odd; **disparità** f inv disparity

disparte: **in ~** aside

dispendio m waste; **dispendioso** expensive

dispensa f stanza larder; mobile cupboard; pubblicazione instalment, Am installment; DIR exemption; **dispensare** dispense; (esonerare) exonerate

disperare despair (di of); **far ~ qu** drive s.o. to despair; **disperarsi** despair; **disperato**

desperate; **disperazione** f despair, desperation

disperdere disperse; energie, sostanze squander; **disperdersi** disperse; **disperso** 1 pp → **disperdere** 2 agg scattered; (sperduto) lost, missing

dispetto m spite; **per ~** out of spite; **a ~ di qc** in spite of sth; **fare i -i a qu** annoy o tease s.o.; **dispettoso** mischievous

dispiacere 1 v/i (causare dolore) upset (a s.o.); (non piacere) displease (a s.o.); **mi dispiace** I'm sorry; **le dispiace se apro la finestra?** do you mind if I open the window? 2 m (rammarico) regret, sorrow; (dolore) sadness; (delusione) disappointment; **-i** pl (preoccupazioni) worries, troubles

display m display

disponibile available; (cortese) helpful, obliging; **disponibilità** f availability; (cortesia) helpfulness

disporre 1 v/t arrange; (stabilire) order 2 v/i (decidere) make arrangements; **~ di qc** have sth (at one's disposal)

dispositivo m device

disposizione f arrangement; (norma) provision; (attitudine) aptitude (a for); **stare / mettere a ~ di qu** be / put at s.o.'s disposal

disposto 1 pp ☞ **disporre 2** agg. ~ **a** ready to, willing to; **essere ben ~ verso qu** be well disposed to s.o.

dispotico despotic

disprezzare despise; **disprezzo** m contempt

disputa f dispute, argument; **disputare 1** v/i argue **2** v/t SP take part in; **disputarsi qc** compete for sth

disseminare scatter, disseminate; fig spread

dissenso m dissent; (dissapore) argument, disagreement

dissenteria f dysentery

dissentire disagree (**da** with)

disservizio m poor service; (inefficienza) inefficiency; (cattiva gestione) mismanagement

dissestato strada uneven; finanze precarious

dissetante thirst-quenching; **dissetare**: ~ **qu** quench s.o.'s thirst; **dissetarsi** quench one's thirst

dissimulare conceal, hide; **dissimulazione** f concealment

dissociarsi dissociate o.s. (**da** from)

dissolvere dissolve; dubbi, nebbia dispel; **dissolversi** dissolve; (svanire) vanish

dissuadere: ~ **qu da fare qc** dissuade s.o. from doing sth, persuade s.o. not to do sth; **dissuaso** pp ☞ **dissuadere**

distaccare detach; SP leave behind; **distaccarsi da persone** detach o.s. (**da** from); **distacco** m detachment (anche fig); (separazione) separation; SP lead

distante distant, far-off; ~ **da** far from; **distanza** f distance (anche fig); **distanziare 1** v/t space out; SP leave behind; (superare) overtake; **distare**: **l'albergo dista 100 metri dalla stazione** the hotel is 100 metres from the station; **quanto dista da qui?** how far is it from here?

distendere (adagiare) lay; gambe, braccia stretch out; muscoli relax; nervi calm; **distendersi** lie down; (rilassarsi) relax

distesa f expanse; **disteso 1** pp ☞ **distendere 2** agg stretched out; (rilassato) relaxed

distinguere distinguish; **distintivo 1** agg distinctive **2** m badge; **distinto 1** pp ☞ **distinguere 2** agg (diverso) different, distinct; (chiaro) distinct; fig distinguished; **-i saluti** yours faithfully; **distinzione** f distinction

distorsione f distortion; MED sprain

distrarre distract; (divertire) entertain; **distrarsi** (non essere attento) get distracted; (svagarsi) take one's mind off things; **distratto** pp ☞

distrarre 2 *agg* absent-minded; **distrazione** *f* absent-mindedness; (*errore*) inattention; (*svago*) amusement; *che distrae da un'attività* distraction

distribuire distribute; *premi* award, present; **distributore** *m* distributor; ~ **di benzina**) (petrol *o Am* gas) pump; ~ **automatico** vending machine; ~ **automatico di biglietti** ticket machine; **distribuzione** *f* distribution; *posta* delivery

distruggere destroy; **distruttivo** destructive; **distrutto** *pp* ☞ **distruggere**, **distruzione** *f* destruction

disturbare disturb; (*dare fastidio a*) bother; (*sconvolgere*) upset; **disturbarsi**: **non si disturbi** please don't bother; **disturbo** *m* trouble, bother; MED **-i pl di circolazione** circulation problems

disubbidiente disobedient; **disubbidire**: ~ **a** disobey

disumano inhuman

disuso: **in ~** in disuse, disused

ditale *m* thimble

dito *m* (*pl* **le dita**) finger; *del piede* toe; **un ~ di vino** a drop of wine

ditta *f* company, firm

dittatore *m* dictator; **dittatura** *f* dictatorship

diurno daytime *attr*; **albergo** *m* ~ place where travellers can have a shower / shave

diva *f* diva

divagare digress

divampare *di rivolta, incendio* break out; *di passione* blaze

divano *m* couch, *Br anche* sofa; ~ **letto** sofa bed

divaricare open (wide)

divario *m* difference

divenire become

diventare become; *rosso, bianco* turn, go

diverbio *m* argument

divergenza *f* divergence; *di opinioni* difference

diversamente differently; (*altrimenti*) otherwise

diversificare 1 *v/t* diversify **2** *v/i e* **diversificarsi** differ; **diversità** *f inv* difference; (*varietà*) diversity

diversivo *m* diversion, distraction

diverso (*differente*) different (**da** from, than); **-i** *pl* several; **da -i giorni** for the past few days

divertente amusing; **divertimento** *m* amusement; **buon ~!** have a good time!, have fun!; **divertire** amuse; **divertirsi** enjoy o.s., have a good time

dividere divide; (*condividere*) share; **dividersi** *di coppia* separate; (*scindersi*) be divided (**in** into)

divieto *m* ban; ~ **di sosta** no parking

divincolarsi twist, wriggle

divinità *f inv* divinity; **divino**

divine

divisa f uniform; FIN currency

divisione f division; **divisorio 1** agg dividing **2** m partition

divo m star

divorare devour

divorziare get a divorce, get divorced; **divorziato** divorced; **divorzio** m divorce

divulgare divulge, reveal; (rendere accessibile) popularize

dizionario m dictionary

DNA m inv (= **acido deossiribonucleico**) DNA (= deoxyribonucleic acid)

do¹ ☞ **dare**

do² m inv MUS C; nel solfeggio della scala doh

dobbiamo ☞ **dovere**

D.O.C., doc (= **Denominazione d'Origine Controllata**) term signifying that a wine is of a certain origin and quality

doccia f shower; **fare la** ~ (take a) shower

docente 1 agg teaching **2** m/f teacher

docile docile

documentario m documentary; **documentarsi** collect information; **documentazione** f documentation; **documento** m document

dodicesimo twelfth; **dodici** twelve

dogana f customs; (dazio) (customs) duty; **doganale** customs attr

doglie fpl: **avere le -e** be in labour o Am labor

dolce 1 agg sweet; carattere, voce, pendio gentle; acqua fresh; clima mild; ricordo pleasant; suono soft **2** m portata dessert; di sapore sweetness; torta cake; **-i** pl sweet things; **dolcezza** f sweetness; di carattere, voce gentleness; di clima mildness; di ricordo pleasantness; di suono softness; **dolciastro** sweetish; fig sugary; **dolcificante** m sweetener; **dolciumi** mpl sweets, Am candy

dolente painful, sore; **dolere** hurt, be painful; **mi duole la schiena** my back hurts

dollaro m dollar

dolo m malice

Dolomiti fpl Dolomites

dolore m pain; **doloroso** painful

doloso malicious

domanda f question; (richiesta) request; FIN demand; **fare una** ~ a qu ask s.o. a question; **domandare 1** v/t per sapere: nome, ora, opinione ecc ask; per ottenere: informazioni, aiuto ecc ask for; ~ **un favore a qu** ask s.o. a favour; ~ **scusa** apologize **2** v/i: ~ **a qu** ask s.o.; ~ **di qu** per sapere come sta ask after s.o.; per parlargli ask for s.o.; **domandarsi** wonder, ask o.s.

domani m/avv tomorrow; ~ **mattina** tomorrow morning;

~ sera tomorrow evening; **a ~!** see you tomorrow!

domare tame; *fig* control

domattina tomorrow morning

domenica *f* Sunday

domestico 1 *agg* domestic; **animale ~** pet **2** *m*, **-a** *f* servant; **donna** maid

domiciliato: ~ a domiciled at; **domicilio** *m* domicile; (*casa*) home

dominante dominant; *idee* prevailing; *classe* ruling; **dominare 1** *v/t* dominate; *materia; passioni* master **2** *v/i* rule (**su** over); *fig*: *di confusione* reign; **dominio** *m* (*controllo*) control, power; *fig* (*campo*) domain, field; INFOR domain

domino *m* mask, domino

donare donate, give; *sangue* give; **donatore** *m*, **-trice** *f* donor; **~ di sangue** blood donor

dondolare 1 *v/t culla* rock **2** *v/i* sway; (*oscillare*) swing; **dondolarsi** *su altalena* swing; *su sedia* rock; *fig* hang around; **dondolo** *m*: *cavallo m* **a ~** rocking horse; **sedia** *f* **a ~** rocking chair

donna *f* woman; *carte da gioco* queen; **~ di servizio** home help

dono *m* gift

dopo 1 *prep* after; **~ di te** after you; **~ mangiato** after eating **2** *avv* (*in seguito*) afterwards, after, *Am* afterward; (*poi*) then; (*più tardi*) later; **il giorno ~** the day after **3** *cong*: **~ che** after; **~ essere uscito ho visto ...** after I left, I saw ...; **dopobarba** *m inv* aftershave; **dopodomani** the day after tomorrow; **dopoguerra** *m inv* post-war period; **dopopranzo** *m* afternoon; **doposci** *m inv* après-ski; **~ pl** *stivali* après-ski boots; **dopotutto** after all

doppiaggio *m di film* dubbing; **doppiare** *film* dub; SP lap; MAR round; **doppiatore** *m*, **-trice** *f* dubber

doppio 1 *agg* double **2** *m* double; SP doubles; **doppiopetto** *m* double-breasted jacket

dorato 1 *pp* ☞ **dorare 2** *agg* gilded; *sabbia, riflessi* golden; GASTR browned

dormicchiare doze

dormiglione *m*, **-a** *f* late riser

dormire sleep; **dormita** *f* (good) night's sleep; **dormitorio** *m* dormitory; **dormiveglia** *m*: **essere nel ~** be only half awake

dorso *m* back; (*di libro*) spine; SP backstroke

dosare measure out; *fig* be sparing with; *parole* weigh; **dose** *f* quantity, amount; MED dose

dosso *m di strada* hump; **togliersi gli abiti di ~** get undressed

dotare provide, supply (*di* with); *fig* provide, endow (*di* with); **dotato** gifted; **~ di** equipped with; **dote** *f* dowry; *fig* gift

dott. (= *dottore*) Dr (= doctor)

dottore *m* doctor (*in* of); **dottoressa** *f* (woman) doctor

dottrina *f* doctrine

dott.ssa (= *dottoressa*) Dr (= doctor)

dove where; *di* **~ sei?** where are you from?; *fin* **~?** how far?; *per* **~ si passa?** which way do you go?; **mettilo ~ vuoi** put it wherever you like

dovere 1 *v/i* have to, must; **non devo dimenticare** I mustn't forget; **deve arrivare oggi** she is supposed to arrive today; **come si deve** (*bene*) properly; *persona* very decent; **doveva succedere** it was bound to happen; **dovresti avvertirlo** you ought to *o* should let him know 2 *v/t denaro* owe 3 *m* duty

dovunque 1 *avv* (*dappertutto*) everywhere; (*in qualsiasi luogo*) anywhere 2 *cong* wherever

dovuto 1 *pp* ☞ *dovere* 2 *agg* due; **~ a** because of, due to

dozzina *f* dozen; **una ~ di uova** a dozen eggs

dragare dredge

drago *m* dragon; **dragoncello** *m* tarragon

dramma *m* drama; **drammatico** dramatic

drastico drastic

dritto 1 *agg* straight 2 *avv* straight (ahead) 3 *m di indumento, tessuto* right side 4 *m*, *-a* F crafty devil F; **drizzare** (*raddrizzare*) straighten; (*erigere*) put up, erect; **~ le orecchie** prick up one's ears; **drizzarsi ~ in piedi** get to one's feet

droga *f* drug; **drogarsi** SP take drugs; **drogato** *m*, *-a* *f* drug addict

drogheria *f* grocer's, *Am* grocery store

dubbio 1 *agg* doubtful; (*equivoco*) dubious 2 *m* doubt; **essere in ~ fra** hesitate between; **mettere qc in ~** doubt sth; **senza ~** without a doubt; **dubbioso** doubtful; **dubitare** doubt (*di* sth); **dubito che venga** I doubt whether he'll come

duca *m* duke; **duchessa** *f* duchess

due two; **a ~ a ~** in twos, two by two; **tutt'e ~** both of them; **duecento** 1 *agg* two hundred 2 *m*: **il Duecento** the thirteenth century

duello *m* duel

duemila two thousand; **duepezzi** *m inv* bikini; *vestito* two-piece (suit)

duna *f* (sand) dune

dunque 1 *cong* so; (*allora*) well (then) 2 *m*: **venire al ~**

come to the crunch

duomo *m* cathedral

duplicato *m* duplicate; **duplice** double; **in ~ copia** in duplicate

durante during; **durare** last; (*conservarsi*) keep, last; **durata** *f* duration, length; **di prodotto** life; **duraturo** last-

ing

duro 1 *agg* hard; *carne, persona* tough; *inverno, voce* harsh; *congegno, meccanismo* stiff; *pane* stale; (*ostinato*) stubborn; **tieni ~!** hang in there! **2** *m* tough guy

durone *m* MED callus

DVD *m inv* DVD

E

e and; **sono le due ~ un quarto** it's (a) quarter past two, *Am* it's a quarter after two

è ☞ **essere**

ebano *m* ebony

ebbe, ebbi ☞ **avere**

ebbene well

ebbrezza *f* drunkenness; *fig* thrill

ebraico 1 *agg* Hebrew; *religione* Jewish **2** *m* Hebrew; **ebreo 1** *m*, **-a** *f* Jew; **2** *agg* Jewish

ecc. (= **eccetera**) etc (= et cetera)

eccedente excess; **eccedere 1** *v/t* exceed, go beyond **2** *v/i* go too far; **~ nel bere** drink too much

eccellente excellent

eccentrico eccentric

eccessivo excessive; **eccesso** *m* excess; **~ di velocità** speeding

eccetera et cetera

eccetto except; **eccezionale** exceptional; **eccezional-**

mente exceptionally; **eccezione** *f* exception

ecchimosi *f inv* bruise

eccitante 1 *agg* exciting **2** *m* stimulant; **eccitare** excite; **eccitarsi** get excited; **eccitazione** *f* excitement

ecclesiastico 1 *agg* ecclesiastical **2** *m* priest

ecco (*qui*) here; (*là*) there; **~ come** this is how; **~ fatto** that's that; **~ tutto** that's all; **~mi** here I am; **~li** here they are; **~ti il libro** here's your book

eclissarsi *fig* slip away; **eclisse** *f*, **eclissi** *f inv* eclipse

eco *m/f* echo

ecografia *f* scan

ecologia *f* ecology; **ecologico** ecological

economia *f* economy; *scienza* economics *sg*; **fare ~** economize (**di** on); **-e** *pl* savings; **economico** economic; (*poco costoso*) economical; **economizzare 1** *v/t* save **2** *v/i* economize (**su** on)

ecosistema *m* ecosystem

eczema *m* eczema

ed and

edera *f* ivy

edicola *f* newspaper kiosk

edificare edify; *fig* edify; **edificio** *m* building; *fig* structure

edile construction *attr*, building *attr*; **edilizia** *f* construction, building; (*urbanistica*) town planning

editore 1 *agg* publishing 2 *m*, **-trice** *f* publisher; (*curatore*) editor; **editoria** *f* publishing; **edizione** *f* edition

educare educate; (*allevare*) bring up; *orecchio*, *mente* train; **educativo** education *attr*; (*istruttivo*) educational; **educato**: (**ben**) ~ well brought-up; **educazione** *f* education; *dei figli* upbringing; (*buone maniere*) (good) manners; ~ **fisica** physical education

effervescente effervescent; *aspirina* soluble

effettivamente in fact; *per rafforzare un'affermazione* really, actually; **effettivo** (*reale*) real, actual; (*efficace*) effective; **effetto** *m* effect; (*impressione*) impression; **fare** ~ (*funzionare*) work; (*impressionare*) make an impression; **-i pl personali** personal effects; **in -i** in fact; **effettuare** carry out; *pagamento* make;

effettuarsi take place; *il servizio non si effettua la domenica* there is no Sunday service

efficace effective

efficiente efficient; (*funzionante*) in working order; **efficienza** *f* efficiency

Egitto *m* Egypt; **egiziano** 1 *agg* Egyptian 2 *m*, **-a** *f* Egyptian; **egizio** ancient Egyptian

egli he

egocentrico egocentric

egoismo *m* selfishness, egoism

egoista 1 *agg* selfish 2 *m/f* selfish person

egr. (= **egregio**) form of address used in correspondence

egregio distinguished; *nelle lettere* ~ **signore** Dear Sir

eguale ☞ **uguale**

ehi! oi!

E.I. (= **Esercito Italiano**) Italian army

elaborare elaborate; *dati* process; *piano* work out; **elaborato** elaborate; **elaboratore** *m*: ~ **elettronico** computer; **elaborazione** *f* elaboration; ~ **elettronica dei dati** electronic data processing; ~ **dei testi** word processing

elastico 1 *agg* elastic; *orari* flexible 2 *m* rubber band

elefante *m* elephant

elegante elegant; **eleganza** *f* elegance

eleggere elect

elementare elementary; **scuola** f ~ primary school, Am elementary school

elemento m element; (*componente*) component; **-i** pl (*rudimenti*) rudiments; (*fatti*) data sg

elemosina f charity; **chiedere l'~** beg

elencare list; **elenco** m list; ~ **telefonico** phone book, telephone directory

eletto 1 pp ▸ **eleggere 2** aggi chosen; **elettore** m, **-trice** f voter

elettrauto m inv auto electrics garage; *persona* automobile electrician; **elettricista** m/f electrician; **elettricità** f electricity; **elettrico** electric

elettrocardiogramma m electrocardiogram; **elettrodo** m electrode; **elettrodomestico** m household appliance; **elettromagnetico** electromagnetic

elettrone m electron; **elettronico** electronic; **libro** ~ e-book, electronic book; **commercio** ~ e-commerce

elettrotecnico 1 aggi electrical **2** m electrical engineer

elevare raise; *costruzioni* erect; (*promuovere*) promote; fig (*migliorare*) better; **elevato** high; fig elevated, lofty

elezione f election

eliambulanza f air ambulance

elica f propeller

elicottero m helicopter

eliminare eliminate; **eliminatoria** f SP heat; **eliminazione** f elimination

eliporto m heliport

élite f élite

elmetto m helmet; **elmo** m helmet

elogio m praise

eloquente eloquent

eludere evade; *sorveglianza, domanda* evade

elvetico Swiss

e-mail f inv e-mail; **inviare un'~ a qc** e-mail s.o., send s.o. an e-mail

emanare 1 v/t give off; *legge* pass **2** v/i emanate, come (**da** from)

emanciparsi become emancipated; **emancipazione** f emancipation

emarginare marginalize; **emarginato** m, **-a** f person on the fringes of society

ematoma m haematoma, Am hematoma

embrione m embryo

emergenza f emergency; **emergere** emerge; (*distinguersi*) stand out; **emerso** pp ▸ **emergere**

emesso pp ▸ **emettere**; **emettere** *luce* give out, emit; *grido, verdetto* give; *calore* give off; FIN issue; TEC emit

emicrania f migraine

emigrante *m/f* emigrant; **emigrare** emigrate; **emigrato** *m*, **-a** *f* person who has emigrated, ex-pat; **emigrazione** *f* emigration

emisfero *m* hemisphere

emissione *f* emission; *di denaro, francobolli* issue; RAD broadcast; **emittente 1** *agg* issuing; (*trasmittente*) broadcasting **2** *f* RAD transmitter; TV channel

emoglobina *f* haemoglobin, *Am* hemoglobin

emorragia *f* haemorrhage, *Am* hemorrhage

emorroidi *fpl* haemorrhoids, *Am* hemorrhoids

emotivo emotional; (*sensibile*) sensitive

emozionante exciting, thrilling; **emozionarsi** get excited; (*commuoversi*) be moved; (*agitato*) nervous; (*commosso*) moved; (*turbato*) upset; **emozione** *f* emotion; (*agitazione*) excitement

emporio *m negozio* department store

emulsione *f* emulsion

enciclopedia *f* encyclopedia

endovenoso intravenous

energetico *consumo* ecc energy *attr*; *alimento* energy-giving; **energia** *f* energy; **energico** strong, energetic

enfasi *f* emphasis

enigma *m* enigma

ennesimo MAT nth; F *per l'-a*

volta for the hundredth time F

enorme enormous

enoteca *f negozio* wine merchant (*specializing in fine wines*)

ente *m* organization; **gli enti locali** the local authorities

entrambi both

entrare (*andare dentro*) go in, enter; (*venire dentro*) come in, enter; *fig* **questo non c'entra** that has nothing to do with it; **~ in una stanza** enter a room, go into / come into a room; **entrata** *f* entrance; *in parcheggio* entrance, way in; *in un paese* entry; FIN **-e** *pl* (*reddito*) income; (*guadagno*) earnings; **~ libera** admission free

entro within

entroterra *m inv* hinterland

entusiasmare enthuse; **entusiasmo** *m* enthusiasm; **entusiasta** enthusiastic

enumerare enumerate

enzima *m* enzyme

epatite *f* hepatitis

epicentro *m* epicentre, *Am* epicenter; *fig* centre, *Am* center

epidemia *f* epidemic

epidermide *f* skin; MED epidermis

Epifania *f* Epiphany

epilessia *f* epilepsy; **epilettico 1** *agg* epileptic **2** *m*, **-a** *f* epileptic

episodio *m* episode

epoca f age; (*periodo*) period, time; *auto* f d'~ vintage car; *mobili* mpl d'~ period furniture

eppure (and) yet

equatore m equator; **equatoriale** equatorial

equazione f equation

equilibrare balance; **equilibrato** balanced; **equilibrio** m balance; fig common sense

equino horse attr

equinozio m equinox

equipaggiamento m equipment; **equipaggio** m crew

équipe f inv team

equitazione f horse riding

equivalente m/agg equivalent

equivoco 1 agg ambiguous; (*sospetto*) suspicious; **F** (*losco*) shady **F 2** m misunderstanding

era f (*epoca*) age, era; GEOL era; ~ *atomica* atomic age; ~ *glaciale* Ice Age

era, erano ☞ *essere*

erba f grass; GASTR -*e* pl herbs; -*e* *aromatiche* herbs; **erbaccia** f weed; **erboristeria** f herbalist's, Am herbalist store

erede m/f heir; *donna* heiress; **eredità** f inheritance; BIO heredity; **ereditare** inherit; **ereditarietà** f heredity; **ereditario** hereditary; **ereditiera** f heiress

eremita m hermit

eretico 1 agg heretical **2** m, -a f heretic

eretto 1 pp ☞ *erigere* **2** agg erect; **erezione** f building; *di pene* erection

ergastolo m life sentence

ergonomico ergonomic

erica f heather

erigere erect; fig (*fondare*) establish, found

eritema m cutaneo rash; ~ *solare* sunburn

ermafrodito m hermaphrodite

ermellino m ermine

ermetico (*a tenuta d'aria*) airtight; fig obscure

ernia f MED hernia; ~ *del disco* slipped disc

ero ☞ *essere*

eroe m hero

erogare denaro allocate; *gas, acqua* supply

eroina f droga heroin; *donna* eroica heroine

erosione f GEOL erosion

erotico erotic; **erotismo** m eroticism

errare wander, roam; (*sbagliare*) be mistaken; **errata corrige** m inv correction; **erroneamente** mistakenly; **errore** m mistake, error; ~ *di ortografia* spelling mistake; ~ *di stampa* misprint, typo; *per* ~ by mistake

erta f: *stare all'~* be on the alert

erudito 1 agg erudite, learned **2** m, -a f erudite person, scholar

eruttare *di vulcano* erupt; **eruzione** *f* eruption; MED rash

es. (= **esempio**) eg (= for example)

esagerare 1 *v/t* exaggerate **2** *v/i* exaggerate; (*eccedere*) go too far; **esagerato** exaggerated; *zelo* excessive; *prezzo* exorbitant; **esagerazione** *f* exaggeration

esalare 1 *v/t odori* give off; **~ il respiro** exhale **2** *v/i* come, emanate (**da** from)

esaltare exalt; (*entusiasmare*) elate; **esaltarsi** become elated; **esaltato 1** *agg* elated; (*fanatico*) fanatical **2** *m* fanatic

esame *m* exam(ination); MED (*test*) test; (*visita*) examination; **esaminare** examine (*anche* MED)

esasperante exasperating; **esasperare** (*inasprire*) exacerbate; (*irritare*) exasperate; **esasperazione** *f* exasperation

esattezza *f* accuracy; **per l'~** to be precise; **esatto 1** *pp* ☞ **esigere 2** *agg* exact; *risposta* correct, right; *in punto* exactly; **~!** that's right!

esaudire grant; *speranze* fulfil, *Am* fulfill

esauriente exhaustive; **esaurimento** *m* exhaustion; MED **svendita** *f* **fino a ~ della merce** clearance sale; **~ ner-**

voso nervous breakdown; **esaurire** exhaust; *merci* run out of; **esaurito** (*esausto*) exhausted; COM sold out; *pubblicazioni* out of print; **esausto** exhausted

esca *f* bait (*anche fig*)

esce ☞ **uscire**

eschimese *agg*, *m/f* Inuit, Eskimo

esclamare exclaim; **esclamazione** *f* exclamation

escludere exclude; **esclusione** *f* exclusion; **esclusiva** *f* exclusive right, sole right; **esclusivo** exclusive; **escluso 1** *pp* ☞ **escludere 2** *agg* excluded; (*impossibile*) out of the question **3** *m*, *-a f* person on the fringes of society

esco ☞ **uscire**

escogitare contrive

escoriazione *f* graze

escrementi *mpl* excrement

escursione *f* trip, excursion; *a piedi* hike; **escursionismo** *m* touring; *a piedi* hiking, walking; **escursionista** *m/f* tourist; *a piedi* hiker, walker

esecutivo *m/agg* executive; **esecutore** *m*, *-trice f* DIR executor; MUS performer; **esecuzione** *f* (*realizzazione*) carrying out; MUS performance; **~** (**capitale**) execution; **eseguire** carry out; MUS perform

esempio *m* example; **per ~, ad ~** for example; **esemplare 1** *agg* exemplary **2** *m* specimen; (*copia*) copy

esentare exempt (*da* from); **esente** exempt; **~ da tasse** tax-free

esercente *m/f* shopkeeper, *Am* storekeeper

esercitare exercise; (*addestrare*) train; *professione* practise; *Am* practice; **esercitarsi** practise, *Am* practice; **esercitazione** *f* exercise

esercito *m* army

esercizio *m* exercise; (*pratica*) practice; (*anno finanziario*) financial year, *Am* fiscal year; FIN *azienda* business; *negozio* shop, *Am anche* store

esibire *documenti* produce; *mettere in mostra* display; **esibirsi** *in uno spettacolo* perform; *fig* show off; **esibizione** *f* exhibition; (*ostentazione*) showing off; (*spettacolo*) performance; **esibizionista** *m/f* show-off; PSI exhibitionist

esigente exacting, demanding; **esigenza** *f* demand; (*bisogno*) need; **esigere** demand; (*riscuotere*) exact

esile slender; *voce* faint

esiliare exile; **esilio** *m* exile

esistente existing; **esistenza** *f* existence; **esistere** exist

esitare hesitate; **esitazione** *f* hesitation

esito *m* result, outcome; FIN sales, turnover

esodo *m* exodus

esofago *m* œsophagus, *Am* esophagus

esonerare exempt (*da* from)

esordiente *m/f* beginner; **esordio** *m* introduction; (*inizio*) beginning; TEA début

esortare (*incitare*) urge; (*pregare*) beg; **esortazione** *f* urging

esotico exotic

espandere expand; **espandersi** expand; (*diffondersi*) spread; **espansivo** FIS, TEC expansive; *fig* warm, friendly

espatriare leave one's country; **espatrio** *m* expatriation

espediente *m* expedient

espellere expel

esperienza *f* experience

esperimento *m* experiment

esperto *m/agg* expert

espirare breathe out, exhale

esplicito explicit

esplodere 1 *v/t colpo* fire **2** *v/i* explode

esplorare explore; **esploratore** *m*, **-trice** *f* explorer; *giovane* **m ~** boy scout

esplosione *f* explosion; **~ demografica** population explosion; **esplosivo** *m/agg* explosive; **esploso** *pp* ☞ *esplodere*

esponente *m/f* exponent; **esporre** expose; (*anche* FOT); *avviso* put up; *in una mostra* exhibit, show; (*riferire*) present; *ragioni, caso* state; *teoria* explain; **esporsi**

expose o.s. (**a** to); (*compromettersi*) compromise o.s.

esportare export; **esportazione** *f* export

esposizione *f* (*mostra*) exhibition; (*narrazione*) presentation; FOT exposure; **esposto 1** *pp* ☞ **esporre 2** *agg* in mostra on show; **~ a** exposed to; *critiche* open to; **~ a sud** south facing **3** *m* statement; (*petizione*) petition

espressione *f* expression; **espressivo** expressive; **espresso 1** *pp* ☞ **esprimere 2** *agg* express **3** *m* posta express letter; FERR express; (*caffè m*) ~ espresso; **per ~** express; **esprimere** express; **esprimersi** express o.s.

espropriare expropriate; **esproprio** *m* expropriation

espulsione *f* expulsion; **espulso** *pp* ☞ **espellere**

essa *pron f persona* she; *cosa, animale* it

essenza *f* essence; **essenziale 1** *agg* essential **2** *m*: **l'~ è** the main thing is

essere 1 *v/i* be; **~ di** (*provenire di*) be o come from; **~ di qu** (*appartenere a*) belong to s.o; **c'è** there is; **ci sono** there are; **sono io** it's me; **cosa c'è?** what's the matter?; **non c'è di che!** don't mention it!; **chi è?** who is it; **sono le tre** it's three o'clock; **siamo in quattro** there are four of us; **se fossi in te** if

I were you; **sarà!** if you say so! **2** *v/aus*: **siamo arrivati alle due** we arrived at two o'clock; **non siamo ancora arrivati** we haven't arrived yet; **è stato investito** he has been run over **3** *m* being

esso *pron m persona* he; *cosa, animale* it

est *m* east; **~ di** (*to the*) east of

estasi *f* ecstasy

estate *f* summer; **in ~, d'~** in (the) summer

estendere extend; **estendersi di territorio** extend; (*allungarsi*) stretch; *fig* (*diffondersi*) spread

estenuante exhausting

esteriore *m/agg* exterior, outside

esterno 1 *agg* external **2** *m* outside; **all'~** on the outside

estero 1 *agg* foreign **2** *m* foreign countries; **all'~** abroad

esteso 1 *pp* ☞ **estendere 2** *agg* extensive; (*diffuso*) widespread; **per ~** in full

estetista *f* beautician

estinguere extinguish, put out; *debito* pay off; **estinguersi** die out; **estinto 1** *pp* ☞ **estinguere 2** *agg* extinct; *debito* paid off **3** *m*, **-a** *f* deceased; **estintore** *m* fire extinguisher; **estinzione** *f* extinction; FIN paying off

estirpare uproot; *dente* extract; *fig* eradicate

estivo summer *attr*

estorcere *denaro* extort; **estorsione** *f* extortion; **estorto** *pp* ☞ **estorcere**

estradizione *f* extradition

estraneo 1 *agg* outside (*a qc* sth) 2 *m*, -**a** *f* stranger; *persona non autorizzata* unauthorized person

estrarre extract; *pistola* pull out; **estratto** 1 *pp* ☞ **estrarre** 2 *m* extract; *documento* abstract; FIN **~ conto** statement (of account); **estrazione** *f* extraction

estremista *m/f* extremist; **estremità** *f inv* extremity; *di corda* end; (*punta*) tip; (*punto superiore*) top; **estremo** 1 *agg* extreme; (*più lontano*) farthest; (*ultimo nel tempo*) last, final 2 *m* (*estremità*) extreme; **gli -i** *pl* di un documento the main points

estro *m* (*ispirazione artistica*) inspiration

estroverso *m* extrovert(ed)

estuario *m* estuary

esuberante (*vivace*) exuberant

esultare rejoice

età *f inv* age; **all'~ di** at the age of; **avere la stessa ~** be the same age; **di mezz'~** middle-aged

eternità *f* eternity; **eterno** eternal; *questione, problema* age-old; **in ~** for ever and ever

eterogeneo heterogen(e)ous

eterosessuale heterosexual

etica *f* ethics *sg*

etichetta *f* label; *cerimoniale* etiquette

etico ethical

etiope *agg*, *m/f* Ethiopian; **Etiopia** *f* Ethiopia

etnico ethnic

etrusco 1 *agg* Etruscan 2 *m*, -**a** *f* Etruscan

ettaro *m* hectare

etto *m* hundred grams; **ettogrammo** *m* hundred grams, hectogram

eucalipto *m* eucalyptus

eucaristia *f* REL Eucharist

euforia *f* euphoria

euro *m inv* euro; **eurodeputato** *m*, -**a** *f* Euro MP; **Europa** *f* Europe; **europeo** 1 *agg* European 2 *m*, -**a** *f* European; **eurovisione** *f* Eurovision

evacuare evacuate; **evacuazione** *f* evacuation

evadere 1 *v/t* evade; (*sbrigare*) deal with 2 *v/i* escape (*da* from)

evaporare evaporate

evasione *f* escape; *fig* escapism; **~ fiscale** *f* tax evasion; **evasivo** evasive; **evaso** 1 *pp* ☞ **evadere** 2 *m*, -**a** *f* fugitive; **evasore** *m*: **~ fiscale** tax evader

evenienza *f* eventuality

evento *m* event

eventuale possible; **eventualità** *f inv* eventuality; **eventualmente** if necessary

fallito

evidente evident; **evidenziatore** *m* highlighter
evitare avoid; ~ **il fastidio a qu** spare s.o. the trouble
evoluto 1 *pp* ☞ **evolvere** 2 *agg* developed; (*progredito*) progressive, advanced; *senza pregiudizi* open-minded;
evoluzione *f* evolution;
evolvere 1 *v/t* develop 2 *v/i*

e **evolversi** evolve, develop
evviva hurray
ex … ex-, former
extra *m/agg* extra
extracomunitario 1 *agg* non-EU 2 *m*, -a *f* non-EU citizen
extraconiugale extramarital
extraeuropeo non-European
extraterrestre *agg*, *m/f* extraterrestrial

F

fa 1 ☞ **fare** 2 *avv*: **5 anni** ~ 5 years ago 3 *m* MUS F; *nel solfeggio della scala* fa(h)
fabbisogno *m* needs
fabbrica *f* plant, factory; **fabbricante** *m/f* manufacturer;
fabbricare manufacture; ARCHI build; *fig* fabricate;
fabbricato *m* building
faccenda *f* matter; **faccende** *fpl* housework
faccia *f* face; (*risvolto*, *aspetto*) facet; (*lato*) side; ~ **tosta** cheek; ~ **a** ~ face to face; **gliel'ha detto in** ~ he told him to his face; **facciata** *f* ARCHI front, façade; *di foglio* side; *fig* (*esteriorità*) appearance
faccio ☞ **fare**
facile easy; *di carattere* easygoing; (*incline*) prone (**a** to); **è** ~ **a dirsi!** easier said than done!; **è** ~ **che venga** he is likely to come; **facilità** *f* ease; (*attitudine*) aptitude,

facility; **facilitare** facilitate; **facilmente** easily
facoltà *f inv* faculty; (*potere*) power; **facoltativo** optional
faggio *m* beech (tree)
fagiano *m* pheasant
fagiolini *mpl* green beans; **fagiolo** *m* bean
fagotto *m* bundle; MUS bassoon; *fig* **far** ~ pack up and leave
fai da te *m inv* do-it-yourself, DIY, *Am* home improvement
fai ☞ **fare**
falciatrice *f* lawn-mower
falco *m* hawk
falegname *m* carpenter
falena *f* moth
falla *f* MAR leak
fallimento *m* failure; FIN bankruptcy; **fallire** 1 *v/t* miss 2 *v/i* fail; FIN go bankrupt; **fallito** 1 *agg* unsuccessful, failed; FIN bankrupt 2 *m* failure; FIN bankruptcy

fallo m fault; (*errore*) error, mistake; SP foul

falò m inv bonfire

falsario m forger; **falsificare** forge; **falso 1** agg false; (*sbagliato*) incorrect, wrong; *oro, gioielli* imitation, fake **F 2** (*falsificato*) forged, fake **F 2** m (*falsità*) falsehood; *oggetto falsificato* forgery, fake **F**

fama f fame; (*reputazione*) reputation

fame f hunger; *aver* ~ be hungry

famiglia f family; **familiare 1** agg family attr, (*conosciuto*) familiar; (*semplice*) informal **2** m/f relative, relation; familiarità f familiarity; familiarizzarsi familiarize o.s.

famoso famous

fanale m light; (*lampione*) street lamp

fanatico **1** agg fanatical **2** m, -a f fanatic

fanciullo m, -a f (young) boy; *ragazza* (young) girl

fango m mud; MED **-ghi** pl mud-baths; **fangoso** muddy

fannullone m, -a f lazy good-for-nothing

fantascienza f science fiction

fantasia f fantasy; (*immaginazione*) imagination; (*capriccio*) fancy; MUS fantasia

fantasma m ghost

fantasticare day-dream (*di* about); **fantastico** fantastic

fantoccio m puppet (*anche* fig)

farabutto m nasty piece of work

faraona f: (*gallina f*) ~ guinea fowl

farcire GASTR stuff; *torta* fill; **farcito** stuffed; *dolce* filled

fard m inv blusher

fardello m bundle; fig burden

fare 1 v/t do; *vestito, dolce, errore* make; *biglietto, benzina* buy, get; ~ *un bagno* have a bath; ~ *il medico* be a doctor; ~ *vedere qc a qu* show sth to s.o.; **farcela** manage; *non c'e la faccio più* I can't take any more; **2 più 2 fa 4** 2 and 2 make(s) 4; **quanto fa?** how much is it?; *far* ~ *qc a qu* get s.o. to do sth **2** v/i: *faccia pure!* go ahead!; *fa freddo / caldo* it's cold / warm

farfalla f butterfly

farina f flour; **farinaceo 1** agg starchy **2** *-cei* mpl starchy foodstuffs

faringe f pharynx; **faringite** f inflammation of the pharynx

farmaceutico pharmaceutical; **farmacia** f pharmacy, Br anche negozio chemist's; **farmacista** m/f pharmacist, Br anche chemist; **farmaco** m drug

faro m MAR lighthouse; AVIA beacon; AUTO headlight

farsi (*diventare*) grow; F (*drogarsi*) shoot up F; *si sta facendo tardi* it's getting late; ~ *male* hurt o.s.

fascia f band; MED bandage; ~

oraria (time) slot; **fasciare** MED bandage; **fasciatura** f (*fascia*) bandage; *azione* bandaging

fascicolo m (*opuscolo*) booklet, brochure; (*incartamento*) file

fascino m fascination, charm

fascio m bundle; *di fiori* bunch; *di luce* beam

fascismo m Fascism; **fascista** agg, m/f Fascist

fase f phase; AUTO stroke; *fig* **essere fuori ~** be out of sorts; **~ di lavorazione** production stage

fastidio m bother, trouble; **dare ~ a qu** bother s.o.; *le dà ~ se ... ?* do you mind if ... ?; **fastidioso** (*irritante*) irritating, annoying; (*irritabile*) irritable

fata f fairy

fatale fatal; **fatalità** f inv fate; (*disavventura*) misfortune

fatica f (*sforzo*) effort; (*stanchezza*) fatigue; *a ~* with a great deal of effort; **faticare** toil; *~ a* find it difficult to; **faticoso** tiring; (*difficile*) laborious

fatto 1 pp ☞ **fare 2** agg done; AGR ripe; **~ a mano** handmade; **~ di legno** made of wood **3** m fact; (*avvenimento*) event; (*faccenda*) affair, business; *di ~* agg real; *avv* in fact, actually; *in ~ di* as regards

fattore m (*elemento*) factor;

AGR farm manager; **~ di protezione antisolare** (sun) protection factor

fattoria f farm; *casa* farmhouse

fattorino m messenger; *per consegne* delivery man

fattura f (*lavorazione*) workmanship; *di abiti* cut; FIN invoice; **fatturare** FIN invoice; **fatturato** m FIN (*giro d'affari*) turnover

fauna f fauna

fava f broad bean

favola f (*fiaba*) fairy tale; (*storia*) story; *morale* fable; (*meraviglia*) dream; **favoloso** fabulous

favore m favour, Am favor; **per ~!** please!; **fare un ~ a qu** do s.o. a favour, Am favor; **favorevole** favourable, Am favorable; **favorire 1** v/t favour, Am favor; (*promuovere*) promote **2** v/i: *vuol ~?* would you care to join me / us?; **favorito** m/agg favourite, Am favorite

fax m inv fax; **faxare** fax

fazione f faction

fazzolettino m: **~ di carta** tissue; **fazzoletto** m handkerchief; *per la testa* headscarf

febbraio m February

febbre f fever; *ha la ~* he has a temperature

fecondare fertilize; **fecondazione** f fertilization; **~ artificiale** artificial insemination

fede f faith; (*fedeltà*) loyalty; *anello* wedding ring; **fedele**

1 agg faithful; (esatto, conforme all'originale) true **2** m REL believer; **i ~ i** pl the faithful pl

federa f pillowcase

federazione f federation

fegato m liver; fig courage, guts F

felce f fern

felice happy; (fortunato) lucky; (felicità) f happiness; **felicitarsi**: **~ con qu per qc** congratulate s.o. on sth

felino feline

felpa f sweatshirt

feltro m felt

femmina f (figlia) girl, daughter; ZO, TEC female; **femminile 1** agg feminine; (da donna) women's **2** m GRAM feminine; **femminilità** f femininity; **femminismo** m feminism; **femminista** m/f feminist

femore m femur

fendinebbia m inv fog lamp o light

fenomeno m phenomenon

feriale: **giorno** m **~** weekday; **ferie** fpl holiday, Am vacation, **andare in ~** go on holiday

ferire wound; in incidente injure; fig hurt; **ferirsi** injure o.s.; **ferita** f wound; in incidente injury; **ferito 1** agg wounded; in incidente injured; fig: sentimenti hurt; orgoglio injured **2** m casualty

fermacarte m inv paperweight

fermacravatta m inv tiepin

fermaglio m clasp; per capelli hair slide, Am barrette; (gioiello) brooch

fermare stop; DIR detain; **fermarsi** stop; (restare) stay, remain; **fermata** f stop; **~ dell' autobus** bus stop

fermentare ferment; **fermento** m yeast; fig ferment

fermo 1 agg still; veicolo stationary; (saldo) firm; mano steady; **star~** (non muoversi) keep still **2** int **~!** (alt!) stop!; (immobile!) keep still!

feroce fierce, ferocious; animale wild; (insopportabile) dreadful

ferragosto m August 15 public holiday; periodo August holidays

ferramenta f hardware; negozio hardware store

ferro m iron; (arnese) tool; **~ da calza** knitting needle; **~ da stiro** iron; **~ di cavallo** horseshoe; GASTR **ai ~i** grilled, Am broiled; **ferrovia** f railway, Am railroad

fertile fertile; **fertilizzante** m fertilizer

fesso m F idiot F; **far~ qu** con s.o F

fessura f (spaccatura) crack; (fenditura) slit, slot

festa f feast; REL di santo feast day; (ricevimento) party; (compleanno) birthday; **~ della mamma / del papà** Mother's / Father's Day;

nazionale national holiday; **festeggiamenti** *mpl* celebrations; **festeggiare** celebrate; *persona* have a celebration for; **festival** *m inv* festival; **festività** *f inv* festival; ~ *pl* celebrations, festivities; **festivo** festive; **giorno** ~ holiday

feto *m* fetus, *Br anche* foetus

fetta *f* slice; **a -e** sliced

fiaba *f* fairy tale

fiacca *f* weariness; (*svogliatezza*) laziness; **battere la** ~ be a shirker

fiaccola *f* torch

fiamma *f* flame; MAR pennant; **fiammante: rosso** *m* ~ fiery red; **nuovo** ~ brand new; **fiammifero** *m* match

fiancheggiare border; *fig* support

fianco *m* side; ANAT hip; **a** ~ side by side; **di** ~ **a qu** beside s.o.

fiasco *m* flask; *fig* fiasco

fiato *m* breath; **senza** ~ breathless; **riprendere** ~ catch one's breath

fibbia *f* buckle

fibra *f* fibre, *Am* fiber; ~ **sintetica** synthetic; **fibroso** fibrous

ficcanaso *m/f* F nosy parker F; **ficcare** thrust; F (*mettere*) shove F; **ficcarsi** get; **dove s'è ficcato?** where can it / he have got to?

fico *m* fig; *albero* fig (tree); ~ **d'India** prickly pear

fidanzamento *m* engagement; **fidanzarsi** get engaged; **fidanzata** *f* fiancée; **fidanzato** *m* fiancé; **i -i pl** the engaged couple *pl*

fidarsi: ~ **di** trust, rely on; **fidato** trustworthy; **fiducia** *f* confidence; **avere** ~ **in qu** have faith in s.o.; **fiduciaria** *f* ~ FIN trust company; **fiducioso** trusting

fienile *m* barn

fieno *m* hay

fiera *f* *mostra* fair

fiero proud

fifa F *f* jitters F; **aver** ~ have the jitters

figlia *f* daughter; **figliastra** *f* stepdaughter; **figliastro** *m* stepson; **figlio** *m* son; **avere -gli** *pl* have children; **essere** ~ **unico** be an only child; **figlioccia** *f* goddaughter; **figlioccio** *m* godson

figura *f* figure; (*illustrazione*) illustration; (*apparenza*) appearance; **far brutta** ~ make a bad impression; **figurare 1** *v/t fig* imagine; **figurati!** just imagine! **2** *v/i* (*apparire*) appear; (*far figura*) make a good impression; **figurato** illustrated; *linguaggio* figurative

fila *f* line, row; (*coda*) queue, *Am* line; **tre giorni di** ~ three days running; **fare la** ~ queue (up), *Am* wait in line; **filare 1** *v/t* spin **2** *v/i di ragionamento* make sense; *di for-*

maggio go stringy; *di veicolo* travel; F *(andarsene)* take off F; **~ diritto** *(comportarsi bene)* behave (o.s.)

filastrocca *f* nursery rhyme

filato 1 *agg (logico)* logical; **andare di ~ a casa** go straight home; **per 10 ore filate** for ten hours on the trot **2** *m* yarn; *per cucire* thread

file *m inv* INFOR file

filetto *m* GASTR fillet

filiale *f* branch; *(società affiliata)* affiliate

filigrana *f su carta* watermark; *in oreficeria* filigree

film *m inv* film, movie; **filmare** film; **filmato** *m* short (film)

filo *m* thread; *metallico* wire; *di lama* edge; *d'erba* blade; **~ interdentale** (dental) floss; **~ spinato** barbed wire; **filone** *m* MIN vein; *pane* French stick; *fig* tradition

filosofia *f* philosophy; **filosofico** philosophical; **filosofo** *m* philosopher

filtrare 1 *v/t* filter **2** *v/i* fig filter out; **filtro** *m* filter

fin → **fine, fino**

finale 1 *agg* final **2** *m* end **3** *f* SP final; **finalista** *m/f* finalist; **finalmente** *(alla fine)* at last; *(per ultimo)* finally

finanza *f* finance; **finanziamento** *m* funding; **finanziare** fund, finance; **finanziario** financial; **finanziere** *m* financier; *(guardia di finanza)* Customs officer; *lungo le co-*

ste coastguard

finché until; *(per tutto il tempo che)* as long as

fine 1 *agg* fine; *(sottile)* thin; *udito, vista* sharp, keen; *(raffinato)* refined **2** *m* aim; **al ~ di ...** in order to ... **3** *f* end; **alla ~** in the end; **fine settimana** *m inv* weekend

finestra *f* window; **finestrino** *m* window

fingere 1 *v/t:* **~ sorpresa** pretend to be surprised **2** *v/i:* **~ di** pretend to; **fingersi** pretend to be

finire finish, end; **finiscila!** stop it!; **finito** finished; *(venduto)* sold out

finlandese 1 *m/agg* Finnish **2** *m/f* Finn; **Finlandia** *f* Finland

fino[1] *agg* fine; *(acuto)* sharp; *oro* pure

fino[2] *prp tempo* till, until; *luogo* as far as; **~ a domani** until tomorrow; **~ a che** *(per tutto il tempo che)* as long as; *(fino al momento in cui)* until; **fin da ieri** since yesterday

fino[3] *avv* even; **fin troppo** more than enough

finocchio *m* fennel

finora so far

finta *f* pretence, *Am* pretense, sham; *SP* feint; **far ~ di** pretend to; **finto 1** *pp* → **fingere 2** *agg* false; *(artificiale)* artificial; *(simulato)* feigned; **finzione** *f* pretence, *Am* pretense

fiocco *m* bow; **~ di neve** snowflake; **-cchi** *pl* **d'avena** oat flakes

fioco weak; *luce* dim

fionda *f* catapult

fioraio *m*, **-a** *f* florist; **fiore** *m* flower; **fig il (fior)** the cream; *nelle carte* **-i** *pl* clubs; **fiorente** flourishing

fiorentino 1 *agg* Florentine **2** *m*, **-a** *f* Florentine; GASTR **alla ~a** with spinach; *bistecca* charcoal grilled **3** *f* GASTR T-bone steak

fiorire flower; *fig* flourish

Firenze *f* Florence

firma *f* signature; **firmare** sign; **firmatario** *m* signatory; **firmato** *abito*, *borsa* designer *attr*

fisarmonica *f* accordion

fiscale tax *attr*, fiscal; *fig spreg* rigid, unbending

fischiare 1 *v/t* whistle; **~ qu** boo s.o. **2** *v/i di vento* whistle; **fischio** *m* whistle

fisco *m* tax authorities, Inland Revenue, *Am* IRS, *Am* Internal Revenue Service

fisica *f* physics; **fisico 1** *agg* physical **2** *m* physicist; ANAT physique

fisionomia *f* face; *fig: di popolo*, *città* appearance; *(carattere)* character

fisioterapia *f* physiotherapy; **fisioterapista** *m/f* physiotherapist

fissare *(fermare)* fix; *(guarda-*

re intensamente) stare at; *(stabilire)* arrange; *(prenotare)* book; **fissarsi** *(stabilirsi)* settle; *(ostinarsi)* set one's mind **(di** on); *(avere un'idea fissa)* become obsessed **(di** with); **fissazione** *f (mania)* fixation **(di** about); **fisso 1** *agg* fixed; *stipendio*, *cliente* regular; *lavoro* permanent **2** *avv* fixedly

fitta *f* sharp pain

fitto *(denso)* thick

fiume *m* river; *fig* flood, torrent

fiutare smell; *cocaina* snort; **~ un imbroglio** smell a rat; **fiuto** *m* sense of smell; *fig* nose

flacone *m* bottle

flagrante flagrant; **cogliere qu in ~** catch s.o. red-handed

flash *m inv* FOT flash; *stampa* newsflash

flauto *m* flute

flemma *f* calm

flessibile flexible; **flessione** *f* bending; GRAM inflection; *(diminuzione)* dip, (slight) drop

flipper *m inv* pinball machine

flirtare flirt

F.lli (= **fratelli**) Bros (= brothers)

floppy disk *m inv* floppy (disk)

flora *f* flora

floscio limp; *muscoli* flabby

flotta *f* fleet

fluido m/agg fluid

fluorescente f fluorescent

flusso m flow

fluttuazione f fluctuation

FMI m (= **Fondo Monetario Internazionale**) IMF (= International Monetary Fund)

foca f seal

focaccia f focaccia; *dolce:* sweet type of bread

foce f mouth

focoso fiery

fodera f *interna* lining; *esterna* cover; **foderare** *all'interno* line; *all'esterno* cover; **fodero** m sheath

foglia f leaf

foglio m sheet

fogna f sewer

folata f gust

folclore m folklore; **folcloristico** folk *attr*

folgorare *di fulmine, idea* strike; *di corrente elettrica* electrocute; ~ **qu con lo sguardo** glare at s.o.

folla f crowd; *fig* host

folle[1] *agg* mad

folle[2] AUTO: *in* ~ in neutral

follia f madness

folto thick

fondale m MAR sea bed; TEA backcloth

fondamentalista m/f fundamentalist; **fondamentale** fundamental; **fondamento** m foundation; *senza* ~ unfounded; **fondare** found; **fondarsi** be based (*su* on); **fondato** founded; **fondato-** re m, **-trice** f founder; **fondazione** f foundation

fondere 1 *v/t* (*liquefare*) melt; *metalli* smelt; *colori* blend **2** *v/i* melt; **fondersi** melt; FIN merge

fondo 1 *agg* deep **2** m bottom; (*sfondo*) background; *terreno* property; FIN fund; SP longdistance; SCI cross-country; *-i pl denaro* funds; *-i neri* illegal earnings; *in* ~ (*profondamente*) in depth; *fig* **in** ~ basically; *in* ~ **alla strada** at the end o bottom of the road; *andare a* ~ (*affondare*) sink; (*approfondire*) get to the bottom (*di* of); **fondotinta** m inv foundation

fonduta f cheese fondue

fonetica f phonetics

fontana f fountain

fonte m/f spring; *fig* source

footing m jogging; *fare* ~ go jogging

forare *di proiettile* pierce; *con il trapano* drill; *biglietto* punch; *pneumatico* puncture; **foratura** f *di pneumatico* puncture

forbici fpl scissors

forchetta f fork

forcina f hairpin

foresta f forest

foresteria f guest rooms; **foristiero 1** *agg* foreign **2** m, **-a** f foreigner

forfait m inv lump sum; **forfettario** flat-rate

forfora f dandruff

forma *f* form; (*sagoma*) shape; TEC (*stampo*) mould; *Am* mold; **essere in ~** be in good form

formaggino *m* processed cheese; **formaggio** *m* cheese

formale formal; **formalità** *f inv* formality

formare shape; **formarsi** form; (*svilupparsi*) develop; **formato** *m* size; **di libro** format; **formattare** INFOR format; **formazione** *f* formation; *fig*: *addestramento* training; SP line-up

formica[1] *f* ZO ant

formica[2]® Formica

formicaio *m* anthill

formicolare *di mano, gamba* tingle; *fig ~ di* teem with; **formicolio** *m sensazione* pins and needles

formidabile (*straordinario*) incredible; (*poderoso*) powerful

formula *f* formula; **formulare** *teoria* formulate; (*esprimere*) express

fornaio *m* baker; *negozio* bakery; **fornello** *m* oven

fornire supply (**qc a qu** s.o. with sth); **fornirsi** get (**di** sth); **fornitore** *m* supplier; **fornitura** *f* supply

forno *m* oven; (*panetteria*) bakery; **~ a microonde** microwave (oven); **al ~** *carne, patate* roast; *mele, pasta* baked

foro[1] *m* (*buco*) hole

foro[2] *m romano* forum; DIR (*tribunale*) (law) court

forse perhaps, maybe

forte **1** *agg* strong; *suono* loud; *pioggia* heavy; *taglia, somma* large; *dolore* severe **2** *avv* (*con forza*) hard; (*ad alta voce*) loudly; (*velocemente*) fast **3** *m* (*fortezza*) fort; **fortezza** *f* MIL fortress

fortuito chance

fortuna *f* fortune; **avere ~** be successful; (*essere fortunato*) be lucky; **buona ~!** good luck!; **per ~** luckily; **fortunatamente** fortunately; **fortunato** lucky, fortunate

foruncolo *m* pimple

forza *f* strength; (*potenza*) power; *muscolare* force; **a ~ di ...** by dint of ...; **per ~** against my / our will; **per ~!** (*naturalmente*) of course!; **~!** come on!; **-e** *pl* (*armate*) MIL (armed) forces; **forzare** force

foschia *f* haze

fosforescente phosphorescent

fossa *f* pit, hole; (*tomba*) grave; **fossato** *m* ditch; *di fortezza* moat; **fossetta** *f* dimple

fossile *m*/*agg* fossil (*attr*)

fosso *m* ditch

foto *f inv* photo

fotocopia *f* photocopy; **fotocopiatrice** *f* photocopier

fotografare photograph; **fotografia** *f arte* photography;

(foto) photograph; **~ a colori** colour photograph; **fotografico** photographic; **macchina f -a** camera; **fotografo** m photographer

fotomontaggio m photomontage

fotoromanzo m graphic novel

fra between; *più persone o cose* among; *temporale* in; **~ questi ragazzi** out of all these boys; **~ l'altro** what's more; **~ breve** in a very short time, soon; **~ sé e sé** to himself / herself

frac m inv tails

fracassare smash; **fracasso** m din; *di oggetti che cadono* crash

fradicio rotten; *(bagnato)* soaking wet

fragile fragile; *persona* frail, delicate

fragola f strawberry

fragore m roar; *di tuono* rumble

fraintendere misunderstand

frammentario fragmentary; **frammento** m fragment

frana f landslide; **franare** collapse

francamente frankly

francese 1 m/agg French **2** m/f Frenchman; *donna* Frenchwoman; **i -i** the French pl; **Francia** f France

franco frank; FIN free; **farla -a** get away with it; **francobollo** m stamp

frangia f fringe, Am bangs

frantumare shatter; **frantumi** mpl splinters; **in ~** in smithereens; **mandare in ~** smash to smithereens

frappé m inv milkshake

frase f sentence; MUS phrase; **~ fatta** set phrase, idiom

frassino m ash (tree)

frastagliato *costa* jagged

frastuono m racket

frate m REL friar, monk

fratellastro m step-brother; *con un genitore in comune* half-brother; **fratello** m brother; **i -i fratello e sorella** brother and sister; **fraterno** brotherly, fraternal

frattaglie fpl GASTR offal; *di pollo* giblets

frattanto meanwhile, in the meantime

frattempo: nel ~ meanwhile, in the meantime

frattura f fracture; **fratturarsi ~ una gamba** break one's leg

frazione f fraction; POL small group; *(borgata)* hamlet

freccia f arrow; AUTO **~ (di direzione)** indicator, Am turn signal

freddo 1 agg cold **2** m cold; **ho ~** I'm cold; **fa ~** it's cold; **freddoloso: essere ~** feel the cold

freezer m inv freezer

fregare rub; F *(imbrogliare)* swindle; F *(rubare)* pinch F; P **me ne frego di quello**

che pensano I don't give a damn what they think F; *fregatura f* F (*imbroglio*) rip-off F; (*ostacolo, contrarietà*) pain F

fregio *m* ARCHI frieze

frenare AUTO brake; *folla, lacrime, risate* hold back; *impulso* restrain; *frenarsi* (*dominarsi*) restrain o.s.; **frenata** *f* braking; **fare una ~** brake; **freno** *m* AUTO brake; *del cavallo* bit; **~ a mano** handbrake, *Am* parking brake

frequentare *luoghi* frequent; *scuola, corso* attend; *persona* associate with; **frequentato** popular; *strada* busy; **frequente** frequent; **di ~** frequently; **frequenza** *f* frequency; *scolastica* attendance; **un'alta ~ di spettatori** a large audience; **con ~** frequently

fresco 1 *agg* fresh; *temperatura* cool **2** *m* coolness; **fa ~** it's cool; **mettere in ~** put in a cool place

fretta *f* hurry; **aver ~** be in a hurry; **non c'è ~** there's no hurry; **frettoloso** hurried; *lavoro* rushed; *persona* in a hurry

fricassea *f* GASTR fricassée

friggere *v/t* fry **2** *v/i* sizzle; **friggitoria** *f* shop that sells deep fried fish etc

frigo *m* fridge, *Am* refrigerator; **frigorifero 1** *agg* cold

attr, *camion* refrigerated **2** *m* refrigerator

frittata *f* GASTR omelette, *Am* omelet; **frittella** *f* fritter; **fritto 1** *pp* ☞ **friggere 2** *agg* fried **3** *m* fried food; **~ misto** assortment of deep-fried food

frittura *f metodo* frying; **~ di pesce** fried fish

frivolo frivolous

frizionare rub; **frizione** *f* friction; AUTO clutch

frizzante *bevanda* fizzy, sparkling

frode *f* fraud

frontale frontal; **scontro ~** head-on collision; **fronte 1** *f* forehead; **di ~** (*a dirimpetto*) opposite, facing; **in presenza di** before; **a confronto di** compared with **2** *m* front; **far ~ agli impegni** face up to one's responsibilities; **fronteggiare** face

frontiera *f* border, frontier

fronzolo *m* frill

frottola *f* F fib F

frugale frugal

frugare 1 *v/i* rummage **2** *v/t* (*cercare con cura*) search, rummage through

frullare GASTR blend, liquidize; *uova* whisk; **frullato** *m* milkshake; **frullatore** *m* liquidizer, blender; **frullino** *m* whisk

frumento *m* wheat

fruscio *m* rustle

frusta *f* whip; GASTR whisk;

frustare whip; **frustino** *m* riding crop

frustante frustrating; **frustrazione** *f* frustration

frutta *f* fruit; ~ **secca** nuts

fruttare 1 *v/t* yield 2 *v/i* fruit; **frutteto** *m* orchard; **fruttivendolo** *m*, **-a** *f* greengrocer; **frutto** *m* fruit; **-i** *pl* **di mare** seafood

FS (= **Ferrovie dello Stato**) Italian State railways

f.to (= **firmato**) signed

fu *☞* **essere**

fucilare shoot; **fucile** *m* rifle

fuga[1] *f* escape; ~ **di gas** gas leak

fuga[2] *f* MUS fugue

fuggifuggi *m inv* stampede; **fuggire** flee; **fuggitivo** *m* fugitive

fuliggine *f* soot

fulminare *di sguardo* glare at; **rimanere fulminato** *da fulmine* be struck by lightning; *da elettricità* be electrocuted; *fig* be thunderstruck; **fulminarsi** *di lampadina* blow; **fulmine** *m* lightning; **fulmineo** fast, rapid

fumare smoke; **fumatore** *m*, **-trice** *f* smoker; **scompartimento** *m* **per** *e* **/** **non** *e* smoking / non-smoking car

fumetto *m* comic strip; **-i** *pl* **per ragazzi** comics

fumo *m* smoke; (*vapore*) steam; ~ **passivo** passive smoking; **fumoso** smoky; *fig* (*oscuro*) muddled

fune *f* rope; (*cavo*) cable

funebre *attr*; *fig* gloomy, funeral

funerale *m* funeral

fungere act (**da** as)

fungo *m* mushroom; MED fungus

funicolare *f* funicular railway

funivia *f* cableway

funzionamento *m* operation, functioning; **funzionare** operate, function; **non** ~ be out of order; *di orologio* have stopped; **funzionario** *m* official, civil servant; **funzione** *f* function; (*carica*) office; REL service; **mettere in** ~ put into operation

fuoco *m* fire; FOT focus; **dar** ~ **a qc** set fire to sth; ~ **fuoco** catch fire; **-chi** *pl* **d'artificio** fireworks; MIL **far** ~ (open) fire; FOT **mettere a** ~ focus

fuorché except

fuori 1 *prp stato* outside, out of; *moto* out of, away from; ~ **città** out of town; ~ **luogo** out of place; ~ **di sé** beside o.s. 2 *avv* outside; *all'aperto* out of doors; SP out; ~**!** out!; **fuoribordo** *m inv* motorboat; *motore* outboard motor; **fuorigioco** *m inv* offside; **essere nel** ~ be offside; **fuoriserie** *f* made to order, custom 2 *f inv* AUTO custom-built model; **fuoristrada** *m inv* off-roader; **fuoriuscita** *f* di gas leakage; **fuor-**

viare 1 *v/i* go astray **2** *v/t* lead astray

furbizia *f* cunning; **furbo** cunning, crafty

furgoncino *m* (small) van; **furgone** *m* van

furia *f* fury, rage; *a ~ di ...* by dint of ...; **furibondo** furious, livid; **furioso** furious; *vento, lotta* violent; **furore** *m* fury, rage; *far ~* be all the rage

furto *m* theft; *~ con scasso* burglary

fusa *fpl*: *fare le ~* purr

fuseaux *mpl* leggings

fusibile *m* EL fuse

fusione *f* fusion; FIN merger

fuso[1] *pp* ☞ *fondere*; *metallo* molten; *burro* melted

fuso[2] *m* spindle; *~ orario* time zone

fusto *m* (*tronco*) trunk; (*stelo*) stem, stalk; *di metallo* drum; *di legno* barrel

futile futile

futuristico futuristic; **futuro** *m/agg* future

G

gabbia *f* cage

gabbiano *m* (sea)gull

gabinetto *m* toilet, *Am* rest room

gaffe *f* blunder, gaffe

gala *f* (*ricevimento*) gala

galante gallant

galera *f* (*prigione*) jail, prison

galla *f*: *venire a ~* (come to the) surface; *fig* come to light; **galleggiante 1** *agg* floating **2** *m* (*boa*) buoy; **galleggiare** float

galleria *f* gallery; *passaggio con negozi* (shopping) arcade; FERR, MIN tunnel; TEA circle, *Am* balcony

Galles *m* Wales; **gallese 1** *m/agg* Welsh **2** *m/f* Welshman; *donna* Welshwoman

gallina *f* hen; **gallo** *m* cock

gallone *m* unità di misura gal-

lon

galoppare gallop; **galoppo** *m* gallop; *al ~* at a gallop

gamba *f* leg; *fig in ~* (*capace*) smart, bright; *persona anziana* sprightly

gamberetto *m* shrimp; **gambero** *m* prawn

gambo *m* di fiore, bicchiere stem; *di pianta, fungo* stalk

gamma *f* range; MUS scale

gancio *m* hook

gara *f* competition; *di velocità* race; *fare a ~* compete

garage *m* inv garage

garantire 1 *v/t* guarantee; (*assicurare*) ensure **2** *v/i* (*farsi garante*) stand guarantor (*per* for); **garantito** guaranteed; **garanzia** *f* guarantee; *essere in ~* be under guarantee

gareggiare compete

gargarismo m gargle; (*collutorio*) mouthwash; **fare i ~i** gargle

garofano m carnation; GASTR **chiodi di ~** cloves

garza f gauze

gas m inv gas; **a ~** gas attr; **~ lacrimogeno** tear gas; **gasato 1** agg bibita fizzy; F (*eccitato*) excited **2** m, **-a** f F bighead F

gasolio m per riscaldamento oil; AUTO diesel

gastrite f gastritis

gastronomia f gastronomy; **gastronomico** gastronomic

gatta f (female) cat; **gattino** m kitten; **gatto** m cat

gay m/agg gay

gazzella f gazelle

gazzetta f gazette

gazzosa f fizzy o Am carbonated drink, Am soda

G.d.F. (= **Guardia di Finanza**) Customs and Excise

gel m inv gel

gelare 1 v/t freeze **2** v/i e gelarsi freeze

gelateria f ice-cream parlour o parlor

gelatina f gelatine; **~ di frutta** fruit jelly

gelato 1 agg frozen **2** m ice cream

gelido freezing

gelo m (*brina*) frost; fig chill

gelosia f jealousy; **geloso** jealous (**di** of)

gelsomino m jasmine

gemellaggio m twinning; **gemello 1** agg twin **2** m di camicia cuff link **3** m, **-a** f twin; ASTR **Gemelli** pl Gemini

gemito m groan

gemma f anche fig gem; BOT bud

gene m BIO gene

genealogia f genealogy; **genealogico** genealogical

generale m/agg general; **in ~** in general; (*natura*) general nature; **le ~** personal details; **generalizzare** generalize; **generalmente** generally; **generare** (*dar vita a*) give birth to; (*causare*) generate, create; *sospetti* arouse; *elettricità, calore* generate; **generatore** m EL generator; **generazione** f generation

genere m kind; BIO genus; GRAM gender; **in ~** generally; **-i alimentari** foodstuffs; **~ umano** mankind, humanity; **generico** generic

genero m son-in-law

generoso generous (**con** to)

genetico genetic; **ingegneria** f **-a** genetic engineering

gengiva f gum

geniale ingenious; **genialità** f genius; (*ingegnosità*) ingeniousness

genio m genius; (*inclinazione*) talent

genitali mpl genitals

genitori mpl parents

gennaio m January

genocidio m genocide

Genova Genoa; **genovese** *m/agg* Genoese

gentaglia *f* scum

gente *f* people *pl*

gentile kind; *nelle lettere* – **Signora** Dear Madam; **gentilezza** *f* kindness

genuino genuine; *prodotto alimentare* traditionally made; *risata* spontaneous

genziana *f* gentian

geografia *f* geography; **geografico** geographic

geologico geological

geometra *m/f* surveyor, *Am* structural engineer; **geometria** *f* geometry

geranio *m* geranium

gerarchia *f* hierarchy

gergo *m* slang; *di una professione anche* jargon

Germania *f* Germany

germe *m* germ; *fig (principio)* seeds; **in** –, in embryo; **germogliare** sprout; **germoglio** *m* shoot

geroglifico *m* hieroglyph

gesso *m* MIN gypsum; MED, *scultura* plaster cast; *per scrivere* chalk

gesticolare gesticulate

gestione *f* management; **gestire** manage

gesto *m* gesture; *con la testa* nod

gestore *m* manager

Gesù *m* Jesus; – **bambino** baby Jesus

gettare throw; *fondamenta* lay; *grido* give, let out; –

via throw away; **gettarsi** throw o.s.; *di fiume* flow (**in** into)

getto *m* jet; **di** – in one go

gettone *m* token; *per giochi* counter; *per giochi d'azzardo* chip

ghetto *m* ghetto

ghiacciaio *m* glacier; **ghiacciato** *lago, stagno* frozen; *bibita* ice-cold; **ghiaccio** *m* ice; *sulla strada* black ice; **ghiacciolo** *m* icicle; *(gelato)* ice lolly, *Am* Popsicle®

ghiaia *f* gravel

ghianda *f* acorn; **ghiandola** *f* gland

ghigliottina *f* guillotine

ghiotto *persona* greedy; *fig: di notizie ecc* avid (**di** for); *(appetitoso)* appetizing

ghirigoro *m* doodle

ghirlanda *f* garland

ghiro *m* dormouse; **dormire come un** – sleep like a log

già already; *(ex)* formerly; –**!** of course!

giacca *f* jacket; – **a vento** windproof jacket

giacché since

giacenza *f per la vendita* stock; *invenduta* unsold goods; *periodo* stock time; – **di cassa** cash in hand; -**e** *pl di magazzino* stock in hand; **giacimento** *m* MIN deposit

giada *f* jade

giallo *m/agg* yellow; **libro** –, **film** – thriller

Giappone *m* Japan; **giapponese** *agg*, *m/f* Japanese

giardinaggio *m* gardening; **giardiniera** *f* gardener; *mobile* plant stand; GASTR (mixed) pickles; **giardiniere** *m* gardener; **giardino** *m* garden; ~ **pubblico** park

gigante *m/agg* giant (*attr*); **gigantesco** gigantic

giglio *m* lily

gilè *m inv* waistcoat, *Am* vest

gin *m inv* gin

ginecologo *m*, -a *f* gynaecologist, *Am* gynecologist

ginepro *m* juniper

ginestra *f* broom

gingillarsi *fidsle*; (*perder tempo*) fool around

ginnastica *f* exercises; *disciplina sportiva* gymnastics; *in palestra* physical education

ginocchio *m* knee; *stare in* ~ be on one's knees, be kneeling

giocare 1 *v/i* play; *d'azzardo, in Borsa* gamble; (*scommettere*) bet; ~ *a* tennis, flipper play **2** *v/t* play; (*ingannare*) trick; **giocarsi** (*perdere al gioco*) gamble away; (*beffarsi*) make fun; *carriera* throw away; **giocatore** *m*, -trice *f* player; *d'azzardo* gambler; **giocattolo** *m* toy; **gioco** *m* game; *il* ~ gambling; ~ *d'azzardo* game of chance; *l'ho detto per* ~ I was joking!; **giocoliere** *m* juggler

gioia *f* joy; (*gioiello*) jewel;

gioielleria *f* jeweller's (shop), *Am* jewelry store; **gioiello** *m* jewel

giornalaio *m*, -a *f* newsagent, *Am* news vendor; **giornale** *m* (news)paper; (*rivista*) magazine; (*registro*) journal; ~ **radio** news (bulletin); **giornaliero** *agg*; *abbonamento* ~ day pass; **giornalino** *m per ragazzi* comic; **giornalismo** *m* journalism; **giornalista** *m/f* journalist, reporter; **giornalistico** journalistic; *agenzia, servizio* news *attr*; **giornata** *f* day; *lo finiremo in* ~ we'll finish it today; **giorno** *m* day; ~ **feriale** weekday, workday; ~ **festivo** (public) holiday; *l'altro* ~ the other day; *a* -*i* (*fra pochi giorni*) in a few days (time); *al* ~ a day; *al* ~ *d'oggi* nowadays; *di* ~ by day

giostra *f* carousel, merry-go-round

giovane 1 *agg* young; (*giovanile*) youthful **2** *m/f* young man, youth; *ragazza* young woman, girl; *i* -*i* young people *pl*, the young *pl*; **giovanotto** *m* young man, youth

giovare (*essere utile*) be useful (*a* to); (*far bene*) be good (*a* for)

Giove *m* Jupiter; **giovedì** *m inv* Thursday

gioventù *f* youth; (*i giovani*) young people *pl*; **giovinezza** *f* youth

gippone m AUTO SUV
giraffa f giraffe
girandola f fuoco d'artificio Catherine wheel, Am pinwheel; (giocattolo) windmill; (banderuola) weather vane; **girare** v/t turn; città, negozi go around; paese travel around; film shoot; (mescolare) mix; FIN endorse **2** v/i turn; rapidamente spin; (andare in giro) wander around; con un veicolo drive around; **mi gira la testa** I feel dizzy; **girarrosto** m GASTR spit; **girasole** m sunflower; **girata** f turn; (passeggiata a piedi) walk, stroll; in macchina drive; FIN endorsement; **girevole** revolving
girino m tadpole
giro m turn; (circolo) circle; (percorso abituale) round; (deviazione) detour; (passeggiata a piedi) walk, stroll; in macchina ride; di pista lap; di motore rev; (viaggio) tour; **nel ~ di una settimana** within a week; **essere in ~** (da qualche parte) be around somewhere; (fuori) be out; **mettere in ~** spread; fig prendere **in ~ qu** pull s.o.'s leg
girocollo m inv: **maglione a ~** crewneck sweater; **gironzolare** hang around; **~ per negozi** wander around the stores; **girovagare** wander around

gita f trip, excursion; **gitante** m/f (day) tripper
giù down; (sotto) below; (da basso) downstairs; fig **essere ~** be down o depressed; di salute be run down; **mandar ~** swallow (anche fig); **su e ~** up and down
giubbotto m sports jacket; **~ di salvataggio** life jacket
giudicare judge; **~ male qu** misjudge s.o.; **lo hanno giudicato colpevole** he has been found guilty; **giudice** m judge; **giudizio** m judg(e)ment; (senno) wisdom; DIR (causa) trial; (sentenza) verdict; **a mio ~** in my opinion
giugno m June
giungere arrive (**a** in, at), reach (**a** sth)
giungla f jungle
giunta f addition; POL junta; **~ comunale** town council; **per ~** in addition, moreover; **giunto** pp ☞ **giungere**
giuramento m oath; **giurare** swear; **giurato 1** agg sworn **2** m member of the jury; **giuria** f jury
giuridico legal; **giurisprudenza** f jurisprudence
giustificare justify; **giustificazione** f justification
giustizia f justice; **giusto 1** agg just, fair; (adatto) right, appropriate; (esatto) correct, right **2** avv correctly; mirare accurately; (proprio, per l'appunto) just; **~!** that's right!

glassa f GASTR icing, Am frosting

gli 1 art mpl the; **avere gli occhi azzurri** have blue eyes 2 pron (a lui) (to) him; (a esso) (to) it; (a loro) (to) them; **dagli i libri** give him / them the books, give the books to him / them

glicemia f glycaemia, Am glycemia

glie: **~la, ~lo, ~li, ~le, ~ne** = pron **gli** or **le** with pron **la, lo, li, le, ne**

globale global; **globalizzazione** f globalization; **globo** m globe; **globulo** m globule; MED corpuscle; **~ rosso** red blood cell

gloria f glory

glossario m glossary

glucosio m glucose

gnocchi mpl (di patate) gnocchi (small potato dumplings)

gnorri m F: **fare lo ~** act dumb F

goal m inv SP goal

gobba f hump; **gobbo 1** agg hunchbacked **2** m hunchback

goccia f drop; **a ~ a ~** little by little; **gocciolare** drip

godere 1 v/t enjoy; **godersela** enjoy o.s. 2 v/i (rallegrarsi) be delighted (di di)

goffo awkward, clumsy

gol m inv SP goal

gola f throat; (ingordigia) greed(iness), gluttony; GEOG gorge; **mal mi di ~** sore throat

golf m inv golf; (cardigan) cardigan; (maglione) sweater

golfo m gulf

goloso greedy; **essere ~ di dolci** have a sweet tooth

golpe m inv coup

gomito m elbow

gomitolo m ball (of wool)

gomma f rubber; per cancellare eraser, Br anche rubber; (pneumatico) tyre, Am tire; **~ da masticare** (chewing) gum; AUTO **~ di scorta** spare tyre; **avere una ~ a terra** have a flat tyre; **gommapiuma®** f foam rubber; **gommista** m tyre o Am tire specialist; **gommone** m rubber dinghy

gondola f gondola; **gondoliere** m gondolier

gonfiare 1 v/t con aria inflate; le guance puff out; fig (esagerare) exaggerate, magnify 2 v/i e **gonfiarsi** swell up; **gonfio** swollen; pneumatico inflated; stomaco bloated; fig puffed up (di with); **gonfiore** m swelling

gonna f skirt

gorgogliare di stomaco rumble; dell'acqua gurgle

gorilla m inv gorilla; F (guardia del corpo) bodyguard, gorilla F

gotico m/agg Gothic

governante 1 f housekeeper **2** m ruler; **governare** POL govern, rule; **governativo** government attr, scuola state *attr*; **governo** *m* government

gozzovigliare make merry

gracchiare *di corvo* caw; *di rane* croak; *di persona* squawk

gracidare croak

gracile (*debole*) delicate

gradazione *f* gradation; (*sfumatura*) shade; **~ alcolica** alcohol(ic) content

gradevole pleasant, agreeable; **gradimento** *m* liking

gradinata *f* flight of steps; *stadio* stand; *a teatro* gallery, balcony; **gradino** *m* step

gradire like; (*desiderare*) wish; *gradisce un po' di vino?* would you like some wine?; **gradito** pleasant; (*bene accetto*) welcome

grado[1] *m* degree; *in una gerarchia*, MIL rank; *in ~ di lavorare* capable of working, fit for work; *per -i* by degrees

grado[2] *m*: *di buon ~* willingly

graduale gradual

graduatoria *f* list

graffa *f* TIP brace

graffiare scratch; **graffio** *m* scratch; **graffiti** *mpl* graffiti *sg o pl*

grafica *f* graphics; **grafico 1** *agg* graphic **2** *m* (*diagramma*) graph; (*disegnatore*) graphic artist

grafologia *f* handwriting analysis, graphology

grammatica *f* grammar; **grammaticale** grammatical

grammo *m* gram(me)

Gran Bretagna *f* Great Britain

gran ☞ **grande**

grana 1 *f* grain; F (*seccatura*) trouble; F *soldi* dough F, cash **2** *m inv* cheese similar to Parmesan

granaio *m* barn

granchio *m* crab

grande big; (*largo*) wide; *fig* (*intenso*, *notevole*) great; (*adulto*) grown-up, big; (*vecchio*) old; **grandezza** *f* (*dimensione*) size; (*larghezza*) width; (*ampiezza*) breadth; (*altezza*) height; *fig* (*eccellenza*) greatness; (*grandiosità*) grandeur

grandinare hail; **grandine** *f* hail

grandioso grand

granducato *m* grand duchy

granello *m* grain; **~ di pepe** peppercorn; **~ di polvere** speck of dust

granita *f* type of ice made of frozen crystals of coffee or fruit syrup

granito *m* granite

grano *m* (*chicco*) grain; (*frumento*) wheat; *fig* grain, ounce

granturco *m* maize, corn

grappa *f* grappa, *brandy made from the remains of the grapes used in wine-making*

grappolo *m* bunch

grassetto *m* TIP bold

grasso 1 *agg* fat; (*unto*) greasy; *cibo* fatty **2** *m* fat;

grassoccio plump

grata f grating

gratella f, **graticola** f GASTR grill, Am broiler

gratifica f bonus

gratin m: **al ~** au gratin; **gratinato** au gratin

gratis free (of charge)

gratitudine f gratitude; **grato** grateful

grattacapo m problem, headache F; **grattacielo** m skyscraper; **grattare** scratch; (raschiare) scrape; (grattugiare) grate; F pinch F; **grattugia** f grater; **grattugiare** grate

gratuito free (of charge); (infondato) gratuitous

gravare 1 v/t burden **2** v/i weigh (**su** on); **grave** (pesante) heavy; (serio) serious; (difficile) hard

gravidanza f pregnancy

gravità f seriousness, gravity; FIS (**forza** f **di**) **~** (force of) gravity

grazia f grace; (gentilezza) favour, Am favor; DIR pardon; **graziare** pardon; **grazie** thank you, thanks; **~ tante**, **~ mille** thank you so much; **~ a** thanks to; **grazioso** charming; (carino) pretty

Grecia f Greece; **greco 1** agg Greek **2** m, **-a** f Greek

gregge m flock

greggio 1 agg (non lavorato) raw, crude **2** m crude (petroleum)

grembiule m apron; **grembo** m lap; **materno** womb; fig bosom

gretto (avaro) narrow-minded; (di mente ristretta) narrow-minded

gridare 1 v/t shout, yell; **~ aiuto** shout for help **2** v/i shout, yell; (strillare) scream; **grido** m shout, cry

grigio grey, Am gray; fig (triste) sad; (scialbo) dreary

griglia f (grata) grating; GASTR grill; **alla ~** grilled

grilletto m trigger

grillo m cricket; fig (capriccio) fancy, whim

grimaldello m lock pick

grinfie fpl fig clutches

grinta f grit; fig determination

grinza f di stoffa crease; **grinzoso** viso wrinkled; (spiegazzato) creased

grissino m bread stick

grondaia f gutter

grondare 1 v/i (colare) pour; (gocciolare) drip; **~ di sudore** be dripping with sweat **2** v/t drip with

groppa f back

groppo m: **avere un ~ alla gola** have a lump in one's throat

grossezza f (dimensione) size; (spessore) thickness; (l'essere grosso) largeness; **grossista** m/f wholesaler; **grosso 1** agg big, large; (spesso) thick; mare rough; sale, ghiaia coarse; **sbagliarsi di ~** make a big mistake;

farla -a make a fine mess **2** *m* bulk; **grossolano** coarse; *errore* serious; **grossomodo** roughly

grotta *f* cave; *artificiale* grotto

grottesco grotesque

groviglio *m* tangle; *fig* muddle

gru *f inv* crane

gruccia *f* crutch; *per vestiti* hanger

grumo *m* clot; *di farina* lump

gruppo *m* group; *~* **sanguigno** blood group

guadagnare earn; *(ottenere)* gain; **guadagno** *m* gain; *(profitto)* profit; *(entrate)* earnings

guaina *f* sheath; *(busto)* corset

guaio *m* trouble; *(danno)* damage; *essere nei -ai* be in trouble

guancia *f* cheek

guanciale *m* pillow

guanto *m* glove; **guantone** *m*: *~ da boxe* boxing glove

guardaboschi *m inv* forest ranger; **guardacoste** *m inv* MAR coastguard; **guardalinee** *m inv* SP assistant referee, linesman; **guardamacchine** *m* car park attendant, *Am* parking lot attendant

guardare 1 *v/t* look at; *(osservare, stare a vedere)* watch; *(custodire)* watch, look after; *(esaminare)* check **2** *v/i* look; *(controllare)* check; *di finestra* overlook *(su* sth); *~ a sud* face south; **guardaroba** *m* cloakroom, *Am* checkroom; *armadio* wardrobe; **guardarsi** look at o.s.; *~ da* beware of; *(astenersi)* refrain from

guardia *f* guard; *~* **forestale** forest ranger; *~* **di finanza** Customs official; *~* **del corpo** bodyguard; *~* **medica, medico** *m* **di** *~* day doctor; *fare la ~* keep guard; *stare in ~* be on one's guard; **guardiano** *m*, *-a f* *(custode)* warden; *(portiere)* caretaker; *(guardia)* guard; *di parco* keeper; *~* **notturno** night watchman; **guardone** *m* voyeur

guardrail *m inv* guardrail

guarigione *f* recovery; *in via di ~* on the mend; **guarire 1** *v/t* cure **2** *v/i* recover; *di ferita* heal

guarnizione *f (abbellimento)* trimming; GASTR garnish; *di rubinetto* washer; AUTO *~* **del freno** brake lining

guastafeste *m/f inv* spoilsport; **guastare** spoil, ruin; *meccanismo* break; **guastarsi** break down; *di tempo* change for the worse; *di cibi* go bad; **guasto 1** *agg* broken; *telefono, ascensore* out of order; AUTO broken down; *cibi* bad; *dente* rotten, decayed **2** *m* fault, failure; AUTO breakdown

guerra *f* war; **guerrafondaio**

m war-monger; **guerriglia** *f* guerriglia warfare; **guerrigliero** *m*, **-a** *f* guerrilla

gufo *m* owl

guida *f* guidance; (*persona, libro*) guide; AUTO driving; **~ telefonica** phone book; **~ turistica** tourist guide; AUTO **~ a destra / a sinistra** right-hand / left-hand

drive; **guidare** guide; AUTO drive; **guidatore** *m*, **-trice** *f* driver

guinzaglio *m* lead, leash

guscio *m* shell

gustare taste; *fig* enjoy; **gusto** *m* taste; (*sapore*) flavour; *Am* flavor; *fig* (*piacere*) pleasure; **buon / cattivo ~** good / bad taste

H

ha[1] (= ***ettaro***) ha (= hectare)

ha[2] → ***avere***

habitat *m inv* BIO habitat

habitué *m/f inv* regular

hacker *m/f inv* INFOR hacker

hai → ***avere***

hall *f inv* foyer

hamburger *m inv* hamburger

handicap *m inv* handicap; **handicappato 1** *agg* disabled, handicapped **2** *m*, **-a** *f* disabled *o* handicapped person

hanno → ***avere***

hard disk *m inv* INFOR hard disk

hardware *m inv* INFOR hardware

harem *m inv* harem

hashish *m inv* hashish

henné *m inv* henna

herpes *m inv* herpes

hinterland *m inv* hinterland

hit parade *f inv* hit parade, charts

ho → ***avere***

hobby *m inv* hobby

hockey *m inv* hockey; **~ su ghiaccio** ice hockey

hostess *f inv* hostess; **~ di terra** (*guida*) member of ground staff

hot dog *m inv* hot dog

hotel *m inv* hotel

I

i *art mpl* the

iceberg *m inv* iceberg

icona *f* icon

idea *f* idea; (*opinione*) opinion; **cambiare ~** change

one's mind; **non avere la minima ~ di qc** not have the slightest idea about sth; **neanche per ~!** of course not!; **ideale** *m/agg* ideal; **idealiz** zare idealize; **ideare** *scherzo, scusa* think up; *metodo, oggetto nuovo* invent; *piano, progetto* devise; **ideatore** *m*, **-trice** *f* originator; *di metodo, oggetto nuovo* inventor

idem ditto

identico identical; **identificare** identify; **identikit** *m inv* Identikit®, *Am* composite drawing; **identità** *f inv* identity

ideologia *f* ideology

idiomatico idiomatic

idiota 1 *agg* idiotic, stupid **2** *m/f* idiot, fool; **idiozia** *f* stupidity; *(assurdità)* nonsense; **un'~** a stupid *o* idiotic thing to do / say

idolo *m* idol

idoneo suitable (**a** for)

idrante *m* hydrant

idratante *della pelle* moisturizing; **idratare** *la pelle* moisturize

idraulico 1 *agg* hydraulic; **impianto** *m* ~ plumbing **2** *m* plumber

idrico water *attr*

idroelettrico hydroelectric; **idrofilo:** **cotone** *m* ~ cotton wool, *Am* absorbent cotton; **idromassaggio** *m* Jacuzzi®, whirlpool; **idroplano** *m* hydroplane

iena *f* hyena

ieri yesterday; ~ **l'altro, l'altro** ~ the day before yesterday; ~ **mattina** yesterday morning

igiene *f* hygiene; **igienico** hy-

gienic; **carta** *f* ~ *-a* toilet paper

ignaro unaware (**di** of); **ignorante** *(non informato)* ignorant; *(incolto)* uneducated; *(maleducato)* rude; **ignoranza** *f* ignorance; **ignorare** *(non considerare)* ignore; *(non sapere)* not know; **ignoto** unknown

il *art m sg* the; ~ **martedì** on Tuesdays; **2 euro ~ chilo** 2 euros a kilo; **mi piace il caffè** I like coffee

illegale illegal

illeggibile illegible

illegittimo illegitimate

illeso unhurt

illimitato unlimited

illogico illogical

illudere deceive; **illudersi** delude o.s.

illuminare light up; *fig* enlighten; **illuminazione** *f* lighting; *fig* flash of inspiration

illusione *f* illusion; **illuso 1** *pp* → **illudere 2** *m/f* (*sognatore*) dreamer

illustrare illustrate; **illustratore** *m*, **-trice** *f* illustrator; **illustrazione** *f* illustration

illustre illustrious

imballaggio *m* operazione packing; *(involucro)* package; **imballare** pack; AUTO ~ **il motore** race the engine

imbambolato *occhi, sguardo* blank; *dal sonno* bleary-eyed

imbarazzante embarrassing; **imbarazzare** embarrass; **im-**

barazzato embarrassed; **imbarazzo** *m* embarrassment; (*disturbo*) trouble; *mettere in ~ qu* embarrass s.o.

imbarcadero *m* landing stage; **imbarcarsi** go on board, embark; **imbarcazione** *f* boat; *~ da diporto* pleasure boat; **imbarco** *m* di passeggeri boarding, embarkation; *di carico* loading; (*banchina*) landing stage

imbattersi: *~ in qu* bump into s.o.

imbattibile unbeatable

imbecille 1 *agg* idiotic, stupid **2** *m/f* imbecile, fool

imbiancare 1 *v/t* whiten; *con pitture* paint; *tessuti* bleach **2** *v/i e* **imbiancarsi** go white; **imbianchino** *m* (house) painter

imboccare *persona* feed; *fig* prompt; *~ una strada* turn into a road; **imboccatura** *f* (*apertura*) opening; (*ingresso*) entrance; MUS mouthpiece; **imbocco** *m* entrance

imboscata *f* ambush

imbottigliare bottle; *di veicoli* hold up

imbottito stuffed; *panino* filled; **imbottitura** *f* stuffing; *di giacca* padding

imbranato clumsy

imbrattare soil; (*macchiare*) stain

imbrogliare 1 *v/t* (*raggirare*) take in; (*truffare*) cheat; *fig* confuse **2** *v/i* cheat; **imbro**-

glio *m* (*truffa*) trick; *fig* (*pasticcio*) mess; **imbroglione** *m*, *-a f* cheat

imbronciato sulky

imbruttire 1 *v/t* make ugly **2** *v/i* get ugly

imbucare *posta* post, *Am* mail

imburrare butter

imbuto *m* funnel

imitare imitate; **imitazione** *f* imitation

immaginare imagine; (*supporre*) suppose; **immaginario** imaginary; **immaginazione** *f* imagination

immagine *f* image

immangiabile inedible

immaturo *persona* immature; (*precoce*) premature; *frutto* unripe

immedesimarsi identify (*in* with)

immediatamente immediately; **immediato** immediate; (*pronto*) prompt

immenso immense

immergere immerse; (*lasciare immerso*) soak; **immergersi** plunge; *di subacqueo, sottomarino* dive; *fig* immerse o.s. (*in* in); **immersione** *f* immersion; *di subacqueo, sottomarino* dive; **immerso 1** *pp ☞* **immergere 2** *agg* immersed

immettere introduce (*in* into); INFOR *dati* enter; (*portare*) lead (*in* into); **immettersi**: *~ in* get into

immigrante *m/f* immigrant; **immigrare** immigrate; **immigrato** *m*, **-a** *f* immigrant; **immigrazione** *f* immigration; (*immigrati*) immigrants; FIN inflow

imminente imminent; *pericolo* impending; *pubblicazione* forthcoming

immischiarsi meddle (**in** with), interfere (**in** in)

immissione *f* introduction; *di manodopera* intake; INFOR *di dati* entry

immobile 1 *agg* motionless **2** *mpl:* **-i** real estate; **immobiliare:** *agente m/f* ~ estate agent, *Am* realtor; *società f* ~ *di compravendita* property company; *di costruzione* construction company

immondizia *f* (*gen pl*) rubbish, *Am* trash

immorale immoral

immortale immortal; **immortalità** *f* immortality

immune MED immune (**a** to); (*esente*) free (**da** from); **immunità** *f* immunity; **immunitario:** *sistema m* ~ immune system; **immunodeficienza** *f* immunodeficiency

immutato unchanged

impacchettare (*confezionare*) wrap (up); (*mettere in pacchetti*) package

impacciare *movimenti* hamper; *persona* hinder; **impacciato** (*imbarazzato*) embarrassed; (*goffo*) awkward; **impaccio** *m* (*ostacolo*) hindrance; (*situazione difficile*) awkward situation; (*imbarazzo*) awkwardness

impacco *m* MED compress

impadronirsi: ~ *di qc* take possession of sth; *fig* master sth

impalcatura *f temporanea* scaffolding; *fig* framework

impallidire *di persona* turn pale

impanare GASTR coat with breadcrumbs; **impanato** in breadcrumbs, breaded

impaperarsi falter

imparare learn (**a** to)

imparentarsi: ~ **con** *qu* become related to s.o.

impari unequal; MAT odd

impartire give

imparziale impartial; **imparzialità** *f* impartiality

impassibile impassive

impastare mix; *pane* knead; **impasto** *m* GASTR dough; (*mescolanza*) mixture

impatto *m* impact

impaurire frighten; **impaurirsi** get frightened

impaziente impatient; **impazienza** *f* impatience

impazzata: *all'~* correre at breakneck speed; *colpire* wildly

impazzire go mad *o* crazy; *far* ~ *qu* drive s.o. mad *o* crazy

impeccabile impeccable

impedire prevent; (*ostruire*) block, obstruct; (*impacciare*) hinder; **~ a qu di fare qc** prevent s.o. from doing sth, keep s.o. from doing sth

impegnare (*dare come pegno*) pawn; (*riservare*) reserve; *spazio, corsia* take up; **impegnarsi** (*prendersi l'impegno*) commit o.s., undertake (**a** to); (*concentrarsi*) apply o.s. (**in** to); **impegnativo** (*che richiede impegno*) demanding; *pranzo, serata, abito* formal; (*vincolante*) binding; **impegnato** (*occupato*) busy; *fig* (*politically*) committed; **sono già ~** I've made other arrangements; **impegno** *m* commitment; (*appuntamento*) engagement; **con ~** in earnest

impensabile unthinkable; **impensato** unexpected

imperante (*dominante*) prevailing

imperativo *m/agg* imperative

imperatore *m*, **-trice** *f* emperor; *donna* empress

impercettibile imperceptible

imperdonabile unforgivable

imperfetto *m/agg* imperfect; **imperfezione** *f* imperfection

impermeabile 1 *agg* waterproof **2** *m* raincoat; **impermeabilizzare** waterproof

impero *m* empire; (*potere*) rule

impersonale impersonal; **impersonare** personify; (*interpretare*) play (the part of)

impertinente impertinent; **impertinenza** *f* impertinence

imperturbabile imperturbable

imperversare rage; *fig*: *di moda* be all the rage

impeto *m* impetus, force; (*accesso*) outburst; (*slancio*) passion; **parlare con ~** speak forcefully; **impetuoso** impetuous

impianto *m operazione* installation; (*apparecchiature*) plant; (*sistema*) system; MED implant; **~ elettrico** wiring; **~ di risalita** ski lift; **~ di riscaldamento** heating system

impiccare hang; **impiccarsi** hang o.s.

impicciarsi ~ di *o* **in qc** interfere *o* meddle in sth; **impiccio** *m* (*ostacolo*) hindrance; (*seccatura*) bother; **essere d'~** be in the way; **essere in un ~** be in trouble

impiegare (*usare*) use; *tempo, soldi* spend; (*metterci*) take; (*assumere*) employ; **ho impiegato un'ora** it took me an hour; **impiegato** *m*, **-a** *f* employee; **~ di banca** bank employee; **impiego** *m* (*uso*) use; (*occupazione*) employment; (*posto*) job

impietosire move to pity; **impietosirsi** be moved to pity

impigliare entangle; **impigliarsi** get entangled

impigrire 1 *v/t* make lazy **2** *v/i* e **impigrirsi** get lazy

implacabile implacable

implicare (*coinvolgere*) implicate; (*comportare*) imply

implicito implicit

implorare implore

impolverato dusty, covered in dust

imponente imposing, impressive

imponibile 1 *agg* taxable **2** *m* taxable income

impopolare unpopular

imporre impose; *prezzo* fix; **imporsi** (*farsi valere*) assert o.s.; (*avere successo*) be successful, become established; (*essere necessario*) be necessary

importante important; **importanza** *f* importance; **senza ~** not important, unimportant; **importare 1** *v/t* FIN, INFOR import **2** *v/i* matter, be important; (*essere necessario*) be necessary; **non importa** it doesn't matter; **non gliene importa niente** he couldn't care less; **importatore** *m*, **-trice** *f* importer; **importazione** *f* import; **importo** *m* amount

importunare (*assillare*) pester; (*disturbare*) bother; **importuno** troublesome; (*domanda, osservazione*) illtimed

impossessarsi: **~ di** seize

impossibile impossible; **im-**

possibilità *f* impossibility

imposta[1] *f* tax; **~ sul reddito** income tax; **~ sul valore aggiunto** value added tax, Am sales tax

imposta[2] *f di finestra* shutter

impostare *lavoro* plan; *problema* set out; *lettera* post, Am mail

imposto *pp* ☞ **imporre**

impostore *m* impostor

impotente powerless; (*inefficace*) ineffectual; MED impotent

impraticabile *strada* impassable

impratichirsi get practice (**in** in)

imprecare curse, swear (**contro** at); **imprecazione** *f* curse

imprecisato *quantità* indeterminate; *motivi, circostanze* not clear; **imprecisione** *f* inaccuracy; **impreciso** inaccurate

impregnare impregnate; (*imbevere*) soak; **impregnarsi** become impregnated (**di** with)

imprenditore *m*, **-trice** *f* entrepreneur; **imprenditoriale** entrepreneurial

impreparato unprepared

impresa *f* (*iniziativa*) enterprise, undertaking; (*azienda*) business, firm

impresario *m* contractor; TEA impresario

impressionante impressive;

(*spaventoso*) frightening; (*sconvolgente*) upsetting, shocking; **impressionare** (*turbare*) upset, shock; (*spaventare*) frighten; (*colpire*) impress; **impressionato** FOT exposed; ~ **favorevolmente** (favourably) impressed; **impressione** *f* impression; (*turbamento*) shock; (*paura*) fright; TIP printing; **impresso** *pp* ➞ **imprimere**

imprevedibile unforeseeable; *persona* unpredictable; **imprevisto 1** *agg* unexpected **2** *m* unforeseen event; **salvo imprevisti** all being well

imprigionare imprison

imprimere impress; *fig: nella mente* fix firmly, imprint; *movimento* impart; TIP print

improbabile unlikely, improbable

impronta *f* impression, mark; (*orma*) footprint; (*traccia*) track; *fig* mark; **-e digitali** fingerprints; **-e genetiche** genetic fingerprints

improprio improper

improvvisamente suddenly; **improvvisare** improvise; **improvvisata** *f* surprise; **improvvisato** improvized, impromptu; **improvviso** sudden; (*inaspettato*) unexpected; **all'~** suddenly; (*inaspettatamente*) unexpectedly

imprudente careless; (*non*

saggio) imprudent, rash; **imprudenza** *f* carelessness; (*mancanza di saggezza*) imprudence, rashness

impugnare grasp; DIR contest; **impugnatura** *f* grip; (*manico*) handle

impulsivo impulsive; **impulso** *m* impulse

impunità *f* impunity

impuntarsi (*ostinarsi*) dig one's heels in

imputato *m*, **-a** *f* accused; **imputazione** *f* charge

imputridire rot

in in; *moto a luogo* to; ~ **casa** at home; *va* ~ **Inghilterra** he is going to England; ~ **italiano** in Italian; ~ **campagna** in the country; *viaggiare* ~ **macchina** travel by car; **nel 1999** in 1999; ~ **vacanza** on holiday

inabile unfit (**a** for); (*disabile*) disabled

inaccessibile inaccessible, out of reach; *fig: persona* unapproachable; *prezzi* exorbitant

inaccettabile unacceptable

inacidire, inacidirsi turn sour

inadatto unsuitable (**a** for)

inadeguato inadequate

inalare inhale; **inalatore** *m* inhaler; **inalazione** *f* inhalation

inalterabile *sentimento* unchangeable; *colore* fast; *metallo* non-tarnish

inalterato unchanged

inamidare starch

inammissibile inadmissible

inanimato inanimate; *(senza vita)* lifeless

inappetenza *f* lack of appetite

inarcare *schiena* arch; *sopracciglia* raise

inaridire 1 *v/t* parch **2** *v/i* dry up

inaspettato unexpected

inasprimento *m (intensificazione)* worsening; *di carattere* embitterment; **inasprire** exacerbate, make worse; *carattere* embitter

inattendibile unreliable

inatteso unexpected

inattività *f* inactivity; **inattivo** *persona, capitale* idle, inactive; *vulcano* dormant

inattuabile *(non fattibile)* impracticable; *(non realistico)* unrealistic

inaugurare *mostra* (officially) open, inaugurate; *lapide* unveil; F *oggetto nuovo* christen F; **inaugurazione** *f di mostra* (official) opening, inauguration; *di lapide* unveiling; F *di oggetto nuovo* christening F

inavvertenza *f* inadvertence

incagliarsi MAR run aground

incalcolabile incalculable

incalzare pursue; *fig:* con richieste ply

incamminarsi set out

incandescente incandescent; *fig* heated

incantare enchant; **incantarsi** *(restare affascinato)* be spellbound; *(sognare a occhi aperti)* be in a daze; TEC jam; **incantato** *per effetto di magia* enchanted; *(trasognato)* in a daze; *(affascinato)* spellbound; **incantesimo** *m* spell; **incantevole** delightful, charming

incanto[1] *m (incantesimo)* spell; **come per ~** as if by magic

incanto[2] *m* COM auction; **mettere all'~** put up for auction

incapace 1 *agg* incapable *(di* of); *(incompetente)* incompetent **2** *m/f* incompetent person; **incapacità** *f (inabilità)* inability; *(incompetenza)* incompetence

incappare: ~ *in nebbia*, *difficoltà* run into

incapricciarsi: ~ *di qu* take a liking to s.o.

incarcerare imprison

incaricare *(dare istruzioni a)* instruct; ~ *qu di fare qc* tell *o* instruct s.o. to do sth; **incaricarsi**: ~ *di qc* see to sth, deal with sth; **incaricato** *m*, **-a** *f (responsabile)* person in charge; *(funzionario)* official; **incarico** *m (compito)* task, assignment; *(nomina)* appointment

incarnare embody

incartare wrap (up) (in paper)

incassare COM (*riscuotere*) cash; *fig*: *colpi, insulti ecc* take; **incasso** *m* (*riscossione*) collection; (*somma incassata*) takings

incastonare set

incastrare fit in; F *fig* (*far apparire colpevole*) frame F; (*mettere in una posizione difficile*) corner F

incastro *m* joint

incatenare chain

incavato hollow; *occhi* deepset

incendiare set fire to; **incendiario** *m*, **-a** *f* arsonist; **incendio** *m* fire; **~ doloso** arson

incenerire reduce to ashes; **inceneritore** *m* incinerator

incenso *m* incense

incensurato irreproachable; DIR **essere ~** have a clean record

incentivare (*incrementare*) boost; **incentivo** *m* incentive

incerata *f* oilcloth

incertezza *f* uncertainty; **incerto 1** *agg* uncertain **2** *m* uncertainty

incessante incessant

incetta *f*: **fare ~ di qc** stockpile sth

inchiesta *f* investigation

inchinarsi bow; *di donna* curtsy; **inchino** *m* bow; *di donna* curtsy

inchiodare 1 *v/t* nail; *coperchio* nail down **2** *v/i* AUTO jam on the brakes

inchiostro *m* ink

inciampare trip (*in* over); **~ in qu** run into s.o.

incidentale (*casuale*) accidental; (*secondario*) incidental; **incidente** *m* (*episodio*) incident; **~ aereo** plane crash; **~ stradale** road accident

incidere[1] *v/i* affect (**su** sth)

incidere[2] *v/t* engrave; (*tagliare*) cut; (*registrare*) record

incinta pregnant

incirca all'~ more or less

incisione *f* engraving; (*acquaforte*) etching; (*taglio*) cut; MED incision; (*registrazione*) recording; **incisivo 1** *agg* incisive **2** *m* (*dente*) incisor

incitare incite

incivile uncivilized; (*villano*) impolite

inclinare 1 *v/t* tilt **2** *v/i*: **~ a** (*tendere a*) be inclined to; **inclinato** tilted; **inclinazione** *f* inclination; **incline** inclined (**a** to)

includere include; (*allegare*) enclose; **inclusivo** inclusive; **incluso 1** *pp* → **includere 2** *agg* included; (*compreso*) inclusive; (*allegato*) enclosed

incoerente (*incongruente*) inconsistent; **incoerenza** *f* inconsistency

incognita *f* unknown quantity; **incognito** *in* incognito

incollare stick; *con colla liquida* glue; **incollarsi** stick (**a** to)

incolore colourless, *Am* colorless

incolpare blame

incolto uneducated; (*trascurato*) unkempt; AGR uncultivated

incolume unharmed; **incolumità** *f* safety

incombente *pericolo* impending; **incombenza** *f* task

incominciare start, begin (**a** to)

incomodare inconvenience; **incomodarsi** put o.s. out

incompatibile incompatible; **incompatibilità** *f* incompatibility

incompetente incompetent; **incompetenza** *f* incompetence

incompiuto unfinished

incompleto incomplete

incomprensibile incomprehensible; **incomprensione** *f* lack of understanding; (*malinteso*) misunderstanding; **incompreso** misunderstood

inconcepibile inconceivable

inconcludente inconclusive; *persona* ineffectual

inconfondibile unmistakable

inconfutabile indisputable

inconsapevole (*ignaro*) unaware

inconscio *m/agg* unconscious

inconsistente insubstantial; *fig* (*infondato*) unfounded; (*vago*) vague

inconsolabile inconsolable

inconsueto unusual

incontentabile hard to please; (*perfezionista*) perfectionist

incontestato undisputed

incontrare *v/t* meet; *difficoltà* encounter **2** *v/i* e **incontrarsi** meet (**con** s.o.)

incontrario: **all'~** the other way round; (*nel modo sbagliato*) the wrong way round

incontrastato undisputed

incontro 1 *m* meeting; **~ di calcio** football match *o* Am game **2** *prp*: **~ a** towards; **andare ~ a qu** go and meet s.o.; *fig* meet s.o. halfway

inconveniente *m* (*svantaggio*) drawback; (*ostacolo*) hitch

incoraggiamento *m* encouragement; **incoraggiante** encouraging; **incoraggiare** encourage

incorniciare frame

incoronare crown

incorporare incorporate

incorreggibile incorrigible

incorrere: **~ in** *sanzioni* incur; *errore* make

incorruttibile incorruptible

incosciente unconscious; (*irresponsabile*) reckless

incoscienza *f* unconsciousness; (*insensatezza*) recklessness

incostante changeable; *negli affetti* fickle

incostituzionale unconstitutional

incredibile incredible

incredulo incredulous, disbelieving

incrementare increase; **incremento** *m* increase, growth

increspare *acque* ripple; *capelli* frizz; *tessuto* gather

incriminare indict

incrociare 1 *v/t* cross **2** *v/i* MAR, AVIA cruise; **incrocio** *m* (*intersezione*) crossing; (*crocevia*) crossroads *sg*, *Am* intersection; *di razze animali* cross(-breed)

incubatrice *f* incubator; **incubazione** *f* incubation

incubo *m* nightmare

incudine *f* anvil

incurabile incurable

incurante heedless (*di* of)

incuriosire: ~ *qu* arouse s.o.'s curiosity

incursione *f* raid; ~ *aerea* air raid

incustodito unattended; *passaggio a livello* unmanned

indaco *m/agg* indigo

indaffarato busy

indagare investigate (*su*, *intorno a* sth); **indagine** *f* research; *della polizia* investigation; ~ *di mercato* market survey

indebitare, indebitarsi get into debt

indebolire weaken

indecente indecent

indecisione *f* indecision, indecisiveness; **indeciso** undecided; *abitualmente* indecisive

indefinito indefinite

indelebile indelible; *colore* fast

indenne *persona* uninjured; *cosa* undamaged; **indennità** *f inv* (*gratifica*) allowance, benefit; (*risarcimento*) compensation; ~ *di trasferta* travel allowance; **indennizzare** compensate (*per* for); **indennizzo** *m* (*compenso*) compensation

indescrivibile indescribable

indesiderato unwanted

indeterminato *tempo* unspecified, indefinite; *quantità* indeterminate

India *f* India; **indiano 1** *agg* Indian **2** *m*, **-a** *f* Indian

indicare show, indicate; *col dito* point at *o* to; (*consigliare*) suggest, recommend; (*significare*) mean; **indicativo** *m* GRAM indicative; **indicato** (*consigliabile*) advisable; (*adatto*) suitable

indicatore 1 *agg* indicative **2** *m* indicator; AUTO ~ *di direzione* indicator, *Am* turn signal; **indicazione** *f* indication; (*direttiva*) direction; (*informazione*) piece of information; MED **-i** *pl* directions (for use); **-i** *pl* **stradali** road signs

indice *m* index; ANAT index finger, forefinger

indicibile indescribable

indietreggiare draw back; *camminando all'indietro* step back; MIL retreat

indietro behind; *tornare, girarsi* back; *essere* ~ *con il lavoro* be behind; *mentalmente* be backward; *di orologio* be slow; *dare* ~ *(restituire)* give back; *tirarsi* ~ draw back; *fig* back out; *all'*~ backwards

indifeso undefended; *(inerme)* defenceless, *Am* defenseless

indifferente indifferent; *non* ~ appreciable, considerable; *per me è* ~ it's all the same to me; **indifferenza** *f* indifference

indigeno 1 *agg* native, indigenous **2** *m*, *-a f* native

indigestione *f* indigestion; **indigesto** indigestible

indignare: ~ *qu* make s.o. indignant; **indignarsi** get indignant (*per* about)

indimenticabile unforgettable

indipendente independent (*da* of); **indipendentemente** independently; ~ *dall'età* regardless of age; **indipendenza** *f* independence

indire *conferenza, elezioni, sciopero* call; *concorso* announce

indiretto indirect

indirizzare direct; *lettera* address; *(spedire)* send; **indirizzario** *m* address book; *per*

spedizione mailing list; **indirizzo** *m* address; *(direzione)* direction; ~ *di posta elettronica* e-mail address

indisciplinato undisciplined

indiscreto indiscreet; **indiscrezione** *f* indiscretion

indiscriminato indiscriminate

indiscusso unquestioned

indiscutibile unquestionable

indispensabile 1 *agg* indispensable, essential **2** *m* essentials

indispettire irritate; **indispettirsi** get irritated; **indispettito** irritated

indisposto *(ammalato)* indisposed

indistinto indistinct

indistruttibile indestructible

indivia *f* endive

individuale individual; **individualista** *m/f* individualist; **individuo** *m* individual

indizio *m* clue; *(segno)* sign; *(sintomo)* symptom; DIR *-i pl* circumstantial evidence

indole *f* nature

indolente indolent

indolore painless

indomani: *l'*~ the next day

indossare *(mettersi)* put on; *(portare)* wear; **indossatore** *m*, *-trice f* model

indotto *pp* ☞ **indurre**

indovinare guess; *futuro* predict; **indovinato** *(ben riuscito)* successful; *(ben scelto)* well chosen; **indovinello** *m* riddle; **indovino** m, -a f fortune-teller

indubbiamente undoubtedly

indugiare 1 v/t partenza delay **2** v/i (tardare) delay; (esitare) hesitate; (attardarsi) linger; **indugio** m delay; **senza ~** without delay

indulgente indulgent; giudice, sentenza lenient; **indulgenza** f indulgence; di giudice, sentenza leniency

indumento m item of clothing; **gli -i** pl clothes

indurire 1 v/t harden **2** v/e indurirsi go hard, harden; **indurito** hardened

indurre induce

industria f industry; (operosità) industriousness; **industriale 1** agg industrial **2** m industrialist; **industrializzazione** f industrialization

ineccepibile irreproachable; ragionamento faultless

inedito unpublished; fig novel

inefficace ineffective

inefficiente inefficient; **inefficienza** f inefficiency

ineguagliabile (senza rivali) unrivalled, Am unrivaled; (senza confronto) incomparable; **ineguale** unequal; (discontinuo) uneven

inequivocabile unequivocal

inerte (inoperoso) idle; (immobile) inert, motionless; (senza vita) lifeless; FIS inert; **inerzia** f inertia, (inattività) inactivity

inesattezza f inaccuracy; **inesatto** inaccurate

inesauribile inexhaustible

inesperienza f inexperience; **inesperto** inexperienced

inesplorato unexplored

inesploso unexploded

inestimabile inestimable; bene invaluable

inetto inept

inevaso pending

inevitabile inevitable

inezia f trifle

infallibile infallible

infame 1 agg (turpe) infamous, foul; spir horrible **2** m/f P (delatore) grass P

infantile letteratura, giochi children's; malattie childhood attr; (immaturo) childish, infantile; **infanzia** f childhood; (primi mesi) infancy (anche fig); (bambini) children pl

infarinare (dust with) flour; **infarinatura** f fig smattering

infarto m cardiaco heart attack

infastidire annoy, irritate

infatti in fact

infatuarsi ~ di qu become infatuated with s.o.

infedele 1 agg unfaithful; traduzione inaccurate **2** m/f REL infidel; **infedeltà** f inv unfaithfulness

infelice unhappy; (inopportuno) unfortunate; (malriuscito) bad; **infelicità** f unhappiness

inferiore 1 *agg* lower; *fig* inferior (**a** to); **essere ~ a qu** be inferior to s.o. **2** *m/f* inferior; (*subalterno*) subordinate; **inferiorità** *f* inferiority; **complesso** *m* **d'~** inferiority complex

infermeria *f* infirmary; **infermiere** *m*, **-a** *f* nurse; **infermo 1** *agg* (*ammalato*) ill; (*invalido*) invalid **2** *m*, **-a** *f* invalid

infernale infernal; **inferno** *m* hell

inferriata *f* grating; (*cancellata*) railings

infestare infest; **infettarsi** become infected; **infettivo** infectious; **infezione** *f* infection

infiammabile flammable; **infiammarsi** become inflamed; **infiammazione** *f* inflammation

inferire *di maltempo, malattie* rage; **~ su** *o* **contro** savagely attack

infilare *fili, corde, ago* thread; (*inserire*) insert, put in; (*indossare*) put on; *strada* take; **infilarsi** *indumento* slip on; (*conficcarsi*) stick; (*introdursi*) slip (**in** into); (*stiparsi*) squeeze (**in** into)

infiltrarsi seep; *fig* infiltrate; **infiltrazione** *f* infiltration; *di liquidi* seepage

infilzare pierce; *perle* thread

infimo lowest

infine (*alla fine*) finally, eventually; (*insomma*) in short

infinità *f* infinity; **ho un'~ di cose da fare** I've got no end of things to do; **infinito 1** *agg* infinite **2** *m* infinity; GRAM infinitive

infischiarsi F: **~ di** not give a hoot about F; **me ne infischio** I couldn't care less F

inflazione *f* inflation

inflessibile inflexible

infliggere inflict; **inflitto** *pp* ☞ **infliggere**

influente influential; **influenza** *f* influence; MED flu, influenza; **influenzabile** easily influenced, impressionable; **influenzare** influence; **influire: ~ su** influence, have an effect on; **influsso** *m* influence

infondato unfounded

infondere *fig* instil, *Am* instill

inforcare *occhiali* put on; *bicicletta* get on, mount

informale informal

informare inform (**di** of); **informarsi** find out (**di, su** about); **informatica** *f* scienza information technology, IT; **informatico 1** *agg* computer attr, IT **2** *m*, **-a** *f* computer scientist, IT specialist

informato informed; **informatore** *m*, **-trice** *f* informant; *della polizia* informer; **informazione** *f* information; **un'~ a** piece of information; **-i** information; **ufficio** *m* **-i** information office

informicolirsi have pins and needles

infortunio *m* accident; **~ sul lavoro** accident at work

infossato *occhi* deep-set, sunken

infrangere break; **infrangibile** unbreakable; **vetro** *m* **~** shatterproof glass

infranto *pp* **~ infrangere**

infrarosso infrared

infrasettimanale midweek

infrastruttura *f* infrastructure

infrazione *f* offence, *Am* offense

infreddatura *f* cold

infuocato (*caldissimo*) scorching; *discorso, tramonto* fiery

infuori: all'~ outwards; **all'~ di** except

infuriarsi fly into a rage; **infuriato** furious

infusione *f*, **infuso** *m* infusion; (*tisana*) herbal tea

ingaggiare (*reclutare*) recruit; *attore, cantante lirico* engage; SP sign (up); (*iniziare*) start, begin; **ingaggio** *m* (*reclutamento*) recruitment; SP signing; (*somma*) fee

ingannare deceive; **~ il tempo** kill time; **inganno** *m* deception, deceit

ingarbugliare tangle; *fig* confuse, muddle; **ingarbugliarsi** *fig* get entangled; *fig* get confused

ingegnarsi do one's utmost

(**a, per** to)

ingegnere *m* engineer; **ingegneria** *f* engineering; **~ genetica** genetic engineering

ingegno *m* (*mente*) mind; (*intelligenza*) brains; (*genio*) genius; (*inventiva*) ingenuity

ingelosire 1 *v/t* make jealous **2** *v/i* be jealous

ingente enormous

ingenuo ingenuous

ingerire swallow

ingessare put in plaster; **ingessatura** *f* plaster

Inghilterra *f* England

inghiottire swallow

ingiallire turn yellow; **ingiallito** yellowed

inginocchiarsi kneel (down)

ingiù: all'~ down(wards)

ingiunzione *f* injunction; **~ di pagamento** final demand

ingiuria *f* insult

ingiustificato unjustified

ingiustizia *f* injustice; **ingiusto** unjust, unfair

inglese 1 *m/agg* English **2** *m/f* Englishman; *donna* Englishwoman *f*

ingoiare swallow

ingolfare, ingolfarsi flood

ingombrante cumbersome, bulky; **ingombrare** *passaggio* block; *stanza, mente* clutter (up); **ingombro 1** *agg passaggio* blocked; *stanza, mente* cluttered (up) **2** *m* hindrance, obstacle; **essere d'~** be in the way

ingordo greedy

ingorgo *m* blockage; ~ *stradale* traffic jam

ingozzare *cibo* devour, gobble up; *persona* stuff (*di* with); **ingozzarsi** stuff o.s (*di* with)

ingranaggio *m* gear; *fig* machine; **ingranare** engage; *fig* F **le cose cominciano a** ~ things are beginning to work out

ingrandimento *m* enlargement; *di azienda, città* expansion, growth; **ingrandire** enlarge; *azienda, città* expand, develop; (*esagerare*) exaggerate; **ingrandirsi** grow

ingrassare 1 *v/t animali* fatten (up); (*lubrificare*) grease **2** *v/i* get fat, put on weight

ingratitudine *f* ingratitude; **ingrato** ungrateful; *lavoro, compito* thankless

ingrediente *m* ingredient

ingresso *m* entrance; (*atrio*) hall; (*accesso*) admittance; INFOR input; ~ *libero* admission free; *vietato l'~* no entry, no admittance

ingrossare 1 *v/t* make bigger; (*gonfiare, accrescere*) swell **2** *v/i* e **ingrossarsi** get bigger; (*gonfiarsi*) swell; **ingrosso:** *all'~* (*all'incirca*) roughly, about; COM wholesale

inguaribile incurable

inguinale groin *attr*; **ernia f ~** hernia; **inguine** *m* ANAT groin

ingurgitare gulp down

inibire prohibit, forbid; PSI inhibit; **inibito** inhibited; **inibizione** *f* PSI inhibition

iniettare inject; ~ *qc a qu* inject s.o. with sth; **iniezione** *f* injection

inimicarsi fall out (*con* with); **inimicizia** *f* enmity

inimmaginabile unimaginable

ininterrotto continuous

iniziale *f* flagg initial; **iniziare** begin, start; *ostilità, dibattito* open; *fig* ~ *a fare qc* begin *o* start doing sth, begin *o* start to do sth

iniziativa *f* initiative; *di mia* ~ on my own initiative

inizio *m* start, beginning; **avere** ~ start, begin; **dare** ~ *a qc* start sth

innaffiare water; **innaffiatoio** *m* watering can

innalzare raise; (*erigere*) erect

innamorarsi fall in love (*di* with); **innamorato 1** *agg* in love (*di* with) **2** *m*, -**a** *f* boyfriend; *donna* girlfriend

innanzi 1 *prp* before; ~ **a** in front of; ~ *tutto* first of all; (*soprattutto*) above all **2** *avv stato in luogo* in front; (*avanti*) forward; (*prima*) before; **d'ora** ~ from now on

innato innate, inborn

innervosire *qu* make s.o. nervous; (*irritare*) get on s.o.'s nerves; **innervosirsi** get nervous; (*irritarsi*) get irritated

innestare BOT, MED graft; EL *spina* insert; AUTO *marcia* engage

inno *m* hymn; **~ nazionale** national anthem

innocente innocent; **innocenza** *f* innocence

innocuo innocuous, harmless

innovativo innovative; **innovazione** *f* innovation

inodore odourless, *Am* odorless

inoffensivo harmless, inoffensive

inoltrare forward; **inoltrarsi** advance, penetrate (**in** into); **inoltrato** late; **inoltre** besides

inondare flood; **inondazione** *f* flood

inopportuno (*inadatto*) inappropriate; (*intempestivo*) untimely; *persona* tactless

inorridire 1 *v/t* horrify **2** *v/i* be horrified; **inorridito** horrified

inosservato unobserved, unnoticed; (*non rispettato*) disregarded; **passare ~** go unnoticed

inossidabile stainless

inquadrare *fotografia* frame; *fig* put into context; **inquadratura** *f* frame

inquietante (*che preoccupa*) worrying; (*che turba*) disturbing; **inquieto** restless; (*preoccupato*) worried; (*adirato*) angry

inquilino *m*, **-a** *f* tenant

inquinamento *m* pollution; **inquinante 1** *agg* polluting; **non ~** environmentally friendly; **sostanza** *f* **~** pollutant **2** *m* pollutant; **inquinare** pollute; DIR *prove* tamper with

insabbiamento *m di porto* silting up; *fig* shelving

insaccati *mpl* sausages

insalata *f* salad; **~ mista** mixed salad; **~ verde** green salad; **insalatiera** *f* salad bowl

insanabile (*incurabile*) incurable; *fig* (*irrimediabile*) irreparable

insanguinato bloodstained

insaponare soap

insapore tasteless; **insaporire** flavour, *Am* flavor

insaputa *all'* **~ di qu** unknown to s.o.

insaziabile insatiable

inscenare stage

inscindibile inseparable

insegna *f* sign; (*bandiera*) flag; (*stemma*) symbol; (*decorazione*) decoration

insegnamento *m* teaching; **insegnante 1** *agg* teaching; **corpo** *m* **~** (teaching) staff **2** *m/f* teacher; **insegnare** teach; **~ qc a qu** teach s.o. sth

inseguimento *m* chase, pursuit; **inseguire** chase, pursue

inseminazione *f* insemination; **~ artificiale** artificial

insemination
insenatura f inlet
insensato 1 agg senseless, idiotic **2** m, -a f fool, idiot
insensibile insensitive (*a* to); *parte del corpo* numb; **insensibilità** f insensitivity; *di parte del corpo* numbness
inseparabile inseparable
inserire insert; (*collegare: in elettrotecnica*) connect; *annuncio* place; **inserirsi** fit in; *in una conversazione* join in; **inserto** m (*pubblicazione*) supplement; **inserviente** m/f attendant
inserzione f insertion; *sul giornale* ad, advertisement
insetticida m insecticide; **insettifugo** m insect repellent; **insetto** m insect
insicurezza f insecurity, lack of security; **insicuro** insecure
insieme 1 avv together; (*contemporaneamente*) at the same time **2** prp: ~ **a**, ~ **con** together with **3** m whole; *di abiti* outfit; **nell'~** on the whole
insignificante insignificant
insinuare insert; fig: *dubbio, sospetto* sow the seeds of; ~ **che** insinuate that; **insinuarsi** penetrate; fig ~ **in** creep into; **insinuazione** f insinuation
insipido insipid
insistente insistent; **insistenza** f insistence; **insiste-**

re insist; (*perseverare*) persevere; ~ **a fare qc** insist on doing sth
insoddisfacente unsatisfactory; **insoddisfatto** unsatisfied; (*scontento*) dissatisfied; **insoddisfazione** f dissatisfaction
insofferente intolerant
insolazione f sunstroke
insolente insolent
insolito unusual
insoluto unsolved; *debito* outstanding; **insolvenza** f insolvency
insomma briefly, in short; ~**!** well, really!
insonne sleepless; **insonnia** f insomnia; **insonnolito** sleepy
insopportabile unbearable, intolerable
insorgere rise (up) (*contro* against); *di difficoltà* come up, crop up
insormontabile insurmountable
insorto 1 pp ☞ **insorgere 2** m rebel
insospettabile above suspicion; (*impensato*) unsuspected; **insospettire 1** v/t: ~ **qu** make s.o. suspicious **2** v/i e **insospettirsi** become suspicious
insperato unhoped for; (*inatteso*) unexpected
inspiegabile inexplicable
inspirare breathe in, inhale
instabile unstable; *tempo*

changeable

installare install; **installazione** f installation

instancabile tireless

insù *all'~* upwards

insuccesso m failure

insufficiente insufficient; (*inadeguato*) inadequate; **insufficienza** f insufficiency; (*inadeguatezza*) inadequacy

insulina f insulin

insulso *fig* (*privo di vivacità*) dull; (*vacuo*) inane; (*sciocco*) silly

insultare insult; **insulto** m insult

insurrezione f insurrection

intaccare (*corrodere*) corrode; *fig* (*danneggiare*) damage; *scorte*, *capitale* make inroads into

intanto (*nel frattempo*) meanwhile; (*per ora*) for the time being; (*invece*) yet; *~ che* while

intasare block; **intasarsi** get blocked; **intasato** blocked

intascare pocket

intatto intact

integrale whole; MAT integral; *edizione* unabridged; *pane* m *~* wholemeal bread, *Am* wholewheat bread; **integrare** integrate; (*aumentare*) supplement; **integrarsi** integrate; **integrazione** f integration; *cassa* f *~* form of income support

intelaiatura f framework

intelletto m intellect; **intellet-**

tuale *agg*, *m/f* intellectual

intelligente intelligent; **intelligenza** f intelligence

intendere (*comprendere*) understand; (*udire*) hear; (*voler dire*) mean; (*avere intenzione*) intend; **s'intende!** of course!; **intendersi** (*capirsi*) understand each other; (*accordarsi*) agree; *~ di qc* know a lot about sth; **intenditore** m, **-trice** f connoisseur, expert

intensificare intensify; **intensificarsi** intensify; **intensità** f *inv* intensity; EL strength; **intensivo** intensive; **intenso** intense

intento 1 *agg* engrossed (*a* in), intent (*a* on) **2** m aim, purpose; **intenzionale** intentional; **intenzione** f intention; *avere l'~ di fare qc* intend to do sth

interagire interact

interamente entirely

interattivo interactive

intercalare 1 *v/t* insert **2** m stock phrase

intercambiabile interchangeable

intercapedine f cavity

intercedere intercede (**presso** with; **per** on behalf of)

intercettare intercept; **intercettazione** f interception; *-i pl* **telefoniche** phone tapping

intercontinentale intercontinental

interdentale: *filo m* ~ (dental) floss

interessante interesting; *in stato* ~ pregnant; **interessare 1** *v/t* interest; *(riguardare)* concern **2** *v/i* matter; **interessarsi** be interested (*a, di* in); *(occuparsi)* take care (*di* of); **interessato 1** *agg* interested (*a* in); *(implicato)* involved (*a* in); *spreg* parere, opinione biased; *persona* self-interested **2** *m*, **-a** *f* person concerned; **interesse** *m* interest; *(tornaconto)* benefit; *per* ~ out of self-interest; *senza* ~ of no interest

interfaccia *f* INFOR interface

interferenza *f* interference; **interferire** interfere

interiezione *f* interjection

interiora *fpl* entrails

interiore *m/agg* interior

interlocutore *m*, **-trice** *f*: *la sua* **-trice** the woman he was talking to

intermediario *m*, **-a** *f* intermediary; **intermedio** intermediate; *bilancio, relazione* interim

interminabile interminable

intermittente intermittent

internazionale international

internet *m* Internet; *navigare su* ~ surf the Net

interno 1 *agg* internal, inside *attr*; GEOG inland; POL, FIN domestic; *fig* inner **2** *m* (*parte interna*) inside, interior; GEOG interior; TELEC exten-

sion; *via Dante n. 6* ~ *9* 6 via Dante, Flat 9; *all'*~ inside

intero whole, entire; *(completo)* complete; *latte m* ~ whole milk; MAT *numero m* ~ integer

interpellare consult

interpretare interpret; *personnagio* play; MUS play, perform; **interpretazione** *f* interpretation; TEA, MUS, *film* performance; **interprete** *m/f* interpreter; *attore, musicista* performer; *fare da* ~ interpret, act as interpreter

interpunzione *f* punctuation

interrogare question; EDU test; **interrogativo 1** *agg* GRAM interrogative; *occhiata* questioning; *punto m* ~ question mark **2** *m* (*domanda*) question; *(dubbio)* doubt; **interrogatorio** *m* questioning; **interrogazione** *f* questioning; *domanda* question; EDU oral (test)

interrompere interrupt; *(sospendere)* break off, stop; *comunicazioni, forniture* cut off; **interrotto** *pp* ☞ **interrompere**; **interruttore** *m* EL switch; **interruzione** *f* interruption

interurbana *f* long-distance (phone) call; **interurbano** intercity; *chiamata f* **-a** long-distance (phone) call

intervallo *m* interval; *di scuola, lavoro* break

intervenire intervene; *(parte-*

cipare) take part, participate (**a** in); MED operate; **intervento** *m* intervention; (*partecipazione*) participation; MED operation; **pronto ~** emergency services

intervista *f* interview; **intervistare** interview; **intervistatore** *m*, **-trice** *f* interviewer

intesa *f* (*accordo*) understanding; (*patto*) agreement; SP team work; **inteso 1** *pp* ☞ **intendere 2** *agg* (*capito*) understood; (*destinato*) intended (**a** to); **siamo ~i?** agreed

intestare *assegno* make out (**a** to); *proprietà* register (**a** in the name of); **intestatario** *m*, **-a** *f di assegno* payee; *di proprietà* registered owner

intestazione *f* heading; *su carta da lettere* letterhead

intestinale intestinal; **intestino** *m* intestine, gut

intimare order

intimidazione *f* intimidation; **intimidire** intimidate

intimità *f* privacy; *di un rapporto* intimacy; **intimo 1** *agg* intimate; (*segreto*) private; (*accogliente*) cosy, Am cozy; *amico* close, intimate **2** *m persona* close friend; (*abbigliamento*) underwear

intingere dip

intitolare call, entitle; (*dedicare*) dedicate (**a** to); **intitolarsi** be called

intollerabile intolerable; **intollerante** intolerable; **intol-**

leranza *f* intolerance

intonacare plaster; **intonaco** *m* plaster

intonarsi (*armonizzare*) go well (**a**, **con** with); **intonato** MUS in tune; **colori** *pl* **-i** colours that go well together

intontito dazed

intoppo *m* (*ostacolo*) hindrance; (*contrattempo*) snag

intorno 1 *prp*: **~ a** around; (*riguardo a*) about **2** *avv* around

intossicare poison; **intossicazione** *f* poisoning; **~ alimentare** food poisoning

intralciare hinder; **intralcio** *m* hindrance

intransigente intransigent

intransitivo intransitive

intraprendente enterprising; **intraprendenza** *f* enterprise; **intraprendere** undertake

intrattabile intractable; *prezzo* fixed, non-negotiable

intrattenere entertain; **~ buoni rapporti con qu** be on good terms with s.o.; **intrattenersi** dwell (**su** on)

intravedere glimpse; *fig* (*presagire*) anticipate, see; **intravisto** *pp* ☞ **intravedere**

intrecciare plait, braid; (*intessere*) weave; **intrecciarsi** intertwine

intreccio *m fig* (*trama*) plot

intricato tangled; *disegno* intricate; *fig* complicated

intrigante scheming; (*affasci-*

nante) intriguing; **intrigo** *m* plot

intrinseco intrinsic

introdurre introduce; (*inserire*) insert; **introdursi** get in; **introduzione** *f* introduction

introito *m* income; (*incasso*) takings

intromettersi interfere; (*interporsi*) intervene

introvabile impossible to find

introverso 1 *agg* introverted **2** *m*, **-a** *f* introvert

intrufolarsi sneak in

intruglio *m* concoction

intruso *m*, **-a** *f* intruder

intuire know instinctively; **intuito** *m* intuition; **intuizione** *f* intuition

inumano inhuman

inumidire dampen, moisten; **inumidirsi** get damp

inutile useless; (*superfluo*) unnecessary, pointless; **inutilizzabile** unusable; **inutilmente** pointlessly, needlessly

invadente 1 *agg* nosy **2** *m/f* busybody

invadere invade; (*occupare*) occupy; (*inondare*) flood

invaghirsi: *~ di* take a liking to

invalido 1 *agg* disabled; DIR invalid **2** *m*, **-a** *f* disabled person

invano in vain

invariato unchanged

invasione *f* invasion (**di** of)

invecchiare 1 *v/t* age **2** *v/i* age, get older; *di vini, cibi* mature; *fig* (*cadere in disuso*) date

invece instead; (*ma*) but; *~ di fare* instead of doing

inveire: *~ contro* inveigh against

invenduto unsold

inventare invent

inventario *m* inventory

inventore *m*, **-trice** *f* inventor; **invenzione** *f* invention

invernale winter *attr*; **sport** *mpl* **-i** winter sports; **inverno** *m* winter; *d'~* in winter

inverosimile improbable, unlikely

inversione *f* (*scambio*) reversal; AUTO *~ di marcia* U-turn

inverso 1 *agg* reverse **2** *m* opposite

invertire reverse; (*capovolgere*) turn upside down; *~ la marcia* turn around

investigare investigate; **investigatore** *m*, **-trice** *f* investigator

investimento *m* investment; *di pedone* running over; **investire** *pedone* run over; FIN, *fig* invest

inviare send; **inviato** *m*, **-a** *f* envoy; *di giornale* correspondent

invidia *f* envy; **invidiare** envy; **invidioso** envious

invincibile invincible

invio *m* dispatch

invisibile invisible

invitante *profumo* enticing; *offerta* tempting; **invitare** invite; **invitato** *m*, -a *f* guest; **invito** *m* invitation

invocare invoke; (*implorare*) beg for

invogliare induce

involontario involuntary

involtini *mpl* GASTR rolled stuffed slices of meat

involucro *m* wrapping

inzaccherare spatter with mud

inzuppare soak; (*intingere*) dip

io 1 *pron* I; **~ stesso** myself; **sono ~!** it's me! **2** *m* *inv* ego

iodio *m* iodine

ionico ARCHI Ionic

iosa: a ~ in abundance

iperattivo hyperactive

ipermercato *m* hypermarket, *Am* supermarket

ipersensibile hypersensitive

ipertensione *f* high blood pressure

ipnosi *f* hypnosis; **ipnotizzare** hypnotize

ipocalorico low-calorie

ipocrisia *f* hypocrisy; **ipocrita 1** *agg* hypocritical **2** *m/f* hypocrite

ipoteca *f* mortgage; **ipotecare** mortgage

ipotesi *f* *inv* hypothesis; **ipotetico** hypothetical; **ipotizzare** hypothesize

ippica *f* (horse) riding; **ippodromo** *m* race-course

ippopotamo *m* hippo(pota-mus)

ira *f* anger

iracheno 1 *agg* Iraqi **2** *m*, -a *f* Iraqi

Iran *m* Iran; **iraniano 1** *agg* Iranian **2** *m*, -a *f* Iranian

Iraq *m* Iraq

irascibile irritable, irascible

iride *f* (*arcobaleno*) rainbow; ANAT, BOT iris

Irlanda *f* Ireland; **irlandese 1** *agg* Irish **2** *m* Irish Gaelic **3** *m/f* Irishman; *donna* Irish-woman

ironia *f* irony; **ironico** ironic(al); **ironizzare** be ironic

IRPEF *f* (= *Imposta sul Reddito delle Persone Fisiche*) income tax

irraggiungibile unattainable

irragionevole unreasonable

irrazionale irrational

irreale unreal

irrealizzabile unattainable

irregolare irregular; **irregolarità** *f* *inv* irregularity

irreparabile irreparable

irreperibile impossible to find

irreprensibile irreproachable

irrequieto restless

irresistibile irresistible

irresponsabile irresponsible

irrestringibile shrink-resistant

irrevocabile irrevocable

irriconoscibile unrecognizable

irrigare irrigate

irrigidire stiffen; *fig disciplina* tighten; **irrigidirsi** stiffen

irrilevante irrelevant

irrimediabile irremediable

irripetibile unrepeatable

irrisorio derisive; *quantità, somma di denaro* derisory; *prezzo* ridiculously low

irritabile irritable; **irritabilità** f irritability; **irritante** irritating; **irritare** irritate; **irritarsi** get irritated

irruzione f: **fare ~ in** burst into; *di polizia* raid

iscritto 1 pp ☞ **iscrivere 2** m, -a f member; *a gare, concorsi* entrant; EDU pupil, student **3** m: **per ~** in writing; **iscrivere** register; *a gare, concorsi* enter (**a** for, in); EDU enrol, *Am* enroll (**a** at); **iscriversi** *in un elenco* register; **~ a** *partito, associazione* join; *gara* enter; EDU enrol at, *Am* enroll at; **iscrizione** f inscription

islamico Islamic

Islanda f Iceland; **islandese 1** m/agg Icelandic **2** m/f Icelander

isola f island; **~ pedonale** pedestrian precinct

isolamento m isolation; TEC insulation; **~ acustico** soundproofing; **isolano** m, -a f islander

isolante 1 agg insulating **2** m insulator; **isolare** isolate; TEC insulate; **isolarsi** isolate o.s., cut o.s. off; **isolato 1**

agg isolated; TEC insulated **2** m outsider; *di case* block

ispettore m, **-trice** f inspector; **ispezionare** inspect; **ispezione** f inspection

ispirare inspire; **ispirarsi** *di artista* get inspiration (**a** from); **ispirazione** f inspiration; *(impulso)* impulse; *(idea)* idea

Israele m Israel; **israeliano** m, -a f Israeli

istallare ☞ **installare**

istantanea f snap; **istantaneo** instantaneous; **istante** m instant; **all'~** instantly

istanza f *(esigenza)* need; *(domanda)* application; DIR petition

isterico hysterical

istigare instigate

istintivo instinctive; **istinto** m instinct

istituire establish; **istituto** m institute; *assistenziale* institution, home; **~ di bellezza** beauty salon; **istituzione** f institution

istmo m isthmus

istruire educate, teach; *(dare istruzioni a, addestrare)* instruct; **istruito** educated; **istruttivo** instructive; **istruttore** m, **-trice** f instructor; **istruzione** f education; *(direttiva)* instruction; **-i** *pl* **per l'uso** instructions (for use)

Italia f Italy; **italiano 1** m/agg Italian; **parla ~?** do you speak Italian? **2** *m*, -a *f* Italian

itinerario *m* route, itinerary

ittico *m* fish

iuta *f* jute

IVA *f* (= *Imposta sul Valore Aggiunto*) VAT (= value-added tax), *Am* sales tax

J

jazz *m* jazz; **jazzista** *m/f* jazz musician

jeans *mpl* jeans

jeep *f inv* jeep

jet-lag *m inv* jet lag

jogging *m* jogging; **fare ~** jog, go for a jog

joint-venture *f inv* joint venture

jolly *m inv* joker

joy-stick *m inv* joystick

judo *m* judo

juke-box *m inv* jukebox

jumbo *m* jumbo

junior *m/agg* junior

K

kamikaze *m inv* suicide bomber

karatè *m* karate

killer *m inv* killer

kit *m inv* kit

kitsch *agg inv*, *m* kitsch

kiwi *m inv* BOT kiwi (fruit)

kmq (= *chilometri quadrati*) km² (= square kilometres)

k.o.: mettere qu ~ knock s.o. out; *fig* trounce s.o.

kolossal *m inv* epic

krapfen *m inv* GASTR doughnut, *Am* donut

L

l (= *litro*) l (= litre)

l' = **lo, la**

là there; **di ~** that way; (*in quel luogo*) in there; (**al**) **di ~ di** on the other side of; **più in ~** further on; **nel tempo** later on

la¹ *art fsg* the; **~ signora Rossi** Mrs Rossi; **~ domenica** on

Sundays; **mi piace la birra** I like beer

la² *pron* **1** *sg* (*persona*) her; (*cosa, animale*) it; **~ prenderò** I'll take it **2** *anche* **La** *sg* you

la³ *m* MUS A; *nel solfeggio della scala* la(h)

labbro *m* lip

labirinto *m* labyrinth

laboratorio *m* lab, laboratory; (*officina*) workshop

laborioso laborious; *persona* hard-working

laburista 1 *agg* Labour **2** *m/f* Labour Party member; *elettore* Labour supporter

lacca *f* lacquer; **laccare** lacquer

laccio *m* tie, (draw)string; **-cci** *pl* **delle scarpe** shoe laces

lacerante *dolore, grido* piercing; **lacero** tattered

lacrima *f* tear; **lacrimare** water; **lacrimevole** heart-rending; *film m* **~** tear-jerker; **lacrimogeno: gas** *m* **~** tear gas

lacuna *f* gap; **lacunoso** incomplete

ladino 1 *agg* South Tyrolean **2** *m*, **-a** *f* South Tyrolean

ladro *m*, **-a** *f* thief

laggiù down there; *distante* over there

laghetto *m* pond

lagna *f* (*lamentela*) whining; *persona* whiner; (*cosa noiosa*) bore; **lagnarsi** complain (*di* about)

lago *m* lake

laguna *f* lagoon

laico 1 *agg* scuola, stato secular **2** *m*, **-a** *f* layman; laywoman

lama *f* blade

lamentarsi complain (*di* about); **lamentela** *f* complaint; **lamento** *m* whimper

lametta *f:* **~** (*da barba*) razor blade

lamiera *f* metal sheet

lamina *f* foil; **~ d'oro** gold leaf

lampada *f* lamp; **lampadario** *m* chandelier; **lampadina** *f* light bulb; **~ tascabile** torch, *Am* flashlight

lampante blindingly obvious

lampeggiare flash; **lampeggiatore** *m* AUTO indicator, *Am* turn signal; FOT flashlight

lampione *m* streetlight

lampo *m* lightning

lampone *m* raspberry

lana *f* wool; **pura ~ vergine** pure new wool

lancetta *f* needle; *di orologio* hand

lancia *f* spear; MAR launch; **lanciare** throw; *prodotto* launch; **~ un'occhiata** glance, take a quick look; **~ un urlo** give a shout, shout; **lanciarsi** rush; **~ contro** throw o.s at, attack; F **~ in un'impresa** embark on a venture

lancinante *dolore* piercing

lancio *m* throwing; *di prodotto* launch; **~ del disco** discus; **~ del giavellotto** javelin; **~ del peso** putting the shot

languore *m* languor; **ho un ~ allo stomaco** I'm feeling peckish

lapide *f* gravestone; *su monumento* plaque

lapis *m inv* pencil

lardo *m* lard

larghezza *f* width, breadth; **largo 1** *agg* wide, broad; (*indumento*) loose, big; (*abbondante*) large, generous **2** *m* width; (*piazza*) square; **andare al** ~ head for the open sea; **farsi** ~ elbow one's way through; **stare alla -a da** keep away from

laringe *f* larynx; **laringite** *f* laryngitis

larva *f* ZO larva

lasagne *fpl* lasagne *sg*

lasciare leave; (*abbandonare*) give up; (*concedere*) let; (*smettere di tenere*) let go of; **lascia andare!**, **lascia perdere!** forget it!; **lasciarsi** separate, split; ~ **andare** let o.s. go

lascito *m* legacy

laser *m inv*, *agg inv* laser

lassativo *m/agg* laxative

lasso *m*: ~ **di tempo** period of time

lassù up there

lastra *f di pietra* slab; *di metallo, ghiaccio, vetro* sheet

latente latent

laterale lateral

laterizio *m* bricks and tiles

latino 1 *agg* Latin; ~**-americano** Latin-American **2** *m* Latin; ~**-americano**, **-a** Latin-American

latitante *m/f* fugitive

latitudine *f* latitude

lato *m* side; **a ~ di**, **di ~ a** beside

latrato *m* barking

latrina *f* latrine

latta *f* can, *Br anche* tin

latte *m* milk; ~ **intero** whole milk; ~ **scremato** skimmed milk; ~ **di soia** soy(a) milk; **latteo** milk *attr*; **Via f Lattea** Milky Way; **latteria** *f* dairy; **lattice** *m* latex; **latticinio** *m* dairy product

lattina *f* can, *Br anche* tin

lattosio *m* lactose

lattuga *f* lettuce

laurea *fpl* degree; ~ **triennale/magistrale** bachelor's/master's degree; **laurearsi** graduate; **laureato** *m*, **-a** *f* graduate

lava *f* lava

lavabile washable; ~ **in lavatrice** machine-washable

lavabo *m* basin

lavaggio *m* washing; ~ **a secco** dry-cleaning

lavagna *f* blackboard, *Am* chalkboard; GEOL slate

lavanda *f* BOT lavender

lavanderia *f* laundry; ~ **a gettone** laundrette, *Am* laundromat®

lavandino *m* basin; *nella cucina* sink

lavapiatti *m/f inv* dishwasher; **lavare** wash; ~ **i panni** do the washing; **lavarsi** wash; ~ **le mani** wash one's hands; ~ **i denti** brush *o* clean one's teeth; **lavastoviglie** *f inv* dishwasher; **lavatrice** *f* washing machine

lavello m basin; *nella cucina* sink

lavorare 1 v/i work **2** v/t *materia prima* process; *legno* carve; *terra* work; *lavorativo:* **giorno** m ~ workday; lavorato legno carved; **lavoratore** m, **-trice** f worker; **lavorazione** f *di materia prima* processing; *di legno* carving; **lavoro** m work; (*impiego*) job; **per** ~ on business; **-i in corso** roadworks, work in progress; **senza** ~ unemployed, out of work

le[1] *art fpl* the

le[2] *pron fsg* to her; *fpl* them; *anche* **Le** you

leader m/f inv leader

leale loyal; **lealtà** f loyalty

lebbroso m, **-a** f leper

lecca-lecca m inv lollipop; **leccare** lick

leccio m holm oak

leccornia f delicacy

lecito legal, permissible

lega f league; *di metalli* alloy

legale 1 *agg* legal **2** m/f lawyer; **legalizzare** legalize

legame m tie, relationship; (*nesso*) link, connection; **legamento** m ANAT ligament; **legare** tie; *persona* tie up; (*collegare*) link; *fig di lavoro* tie down

legge f law; *fuori* ~ illegal

leggenda f legend; *di carta geografica ecc* key; **leggendario** legendary

leggere read

leggerezza f lightness; *fig* casualness; **con** ~ thoughtlessly; **leggero** light; (*lieve, di poca importanza*) slight; (*superficiale*) thoughtless; *caffè* weak; **alla** ~**a** lightly

leggibile legible

leggio m lectern; MUS music stand

legislativo legislative; **legislatura** f *periodo* term of parliament

legittimare approve; **legittimo** legitimate

legna f (fire)wood; **legname** m timber; **legno** m wood; **di** ~ wooden

legumi mpl peas and beans; *secchi* pulses

lei *pron fsg soggetto* she; *oggetto, con preposizione* her; ~ **stessa** herself; *anche* **Lei** you; **dare del** ~ **a qu** address s.o. as 'lei'

lembo m *di gonna* hem, bottom; *di terra* stip

lente f lens; **-i** pl glasses, spectacles; **-i** pl (**a contatto**) contact lenses, contacts F; ~ **d'ingrandimento** magnifying glass

lenticchia f lentil

lentiggine f freckle

lento slow; (*allentato*) slack; *abito* loose

lenza f fishing rod

lenzuolo m sheet

leone m lion; ASTR **Leone** Leo; **leonessa** f lioness

leopardo m leopard

lepre f hare

lesbica f lesbian

lesionare damage; **lesione** f MED injury

lessare boil

lessico m vocabulary; (*dizionario*) glossary

lesso 1 *agg* boiled **2** m boiled beef

letale lethal

letame m manure, dung

letargo m lethargy

lettera f letter; **alla ~** to the letter; FIN **~ di cambio** bill of exchange; **letterale** literal; **letterario** literary; **letteratura** f literature

lettino m cot, Am crib; *dal medico* bed; *dallo psicologo* couch

letto 1 m bed; **~ a una piazza** single bed; **~ matrimoniale** double bed; **~i** pl **a castello** bunk beds; **andare a ~** go to bed

letto 2 pp **~ leggere**

lettore m, **-trice** f reader; *all'università* lecturer in a foreign language; INFOR disk drive; **~ compact disc**, **~ CD** CD player

lettura f reading

leucemia f leukaemia, Am leukemia

leva f lever; MIL call-up, Am draft; (*alzare*) raise, lift; (*togliere*) take, (re)move; (*rimuovere*) take out, remove; *macchia* remove, get out; *dente* take out, extract; **~ l'ancora** weigh anchor; **levarsi** get up, rise; *di sole* rise, come up; *indumento* take off; **levata** f *di posta* collection; **levatrice** f midwife

levigare smooth down; **levigato** smooth

lezione f lesson; *all'università* lecture

li *pron* mpl them

lì there; **~ per ~** there and then

libanese *agg*, m/f Lebanese; **Libano** m (the) Lebanon

libbra f pound

libellula f dragon-fly

liberale *agg* generous; POL liberal **2** m/f liberal; **liberalizzare** liberalize; **liberalizzazione** f liberalization; **liberamente** freely; **liberare** release, free; (*sgomberare*) empty; *stanza* vacate; **liberarsi ~ di** get rid of; **liberazione** f release; *di nazione* liberation; **libero** free; **libertà** f inv freedom, liberty

Libia f Libya; **libico 1** *agg* Libyan **2** m, **-a** f Libyan

libreria f bookshop, Am bookstore; (*biblioteca*) library; *mobile* bookcase

libretto m booklet; MUS libretto; **~ degli assegni** cheque book, Am check book; AUTO **~ di circolazione** registration document; **~ di risparmio** bank book

libro m book

licenza f FIN licence, Am license; MIL leave; EDU school leaving certificate; **~ di costruzione** building permit; **~ di esercizio** trading licence; **licenziamento** m dismissal; **licenziare** dismiss; **licenziarsi** resign

liceo m high school

lido m beach

lieto happy; **~ di conoscerla** nice o pleased to meet you

lieve light; (di poca gravità) slight, minor; sorriso, rumore faint

lievitare rise; fig rise, be on the increase; **lievito** m yeast; **~ in polvere** baking powder

lilla m/agg lilac

lima f file; **limetta** f emery board; di metallo nail file

limitare limit (**a** to); **limitato** limited; **limitazione** f limitation; **~ delle nascite** birth control; **senza -i** without restriction; **limite** m limit; (confine) boundary; **~ di velocità** speed limit; **al ~** at most, at the outside

limitrofo bordering

limonata f lemonade; **limone** m lemon; (albero) lemon tree

limpido clear; acqua crystalclear

lince f lynx

linciare lynch

linea f line; **~ dell'autobus** bus route; **mantenere la ~**

keep one's figure; TELEC **restare in ~** stay on the line, not hang up; INFOR **in ~** on line

lineamenti mpl (fisionomia) features

lineare linear

lineetta f dash

linfonodo m lymph node

lingotto m ingot

lingua f tongue; (linguaggio) language; **~ madre** mother tongue; **~ straniera** foreign language; **linguaggio** m language

lino m BOT flax; tessuto linen

liofilizzato freeze-dried

lipidico: a basso contenuto ~ low-fat

liposuzione f liposuction

liquidare (pagare) pay; merci clear; azienda liquidate; fig: questione settle; problema dispose of; persona F dispose of F; **liquidazione** f liquidation; **~ totale** clearance sale; **liquidità** f liquid assets, liquidity; **liquido** m/agg liquid

liquirizia f liquorice

liquore m liqueur

lira f lira

lirica f lyric poem; MUS **la ~** opera; **lirico** lyric; cantante opera attr

lisca f fishbone

lisciare smooth; (accarezzare) stroke; capelli straighten; **liscio** smooth; bevanda straight, neat

liso worn

lista f (*elenco*) list; (*striscia*) strip; **~ d'attesa** waiting list; **~ dei vini** wine list

listino m: **~ di borsa** share index; **~ prezzi** price list

lite f quarrel, argument; **litigare** quarrel, argue; **litigio** m quarrel, argument

litografia f lithography

litorale 1 agg coastal **2** m coast; **litoranea** f coast road; **litoraneo** coast attr, coastal

litro m litre, Am liter

liuto m lute

livella f level; **livello** m level

livido 1 agg livid; *braccio, viso* black and blue; *occhio* black; *per il freddo* blue **2** m bruise

lo 1 art msg the **2** pron msg him; *cosa, animale* it; **non ~ so** I don't know

lobo m lobe

locale 1 agg local **2** m room; *luogo pubblico* place; FERR local train; **località** f inv town; **~ balneare** seaside resort; **localizzare** localize; (*reperire*) locate

locandina f TEA bill

locatario m, -a f tenant; **locatore** m, -**trice** f landlord; *donna* landlady; **locazione** f rental

locomotiva f locomotive; **locomozione** f locomotion; **mezzo** m **di ~** means of transport

locuzione f fixed expression

lodare praise; **lode** f praise

loggia f loggia

loggione m TEA gallery

logica f logic; **logico** logical

logorare wear out; **logorio** m wear and tear; **logoro** *indumento* worn (out)

lombaggine f lumbago

Lombardia f Lombardy; **lombardo 1** agg of Lombardy **2** m, -**a** f native of Lombardy

lombata f loin

lombo m loin

lombrico m earthworm

Londra f London

longevo long-lived

longitudine f GEOG longitude

lontananza f distance; *tra persone* separation; **lontano 1** agg far; *nel tempo* far-off; *passato, futuro, parente* distant **2** avv far (away); **da ~** from a distance; **abita molto ~?** do you live very far away?

lontra f otter

loquace talkative

lordo dirty; *peso, reddito ecc* gross

loro 1 pron soggetto they; *oggetto* them; *forma di cortesia* you **2** possessivo their; *forma di cortesia* your; **il ~ amico** their / your friend; **i ~ genitori** their / your parents **3** pron: **il ~** theirs; *forma di cortesia* yours

lotta f struggle; SP wrestling; *fig* fight; **lottare** wrestle, struggle (**con** with); *fig* fight (**contro** against; **per** for);

lottatore *m* wrestler

lotteria *f* lottery

lotto *m* lottery; *di terreno* plot

lozione *f* lotion; ~ *dopobarba* aftershave

L.st. (= *lira sterlina*) £ (= pound)

lubrificante *m* lubricant; AUTO lubricating oil; **lubrificare** lubricate

lucchetto *m* padlock

luccicare sparkle

luccio *m* pike

lucciola *f* glowworm

luce *f* light; *fig far* ~ *su qc* shed light on sth; AUTO *-i pl di posizione* side lights; *-i pl posteriori* rear lights

lucente shining

lucertola *f* lizard

lucidare polish; *disegno* trace; **lucido 1** *agg superficie* shiny; FOT glossy; *persona* lucid **2** *m* polish; *disegno* transparency; ~ *da scarpe* shoe polish

lucro *m*: *a scopo di* ~ profit-making

luglio *m* July

lugubre sombre, *Am* somber

lui *pron msg soggetto* he; *oggetto* him; *a* ~ to him; ~ *stesso* himself

lumaca *f* slug

luminosità *f* luminosity; FOT

speed; **luminoso** luminous; *stanza* bright

luna *f* moon; ~ *crescente* / *calante* crescent / waning moon; ~ *piena* full moon; ~ *di miele* honeymoon; **luna-park** *m inv* amusement park

lunario *m*: *sbarcare il* ~ make ends meet

lunatico moody

lunedì *m inv* Monday

lunghezza *f* length; **lungo 1** *agg* long; *caffè* weak; *a* ~ for a long time; *fig alla -a* in the long run; *andare per le -ghe* drag on; *di gran -a* by far **2** *prp* along; (*durante*) throughout; **lungolago** *m* lakeside; **lungomare** *m inv* sea front

lunotto *m* AUTO rear window

luogo *m* place; ~ *di nascita* birthplace, place of birth; *avere* ~ take place, be held; *fuori* ~ out of place; *in primo* ~ in the first place

lupo *m* wolf

lurido filthy

lusingare flatter

lussazione *f* dislocation

lusso *m* luxury; *albergo m di* ~ luxury hotel; **lussuoso** luxurious

lustrare polish

lutto *m* mourning

M

ma but; *(eppure)* and yet; **~ va!** nonsense!

maccheroni mpl macaroni sg

macchia f spot; *di sporco* stain; *(bosco)* scrub; **macchiare** stain; **macchiato** stained; **caffè** m **~** espresso with a splash of milk

macchina f machine; *(auto)* car; fig machinery; **~ fotografica** camera; **~ da cucire** sewing machine; **~ da scrivere** typewriter; **macchinario** m machinery

macedonia f: **~ (di frutta)** fruit salad

macellaio m, **-a** f butcher; **macelleria** f butcher's

macerie fpl rubble

macigno m boulder

macinacaffè m inv coffee mill; **macinapepe** m inv pepper mill; **macinare** mill, grind

macrobiotica f health food; **negozio** m **di ~** health food store; **macrobiotico** macrobiotic

Madonna f Madonna, Our Lady; **madonnaro** m pavement artist specializing in sacred images

madre f mother; **madrelingua** f mother tongue **2** m/f native speaker; **madreperla** f mother-of-pearl; **madrina** f godmother

maestà f majesty

maestrale m north-west wind

maestro m agg *(principale)* main **2** m master; MUS, PITT maestro, master **3** m, **-a** f teacher; **~ di nuoto** swimming teacher o instructor; **~ di sci** ski instructor

mafia f Mafia

maga f witch

magari 1 avv maybe, perhaps **2** int **~!** if only! **3** cong **~ venisse** if only he would come

magazzino m warehouse; *di negozio* stock room; *(emporio)* factory shop; **grandi -i** pl department store

maggio m May

maggioranza f majority; **maggiore 1** agg bigger; *(più vecchio)* older; MUS major; **il ~** the biggest; **figlio** the oldest; **artista** the greatest; **la maggior parte di ...** most of the ..., the majority of the ...; **andare per la ~** be a crowd pleaser **2** m MIL major; **maggiorenne** adult attr; **maggioritario** majority; POL **sistema** m **~** first-past-the-post system

magia f magic; **magico** magic(al)

magistrato DIR m magistrate

maglia f top; *(maglione*

sweater; SP shirt, jersey; *ai ferri* stitch; **lavorare a ~** knit; **maglieria** *f* knitwear; **maglietta** *f* T-shirt; **maglione** *m* sweater

magnetico magnetic

magnifico magnificent

magnolia *f* magnolia

mago *m* wizard; *i re -gi* the Three Wise Men, the Magi

magro thin; *cibo* low-fat; *fig: consolazione* small; *guadagno* meagre, *Am* meager

mai *F* never; *(qualche volta)* ever; *~ più* never again; *più che ~* more than ever; *se ~* if ever; *dove / perché ~?* where / why on earth?

maiale *m* pig, *Am* hog; *(carne f di)* ~ pork

maiolica *f* majolica

maionese *f* mayonnaise

mais *m* maize

maiuscola *f* capital (letter); **maiuscolo** capital

mal *F* **male**

malandato dilapidated; *persona* poorly

malanno *m* misfortune; *(malattia)* illness

malapena: a ~ hardly

malato 1 *agg* ill; **essere ~ di cuore** have heart problems; **~ di mente** mentally ill **2** *m*, **-a** *f* sick person; **malattia** *f* illness; **essere / mettersi in ~** be / go on sick leave

malavita *f* underworld

malavoglia *f* unwillingness, reluctance; *di ~* unwillingly,

reluctantly

malconcio the worse for wear; *persona* not very well

maldestro awkward, clumsy

male 1 *m* evil; *che c'è di ~* where's the harm in it?; *andare a ~* go bad; MED *mal di gola* sore throat; *mal di testa* headache; *mal di denti* toothache; *mal di mare* seasickness; *far ~ a qu* hurt s.o.; *mi fa ~ il braccio* my arm hurts; *il cioccolato mi fa ~* chocolate doesn't agree with me; *fare ~ alla salute* be bad for you; *farsi ~* hurt o.s. **2** *avv* badly; *capire ~* misunderstand; *meno ~!* thank goodness!; *stare ~ (essere malato)* be ill; *(essere giù)* be depressed; *il giallo mi sta ~* yellow doesn't suit me

maledetto 1 *pp F* **maledire 2** *agg* damn(ed); **maledire** curse; **maledizione** *f* curse; *~! * damn!

maleducato bad-mannered

malessere *m* indisposition; *fig* malaise

malfamato disreputable

malfatto *cosa* badly made; **malfattore** *m* criminal

malformazione *f* malformation

malgoverno *m* misgovernment

malgrado 1 *prp* in spite of; *mio ~* against my will **2** *cong* although

maligno malicious, spiteful;

MED malignant

malinconia *f* melancholy; **malinconico** melancholic

malincuore: *a* ~ reluctantly, unwilling

malintenzionato 1 *agg* shady, suspicious **2** *m*, *-a f* shady character

malinteso *m* misunderstanding

malizioso malicious; *sorriso* mischievous

malloppo *m* (*refurtiva*) loot

malmenare mistreat

malnutrito under-nourished; **malnutrizione** *f* malnutrition

malore *m*: **è stato colto da un** ~ he was suddenly taken ill

malsano unhealthy

maltempo *m* bad weather

malto *m* malt

maltrattare ill-treat

malumore *m* bad mood; **essere di** ~ be in a bad mood

malvagio evil, wicked

malvisto unpopular

malvivente *m* lout

malvolentieri unwillingly, reluctantly

mamma *f* mother, mum; ~ **mia!** goodness!

mammella *f* breast

mammifero *m* mammal

mammografia *f* mammography

manager *m/f* manager; **manageriale** managerial, management *attr*

mancanza *f* lack (**di** of); (*er-*

rore) oversight

mancare 1 *v/i* be missing; *di coraggio* fail; (*euph: morire*) pass away; **a qu manca qc** s.o. lacks sth; **mi manchi molto** I miss you a lot; **mi mancano 10 euro** I'm 10 euros short; **mancano tre mesi a Natale** it's three months to Christmas; **mi mancano le parole** words fail me; **c'è mancato poco che cadesse** he almost fell; **ci mancherebbe altro!** no way!, you must be joking!; ~ **di qc** (*non avere*) lack sth, be lacking in sth **2** *v/t* miss; **mancato** *occasione* missed, lost; *tentativo* unsuccessful

mancia *f* tip; **manciata** *f* handful

mancino 1 *agg* left-handed; *fig* **colpo** *m* ~ dirty trick **2** *m*, *-a f* left-hander

mandante *m/f* DIR client; **mandare** send; ~ **qu a prendere qc** send s.o. for sth; *fig* ~ **giù** digest, take in

mandarino *m* BOT mandarin (orange)

mandato *m* POL mandate; DIR warrant; ~ **bancario** banker's order; ~ **d'arresto** arrest warrant

mandibola *f* jaw

mandolino *m* mandolin

mandorla *f* almond; **mandorlo** *m* almond tree

mandria *f* herd

maneggevole manageable; **maneggiare** handle (*anche fig*); **maneggio** *m* handling; *per cavalli* riding school

manesco a bit too ready with one's fists

manette *fpl* handcuffs

manganello *m* truncheon, *Am* night stick

mangereccio edible

mangiabile edible; **mangia-cassette** *m inv*, **mangiana-stri** *m inv* cassette player; **mangiare 1** *v/t* eat; *fig* squander; **mangiarsi le parole** mumble **2** *m* food; **mangime** *m* fodder; **mangiuc-chiare** snack

mango *m* mango

mania *f* mania

manica *f* sleeve; **senza -che** sleeveless

Manica *f*: **la ~** the (English) Channel

manicaretto *m* delicacy

manichino *m* dummy

manico *m* handle

manicomio *m* mental home

manicure *f inv* manicure; *(persona)* manicurist

maniera *f (modo)* way, manner; *(stile)* manner; **-e** *pl* manners

manifestante *m/f* demonstrator; **manifestare 1** *v/t (esprimere)* express; *(mostrare)* show **2** *v/i* demonstrate; **manifestarsi** appear, show up; *di malattia* manifest itself; **manifestazione** *f* expres-sion; *il mostrare* show; **~ di protesta** demonstration, demo F; **~ sportiva** sporting event; **manifesto 1** *agg* obvious **2** *m* poster

maniglia *f* handle; *di autobus, metro* strap

manipolare manipulate; *vino* adulterate; **manipolato geneticamente** genetically modified

mano *f* hand; **fuori ~** out of the way; *fig* **alla ~** approachable; **di seconda ~** second-hand; **dare una ~ a qu** give s.o. a hand; **tenersi per ~** hold hands; **man ~ che** as (and when); **manodopera** *f* labour, *Am* labor

manomettere tamper with

manopola *f* knob

manoscritto *m* manuscript

manovale *m* hod carrier

manovella *f* starting handle

manovra *f* manoeuvre, *Am* maneuver; **manovrare 1** *v/t* TEC operate; FERR shunt; *fig* manipulate **2** *v/i* manoeuvre, *Am* maneuver

mansarda *f locale* attic

mantello *m (cappa)* cloak; *di animale* coat; *(strato)* layer

mantenere keep; *in buono stato* maintain; **mantenersi in forma** keep in shape; **mantenimento** *m* maintenance; *di famiglia* keep

Mantova *f* Mantua; **mantovano 1** *agg* Mantuan **2** *m*, **-a** *f* Mantuan

manuale *m/agg* manual

manubrio *m* handlebars

manutenzione *f* maintenance

manzo *m* steer, bullock; *carne* beef

mappa *f* map; **mappamondo** *m* globe

maratona *f* marathon; **maratoneta** *m/f* marathon runner

marca *f* brand, make; (*etichetta*) label; *~ da bollo* revenue stamp; **marcare** mark; *goal* score; **marcato** *accento*, *lineamenti* strong

marchio *m* COM brand; *~ depositato* registered trademark

marcia *f* march; SP walk; TEC AUTO gear; *~ indietro* reverse; **marciapiede** *m* pavement, *Am* sidewalk; **marciare** march

marcio bad, rotten; (*corrotto*) corrupt; **marcire** rot *anche fig*

mare *m* sea; *in alto ~* on the high seas; **marea** *f* tide; *fig una ~ di* loads of; *alta ~* high tide; *bassa ~* low tide; **mareggiata** *f* storm; **maremoto** *m* tidal wave

margarina *f* margarine

margherita *f* daisy

margine *m* margin; (*orlo*) edge, brink

marina *f* coast(line); MAR navy; PITT seascape; **marinaio** *m* sailor

marinare GASTR marinate; F

~ la scuola play truant, *Am* play hooky; **marinato** GASTR marinated

marino sea *attr*, marine

marionetta *f* puppet, marionette

marito *m* husband

marittimo maritime

marmellata *f* jam, *Am* jelly; *~ di arance* marmalade

marmitta *f* AUTO silencer, *Am* muffler

marmo *m* marble

marocchino 1 *agg* Moroccan **2** *m*, *-a f* Moroccan; **Marocco** *m* Morocco

marrone 1 *agg* (chestnut) brown **2** *m* colore (chestnut) brown; (*castagno*) chestnut

marsala *m* Marsala, *dessert wine*

Marte *m* Mars

martedì *m inv* Tuesday; *~ grasso* Shrove Tuesday, *Am* Mardi Gras

martello *m* hammer

martire *m/f* martyr; **martirio** *m* martyrdom

marzapane *m* marzipan

marziano *m* Martian

marzo *m* March

mascara *m inv* mascara

mascarpone *m* mascarpone

mascella *f* jaw

maschera *f* mask; *in teatro* usher; *donna* usherette; *~ antigas* gas mask; **mascherare** mask; *fig* camouflage, conceal; **mascherarsi** put on a mask; (*travestirsi*) dress up

165

mazza

(**da** as)

maschile spogliatoio, *abito* men's; *caratteristica* male; GRAM masculine; **maschilista** *m/agg* sexist; **maschio 1** *agg* male; **hanno tre figli -i** they have three sons o boys **2** *m* (*ragazzo*) boy; (*uomo*) man; ZO male; **mascolino** masculine

mascotte *f inv* mascot

mass media *mpl* media

massa *f* mass; EL earth; Am ground

massacrare massacre; **massacro** *m* massacre

massaggiare massage; **massaggiatore** *m*, **-trice** *f* masseur; *donna* masseuse; **massaggio** *m* massage

massaia *f* housewife

massiccio 1 *agg* massive; *oro, noce ecc* solid **2** *m* massif

massima *f* saying, maxim; *temperatura* maximum; **in linea di ~** generally speaking; **massimo 1** *agg* greatest, maximum **2** *m* maximum; **al ~** at most

masso *m* rock

masticare chew

mastice *m* mastic; (*stucco*) putty

mastino *m* mastiff

mastodontico gigantic

masturbare, masturbarsi masturbate

matematica *f* mathematics, maths, *Am* math; **matematico 1** *agg* mathematical **2** *m*,

-a *f* mathematician

materassino *m* airbed; **materasso** *m* mattress

materia *f* matter; (*materiale*) material; (*disciplina*) subject; **~ prima** raw material; **materiale 1** *agg* material; (*rozzo*) coarse, rough **2** *m* material; TEC equipment

maternità *f inv* motherhood; *in ospedale* maternity; **materno** maternal; **scuola** *f* **-a** nursery school

matita *f* pencil

matrice *f* matrix

matricola *f* register; *all'università* first-year student

matrigna *f* stepmother

matrimoniale matrimonial; **matrimonio** *m* marriage; *rito* wedding *attr*

mattina *f* morning; **di ~** in the morning; **mattinata** *f* morning; TEA matinée; **mattiniero: essere ~** be an early bird; **mattino** *m* morning

matto 1 *agg* mad, crazy (**per** about) **2** *m*, **-a** *f* madman, lunatic; *donna* madwoman, lunatic; **mi piace da -i andare al cinema** I'm mad about the cinema

mattone *m* brick; **mattonella** *f* tile

maturare *interessi* accrue; **maturità** *f* maturity; *diploma: A* levels, *Am* final exams

maturo *frutto* ripe; *persona* mature

mazza *f* club; (*martello*)

sledgehammer; *da baseball* bat; ~ *da golf* golf club

mazzo *m* bunch; ~ *di carte* pack *o* deck of cards

me (= **mi** before **lo, la, li, le, ne**) me; **dammelo** give me it, give it to me; **per** ~ for me

meccanica *f* mechanics; *di orologio* mechanism; **meccanicamente** mechanically; **meccanico 1** *agg* mechanical **2** *m* mechanic; **meccanismo** *m* mechanism

mecenate *m/f* sponsor

mèche *f inv* streak, highlight

medaglia *f* medal

medesimo (very) same

media *f* average; **in** ~ on average; **mediano 1** *agg* central, middle **2** *m* SP half-back; **mediante** by (means of); **mediatore** *m*, **-trice** *f* mediator; **mediazione** *f* mediation

medicare *persona* treat; *ferita* clean, disinfect; **medicazione** *f* treatment; (*bende*) dressing; **medicina** *f* medicine; **medicinale 1** *agg* medicinal **2** *m* medicine; **medico 1** *agg* medical **2** *m* doctor; ~ *di guardia* duty doctor

medievale medieval

medio 1 *agg* middle *attr*, *statura*, *rendimento* average **2** *m* middle finger

mediocre mediocre

medioevo *m* Middle Ages

meditare 1 *v/t* think about; (*progettare*) plan **2** *v/i* medi-

tate; (*riflettere*) think; ~ *su qc* think about sth; **meditazione** *f* meditation; (*riflessione*) reflection

mediterraneo *m/agg* Mediterranean

medium *m/f inv* medium

medusa *f* ZO jellyfish

meglio 1 *avv* better; ~*!*, *tanto* ~*!* good!; **alla** ~ to the best of one's ability **2** *agg* better; *superlativo* best **3** *m* best; *fare del proprio* ~ do one's best **4** *f avere la* ~ *su* get the better of

mela *f* apple

melagrana *f* pomegranate

melanzana *f* aubergine, *Am* eggplant

melma *f* mud

melo *m* apple (tree)

melodia *f* melody

melodrammatico melodramatic

melone *m* melon

membrana *f* membrane; ~ *del timpano* eardrum

membro *m* ANAT limb; *persona* member

memorabile memorable; **memoria** *f* memory; **a** ~ by heart; **-e** *pl* memoirs; **memorizzare** memorize; INFOR save

menare lead; F (*picchiare*) hit

mendicante *m/f* beggar; **mendicare 1** *v/t* beg for **2** *v/i* beg

menefreghismo *m* couldn't--care-less attitude

meningite f meningitis
meno 1 avv less; superlativo least; MAT minus; **il ~ possibile** as little as possible; **a ~ che** unless; **per lo ~** at least; **sono le sei ~ un quarto** it's a quarter to six; **sono le sei e un quarto** it's a quarter of six; **sempre ~** less and less; **fare a ~ di qc** do without sth **2** prp except; **menomato** damaged; (handicappato) disabled
mensa f di azienda canteen; MIL mess
mensile m/agg monthly; **mensilità** f inv salary
mensola f bracket
menta f mint
mentale mental; **mentalità** f inv mentality; **mentalmente** mentally; **mente** f mind; **avere in ~ di fare qc** be thinking about doing sth; **tenere a ~ qc** bear sth in mind; **non mi viene in ~ il nome di ...** I can't remember the name of ...
mentire lie
mento m chin
mentre while
menù m inv menu (anche INFOR)
menzionare mention
menzogna f lie
meraviglia f wonder; **a ~** wonderfully; **meravigliare** astonish; **meravigliarsi: ~ di** be astonished by; **meravigliato** astonished; **meraviglioso** marvellous, Am marvelous, wonderful

mercante m merchant; **mercantile 1** agg nave cargo attr; porto commercial **2** m cargo ship; **mercanzia** f merchandise
mercato m market; **~ coperto** indoor market; **~ delle pulci** flea market; **a buon ~** cheap, inexpensive
merce f goods
merceria f haberdashery, Am notions
mercoledì m inv Wednesday; **~ delle Ceneri** Ash Wednesday
mercurio m mercury; AST **Mercurio** Mercury
merda P shit P
merenda f snack
meridiana f sundial; **meridiano 1** agg midday attr **2** m meridian
meridionale 1 agg southern **2** m/f southerner; **meridione** m south; **il Meridione** southern Italy
meringa f meringue
meritare 1 v/t deserve **2** v/i: **un libro che merita** a worthwhile book; **merito** m merit; **in ~ a** as regards; **per ~ suo** thanks to him
merletto m lace
merlo m ZO blackbird
merluzzo m cod
meschino mean; (infelice) wretched
mescolanza f mixture; **mescolare** mix; insalata toss;

caffè stir; **mescolarsi** mix, blend

mese *m* month

messa[1]: ~ *in piega* set; ~ *in scena* production

messa[2] *f* REL mass

messaggino *m* text, text message; **messaggio** *m* message

messicano *agg* Mexican **2** *m*, -a *f* Mexican; **Messico** *m* Mexico

messinscena *f* production; *fig* act

messo *pp* ☞ **mettere**

mestiere *m* trade; (*professione*) profession

mestolo *m* ladle

mestruazione *f* menstruation

meta *f* destination; SP try; *fig* goal, aim

metà *f inv* half; *punto centrale* middle, centre, *Am* center; *a ~ prezzo* half price; *a ~ strada* halfway; *fare a ~* go halves (*di* on)

metabolismo *m* metabolism

metadone *m* methadone

metafora *f* metaphor; **metaforico** metaphorical

metallico metallic; **metallizzato** metallic; **metallo** *m* metal

metamorfosi *f inv* metamorphosis

metano *m* methane; **metanodotto** *m* gas pipeline

meteora *f* meteor; **meteorite** *m o f* meteorite; **meteorolo-**

gico meteorological, weather *attr*

meticoloso meticulous

metodico methodical; **metodo** *m* method

metrico metric

metro *m* metre, *Am* meter; ~ *quadrato* square metre; ~ *cubo* cubic metre

metrò *m inv* (*metropolitana*) underground, *Am* subway

metronotte *m inv* night watchman

metropoli *f inv* metropolis; **metropolitana** *f* underground, *Am* subway

mettere put; *vestito* put on; ~ *in moto* start (up); ~ *in ordine* tidy up; *mettiamo che ...* let's assume that ...; **mettersi** *abito, cappello ecc* put on; ~ *a sedere* sit down; AVIA, AUTO ~ *la cintura* fasten one's seat belt; ~ *a fare qc* start to do sth

mezzaluna *f* half moon; GASTR *two-handled chopper*; **mezzanotte** *f* midnight; **mezzo 1** *agg* half; **mezz'ora** half-hour; *le sei e ~* half past six, *Am* six thirty; ~ *chilo* a half kilo; *di -a età* middle-aged **2** *avv* half **3** *m* (*parte centrale*) middle; (*metà*) half; (*strumento*) means *sg*; (*veicolo*) means *sg* of transport; *per ~ di* by means of; *in ~* a between; *in ~ a quei documenti* in the middle of those papers, among those papers;

in ~ *alla stanza* in the middle of the room; *nel* ~ *di* in the middle of; *giusto* ~ happy medium; **mezzobusto** *m* half-length photograph / portrait; **mezzofondo** *m* middle distance; **mezzogiorno** *m* midday; GEOG **Mezzogiorno** south (of Italy)

mi[1] *m* MUS E; *nel solfeggio della scala* me, mi

mi[2] *pron* me; *riflessivo* myself; *eccomi* here I am

miagolare miaow; **miagolio** *m* miaowing

mica: *non ho* ~ *finito* I'm nowhere near finished; *non è* ~ *vero* there's not the slightest bit of truth in it; ~ *male* not bad at all

miccia *f* fuse

micidiale *veleno, clima* deadly; *fatica, sforza* exhausting

micio F *m* (pussy) cat

micosi *f inv* mycosis

microbiologia *f* microbiology

microbo *m* microbe

microchip *m inv* microchip

microcamera *f* miniature camera

microchirurgia *f* microsurgery

microfilm *m inv* microfilm

microfono *m* microphone, mike F

microonda *f* microwave; *forno m a* -e microwave (oven)

microprocessore *m* micro-

processor

microscopico microscopic; **microscopio** *m* microscope

midollo *m* marrow; ~ *spinale* spinal cord

miei *mpl di* **mio** my

miele *m* honey

mietere harvest

migliaio *m* thousand; *un* ~ a *o* one thousand; *a migliaia* in their thousands

miglio[1] *m misura* mile

miglio[2] *m grano* millet

miglioramento *m* improvement; **migliorare** 1 *v/t* improve 2 *v/i e* **migliorarsi** improve, get better; **migliore** better; *il* ~ the best

mignolo *m* (*o* **dito** ~) little finger; *del piede* little toe

-**mila** thousand; *due*~ two thousand

milanese 1 *agg* of Milan **2** *m/f* inhabitant of Milan; **Milano** *f* Milan

miliardario *m*, -*a* *f* billionaire, multimillionaire; **miliardo** *m* billion; **milionario** *m*, -*a* *f* millionaire; *donna* **milionairess**; **milione** *m* million

militare 1 *agg* military **2** *m* soldier; **milite** *m* soldier; **militesente** exempt from military service; **milizia** *f* militia

mille a thousand

millefoglie *m inv* vanilla slice; **millennio** *m* millennium; **millepiedi** *m inv* millipede; **millesimo** thousandth

milligrammo *m* milligram(me)

millimetro *m* millimetre, *Am* millimeter

milza *f* spleen

mimetizzare MIL camouflage; **mimetizzarsi** camouflage o.s.

mimo *m* mime

mina *f* mine; *di matita* lead

minaccia *f* threat; **minacciare** threaten; **minaccioso** threatening

minareto *m* minaret

minato: *campo m ~* minefield; **minatore** *m* miner

minatorio threatening

minerale *m/agg* mineral

minestra *f* soup; *~ di verdura* vegetable soup; **minestrina** *f* clear soup, broth; **minestrone** *m* minestrone

miniatura *f* miniature

miniera *f* mine (*anche fig*)

minigolf *m inv* minigolf

minigonna *f* mini(skirt)

minimizzare minimize; **minimo 1** *agg* least, slightest; *prezzo* lowest; *salario, temperatura* minimum **2** *m* minimum

ministero *m* ministry; **ministro** *m* minister; *~ degli Esteri* Foreign Secretary, *Am* Secretary of State; *~ degli Interni* Home Secretary, *Am* Secretary of the Interior; *primo ~* Prime Minister; *consiglio m dei -i* Cabinet

minoranza *f* minority

minorato 1 *agg* severely handicapped **2** *m*, **-a** *f* severely handicapped person

minore 1 *agg* minor; *di età* younger; *distanza* shorter; *più piccolo* smaller **2** *m/f*: *vietato ai -i di 18 anni* no admittance to those under 18 years of age; *film* X-rated; **minorenne 1** *agg* underage **2** *m/f* minor

minuscola *f* small letter, lower case letter; **minuscolo** tiny, miniscule

minuto 1 *agg* tiny, minute; *descrizione* detailed **2** *m* minute; **minuzioso** *descrizione* detailed; *ricerca* meticulous

mio 1 *agg* my; *un ~ amico* a friend of mine, one of my friends **2** *pron*: *il ~* mine; *i miei* my parents

miope short-sighted; **miopia** *f* short-sightedness, myopia

mira *f* aim; (*obiettivo*) target; *prendere la ~* take aim; *fig prendere di ~ qu* have it in for s.o.

miracolo *m* miracle; *per ~* by a miracle, miraculously

miraggio *m* mirage

mirare aim (*a* at)

mirino *m* MIL sight; FOT viewfinder

mirtillo *m* blueberry

mirto *m* myrtle

miscela *f* mixture; *di caffè, tabacco* blend; **miscelatore** *m* GASTR mixer; *rubinetto* mixer tap

mischia *f* (*rissa*) scuffle; SP,

(*folla*) scrum; **mischiare** mix; *carte* shuffle; **mischiarsi** mix; **miscuglio** *m* mixture

miseria *f* (*povertà*) poverty; **costare una ~** cost next to nothing; F **porca ~!** damn and blast! F; **misero** wretched

missile *m* missile

missionario *m*, -**a** *f* missionary; **missione** *f* mission

misterioso mysterious; **mistero** *m* mystery

mistico mystic(al)

misto 1 *agg* mixed **2** *m* mixture; **~ lana** wool mix

misura *f* measurement; (*taglia*) size; (*provvedimento*), *fig* measure; **su ~** made to measure; **misurare** measure; *vestito* try on; **misurino** *m* measuring spoon

mite mild; *condanna* light

mito *m* myth; **mitologia** *f* mythology; **mitologico** mythological

mitra *m inv*, **mitragliatrice** *f* machine gun

mitt. (= **mittente**) from

mittente *m/f* sender

mixare mix

M.M. (= **Marina Militare**) Italian navy

mobile 1 *agg* mobile; *ripiano*, *pannello* removeable **2** *m* piece of furniture; **-i** *pl* furniture; **mobilia** *f* furnishings; **mobilificio** *m* furniture factory; **mobilitare** mobilize

moca *m* mocha

mocassino *m* moccasin

moda *f* fashion; **alla ~** fashionable, in fashion; *vestirsi* fashionably; **fuori ~** out of fashion, unfashionable

modalità *f inv* method

modella *f* model; **modellare** model; **modello 1** *agg* model **2** *m* model; *di vestito* style; (*formulario*) form

modem *m inv* INFOR modem

moderare moderate; **moderato** moderate; **moderazione** *f* moderation

modernizzare modernize; **moderno** modern

modestia *f* modesty; **modesto** modest; *prezzo* very reasonable

modico reasonable

modifica *f* modification; **modificare** modify

modo *m* (*maniera*) way, manner; (*mezzo*) way; **~ di dire** expression; **per ~ di dire** so to speak; **a ~ mio** in my own way; **di ogni ~** anyway, anyhow; **di ~ che** so that; **in che ~?** how?

modulo *m* form; (*elemento*) module

mogano *m* mahogany

moglie *f* wife

molare 1 *v/t* grind **2** *m* molar

mole *f* (*grandezza*) size

molecola *f* molecule

molestare bother; *sessualmente* sexually harass; **molestia** *f* bother, nuisance; **~ sessuale** sexual harassment

molla f spring; fig spur; **-e** pl tongs; **mollare** corda release, let go; F schiaffo, ceffone give; F fidanzato dump; ~ **la presa** let go

molle soft; (bagnato) wet

molletta f hairgrip; da bucato clothes peg, Am clothes pin

mollica f crumb

mollusco m mollusc, Am mollusk

molo m pier

molteplice multifaceted

moltiplicare, moltiplicarsi multiply

molto 1 agg a lot of; con nomi plurali ts a lot of, many **2** avv a lot; con aggettivi very; ~ **meglio** much better, a lot better; **da** ~ for a long time; **fra non** ~ before long

momentaneo momentary, temporary; **momento** m moment; **dal** ~ **che** causale since; **a** ~**i** sometimes; **per il** ~ for the moment; **sul** ~ at the time

monaca f nun; **monaco** m monk

monarchia f monarchy

monastero m monastery; di monache convent

mondano society attr; (terreno) worldly; **fare vita -a** go out

mondare frutta peel

mondiale 1 agg world attr; fenomeno, scala worldwide; **di fama** ~ world-famous **2** m: **i -i di calcio** the World Cup;

mondo m world; **il più bello del** ~ the most beautiful in the world

monello m, **-a** f little devil

moneta f coin; (valuta) currency; (denaro) money; (spiccioli) change; **monetario** monetary; **Fondo** m ~ **internazionale** International Monetary Fund

mongolfiera m hot-air balloon

monolocale m bedsit

monopattino m child's scooter

monopolio m monopoly; **monopolizzare** monopolize

monoposto m single-seater

monotonia f monotony; **monotono** monotonous

monouso disposable, throwaway

montacarichi m inv hoist

montaggio m TEC assembly; di film editing

montagna f mountain; fig **-e russe** rollercoaster; **montagnoso** mountainous; **montanaro** m, **-a** f mountain dweller

montare 1 v/t go up, climb; cavallo get onto, mount; TEC assemble; film edit; GASTR whip **2** v/i go up; venire come up; ~ **in macchina** get into; ~ **su scala** climb; pullman get on

montarsi ~ **la testa** get bigheaded

montatura f di occhiali frame;

di gioiello mount; *fig* frame-up F

monte *m* mountain (*anche fig*); **a ~** upstream; *fig* **mandare a ~** ruin

montone *m* ram; *pelle, giacca* sheepskin

montuoso mountainous

monumento *m* monument

moquette *f* fitted carpet

mora *f* BOT *del gelso* mulberry; *del rovo* blackberry

morale 1 *agg* moral **2** *f* morals; *di favola ecc* moral **3** *m* morale; **essere giù di ~** be feeling a bit down

morbido soft

morbillo *m* measles *sg*

morbo *m* disease; **morboso** *fig* unhealthy; **curiosità** *f* morbid

mordere bite

morena *f* moraine

morfina *f* morphine

moribondo dying

morire die; *fig* **~ di paura** be scared to death

mormorare murmur; (*bisbigliare, lamentarsi*) mutter; **mormorio** *m* murmuring; (*brontolio*) muttering

morsetto *m* TEC clamp; EL terminal

morsicare bite; **morso 1** *pp* **mordere 2** *m* bite; *di cibo* bit, mouthful; *per cavallo* bit

mortale *malattia* fatal; *offesa, nemico* deadly; *uomo* mortal; **mortalità** *f* mortality

morte *f* death

mortificare mortify

morto 1 *pp* **morire 2** *agg* dead; **stanco ~** dead tired **3** *m*, **-a** *f* dead man; *donna* dead woman; **i -i** *pl* the dead *pl*

mortorio *m*: F **essere un ~** be deadly boring

mosaico *m* mosaic

mosca *f* fly

moscato 1 *agg* muscat **2** *m* muscatel

moscerino *m* gnat, midge

moschea *f* mosque

moscio thin, flimsy; *fig* washed out

moscone *m* ZO bluebottle; (*imbarcazione*) pedalo

mossa *f* movement; *fig e di judo, karate* move; **mosso 1** *pp* **muovere 2** *agg mare* rough

mostarda *f* mustard

mosto *m* must, unfermented grape juice

mostra *f* show; (*esposizione*) exhibition; *fig* **mettere in ~** show off; **mostrare** (*indicare*) point out; **mostrarsi** appear

mostro *m* monster; **mostruoso** monstrous

motel *m inv* motel

motivare cause; *personale* motivate; (*spiegare*) explain; **motivazione** *f* (*spiegazione*) explanation; (*stimolo*) motivation; **motivo** *m* reason; MUS theme, motif; *su tessuto* pattern; **per quale ~?** for what reason?

moto¹ *m* movement; **fare ~** get some exercise; **mettere in ~ motore** start (up)

moto² *f* (motor)bike

motocicletta *f* motorcycle; **motociclista** *m/f* motorcyclist; **motociclo** *m* motorcycling

motore *m* engine; **accendere il ~** start the engine; **motorino** *m* moped; **motorizzato** motorized; **F sei ~** have you got wheels? F

motoscafo *m* motorboat

motto *m* motto

mouse *m inv* INFOR mouse

movente *m* motive

movimento *m* movement; **(vita)** life

mozione *f* motion; **~ di fiducia** vote of confidence

mozzarella *f* mozzarella

mozzicone *m* cigarette end, (cigarette) stub

mozzo *m* TEC hub

mq (= **metro quadrato**) sq m, m² (= square metre)

mucca *f* cow

mucchio *m* pile

muco *m* mucus

muffa *f* mould, *Am* mold; **fare la ~** go mouldy

mugolare whine

mulattiera *f* mule track

mulatto *m*, **-a** *f* mulatto

mulinello *m* su canna da pesca reel; **vortice d'acqua** eddy

mulino *m* mill; **~ a vento** windmill

mulo *m* mule

multa *f* fine; **multare** fine

multiculturale multicultural

multimediale multimedia

multinazionale *f* agg multinational

multiplo multiple

multisala *m inv* multiplex

multiuso multipurpose

mungere milk

municipale municipal; **municipio** *m* town council, municipality; **edificio** town hall

munire: ~ di supply with; **munizioni** *fpl* ammunition

muovere 1 *v/t* move **2** *v/i partire* move off **(da** from); **~ incontro a qu** move towards s.o.; **muoversi** move; F **(sbrigarsi)** get a move on F

murare *(chiudere)* wall up; **muratore** *m* bricklayer; **muratura** *f* brickwork

murena *f* moray eel

muro *m* wall; **le -a** *fpl* the (city) walls

muschio *m* BOT moss

muscolare muscular; **strappo** *m* ~ strained muscle; **muscolo** *m* muscle; **muscoloso** muscular

museo *m* museum; **~ etnologico** folk museum; **~ d'arte** art gallery

museruola *f* muzzle

musica *f* music; **musicale** musical; **musicista** *m/f* musician

muso *m* di animale muzzle; **tenere il ~ a qu** be in a huff with s.o.; **musone** *m* sulker

musulmano 1 *agg* Muslim **2** *m*, **-a** *f* Muslim

muta *f* di cani pack; SP wetsuit

mutamento *m* change

mutande *fpl* di donna panties; di uomo (under)pants, *Am* briefs; **mutandine** *fpl* panties; ~ **(da bagno)** (swimming) trunks, *Am* swimsuit

mutare change

mutilato *m* disabled ex-serviceman

muto 1 *agg* dumb; (*silenzioso*) silent, dumb; *film m* ~ silent movie **2** *m*, **-a** *f* mute

mutua *f* fund that pays out sickness benefit; **medico** *m* **della ~a** a doctor recognized by the 'mutua'; **mutuato** *m*, **-a** *f* person entitled to sickness benefit

mutuo 1 *agg* mutual **2** *m* mortgage

N

n. (= **numero**) No. (= number)

nacchere *fpl* castanets

nafta *f* naphtha

nano 1 *agg* dwarf **2** *m*, **-a** *f* dwarf

napoletano 1 *agg* Neapolitan **2** *m*, **-a** *f* Neapolitan; **Napoli** *f* Naples

nappa *f* tassel; pelle nappa (type of soft leather)

narcotico *m* narcotic

narice *f* nostril

narrare tell, narrate; **narratore, -trice** *f* narrator

nascere be born; BOT, di sole come up; fig develop; **sono nato a Roma** I was born in Rome; **nascita** *f* birth

nascondere hide; **nascondersi** hide; **nascondiglio** *m* hiding place; **nascosto 1** *pp* ☞ **nascondere 2** *avv*: di ~ in secret; di ~ a qu unbeknownst to s.o.

nasello *m* pesce hake

naso *m* nose

nastro *m* tape; per capelli, di decorazione ribbon; ~ **adesivo** adhesive tape, Sellotape®, *Am* Scotch tape®

Natale *m* Christmas; **buon ~!** Merry Christmas!; **natalità** *f* birth rate; **natalizio** Christmas

natante 1 *agg* floating **2** *m* boat

nativo 1 *agg* native **2** *m*, **-a** *f* native

NATO *f* (= **Organizzazione del Trattato nord-atlantico**) NATO (= North Atlantic Treaty Organization)

nato ☞ **nascere**

natura *f* nature; PITT ~ **morta** still life; **naturale** natural; **naturalezza** *f* naturalness; **con ~** naturally; **naturaliz-**

zare: **è naturalizzato ameri-cano** he's a naturalized American; **naturalmente** naturally

naufragare *di nave* be wrecked; *di persona* be shipwrecked; *fig* be ruined; **naufragio** *m* shipwreck; *fig* ruin; **fare ~ di nave** be wrecked; *di persona* be shipwrecked; **naufrago** *m*, **-a** *f* survivor of a shipwreck

nausea *f* nausea; **avere la ~** feel sick, *Am* feel nauseous; **nauseare** nauseate (*anche fig*)

nautico nautical

navale naval; **cantiere** *m* **~** shipyard

navata *f* ARCHI: **~ centrale** nave; **~ laterale** aisle

nave *f* ship; **~ da carico** cargo ship; **~ passeggeri** passenger ship; **~ traghetto** ferry; **navetta 1** *agg inv:* **bus** *m* **~** shuttle bus **2** *f* shuttle; **~ spaziale** space shuttle

navigabile navigable; **navigare** sail; INFOR navigate; **~ in Internet** surf the Net; **navigatore** *m* navigator

nazionale 1 *agg* national **2** *f* national team; **nazionalismo** *m* nationalism; **nazionalista** *m/f* nationalist; **nazionalità** *f inv* nationality; **nazione** *f* nation

ne 1 *pron* (*di lui*) about him; (*di lei*) about her; (*di loro*) about them; (*di ciò*) about

it; **~ sono contento** I'm happy about it; **~ ho abbastanza** I have enough **2** *avv* from there; **~ vengo adesso** I've just come back from there

né ... ~ ... neither ... nor; **non l'ho trovato ~ a casa ~ in ufficio** I couldn't find him either at home or in the office

neanche neither; **neanch'io** neither am I, me neither; **non l'ho ~ visto** I didn't even see him

nebbia *f* fog; **nebbioso** foggy

nebulosa *f* AST nebula

necessaire *m inv:* **~ (da viaggio)** beauty case; **necessario 1** *agg* necessary **2** *m:* **il ~ per vivere** the basic necessities; **necessità** *f inv* need; **in caso di ~** if need be; **per ~** out of necessity

nefrite *f* MED nephritis

negare deny; (*rifiutare*) refuse; **negativa** *f* negative; **negativo** *m/agg* negative; **negato: essere ~ per qc** be hopeless at sth

negli = in and *art* **gli**

negligente careless, negligent; **negligenza** *f* carelessness, negligence

negoziante *m/f* shopkeeper, *Am* storekeeper; **negoziare** negotiate FIN **~ in** trade in; **negoziato** *m* negotiation; **-i** *pl* **di pace** peace negotiations; **negozio** *m* shop, *Am* store

negro 1 *agg* black **2** *m*, **-a** *f*

black (man / woman)

nei, nel, nell', nella, nelle, nello = in and *art* **i, il, l', la, le, lo**

nemico 1 *agg* enemy *attr* **2** *m*, **-a** *f* enemy

nemmeno neither; **~ io** me neither; **~ per idea!** don't even think about it!

neo *m* mole; *fig* flaw

neonato *m*, **-a** *f* infant, new-born baby

neppure not even; **non ci va-do-~ io** I'm not going - neither am I, me neither

nero 1 *m/agg* black (*anche fig*) **2** *m*, **-a** *f* black (man / woman)

nervo *m* nerve; **dare sui -i a qu** get on s.o.'s nerves; **nervosismo** *m* nervousness; **nervoso 1** *agg* nervous; (*irritabile*) edgy **2** *m* F: **mi viene il ~** this is getting on my nerves

nespola *f* medlar; **nespolo** *m* medlar (tree)

nessuno 1 *agg* no; **non chiamare in nessun caso** don't call in any circumstances; **c'è -a notizia?** is there any news? **2** *pron* nobody, no one; **hai visto ~?** did you see anyone or anybody?

nettezza *f* cleanliness; **-a urbana** cleansing department; **netto** clean; (*chiaro*) clear; *reddito, peso* net

neurologico neurological; **neurologo** *m*, **-a** *f* neurologist

neutrale neutral; **neutralizzare** neutralize; **neutro** neutral; GRAM neuter

neve *f* snow; **nevicare** snow; **nevicata** *f* snowfall

nevralgia *f* neuralgia; **nevralgico** neuralgic; **punto** *m* **~** specially painful point; *fig* weak point

nevrotico 1 *agg* neurotic; F short-tempered **2** *m*, **-a** *f* neurotic

nicchia *f* niche

nicotina *f* nicotine

nido *m* nest

niente 1 *pron* nothing **2** *avv* nothing; **non ho ~ I** don't have anything, I have nothing; **non ho per ~ fame** I'm not at all hungry; **non fa niente** it doesn't matter; **niente(di)meno** no less; ~ **!** that's incredible!

ninfea *f* water-lily

nipote *m/f* *di zio* nephew; *donna, ragazza* niece; *di nonno* grandson; *donna, ragazza* granddaughter

nitido clear; FOT sharp

nitrire neigh

NO (= **nord-ovest**) NW (= northwest)

no no; **come ~!** of course!; **se ~** otherwise; **dire di ~** say no; **credo di ~** I don't think so

nobile 1 *agg* noble **2** *m/f* aristocrat; **nobiltà** *f* nobility

nocca *f* knuckle

nocciola *f* hazelnut; (*color m*) **~** hazel; **nocciolina** *f*: ~

(*americana*) peanut

nocciolo[1] *m albero* hazel (tree)

nocciolo[2] *m di frutto* stone; *di questione* kernel

noce 1 *m* walnut (tree); *legno* walnut **2** *f* walnut; ~ *di cocco* coconut; ~ *moscata* nutmeg; **nocepesca** *f* nectarine

nocivo harmful

nodo *m* knot; *fig* crux; FERR junction

no-global *m/f inv* anti-globalist

noi *pron soggetto* we; *con prp* us; *a* ~ to us; *con* ~ with us

noia *f* boredom; *-e pl* trouble; *dar* ~ *a qu* annoy s.o.; **noioso** boring; (*molesto*) annoying

noleggiare rent, *Br anche* hire; (dare a noleggio) rent out, *Br* hire out; **noleggio** *m* rent, *Br anche* hire; **nolo** *m* rent, *Br anche* hire; **prendere a** ~ rent; **dare a** ~ rent out

nome *m* name; GRAM noun; ~ *di battesimo* Christian name; ~ *e cognome* full name; *in* ~ *di* in the name of

nomina *f* appointment; **nominare** (*menzionare*) mention; *a un incarico* appoint (*a* to)

non not; ~ *ho fratelli* I don't have any brothers, I have no brothers

non stop *inv* nonstop

non vedente *m/f* blind person

nonché let alone; (*e anche*) as well as

noncurante nonchalant; ~ *di* heedless of

nondimeno nevertheless

nonno *m*, **-a** *f* grandfather; *donna* grandmother; *-i pl* grandparents

nonnulla *m inv* trifle

nono ninth

nonostante despite; *ciò* ~ however

nontiscordardimé *m inv* forget-me-not

nord *m* north; *a*(*l*) ~ *di* (to the) north of; **nordest** *m* northeast; **nordico** northern; *lingue* Nordic; **nordovest** *m* north-west

norma *f* (*precetto*) rule; TEC standard; *a* ~ *di legge* up to standard; **normale** normal; **normalità** *f* normality

norvegese *agg*, *m/f* Norwegian; **Norvegia** *f* Norway

nostalgia *f* nostalgia; *avere* ~ *di casa* feel homesick; *avere* ~ *di qu* miss s.o.

nostrano local, home *attr*

nostro 1 *agg* our; *i* ~ *i genitori* our parents; *un* ~ *amico* a friend of ours **2** *pron*: *il* ~ ours

nota *f* note; FIN bill; ~ *spese* expense account; *prendere* ~ *di qc* make a note of sth; *situazione* take note of sth; **notaio** *m* notary (public);

nuvoloso

notare (*osservare*) notice; (*annotare*) make a note of; con *segni* mark; notarile notarial; notevole (*degno di nota*) notable, noteworthy; (*grande*) considerable; notificare *qc* (**a** on)

notizia *f* piece of news; *avere* **-e di** *qu* have news of s.o., hear from s.o.; notiziario *m* RAD, TV news *sg*

noto well-known; rendere ~ announce; notorietà *f* fame; *spreg* notoriety

nottambulo *m*, -a *f* night owl; nottata *f* night; *fare la* ~ stay up all night; notte *f* night; *di* ~ at night; **buona** ~! good night!; notturno night(-time) *attr, animale* nocturnal

novanta ninety; novantesimo ninetieth; nove nine; novecento **1** *agg* nine hundred **2** *m*: **il Novecento** the twentieth century

novella *f* short story

novembre *m* November

novità *f inv* novelty; (*notizia*) piece of news

nozione *f* notion, idea; *-i pl di base* rudiments

nozze *fpl* wedding; ~ *d'argento* silver wedding (anniversary)

ns. (= *nostro*) our(s), *used in correspondence*

nube *f* cloud; nubifragio *m* cloudburst

nubile single, unmarried

nuca *f* nape of the neck

nucleare nuclear; nucleo *m* FIS nucleus (*anche fig*)

nudismo *m* naturism, nudism; nudista *m/f* naturist, nudist; nudo **1** *agg* nude, naked; (*spoglio*) bare **2** *m* PITT nude

nulla nothing; *è una cosa da* ~ it's nothing; *per* ~ for nothing; nullaosta *m*: *fig ottenere il* ~ get the green light; nullo invalid; *gol* disallowed; *voto* spoiled

numerale *m* numeral; numerare number; numerato numbered; numero *m* number; *arabo, romano* numeral; *di scarpa* size; ~ *di targa* registration number, *Am* license number; ~ *di telefono* phone number; ~ *di volo* flight number; ~ *verde* 0800 number, *Am* toll-free number; F *dare i* -*i* talk nonsense; numeroso numerous; *famiglia, classe* large

nuocere: ~ **a** harm

nuora *f* daughter-in-law

nuotare swim; nuotata *f* swim; nuoto *m* swimming

nuovamente again; nuovo **1** *agg* new; *di* ~ again **2** *m*: *che c'è di* ~? what's new?

nutriente nourishing; nutrimento *m* food; nutrire feed; nutrirsi: ~ *di* live on; nutritivo nutritious

nuvola *f* cloud; *fig cadere dalle* -*e* be taken aback; nuvoloso cloudy

O

O (= *ovest*) W (= west)

o or; ~ ... ~ either ... or

oasi *f inv* oasis

obbedire ☞ **ubbidire**

obbligare ~ **qu a fare qc** oblige s.o. to do sth; **obbligatorio** obligatory; **obbligazione** *f* obligation; FIN bond; **obbligo** *m* obligation; **d'~** obligatory

obesità *f* obesity; **obeso** obese

obiettare object (**a** to); **obiettivo 1** *agg* objective **2** *m* aim, objective; FOT lens; **obiettore** *m*: **~ di coscienza** conscientious objector; **obiezione** *f* objection

obliquo oblique

obliterare *biglietto* punch

oblò *m inv* MAR porthole

oca *f* goose; *fig* silly woman

occasionale casual; **occasionalmente** occasionally; **occasione** *f* (*opportunità*) opportunity, chance; (*evento*) occasion; (*affare*) bargain; **automobile** *f* **d'~** second-hand car; **cogliere l'~** seize the opportunity; **all'~** if necessary; **in ~ di** on the occasion of

occhiaie *fpl* bags under the eyes

occhiali *mpl* glasses; ~ **da sole** sunglasses; **occhiata** *f* look; **dare un'~ a** have a look at; (*sorvegliare*) keep an eye on; **occhiello** *m* buttonhole; **occhio** *m* eye; **a ~ nudo** to the naked eye; **a ~ e croce** roughly; **dare nell'~** attract attention; **a quattr'~i** in private

occidentale western; **occidente** *m* west; **a ~ di** (to the) west of

occorrente 1 *agg* necessary **2** *m* necessary materials; **occorrenza** *f*: **all'~** if necessary, if need be; **occorrere** be necessary; (*accadere*) occur; **mi occorre** I need; **non occorre!** there's no need!

occupare *spazio* take up, occupy; *tempo* occupy, fill; *posto* have; *persona* keep busy; **occuparsi** take care (**di** of), deal (**di** with); **occupati degli affari tuoi!** mind your own business!; **occupato** TELEC busy, *Br anche* engaged; *posto, appartamento* taken; *gabinetto* engaged, *Am* occupied; *persona* busy; *città, nazione* occupied; **occupazione** *f* di *città, paese* occupation; (*attività*) pastime; (*impiego*) job

oceano *m* ocean; **Oceano Atlantico** Atlantic Ocean; **Oceano Pacifico** Pacific

Ocean
oculista *m/f* ophthalmologist
od = **o** (*before a vowel*)
odiare hate, detest
odierno modern-day *attr*, today's *attr*
odio *m* hatred; **odioso** hateful, odious
odontotecnico *m*, **-a** *f* dental technician
odorare smell (**di** *of*); **odorato** *m* sense of smell; **odore** *m* smell, odour, *Am* odor; **-i** *pl* GASTR herbs
offendere offend; **offendersi** take offence *o Am* offense; **offensiva** *f* offensive; **offensivo** offensive
offerente *m* bidder; **maggior ~** highest bidder; **offerta** *f* offer; FIN supply; REL offering; (*dono*) donation; *in asta* bid; **~ d'impiego** job offer; **~ speciale** special offer
offesa *f* offence, *Am* offense; **offeso** *pp* ☞ **offendere**
officina *f* workshop; *per macchine* garage
offrire offer; **ti offro da bere** I'll buy you a drink; **posso offrirti qualcosa?** can I get you anything?
oggettivo objective; **oggetto** *m* object
oggi today; **d'~** of today; **da ~ in poi** from now on; **~ stesso** this very day; **~ come ~** at the moment; **~ pomeriggio** this afternoon; **oggigiorno** nowadays

ogni every; **~ tanto** every so often; **~ sei giorni** every six days; **Ognissanti** *m inv* All Saints' Day; **ognuno** everyone, everybody
Olanda *f* Holland; **olandese 1** *agg m* Dutch **2** *m/f* Dutchman; *donna* Dutchwoman
oleandro *m* oleander
oleoso oily
olfatto *m* sense of smell
oliera *f* type of cruet for oil and vinegar bottles
Olimpiadi *fpl* Olympic Games, Olympics; **~ invernali** Winter Olympics
olio *m* oil; **~ extra-vergine d'oliva** extra-virgin olive oil; **~ solare** suntan oil
oliva *f* olive; **olivo** *m* olive (tree)
oltraggio *m* offence, *Am* offense, outrage
oltre 1 *prp* after, past; (*più di*) over; **vai ~ il semaforo** go past the traffic lights; **~ a** apart from **2** *avv nello spazio* further; *nel tempo* longer
omaggio *m* homage; (*dono*) gift; **copia (in) ~** free *o* complimentary copy; **essere in ~ con** come free with
ombelico *m* navel
ombra *f* shadow; *zona non illuminata* shade; **all'~** in the shade; **ombrello** *m* umbrella; **ombrellone** *m* parasol; *sulla spiaggia* beach umbrella; **ombretto** *m* eye shadow
omeopatico 1 *agg* homeo-

pathic **2** *m*, **-a** *f* homeopath

omero *m* humerus

omesso *pp* ☞ **omettere**; omettere omit, leave out

omicida 1 *agg* murderous **2** *m/f* murderer; **omicidio** *m* murder

omogeneizzato *m* baby food; **omogeneo** homogenous

omonimo 1 *agg* of the same name **2** *m* homonym **3** *m*, **-a** *f* namesake

omosessuale *agg*, *m/f* homosexual

on. (= **onorevole**) Hon (= honourable)

onda *f* wave; **-e** *pl* **corte** short wave; **-e** *pl* **lunghe** long wave; **-e** *pl* **medie** medium wave; RAD **andare in ~** go on the air; **onda** *f* wave; **~ di caldo** heat wave; **~ di freddo** cold spell; **ondeggiare** *di barca* rock; *di bandiera* flutter; **ondulato** *capelli* wavy; *superficie* uneven; *cartone, lamiera* corrugated

onestà *f* honesty; **onesto** honest; *prezzo, critica* fair

onice *m* onyx

onomastico *m* name day

onorare be a credit to; **~ qu di qc** honour *o Am* honor s.o. with sth; **onorario 1** *agg* honorary **2** *m* fee; **onore** *m* honour, *Am* honor; **in ~ di** in honour of; **onorevole 1** *agg* honourable, *Am* honorable **2** **Onorevole** *m/f*

Member of Parliament

ONU *f* (= **Organizzazione delle Nazioni Unite**) UN (= United Nations)

opaco opaque; *calze, rossetto* dark

opera *f* work; MUS opera; **~ d'arte** work of art; **mettersi all'~** set to work; **operaio 1** *agg* working **2** *m*, **-a** *f* worker; **~ specializzato** skilled worker; **operare 1** *v/t cambiamento* make; *miracoli* work; MED operate on **2** *v/i* act; **operativo** operational; *ricerca* applied; *ordine* operative; **piano** *m* **~** plan of operations; **operatore** *m*, **-trice** *f* operator; *televisivo, cinematografico* cameraman; **~ di Borsa** market trader; **~ sociale** social worker; **~ turistico** tour operator; **operazione** *f* operation

opinione *f* opinion

oppio *m* opium

opporre offer; **opporsi** be opposed

opportunista *m/f* opportunist; **opportunità** *f inv* opportunity; *di decisione* timeliness; **opportuno** suitable

opposizione *f* opposition; **opposto 1** *pp* ☞ **opporre 2** *agg* opposite **3** *m* POL opposition

oppressione *f* oppression; **oppresso 1** *pp* ☞ **opprimere 2** *agg* oppressed; **opprimere** oppress

oppure or (else)

optare: **~ per** choose, opt for

opuscolo *m* brochure

opzione *f* option

ora[1] *f* time; *unità di misura* hour; *che ~ è?, che -e sono?* what's the time?; **~ legale** daylight saving time; **~ locale** local time; **~ di punta** rush hour; **TELEC** peak time; *di buon'~* early

ora[2] **1** *avv* now; **per ~** for the moment, for the time being; **~ come ~** at the moment; *d'~ in poi* from now on **2** *cong* now

orale *m/agg* oral

orario 1 *agg tariffa* hourly; *velocità* per hour **2** *m di treno, bus* timetable, *Am* schedule; *di negozio* business hours; *al lavoro* hours of work; **~ di apertura / chiusura** opening / closing time; *in ~* on time

orata *f* bream

orbita *f* AST orbit; ANAT eyesocket; *in ~* in orbit

orchestra *f* orchestra; *luogo* (orchestra) pit

orchidea *f* orchid

ordigno *m* device

ordinale *m/agg* ordinal

ordinamento *m* rules and regulations; **~ sociale** rules governing society; **ordinare** order; *stanza* tidy up

ordinario ordinary; *mediocre* pretty average

ordinato tidy; **ordinazione** *f* order; **ordine** *m* order; **mettere in ~** tidy up; *di prim'~* first-rate; **~ del giorno** agenda; *l'~ dei medici* the medical association

orecchino *m* earring; **orecchio** *m* ear; MUS **a ~** by ear; **orecchioni** *mpl* mumps *sg*

oreficeria *f* goldsmith work; *(gioielleria)* jeweller's, *Am* jewelry store

orfano 1 *agg* orphan **2** *m*, *-a f* orphan; **orfanotrofio** *m* orphanage

organismo *m* organism; *fig* body

organizzare organize; **organizzazione** *f* organization

organo *m* organ

orgasmo *m* orgasm

orgoglio *m* pride; **orgoglioso** proud

orientale 1 *agg* eastern; *(dell'Oriente)* Oriental **2** *m/f* Oriental

orientamento *m*: **senso m d'~** sense of direction; **~ professionale** professional advice; **orientarsi** get one's bearings

oriente *m* east; *l'Oriente* the Orient; *Medio Oriente* Middle East; *Estremo Oriente* Far East; **ad~ di** (to the) east of

origano *m* oregano

originale *m/agg* original; **originalmente** originally; **originario** original; **essere ~**

di come from; *popolo* originate in; **origine** *f* origin; **in ~** originally

origliare eavesdrop

orizzontale horizontal; **orizzonte** *m* horizon

orlo *m* edge; *di vestito* hem

orma *f* footprint; *fig* **seguire le -e di qu** follow in s.o.'s footsteps

ormai by now

ormonale hormonal; **ormone** *m* hormone

ornamentale ornamental; **ornamento** *m* ornament; **ornare** decorate

oro *m* gold; **d'~** (made of) gold

orologiaio *m* (clock- and) watch-maker; **orologio** *m* clock; *da polso* watch

oroscopo *m* horoscope

orrendo horrendous

orribile horrible

orrore *m* horror (**di** of)

orsacchiotto *m* bear cub; *giocattolo* teddy (bear)

orso *m* bear; *fig* hermit; **~ bianco** polar bear

ortaggio *m* vegetable

ortica *f* nettle; **orticaria** *f* nettle rash

orto *m* vegetable garden, kitchen garden; **~ botanico** botanical gardens

ortodosso orthodox

ortografia *f* spelling

ortopedico 1 *agg* orthopaedic, *Am* orthopedic **2** *m*, **-a** *f* orthopaedist, *Am* orthopedist

orzaiolo *m* stye

orzo *m* barley

osceno obscene

oscillare *di corda* sway, swing; *di barca* rock; FIS oscillate; *fig*: *di persona* waver; *di prezzi* fluctuate

oscurare obscure; *luce* block out; **oscurità** *f* darkness; *fig* obscurity; **nell'~** in the dark; **oscuro 1** *agg* dark; (*sconosciuto*) obscure **2** *m*: **essere all'~ di qc** be in the dark about sth

ospedale *m* hospital

ospitale hospitable; **ospitalità** *f* hospitality; **ospitare** put up; **ospite** *m/f* guest; *chi ospita* host; *donna* hostess; **ospizio** *m* old folk's home

osservare (*guardare*) look at, observe; (*notare*) see, observe; (*far notare*) point out; (*seguire*) obey; **~ una dieta** keep to a diet; **osservatore** *m*, **-trice** *f* observer; **osservatorio** *m* AST observatory; **osservazione** *f* observation

ossessione *f* obsession (**di** with); **avere l'~ di** be obsessed with; **ossessivo** obsessive

ossia or rather

ossidare tarnish

ossigeno *m* oxygen

osso *m* bone; **~ sacro** sacrum; **in carne e -a** in the

flesh; **ossobuco** m marrow-
bone; GASTR ossobuco, *stew
made with knuckle of
veal*

ostacolare hinder; **ostacolo**
m obstacle; *nell'atletica* hurdle; *nell'equitazione* fence,
jump; *fig* stumbling block,
obstacle

ostaggio m hostage; **prendere qu in ~** take s.o. hostage

ostello m: **~ della gioventù**
youth hostel

osteoporosi f osteoporosis

osteria f inn

ostetrica f obstetrician; (*levatrice*) midwife; **ostetrico 1**
agg obstetric(al) **2** m obstetrician

ostia f Host

ostile hostile; **ostilità** f inv
hostility

ostinarsi dig one's heels in; **~
a fare qc** persist in doing sth;
ostinato obstinate

ostrica f oyster

ostruire block, obstruct;
ostruito blocked

otite f ear infection

otorinolaringoiatra m/f ear,
nose and throat specialist

ottagono octagon; **ottanta**
eighty; **ottantesimo** eighti-

eth; **ottavo** eighth

ottenere get, obtain; *fig* obtain; **ottengo**
☞ **ottenere**

ottica f optics; *fig* viewpoint; **ottico 1** *agg* optical **2** m optician

ottimismo m optimism; **ottimista** m/f optimist

ottimizzare optimize; **ottimo**
excellent

otto eight

ottobre m October

ottocento 1 *agg* eight hundred **2** m: **l'Ottocento** the
nineteenth century

ottone m brass; MUS **~i** pl brass

otturare block; *dente* fill; **otturatore** m FOT shutter; **otturazione** f blocking; *di dente* filling

ottuso obtuse

ovaia f ANAT ovary

ovale m/agg oval

overdose f inv overdose

ovest m west; **a(l) ~ di** (to the)
west of

ovini mpl sheep

ovunque everywhere

ovvero or rather; (*cioè*) that is

ovvio obvious

ozio m laziness, idleness

ozono m ozone; **la fascia d'~**
the ozone layer

P

pacato calm, unhurried

pacchetto *m* package; *di sigarette, biscotti* packet

pacchiano vulgar, in bad taste

pacco *m* parcel, package; ~ **postale** parcel

pace *f* peace; *lasciare in ~ qu* leave s.o. alone *o* in peace

pacifista *m/f* pacifist

padano of the Po; *pianura f -a* Po Valley

padella *f di cucina* frying pan

padiglione *m* pavilion; ~ *auricolare* auricle

Padova *f* Padua; **padovano 1** *agg* Paduan **2** *m, -a* Paduan

padre *m* father; **padrino** *m* godfather; **padronanza** *f* control; *(conoscenza)* mastery; ~ *di sé* self-control; **padrone** *m, -a f* boss; *(proprietario)* owner; *di cane* master; *donna* mistress; ~ *di casa* man *o* lady of the house; *per inquilino* landlord; *donna* landlady

paesaggio *m* scenery; PITT, GEOG landscape; **paesaggista** *m/f* PITT landscape painter; **paese** *m* country; *(villaggio)* village; *(territorio)* region; *i Paesi Bassi pl* the Netherlands; *-i pl in via di sviluppo* developing countries

paga *f* pay; **pagabile** payable; **pagamento** *m* payment; **pagare 1** *v/t* pay for; *conto, fattura* pay; *gliela faccio ~* he'll pay for this **2** *v/i* pay

pagella *f* report, *Am* report card

paghetta *f* pocket money

pagina *f* page; *-e gialle* Yellow Pages; ~ *web* webpage

paglia *f* straw

paio *m*: *un ~ di* a pair of; *un ~ di volte* a couple of times

pala *f* shovel; *di elica, turbina* blade

palasport *m inv* indoor sports arena

palato *m* palate

palazzina *f* luxury home; **palazzo** *m* palace; *(edificio)* building; *con appartamenti* block of flats, *Am* apartment block; ~ *di giustizia* courthouse; ~ *dello sport* indoor sports arena

palco *m* dais; TEA stage; **palcoscenico** *m* stage

palese obvious

Palestina *f* Palestine; **palestinese** *agg, m/f* Palestinian

palestra *f* gym

paletta *f* shovel; *per la spiaggia* spade; **paletto** *m* tent peg

palla *f* ball; ~ *di neve* snowball; **pallacanestro** *f* basketball; **pallanuoto** *f* water polo; **pallavolo** f volley ball

palliativo m palliative

pallido pale

pallina f di vetro marble; **~ da golf** golf ball; **~ da tennis** tennis ball; **pallino** m nel biliardo cue ball; nelle bocce jack; munizione pellet; fig **avere il ~ della pesca** be mad about fishing; **a -i** pl spotted; **palloncino** m balloon; **pallone** m ball; (calcio) football, soccer; AVIA balloon; **pallottola** f pellet; di pistola bullet

palma f palm

palmare m PDA

palmo m hand's breadth; ANAT palm

palo m pole; nel calcio (goal-)post

palombaro m diver

palpare feel; MED palpate

palpebra f eyelid

paltò m inv overcoat

palude f swamp; **paludoso** swampy; **palustre** swampy; pianta swamp attr

panca f bench; in chiesa pew

pancarré m sliced loaf

pancetta f pancetta, cured belly of pork

panchetto m footstool; **panchina** f bench

pancia f m stomach; **mal m di ~** stomach-ache; **panciotto** m waistcoat, Am vest

pancreas m inv pancreas

pane m bread; **~ integrale** wholemeal o Am whole-

wheat bread; **panetteria** f bakery; **panettiere** m/f baker; **panettone** m panettone, cake made with candied fruit

panfilo m yacht; **~ a motore** motor yacht

pangrattato m breadcrumbs

panico m panic

paniere m basket

panificio m bakery

panino m roll; **~ imbottito** filled roll; **paninoteca** f sandwich shop

panna f cream; **~ montata** whipped cream

panne f: **essere in ~** have broken down

pannello m panel; **~ solare** solar panel

panno m (pezzo di stoffa) cloth; per donne sanitary towel; **-i** pl clothes; **se fossi nei tuoi -i** if I were in your shoes

pannocchia f cob

pannolino m nappy, Am diaper; per bambini sanitary towel, Am sanitary napkin

panorama m panorama; fig overview

pantaloncini mpl shorts; **pantaloni** mpl trousers, Am pants

pantera f ZO panther

pantofola f slipper

papà m inv daddy, dad

papa m Pope

papavero m poppy

papera f fig (errore) slip of the tongue

papero m, **-a** f gosling

papillon m inv bow tie

pappa f food

pappagallo m parrot

paprica f paprika

parabola f TV satellite dish

parabrezza m inv windscreen, Am windshield

paracadute m inv parachute; **paracadutista** m/f parachutist

paracarro m post

paradiso m heaven, paradise

paradossale paradoxical; **paradosso** m paradox

parafango m AUTO wing; di bici mudguard

parafulmine m lightning rod

paraggi mpl neighbourhood, Am neighborhood; **nei ~ di** (somewhere) near

paragonare compare; **paragone** m comparison

paragrafo m paragraph

paralisi f paralysis; **paralizzare** paralyze

parallela f parallel line; **-e** pl parallel bars; **parallelo** m/agg parallel

paralume m lampshade

parametro m parameter

paranoia f paranoia; **paranoico** paranoid

paranormale m/agg paranormal

paraocchi mpl blinkers (anche fig)

parapetto m parapet; MAR rail

paraplegico 1 agg paraplegic **2** m, **-a** f paraplegic

parare 1 v/t ornare decorate; proteggere shelter; occhi shield; scansare parry **2** v/i save

parassita m/f parasite (anche fig)

parata f parade

paraurti m inv bumper

parcheggiare park; **parcheggio** m parking; luogo car park, Am parking lot

parchimetro m parking meter

parco m park; **~ naturale** nature reserve

parecchio 1 agg a lot of **2** pron **parecchi** mpl, **parecchie** fpl quite a few **3** avv quite a lot

pareggiare 1 v/t even up; (uguagliare) match; conto balance **2** v/i SP draw, Am tie; **pareggio** m SP draw, Am tie

parente m/f relative

parentesi f bracket, Am parenthesis

parere 1 v/i seem, appear; **che te ne pare?** what do you think?; **non ti pare?** don't you think?; **a quanto pare** by all accounts **2** m opinion; **a mio ~** in my opinion

parete f wall

pari 1 agg equal; numero even; **alla ~** the same; SP **finire alla ~** end in a draw o Am tie **2** m (social) equal, peer

Parigi Paris; **parigino** Parisian

parità f equality, parity; **~ di diritti** equal rights; **a ~ di condizioni** all things being equal

parlamentare 1 agg Parliamentary **2** v/i negotiate **3** m/f Member of Parliament, MP; **parlamento** m Parliament

parlare talk, speak (**a qu** to s.o.; **di qc** about sth); **parla inglese?** do you speak English?

parmigiano m formaggio Parmesan

parodia f parody

parola f word; facoltà speech; **~ d'ordine** password; **-e** pl **crociate** crossword; **~ chiave** keyword; **essere di ~** keep one's word; **parolaccia** f swear word

parquet m parquet floor

parrocchia f parish; **parroco** m parish priest

parrucca f wig; **parrucchiere** m, **-a** f hairdresser; **~ per signora** ladies' hairdresser

part time 1 agg part-time **2** avv part time

parte f part; (porzione) portion; (lato) side; DIR party; **prendere ~ a** take part in; **a ~** separate; **mettere da ~ qc** put sth aside; **da nessuna ~** nowhere; **da tutte le -i** everywhere; **da ~ mia** regalo ecc from me; **in ~** in part, partly

partecipante m/f participant;

partecipare 1 v/t announce **2** v/i: **~ a gara** take part in; dolore, gioia share; **partecipazione** f (intervento) participation; (annunzio) announcement; FIN holding; **~ agli utili** profit-sharing

partenza f departure; SP start

participio m participle

particolare 1 agg particular; segretario private; **in ~** in particular **2** m particular, detail; **particolareggiato** detailed; **particolarità** f inv special nature

partigiano m, **-a** f partisan

partire leave; AUTO, SP start

partita f SP match; di carte game; di merce shipment; **~ IVA** VAT registration number

partito m POL party

partner m/f inv partner

parto m birth; **partorire** give birth to

parziale partial; fig biased

Pasqua f Easter; **pasquale** Easter attr; **Pasquetta** f Easter Monday

passaggio m passage; in macchina lift, Am ride; atto passing; SP pass; **essere di ~** be passing through; **~ a livello** level crossing, Am grade crossing; **dare un ~ a qu** give s.o. a lift; **passante** m/f passer-by; **passaporto** m passport; **passare 1** v/i (trasferirsi) go (in into); SP pass; di legge be passed; di *tempo* go by, pass; *~ da / per Milano* go through Milan; *~ dal panettiere* drop by the baker's; *mi è passato di mente* it slipped my mind; *~ per imbecille* be taken for a fool **2** *v/t confine* cross; *(sorpassare)* overstep; *(porgere)* pass; *(trascorrere)* spend; TELEC *ti passo Claudio* here's Claudio; **passata** *f* quick wipe; GASTR *~* *(di pomodoro)* passata, sieved tomato pulp; **passatempo** *m* pastime, hobby; **passato 1** *agg* past; *alimento* puréed; *l'anno ~* last year **3** *m* past; GASTR purée

passeggero 1 *agg* passing, short-lived **2** *m*, *-a f* passenger; **passeggiare** stroll, walk; **passeggiata** *f* stroll, walk; *(percorso)* walk; **passeggino** *m* pushchair, *Am* baby buggy; **passeggio** *m*: *andare a ~* go for a walk

passe-partout *m inv chiave* master key

passerella *f* (foot)bridge; MAR gangway; AVIA ramp; *per sfilate* catwalk, *Am* runway

passero *m* sparrow

passionale passionate; *delitto* of passion; **passione** *f* passion; REL Passion

passivo 1 *agg* passive **2** *m* GRAM passive; FIN liabilities

passo *m* step; *(impronta)* footprint; *di libro* passage;

GEOG pass; *~* **carrabile** driveway; **fare due -i** go for a walk *o* a stroll; *fig* **fare il primo ~** take the first step

pasta *f* paste; *(pastasciutta)* pasta; *(impasto)* dough; *(dolce)* pastry; *~* **frolla** shortcrust pastry; *~* **sfoglia** puff pastry; **pastasciutta** *f* pasta; **pastella** *f* batter

pastello *m* pastel

pasticca *f* pastille

pasticceria *f* pastries, cakes; *negozio* cake shop; **pasticcino** *m* pastry; **pasticcio** *m* GASTR pie; *fig* mess; *essere nei -i* be in a mess

pastiglia *f* MED tablet, pill

pasto *m* meal

pastore 1 *m*, *-a f* shepherd **2** *m* REL: *~* *(evangelico)* pastor; **pastorizzato** pasteurized

patata *f* potato; *-e pl fritte* (French) fries; **patatine** *fpl* crisps, *Am* chips; *(fritte)* French fries

patente *f*: *~* *(di guida)* driving licence, *Am* driver's license

paternità *f* paternity; **paterno** paternal, fatherly

patetico pathetic

patire 1 *v/i* suffer *(di* from) **2** *v/t* suffer (from); **patito 1** *agg* of suffering **2** *m*, *-a f* fan

patria *f* homeland

patrigno *m* stepfather

patrimonio *m* estate; *~* **artistico** artistic heritage

patriottismo *m* patriotism

patrocinio *m* support, patronage

patrono *m*, **-a** *f* REL patron saint

patteggiare negotiate

pattinaggio *m* skating; **~ su ghiaccio** ice skating; **pattinare** skate; AUTO skid; **pattinatore** *m*, **-trice** *f* skater; **pattino** *m* SP skate; **~ a rotelle** roller skate; **~ in linea** roller blade

patto *m* pact; **a ~ che** on condition that

pattuglia *f* patrol

pattumiera *f* dustbin, *Am* trashcan

paura *f* fear; **avere ~ di** be frightened of; **mettere ~ a qu** frighten s.o.; **pauroso** fearful; (*che fa paura*) frightening

pausa *f* pause; **durante il lavoro** break

pavimento *m* floor

pavone *m* peacock

pazientare be patient; **paziente** *agg*, *m/f* patient; **pazienza** *f* patience

pazzesco crazy; **pazzia** *f* madness; **pazzo 1** *agg* mad, crazy; **andare ~ per** be mad *o* crazy about **2** *m*, **-a** *f* madman; **donna** madwoman

p.c. (= **per conoscenza**) cc (= carbon copy)

peccare sin; **~ di** be guilty of; **peccato** *m* sin; (*che*) **~!** what a pity!

pecora *f* sheep

pecorino *m/agg*: (**formaggio** *m*) **~** pecorino (*ewe's milk cheese*)

peculiarità *f inv* special feature, peculiarity

pedaggio *m* toll

pedalare pedal; **pedale** *m* pedal; **pedalò** *m inv* pedalo

pedana *f* footrest; SP springboard

pedata *f* kick; **impronta** footprint

pediatra *m/f* paediatrician, *Am* pediatrician

pedicure 1 *m/f* chiropodist, *Am* podiatrist **2** *m inv* pedicure

pedina *f* draughtsman, *Am* draftsman; *fig* cog in the wheel; **pedinare** shadow, follow

pedofilo *m*, **-a** *f* paedophile, *Am* pedophile

pedonale pedestrian; **pedone** *m* pedestrian

peggio 1 *avv* worse **2** *m*: **il ~ è che** the worst of it is that; **avere la ~** get the worst of it; **peggioramento** *m* deterioration, worsening; **peggiorare 1** *v/t* make worse, worsen **2** *v/i* get worse, worsen; **peggiore** worse; *superlativo* worst; **il ~** the worst

pelare peel; **pollo** pluck; *fig* fleece F

pelle *f* skin; **avere la ~ d'oca** have gooseflesh

pellegrinaggio *m* pilgrimage; **pellegrino** *m*, -a *f* pilgrim

pelletteria *f* leatherwork

pellicano *m* pelican

pelliccia *f* fur; *cappotto* fur coat

pellicola *f* film

pelo *m* hair, coat; (*pelliccia*) coat; *fig* **per un ~** by the skin of one's teeth

pena *f* (*sofferenza*) pain, suffering; (*punizione*) punishment; **~ di morte** death penalty; **stare in ~ per qu** worry about s.o.; **non ne vale la ~** it's not worth it; **mi fa ~** I feel sorry for him / her; **penale 1** *agg* criminal; *codice penale* 2 *f* penalty; **penalità** *f inv* penalty; **penalizzare** penalize

pendenza *f* slope; **pendere** hang; (*essere inclinato*) slope; **pendio** *m* slope

pendolare *m/f* commuter

pendolo *m* pendulum

pene *m* penis

penetrante *dolore, freddo* piercing; *fig*: *sguardo* piercing, penetrating; *analisi* penetrating; **penetrare 1** *v/t* penetrate **2** *v/i*: **~ in** enter

penisola *f* peninsula

penitenza *f* REL penance; *in gioco* forfeit; **penitenziario** *m* prison

penna *f* pen; *di uccello* feather; **~ stilografica** fountain pen; **pennarello** *m* felt-tip (pen); **pennello** *m* brush

penombra *f* half-light

penoso painful

pensare think; **~ a** think about *o* of; **~ a fare qc** (*ricordarsi di*) remember to do sth; **~ di fare qc** think of doing sth; *ci penso io* I'll take care of it; **pensiero** *m* thought; (*preoccupazione*) worry; **stare in ~** be worried (**per** about); **pensieroso** pensive

pensile hanging

pensilina *f* shelter

pensionamento *m* retirement; **pensionato** *m*, -a *f* pensioner, retired person; *alloggio* boarding house; **pensione** *f* pension; *albergo* boarding house; **~ completa** full board; **mezza ~** half board; **andare in ~** retire

Pentecoste *f* Pentecost, *Br anche* Whitsun

pentirsi *di peccato* repent; **~ di aver fatto qc** be sorry for doing sth

pentola *f* pot, pan

penultimo last but one, penultimate

penzolare dangle; **penzoloni** dangling

pepare pepper; **pepato** peppered; **pepe** *m* pepper; **peperone** *m* pepper

per for; *mezzo* by; **~ qualche giorno** for a few days; **~ tutta la notte** throughout the night; **dieci ~ cento** ten per cent; **uno ~ uno** one by one; **~ fare qc** (in order) to do sth; **stare ~** be about to

pera f pear

peraltro however

perbene 1 agg respectable **2** avv properly

percento 1 m percentage **2** avv per cent; **percentuale** f agg percentage

percepire perceive; (riscuotere) cash

perché because; (affinché) so that; **~?** why?

perciò so, therefore

percorrere distanza cover; strada, fiume travel along; **percorso 1** pp ☞ **percorrere 2** m (tragitto) route

percossa f blow; **percosso** pp ☞ **percuotere**; **percuotere** strike

percussione f percussion; MUS **-i** pl percussion

perdere v/t lose; treno, occasione miss; **~ tempo** waste time **2** v/i lose; di rubinetto, tubo leak; **perdersi** get lost; **~ d'animo** lose heart; **mi sono perduto** I'm lost; **perdita** f loss; di gas, d'acqua leak; **~ di tempo** waste of time; **perditempo 1** m/f inv idler **2** m inv waste of time

perdonare forgive; **perdono** m forgiveness

perenne eternal; BOT perennial

perfettamente perfectly; **perfetto** perfect; **perfezionamento** m perfection, further improvement; **corso di ~** further training; **per-**

fezionare perfect; **perfezione** f perfection; **perfezionista** m/f perfectionist

perfido treacherous

perfino even

perforare drill through

pergolato m pergola

pericolante on the verge of collapse; **pericolo** m danger; (rischio) risk; **fuori ~** out of danger; **pericoloso** dangerous

periferia f periphery; di città outskirts; **periferico** peripheral; quartiere outlying; IN-FOR **unità** f inv **-a** peripheral

perifrasi f inv circumlocution

periodico 1 agg periodic **2** m periodical; **~ mensile** monthly; **periodo** m period

peripezia f misadventure

perito 1 agg expert **2** m, **-a** f expert

peritonite f peritonitis

perizia f skill, expertise; esame examination (by an expert)

perla f pearl; **perlina** f bead

perlomeno at least

perlopiù usually

perlustrare patrol

permaloso easily offended, touchy

permanente 1 agg permanent **2** f perm; **permanenza** f permanence; **in un luogo** stay

permesso 1 pp ☞ **permettere 2** m permission; (breve licenza) permit; MIL leave; **~**

di soggiorno residence permit; (*è*) ~? may I?; **permettere** allow, permit; **permettersi** afford

pernacchia *f* F raspberry F, *Am* bronx cheer F

perno *m* pivot

pernottamento *m* night, overnight stay

però but

pero *m* pear (tree)

perpendicolare *f/agg* perpendicular

perplesso perplexed

perquisire search; **perquisizione** *f* search; ~ **personale** body search; **mandato** *m* **di** ~ search warrant

persecuzione *f* persecution; **mania** *f* **di** ~ persecution complex; **perseguitare** persecute; **perseguitato** m: ~ **politico** person persecuted for their political views

perseverante persevering; **perseveranza** *f* perseverance; **perseverare** persevere

persiana *f* shutter

persino ☞ **perfino**

persistente persistent; **persistere** persist

perso *pp* ☞ **perdere**

persona *f* person; **a** (*o* **per**) ~ a head, each; **in** ~, **di** ~ in person; **personaggio** *m* character; (*celebrità*) personality; **personale 1** *agg* personal **2** *m* staff, personnel; **personalità** *f inv* personality; **personalmente** personally

perspicace shrewd

persuadere persuade, convince; ~ **qu a fare qc** persuade s.o. to do sth; **persuasivo** persuasive; **persuaso** *pp* ☞ **persuadere**

pertanto and so, therefore

pertinente relevant, pertinent

perturbazione *f* disturbance

Perù *m* Peru; **peruviano 1** *agg* Peruvian **2** *m*, **-a** *f* Peruvian

pervenire arrive; **far** ~ send

p.es. (= **per esempio**) eg (= for example)

pesante heavy; *fig: libro, film* boring; **pesantezza** *f* heaviness; ~ **di stomaco** indigestion; **pesapersone** *f inv* scales; *in negozio ecc* weighing machine; **pesare** weigh

pesca[1] *f frutto* peach

pesca[2] *f* fishing

pescare fish for; (*prendere*) catch; *fig* dig up; *ladro, svaligiatore ecc* catch (red-handed); **pescatore** *m* fisherman; **pesce** *m* fish; ~ **d'aprile** April Fool; ASTR **Pesci** *pl* Pisces; **pescecane** *m* shark; **peschereccio** *m* fishing boat; **pescheria** *f* fishmonger's, *Am* fish store; **pescivendolo** *m*, **-a** *f* fishmonger, *Am* fish seller

pesco *m* peach (tree)

peso *m* weight; **a** ~ by weight

pessimismo *m* pessimism; **pessimista 1** *agg* pessimistic **2** *m/f* pessimist

pessimo very bad, terrible

pestaggio *m* F going-over F; **pestare** *carne, prezzemolo* pound; *con piede* step on; *(picchiare)* beat up

peste *f* plague; *persona* pest F

pesticida *m* pesticide

pesto *m* pesto, *paste of basil, olive oil and pine nuts*

petalo *m* petal

petardo *m* fire-cracker

peto *m* fart F

petroliera *f* (oil) tanker; **petrolifero** oil *attr*; **petrolio** *m* oil, petroleum

pettegolezzo *m* piece of gossip; **pettegolo 1** *agg* gossipy **2** *m*, **-a** *f* gossip

pettinare comb; **pettinarsi** comb one's hair; **pettinatura** *f* hairstyle, hairdo; **pettine** *m* comb

petto *m* chest; *(seno)* breast; **~ di pollo** chicken breast; **a doppio ~** double-breasted

pezza *f* cloth; *(toppa)* patch

pezzo *m* piece; *di motore* part; **da / per un ~** for a long time; **~ di ricambio** spare (part); **andare in -i** break into pieces

piacere 1 *v/i*: **le piace il vino?** do you like wine?; **non mi piace il cioccolato** I don't like chocolate; **mi piacerebbe saperlo** I'd really like to know F *2 m* pleasure; *(favore)* favour, *Am* favor; **~!** pleased to meet you!; **mi fa ~** I'm happy to; **con ~** with pleasure; **per ~** please; **piacevole** pleasant; **piacimento**: **a ~** as much as you like

piaga *f* *(ferita)* wound

piallare plane

pianerottolo *m* landing

pianeta *m* planet

piangere 1 *v/i* cry, weep **2** *v/t* mourn

pianificare plan

pianista *m/f* pianist; **piano 1** *agg* flat **2** *avv* (*adagio*) slowly; (*a voce bassa*) quietly **3** *m* plan; (*pianura*) plane; *di edificio* floor; MUS piano; **~ rialzato** mezzanine; **primo ~** foreground; FOT close-up; **pianoforte** *m* piano

pianta *f* plant; *di città* map; *del piede* sole; **piantare** plant; *chiodo* hammer in; F **piantala!** cut it out! F; **F ~ qu** dump s.o. F

pianterreno *m* ground floor, *Am* first floor

pianto 1 *pp* *☞* **piangere 2** *m* crying, weeping; (*lacrime*) tears

pianura *f* plain

piastra *f* plate; **piastrella** *f* tile

piattaforma *f* platform; **~ di lancio** launch pad; **piattino** *m* saucer; **piatto 1** *agg* flat **2** *m* plate; GASTR dish; MUS **-i** *pl* cymbals; **primo ~** first course; **~ del giorno** day's special

piazza *f* square; COM market (place); **piazzale** *m* large square; *in autostrada* toll-booth area; **piazzare** place, put; (*vendere*) sell; **piazzola** *f* small square; **~ di sosta** lay-by

piccante spicy, hot

picchiare beat

piccione *m* pigeon

picco *m* peak; MAR **colare a ~** sink

piccolo 1 *agg* small, little; *di statura* short **2** *m*, **-a** *f* child; **la gatta con i suoi -i** the cat and her young; **da ~ as** a child

piccozza *f* ice axe, *Am* ice ax

picnic *m inv* picnic

pidocchio *m* louse

piede *m* foot; **a -i** on foot; **stare in -i** stand; **a -i nudi** barefoot, with bare feet

piedistallo *m* pedestal

piega *f* wrinkle; *di pantaloni* crease; *di gonna* pleat; **piegare 1** *v/t* bend; (*ripiegare*) fold **2** *v/i* bend; **piegarsi** bend; *fig* **~ a** comply with; **pieghevole sedia** folding

Piemonte *m* Piedmont; **piemontese** *agg*, *m/f* Piedmontese

piena *f* flood; *a teatro* full house; **pieno 1** *agg* full (*di* of); (*non cavo*) solid **2** *m*: AUTO **fare il ~** fill up

pietà *f* pity (*di* for); PITT pietà; **avere ~ di qu** take pity on s.o.

pietanza *f* dish

pietra *f* stone; **pietrina** *f* flint; **pietroso** stony

pigiama *m* pyjamas, *Am* pa-

jamas

pigiare crush

pigliare catch

pigna *f* pinecone

pignolo *m* pedantic

pigrizia *f* laziness; **pigro** lazy

pila *f* EL battery; (*catasta*) pile

pilastro *m* pillar

pillola *f* pill; **prendere la ~** be on the pill

pilone *m* pier; EL pylon

pilota *m/f* AVIA, MAR pilot; AUTO driver; **pilotare** pilot; AUTO drive

pinacoteca *f* art gallery

pineta *f* pine forest

ping-pong *m* ping-pong

pinna *f di pesce* fin; SP flipper

pino *m* pine; **pinolo** *m* pine nut

pinza *f* pliers; **pinzare** staple; **pinzatrice** *f* stapler; **pinzette** *fpl* tweezers

pioggia *f* rain

piombare fall; *precipitarsi* rush (**su** at); **mi è piombato in casa** he dropped in unexpectedly; **piombino** *m* sinker; **piombo** *m* lead

pioppo *m* poplar

piovere rain; **piovigginare** drizzle; **piovoso** rainy

piovra *f* octopus

pipa *f* pipe

pipì *f* pee F; F **fare la ~** go for a pee F

pipistrello *m* bat

piramide *f* pyramid

pirata *m* pirate

pirofila *f* oven-proof dish

piroscafo *m* steamer

pisciare P piss P

piscina *f* (swimming) pool; **~ coperta** indoor pool

pisello *m* pea

pisolino *m* nap

pista *f* di atletica track; (*traccia*) trail; **~ d'atterraggio** runway; **~ da ballo** dance floor; **~ da sci** ski slope; **~ ciclabile** bike path

pistacchio *m* pistachio

pistola *f* pistol

pittore *m*, **-trice** *f* painter; **pittura** *f* painting; **pitturare** paint

più 1 *avv* more (*di*, *che* than); *superlativo* most; MAT plus; **~ grande** bigger; **il ~ grande** the biggest; **di ~** more; **non ~** no more; *tempo* no longer; **~ o meno** more or less; **per di ~** what's more; **mai ~** never again; **al ~ presto** as soon as possible; **al ~ tardi** at the latest **2** *agg* more; *superlativo* most; **~ volte** several times **3** *m* most; **per lo ~** mainly; **i ~**, **le ~** the majority

piuma *f* feather

piumino *m* down; *giacca* quilted jacket

piumone® *m* Continental quilt, duvet

piuttosto rather

pizza *f* pizza; **pizzaiolo** *m* pizza maker; **pizzeria** *f* pizzeria

pizzicare 1 *v/t* braccio, *persona* pinch; F *ladro* catch (redhanded) **2** *v/i* pinch; **pizzico**

m pinch; **pizzicotto** *m* pinch

pizzo *m* (*merletto*) lace

placare placate; *dolore* ease

placca *f* plate; (*targhetta*) plaque; **~ dentaria** plaque; **placcare** plate; *nel rugby* tackle; **placcato d'oro** gold-plated

planetario 1 *agg* planetary **2** *m* planetarium

plasma *m* plasma; **~ sanguigno** blood plasma; plasma-re mould, *Am* mold

plastica *f* plastic; MED plastic surgery; **plastico 1** *agg* plastic **2** *m* ARCHI scale model; **esplosivo** *m* **al ~** plastic bomb

plastilina® *f* Plasticine®

platano *m* plane (tree)

platea *f* TEA stalls

platino *m* platinum

plausibile plausible

plenilunio *m* full moon

plettro *m* plectrum

pleurite *f* pleurisy

plico *m* envelope

plurale *m*/agg plural

plutonio *m* plutonium

pneumatico 1 *agg* pneumatic **2** *m* tyre, *Am* tire

po': un ~ a little (*di* sth), a little bit (*di* of); **un bel ~** quite a lot

poco 1 *agg* little; *con nomi plurali* few **2** *avv* not much; *con aggettivi* not very; **senti un po'!** just listen!; **a ~ a ~** little by little, gradually; **~ fa** a little while ago; **fra ~**

in a little while, soon; **~ dopo** a little while later, soon after; **per ~** cheap; (*quasi*) almost, nearly

podere *m* farm

podio *m* podium

podismo *m* walking

poesia *f* poetry; *componimento* poem; **poeta** *m*, **-essa** *f* poet; **poetico** poetic

poggiare lean; (*posare*) put, place; **poggiatesta** *m inv* head rest

poi then; **d'ora in ~** from now on

poiché since

polacco 1 *m/agg* Polish **2** *m*, **-a** *f* Pole

polare Polar; **circolo** *m* **~ artico / antartico** Arctic / Antarctic circle

polemica *f* argument; **polemico** argumentative; **polemizzare** argue

polenta *f* polenta, *kind of porridge made from cornmeal*

policlinico *m* general hospital

poliglotta 1 *agg* multilingual **2** *m/f* polyglot

poligono *m* MAT polygon; MIL **~ di tiro** firing range

poliomielite *f* poliomyelitis

polipo *m* polyp

politica *f* politics; (*strategia*) policy; **politico 1** *agg* political **2** *m*, **-a** *f* politician

polizia *f* police; **poliziesco** police *attr*; **romanzo** *m* **~** detective story; **poliziotto 1** *m*

policeman **2** *agg*: **donna** *f* **-a** policewoman; **cane** *m* **~** police dog

polizza *f* policy

pollame *m* poultry

pollice *m* thumb; *unità di misura* inch

polline *m* pollen

pollo *m* chicken

polmone *m* lung; **polmonite** *f* pneumonia

polo¹ *m* GEOG pole; **~ nord** North Pole; **~ sud** South Pole

polo² **1** *m* SP polo **2** *f inv* polo shirt

Polonia *f* Poland

polpa *f* flesh; *di manzo, vitello* meat

polpaccio *m* calf

polpastrello *m* fingertip

polpetta *f* di carne meatball; **polpettone** *m* meat loaf

polpo *m* octopus

polsino *m* cuff; **polso** *m* ANAT wrist; *di camicia* cuff; *pulsazione* pulse

poltiglia *f* mush

poltrire laze around

poltrona *f* armchair; TEA stall (seat)

poltrone *m*, **-a** *f* lazybones *sg*

polvere *f* dust; (*sostanza polverizzata*) powder; **latte** *m* **in ~** powdered milk; **polverina** *f* powder; **polveroso** dusty

pomata *f* cream

pomello *m* cheek; *di porta* knob

pomeridiano afternoon *attr*; **pomeriggio** *m* afternoon; *di ~*, *nel ~* in the afternoon

pomice *f/agg*: (**pietra** *f*) *~* pumice (stone)

pomo *m* knob; *~ d'Adamo* Adam's apple

pomodoro *m* tomato

pompa¹ *f* pomp; **impresa** *f di -e funebri* undertaker's, *Am* mortician

pompa² *f* TEC pump

pompelmo *m* grapefruit

pompiere *m* fireman; *-pl* fire brigade, *Am* fire department

pone ☞ **porre**

ponente *m* west

pongo ☞ **porre**

ponte *m* bridge; ARCHI scaffolding; MAR deck; *fare il ~* make a long weekend of it

pontefice *m* pontiff

ponteggio *m* scaffolding

pontificio papal; **Stato** *m ~* Papal States

pontile *m* jetty

pop: **musica** *f ~* pop (music)

popolare 1 *agg* popular; *quartiere* working-class; *ballo m ~* folk dance **2** *v/t* populate; **popolarità** *f* popularity; **popolato** populated; (*abitato*) inhabited; (*pieno*) crowded; **popolazione** *f* population; **popolo** *m* people

poppa *f* MAR stern

porcellana *f* porcelain, china

porcellino *m* piglet; *~ d'India* guinea-pig

porcheria *f* disgusting thing; *è una ~* it's disgusting; *-e pl* junk food; **porchetta** *f* suckling pig, *roasted whole in the oven*

porcile *m* pigsty, *Am* pigpen

porcino *m* cep

porco *m* pig; **porcospino** *m* porcupine

porgere *mano*, *oggetto* hold out; *aiuto*, *saluto* ecc offer

porno *m/agg* F porn F; **pornografico** pornographic

poro *m* pore

porre place, put; *domanda* ask; *poniamo che ...* let's suppose that ...

porro *m* leek; MED wart

porta *f* door

portabagagli *m inv* luggage rack; AUTO roof rack; **portacenere** *m inv* ashtray; **portachiavi** *m inv* keyring; **portafinestra** *f* French window; **portafoglio** *m* wallet; **portafortuna** *m inv* good luck charm

portale *m* door; INFOR portal

portamonete *m inv* purse; **portaombrelli** *m inv* umbrella stand; **portapacchi** *m inv di macchina* roof rack; *di bicicletta* carrier; **portapenne** *m inv* pencil case

portare (*trasportare*) carry; (*accompagnare*) take; (*avere addosso*) wear; (*condurre*) lead; *~ via* take away; *mi ha portato un regalo* he brought me a present; *por-*

tale un regalo take her a present; *essere portato per qc / per fare qc* have a gift for sth / for doing sth

portasci *m inv* AUTO ski rack

portata *f* GASTR course; *di cannocchiale* range; *alla ~ di film, libro ecc* suitable for; *a ~ di mano* within reach

portatile portable; (*computer* *m*) ~ portable (computer); (*telefono* *m*) ~ mobile (phone), *Am* cell(ular) phone

portatore *m*, **-trice** *f* bearer; *di malattia* carrier

portauovo *m inv* eggcup

portavoce *m/f inv* spokesperson

portico *m* porch; **-i** *pl* arcades

portiera *f* door; **portiere** *m* doorman; (*portinaio*) caretaker; SP goalkeeper

portinaio *m*, **-a** *f* caretaker; **portineria** *f* caretaker's flat, *Am* superintendent's apartment

porto[1] *pp* ☞ *porgere*

porto[2] *m posta* postage; ~ *d'armi* gun licence *o Am* license

porto[3] *m* MAR port

Portogallo *m* Portugal; **portoghese** *agg*, *m/f* Portuguese

portone *m* main entrance

porzione *f* share; GASTR portion

posa *f di cavi, tubi* laying; FOT exposure; FOT *mettersi in* ~

pose; **posacenere** *m inv* ashtray; **posare 1** *v/t* put, place **2** *v/i* pose; ~ *su* rest on; *fig* ~ *da* intellettuale pose as an intellectual; *posarsi* alight; **posate** *fpl* cutlery, *Am* flatware

positivo positive

posizione *f* position

possedere own, possess; **possessivo** possessive; **possesso** *m* possession

possiamo ☞ *potere*

possibile 1 *agg* possible; *il più presto* ~ as soon as possible **2** *m:* **fare il** ~ do everything one can; **possibilità** *f inv* possibility; (*occasione*) opportunity, chance; **possibilmente** if possible

posso ☞ *potere*

posta *f* mail, *Br anche* post; (*ufficio postale*) post office; ~ *aerea* airmail; *per* ~ by post; INFOR ~ *elettronica* e-mail; ~ *lumaca* snail mail; **postale** postal

postdatare postdate

posteggiare park; **posteggio** *m* carpark, *Am* parking lot; ~ *dei taxi* rank, *Am* cab stand

posteriore back *attr*, rear *attr*; (*successivo*) later

posticipare postpone; **posticipato:** *pagamento m* ~ payment in arrears

postino *m*, **-a** *f* postman, *Am* mailman; *donna* postwoman, *Am* mailwoman

posto[1] *pp* ☞ **porre**; ~ **che** supposing that

posto[2] *m* place; (*lavoro*) job, position; **mettere a ~ stanza** tidy up; ~ **macchina** parking space; ~ **finestrino / corridoio** window / aisle seat; ~ **a sedere** seat; ~ **di polizia** police station; **vado io al ~ tuo** I'll go in your place, I'll go instead of you; **fuori ~** out of place

postoperatorio postoperative

postumo posthumous

potabile fit to drink; **acqua f ~** drinking water

potare prune

potente powerful; (*efficace*) potent; **potenza f** power; ~ **mondiale** world power; ~ **del motore** engine power; **potenziare** strengthen

potere 1 *v/i* can, be able to; **non posso andare** I can't go; **non ho potuto farlo** I couldn't do it, I wasn't able to do it; **può darsi** perhaps, maybe **2** *m* power

poveraccio *m*, **-a f** poor thing; **poveretto** *m*, **poverino** *m* poor man; **povero 1** *agg* poor **2** *m*, **-a f** poor man; **donna** poor woman; **i -i** *pl* the poor *pl*; **povertà f** poverty

pozzanghera f puddle

pozzo *m* well; ~ **petrolifero** oil well

PP.TT. (= **Poste e Telecomunicazioni**) Italian Post Office

pranzare have lunch; **la sera** have dinner; **pranzo** *m* lunch; **la sera** dinner

prassi f *inv* standard procedure

pratica f practice; (*esperienza*) experience; (*atto*) file; **mettere in ~** put into practice; **-che** *pl* papers; **in ~** in practice; **avere ~ di qc** have experience of sth; **praticabile sport** which can be done; **strada** passable; **praticantato** *m* apprenticeship; **praticare** *profession* practise; **locale** frequent; ~ **molto sport** do a lot of sport; **pratico** practical; **essere ~ di conoscere bene** know a lot about

prato *m* meadow

preavviso *m* notice

precauzione f caution; **-i** *pl* precautions

precedente 1 *agg* preceding **2** *m* precedent; **avere dei -i penali** have a record; **precedenza f** precedence; **avere la ~** AUTO have right of way; **dare la ~** AUTO give way, *Am* yield; **precedere** precede

precipitare 1 *v/t* throw; *fig* rush **2** *v/i* fall, plunge; **precipitarsi** (*affrettarsi*) rush; **precipitazione f** (*fretta*) haste; **-i pl atmosferiche** atmospheric precipitation; **precipitoso** hasty

precipizio *m* precipice

precisamente precisely; **precisare** specify; **precisione** *f* precision; **con ~** precisely; **preciso** accurate; *persona* precise

precoce precocious; *pianta* early

precotto *m* ready-made, pre-cooked

preda *f* prey

predica *f* sermon

prediletto 1 *pp* ☞ **prediligere 2** *agg* favourite, *Am* favorite; **prediligere** prefer

predire predict

predisporre draw up in advance; **~ a** encourage; **predisposto** *pp* ☞ **predisporre**

predominare predominate; **predominio** *m* predominance

prefabbricato 1 *agg* prefabricated **2** *m* prefabricated building

prefazione *f* preface

preferenza *f* preference; **preferenziale** preferential; **preferire** prefer

preferito favourite, *Am* favorite

prefettura *f* prefecture

prefiggersi set o.s.; **prefisso 1** *pp* ☞ **prefiggersi 2** *m* TELEC code

pregare beg (**di fare** to do); *divinità* pray to; **ti prego di ascoltarmi** please listen to me

preghiera *f* request; REL prayer

pregiato *pietra* precious

pregio *m* (*qualità*) good point

pregiudicato *m*, **-a** *f* previous offender; **pregiudizio** *m* prejudice

prego please; **~?** I'm sorry (what did you say)?; **grazie! – ~!** thank you! – you're welcome!, not at all!

preistoria *f* prehistory; **preistorico** prehistoric

prelavaggio *m* pre-wash

prelevamento *m di sangue, campione* taking; FIN withdrawal; **~ in contanti** cash withdrawal; **prelevare** *sangue, campione* take; *denaro* withdraw

prelibato exquisite

prelievo *m* (*prelevamento*) taking; FIN withdrawal; **~ del sangue** blood sample

pre-maman 1 *agg* maternity *attr* **2** *m inv* maternity dress

prematuro premature

premeditato premeditated

premere press

premessa *f* introduction

premesso *pp* ☞ **premettere**; **premettere** say first

premiare give an award *o* prize to; *onestà, coraggio* reward; **premiazione** *f* awards ceremony; **premio** *m* prize, award; FIN premium

premura *f* (*fretta*) hurry, rush; **mettere ~ a qu** hurry s.o. along; **premuroso** attentive

prenatale prenatal

prendere 1 v/t take; *malattia, treno* catch; *cosa prendi?* what will you have; *anda-re / venire a ~ qu* fetch s.o.; *~ il sole* sunbathe; *pren-dersela* get upset (*per* about; *con* with); *che ti prende?* what's got into you? **2** v/i: *~ a destra* turn right; **prendisole** m inv sundress

prenotare book, reserve; **prenotazione** f booking, reservation

preoccupare worry; **preoc-cuparsi** worry; **preoccupa-to** worried; **preoccupazio-ne** f worry

preparare prepare; **preparar-si** get ready (*a* to), prepare (*a* to); **preparativi** mpl preparations; **preparazione** f preparation

preposizione f preposition

prepotente domineering; *bi-sogno* pressing

presa f grip, hold; EL *~ di cor-rente* socket, Am outlet; *es-sere alle -e con qc* be grappling with sth

presagio m omen

presbite far-sighted

prescindere: *~ da* have nothing to do with

prescritto pp ☞ **prescrivere;** **prescrivere** prescribe

presentare *documenti, biglietto* show, present; *domanda* submit; *scuse* make; TEA pre-sent; (*contenere*) contain; (*far* *conoscere*) introduce (*a* to);

presentarsi look; (*esporre*) show itself; *occasione* occur; **presentatore** m *-trice* f pre-senter; **presentazione** f presentation; *di richiesta* submission; *fare le ~i* make the introductions; **presente 1** agg present; *hai ~ il nego-zio … ?* do you know the shop … ? **2** m present; *i -i* pl those present

presentimento m premonition

presenza f presence; *alla* (*o* *in*) *~ di* in the presence of

presepe m, **presepio** m nativity (scene)

preservare protect, keep (*da* from); **preservativo** m condom

presidente m/f chairman; POL President; *~ del Consi-glio* (*dei ministri*) Prime Minister

preso pp ☞ **prendere**

pressappoco more or less

pressione f pressure; *far ~ su* put pressure on, pressure

presso 1 prp (*vicino a*) near; *nella sede di* on the premises of; *posta* care of; *vive ~ i ge-nitori* he lives with his par-ents; *lavoro ~ la FIAT* I work for Fiat **2** m: *nei ~ di* in the vicinity of; *pressoché* al-most

prestare lend; *~ ascol-to / aiuto a qu* listen to / help s.o.; **prestarsi** offer one's services; (*essere adatto*) lend itself (*a* to); prestazione *f* service; prestito *m* loan; in ~ on loan; dare in ~ lend; prendere in ~ borrow

presto (*fra poco*) soon; (*in fretta*) quickly; (*di buon'ora*) early; a ~! see you soon!; far ~ be quick

presumere presume; presuntuoso presumptuous

prete *m* priest

pretendere claim; pretesa *f* pretension

pretesto *m* pretext

pretura *f* magistrates' court, *Am* circuit court

prevalenza *f* prevalence; in ~ prevalently; prevalere prevail

prevedere foresee, predict; *tempo* forecast; *di legge* provide for; prevedibile predictable

prevendita *f* advance sale

prevenire *domanda, desiderio* anticipate; (*evitare*) prevent; preventivo 1 *agg* preventive 2 *m* estimate; prevenzione *f* prevention

previdenza *f* foresight; ~ sociale social security, *Am* welfare

previsione *f* forecast; -*i pl del tempo* weather forecast; previsto *pp* → prevedere

prezioso precious

prezzemolo *m* parsley

prezzo *m* price; a buon ~ cheap

prigione *f* prison; prigioniero *m*, -a *f* prisoner

prima[1] *avv* before; (*in primo luogo*) first; ~ di before; ~ di fare qc before doing sth; ~ o poi sooner or later; ~ che before; quanto ~ as soon as possible

prima[2] *f* FERR first class; AUTO first; TEA first night

primavera *f* spring

primitivo primitive; (*iniziale*) original

primizia *f* early crop

primo 1 *agg* first 2 *m*, -a *f* first; ai -i del mese at the beginning of the month; sulle -e in the beginning, at first 3 *m* GASTR first course, starter; primogenito 1 *agg* firstborn 2 *m*, -a *f* first-born

principale 1 *agg* main 2 *m* boss

principato *m* principality; principe *m* prince; principessa *f* princess

principiante *m/f* beginner; principio *m* start, beginning; (*norma*) principle; al ~ at the start, in the beginning; per ~ as a matter of principle

privare deprive (*di* of); privarsi deprive o.s. (*di* of)

privatizzare privatize; privato 1 *agg* private; in ~ in private 2 *m* private citizen

privilegiare favour, *Am* favor, prefer; privilegiato privileged; privilegio *m* privilege

privo: **~ di** lacking in; **~ di grassi** fat-free

pro 1 *m inv*: **i ~ e i contro** the pros and cons; **a che ~?** what's the point? 2 *prp* for; **~ capite** per capita, each

probabile probable; probabilità *f inv* probability

problema *m* problem

proboscide *f* trunk

procedere carry on; *fig (agire)* proceed; procedimento *m* process

procedura *f* procedure; DIR proceedings

processare try

processione *f* procession

processo *m* process; DIR trial

procinto *m*: **essere in ~ di** be about to

proclamare proclaim

procura *f* power of attorney; **Procura di Stato** public prosecutor's office; **per ~** by proxy; procurare *(causare)* cause; **~ qc a qu** cause s.o. sth; procurarsi get hold of; procuratore *m*, -trice *f* person with power of attorney; DIR lawyer for the prosecution; **~ generale** Attorney General

prodotto 1 *pp* ☞ **produrre** 2 *m* product; produco ☞ **produrre**; produrre produce; *danni* cause; produttivo productive; produttore *m*, -trice *f* producer; produzione *f* production

prof. ssa (= **professoressa**)

Prof. (= Professor)

profanare desecrate

professionale professional; *scuola, corso* vocational; professione *f* profession; professionista *m/f* professional; **libero ~** self-employed person

professore *m*, -essa *f* teacher; *d'università* professor

proficuo profitable

profilattico prophylactic

profilo *m* profile

profitto *m (vantaggio)* advantage

profondità *f inv* depth; FOT **~ di campo** depth of field; profondo deep

profugo *m*, -a *f* refugee

profumare perfume; profumeria *f* perfume shop; profumo *m* perfume

progettare plan; progetto *m* design; *di costruzione* project; **~ di legge** bill

prognosi *f inv* prognosis

programma *m* programme, *Am* program; INFOR program; **~ televisivo** TV programme; **avere in ~** have planned; programmare plan; INFOR program; programmatore *m*, -trice *f* programmer; programmazione *f* programming; FIN **~ economica** economic planning; INFOR **linguaggio *m* di ~** programming language

progredire progress; progressivo progressive; progresso *m* progress; *fare -i* make progress

proibire ban, prohibit; ~ *a qu di fare qc* forbid s.o. to do sth

proiettare throw; *film* screen, show; *fig* project; **proiettile** *m* projectile

proiettore *m* projector; ~ *per diapositive* slide projector

proletario 1 *agg* proletariat **2** *m* proletarian

pro loco *f inv* local tourist board

prologo *m* prologue

prolunga *f* EL extension cord; **prolungare** extend; *nel tempo* prolong, extend; **prolungarsi** *di strada* extend; *di riunione* go on

promemoria *m inv* memo

promessa *f* promise; **promesso** *pp* ☞ **promettere**; **promettere** promise; ~ *bene* look promising

promontorio *m* promontory, headland

promosso *pp* ☞ **promuovere**; **promozione** *f* promotion; EDU year; ~ *delle vendite* sales promotion; **promuovere** promote; EDU move up

pronome *m* pronoun

prontezza *f* readiness, promptness; *(rapidità)* speediness, promptness; ~ *di spirito* quick thinking; **pronto** *(preparato)* ready (*a fare qc* to do sth; *per qc*

for sth); TELEC ~*!* hello!; ~ *soccorso* first aid; *in ospedale* accident and emergency, A&E

pronuncia *f* pronunciation; **pronunciare** pronounce; **pronunciarsi** give an opinion (*su* on)

propaganda *f* propaganda; **propagare** propagate; *fig* spread; **propagarsi** spread (*anche fig*)

propenso inclined (*a fare qc* to do sth)

propongo ☞ **proporre**; **proporre** propose; **proporsi** stand (*come* as); ~ *di fare qc* intend to do sth

proporzionato in proportion (*a* to); **proporzione** *f* proportion; *in* ~ in proportion (*a, con* to)

proposito *m* intention; *a* ~ by the way; *a* ~ *di* about, with reference to; *di* ~ on purpose

proposizione *f* GRAM sentence

proposta *f* proposal; **proposto** *pp* ☞ **proporre**

proprietà *f inv* property; *diritto* ownership; **proprietario** *m*, *-a f* owner

proprio 1 *agg* own; *(caratteristico)* typical; *(adatto)* proper; *nome m* ~ proper noun; *amor m* ~ pride **2** *avv* (*davvero*) really **3** *m* (*beni*) personal property; *lavorare in* ~ be self-employed

propulsore *m* propeller

prora *f* prow

proroga *f* postponement; (*prolungamento*) extension; **prorogare** (*rinviare*) postpone; (*prolungare*) extend

prosa *f* prose

prosciogliere release; DIR acquit

prosciugare drain; *di sole* dry up

prosciutto *m* ham; **~ cotto** cooked ham; **~ crudo** salted air-dried ham

proseguimento *m* continuation; **proseguire 1** *v/t* continue **2** *v/i* continue, carry on

prospettiva *f* perspective; (*panorama*) view; (*possibilità*) prospect; *fig* point of view

prospetto *m disegno* elevation; (*facciata*) facade; (*tabella*) table

prossimamente shortly, soon; **prossimità** *f inv* proximity; **in ~ di** near; **prossimo 1** *agg* close; **la ~a volta** the next time **2** *m* fellow human being

prostituta *f* prostitute

protagonista *m/f* protagonist

proteggere protect (*da* from)

proteina *f* protein

protesi *f inv* prosthesis; **~ dentaria** false teeth

protesta *f* protest; **protestante** *agg*, *m/f* Protestant; **protestare** protest

protetto *pp* ☞ **proteggere**; **protezione** *f* protection

prova *f* (*esame*) test; (*tentativo*) attempt; (*testimonianza*) proof; *di abito* fitting; SP heat; TEA **-e** *pl* rehearsal; TEA **-e** *pl* **generali** dress rehearsal; **mettere alla ~** put to the test; **provare** test, try out; *vestito* try (on); (*dimostrare*) prove; TEA rehearse; **~ a fare qc** try to do sth

provengo ☞ **provenire**; **provenienza** *f* origin; **provenire come** (*da* from); **proventi** *mpl* income

proverbio *m* proverb

provetta *f* test-tube

provincia *f* province; **provinciale 1** *agg* provincial **2** *m/f* provincial **3** *f* A road, *Am* highway

provino *m* screen-test; (*campione*) sample

provocante provocative; **provocare** (*causare*) cause; (*sfidare*) provoke; *invidia* arouse

provvedere 1 *v/t* provide (*di* with) **2** *v/i*: **~ a** take care of; **provvedimento** *m* measure

provvigione *f* commission

provvisorio provisional

provvista *f*: **fare ~ di qc** stock up on sth; **provvisto 1** *pp* ☞ **provvedere 2** *agg*: **essere ~ di** be provided with

prozio *m*, **-a** *f* great-uncle; *donna* great-aunt

prua *f* prow

prudente careful, cautious;

prudenza *f* care, caution

prudere *mi prude la mano* my hand itches

prugna *f* plum; *~ secca* prune

prurito *m* itch

P.S. (= *Pubblica Sicurezza*) police; (= *post scriptum*) PS (= post scriptum)

pseudo ... pseudo ...

pseudonimo *m* pseudonym

psicanalisi *f* psychoanalysis; psicanalista *m/f* psychoanalyst

psiche *f* psyche

psichiatra *m/f* psychiatrist

psicologia *f* psychology; psicologico psychological; psicologo *m*, -a *f* psychologist

psicosi *f inv* psychosis

psicoterapia *f* psychotherapy

P.T.P. (= *Posto Telefonico Pubblico*) public telephone

pubblicare publish; pubblicazione *f* publication; *-i pl* (*matrimoniali*) banns; pubblicità *f inv* publicity; *annuncio* advert; *fare ~ a evento* publicize; pubblicitario 1 *agg* advertising 2 *m*, -a *f* publicist; pubblico 1 *agg* public 2 *m* public; (*spettatori*) audience; *in ~* in public

pube *m* pubis

pubertà *f* puberty

pudore *m* modesty

pugilato *m* boxing; pugile *m* boxer

pugnalare stab; pugnale *m* dagger

pugno *m* fist; (*colpo*) punch; *quantità* handful; *fare a -i* come to blows

pulce *f* flea

pulcino *m* chick

puledro *m*, -a *f* colt; *femmina* filly

pulire clean; pulito clean; *fig* cleaned-out; pulitura *f* cleaning; *~ a secco* dry cleaning; pulizia *f* cleanliness; *fare le -e* do the cleaning

pullman *m inv* bus, *Br anche* coach

pullover *m inv* pullover

pullulare *~ di* be swarming with

pulpito *m* pulpit

pulsante *m* button; pulsazione *f* pulsation

pungere prick; *di ape* sting; pungiglione *m* sting

punibile punishable (*con* by); punire punish; punizione *f* punishment; SP (*calcio m di*) *~* free kick

punta *f* di spillo, coltello point; *di dita, lingua* tip; GEOG peak; *fig* touch, trace; puntare 1 *v/t* aim (*su* to); (*dirigere*) point (*verso* at); (*scommettere*) bet (*su* on); *fig ~ i piedi* dig one's heels in 2 *v/i*: *~ a* success aspire to; puntata *f* instalment, *Am* instalment; (*scommessa*) bet

punteggiatura *f* punctuation; punteggio *m* score

puntiglioso punctilious

puntina *f di giradischi* stylus; ~ **(da disegno)** drawing pin, *Am* thumbtack; **puntino** *m* dot; **a ~** perfectly; **punto 1** *pp* ~ **pungere 2** *m* point; MED, *(maglia)* stitch; ~ **di vista** point of view; ~ **cardinale** point of the compass; *fino a che ~ sei arrivato?* how far have you got?; *alle dieci in ~* at ten o'clock exactly *o* on the dot; ~ *(fermo)* full stop, *Am* period; *due -i* colon; ~ **e virgola** semi-colon; ~ **esclamativo** exclamation mark, *Am* exclamation point; ~ **interrogativo** question mark; *essere sul ~ di fare qc* be on the point of doing sth

puntuale punctual; **puntualità** *f* punctuality; **puntualizzare** make clear

puntura *f di ape* sting; *di ago* prick

punzecchiare prick; *fig (provocare)* tease

può, puoi ☞ **potere**

pupazzo *m* puppet; ~ **di neve** snowman

pupilla *f* pupil

purché provided

pure 1 *cong* even if; *(tuttavia)* (and) yet **2** *avv* too, as well; *pur di* in order to; *venga ~ avanti!* do come in!

purè *m inv* purée

purga *f* purge; **purgante** *m* laxative

puro pure

purtroppo unfortunately

pus *m* pus

pustola *f* pimple

puttana *f* P whore

puzza *f* stink; **puzzare** stink *(di* of); **puzzo** *m* stink; **puzzola** *f* ZO polecat; **puzzolente** stinking

p.v. (= *prossimo venturo*) next

Q

q (= *quintale*) 100 kilos

qua here; *passa di ~* come this way; *al di ~ di* on this side of

quaderno *m* exercise book

quadrante *m* quadrant; *di orologio* dial

quadrare *di conti* balance; *fig i conti non quadrano* there's something fishy going on; **quadrato** *m/agg*

square

quadrifoglio *m* four-leaf clover

quadro 1 *agg* square **2** *m* painting; picture; MAT square; *a -i* check *attr*, *Am* checkered; **quadruplo** *m/agg* quadruple

quaggiù down here

quaglia *f* quail

qualche a few; *(un certo)*

some; *interrogativo* any; **~ co-sa** something; **~ volta** sometime; *alcune volte* a few times; *a volte* sometimes; **in ~ luogo** somewhere; **in ~ modo** somehow

qualcosa something; *interrogativo* anything, something; *qualcos'altro* something else; **~ da mangiare** something to eat; **~ di bello** something beautiful

qualcuno someone, somebody; *in interrogazioni anche* anyone, anybody; **c'è ~?** is anybody there ?

quale 1 *agg* what; **~ libro vuoi?** which book do you want? **2** *pron:* **prendi un libro – ~?** take a book – which one?; **il / la ~** *persona* who, that; *cosa* which, that; **la persona della ~ stai parlando** the person you're talking about **3** *avv* as

qualifica *f* qualification; **qualificare** qualify; (*definire*) describe; **qualificarsi** give one's name (*come* as); *a esame*, *gara* qualify; **qualificato** qualified

qualità *f inv* quality; **di prima ~** top quality

qualora in the event that

qualsiasi any; *non importa quale* whatever; **~ persona** anyone; **~ cosa faccia** whatever I do

qualunque any; **uno ~** any one; **~ cosa** anything; **~ co-**

sa faccia whatever I do; **in ~ stagione** whatever the season

qualvolta: ogni ~ every time that

quando when; **da ~?** how long?; **~ vengo** when I come; *ogni volta che* whenever I come

quantità *f inv* quantity, amount; **quantitativo** *m* quantity, amount

quanto 1 *agg* how much; **con nomi plurali** how many; **tutti -i pl** every single one *sg;* **-i ne abbiamo oggi?** what is the date today? **2** *avv:* **~ dura ancora?** how long will it go on for?; **~ a me** as for me; **~ costa?** how much is it; **in ~** since, because; **per ~ ne sappia** as far as I know

quaranta forty

quarantena *f* quarantine

quarantenne1 *agg* forty or so **2** *m/f* person in his / her forties; **quarantesimo** fortieth

quaresima *f* Lent

quarta *f* AUTO fourth (gear)

quartiere *m* district; MIL quarters; **~ generale** headquarters

quarto 1 *agg* fourth **2** *m* fourth; (*quarta parte*) quarter; **~ d'ora** quarter of an hour

quarzo *m* quartz

quasi almost; **~ mai** hardly ever

quassù up here

quattordicesimo fourteenth; **quattordici** fourteen
quattrini *mpl* money
quattro four; *farsi in ~ per fare qc* go to a lot of trouble to do sth; **quattrocchi**: *a ~* in private; **quattrocento 1** *agg* four hundred **2** *m*: *il Quattrocento* the fifteenth century; **quattromila** four thousand

quegli, quei ☞ *quello*
quello 1 *agg* that, *pl* those **2** *pron* that (one), *pl* those (ones); *~ che* the one that; *tutto ~ che* all (that), everything (that)
quercia *f* oak
querela *f* legal action; *sporgere ~ contro qc* take legal action against s.o.
quesito *m* question
questi ☞ *questo*
questionario *m* questionnaire; **questione** *f* question; *è fuori ~* it is out of the question
questo 1 *agg* this, *pl* these **2** *pron* this (one), *pl* these (ones); *~ qui* this one here; *per ~* for that reason; *-a*

poi! well I'm blowed
questore *m* chief of police; **questura** *f* police headquarters
qui here; *~ vicino* near here; *passa di ~!* come this way!; *di ~ a un mese* a month from now
quiete *f* peace and quiet
quindi 1 *avv* then **2** *cong* therefore
quindicesimo fifteenth; **quindici** fifteen; **quindicina** *f: una ~* about fifteen; quinta *f* AUTO fifth (gear); TEA *le -e* the wings; **quintale** *m* hundred kilos; **quinto** fifth
quota *f* share, quota; (*altitudine*) altitude; quotare (*valutare*) value; FIN **quotate in borsa** listed *o* quoted on the Stock Exchange; **quotato** respected; **quotazione** *f di azioni* value, price; *~ d'acquisto* bid price; *~ di vendita* offer price
quotidianamente daily; **quotidiano 1** *agg* daily **2** *m* daily (newspaper)
quoziente *m*: *~ d'intelligenza* IQ

R

rabarbaro *m* rhubarb
rabbia *f* rage; (*stizza*) anger; MED rabies *sg*; *fare ~ a qu* make s.o. angry
rabbino *m* rabbi

rabbioso *gesto, sguardo* of rage; *cane* rabid
rabbrividire shudder; *per paura* shiver
raccapricciante appalling

raccattare (*tirar su*) pick up

racchetta *f* racquet; ~ **da sci** ski pole

raccogliere (*tirar su*) pick up; (*radunare*) gather; AGR harvest; raccoglitore *m* ring binder; ~ **del vetro** bottle bank; raccolgo → **raccogliere**; raccolta *f* collection; AGR harvest; **fare la ~ di francobolli** collect stamps; raccolto 1 *pp* → **raccogliere** 2 *m* harvest

raccomandabile: *un tipo poco* ~ a shady character; raccomandare 1 *v/t* recommend 2 *v/i*: ~ **a qu di fare qc** tell s.o. to do sth; raccomandata *f* recorded delivery (letter); *Am* certified mail; raccomandazione *f* recommendation

raccontare tell; racconto *m* story

raccordo *m* TEC connection; **strada** slip road, *Am* ramp; ~ **anulare** ring road, *Am* beltway

radar *m inv* radar

raddoppiare double; *sforzi* redouble

raddrizzare straighten

radere shave; *sfiorare* skim; ~ **al suolo** raze to the ground; radersi shave

radiare strike off

radiatore *m* radiator

radicale radical; *radice f* root; ~ **quadrata** square root

radio *f inv* radio; (*stazione*) ra-

dio station; radioascoltatore *m*, -trice *f* (radio) listener; radioattività *f* radioactivity; radioattivo radioactive; radiocronaca *f* (radio) commentary; radiofonico radio *attr*; radiografia *f* X-ray; radiosveglia *f* clock radio; radiotaxi *m inv* taxi, cab; radiotelefono *m* radio; radioterapia *f* radiation treatment; radiotrasmittente *f* apparecchio radio transmitter; *stazione* radio station

rado pettine wide-toothed; *alberi, capelli* sparse; *di* ~ seldom

radunare, radunarsi collect, gather; raduno *m* rally

rafano *m* horseradish

rafferno pane stale

raffica *f* gust; *di mitragliatrice* burst

raffigurare represent

raffinatezza *f* refinement; raffinato *fig* refined; raffineria *f* refinery

rafforzare strengthen

raffreddare cool; raffreddarsi cool down; MED catch cold; raffreddato: **essere** ~ have a cold; raffreddore *m* cold; ~ **da fieno** hay fever

rag. (= *ragioniere*) accountant

ragazza *f* girl; **la mia** ~ my girlfriend

ragazzo *m* boy; **il mio** ~ my boyfriend

raggio *m* ray; MAT radius; ~

d'azione range; *fig* duties; **-i** *pl* **X** X-rays

raggirare fool, take in; **raggiro** *m* trick

raggiungere *luogo* reach, get to; *persona* join; *scopo* achieve

raggomitolarsi curl up

raggrinzito wrinkled

ragionamento *m* reasoning; **ragionare** reason; **ragione** *f* reason; *(diritto)* right; **aver ~** be right; **dare ~ a qu** admit that s.o. is right; **ragioneria** *f* book-keeping; EDU *high school specializing in business studies*; **ragionevole** reasonable; **ragioniere** *m*, **-a** *f* accountant

ragnatela *f* spider's web; **ragno** *m* spider

ragù *m inv* meat sauce for pasta

rallegramenti *mpl* congratulations; **rallegrare** cheer up; **rallegrarsi** cheer up; **~ con qu di qc** congratulate s.o. on sth

rallentare slow down; **rallentatore**: **al ~** in slow motion

ramanzina *f* lecture

rame *m* copper

rammaricarsi be disappointed (**di** at)

rammendare darn

ramo *m* branch; **ramoscello** *m* twig

rampa *f* flight; **~ d'accesso** slip road, *Am* ramp; **rampicante 1** *agg* climbing; **pianta**

f ~ climber **2** *m* climber

rampone *m* crampon

rana *f* frog

rancore *m* rancour, *Am* rancor

randagio stray

rango *m* rank

rannicchiarsi huddle up

rannuvolarsi cloud over

ranocchio *m* frog

rapa *f* turnip

rapace 1 *m* bird of prey **2** *agg* *fig* predatory

rapida *f* rapids; **rapidità** *f* speed, rapidity; **rapido 1** *agg* quick, fast; *crescita, aumento* rapid **2** *m* *(treno)* **~** intercity train

rapimento *m* abduction, kidnapping

rapina *f* robbery; **rapinare** rob; **rapinatore** *m*, **-trice** *f* robber

rapire abduct, kidnap; **rapitore** *m*, **-trice** *f* abductor, kidnapper

rappacificazione *f* reconciliation

rapporto *m* *(resoconto)* report; *(relazione)* relationship; *(nesso)* connection; **in ~ a** in connection with

rappresentante *m/f* representative; **rappresentanza** *f* agency; **~ esclusiva** sole agency; **rappresentare** represent; TEA perform; **rappresentazione** *f* representation; TEA performance

rarità *f inv* rarity; **raro** rare

rasare shave; **rasatura** f shaving

raschiare scrape; *ruggine, sporco* scrape off; **raschiarsi: ~ la gola** clear one's throat

rasentare (*sfiorare*) scrape; fig (*avvicinarsi*) verge on; **~ il muro** hug the wall; **rasente: ~ a** very close to

rasoio m razor

rassegna f festival; *di pittura ecc* exhibition; **passare in ~** review; **rassegnarsi** resign o.s (**a** to)

rasserenarsi *di tempo* clear up

rassicurare reassure

rassomigliare: ~ a look like, resemble; **rassomigliarsi** look like o resemble each other

rastrellare rake; fig comb; **rastrelliera** f rack; **~ per biciclette** bike rack; **rastrello** m rake

rata f instalment, *Am* installment; **a~e** in instalments; **rateale: pagamento ~** payment in instalments o *Am* installments; **vendita f ~** hire purchase, *Am* installment plan

ratto m ZO rat

rattoppare patch; **rattoppo** m patch

rattrappito stiff

rattristare sadden; **rattristarsi** become sad

raucedine f hoarseness; **rau-**

co hoarse

ravanello m radish

ravioli mpl ravioli sg

ravvicinare come closer; (*riappacificare*) reconcile

ravvivare revive

razionale rational; **razionare** ration; **razione** f ration

razza f race; fig sort, kind; ZO breed

razzia f raid

razziale racial; **razzismo** m racism; **razzista** agg, m/f racist

razzo m rocket

re m inv king; MUS D

reagire react (**a** to)

reale (*vero*) real; (*regale*) royal; **realista** m/f realist

realizzabile feasible; **realizzare** realize; *progetto* carry out; **realizzarsi** *di sogno* come true; *di persona* find, find fulfilment o *Am* fulfillment

realmente really; **realtà** f inv reality; **in ~** in fact, actually

reato m (*criminale*) offence o *Am* offense

reattore m AVIA jet engine; *aereo* jet; **~ nucleare** nuclear reactor; **reazione** f reaction

recapitare deliver; **recapito** m delivery; (*indirizzo*) address; **~ telefonico** phone number

recarsi go

recensione f review; **recensire** review

recente recent; **recentemen-**

te recently
recintare enclose; **recinto** *m* enclosure; *steccato* fence
recipiente *m* container, recipient
reciproco mutual, reciprocal
recita *f* performance; **recitare 1** *v/t* recite; TEA play (the part of); *preghiera* say **2** *v/i* act
reclamare 1 *v/i* complain **2** *v/t* claim
réclame *f inv* advert; **reclamizzare** advertise
reclamo *m* complaint
reclusione *f* seclusion
record *m inv* record
recuperare ☞ **ricuperare**
redatto *pp* ☞ **redigere**; **redattore** *m*, **-trice** *f* editor; *di articolo* writer; **~ capo** editor-in-chief
reddito *m* income
redigere *testo*, *articolo* write; *lista* draw up
redini *fpl* reins
referendum *m inv* referendum
referenza *f* reference
referto *m* (official) report
refettorio *m* refectory
refurtiva *f* stolen property
regalare give; **regalino** *m* little gift *o* present; **regalo** *m* gift, present
regata *f* (boat) race
reggere 1 *v/t* (*sostenere*) support; (*tenere in mano*) hold; (*sopportare*) bear **2** *v/i di ragionamento* stand up; **reg-**

gersi stand
reggia *f* palace
reggipetto *m*, **reggiseno** *m* bra, *Am* brassiere
regia *f* production; *di film* direction
regime *m* régime; MED diet
regina *f* queen
regionale regional; **regione** *f* region
regista *m/f* director; TEA producer
registrare record; (*rilevare*) show, register; **registratore** *m*: **~** (**a cassetta**) cassette recorder; **registrazione** *f* recording; **registro** *m* register
regno *m* kingdom; *periodo* reign
regola *f* rule; **in ~** in order; **regolabile** adjustable; **regolamento** *m* regulation; **regolare 1** *v/t* regulate; *spese* cut down on; TEC adjust; *questione* sort out; *conto*, *debito* settle **2** *agg* regular
regredire regress
relativo relative (**a** to); (*corrispondente*) relevant; **relatore** *m*, **-trice** *f* speaker; **relazione** *f* relationship; (*esposizione*) report; **avere una ~ con qu** have a relationship with s.o.
religione *f* religion; **religiosa** *f* nun; **religioso 1** *agg* religious **2** *m* monk
relitto *m* wreck
remare row; **remo** *m* oar
remoto remote

remunerare pay; remunerazione f payment, remuneration

rendere (restituire) give back, return; (fruttare) yield; senso, idea render; ~ felice make happy; rendimento m di macchina, impiegato performance; rendita f income

rene m kidney

reparto m department

repentaglia: mettere a ~ risk, endanger

reperibile available; difficilmente ~ difficult to find; reperire find; reperto m find; DIR exhibit

replica f replica; TV, TEA repeat; (risposta) answer, reply; replicare repeat; (ribattere) reply, answer

reportage m inv report

repressopp ☞ reprimere; reprimere repress

repubblica f republic

reputare consider; reputarsi consider o.s.; reputazione f reputation

requisire requisition; requisito m requirement

resa f surrender; (restituzione) return; ~ dei conti settling of accounts

residence m inv block of service flats o Am apartments; residente resident; residenza f (official) address; (sede) seat; (soggiorno) stay; residenziale residential; zona f ~ residential area

residuo m remainder

resina f resin

resistente sturdy, strong; resistere al freddo ecc stand up to; (opporsi) resist

reso pp ☞ rendere

resoconto m report

respingere richiesta reject, turn down; nemico, attacco repel; respintopp ☞ respingere

respirare 1 v/t breathe (in) 2 v/i breathe; fig draw breath; respiratore m respirator; per apnea snorkel; respirazione f breathing; ~ artificiale artificial respiration; respiro m breathing; trattenere il ~ hold one's breath

responsabile responsible (di for); DIR liable (di for); responsabilità f inv responsibility; DIR liability

ressa f crowd

restare stay, remain; (avanzare) be left; ~ indietro stay behind; ~ perplesso / vedovo be puzzled / widowed

restaurare restore; restauro m restoration

restituire return; salute restore

resto m rest, remainder; (soldi) change; -i pl remains; del ~ anyway, besides

restringere narrow; vestito take in; restringersi di strada narrow; di stoffa shrink

rete f per pescare ecc net; SP goal; INFOR, TELEC, FERR

network

retina f ANAT retina

retribuire pay; **retribuzione** f payment

retroattivo retroactive

retrobottega m inv back shop

retrocedere retreat; fig lose ground

retrodatare backdate

retromarcia f AUTO reverse (gear)

retroscena mpl fig background

retrospettivo mostra retrospective

retroterra m inv hinterland

retrovisivo: specchietto m ~ rearview mirror

retta[1] f somma fee

retta[2] f MAT straight line

retta[3] f: dare ~ a qu listen to s.o.

rettangolare rectangular; **rettangolo** m rectangle

rettificare correct

rettile m reptile

rettilineo straight

rettore m rector

reumatismo m rheumatism

revisionare conti audit; automobile MOT; testo revise; **revisione** f di conti audit; di automobile MOT; di testo revision

revoca f repeal; **revocare** repeal

ri- re-

riabilitazione f rehabilitation

riacquistare get back, regain; casa buy back

riagganciare TELEC hang up

riallacciare refasten; TELEC reconnect

rialzare (alzare di nuovo) pick up; (aumentare) raise, increase; **rialzo** m rise, increase

rianimare speranze, entusiasmo revive; (rallegrare) cheer up; MED resuscitate; **rianimazione** f resuscitation; **centro** m **di** ~ intensive care unit

riapertura f reopening; **riaprire** reopen

riassumere re-employ; (riepilogare) summarize; **riassunto 1** pp → **riassumere 2** m summary

riavere get back, regain

ribaltabile folding; **ribaltare** overturn

ribassare 1 v/t lower 2 v/i fall, drop; **ribasso** m fall, drop; (sconto) discount

ribattere (replicare) answer back; (insistere) insist

ribellarsi rebel (a against); **ribelle 1** agg rebellious 2 m/f rebel; **ribellione** f rebellion

ribes m inv currant; ~ **nero** blackcurrant; ~ **rosso** redcurrant

ribrezzo m horror; **fare** ~ a disgust

ricadere fall; (cadere di nuovo) fall back; fig relapse; **ricaduta** f relapse

ricamare embroider

ricambiare change; (contrac-

cambiare) return, reciprocate; **ricambio** *m* change; (*sostituzione*) replacement; *pezzo* (spare) part

ricamo *m* embroidery

ricapitolare sum up, recapitulate

ricaricare *batteria* recharge

ricattare blackmail; **ricatto** *m* blackmail

ricavare derive; *denaro* get; **ricavato** *m di vendita* proceeds

ricchezza *f* wealth

riccio[1] *m* ZO hedgehog; **~ di mare** sea urchin

riccio[2] **1** *agg* curly **2** *m* curl

ricciolo *m* curl

ricco 1 *agg* rich; **~ di** rich in **2** *m*, **-a** *f* rich man / woman

ricerca *f* research; *di persona scomparsa, informazione* search (*di* for); EDU project; **alla ~ di** in search of; **ricercare** (*cercare di nuovo*) look again for; (*cercare con cura*) search for; **ricercato 1** *agg* oggetto, *artista* sought-after **2** *m* man wanted by the police

ricetta *f* prescription; GASTR recipe

ricevere receive; *di medico* see patients; **ricevimento** *m* receipt; *festa* reception; **ricevitore** *m* receiver; **ricevuta** *f* receipt

richiamare (*chiamare di nuovo*) call again; (*chiamare indietro*) call back; (*attirare*)

draw; *fig* (*rimproverare*) reprimand

richiedere ask for again; (*necessitare di*) take, require; *documento* apply for; **richiesta** *f* request (*di qc* for sth); **a** (*o* **su**) **~ di** at the request of; **richiesto** *pp* ☞ **richiedere**

riciclare recycle; **riciclabile** recyclable

ricompensa *f* reward; **ricompensare** reward (**qu di qc** s.o. for sth)

riconciliarsi be reconciled

riconoscente grateful; **riconoscenza** *f* gratitude; **riconoscere** recognise; **riconoscimento** *m* recognition

riconquistare reconquer

ricordare remember; (*menzionare*) mention; **~ qc a qu** remind s.o. of sth; **ricordarsi** remember (**di qc** sth; **di fare qc** to do sth); **ricordo** *m* memory; *oggetto* memento; **~ (di viaggio)** souvenir

ricorrenza *f* recurrence; *di evento* anniversary; **ricorrere** *di data, di festa* take place; **~ a qu** turn to s.o.; **~ a qc** have recourse to sth; **ricorso 1** *pp* ☞ **ricorrere 2** *m* DIR appeal; **avere ~ a** avvocato, *medico* see

ricostruire rebuild; *fig* reconstruct; **ricostruzione** *f* rebuilding; *fig* reconstruction

ricotta *f* ricotta, *soft cheese made from ewe's milk*

ricoverare admit; **ricovero** *m*

in ospedale admission; (*refugio*) shelter

ricreazione *f* recreation; *nelle scuole* break, *Am* recess

ricredersi change one's mind

ricuperare 1 *v/t* get back, recover; *libertà, fiducia* regain; *spazio* gain; *tempo* make up **2** *v/i* catch up; **ricupero** *m* recovery; ~ *del centro storico* development of the old town; ~ *di debiti* debt collection; EDU *corso m di* ~ remedial course; *materiale m di* ~ scrap; SP *partita f di* ~ scheduled match

ridare (*restituire*) give back, return; *fiducia, forze* restore

ridere laugh (*di* at)

ridicolo 1 *agg* ridiculous **2** *m* ridicule

ridimensionare downsize; *fig* get into perspective

ridotto 1 *pp* ☞ *ridurre* **2** *agg*: *a prezzi -i* at reduced prices; **riduco** ☞ *ridurre*; **ridurre** reduce (*a* to); *prezzi* reduce, cut; *personale* reduce, cut back; **ridursi** decrease; ~ *a fare qc* be reduced to doing sth; ~ *male* be in a bad way; ~ *in miseria* ruin o.s.; **riduzione** *f* reduction, cut

riempire fill (up); *formulario* fill in

rientrare come back; *a casa* come home; *questo non rientrava nei miei piani* that didn't come in to the plan; **rientro** *m* return; *al tuo* ~

when you get back

rifare do again; (*rinnovare*) do up; *stanza* tidy up; *letto* make; **rifarsi** rebuild; *casa* renovate; *guardaroba* replace; ~ *di qc* make up for sth

riferimento *m* reference; **riferire** report; **riferirsi**: ~ *a* refer to

rifiutare, rifiutarsi refuse; **rifiuto** *m* refusal; *-i pl* waste, refuse; (*spazzatura*) rubbish

riflessione *f anche* FIS reflection; **riflessivo** thoughtful; GRAM reflexive; **riflesso 1** *pp* ☞ *riflettere* **2** *m* reflection; (*gesto istintivo*) reflex (movement); **riflettere 1** *v/t* reflect **2** *v/i* think; ~ *su qc* think about sth, reflect on sth; **riflettersi** be reflected; **riflettore** *m* floodlight

riforma *f* reform; **riformare** (*rifare*) re-shape, re-form; (*cambiare*) reform; MIL declare unfit

rifornimento *m* AVIA refuelling, *Am* refueling; *-i pl* supplies; *fare* ~ *di cibo* stock up on food; *fare* ~ *di benzina* fill up; **rifornire** *macchina* fill up; *frigo* restock, fill up (*di* with); ~ *il magazzino* restock; **rifornirsi** stock up (*di* on)

rifugiarsi take refuge; **rifugiato** *m*, -a *f* refugee; **rifugio** *m* shelter; ~ *alpino* mountain hut

riga

riga f line; (*fila*) row; (*regolo*) rule; *in stoffa* stripe; *nei capelli* parting, Am part; *stoffa f a -ghe* striped fabric

rigatoni mpl rigatoni sg

rigenerare regenerate; **rigenerazione** f regeneration

rigetto m MED rejection; fig mental block

rigido (*duro*) rigid; *muscolo, articolazione* stiff; *clima* harsh; fig harsh

rigirare 1 v/i walk around **2** v/t turn over and over; *denaro* launder; **~** *il discorso* change the subject; **rigirarsi** turn around; *nel letto* toss and turn

rigoglioso lush, luxuriant

rigore m *di clima* harshness; (*severità*) strictness; SP (*calcio m di*) **~** penalty (kick); **rigoroso** rigorous

riguardare look at again; (*rivedere*) review, look at; (*riferirsi*) be about; *non ti riguarda* it doesn't concern you; **riguardarsi** take care of o.s.; *riguardo m* (*attenzione*) care; (*rispetto*) respect; **~** *a* as regards

rilasciare release; *documento* issue; **rilascio** m release; *di passaporto* issue

rilassare, rilassarsi relax; **rilassato** relaxed

rilegare *libro* bind

rilevare (*ricavare*) find; (*osservare*) notice; *ditta* buy up

rilievo m relief; fig **dare ~ a** *qc, mettere qc in* **~** emphasize o highlight sth

rima f rhyme; **far ~** rhyme

rimandare send again; (*restituire*) send back; *palla* return; (*rinviare*) postpone

rimanente 1 agg remaining **2** m rest, balance; (*avanzare*) be left (over); **rimanerci male** be hurt; **rimango** *☞* **rimanere**

rimarginare, rimarginarsi heal

rimasto pp *☞* **rimanere**

rimbalzare bounce

rimboccare *coperte* tuck in *piu*; **rimboccarsi le maniche** roll up one's sleeves

rimborsare reimburse, pay back; **rimborso** m reimbursement, repayment; **~** *spese* reimbursement of expenses

rimboschire reforest

rimediare 1 v/i: **~** *a* make up for, remedy **2** v/t find, scrape together; **rimedio** m remedy; MED medicine

rimescolare mix again; *più volte* mix thoroughly; *caffè* stir again

rimessa f *di auto* garage; *degli autobus* depot; SP **~** *laterale* throw-in

rimettere put back, return; (*affidare*) refer; (*vomitare*) bring up; **~** *a posto* put back; *ci ho rimesso molti soldi* I lost a lot of money; **rimetter-**

si *di tempo* improve; **~ da qc** get over sth

rimodernare modernize

rimorchiare AUTO tow (away); **rimorchiatore** *m* MAR tug; **rimorchio** *m* AUTO tow; *veicolo* trailer

rimorso *m* remorse

rimozione *f* removal

rimpatriare 1 *v/t* repatriate **2** *v/i* go home

rimpiangere regret (**di avere fatto qc** doing sth); *tempi passati, giovinezza* miss; **rimpianto 1** *pp* ☞ **rimpiangere 2** *m* regret

rimpiazzare replace

rimpicciolire 1 *v/t* make smaller **2** *v/i* become smaller, shrink

rimproverare scold; *impiegato* reprimand; **~ qc a qu** reproach s.o. for sth; **rimprovero** *m* scolding

rimuovere remove; (*muovere di nuovo*) move again

rinascere be born again; *di passione, speranza* be revived; *fig* **sentirsi ~** feel rejuvenated; **Rinascimento** *m* Renaissance

rincarare 1 *v/t* increase, put up; **~ la dose** make matters worse **2** *v/i* increase in price; **rincaro** *m* price increase

rincasare *venire* come home; *andare* go home

rinchiudere shut up; **rinchiudersi** shut o.s. up

rincorrere run after; **rincorsa**

f run-up; **rincorso** *pp* ☞ **rincorrere**

rincrescere: **mi rincresce** I'm sorry

rinfacciare: **~ qc a qu** cast sth up to s.o.

rinforzare strengthen; **rinforzo** *m* reinforcement; MIL **-i** *pl* reinforcements

rinfrescare cool down; **rinfrescarsi** freshen up; **rinfresco** *m* buffet (party)

rinfusa: alla ~ any which way, all higgledy-piggledy

ringhiare growl

ringhiera *f* railing

ringiovanire 1 *v/t* make feel younger; *di aspetto* make look younger **2** *v/i* feel younger; *di aspetto* look younger

ringraziamento: **un ~** a word of thanks; **i miei -i** *pl* my thanks; **ringraziare** thank (**di** for)

rinnovare renovate; *guardaroba* replace; *abbonamento* renew; (*ripetere*) renew, repeat; **rinnovarsi** be repeated; **rinnovo** *m* renovation; *di guardaroba* replacement; *di abbonamento* renewal; *di richiesta* repetition

rintracciare track down

rinuncia *f* renunciation (**a** of); **rinunciare** give up (**a** sth)

rinvenire 1 *v/t* recover; *resti* discover **2** *v/i* regain consciousness, come round

rinviare (*mandare indietro*) return; (*posticipare*) postpone; *a letteratura* refer; **rinvio** *m* return; *di riunione* postponement; *in un testo* cross-reference

rione *m* district

riordinare tidy up

riorganizzare reorganize

riparare 1 *v/t* (*proteggere*) protect (*da* from); (*aggiustare*) repair; *un torto* make up for **2** *v/i* escape; **ripararsi** *dalla pioggia* take shelter (*da* from); **riparato** sheltered; **riparazione** *f* repair; *fig di torto* putting right; **riparo** *m* shelter; **mettersi al ~** take shelter

ripartire 1 *v/i* leave again

ripartire² *v/t* divide up

ripassare 1 *v/i* ☞ **passare 2** *v/t col ferro* iron; *lezione* revise; *Am* review

ripensamento *m*: **avere un ~** have second thoughts; **ripensare**: **~ a qc** think about sth again; **ci ho ripensato** I've changed my mind

ripetere repeat; **ripetizione** *f* repetition; **dare -i a qu** tutor s.o.

ripido steep

ripiegare 1 *v/t* fold up again **2** *v/i* fall back; **ripiego** *m* makeshift (solution)

ripieno 1 *agg* full; GASTR stuffed **2** *m* stuffing

riporre put away; *speranze*

place

riportare take back; (*riferire*) report; *vittoria, successo* achieve; MAT carry over; *danni* sustain

riposarsi rest; **riposo** *m* rest

ripostiglio *m* boxroom, storeroom

riprendere take again; (*prendere indietro*) take back; *lavoro* go back to; FOT record; **~ a fare qc** start doing sth again; **riprendersi**: **~ da qc** get over sth; **ripresa** *f* resumption; *di vestito* alteration; *film* shot; AUTO acceleration; **a più -e** several times

riproduco ☞ **riprodurre**; **riprodurre** reproduce; **riprodursi** *di animali* breed, reproduce; *di situazione* happen again; **riproduzione** *f* reproduction; **~ vietata** copyright

riprovare 1 *v/t* feel again; *vestito* try on again **2** *v/i* try again

ripugnante disgusting, repugnant; **ripugnare**: **~ a qu** disgust s.o.

ripulire clean again; (*rimettere in ordine*) tidy (up)

risa *fpl* laughter

risalire 1 *v/t scale* go back up **2** *v/i* (*rincarare*) go back up; **~ a** go back to; **risalita** *f* ascent; **impianti** *mpl di* **~** ski lifts

risaltare stand out; **risalto**:

mettere in ~, dare ~ a highlight

risanamento *m* redevelopment; FIN improvement

risarcimento *m* compensation; **risarcire** *persona* compensate (*di* for); *danno* compensate for

risata *f* laugh

riscaldamento *m* heating; ~ *della temperatura terrestre* global warming

riscaldare heat *o* warm up; **riscaldarsi** warm o.s.

rischiararsi clear (up); *di cielo* clear (up); ~ *in volto* cheer up

rischiare 1 *v/t* risk **2** *v/i*: ~ *di sbagliare* risk making a mistake; **rischio** *m* risk; **rischioso** risky

riscontrare (*confrontare*) compare; (*controllare*) check; (*incontrare*) come up against; *errori* come across

riscuotere FIN *soldi* draw; *assegno* cash; *fig* earn

risentimento *m* resentment; **risentire 1** *v/t* hear again **2** *v/i* feel the effects; **risentirsi** TELEC talk again; (*offendersi*) take offence *o* Am offense

riserva *f* reserve; *fig* reservation; AUTO *essere in ~* be running out of fuel; *fare ~ di* stock up on; **riservare** keep; (*prenotare*) book, reserve; **riservarsi** reserve; *mi riservo di non accettare*

I reserve the right not to accept; **riservato** reserved; (*confidenziale*) confidential

risiedere be resident, reside

riso[1] **1** *pp* ☞ *ridere* **2** *m* laughing

riso[2] *m* rice

risolto *pp* ☞ *risolvere*; **risoluto** determined; **risoluzione** *f* resolution; (*soluzione*) solution; *di contratto* cancellation; *prendere una ~* make a decision; **risolvere** solve; (*decidere*) resolve; **risolversi** be solved; (*decidersi*) decide, resolve; ~ *in nulla* come to nothing

risorgere rise; *fig*: *di industria ecc* experience a rebirth; **Risorgimento** *m* Risorgimento, *the reunification of Italy*

risorsa *f* resource

risotto *m* risotto

risparmiare save; *fig* spare; **risparmio** *m* saving; ~ *-i pl* savings

rispettare respect; *legge, contratto* abide by; **rispettivo** respective; **rispetto 1** *m* respect **2** *prp*: ~ *a* (*confronto a*) compared with; (*in relazione a*) as regards

risplendere shine, glitter

rispondere answer (*a* sth), reply (*a* to); (*reagire*) respond; *saluto* acknowledge; ~ *di qc* be accountable for sth (*a* to); **risposta** *f* answer, reply; (*reazione*) response

rissa *f* brawl

ristabilire *ordine* restore; *regolamento* re-introduce; **ristabilirsi** recover

ristampa *f* reprint

ristorante *m* restaurant

ristretta caffè *m inv* ∼ very strong coffee

ristrutturare restructure; **ristrutturazione** *f* restructuring

risultare result; (*rivelarsi*) turn out; **risultato** *m* result

risurrezione *f* REL Resurrection

risvegliare, risvegliarsi *fig* reawaken

ritardare 1 *v/t* delay **2** *v/i* be late; *di orologio* be slow; **ritardatario** *m*, **-a** *f* latecomer; **ritardo** *m* delay; **essere in** ∼ be late

ritenere (*credere*) believe; **ritenersi si ritiene molto intelligente** he thinks he is very intelligent; **ritenuta** *f* deduction (*su* from)

ritirare withdraw, pull back; (*tirare di nuovo*) throw again; *proposta* withdraw; (*prelevare*) collect; **ritirarsi** (*restringersi*) shrink; ∼ **da gara, esame ecc** withdraw from; **ritiro** *m* withdrawal

ritmo *m* rhythm

rito *m* ceremony

ritoccare touch up

ritornare *venire* get back, come back, return; *andare* go back, return; *su argomento* go back (**su** over); ∼ **verde**

turn green again

ritornello *m* refrain

ritorno *m* return; **essere di** ∼ be back

ritrarre pull away; PITT paint

ritrattare retract

ritratto *m* portrait

ritrovare find; (*riacquistare*) regain; **ritrovarsi** meet again; (*capitare*) find o.s.; (*orientarsi*) get one's bearings; **ritrovo** *m* meeting; *luogo* meeting place

riunione *f* meeting; *di amici, famiglia* reunion; **riunire** gather; **riunirsi** meet

riuscire succeed; (*essere capace*) manage; **non riesco a capire** I can't understand; ∼ **in qc** be successful in sth; **riuscita** *f* success; **riuscito** successful

riutilizzare re-use

riva *f* shore

rivale *m*/*f*, *agg* rival *attr*; **rivalità** *f inv* rivalry

rivalutare revalue; *persona* change one's mind about

rivedere see again; (*ripassare*) review, look at again; (*verificare*) check

rivelare reveal

rivendere resell

rivendicare demand

rivendita *f negozio* retail outlet; **rivenditore** *m*, **-trice** *f* retailer; ∼ **specializzato** dealer

rivestimento *m* covering; **rivestire** (*foderare*) cover; *ruo-*

rotella

lo play; *carica* fill

rivincita *f* return game; **prendersi la ~** get one's revenge

rivista *f* magazine; TEA revue; MIL review

rivolgere turn; *domanda* address (**a qu** to s.o.); **~ la parola a qu** speak to s.o., address s.o; **rivolgersi: ~ a qu** apply to s.o. (**per** for)

rivolta *f* revolt; **rivoltare** turn; (*mettere sottosopra*) turn upside down; (*disgustare*) revolt; **rivoltella** *f* revolver; **rivoluzione** *f* revolution

rizzare put up; *bandiera* raise; *orecchie* prick up; **rizzarsi** straighten up; **mi si sono rizzati i capelli in testa** my hair stood on end

roba *f* things, stuff; **~ da matti!** would you believe it!

robot *m inv* robot; *da cucina* food processor

robusto sturdy

rocca *f* fortress

roccia *f* rock; **roccioso** rocky

rock *m inv* MUS rock

roco hoarse

rodaggio *m* running in; *fig* **sono ancora in ~** I'm still finding my feet

rodere gnaw at; **rodersi: ~ dalla gelosia** be eaten up with jealousy; **roditore** *m* rodent

rogna *f* F *di cane* mange; *problema* hassle

rognone *m di animale* kidney

Roma *f* Rome

Romania *f* Romania

romanico Romanesque; **romano 1** *agg* Roman **2** *m*, **-a** *f* Roman

romantico 1 *agg* romantic **2** *m*, **-a** *f* romantic

romanzo 1 *agg* Romance **2** *m* novel; **~ giallo** thriller

rombo[1] *m* rumble

rombo[2] *m* MAT rhombus

romeno 1 *agg* Romanian **2** *m*, **-a** *f* Romanian

rompere 1 *v/t* break; F **~ le scatole a qu** get on s.o.'s nerves F **2** *v/i* F be a pain F; **rompersi** break; **~ un braccio** break one's arm

rompicapo *m inv* puzzle; (*problema*) headache

rondine *f* swallow

ronzare buzz; **ronzio** *m* buzzing

rosa 1 *f* rose **2** *m/agg inv* pink; **rosario** *m* REL rosary; **rosato** *m* rosé; **rosmarino** *f* rosemary

rosolare brown

rosolia *f* German measles *sg*

rosone *m* ARCHI rose window

rospo *m* toad

rossetto *m* lipstick

rosso 1 *agg* red **2** *m* red; **~ d'uovo** egg yolk; **passare col ~** go through a red light

rosticceria *f* rotisserie (*shop selling roast meat*)

rotaia *f* rail

rotatoria *f* roundabout, *Am* traffic circle

rotella *f* castor

rotolare roll; **rotolarsi** roll (around); **rotolino** m FOT film; **rotolo** m roll; FOT film; *andare a -i* go to rack and ruin

rotondo round

rotta f MAR, AVIA course

rottame m wreck

rotto 1 pp ☞ **rompere 2** agg broken; **rottura** f breaking; F *tra innamorati* break-up; F *che ∼!* what a pain! F

rotula f kneecap

roulotte f inv caravan, Am trailer

routine f routine

rovesciare *liquidi* spill; *oggetto* knock over; (*capovolgere*) overturn; **rovesciarsi** overturn, capsize; **rovescio** reverse; *in tennis* backhand; *mettersi una maglia al ∼* put a sweater on inside out

rovina f ruin; *andare in ∼* go to rack and ruin; **rovinare** ruin; **rovinarsi** ruin o.s.

rovo m bramble

rozzo rough

ruba: *andare a ∼* sell like hot cakes; **rubare** steal

rubinetto m tap, Am faucet

rubino m ruby

rubrica f *di libro* table of contents; *quaderno* address book; *di giornale* column; TV report

rudere m ruin

rudimentale rudimentary

ruga f wrinkle, line

ruggine f rust

ruggire roar

rugiada f dew

rullino m FOT film; **rullo** m roll

rum m rum

rumore m noise; **rumoroso** noisy

ruolo m role

ruota f wheel; *∼ di scorta* spare wheel

rupe f cliff

rupestre rock attr; *arte* f *∼* wall painting

ruscello m stream

russare snore

Russia f Russia; **russo 1** agg Russian **2** m, *-a* f Russian

rustico rural, rustic; fig unsophisticated

ruttare belch; **rutto** m belch

ruvido rough

ruzzolare fall; **ruzzolone** m fall; *fare un ∼* fall

S

S. (= **santo**) St (= Saint)

sa ☞ **sapere**

sabato m Saturday

sabbia f sand; **sabbioso** sandy

sabotaggio m sabotage; **sabotare** sabotage

sacca f bag; ANAT, BIO sac

saccheggiare sack; **spir** raid

sacchetto m bag; **sacco** m sack; fig **F un ~ di** piles of F; **costa un ~** it costs a fortune; **~ a pelo** sleeping bag; **saccopelista** m/f backpacker

sacerdote m priest

sacramento m sacrament

sacrificare sacrifice; **sacrificarsi** sacrifice o.s.; **sacrificio** m sacrifice

sacro sacred

sadico 1 agg sadistic **2** m, -a f sadist

safari m inv safari

saggio[1] **1** agg wise **2** m wise man, sage

saggio[2] m test; (campione) sample; scritto essay; (di danza, musica end of term show

Sagittario m ASTR Sagittarius

sahariana f safari jacket

sala f room; (soggiorno) living room; **~ da pranzo** dining room; **~ giochi** amusement arcade; **~ operatoria** (operating) theatre, Am operating room

salame m salami

salamoia f: **in ~** in brine

salariale agg attr; **salario** m salary, wages

salatino m savoury, Am savory; **salato** savoury, Am savory; **acqua** salt; **cibo** salted; F (caro) steep F; **troppo ~** salty

saldare weld; **ossa** set; **fattura** pay; **saldo 1** agg steady, secure **2** m payment; **in svendita** sale item; (resto) balance; **-i** pl **di fine stagione** end-of-season sales

sale m salt

salgo ☞ **salire**

salice m willow; **~ piangente** weeping willow

saliera f salt cellar; **salina** f salt works

salire 1 v/i climb; di livello, prezzi, temperatura rise; **~ in macchina** get in; **~ su** scala climb; treno, autobus get on **2** v/t scale climb; **salita** f climb; strada slope; **strada f in ~** steep street

saliva f saliva

salma f corpse, body

salmastro 1 agg briny **2** m salt

salmone m salmon; **~ affumicato** smoked salmon

salone m living room; (esposi-

zione) show
salotto *m* lounge
salpare sail
salsa *f* sauce; ~ *di pomodoro* tomato sauce
salsiccia *f* sausage
saltare 1 *v/t* jump; (*omettere*) skip; ~ (*in padella*) sauté **2** *v/i* jump; *di bottone* come off; *di fusibile* blow; F *di impegno* be cancelled *o Am* canceled; ~ *fuori* turn up
saltellare hop
salto *m* jump; (*dislivello*) change in level; ~ *in alto* high jump; ~ *in lungo* long jump, *Am* broad jump; *faccio un* ~ *da te* I'll drop in
saltuariamente occasionally; **saltuario** occasional
salumeria *f* shop that sells '*salumi*'; **salumi** *mpl* cold meat
salutare 1 *agg* healthy **2** *v/t* say hello to, greet; **salute** *f* health; ~*!* cheers!; **saluto** *m* wave; *tanti* -*i* greetings
salvagente *m inv* lifebelt; (*giubbotto*) life jacket; *per bambini* ring; (*isola spartitraffico*) traffic island; **salvaguardare** protect, safeguard; **salvaguardia** *f* protection; **salvare** save, rescue; **salvataggio** *m* salvage; *barca f di* ~ lifeboat; **salve!** hello!; **salvezza** *f* salvation
salvia *f* sage
salvietta *f* napkin
salvo 1 *agg* safe **2** *prp* except;

~ *che* unless; ~ *imprevisti* all being well **3** *m*: *mettersi in* ~ take shelter
San = *Santo*
sandalo *m* sandal; BOT sandalwood
sangue *m* blood; *a* ~ *freddo* in cold blood; GASTR *al* ~ rare; **sanguigno: *gruppo*** *m* ~ blood group; **sanguinare** bleed; **sanguinoso** bloody; **sanguisuga** *f* leech
sanità *f* health; *amministrazione* health care; **sanitario** health *attr*; **assistenza** *f* -*a* health care
sanno ☞ *sapere*
sano healthy; ~ *e salvo* safe and sound
santo 1 *agg* holy **2** *m*, -*a f* saint; *davanti al nome* St
santuario *m* sanctuary
sanzione *f* sanction
sapere 1 *v/t* know; (*essere capace di*) be able to; (*venire a*) ~ hear; *sai nuotare?* can you swim? *lo so* I know **2** *v/i*: *far* ~ *qc a qu* let s.o. know sth; ~ *di* (*avere sapore di*) taste of **3** *m* knowledge
sapone *m* soap; **saponetta** *f* toilet soap
sapore *m* taste; -*i pl* aromatic herbs; **saporito** tasty
saracinesca *f* roller shutter
sarcastico sarcastic
sarcofago *m* sarcophagus
Sardegna *f* Sardinia
sardina *f* sardine
sardo 1 *agg* Sardinian **2** *m*, -*a*

f Sardinian

sarò ► *essere*

sarto *m*, **-a** *f* tailor; *per donne* dressmaker; **sartoria** *f* tailor's; *per donne* dressmaker's

sasso *m* stone

sassofono *m* saxophone

satellite *m* satellite

satira *f* satire; **satirico** satirical

saturo saturated

sauna *f* sauna

sazietà *f*: **mangiare a ~** eat one's fill; **sazio** full (up)

sbadato absent-minded

sbadigliare yawn; **sbadiglio** *m* yawn

sbagliare 1 *v/i e* **sbagliarsi** make a mistake **2** *v/t* make a mistake in; TELEC **sbagliare ~** dial the wrong number; **~ strada** go the wrong way; **sbagliato** wrong; **sbaglio** *m* mistake; **per ~** by mistake

sbalordire amaze; **sbalorditivo** amazing

sbalzare throw; **sbalzo** *m* jump; **~ di temperatura** sudden change in temperature

sbandare AUTO skid; FERR, *fig* go off the rails; **sbandata** *f* AUTO skid; F **prendersi una ~ per qu** get a crush on s.o.

sbarazzare clear; **sbarazzarsi**: **~ di** get rid of

sbarcare 1 *v/t merci* unload; *persone* disembark **2** *v/i* disembark; **sbarco** *m di merci* unloading; *di persone* disembarkation

sbarra *f* bar

sbarramento *m* fence; (*ostacolo*) barrier; **sbarrare** bar; *assegno* cross; *occhi* open wide; **sbarrato** *assegno* crossed; *occhi* wide open

sbattere 1 *v/t porta* slam, bang; (*urtare*) bang; GASTR beat **2** *v/i* bang

sberla *f* F slap

sbiadire fade; **sbiadito** faded

sbilanciarsi lose one's balance; *fig* commit o.s.

sbizzarrirsi indulge o.s.

sbloccare clear; *macchina* unblock; *prezzi* deregulate

sboccare: **~ in** *di fiume* flow into; *di strada* lead to

sbocciare open (out)

sbocco *m di situazione* way out

sbornia *f* F: **prendersi una ~** get drunk

sborsare F cough up F

sbottonare unbutton; **sbottonarsi**: **~ la giacca** unbutton one's jacket

sbraitare shout, yell

sbranare tear apart

sbriciolarsi crumble

sbrigare attend to; **sbrigarsi** hurry up; **sbrigativo** (*rapido*) hurried, rushed; (*brusco*) brusque

sbrinare *frigorifero* defrost; **sbrinatore** *m* defrost control

sbrogliare untangle; **sbrogliarsela** sort things out

sbronza *f* F hangover; **sbronzarsi** F get drunk; **sbronzo** F tight F

sbucare emerge; **da dove sei sbucato?** where did you spring from?

sbucciare *frutta, patate* peel; **sbucciarsi le ginocchia** skin one's knees; **sbucciatura** *f* graze

scabroso rough, uneven; *fig* offensive

scacchiera *f* chessboard

scacciare chase away

scacco *m* (chess) piece; **-cchi** *pl* chess; **a -cchi** checked, *Am* checkered

scadente 1 ☞ **scadere** 2 *agg* second-rate; **scadenza** *f* deadline; **su** *alimento* best before date; **scadere di passaporto** expire; **di cambiale** fall due; (*perdere valore*) decline (in quality); **scaduto** expired; *alimento* past its sell-by date

scaffale *m* shelves

scaglia *f* flake; *di legno* chip; *di pesce* scale

scagliare hurl; **scagliarsi: ∼ contro** attack

scala *f* staircase; GEOG, MUS scale; **∼ (a pioli)** ladder; **∼ mobile** escalator; *disegno m in* ∼ scale drawing; **fare le -e** climb the stairs; **scalare** climb; **scalata** *f* climb; **∼ al successo** rise to fame; **scalatore** *m*, **-trice** *f* climber

scaldabagno *m* water heater; **scaldare** heat (up); **scaldarsi** warm up; *fig* get worked up

scalinata *f* steps; **scalino** *m* step

scalo *m* AVIA stop; MAR port of call; **fare ∼ a** call at

scalogna *f* bad luck; **portare ∼** be unlucky; **scalognato** unlucky

scaloppina *f* escalope

scalpello *m* chisel

scalzo barefoot

scambiare (*confondere*) mistake (**per** for); (*barattare*) exchange, swap F (**con** with); **scambio** *m* exchange; *di persona* mistake; FERR points; **-i** *pl* **commerciali** trade

scampagnata *f* day out in the country

scampanellata *f* ring

scampi *mpl* scampi

scampo *m* escape, way out

scampolo *m* remnant

scandagliare sound; *fig* sound out

scandalistico scandal-mongering; **scandalizzare** scandalize; **scandalizzarsi** be scandalized (**di** by); **scandalizzato** scandalized; **scandalo** *m* scandal; **scandaloso** scandalous

scandinavo 1 *agg* Scandinavian 2 *m*, **-a** *f* Scandinavian

scanner *m inv* INFOR scanner; **scannerizzare** INFOR scan

scansare (*allontanare*) move;

(*evitare*) avoid; **scansarsi** move out of the way

scansione f scan

scantinato m cellar

scapito: *a ~ di* to the detriment of

scapola f shoulder blade, ANAT scapula

scapolo 1 agg single, unmarried **2** m bachelor

scappamento m TEC exhaust

scappare (*fuggire*) run away; (*affrettarsi*) rush, run

scappatella f di bambino escapade; *fare delle -lle* get into mischief

scappatoia f way out

scarabocchiare scribble; **scarabocchio** m scribble

scarafaggio m cockroach

scaraventare throw, hurl; **scaraventarsi** throw o hurl o.s. (*contro* at)

scarcerare release; **scarcerazione** f release

scarica f discharge; **scaricamento** m INFOR download; **scaricare** unload; *batteria* run down; *responsabilità nocive* dump; *responsabilità* offload; INFOR download; **scaricarsi** di batteria run down; **scarico 1** agg camion empty; *batteria* run-down **2** m di merci unloading; *luogo* dump; *divieto di ~* no dumping

scarlattina f scarlet fever

scarpa f shoe

scarpata f (*burrone*) escarp-

ment

scarpinata f trek

scarpone m (heavy) boot; ~ *da sci* ski boot

scarseggiare become scarce; *~ di qc* be short of sth; **scarso** scarce, in short supply; *quattro chilometri -si* barely four kilometres

scartare (*svolgere*) unwrap; (*eliminare*) reject; **scarto** m rejection; (*cosa scartata*) reject

scassare F ruin, wreck; **scassarsi** F give up the ghost F; **scassato** F done for F

scassinare force open; **scasso** m forced entry; *furto m con ~* breaking and entering

scatenare fig unleash; **scatenarsi** di tempesta break; di collera break out; di persona let one's hair down

scatola f box; di tonno, piselli can, Br anche tin; *in ~ cibo* canned, Br anche tinned

scattare 1 v/t FOT take **2** v/i go off; di serratura catch; (*arrabbiarsi*) lose one's temper; di atleta put on a spurt; **scatto** m click; SP spurt; FOT exposure; di foto taking; TELEC unit; *uno ~ di rabbia* an angry gesture

scavalcare muro climb (over)

scavare con pala dig; con trivella excavate; **scavi** mpl archeologici dig

scegliere choose, select;

scelgo ☞ **scegliere**; **scelta** f choice, selection; **di prima ~** first-rate; **scelto1** pp ☞ **scegliere** 2 agg handpicked; **merce, pubblico** selected

scemo agg stupid, idiotic 2 m, -a f idiot

scena theatre, Am theater; (scenata) scene; **scenata** f scene

scendere 1 v/i andare go down, descend; venire come down, descend; da cavallo get down, dismount; dal treno, dall'autobus get off; dalla macchina get out; di temperatura, prezzi go down, drop 2 v/t: ~ **le scale** andare go down the stairs; venire come down the stairs

sceneggiatura f screenplay

scenografo m, -a f set designer

scettico agg sceptical, Am skeptical 2 m, -a f sceptic, Am skeptic

scheda f card; (formulario) form; ~ **telefonica** phonecard; **schedario** m file; **schedina** f pools coupon

scheggia f sliver

scheletro m skeleton

schema m diagram; (abbozzo) outline; **schematico** general; disegno schematic

scherma f fencing

schermo m screen; (riparo) shield; ~ **piatto** flat screen; ~ **a contatto** touchscreen

scherzare play; (burlare)

joke; **scherzo** m joke; **-i a parte** joking aside; **per ~** fare, dire qc as a joke

schiaccianoci m inv nutcrackers; **schiacciare** 1 v/t crush; **noce** crack 2 v/i SP smash the ball; **schiacciato** crushed, squashed

schiaffeggiare slap; **schiaffo** m slap

schiamazzo m yell, scream

schiantare, **schiantarsi** crash

schiarire lighten; **schiarirsi** brighten up; **schiarita** f bright spell

schiavitù f slavery; **schiavo1** agg: **essere ~ di** be a slave to 2 m, -a f slave

schiena f back; **mal m di ~** back ache; **schienale** m di sedile back

schiera f group; **a ~** in ranks; **schierarsi ~ in favore di qu** come out in favour o Am favor of s.o.

schietto pure; fig frank

schifezza **che ~!** how disgusting!; **schifo** m disgust; **fare ~ a qu** disgust s.o.; **schifoso** disgusting; (pessimo) dreadful

schiuma f foam; ~ **da bagno** bubble bath; ~ **da barba** shaving foam

schivare avoid, dodge F; **schivo** shy

schizzare 1 v/t (spruzzare) squirt; (abbozzare) sketch 2 v/i squirt; (saltare) jump

scollatura

schizzinoso fussy

schizzo *m* squirt; *(abbozzo)* (lightning) sketch

sci *m inv* ski; *attività* skiing; ~ **acquatico** water ski / skiing; ~ **di fondo** cross-country ski / skiing

sciacquare rinse

sciagura *f* disaster; **sciagurato** unfortunate

scialle *m* shawl

scialuppa *f* dinghy; ~ **di salvataggio** lifeboat

sciame *m* swarm

sciare ski

sciarpa *f* scarf

sciatica *f* sciatica

sciatore *m*, **-trice** *f* skier

sciatto untidy, sloppy

scientifico scientific; **scienza** *f* science; **scienziato** *m*, **-a** *f* scientist

scimmia *f* monkey; **scimmiottare** ape

scimpanzè *m inv* chimpanzee, chimp F

scintilla *f* spark; **scintillante** sparkling; **scintillare** sparkle

sciocchezza *f (idiozia)* stupidity; **sciocco 1** *agg* silly **2** *m*, **-a** *f* silly thing

sciogliere untie; *capelli* let down; *neve* melt; *dubbio*, *problema* clear up; **sciogliersi** *di corda*, *nodo* come undone; *di burro*, *neve* melt; **scioglilingua** *m inv* tongue-twister

scioltezza *f* nimbleness; *fisica*

agility

sciolto 1 *pp* ☞ **sciogliere 2** *agg ghiaccio* melted

scioperare strike; **sciopero** *m* strike; **fare** ~ go on strike

sciovia *f* ski-lift

scippatore *m*, **-trice** *f* bag-snatcher; **scippo** *m* bag-snatching

sciocco *m* sirocco

sciroppo *m* syrup

scissione *f* splitting

sciupare *(logorare)* wear out; *salute* ruin; *tempo*, *denaro* waste; **sciupato** *persona* drawn; *cosa* worn out

scivolare slide; *(cadere)* slip; **scivolo** *m* slide; *gioco* chute; **scivoloso** slippery

sclerosi *f inv* MED sclerosis; ~ **multipla** multiple sclerosis, MS

scocciare F bother, hassle F; **scocciatore** F *m*, **-trice** *f* pest F, nuisance; **scocciatura** F *f* nuisance

scodella *f* bowl

scogliera *f* cliff; **scoglio** *m* rock

scoiattolo *m* squirrel

scolapasta *m inv* colander; **scolare** drain

scolaro *m*, **-a** *f* schoolboy; *ragazza* schoolgirl; **scolastico** school *attr*

scoliosi *f inv* curvature of the spine

scollato low-necked; *donna* wearing a low neckline; **scollatura** *f* neck(line)

scollo *m* neck

scolo *m* drainage

scolorire, scolorirsi fade; **scolorito** faded

scolpire *statua* sculpt; *legno* carve; *fig* engrave

scommessa *f* bet; **scommesso** *pp* ☞ **scommettere**; **scommettere** bet

scomodare disturb; **scomodarsi** put o.s. out; **non si scomodi** please don't go to any bother; **scomodo** uncomfortable; *(non pratico)* inconvenient

scomparire disappear; **scomparsa** *f* disappearance; **scomparso** *pp* ☞ **scomparire**

scompartimento *m* compartment

scompigliare *persona* ruffle the hair of; *capelli* ruffle; **scompiglio** *m* confusion

scomporre break down; **scomporsi**: **senza~** without showing any emotion

sconcertante disconcerting

sconcio indecent; *parola* filthy

sconclusionato incoherent

sconfiggere defeat

sconfinato vast, boundless

sconfitta *f* defeat; **sconfitto** *pp* ☞ **sconfiggere**

sconforto *m* discouragement

scongelare thaw

scongiurare beg; *pericolo* avert

sconosciuto 1 *agg* unknown

2 *m*, **-a** *f* stranger

sconsigliare advise against; **~ qc a qu** advise s.o. against sth

scontare FIN deduct, discount; *pena* serve; **scontato** discounted; *(previsto)* expected; **~ del 30%** with a 30% discount

scontento 1 *agg* unhappy, not satisfied *(di* with) **2** *m* unhappiness, dissatisfaction

sconto *m* discount

scontrarsi collide *(con* with); *fig* clash *(con* with)

scontrino *m* receipt

scontro *m* AUTO collision; *fig* clash; **scontroso** unpleasant, disagreeable

sconvolgente upsetting, distressing; *di un'intelligenza~* incredibly intelligent; **sconvolgere** upset; **sconvolto 1** *pp* ☞ **sconvolgere 2** *agg paese* in upheaval

scopa *f* broom; **scopare** sweep; P shag P

scoperchiare *pentola* take the lid off

scoperta *f* discovery; **scoperto 1** *pp* ☞ **scoprire 2** *agg*: **assegno** *m* **~** dud cheque **3** *m*: **allo ~** in the open

scopo *m* aim, purpose; **allo ~ di fare qc** in order to do sth

scoppiare *di bomba* explode; *di palloncino, pneumatico* burst; **~ in lacrime** burst into tears; **~ a ridere** burst out laughing; **scoppio** *m* explo-

sion; *di palloncino* bursting;
fig outbreak

scoprire *contenitore* take the
lid off; (*denudare*) uncover;
piani, verità discover

scoraggiare   discourage;
scoraggiarsi become discouraged, lose heart; **scoraggiato** discouraged

scorciatoia *f* short cut

scordare, scordarsi *di* forget; **scordato** MUS out of
tune

scoreggia *f* F fart F; **scoreggiare** F fart F

scorgere see, make out

scoria *f* waste

scorpione *m* scorpion; ASTR
Scorpione Scorpio

scorrere 1 *v/i* flow, run; *di
tempo* go past, pass 2 *v/t giornale* skim

scorretto (*errato*) incorrect;
(*non onesto*) unfair

scorrevole sliding; *stile*
flowing

scorso 1 *pp* ☞ **scorrere** 2
agg: **l'anno** ~ last year

scorta *f* escort; (*provvista*)
supply; **scortare** escort

scortese rude, discourteous;
scortesia *f* rudeness

scorto *pp* ☞ **scorgere**

scorza *f* peel; *fig* exterior

scossa *f* shake; ~ **di terremoto** (earth) tremor; ~ **elettrica**
electric shock; **scosso** *pp* ☞
scuotere

scostare move away (**da**
from); **scostarsi** move

(aside)

scottare 1 *v/t* burn; GASTR
verdure blanch 2 *v/i* burn;
scotta! it's hot!; **scottato**
verdure blanched; **scottatu-
ra** *f* burn

Scozia *f* Scotland; **scozzese**
1 *agg* Scottish 2 *m/f* Scot

screditare discredit

scremato skimmed

screpolare,   screpolarsi
crack; **screpolatura** *f* crack

scricchiolare creak; **scric-
chiolio** *m* creak

scritta *f* inscription; **scritto** 1
pp ☞ **scrivere** 2 *m* writing;
scrittore *m*, **-trice** *f* writer;
scrittura *f* writing; REL
scripture

scrivania *f* desk; **scrivere**
write; (*annotare*) write down;
come si scrive ... ? how do
you spell ... ?

scroccare F scrounge F

scrollare shake; ~ **le spalle**
shrug (one's shoulders)

scrosciare *di pioggia* fall in
torrents

scrupolo *m* scruple; **scrupo-
losità** *f* scrupulousness;
scrupoloso scrupulous

scrutare look at intently; *ori-
zonte* scan

scrutinio *m* POL counting;
EDU *teachers' meeting to discuss pupils' performance*

scucire unpick; F **scuci i soldi!** cough up! F; **scucirsi**
come apart at the seams

scuderia *f* stable

scudetto *m* SP championship; **scudo** *m* shield

sculacciare spank

scultore *m*, **-trice** *f* sculptor; **scultura** *f* sculpture

scuola *f* school; **~ media** secondary school; **~ superiore** high school; **~ guida** driving school; **andare a ~** go to school

scuotere shake

scure *f* axe, *Am* ax

scurire darken; **scuro** dark

scusa *f* excuse; **chiedere ~** apologize; **scusare** forgive; *(giustificare)* excuse; **mi scusi** I'm sorry; **scusi, scusa** excuse me; **scusarsi** apologize

sdebitarsi pay one's debts

sdegno *m* moral indignation

sdentato toothless

sdoganare clear through customs

sdolcinato sloppy

sdraiarsi lie down; **sdraiato** lying down; **sdraio** *m*: *(sedia f a)* **~** deck chair

sé oneself; *lui* himself; *lei* herself; *loro* themselves; *esso, essa* itself; *da* **~** (by) himself / herself / themselves

se[1] *cong* if; **~ mai** if need be; **~ mai arrivasse ...** should he arrive ...; **come ~** as if; **~ no** if not now

se[2] *pron* = **si** in front of *lo, la, li, le, ne*

sebbene even though

secca *f* shallows

seccante *fig* annoying; **seccare 1** *v/t* dry; *fig* annoy **2** *v/i* dry; **seccarsi** dry; *fig* get annoyed; **seccatore** *m*, **-trice** *f* nuisance, pest F; **seccatura** *f* nuisance

secchio *m* bucket

secco dry; *fiori, pomodori* dried; *tono* curt

secolo *m* century

seconda *f* AUTO second (gear); FERR second class; EDU second year; **secondario** secondary; **secondo 1** *agg* second; **di -a mano** second-hand; **~ fine** ulterior motive **2** *prp* according to; **~ me** in my opinion **3** *m* second; GASTR main course

sedano *m* celery

sedare calm (down); **sedativo** *m* sedative

sede *f* headquarters

sedentario sedentary; **sedere 1** *m* F rear end F **2** *v/i e* **sedersi** sit down; **sedia** *f* chair; **~ a dondolo** rocking chair; **~ a rotelle** wheelchair

sedicesimo sixteenth; **sedici** sixteen

sedile *m* seat

seducente attractive; **sedurre** seduce; *(attrarre)* attract

seduta *f* session; **seduto** seated

seduzione *f* seduction

sega *f* saw

segale *f* rye

segare saw; **segatura** *f* sawdust

seggio m seat; ~ **(elettorale)** polling station; **seggiola** f chair; **seggiolino** m di bicicletta child's seat; **seggiolone** m high chair; **seggiovia** f chair lift

segnalare signal; (annunciare) report; **segnale** m signal; (segno) sign; ~ **d'allarme** alarm; **segnaletica** f signs; **segnalibro** m bookmark; **segnare** (marcare) mark; (annotare) note down; SP score; **segno** m sign; (traccia) mark, trace; (cenno) gesture, sign

segretaria f secretary; **segretario** m secretary; **segreteria** f carica secretaryship; ufficio administrative office; attività secretarial duties; ~ **telefonica** answering machine, voicemail

segreto m/agg secret

seguace m/f disciple, follower; **seguente** next, following; **seguire** 1 v/t follow; corso take 2 v/i follow (**a qc** sth); **seguito** m persone retinue; (sostenitori) followers; di film sequel; **di** ~ one after the other, in succession; **in** ~ after that

sei[1] → **essere**

sei[2] six

seicento 1 agg six hundred 2 m: **il Seicento** the seventeenth century

selciato m paving

selezione f selection

self-service m inv self-service (café)

sella f saddle; **sellino** m saddle

seltz m: **acqua f di** ~ soda (water)

selvaggina f game; **selvaggio** 1 agg animale, fiori wild; tribù, omicidio savage 2 m, -a f savage; **selvatico** wild

semaforo m traffic lights

sembrare seem; (assomigliare a) look like

seme m seed

semestre m six months; EDU term, Am semester

semicerchio m semi-circle; **semicircolare** semi-circular

semifinale f semi-final

semifreddo m soft ice cream

seminare sow

seminario m seminar

seminudo half-naked

seminuovo practically new

semolino m semolina

semplice simple; (non doppio) single; (spontaneo) natural; **semplicità** f simplicity; **semplificare** simplify

sempre always; **per** ~ for ever; ~ **più** more and more; ~ **più vecchio** older and older; **piove** ~ **di più** the rain's getting heavier and heavier; ~ **che** as long as

senape f mustard

senato m senate; **senatore** m, -trice f senator

senno m common sense; **uscire di** ~ lose one's mind;

(*arrabbiarsi*) lose control
seno *m* breast
sensato sensible
sensazionale sensational;
sensazione *f* sensation,
feeling; (*impressione*) feeling; **fare ~** cause a sensation
sensibile sensitive; (*evidente*)
significant; **sensibilità** *f* sensitivity; **sensibilizzare** make
more aware (**a** of)
senso *m* sense; (*significato*)
meaning; (*direzione*) direction; **buon ~** common sense;
~ unico one way; **~ vietato**
no entry; **in ~ orario** clockwise; **perdere i -i** faint; **sensore** *m* TEC sensor
sensuale sensual
sentenza *f* DIR verdict
sentiero *m* path
sentimentale sentimental;
sentimento *m* feeling, sentiment
sentire feel; (*udire*) hear;
(*ascoltare*) listen to; *odore*
smell; *cibo* taste; **sentirsi**
feel; **sentirsela di fare qc**
feel up to doing sth
senza without; **senz'altro**
definitely; **~ di me** without
me; **~ ridere** without laughing; **senzatetto** *m/f inv*
homeless person; **i -i** *pl* the
homeless *pl*
separare separate; **separarsi**
separate, split up F; **separazione** *f* separation
sepolto *pp* ☞ **seppellire**; **sepoltura** *f* burial; **seppellire**

bury
seppia *f* cuttlefish
seppure even if
sequestrare confiscate; DIR
impound, seize; (*rapire*)
kidnap; **sequestro** *m* kid-
nap(ping); DIR impounding,
seizure
sera *f* evening; **di ~** in the eve-
nings; **serale** evening *attr*;
serata *f* evening; **festa** party
serbatoio *m* tank
Serbia *f* Serbia
serbo[1] **1** *agg* Serbian **2** *m*, -a *f*
Serb
serbo[2] *m*: **avere qc in ~** have
sth in store
serenata *f* serenade
sereno serene; *fig* relaxed,
calm
sericoltura *f* silk-worm farming
serie *f inv* series *sg*
serietà *f* seriousness; **serio 1**
agg serious; (*affidabile*) reliable **2** *m*: **sul ~** seriously
serpe *f* grass snake; **serpente**
m snake
serra *f* greenhouse
serramanico *m*: **coltello** *m* **a**
~ flick knife, *Am* switch-
blade
serranda *f* shutter; **serrare**
close; *denti, pugni* clench;
serratura *f* lock
servire 1 *v/i* be useful; **non mi**
serve I don't need it; **a che**
serve questo? what's this
for? **2** *v/t* serve; **~ da bere**
a qu pour s.o. a drink; **ser-**

virsi (*usare*) use (**di** sth); **prego, si serva!** a tavola please help yourself!

servizio m service; (*favore*) favour, Am favor; (*dipartimento*) department; *in giornale* feature (story); **~ militare** military service; **~ da tavola** dinner service; **fuori ~** out of order; **in ~** on duty; **-zi** pl (*igienici*) toilets, Am rest room

servofreno m servo brake; **servosterzo** m power steering

sesamo m sesame

sessanta sixty; **sessantenne** sixty-year-old; **sessantesimo** sixtieth; **sessantina** f: **una ~** about sixty (**di** sth)

sesso m sex; **sessuale** sexual

sesto sixth

seta f silk

sete f thirst; **aver ~** be thirsty

setta f sect

settanta seventy; **settantenne** seventy-year-old; **settantesimo** seventieth; **settantina** f: **una ~** about seventy (**di** sth)

settare macchina, computer set up

sette seven; **settecento 1** agg seven hundred **2** m: **il Settecento** the eighteenth century

settembre m September

settentrionale 1 agg northern **2** m/f northerner; **settentrione** m north

setticemia f septicaemia, Am septicemia

settimana f week; **~ santa** Easter week, Holy week; **settimanale** m/agg weekly

settimo seventh

settore m sector

severo severe

sezione f section

sfaccendata f backbreaking job

sfacciato cheeky, Am fresh

sfamare feed

sfarzo m splendour, Am splendor

sfarzoso magnificent

sfasciare smash; **sfasciarsi** smash

sfavore m disadvantage; **sfavorevole** unfavourable, Am unfavorable

sfera f sphere

sfida f challenge; **sfidare** challenge

sfiducia f distrust

sfigurare 1 v/t disfigure **2** v/i look out of place; **sfigurato** disfigured

sfilare 1 v/t unthread; (*togliere*) take off **2** v/i parade; **sfilata** f: **~ di moda** fashion show

sfinimento m exhaustion; **sfinito** exhausted

sfiorare brush; *argomento* touch on

sfitto empty, not rented

sfocato foto blurred, out of focus

sfociare flow

sfogare *rabbia, frustrazione* vent, get rid of (**con, su** on); **sfogarsi** vent one's feelings; **~ con qu** confide in s.o.

sfoglia *pasta f* **~** puff pastry; **sfogliare** *libro* leaf through

sfogo *m* outlet; MED rash

sfoltire thin

sfondare break; *porta* break down; *pavimento* break through

sfondo *m* background

sformare stretch out of shape; **sformato** *m* GASTR soufflé

sfortuna *f* bad luck, misfortune; **sfortunatamente** unfortunately; **sfortunato** unlucky, unfortunate

sforzare strain; **sforzarsi** try very hard; **sforzo** *m* effort; *fisico* strain; **fare uno ~** make an effort

sfrattare evict; **sfratto** *m* eviction

sfregare rub

sfruttamento *m* exploitation; **sfruttare** exploit

sfuggire (*scampare*) escape (**a** from); **mi è sfuggito di mente** it slipped my mind; **sfuggita di ~** in passing

sfumatura *f* nuance; *di colore* shade

sfuriata *f* (angry) tirade

sfuso loose; *vino* in bulk

sgabello *m* stool

sgabuzzino *m* cupboard

sgambetto *m*: **fare lo ~ a qu** trip s.o. up

sganciare unhook; F *soldi* fork out F; **sganciarsi** come unhooked

sgarbato rude

sgobbare slave; **sgobbone** *m, -a f* F swot F

sgocciolare drip

sgomberare ☞ **sgombrare**; **sgombrare** *strada, stanza* clear; *ostacolo* remove

sgombro¹ *agg strada, stanza* empty

sgombro² *m* mackerel

sgomentarsi be frightened

sgonfiare 1 *v/t* let the air out of **2** *v/i e* **sgonfiarsi** become deflated; **il braccio si è sgonfiato** the swelling in the arm has gone down; **sgonfio** flat; MED not swollen

sgradevole unpleasant

sgradito unwelcome

sgranchire, sgranchirsi ~ le gambe stretch one's legs

sgraziato awkward

sgridare scold, tell off F

sguaiato raucous

sguardo *m* look; (*occhiata*) glance

sguazzare splash about; *fig* F **~ nei soldi** be rolling in it F

sgusciare 1 *v/t* shell **2** *v/i* slip away; **mi è sgusciato di mano** it slipped out of my hand

shampoo *m inv* shampoo

shock *m inv* shock

sì yes; **dire di ~** say yes; **penso di ~** I think so

si[1] *pron* oneself; *lui* himself; *lei* herself; *esso, essa* itself; *loro* themselves; *reciproco* each other; **spazzolarsi i capelli** brush one's hair; **~ dice** they say; **cosa ~ può dire?** what can one say?, what can I say?

si[2] *m* MUS B

sia ~ ... ~ ... both ... and ...; (*o l'uno o l'altro*) either ... or ...; **~ che ... ~ che ...** whether ... or whether ...

siamo ☞ **essere**

sibilare hiss; *di vento* whistle

sicario *m* hired killer, hit man F

sicché (and) so

siccità *f inv* drought

siccome since

Sicilia *f* Sicily; **siciliano 1** *agg* Sicilian **2** *m, -a f* Sicilian

sicura *f* safety catch

sicurezza *f* security; (*protezione*) safety; (*certezza*) certainty; **sicuro 1** *agg* safe; (*certo*) sure; **~ di sé** sure of o.s.; **di ~** definitely **2** *m*: **mettere al ~** put in a safe place

sidro *m* cider

siedo ☞ **sedere**

siepe *f* hedge

siero *m* MED serum; **sieropositivo** HIV positive

siesta *f* siesta

siete ☞ **essere**

sig. (= **signore**) Mr (= mister)

sigaretta *f* cigarette; **sigaro** *m* cigar

sigg. (= **signori**) Messrs

sigillare seal; **sigillo** *m* seal

sigla *f* initials *pl*; *musicale* theme (tune)

sig.na (= **signorina**) Miss, Ms

significare mean; **significato** *m* meaning

signora *f* lady; **mi scusi, ~!** excuse me!; **la ~ Rossi** Mrs Rossi; **-e e signori** ladies and gentlemen

signore *m* gentleman; **mi scusi, ~!** excuse me!; **il signor Rossi** Mr Rossi; **i -i Rossi** Mr and Mrs Rossi

signorina *f* young lady; **la ~ Rossi** Miss Rossi

sig.ra (= **signora**) Mrs

silenziatore *m* silencer, *Am* muffler

silenzio *m* silence; **silenzioso** silent

sillaba *f* syllable

siluro *m* MAR torpedo

simboleggiare symbolize; **simbolico** symbolic; **simbolismo** *m* symbolism; **simbolo** *m* symbol

simile similar

simmetria *f* symmetry; **simmetrico** symmetrical

simpatia *f* liking; (*affinità*) sympathy; **simpatico** likeable; **simpatizzare** become friends

simulare feign; TEC simulate; **simulazione** *f* pretence, *Am* pretense; TEC simulation

sinagoga *f* synagogue

sinceramente sincerely; (*in verità*) honestly; **sincerità** *f* sincerity; **sincero** sincere

sindacalista *m/f* trade unionist, *Am* labor unionist; **sindacato** *m* trade union; *Am* labor union

sindaco *m* mayor

sinfonia *f* symphony; **sinfonico** symphonic

singhiozzare sob; **singhiozzo** *m*: **avere il ~** have hiccups; **-zi** *pl* sobs

single *m/f inv* single

singolare 1 *agg* singular; (*insolito*) unusual; (*strano*) strange **2** *m* singular; SP singles; **singolo 1** *agg* individual; *camera, letto* single **2** *m* individual; SP singles

sinistra *f* left; **a ~** on the left; *andare* to the left; **sinistro 1** *agg* left, left-hand; *fig* sinister **2** *m* accident

sino ☞ *fino*

sinonimo 1 *agg* synonymous **2** *m* synonym

sintesi *f inv* synthesis; (*riassunto*) summary; **sintetico** synthetic; (*riassunto*) brief; **sintetizzare** synthesize; (*riassumere*) summarize

sintomo *m* symptom

sintonia *f* RAD tuning; *fig* **essere in ~** be on the same wavelength (**con** as); **sintonizzare** RAD tune; **sintonizzarsi** tune in (**su** to)

sinusite *f* sinusitis

sipario *m* curtain

sirena *f* siren; *mitologica* mermaid; **~ d'allarme** alarm

siringa *f* MED syringe

sismico seismic

sistema *m* system; **sistemare** put; (*mettere in ordine*) arrange; *casa* do up; **sistemarsi** tidy o.s. up; (*trovare casa, sposarsi*) settle down; **sistemazione** *f* place; (*lavoro*) job; *in albergo* accommodation, *Am* accommodations

sito site; **in ~** on the premises

situato: **essere ~** be situated; **situazione** *f* situation

sito web *m* website

slacciare undo

slalom *m* slalom

slanciato slender

slancio *m* impulse

slavo 1 *agg* Slav, Slavonic **2** *m*, **-a** *f* Slav

sleale disloyal

slegare untie

slip *m inv* underpants, *Am* briefs; *da donna* panties

slitta *f* sledge

slittino *m* sled; SP bobsleigh

slogan *m inv* slogan

slogare dislocate; **slogarsi**: **~ una caviglia** sprain one's ankle; **slogatura** *f* sprain

sloggiare move out

Slovacchia *f* Slovakia; **slovacco1** *agg* Slovak(ian) **2** *m*, **-a** *f* Slovak(ian)

Slovenia *f* Slovenia; **sloveno 1** *agg* Slovene **2** *m*, **-a** *f* Slovene

smacchiare take the stains out of; **smacchiatore** *m* stain remover

smagliatura *f* ladder, *Am* run; MED stretch mark

smaltire dispose of

smalto *m* enamel; *per ceramiche* glaze; ~ *per unghie* nail varnish

smantellare dismantle

smarrimento *m* loss; **smarrire** lose; **smarrirsi** get lost; **smarrito 1** *pp* ☞ **smarrire 2** *agg* lost

smascherare unmask

smemorato forgetful

smentire prove to be wrong; **smentita** *f* denial

smeraldo *m/agg* emerald

smesso *pp* ☞ **smettere**; **smettere 1** *v/t* stop; *abiti* stop wearing **2** *v/i* stop (*di fare qc* doing sth)

smilitarizzare demilitarize

sminuire *problema* downplay; *persona* belittle

smisurato boundless

smontabile which can be taken apart, *Am* knockdown; **smontare 1** *v/i da cavallo* dismount **2** *v/t* dismantle

smorfia *f* grimace; **smorfioso** affected

smorzare *colore* tone down; *luce* dim; *entusiasmo* dampen

SMS *m inv* text, text message; *mandare un ~ a qc* text s.o., send s.o. a text

smuovere shift, move

snello slim, slender

snervante irritating

snob 1 *agg* snobbish **2** *m/f inv* snob

SO (= *sud-ovest*) SW (= southwest)

so ☞ *sapere*

sobborgo *m* suburb

sobrio sober

Soc. (= *società*) Co (= company); soc. (= society)

socchiudere half-close; **socchiuso 1** *pp* ☞ **socchiudere 2** *agg* half-closed; *porta* ajar

soccorrere help; **soccorritore** *m* rescue worker; **soccorso 1** *pp* ☞ **soccorrere 2** *m* rescue; *pronto* ~ first aid; ~ *stradale* breakdown service, *Am* wrecking service

sociale social; **socialismo** *m* socialism; **socialista** *agg*, *m/f* socialist; **socializzare** socialize

società *f inv* company; (*associazione*) society; ~ *per azioni* joint stock company

socievole sociable

socio *m*, **-a** *f* member; FIN partner

soddisfacente satisfying; **soddisfare** satisfy; **soddisfatto 1** *pp* ☞ **soddisfare 2** *agg* satisfied; *essere* ~ *di qu* be satisfied with s.o.; **soddisfazione** *f* satisfaction

sodo *uovo* hard-boiled

sofà *m inv* sofa

sofferenza *f* suffering

soffermarsi dwell (*su* on)

sofferto *pp* ☞ **soffrire**

soffiare blow; F swipe; **soffiarsi**: ~ *il naso* blow one's

nose
soffice soft
soffio *m* puff
soffitta *f* attic
soffitto *m* ceiling
soffocante suffocating; **sof-focare** suffocate
soffriggere fry gently
soffrire 1 *v/t* suffer; *persone* bear, stand **2** *v/i* suffer (*di* from)
soffritto *pp* ☞ **soffriggere**
sofisticato sophisticated
software *m inv* software
soggettivo subjective; **sog-getto 1** *agg* subject; *essere* ~ *a qc* suffer from sth **2** *m* GRAM subject; **soggezione** *f* subjection
soggiornare stay; **soggiorno** *m* stay
soglia *f* threshold
sogliola *f* sole
sognare, sognarsi dream (*di* about, of); **sognatore** *m*, **-trice** *f* dreamer; **sogno** *m* dream
soia *f* soya
sol *m inv* MUS G
solaio *m* attic, loft
solamente only
solare solar
solco *m* furrow
soldato *m* soldier
soldi *mpl* money
sole *m* sun; *c'è il* ~ it's sunny; *prendere il* ~ sunbathe; **so-leggiato** sun-dried
solenne solemn
solere: ~ *fare* be in the habit

of doing
soletta *f* insole
solidale *fig* in agreement; **so-lidarietà** *f* solidarity
solido solid; (*robusto*) sturdy
solista *m/f* soloist
solitario 1 *agg* solitary; *luogo* lonely **2** *m* solitaire; *gioco* patience, *Am* solitaire
solito 1 *agg* usual, same **2** *m di* ~ usually; *come al* ~ as usual
solitudine *f* solitude
sollecitare (*stimolare*) urge; *risposta* ask for
solletico *m* tickling; *fare il* ~ *a qu* tickle s.o.; *soffrire il* ~ be ticklish
sollevamento *m* lifting; (*in-surrezione*) rising; ~ *pesi* weightlifting; **sollevare** lift; *obiezione* bring up; **sollevar-si** *di popolo* rise up; AVIA climb
sollievo *m* relief
solo 1 *agg* lonely; (*non accom-pagnato*) alone; (*unico*) only; MUS solo; *da* ~ by myself / yourself etc, on my / your etc own **2** *avv* only **3** *m* MUS solo
solstizio *m* solstice
soltanto only
solubile soluble; **soluzione** *f* solution; **solvente 1** *agg* FIN solvent **2** *m* CHIM solvent
somigliante similar; **somi-glianza** *f* resemblance; **so-migliare**: ~ *a qu* resemble s.o.

somma *f* (*addizione*) addition; (*risultato*) sum; (*importo*) amount, sum; **sommare** add; **sommario 1** *agg* summary; **2** *m* summary; *di libro* table of contents; **sommato: tutto ~** all things considered

sommergere submerge; *fig* overwhelm (*di* with); **sommergibile** *m* submarine; **sommerso** *pp* ☞ *sommergere*

somministrare MED administer

sommossa *f* uprising

sondaggio *m*: **~ (d'opinione)** (opinion) poll

sondare sound; *fig* test

sonnambulo *m*, **-a** *f* sleepwalker; **sonnecchiare** doze; **sonnifero** *m* sleeping pill; **sonno** *m* sleep; **aver ~** be sleepy; **sonnolenza** *f* drowsiness

sono ☞ *essere*

sonoro sound *attr*, *risa*, *applausi* loud; **colonna** *f* **-a** sound-track

sontuoso sumptuous

soppesare weigh; *fig* weigh up

sopportabile bearable, tolerable; **sopportare** *peso* bear; *fig* bear, stand F

soppressione *f* deletion; *di regola* abolition; **soppresso** *pp* ☞ *sopprimere*; **sopprimere** delete; *regola* abolish

sopra 1 *prp* on; (*più in alto di*) above; **l'uno ~ l'altro** one on top of the other; **i bambini ~ cinque anni** children over five; **al di ~ di qc** over sth **2** *avv* on top; (*al piano superiore*) upstairs; *vedi* **~** see above

soprabito *m* (over)coat

sopracciglio *m* eyebrow

sopraccoperta *f di letto* bedspread; *di libro* dustjacket

sopraffare overwhelm

sopraggiungere *di persona* turn up; *di difficoltà* come up

sopralluogo *m* inspection (of the site)

soprammobile *m* ornament

soprannaturale supernatural

soprannome *m* nickname

soprannumero: in ~ overcrowded

soprano *m soprano*; **mezzo ~** mezzo(-soprano)

soprappensiero ☞ *sovrapensiero*

soprattassa *f* surcharge

soprattutto particularly, above all

sopravvalutare overvalue; *fig* overestimate

sopravvento *m*: **avere** *o* **prendere il ~** have the upper hand

sopravvissuto 1 *agg* surviving **2** *m*, **-a** *f* survivor; **sopravvivenza** *f* survival; **sopravvivere** survive, outlive (**a qu** s.o.)

soprintendente *m/f* supervisor

sopruso *m* abuse of power

soqquadro *m*: **mettere a ~** turn upside down

sorbetto *m* sorbet

sorbirsi put up with

sordina *f* mute; **in ~** in secret, on the quiet

sordità *f* deafness; **sordo** deaf; **sordomuto** deaf and dumb

sorella *f* sister; **sorellastra** *f* stepsister

sorgente *f* spring; *fig* source; **sorgere** *di sole* rise, come up; *fig* arise, come up

sorpassare go past; AUTO pass, *Br anche* overtake; *fig* exceed; **sorpassato** out of date; **sorpasso** *m*: **fare un ~** pass, *Br anche* overtake

sorprendente surprising; **sorprendere** surprise; (*cogliere sul fatto*) catch; **sorpresa** *f* surprise; **sorpreso** *pp* ☞ **sorprendere**

sorridere smile; **sorriso 1** *pp* ☞ **sorridere 2** *m* smile

sorseggiare sip

sorso *m* mouthful

sorta *f* sort, kind

sorte *f* fate; **tirare a ~** draw lots; **sorteggiare** draw

sorto *pp* ☞ **sorgere**

sorveglianza *f* supervision; *di edificio* security; **sorvegliare** supervise; *bagagli ecc* look after

sorvolare 1 *v/t* AVIA fly over **2** *v/i fig*: **~ su** skim over; (*omettere*) skip

sosia *m inv* double

sospendere suspend; (*appendere*) hang; **sospensione** *f* suspension; **sospeso 1** *pp* ☞ **sospendere 2** *agg* hanging; *fig*: *questione* pending; **tenere in ~** *persona* keep in suspense

sospettare suspect; **~ qu** o **di qu** suspect s.o.; **sospetto 1** *agg* suspicious **2** *m*, **-a** *f* suspect; **sospettoso** suspicious

sospirare 1 *v/i* sigh **2** *v/t* long for; **sospiro** *m* sigh

sosta *f* stop; (*pausa*) break, pause; **divieto di ~** no parking

sostantivo *m* noun

sostanza *f* substance

sostare stop

sostegno *m* support

sostenere support; (*affermare*) maintain; **sostengo** ☞ **sostenere**; **sostenitore** *m*, **-trice** *f* supporter

sostituibile replaceable; **sostituire**: **~ X con Y** replace X with Y, substitute Y for X; **sostituto** *m*, **-a** *f* substitute, replacement; **sostituzione** *f* substitution, replacement

sottaceti *mpl* pickles

sottana *f* slip, underskirt; (*gonna*) skirt; REL cassock

sotterraneo 1 *agg* underground **2** *m* cellar

sotterrare bury

sottile fine; *fig* subtle; *udito* keen

sottintendere imply; **sottinteso** 1 *pp* ☞ **sottintendere** 2 *m* allusion

sotto 1 *prp* under; **5 gradi ~ zero** 5 degrees below (zero); **al di ~ di qc** under sth 2 *avv* below; *(più in basso)* lower down; *(al di sotto)* underneath; *(al piano di ~)* downstairs

sottobanco under the counter

sottobraccio: camminare ~ walk arm-in-arm; **prendere qu ~** take s.o.'s arm

sottocchio: tenere ~ qc keep an eye on sth

sottoesposto FOT underexposed

sottofondo *m* background

sottolineare *anche fig* underline

sottomarino 1 *agg* underwater *attr* 2 *m* submarine

sottomesso 1 *pp* ☞ **sottomettere** 2 *agg* submissive; *popolo* subject *attr*; **sottomettere** submit; *popolo* subdue

sottopassaggio *m* underpass

sottoporre submit; **sottoporsi: ~ a** undergo

sottoscritto 1 *pp* ☞ **sottoscrivere** 2 *m* undersigned; **sottoscrivere** *documento* sign; *teoria* subscribe to; *abbonamento* take out; **sottoscrizione** *f* signing; *(abbonamento)* subscription

sottosopra *fig* upside-down

sottosuolo *m* subsoil

sottosviluppato underdeveloped

sottovalutare undervalue; *persona* underestimate

sottoveste *f* slip, underskirt

sottovoce quietly, sotto voce

sottrarre MAT subtract; *denaro* embezzle; **sottrarsi: ~ a qc** avoid sth; **sottratto** *pp* ☞ **sottrarre**; **sottrazione** *f* MAT subtraction; *di denaro* embezzlement

souvenir *m inv* souvenir

sovrabbondante overabundant

sovraccarico 1 *agg* overloaded (**di** with) 2 *m* overload

sovrano 1 *agg* sovereign 2 *m*, **-a** *f* sovereign

sovrappensiero: essere ~ be lost in thought

sovrappeso 1 *agg* overweight 2 *m* excess weight

sovrappopolato overpopulated

sovrapporre overlap

sovrastare overlook, dominate

sovrintendente *m/f* ☞ **soprintendente**

sovrumano superhuman

sovvenzionare give a grant to; **sovvenzione** *f* grant

sovversivo subversive

S.P. (= **Strada Provinciale**) A road, *Am* highway

S.p.A. *f* (= **Società per Azio-**

nl) joint stock company

spaccare break in two; *legna* split, chop; **spaccarsi** break in two

spacciare *droga* deal in, push F; **spacciarsi: ~ per** pass o.s. off as; **spacciatore** *m*, **-trice** *f di droga* dealer; **spaccio** *m di droga* dealing; *negozio* general store

spacco *m in gonna* slit; *in giacca* vent; **spaccone** *m*, **-a** *f* braggart

spada *f* sword

spaesato disoriented, confused

spaghetti *mpl* spaghetti *sg*

Spagna *f* Spain; **spagnolo 1** *m/agg* Spanish **2** *m*, **-a** *f* Spaniard

spago *m* string

spalancare open wide

spalla *f* shoulder; *era di -e* he had his back to me

spalliera *f* wallbars

spallina *f* shoulder pad

spalmare spread

spalti *mpl* terraces

spandere spread; **spandersi** spread; **spanto** *pp* ☞ **spandere**

sparare 1 *v/i* shoot (*a* at) **2** *v/t:* ~ *un colpo* fire a shot; **sparatoria** *f* gunfire

sparecchiare clear

spareggio *m* SP play-off

spargere spread; *lacrime, sangue* shed

sparire disappear; **sparizione** *f* disappearance

sparo *m* (gun)shot

sparpagliare scatter

sparso 1 *pp* ☞ **spargere 2** *agg* scattered

spartire divide (up); split; **spartito** *m* score; **spartitraffico** *m* traffic island

spasimante *m/f* admirer

spasmo *m* MED spasm

spasso *m* fun; *andare a* ~ go for a walk; *è uno* ~ he / it's a good laugh; **spassoso** very funny

spavaldo cocky, over-confident

spaventapasseri *m inv* scarecrow; **spaventare** frighten, scare; **spaventarsi** be frightened, be scared; **spavento** *m* fright, scare; **spaventoso** frightening

spaziale space *attr*

spazientirsi get impatient

spazio *m* space; **spazioso** spacious

spazzaneve *m inv* snowplough, *Am* snowplow; **spazzare** sweep; **spazzatura** *f* rubbish, *Am* garbage; **spazzino** *m*, **-a** *f* street sweeper; **spazzola** *f* brush; **spazzolare** brush; **spazzolino** *m* brush; ~ *da denti* toothbrush

specchiarsi look at o.s.; *(riflettersi)* be mirrored; **specchietto** *m* mirror; *(prospetto)* table; AUTO ~ *retrovisore* rear-view mirror; **specchio** *m* mirror

speciale special; **specialista** *m/f* specialist; **specialità** *f inv* speciality, *Am* speciality; **specializzarsi** specialize; **specialmente** especially

specie 1 *f inv* species *sg*; **una ~ di** a sort *o* kind of **2** *avv* especially

specificare specify; **specifico** specific

speculatore *m*, **-trice** *f* speculator; **speculazione** *f* speculation

spedire send; **spedizione** *f* dispatch; *di merce* shipping; *(viaggio)* expedition; **spedizioniere** *m* courier

spegnere put out; *luce, motore, radio* turn off, switch off; **spegnersi** *di fuoco* go out; *di motore* stop

spellare skin; **spellarsi** peel

spendere spend; *fig* invest

spennare *pollo* pluck

spensierato carefree

spento *pp* ☞ **spegnere**

speranza *f* hope; **sperare 1** *v/t* hope for **2** *v/i* trust (**in** in)

sperduto lost; *luogo* isolated

sperimentare try; *in laboratorio* test; *fig: fatica, dolore* feel; *droga* experiment with

sperma *m* sperm

sperperare fritter away, squander

spesa *f* expense; **fare la ~** do the shopping; **fare -e** *o* **go shopping**; **a proprie -e** at one's own expense

spesso 1 *agg* thick **2** *avv* often, frequently; **spessore** *m* thickness

spett. (= **spettabile**) Messrs; *in lettera* **Spett. Ditta** Dear Sirs

spettacolare spectacular; **spettacolo** *m* show; *(panorama)* spectacle, sight; **~ teatrale** show

spettare: **questo spetta a te** this is yours; **non spetta a te giudicare** it's not up to you to judge

spettatore *m*, **-trice** *f* spectator; *TEA* member of the audience

spettinare: **~ qu** ruffle s.o.'s hair

spettro *m* ghost; *FIS* spectrum

spezie *fpl* spices

spezzare break in two; **spezzarsi** break; **spezzatino** *m* stew; **spezzato 1** *agg* broken (in two) **2** *m* co-ordinated two-piece suit; **spezzettare** break up

spia *f* spy; *TEC* pilot light; **fare la ~** tell, sneak

spiacente: **essere ~** be sorry; **spiacere**: **mi spiace** I am sorry

spiacevole unpleasant

spiaggia *f* beach

spiare spy on

spiazzo *m* empty space

spiccato strong

spicchio *m di frutto* section; **~ d'aglio** clove of garlic

spicciarsi hurry up

spiccioli *mpl* (small) change

spiedo *m* spit; **allo ~** spit-roasted

spiegare (*stendere*) spread; (*chiarire*) explain; **spiegarsi** explain what one means; **spiegazione** *f* explanation

spiegazzare crease

spietato pitiless

spiga *f di grano* ear; **spigato** herring-bone *attr*

spigliato confident

spigola *f* sea bass

spigolo *m* corner

spilla *f gioiello* brooch; **~ da balia** safety pin

spillo *m* pin

spina *f* BOT thorn; ZO spine; *di pesce* bone; EL plug; ANAT **~ dorsale** spine

spinaci *mpl* spinach

spinale spinal

spinello F *m* joint F

spingere push; *fig* drive

spinoso thorny

spinta *f* push

spinterogeno *m* AUTO distributor

spinto *pp* ☞ **spingere**

spionaggio *m* espionage

spiraglio *m* crack; *di luce, speranza* glimmer

spirale *f* spiral; *contraccettivo* coil

spirare blow; *fig* die

spirito *m* spirit; (*disposizione*) mind; (*umorismo*) wit; **spiritoso** witty; **spirituale** spiritual

splendente bright; **splendere** shine; **splendido** wonder-ful, splendid

spogliare undress; (*rubare*) rob; **spogliarello** *m* strip-tease; **spogliarsi** undress, strip; **spogliatoio** *m* dressing room, locker room; **spoglio** bare

spola *f:* **fare la ~ da un posto all'altro** shuttle backwards and forwards between two places

spolverare dust

sponda *f di letto* edge, side; *di fiume* bank; *nel biliardo* cushion

sponsor *m inv* sponsor; **sponsorizzare** sponsor

spontaneo spontaneous

sporadico sporadic

sporcare dirty; **sporcarsi** get dirty; **sporcizia** *f* dirt; **sporco 1** *agg* dirty **2** *m* dirt

sporgere 1 *v/t* hold out; *denuncia* make **2** *v/i* jut out; **sporgersi** lean out

sport *m inv* sport

sportello *m* door; **~ automatico** ATM, cash dispenser

sportivo 1 *agg* sports *attr, persona* sporty **2** *m, ~a f* sportsman; *donna* sportswoman

sporto *pp* ☞ **sporgere**

sposa *f* bride; **sposare** marry; **sposarsi** get married; **sposato** married; **sposo** *m* bridegroom; **-i** *pl* newlyweds

spostare (*trasferire*) move, shift; (*rimandare*) postpone; **spostarsi** move

spranga *f* bar; **sprangare** bar

sprecare waste, squander; **spreco** m waste

spregevole despicable

spremere squeeze; **spremimoni** m inv lemon squeezer; **spremuta** f juice; **~ d'arancia** orange juice

sprofondare sink

sproporzionato out of proportion (**a** to)

sproposito m blunder; **costare uno ~** cost a fortune; **a ~** out of turn

sprovveduto inexperienced

sprovvisto: ~ di lacking; **alla -a** unexpectedly

spruzzare spray; **spruzzatore** m spray; **spruzzo** m spray; **di fango** splatter

spudorato shameless

spugna f sponge

spuma f foam; **spumante:** **(vino m) ~** sparkling wine

spuntare stick out; BOT come up; **di sole** appear; **di giorno** break

spuntino m snack

spunto m suggestion; **prendere ~ da** be inspired by

sputare v/i spit **2** v/t spit out; **sputo** m spittle

squadra f **strumento** set square; **(gruppo)** squad; SP team

squalifica f disqualification; **squalificare** disqualify

squallido squalid; **squallore** m squalor

squalo m shark

squama f flake; **di pesce** scale

squarcio m in **stoffa** rip, tear; in **nuvole** break

squilibrato agg insane **2** m, -a f lunatic; **squilibrio** m imbalance

squillare ring; **squillo** m ring

squisito cibo delicious

sradicare uproot; fig (eliminare) eradicate; persona, pianta uproot

S.r.l. f (= **Società a responsabilità limitata**) Ltd (= limited)

SS. (= **santi**) Saints

stabile 1 agg steady; (duraturo) stable; tempo settled **2** m building

stabilimento m (fabbrica) plant, Br factory

stabilire data, obiettivi, record set; (decidere) decide, settle; **stabilirsi** settle; **stabilità** f steadiness; di relazione, moneta stability

staccare remove, detach; EL unplug

stadio m stage; SP stadium

staffa f stirrup; **perdere le -e** blow one's top

staffetta f SP relay; **corsa f a ~** relay race

stage m inv training period

stagionale seasonal; **stagionare** age, mature; legno season; **stagionato** aged, mature; legno seasoned; **stagione** f season; **alta ~** high season; **bassa ~** low season

stagnante stagnant

stagno 1 m pond; TEC tin **2**

agg watertight

stalla *f per bovini* cowshed; *per cavalli* stable

stamani, stamattina this morning

stambecco *m* ibex

stampa *f* press; *tecnica* printing; FOT print; *posta* **-e** *pl* printed matter; **stampante** *f* INFOR printer; **~ a getto di inchiostro** ink-jet printer; **stampare** print; **stampatello** *m* block letters; **stampato** *m* INFOR printout, hard copy

stampella *f* crutch

stampo *m* mould, *Am* mold

stancare tire (out); **stancarsi** get tired, tire; **stanchezza** *f* tiredness; **stanco** tired; **~ morto** dead beat

stanghetta *f* leg

stanotte tonight; (*la notte scorsa*) last night

stanza *f* room

stanziare *somma di denaro* allocate, earmark

stanzino *m* boxroom

stappare take the top off

stare be; (*restare*) stay; (*abitare*) live; **~ in piedi** stand; **~ bene** be well; *di vestiti* suit; **~ per fare qc** be about to do sth; **lascialo ~** let him be; **~ telefonando** be making a phonecall; **come sta?** how are you?, how are things?; **ben ti sta!** serves you right!

starnutire sneeze; **starnuto** *m* sneeze

stasera this evening, tonight

statale 1 *agg* state *attr* **2** *m/f* civil servant **3** *f* main road; **Stati Uniti d'America** *mpl* United States of America, USA

statistica *f* statistics

stato 1 *pp* **~ essere** *e* **stare 2** *m anche* POL state; **~ civile** marital status

statua *f* statue

statunitense 1 *agg* US *attr*, American **2** *m/f* US citizen

statura *f* height; *fig* stature

stavolta this time

stazionario stationary; **stazione** *f* station; **~ di servizio** service station; **~ balneare** seaside resort; **~ termale** spa

stecca *f di biliardo* cue; *di sigarette* carton; MED splint; MUS wrong note; **stecchino** *m* toothpick

stella *f* star; **~ di mare** starfish

stelo *m* stem, stalk

stemma *m* coat of arms

stendere spread; *braccio* stretch out; *biancheria* hang up; *verbale* draw up; **stendersi** stretch out; **stendibiancheria** *m inv* clothes dryer

stenodattilografa *f* shorthand typist

stentare: ~ a fare qc find it hard to do sth; **stento: a ~** with difficulty

stereo *m inv* stereo

stereotipo 1 *agg* stereotypical **2** *m* stereotype

sterile sterile; **sterilità** f sterility; **sterilizzare** sterilize; **sterilizzazione** f sterilization

sterlina f sterling

sterminare exterminate

sterminato vast

sterminio m extermination

sterno m breastbone, ANAT sternum

sterzare steer; **sterzata** f swerve; **sterzo** m AUTO steering

steso pp ☞ **stendere**

stesso same; **lo ~, la stessa** the same one; **è lo ~** it's all the same; **oggi ~** this very day; **io ~** myself; **se ~** himself

stile m style

stilografica f fountain pen

stima f (ammirazione) esteem; (valutazione) estimate; **stimare** persona esteem; oggetto value; (ritenere) consider; **stimato** value

stimolante 1 agg stimulating **2** m stimulant; **stimolare** stimulate

stinco m shin

stingere, **stingersi** fade; **stinto** pp ☞ **stingere**

stipare cram; **stipato** crammed (**di** with)

stipendiato m, -a f salary-earner; **stipendio** m salary

stipulare stipulate

stiramento m MED pulled muscle

stirare iron; **stirarsi** pull; **stiro:** **ferro** m **da ~** iron; **non ~**

non-iron

stirpe f (origine) birth

stitichezza f constipation

stivale m boot; **-i** pl **di gomma** wellingtons, Am rubber boots

sto ☞ **stare**

stoccafisso m stockfish (air-dried cod)

stoffa f material

stomaco m stomach

stonare di cantante sing out of tune; fig be out of place; di colori clash; **stonato** tone deaf; nota false; strumento out of tune

stop m inv AUTO brake light; cartello stop sign; **stoppare** stop

storcere twist; **~ il naso** make a face; **storcersi** bend; **~ un piede** twist one's ankle

stordimento m dizziness; **stordire** stun; **stordito** stunned

storia f history; (narrazione) story; **non far -e!** don't make a scene!; **storico 1** agg historical; (memorabile) historic **2** m, -a f historian

stormo m di uccelli flock

storpio 1 agg crippled **2** m -a f cripple

storta f: **prendere una ~** twist one's ankle; **storto** crooked

stoviglie fpl dishes

strabico cross-eyed; **strabismo** m strabismus

stracarico overloaded

stracciare tear up

stracciatella f type of soup; *gelato* chocolate chip

stracciato in shreds

straccio m *per pulire* cloth; *per spolverare* duster

strada f road; **per ~** down the road; *sono (già) per ~* I'm on my way; *a metà ~* halfway; **stradale** road *attr*; **stradario** m street-finder, street map

strafare exaggerate

strage f slaughter

stragrande: *la ~ maggioranza* the vast majority

strangolare strangle

straniero 1 *agg* foreign 2 *m*, -*a* f foreigner

strano strange

straordinario 1 *agg* special; *(eccezionale)* extraordinary 2 *m* overtime

strapazzare treat badly; **strapazzarsi** overdo it; **strapazzo** m strain; *essere uno ~* be exhausting; *da ~* third-rate

strapieno crowded

strapiombo: *a ~* overhanging

strappare tear, rip; *(staccare)* tear down; *(togliere)* snatch (*a qu* from s.o.); **strappo** m tear, rip; MED torn ligament

straripare overflow its banks

strascico m train; *fig* after-effects

stratagemma m stratagem

strategia f strategy; **strategico** strategic

strato m layer

stravagante extravagant

stravecchio ancient

stravedere: *~ per qu* worship s.o.

stravolgere change radically; *(travisare)* twist; *(stancare)* exhaust; **stravolto** 1 *pp* ☞ **stravolgere** 2 *agg (stanco)* exhausted

strazio m: *era uno ~* it was painful

strega f witch; **stregone** m wizard

stremare exhaust; **stremato** exhausted

stress m *inv* stress; **stressante** stressful; **stressare** stress

stretta f hold; *~ di mano* handshake; *mettere qu alle -e* put s.o. in a tight corner; **strettamente** closely; **tenere qc ~ (in mano)** clutch sth (in one's hand); **stretto** 1 *pp* ☞ **stringere** 2 *agg* narrow; *vestito* too tight; *lo ~ necessario* the bare minimum 3 *m* GEOG strait; **strettoia** f bottleneck

stridere *di porta* squeak; *di colori* clash

stridulo shrill

strillare scream; **strillo** m scream

striminzito skimpy

strimpellare strum

stringa f lace

stringere 1 *v/t* make narrower; *abito* take in; *vite* tighten; *~ amicizia* become friends 2 *v/i di tempo* press; **stringersi** *intorno a tavolo*

squeeze up
striscia f strip; *dipinta* stripe; *-sce pl* **pedonali** zebra crossing, *Am* crosswalk; **a** *-sce* striped
strisciare 1 v/t *piedi* scrape; *(sfiorare)* brush, smear *(contro* against) **2** v/i crawl; **striscio** m MED smear
striscione m banner
strizzare wring; **~** *l'occhio a qu* wink at s.o.
strofa f verse
strofinaccio m dish towel; **strofinare** rub
stroncare *vita* snuff out; F *idea* shoot down
stropicciare crush, wrinkle
strozzare strangle
strozzino m, -a f *loan* shark F
strumentalizzare make use of; *strumento* m instrument
strutto m lard
struttura f structure
struzzo m ZO ostrich
stuccare plaster; **stucco** m plaster
studente m, -essa f student; **studiare** study; **studio** m study; *di artista*, RADIO, TV studio; *di professionista* office; *di medico* surgery, *Am* office
stufa f stove; **~** **elettrica** / **a gas** electric / gas heater
stufare GASTR stew; *fig* bore; **stufarsi** get bored *(di* with); **stufato** m stew; **stufarsi** **~** **di qc** be bored with sth
stuolo m host
stupefacente 1 agg amazing,

stupefying **2** m narcotic; **stupefatto** amazed, stupefied; **stupendo** stupendous
stupidaggine f stupidity; **stupidità** f stupidity; **stupido 1** agg stupid **2** m, -a f idiot
stupire 1 v/t amaze **2** v/i e **stupirsi** be amazed; **stupore** m amazement
stuprare rape; **stupro** m rape
sturare clear, unblock
stuzzicadenti m inv toothpick
stuzzicare tease; *appetito* whet
su 1 prp on; *argomento* about; *(circa)* about; *sul tavolo* on the table; *sul mare* by the sea; *sui trecento euro* about three hundred euros; *nove volte* **~** *dieci* nine times out of ten **2** avv up; *(al piano di sopra)* upstairs; **~!** come on!; *guardare in* **~** look up
sub m/f inv skin diver
subacqueo 1 agg underwater **2** m, -a f skin diver
subaffittare sublet; **subaffitto** m sublet
subentrare: ~ **a qu** take s.o.'s place
subire *danni, perdita* suffer
subito immediately
suburbano suburban
succedere *(accadere)* happen; **~** **a in carica** succeed; **successione** f succession; **successivo** successive
successo 1 pp ↩ **succedere 2** m success; *di* **~** successful;

successore *m* successor

succhiare suck; succo *m* juice; ~ **d'arancia** orange juice

succursale *f* branch

sud *m* south; **a(l)~ di** (to the) south of; **~ ovest** south-west; **~ est** south-east; **a ~ di** (to the) south of

sudare perspire, sweat; sudato sweaty

suddividere subdivide

sudicio 1 *agg* dirty 2 *m* dirt; sudiciume *m* dirt

sudore *m* perspiration, sweat

sufficiente sufficient; sufficienza *f* sufficiency; **a ~** enough

suffragio *m* suffrage

suggerimento *m* suggestion; suggerire suggest; TEA prompt; **suggeritore** *m* TEA prompter; suggestionare influence; suggestivo picturesque

sughero *m* cork

sugli = **su** and **gli**

sugo *m* sauce; *di arrosto* juice

sui = **su** and **i**

suicida *m/f* suicide (victim); suicidarsi commit suicide, kill o.s.; **suicidio** *m* suicide

suino pork *attr*

sul = **su** and **il**

sull', sulla, sulle, sullo = **su** and *art* **l', la, le, lo**

suo 1 *agg* ~ *di lui* his; *di lei* her; *di cosa* its; **il ~ maestro** his / her teacher; **questo libro è ~** this is his / her book

◇ *forma di cortesia* your; **il ~, la sua, i suoi, la sue** your 2 *pron*: **il ~, la sua, i suoi, le sue** *di lui* his; *di lei* hers; *di cosa* its; *forma di cortesia* yours

suocera *f* mother-in-law; suocero *m* father-in-law; *-i pl* mother- and father-in-law, in-laws F

suola *f* sole

suolo *m* ground; (*terreno*) soil

suonare 1 *v/t* play; *campanello* ring 2 *v/i* play; *alla porta* ring; suono *m* sound

suora *f* REL nun

super *f inv* F 4-star; *Am* premium

superare go past; *fig* overcome; *esame* pass

superbo haughty

superficiale superficial; superficie *f* surface

superfluo superfluous

superiore 1 *agg* top; *qualità* superior 2 *m* superior; superiorità *f* superiority

superlativo *m/agg* superlative

supermarket *m inv*, supermercato *m* supermarket

superstite 1 *agg* surviving 2 *m/f* survivor

superstizione *f* superstition; superstizioso superstitious

superstrada *f* motorway, *Am* highway

suppergiù about

supplementare supplementary; supplemento *m* supplement; **supplente** m/f replacement; EDU supply teacher

supplicare beg

suppongo ☞ **supporre**; **supporre** suppose

supporto m TEC support

supposizione f supposition

supposta f MED suppository

supposto pp ☞ **supporre**

suppurare MED suppurate

surf m inv surfboard; **fare ~** surf, go surfing; **surfista** m/f surfer

surgelato 1 agg frozen **2** m: **-i** pl frozen food

suscettibile touchy

suscitare arouse

susina f plum

sussidio m grant, allowance

sussultare start, jump; **sussulto** m start, jump

sussurrare whisper

svagarsi take one's mind off things; **svago** m distraction

svaligiare burgle, Am burglarize

svalutare devalue; **svalutazione** f devaluation

svanire vanish

svantaggio m disadvantage; **svantaggioso** disadvantageous

svariato varied

svedese 1 m/agg Swedish **2** m/f Swede

sveglia f alarm clock; **sve-**

gliare wake (up); **svegliarsi** waken up; **sveglio** awake; fig alert

svelare segreto reveal

svelto quick; **alla ~** quickly

svendere sell at a reduced price; **svendita** f clearance

svenire faint

sventolare wave

svenuto pp ☞ **svenire**

svestire undress; **svestirsi** get undressed, undress

Svezia f Sweden

sviare deflect; fig divert

svignarsela slip away

sviluppare develop; **svilupparsi** develop; **sviluppato** developed; **sviluppo** m development

svincolo m di strada junction

svista f oversight

svitare unscrew; **svitato** unscrewed; fig F **essere ~** have a screw loose F

Svizzera f Switzerland; **svizzero 1** agg Swiss **2** m, **-a** f Swiss

svogliato lazy

svolgere rotolo unwrap; tema develop; attività carry out; **svolgersi** happen; di film be set

svolta f turning; fig turning point; **svoltare ~ a destra** turn right; **svolto** pp ☞ **svolgere**

svuotare empty

T

tabaccheria f tobacconist's, *Am* tobacco store; **tabacco** m tobacco

tabella f table; **tabellina** f multiplication table

tabellone m board; *per avvisi* notice board, *Am* bulletin board

tabù m/*ag* inv taboo

tabulato m printout

taccagno mean, stingy F

tacchino m turkey

tacco m heel

taccuino m notebook

tacere 1 v/t keep quiet about, say nothing about **2** v/i not say anything, be silent

tachicardia f tachycardia

tachimetro m speedometer

taciturno taciturn

tafano m ZO horsefly

tafferuglio m scuffle

taglia f (*misura*) size; **~ unica** one size; **tagliacarte** m inv paper-knife; **tagliando** m coupon; AUTO service; **tagliare** cut; *albero* cut down; *legna* chop; **tagliarsi i capelli** have one's hair cut; *fig* **~ la strada a qu** cut in front of s.o.; **tagliarsi** cut o.s.; **mi sono tagliata un dito** I've cut my finger; **tagliatelle** fpl tagliatelle sg; **tagliente** sharp; **tagliere** m chopping board; **taglierini** mpl type of noo-

dles; **taglio** m cut

tailleur m inv suit

talco m talcum powder

tale such a; **-i** pl such; **~ e quale** just like; **un ~** someone

talento m talent

talloncino m coupon

tallone m heel

talmente so

talora sometimes

talpa f mole

talvolta sometimes

tamburo m drum

tamponamento m AUTO collision; **~ a catena** multi-vehicle pile-up; **tamponare** *falla* plug; AUTO collide with; **tampone** m MED swab; *per donne* tampon; *per timbri* (ink) pad

tana f den

tandem m inv tandem

tangente f MAT tangent; F (*bustarella*) bribe; **tangenziale** f ring road

tanica f container

tanto 1 *agg* so much; **-i** pl so many; **-i saluti** best wishes; **-e grazie** thank you so much **2** *pron* many **3** *avv* (*così*) so; *con verbi* so much; **di ~ in ~** from time to time; **~ quanto** as much as; **è da ~ (tempo) che non lo vedo** I haven't seen him for a long time

tappa f stop; di viaggio stage; **tappare** plug; bottiglia put the cork in; **tapparella** f rolling shutter

tappeto m carpet

tappezzare (wall)paper; **tappezzeria** f wallpaper; di sedili upholstery

tappo m cap, top; di sughero cork; di lavandini, vasche plug

tarchiato stocky

tardare 1 v/t delay **2** v/i be late; **tardi** later; **più** ~ later (on); **al più** ~ at the latest; **a più** ~! see you!; **far** ~ (arrivare in ritardo) be late; (stare alzato) stay up late; in ufficio work late; **tardo** late

targa f nameplate, AUTO numberplate, Am license plate; **targhetta** f tag; su porta nameplate

tariffa f rate; nei trasporti fare

tarlato worm-eaten

tarlo m woodworm

tarma f (clothes) moth

tartaro m tartar

tartaruga f tortoise; aquatica turtle

tartina f canapé

tartufo m truffle

tasca f pocket; **tascabile 1** agg pocket attr **2** m paperback

tassa f tax; **tassametro** m meter; **tassare** tax

tassello m nel muro plug

tassista m/f taxi driver, cab driver

tasso m FIN rate; ~ **d'interesse** interest rate

tastare feel; fig ~ **il terreno** see how the land lies

tastiera f keyboard; **tasto** m key

tattica f tactics

tatto m (senso) touch; fig tact

tatuaggio m tattoo

tavola f table; (asse) plank, board; in libro plate; ~ **calda** snackbar; **mettersi a** ~ sit down to eat; **tavoletta** f: ~ **di cioccolata** bar of chocolate; **tavolo** m table

taxi m inv taxi, esp Am cab

tazza f cup; **tazzina** f espresso cup

tè m inv tea; ~ **freddo** iced tea

te you

teatrale theatre attr, Am theater attr; fig theatrical; **rappresentazione** f ~ play; **teatro** m theatre, Am theater; ~ **lirico** opera (house)

tecnica f technique; (tecnologia) technology; **tecnico 1** agg technical **2** m technician; **tecnologia** f technology; **alta** ~ high tech; **tecnologico** technological

tedesco 1 m/agg German **2** m, -a f German

tegame m (sauce)pan

teglia f baking tin

tegola f tile

teiera f teapot

tela f cloth; PITT canvas; ~ **cerata** oilcloth

telaio m loom; di automobile

chassis; *di bicicletta, finestra* frame

telecamera *f* television camera

telecomando *m* remote control

telecomunicazioni *fpl* telecommunications, telecomms

teleferica *f* cableway

telefilm *m inv* television film

telefonare (tele)phone, call (**a qu** s.o.); **telefonata** *f* (tele)phone call; **fare una ~ a qu** phone *o* call s.o.; **telefonico** (tele)phone *attr;* **telefonino** *m* mobile (phone), *Am* cell(ular) phone; **telefono** *m* (tele)phone; **~ a scheda** (**magnetica**) cardphone; **~ cellulare** mobile phone, *Am* cellular phone

telegiornale *m* news *sg*

telelavoro *m* teleworking

teleobiettivo *m* telephoto lens

telepatia *f* telepathy

teleschermo *m* TV screen

telescopio *m* telescope

telespettatore *m*, **-trice** *f* TV viewer

televisione *f* television, TV; **televisivo** television *attr,* TV *attr;* **televisore** *m* television (set), TV (set)

tema *m* theme, subject

temere be afraid *o* frightened of

temperamatite *m inv* pencil sharpener

temperamento *m* temperament

temperare *acciaio* temper; *matita* sharpen; **temperato** *acciaio* tempered; *clima* temperate

temperatura *f* temperature; **~ ambiente** room temperature

tempesta *f* storm

tempia *f* temple

tempio *m* temple

tempo *m* time; *meteorologico* weather; **~ libero** free time; **a ~ pieno** full-time; **in ~ in** time; **un ~** once, long ago; **lavora da molto ~** he has been working for a long time; **fa bel / brutto ~** the weather is lovely / nasty

temporale *m* thunderstorm; **temporaneo** temporary

tenace tenacious

tenaglie *fpl* pincers

tenda *f* curtain; *da campeggio* tent

tendenza *f* tendency; **tendere 1** *v/t elastico, muscoli* stretch; *corde del violino* tighten; *mano* hold out; *fig: trappola* lay; **2** *v/i:* **~ a** (*aspirare a*) aim at; (*essere portati a*) tend to; (*avvicinarsi a*) verge on

tendina *f* net curtain

tendine *m* tendon

tenente *m* lieutenant

tenere 1 *v/t* hold; (*conservare, mantenere*) keep; (*gestire*) run; *conferenza* give; **~ d'oc-**

chio keep an eye on **2** *v/i* hold (on); **~ a** *(dare importanza a)* care about; SP support

tenero tender; *pietra, legno* soft

tenersi *(reggersi)* hold on (**a** to); *(mantenersi)* keep o.s.; **~ in piedi** stand (up)

tengo ☞ **tenere**

tennis *m* tennis; **~ da tavolo** table tennis; **tennista** *m/f* tennis player

tenore *m* MUS tenor

tensione *f* voltage; *fig* tension

tentare try, attempt; *(allettare)* tempt; **tentativo** *m* attempt; **tentazione** *f* temptation

tenuta *f* *(capacità)* capacity; *(resistenza)* stamina; *(divisa)* uniform; *(abbigliamento)* outfit; AGR estate

teologo *m*, **-a** *f* theologian

teorema *m* theorem; **teoria** *f* theory; **teorico** theoretical

tepore *m* warmth

teppista *m/f* hooligan

terapia *f* therapy

tergicristallo *m* AUTO windscreen *o* Am windshield wiper

termale thermal; **terme** *fpl* baths

terminal *m inv* AVIA terminal; **terminale** *m/agg* end; **terminare** *v/t* end, terminate; **termine** *m* end; *(confine)* limit; FIN *(scadenza)* deadline; *(parola)* term; **a breve / lungo ~** in the short / long term

termocoperta *f* electric blanket

termometro *m* thermometer

termos *m inv* thermos®

termosifone *m* radiator

termostato *m* thermostat

terra *f* earth; *(regione, proprietà, terreno agricolo)* land; *(superficie del suolo)* ground; *(pavimento)* floor; **a ~** on the ground; AVIA, MAR **scendere a ~** get off; **terracotta** *f* terracotta; **terraferma** *f* dry land, terra firma

terrazza *f*, **terrazzo** *m* balcony, terrace

terremoto *m* earthquake

terreno 1 *agg* earthly; *piano ~* ground, Am first **2** *m* *(superficie)* ground; *(suolo, materiale)* soil; *(appezzamento)* plot of land; *fig* *(settore, tema)* field, area; **terrestre** terrestrial

terribile terrible

terrina *f* bowl

territorio *m* territory

terrore *m* terror; **terrorismo** *m* terrorism; **terrorista** *m/f* terrorist; **terrorizzare** terrorize

terza *f* AUTO third (gear); **terziario** *m* tertiary sector, services; **terzino** *m* SP back; **terzo** third

teschio *m* skull

tesi *f inv*: **~ (di laurea)** thesis

teso 1 *pp* ☞ **tendere 2** *agg* taut; *fig* tense

tesoro *m* treasure; *(tesoreria)*

treasury
tessera f card
tessile 1 agg textile **2 -i** mpl textiles
tessuto m fabric, material
test m inv test
testa f head; **a ~** a head; **essere in ~** lead, be ahead
testamento m will
testardo stubborn
testata f (giornale) newspaper; di letto headboard
teste m/f witness
testicolo m testicle
testimone m/f witness; **testimoniare 1** v/i testify, give evidence **2** v/t fig testify to; DIR **~ il falso** commit perjury
testo m text
tetano m tetanus
tetro gloomy
tetto m roof; **tettoia** f roof
Tevere m Tiber
TG m (= **Telegiornale**) TV news sg
thermos ☞ **termos**
ti you; riflessivo yourself
tibia f shinbone, tibia
tic m inv di orologio tick; MED tic
ticket m inv MED prescription charge
tiene ☞ **tenere**
tiepido lukewarm, tepid
tifo m MED typhus; fig **fare il ~ per** be a fan o supporter of; **tifoso** m, **-a** f fan, supporter
tigre f tiger
timbrare stamp; **timbro** m stamp; MUS timbre; **~ posta-**

le postage stamp
timidezza f shyness, timidity; **timido** shy, timid
timo m BOT thyme
timone m MAR, AVIA rudder
timore m fear
timpano m MUS kettledrum; ANAT eardrum
tingere dye
tinta f (colorante) dye; (colore) colour, Am color; **tintarella** f (sun)tan
tinto pp ☞ **tingere**
tintoria f dry-cleaner's
tintura f dyeing; (colorante) dye; **~ di iodio** iodine
tipico typical
tipo m sort, type; F fig guy
tipografia f printing; stabilimento printer's
tir m heavy goods vehicle, Am truck
tiranno m tyrant
tirare 1 v/t (tendere) stretch; (lanciare) throw; (sparare) fire; (tracciare) draw; **~ giù** take out; **~ su** da terra pick up; bambino bring up; **~ giù** take down **2** v/i pull; di abito be too tight; di vento blow; (sparare) shoot; **tirarsi: ~ indietro** back off; fig back out; **tiratura** f di libro print run; di giornale circulation
tirchio 1 agg mean **2** m, **-a** f miser, skinflint F
tiro m (lancio) throw; (sparo) shot; **~ con l'arco** archery
tirocinante m/f trainee; **tiro-**

cinio *m* training

tiroide *f* thyroid

tirolese *agg*, *m/f* Tyrolean, Tyrolese; **Tirolo** *m* Tyrol

tisana *f* herbal tea, tisane

titolare *m/f* owner; **titolo** *m* title; *dei giornali* headline; FIN security; **~ di studio** qualification

titubare hesitate

tizio *m*, -a *f*: **un ~** somebody, some man; **una -a** somebody, some woman

toccare **1** *v/t* touch; (*riguardare*) be about **2** *v/i* happen (**a** to); **tocca a me** it's my turn; **mi tocca partire** I have to go; **tocco** *m* touch

togliere take (away), remove; (*eliminare*) take off; (*revocare*) lift; *dente* take out, extract; **~ di mezzo** get rid of; **togliersi** *giacca* take off, remove; (*spostarsi*) take o.s. off; **~ dai piedi** get out of the way; **tolgo** ☞ **togliere**

tollerante tolerant; **tollerare** tolerate

tolto *pp* ☞ **togliere**

tomba *f* grave

tombola *f* bingo

tonaca *f* habit

tonalità *f inv* tonality

tondo round

tonfo *m in acqua* splash

tonificare tone up

tonnellata *f* tonne

tonno *m* tuna

tono *m* tone

tonsille *fpl* ANAT tonsils; ton-

sillite *f* tonsillitis

topazio *m* topaz

topo *m* mouse; **Topolino** *m* Mickey Mouse

toppa *f* (*serratura*) keyhole; (*rattoppo*) patch

torace *m* chest

torbido *liquido* cloudy

torcere twist; *biancheria* wring; **torchio** *m* press

torcia *f* torch

torcicollo *m* stiff neck

tordo *m* thrush

torinese of Turin; **Torino** *f* Turin

tormenta *f* snowstorm; **tormentare** torment; **tormentarsi** torment o.s.

tornaconto *m* benefit

tornante *m* hairpin bend

tornare *venire* come back, return; *andare* go back, return; (*quadrare*) balance; **~ utile** prove useful

torneo *m* tournament

tornio *m* lathe

toro *m* bull; ASTR *Toro* Taurus

torre *f* tower

torrefazione *f* roasting

torrente *m* stream

torrido torrid

torrone *m* nougat

torso *m* torso

torsolo *m* core

torta *f* cake; **tortellini** *mpl* tortellini *sg*

torto *m* wrong; **aver ~** be wrong; **a ~** wrongly

tortora *f* turtledove

tortuoso (*sinuoso*) winding;

(ambiguo) devious

tortura *f* torture; **torturare** torture

tosaerba *f o m* lawnmower; **tosare** *pecore* shear

Toscana *f* Tuscany; **toscano** Tuscan

tosse *f* cough; **aver la ~** have a cough

tossico 1 *agg* toxic **2** *m*, -a *f* F druggie F; **tossicodipendente** *m/f* drug addict; **tossicodipendenza** *f* drug addiction; **tossicomane** *m/f* drug addict

tossire cough

tostapane *m* toaster; **tostare** *pane* toast; *caffè* roast

totale *m/agg* total; **totalità** *f* (*interezza*) totality; **nella ~ dei casi** in all cases

totip *m* competition similar to football pools, based on horse racing

totocalcio *m* competition similar to football pools

tovaglia *f* tablecloth; **tovagliolo** *m* napkin, serviette

tozzo 1 *agg* stocky **2** *m di pane* crust

tra ☞ **fra**

traballare stagger; *di mobile* wobble

traboccare overflow (*anche fig*)

traccia *f* (*orma*) footprint; *di veicolo* track; (*indizio*) clue; (*segno*) trace; (*abbozzo*) sketch; **tracciare** *linea* draw; (*delineare*) outline; (*abbozza-*

re) sketch

trachea *f* windpipe

tracolla *f* (*shoulder*) strap; **a ~** slung over one's shoulder; **borsa** *f* **a ~** shoulder bag

tradimento *m* betrayal; **tradire** betray; *coniuge* be unfaithful to; **tradirsi** give o.s. away; **traditore 1** *agg* (*infedele*) unfaithful **2** *m*, **-trice** *f* traitor

tradizionale traditional; **tradizione** *f* tradition

tradotto *pp* ☞ **tradurre**; **tradurre** translate (*in* into); **traduttore** *m*, **-trice** *f* translator; **traduzione** *f* translation

trafficante *m/f spreg* dealer; **~ di droga** drug dealer; **trafficare** deal, trade (*in* in); *spreg* traffic (*in* in); (*armeggiare*) tinker; (*affaccendarsi*) bustle about; **traffico** *m* traffic

traforo *m* tunnel

tragedia *f* tragedy

traghetto *m* ferry

tragico tragic

tragitto *m* journey

traguardo *m* finishing line

traiettoria *f* trajectory

trainare (*rimorchiare*) tow; *di animali* pull, draw; **traino** *m* towing; *veicolo* vehicle on tow; **a ~** on tow

tralasciare (*omettere*) omit, leave out; (*interrompere*) interrupt

traliccio *m* EL pylon; TEC trellis

tram *m inv* tram

trama f fig plot

tramandare hand down

tramare fig plot

trambusto m (confusione) bustle; (tumulto) commotion

tramezzino m sandwich

tramite 1 m (collegamento) link; (intermediario) go-between **2** prp through

tramontana f north wind

tramontare set; **tramonto** m sunset; fig decline

trampolino m diving board; SCI ski jump

tranello m trap

tranne except

tranquillante m tranquillizer, Am tranquilizer; **tranquillità** f peacefulness, tranquility; **tranquillizzare** ~ **qu** set s.o.'s mind at rest; **tranquillo** calm, peaceful

transatlantico 1 agg transatlantic **2** m liner

transazione f DIR settlement; FIN transaction

transenna f barrier

transgenico genetically modified

transitabile strada passable

transitivo GRAM transitive

transito m transit; **divieto di** ~ no thoroughfare

trantran m F routine

tranviere m (manovratore) tram driver; (controllore) tram conductor

trapanare drill; **trapano** m drill

trapezio m trapeze; **trapezi-**

sta m/f trapeze artist

trapiantare transplant; **trapianto** m transplant

trappola f trap

trapunta f quilt

trarre conclusioni draw; **vantaggio** derive

trasalire jump

trasandato scruffy; **lavoro** slipshod

trasbordo m transfer

trascinare drag; (travolgere) sweep away; fig (entusiasmare) carry away

trascorrere 1 v/t spend **2** v/i pass, go by; **trascorso** pp ☞ **trascorrere**

trascrivere transcribe

trascurabile unimportant; **trascurare** neglect; (tralasciare) ignore; **trascurato** careless, negligent; (trasandato) slovenly; (ignorato) neglected

trasferibile transferable; **trasferimento** m transfer; **trasferire** transfer; **trasferirsi** move; **trasferta** f transfer; SP away game

trasformare transform; TEC process; **trasformarsi** change, turn (**in** into); **trasformatore** m transformer; **trasformazione** f transformation

trasfusione f transfusion

trasgredire disobey; **trasgressore** m transgressor

traslocare move; **trasloco** m move

trasmettere pass on; RAD, TV broadcast, transmit; **trasmissione** f transmission; RAD, TV broadcast, transmission; (*programma*) program, *Am* program

trasparente 1 *agg* transparent **2** *m* transparency

trasportare transport; **trasporto** *m* transport; **-i pl pubblici** public transport, *Am* mass transit

trasversale 1 *agg* transverse **2** f MAT transversal

tratta f trade; FIN draft

trattamento *m* treatment; **trattare 1** v/t treat; TEC treat, process; FIN deal in; (*negoziare*) negotiate **2** v/i deal; ∼ **di** be about; **trattarsi: di che si tratta?** what's it about?; **trattative** fpl negotiations, talks; **trattato** *m* treatise; DIR, POL treaty

trattenere (*far restare*) keep, hold; (*far perder tempo*) hold up; (*frenare*) restrain; *fiato, respiro* hold; *lacrime* hold back; *somma* withhold; **trattenersi** (*rimanere*) stay; (*frenarsi*) restrain o.s.; ∼ **dal fare qc** refrain from doing sth; **trattenuta** f deduction

trattino *m* dash; *in parole composte* hyphen; **tratto 1** pp ☞ **trarre 2** *m* di spazio, tempo stretch; *di penna* stroke; (*linea*) line; **a un** ∼ all of a sudden; **-i pl** (*lineamenti*) features

trattore *m* tractor

trattoria f restaurant

trauma *m* trauma; **traumatico** traumatic

travaglio *m* MED labour, *Am* labor

travasare decant

trave f beam

traversa f crossbeam; **traversare** cross; **traversata** f crossing; **traverso:** *andare di* ∼ *di cibi* go down the wrong way

travestire disguise; **travestirsi** disguise o.s., dress up (*da* as); **travestito** *m* transvestite

travolgere carry away (*anche fig*); *con un veicolo* run over; **travolto** pp ☞ **travolgere**

trazione f TEC traction; AUTO ∼ *anteriore / posteriore* front- / rear-wheel drive

tre three

treccia f plait

trecento 1 *agg* three hundred **2** *m*: *il Trecento* the fourteenth century; **tredicesimo** thirteenth; **tredici** thirteen

tregua f truce; *fig* break, let-up

trekking *m* hiking

tremare tremble, shake (*di, per* with)

tremendo terrible, tremendous

tremila three thousand

treno *m* train; *in* ∼ by train

trenta thirty; **trentenne** agg, m/f thirty-year-old; **trentesimo** thirtieth; **trentina:** *una* ∼

about thirty

treppiedi *m inv* tripod

triangolare triangular; **triangolo** *m* triangle; AUTO warning triangle

tribù *f inv* tribe

tribuna *f* platform; **tribunale** *m* court

tributo *m* tax; *fig* tribute

tricheco *m* walrus

triciclo *m* tricycle

tricolore *m* Italian flag

triennale *contratto* three-year; *mostra* three-yearly; **triennio** *m* three-year period

trifoglio *m* clover

triglia *f* red mullet

trillo *m* trill

trimestrale quarterly

trincea *f* trench

trio *m* trio

trionfare triumph (**su** over); **trionfo** *m* triumph

triplicare triple; **triplo 1** *agg* triple **2** *m*: **il ~** three times as much (**di** as)

trippa *f* tripe

triste sad; **tristezza** *f* sadness

tritare mince, *Am* ground meat; **tritatutto** *m inv* mincer, *Am* meat grinder

triturare grind

trivella *f* drill

triviale trivial

trofeo *m* trophy

tromba *f* MUS trumpet; **~ d'aria** whirlwind; **~ delle scale** stairwell

trombone *m* trombone

trombosi *f* thrombosis

troncare cut off; *fig* break off

tronco *m* ANAT, BOT trunk; FERR section

trono *m* throne

tropicale tropical; **tropici** *mpl* tropics

troppo 1 *agg* too much; **-i** *pl* too many **2** *avv* too much; **con ~** too; **è ~ tardi** it's too late

trota *f* trout

trottare trot; **trotto** *m* trot

trovare find; (*inventare*) find, come up with; **andare a ~ qu** (go and) see s.o.; **trovarsi** be; **~ bene** be happy; **trovata** *f* good idea

truccare make up; *motore* soup up F; *partita, elezioni* fix; **truccarsi** put on one's make-up; **trucco** *m* make-up; (*inganno, astuzia*) trick

truffa *f* fraud; **truffare** defraud (**di** of); **truffatore** *m*, **-trice** *f* trickster, con artist F

truppa *f* troops

tu you; **dammi del ~** call me 'tu'

tubatura *f*, **tubazione** *f* pipes, piping

tubercolosi *f* tuberculosis

tubetto *m* tube

tubo *m* pipe; *flessibile* hose; AUTO **~ di scappamento** exhaust (pipe)

tuffarsi (*immergersi*) dive; (*buttarsi dentro*) throw o.s. (*anche fig*); **tuffo** *m* dip; SP dive

tugurio m hovel
tulipano m tulip
tumore m tumour, Am tumor
tumulto m riot
tunica f tunic
Tunisia f Tunisia; **tunisino 1** agg Tunisian **2** m, -a f Tunisian
tunnel m inv tunnel
tuo 1 agg your; **il ~ amico** your friend; **un ~ amico** a friend of yours **2** pron: **il ~** yours
tuonare thunder; **tuono** m thunder
tuorlo m yolk
turbante m turban
turbare upset, disturb; **turbolenza** f turbulence
turchese m/agg turquoise
Turchia f Turkey; **turco 1** m/agg Turkish **2** m, -a f Turk
turismo m tourism; **turista**

m/f tourist; **turistico** tourist attr
turno m turn; di lavoro shift; **a ~ in** turn; **~ di riposo** rest day; **darsi il ~** take turns
tuta f da lavoro overalls; **~ da ginnastica** track suit, Am sweats; **~ da sci** ski suit
tutela f protection; DIR guardianship; **tutelare** protect; **tutore** m, **-trice** f guardian
tuttavia still
tutto 1 agg whole; **-i, -e** pl all; **~ il libro** the whole book; **-i i giorni** every day; **-i e tre** all three; **noi -i** all of us **2** avv all; **era ~ solo** he was all alone; **del ~** quite; **in ~** altogether, in all **3** pron all; **gente** everybody, everyone; **cose** everything
tuttora still
TV f inv TV

U

ubbidiente obedient; **ubbidire** obey
ubriacare: **~ qu** get s.o. drunk; **ubriacarsi** get drunk; **ubriaco 1** agg drunk **2** m, **-a** f drunk
uccello m bird
uccidere kill; **uccidersi** kill o.s.; **ucciso** pp ☞ **uccidere**
udienza f audience; DIR hearing; **udire** hear; **udito** m hearing
Ue f (= **Unione europea**) EU

(= European Union)
ufficiale 1 agg official **2** m official; MIL officer; **ufficio** m office; **~ cambi** bureau de change; **~ postale** post office; **~ turistico** tourist information office; **ufficioso** unofficial
ufo m UFO
uguaglianza f equality; **uguagliare** make equal; (livellare) level; (essere pari a) equal; **uguale** equal; (lo stes-

so) the same; *terreno* level
ulcera *f* ulcer
ulteriore further
ultimamente recently; **ultimare** complete; **ultimatum** *m inv* ultimatum; **ultimo 1** *agg* last; (*più recente*) latest; **~ piano** top floor **2** *m*, **-a** *f* last; **fino all'~** till the end
ultrasuono *m* ultrasound
ultravioletto ultraviolet
ululare howl
umanità *f* humanity; **umanitario** humanitarian; **umano** human; *trattamento ecc* humane
umidificatore *m* humidifier; **umidità** *f* dampness; *di clima* humidity; **umido 1** *agg* damp **2** *m* dampness; GASTR **in ~** stewed
umile (*modesto*) humble; *mestiere* menial; **umiliante** humiliating; **umiliare** humiliate; **umiliazione** *f* humiliation; **umiltà** *f* humility
umore *m* mood; **di buon ~** in a good mood; **di cattivo ~** in a bad mood
umorismo *m* humour, *Am* humor
un, una ☞ **uno**
unanime unanimous; **unanimità** *f* unanimity; **all'~** unanimously
uncinetto *m* crochet hook; **uncino** *m* hook
undicesimo eleventh; **undici** eleven
ungere grease

ungherese *agg*, *m/f* Hungarian; **Ungheria** *f* Hungary
unghia *f* nail
unico only; (*senza uguali*) unique
unifamiliare: **casa ~** detached house
unificazione *f* unification
uniformare standardize; **uniformarsi**: **~ a** conform to; *regole* comply with; **uniforme** *f* agg uniform
unione *f* union; *fig* unity; **Unione europea** European Union; **unire** unite; (*congiungere*) join; **unirsi** unite; **unità** *f inv* unit; INFOR **~ disco** disk drive; **~ di misura** unit of measurement; **unito** united
universale universal; **università** *f inv* university; **universitario 1** *agg* university *attr* **2** *m*, **-a** *f* university student; (*professore*) university lecturer; **universo** *m* universe
uno 1 *art* a; *before a vowel or silent h* an; **un uovo** an egg **2** *agg* a, one **3** *m* one; **~ e mezzo** one and a half **4** *pron* one; **a ~ a ~** one by one; **l'un l'altro** each other, one another
unto 1 *pp* ☞ **ungere 2** *agg* greasy **3** *m* grease
uomo *m* man; **~ d'affari** businessman; **da ~** *abbigliamento ecc* for men, men's
uovo *m* egg; **~ alla coque** soft-boiled egg; **~ di Pasqua** Easter egg; **~ al tegame**

fried egg; **-a** pl **strapazzate** scrambled eggs

uragano m hurricane

uranio m uranium

urbano urban; fig urbane

urgente urgent; **urgenza** f urgency; **in caso d'~** in an emergency

urina f urine

urlare scream; **urlo** m scream

urna f urn; **elettorale** ballot box

urrà! hooray!

urtare bump into; fig offend

urto m bump; (scontro) collision

usa: **~ e getta** disposable, throw-away

usanza f custom, tradition; **usare 1** v/t use **2** v/i use; (essere di moda) be in fashion; **usato** used; (di seconda mano) second-hand

uscire come out; (andare fuo-ri) go out; **uscita** f exit, way out; **~ di sicurezza** emergency exit

usignolo m nightingale

uso m use; (abitudine) custom; **fuori ~** out of use; **per ~ esterno** not to be taken internally

ustionarsi burn o.s.; **ustione** f burn

usuale usual

usufruire: **~ di qc** have the use of sth

usuraio m loan shark

utensile m utensil

utente m/f user

utero m womb

utile 1 agg useful **2** m FIN profit; **utilità** f usefulness; **utilitaria** f economy car; **utilizzare** use; **utilizzazione** f use

utopia f utopia

uva f grapes; **~ passa** raisins pl; **~ spina** gooseberry

V

V. (= via) St (= street)

va ☞ **andare**

vacanza f holiday, Am vacation; **andare in ~** go on holiday

vacca f cow

vaccinare vaccinate; **vaccinazione** f vaccination; **vaccino** m vaccine

vado ☞ **andare**

vagabondo 1 agg (girovago) wandering; (fannullone) idle

2 m, **-a** f (giramondo) wanderer; (fannullone) idler, layabout F; (barbone) tramp, Am hobo; **vagare** wander (aimlessly)

vagina f ANAT vagina

vaglia m inv: **~ (postale)** postal order

vago vague

vagone m carriage, car; per merci wagon; **~ letto** sleeper; **~ ristorante** dining car

vegetariano

vai ☞ *andare*

valanga *f* avalanche

valere be worth; (*essere valido*) be valid; *far ~ diritti, autorità* assert; *valersi: ~ di qc* avail o.s. of sth; *valevole* valid

valgo ☞ *valere*

valico *m* pass

validità *f* validity; *valido* valid; *persona* fit

valigia *f* suitcase; *fare le -e* pack

valle *f* valley

valore *m* value; (*coraggio*) bravery, valour, *Am* valor; *-i pl* securities; *di ~* valuable; (*far risaltare*) show off

valorizzare increase the value of; (*far risaltare*) show off

valuta *f* currency; *valutare* value

valvola *f* valve; EL fuse

valzer *m inv* waltz

vandalo *m* vandal

vanga *f* spade

vangelo *m* gospel

vaniglia *f* vanilla

vanità *f* vanity; *vanitoso* vain

vanno ☞ *andare*

vano 1 *agg* minacce, promesse empty; (*inutile*) vain 2 *m* (*spazio vuoto*) hollow; (*stanza*) room

vantaggio *m* advantage; *in gara* lead; *vantaggioso* advantageous

vantarsi boast (*di* about)

vapore *m* vapour, *Am* vapor; MAR steamer; *~* (*acqueo*) steam; *vaporetto m* water bus; *vaporoso* floaty; (*vago*) woolly, *Am* wooly

variabile 1 *agg* changeable 2 *f* MAT variable; *variare* vary; *variazione f* variation

varice *f* varicose vein

varicella *f* chickenpox

varietà 1 *f inv* variety 2 *m inv* variety, *Am* vaudeville; (*spettacolo o dì*) ~ (*variety o Am* vaudeville) show; *vario* varied; *-ri pl* various

variopinto multicoloured, *Am* multicolored

vasca *f* (*serbatoio, cisterna*) tank; (*lunghezza di piscina*) length; *di fontana* basin; *~* (*da bagno*) bath, (bath)tub

vaselina *f* vaseline

vasellame *m* dishes

vaso *m* pot; ANAT vessel

vassoio *m* tray

vasto vast

V.d.F. (= *vigili del fuoco*) fire brigade, *Am* fire department

ve = *vi* (*before lo, la, li, le, ne*)

vecchiaia *f* old age; *vecchio* 1 *agg* old 2 *m*, -a *f* old man; *donna* old woman

vece *f: fare le -i di qu* take s.o.'s place

vedere see; *far ~* show

vedovo 1 *agg* widowed 2 *m*, -a *f* widower; *donna* widow

veduta *f* view (*su* of)

vegetale 1 *agg* vegetable *attr*; *vita* plant *attr* 2 *m* vegetable; *vegetariano* 1 *agg* vegetarian *attr* 2 *m*, -a *f* vegetarian;

vegetazione f vegetation

vegeto *vecchio* spry; *vivo e ~* hale and hearty

veglia f (*l'essere svegli*) wakefulness; (*il vegliare*) vigil

veicolo m vehicle

vela f sail; *attività* sailing

veleno m poison; *di animali* venom (*anche fig*); **velenoso** poisonous; *fig* venomous

veliero m sailing ship

velina: *carta f ~ per imballaggio* tissue paper

velista m/f sailor

velluto m velvet; *~ a coste* corduroy

velo m veil

veloce fast, quick; **velocemente** quickly; **velocità** f inv speed

vena f vein

vendemmia f (grape) harvest; **vendemmiare** harvest

vendere sell

vendetta f revenge; **vendicare** avenge; **vendicarsi** get one's revenge (*di qu* on s.o.; *di qc* for sth)

vendita f sale; **venditore** m, **-trice** f salesman; *donna* saleswoman

venerare revere

venerdì m inv Friday; *Venerdì Santo* Good Friday

Venere f Venus

Venezia f Venice; **veneziano 1** agg Venetian **2** m, **-a** f Venetian

vengo ☞ **venire**; **venire** come; (*riuscire*) turn out; *come ausiliare* be; *mi sta venendo fame* I'm getting hungry

ventaglio m fan

ventenne agg, m/f twenty-year-old; **ventesimo** twentieth; **venti** twenty

ventilatore m fan

ventina f: *una ~* about twenty; **ventiquattrore** f inv valigetta overnight bag

vento m wind; *c'è ~* it's windy; **ventoso** windy

ventre m stomach

venuta f arrival; **venuto** pp ☞ **venire**

veramente really

veranda f veranda

verbale 1 agg verbal **2** m record; *di riunione* minutes

verbo m GRAM verb

verde 1 agg green **2** m green; POL *i -i* pl the Greens

verdura f vegetables

vergine 1 agg virgin attr **2** f virgin; ASTR *Vergine* Virgo

vergogna f shame; (*timidezza*) shyness; **vergognarsi** be ashamed; (*essere timido*) be shy; **vergognoso** ashamed; (*timido*) shy; *azione* shameful

verifica f check; **verificare** check; **verificarsi** (*accadere*) occur, take place; (*avverarsi*) come true

verità f inv truth

verme m worm

vermut m vermouth

vernice f paint; *trasparente*

varnish; *pelle* patent leather; **~ fresca** wet paint; **vernicia-re** paint; *con vernice traspa-rente* varnish

vero 1 *agg* true; *(autentico)* re-al; *sei contento, ~?* you're happy, aren't you?; *ti piace il gelato, ~?* you like ice cream, don't you? **2** *m* truth

veronese 1 *agg* of Verona **2** *m/f* inhabitant of Verona

verosimile likely

verruca *f* wart

versamento *m* payment

versante *m* slope

versare *vino* pour; *denaro* pay; *(rovesciare)* spill

versione *f* version; *(traduzio-ne)* translation

verso 1 *prp* towards; *andare ~ casa* head for home; *~ le ot-to* about eight o'clock **2** *m* di *poesie* verse

vertebra *f* vertebra; **vertebra-le: colonna** *f* **~** spinal col-umn

verticale 1 *agg* vertical **2** *f* ver-tical (line); *in ginnastica* handstand

vertice *m* summit

vertigine *f* vertigo, dizziness; *ho le ~ i* I feel dizzy; **vertigi-noso** *altezza* dizzy; *prezzi* sky-high; *velocità* breakneck

verza *f* savoy (cabbage)

vescica *f* ANAT bladder

vescovo *m* bishop

vespa *f* ZO wasp; *(scooter)* Vespa® scooter; **vespista** *m/f* Vespa® rider

vestaglia *f* dressing gown, *Am* robe

veste *f* fig *(capacità, funzione)* capacity; *in ~ ufficiale* in an offical capacity; **vestiario** *m* wardrobe; **vestire** dress; *(portare)* wear; **vestirsi** get dressed; *in un certo modo* dress; **~ da** *(travestirsi)* dress up as; **vestito** *m* da *uomo* suit; *da donna* dress; *(capo di vestiario)* item of clothing, garment; *-i pl* clothes; *-i pl* **da uomo** menswear

veterinario *m*, *-a* *f* veterinary surgeon, vet *F*

veto *m* veto; *porre il ~ a* veto

vetrata *f* *finestra* large win-dow; *porta* glass door; *di chiesa* stained-glass window; **vetrina** *f* (shop) window; *mobile* display cabinet; *di museo, di negozio* fig showcase; **vetrini-sta** *m/f* window dresser; **ve-tro** *m* glass; *di finestra, porta* pane; **di ~** glass *attr*

vetta *f* top; *di montagna* peak

vettura *f* AUTO car; FERR car-riage, car

vi 1 *pron* you; *riflessivo* your-selves; *reciproco* each other **2** *avv ☞* **ci**

via 1 *f* street, road; fig way; *per ~ di* by; *(a causa di)* because of **2** *m* off, starting signal; SP *dare il ~* give the off **3** *avv* away; *andar ~* go away, leave; **e così ~** and so on; **~!** go away!; *(suvvia)* come on! **4** *prp* via, by way of

viabilità *f* road conditions; (*rete stradale*) road network; (*traffico stradale*) road traffic

viadotto *m* viaduct

viaggiare travel; **viaggiatore** *m*, **-trice** *f* traveller, *Am* traveler; **viaggio** *m* journey; **~ di nozze** honeymoon; **~ d'affari** business trip; **~ di studio** study trip; **essere in ~** be away, be travelling

viale *m* avenue

viavai *m inv* coming and going

vibrare vibrate; **vibrazione** *f* vibration

vice *m/f inv* deputy

vice- *prefisso* vice-

vicedirettore *m* assistant manager

vicenda *f* (*episodio*) event; (*storia*) story; **a ~** (*a turno*) in turn; (*scambievolmente*) each other, one another

viceversa vice versa

vicinanza *f* nearness, proximity; **-e** *pl* neighbourhood, *Am* neighborhood, vicinity; **vicinato** *m* neighbourhood, *Am* neighborhood, (*persone*) neighbours, *Am* neighbors; **vicino 1** *agg* near, close; **~** *a* near, close to; (*accanto a*) next to; **da~** *esaminare* closely; *visto* close up **2** *avv* nearby, close by **3** *m*, **-a** *f* neighbour, *Am* neighbor

vicolo *m* lane; **~ cieco** dead end

videata *f* INFOR display

video *m* video; **F** (*schermo*) screen; **videocamera** *f* videocamera, camcorder; **videocassetta** *f* video (cassette); **videogioco** *m* video game; **videoregistratore** *m* video (recorder); **videoteca** *f* video library; *negozio* video shop *o Am* store; **videotel** *m inv* Italian Videotex®; **videotelefono** *m* videophone

vietare forbid; **~ a qu di fare qc** forbid s.o. to do sth; **vietato** forbidden; **~ fumare** no smoking

vigilanza *f* vigilance; **sotto ~** under surveillance; **vigile 1** *agg* watchful **2** *m/f*: **~** (*urbano*) local police officer; **~ del fuoco** firefighter; **vigilia** *f* night before, eve; **~ di Natale** Christmas Eve

vigliacco 1 *agg* cowardly **2** *m*, **-a** *f* coward

vigna *f* (small) vineyard; **vigneto** *m* vineyard

vignetta *f* cartoon

vigore *m* vigour, *Am* vigor

vile 1 *agg* vile; (*codardo*) cowardly **2** *m* coward

villa *f* villa

villaggio *m* village; **~ turistico** holiday village

villeggiatura *f* holiday, *Am* vacation

villino *m* house

vincere *v/t* win; *avversario* defeat, beat; *difficoltà* overcome **2** *v/i* win; **vincita** *f* win; **vincitore** *m*, **-trice** *f* winner

vincolare bind; *capitale* tie up; **vincolo** *m* bond

vino *m* wine; **~ bianco** white wine; **~ rosso** red wine

vinto *pp* ☞ **vincere**

viola 1 *m/agg inv* purple **2** *f* MUS violet; BOT violet

violare violate; *legge* break; **violazione** *f* violation; *di leggi, accordi* breach; **~ di domicilio** unlawful entry

violentare rape; **violento** violent; **violenza** *f* violence

violino *m* violin; **violoncello** *m* cello

vipera *f* viper

virgola *f* comma; MAT decimal point

virile manly, virile

virtù *f inv* virtue

virus *m inv* virus

vischio *m* mistletoe

viscido slimy

viscosa *f* viscose

visibile visible; **visibilità** *f* visibility

visiera *f di berretto* peak; *di casco* visor

visione *f* sight, vision

visita *f* visit; **~ medica** medical (examination); **far ~ a qu** visit s.o.; **visitare** visit; MED examine; **visitatore** *m*, **-trice** *f* visitor

visivo visual

viso *m* face

visone *m* mink

vissuto *pp* ☞ **vivere**

vista *f* sight; *(veduta)* view; **a prima ~** at first sight; **conoscere qu di ~** know s.o. by sight; *fig* **perdere qu di ~** lose touch with s.o.; **visto 1** *pp* ☞ **vedere**; **~ che** seeing that **2** *m* visa; **vistoso** eye-catching

visuale 1 *agg* visual **2** *f (veduta)* view

vita *f* life; *(durata della vita)* lifetime; ANAT waist; **vitale** vital; *persona* lively

vitamina *f* vitamin

vite[1] *f* TEC screw

vite[2] *f* AGR vine

vitello *m* calf; GASTR veal

viticoltura *f* vinegrowing

vitreo *fig: sguardo* glazed

vittima *f* victim

vitto *m* diet food; **~ e alloggio** bed and board

vittoria *f* victory

viva voce *m inv* speakerphone, hands-free phone

vivace lively; *colore* bright

vivaio *m di pesci* tank; *di piante* nursery; *fig* breeding ground

vivanda *f* food

vivente living; **vivere 1** *v/i* live *(di* on) **2** *v/t (passare, provare)* experience; *vita* live, lead; **viveri** *mpl* food (supplies)

vivisezione *f* vivisection

vivo 1 *agg (in vita)* alive; *(vivente)* living; *colore* bright; **farsi ~** get in touch; *(arrivare)* turn up **2** *m*: **dal ~ trasmissione** live; **i -i** *pl* the living *pl*

viziare *persona* spoil; **viziato** *persona* spoiled; **aria** *f* -**a** stale air; **vizio** *m* vice; (*cattiva abitudine*) (bad) habit; (*dipendenza*) addiction; **vizioso** *persona* dissolute; *circolo m* ~ vicious circle

v.le (= *viale*) St (= *street*)

vocabolario *m* vocabulary; (*dizionario*) dictionary; **vocabolo** *m* word

vocale 1 *agg* vocal **2** *f* vowel

vocazione *f* vocation

voce *f* voice; *fig* rumour, *Am* rumor; *in dizionario, elenco* entry

voglia *f* (*desiderio*) wish, desire; (*volontà*) will; *sulla pelle* birthmark; *avere ~ di fare qc* feel like doing sth; *contro ~*, *di mala ~* unwillingly; **voglio** ☞ **volere**

voi you; *riflessivo* yourselves; *reciproco* each other

volano *m* shuttlecock

volante 1 *agg* flying **2** *m* AUTO (steering) wheel; **volantino** *m* leaflet; **volare** fly

volentieri willingly; ~! with pleasure!

volere 1 *v/t & v/i* want; *vorrei ... I* would *o* I'd like ...; *vorrei partire* I'd like to leave; ~ *dire* mean; ~ *bene a qu* (*amare*) love s.o.; *ci vogliono dieci mesi* it takes ten months; *senza ~* without meaning to **2** *m* will

volgare vulgar

volgere *v/t*: ~ *le spalle* turn

one's back **2** *v/i*: ~ *al termine* draw to a close

volo *m* flight; (*caduta*) fall; ~ *di linea* scheduled flight; *fig afferrare qc al* ~ be quick to grasp sth

volontà *f* will; *a* ~ as much as you like; *buona* ~ goodwill; **volontariato** *m* voluntary work; **volontario 1** *agg* voluntary **2** *m*, -**a** *f* volunteer

volpe *f* fox; *femmina* vixen

volt *m inv* volt

volta *f* time; (*turno*) turn; ARCHI vault; *una* ~ once; *due* ~*e* twice; *qualche* ~ sometimes; *poco per* ~ little by little; *un'altra* ~ (*ancora una volta*) one more time; *lo faremo un'altra* ~ we'll do it some other time

voltaggio *m* voltage

voltare turn; ~ *a destra* turn right; **voltarsi** turn (round)

volto¹ *m* face

volto² *pp* ☞ **volgere**

volume *m* volume; **voluminoso** bulky

vomitare vomit; **vomito** *m* vomit

vongola *f* ZO, GASTR clam

vortice *m* whirl; *in acqua* whirlpool; *di vento* whirlwind

vostro 1 *agg* your; *i* -*i amici* your friends **2** *pron*: *il* ~ yours; *questi libri sono* -*i* these books are yours

votare vote; **votazione** *f* vote; **voto** *m* POL vote; EDU mark,

Am grade; REL vow
v.r. (= *vedi retro*) see over
v.s. (= *vedi sopra*) see above
Vs. (= *vostro*) your
V.U. (= *Vigili Urbani*) police
vulcanico volcanic; **vulcano**
m volcano
vulnerabile vulnerable

vuole ☞ *volere*
vuotare empty; **vuotarsi**
empty; **vuoto 1** *agg* empty;
(*non occupato*) vacant **2** *m*
(*spazio*) empty space; (*recipiente*) empty; FIS vacuum;
fig void; **andare a ~** fall
through

W

W (= *watt*) W (= watt); (= *viva*)
walkman *m inv* Walkman®
watt *m inv* watt
WC *m inv* WC
week-end *m inv* weekend

western *m inv* Western
whisky *m inv* whisky
windsurf *m inv* (*tavola*) sail-
board; *attività* windsurfing;
fare ~ go windsurfing

X

X, x *f* x; **raggi** *mpl* **~** X-rays
xenofobia *f* xenophobia

xilofono *m* xylophone

Y

yacht *m inv* yacht
yoga *m* yoga

yogurt *m inv* yoghurt

Z

zafferano *m* saffron
zaffiro *m* sapphire
zaino *m* rucksack, backpack
zampa *f* ZO (*piede*) paw; *di uccello* claw; (*arto*) leg; GASTR
di maiale trotter

zampillare gush; **zampillo** *m*
spurt
zampone *m* GASTR stuffed
pig's trotter
zanzara *f* mosquito; **zanza-
riera** *f* mosquito net; *su fine-*

stre insect screen

zappa *f* hoe; **zappare** hoe

zapping *m inv*: **fare lo ~** zap, channel-punch

zattera *f* raft

zebra *f* zebra

zecca[1] *f* ZO tick

zecca[2] *f* Mint

zelo *m* zeal

zenzero *m* ginger

zeppo: *pieno* **~** crammed (*di* with)

zerbino *m* doormat

zero *m* zero; *nel tennis* love; *nel calcio* nil; **2 gradi sotto ~** 2 degrees below zero

zigomo *m* cheekbone

zigzag *m inv* zigzag

zimbello *m* decoy; *fig* laughing stock

zinco *m* zinc

zingaro *m*, **-a** *f* gipsy

zio *m*, **-a** *f* uncle; *donna* aunt

zitto quiet; **sta ~!** be quiet!

zoccolo *m* clog; ZO hoof

zodiacale: **segni** *mpl* **-i** signs of the Zodiac

zolfo *m* sulphur, *Am* sulfur

zona *f* zone, area; **~ disco** short-stay parking area; **~ industriale** industrial area; **~ pedonale** pedestrian precinct

zoo *m inv* zoo

zoppicare limp; *di mobile* wobble

zoppo lame; (*zoppicante*) limping; *mobile* wobbly

zucca *f* marrow; *fig* F (*testa*) nut F

zuccherare sugar; **zucchero** *m* sugar

zucchini *mpl* courgettes, *Am* zucchini(s)

zuffa *f* scuffle

zuppa *f* soup; **~ inglese** trifle

zuppo soaked

English-Italian
Inglese-Italiano

A

a [ə] un *m*, una *f*; *masculine before s + consonant, gn, ps, x, y, z* uno; *feminine before vowel* un'; *five flights ~ day* cinque voli al giorno

aback [ə'bæk]: *taken ~* preso alla sprovvista

abandon [ə'bændən] abbandonare; *scheme* rinunciare a

abate [ə'beɪt] *of storm* calmarsi

abbey ['æbɪ] abbazia *f*

abbreviate [ə'briːvɪeɪt] abbreviare; **abbreviation** abbreviazione *f*

abdicate ['æbdɪkeɪt] abdicare

abdomen ['æbdəmən] addome *m*

abduct [əb'dʌkt] sequestrare

♦ **abide by** [ə'baɪd] attenersi a

ability [ə'bɪlətɪ] abilità *f inv*

ablaze [ə'bleɪz] in fiamme

able ['eɪbl] (*skilful*) capace; *be ~ to do sth* poter fare qc

abnormal [æb'nɔːml] anormale

aboard [ə'bɔːd] **1** *prep* a bordo di **2** *adv* a bordo

abolish [ə'bɒlɪʃ] abolire; **abolition** abolizione *f*

abort [ə'bɔːt] annullare; *program* interrompere; **abortion** aborto *m*; *have an ~* abortire; **abortive** fallito

about [ə'baʊt] **1** *prep* (*concerning*) su; *talk ~ sth* parlare di qc; *be angry ~ sth* essere arrabbiato per qc; *what's it ~?* of book, film di cosa parla?; *of complaint, problem* di cosa si tratta? **2** *adv* (*roughly*) intorno a; (*nearly*) quasi; *it's ~ ready* è quasi pronto; *be ~ to ...* (*be going to*) essere sul punto di ...; *be ~* (*somewhere near*) essere nei paraggi; *there are a lot of people ~* c'è un sacco di gente qui

above [ə'bʌv] sopra; *on the floor ~* al piano di sopra; **above-mentioned** suddetto

abrasive [ə'breɪsɪv] *personality* ruvido

abreast [ə'brest] fianco a fianco; *keep ~ of* tenere al corrente di

abridge [ə'brɪdʒ] ridurre

abroad [ə'brɔːd] all'estero

abrupt [ə'brʌpt] brusco

abscess ['æbsɪs] ascesso *m*

absence ['æbsəns] assenza f;
absent assente; **absentee**
assente m/f; **absenteeism**
assenteismo m; **absent-
minded** distratto

absolute ['æbsəlu:t] assoluto;
idiot totale; **absolutely** assolutamente; **absolution** REL
assoluzione f; **absolve** assolvere

absorb [əb'sɔ:b] assorbire;
absorbent assorbente; **ab-
sorbing** avvincente

abstain [əb'steɪn] *from voting*
astenersi; **abstention** *in voting* astensione f

abstract ['æbstrækt] astratto

absurd [əb'sɜ:d] assurdo; **absurdity** assurdità f inv

abundance [ə'bʌndəns] ab-
bondanza f; **abundant** abbondante

abuse¹ [ə'bju:s] n abuso m;
(*ill treatment*) maltrattamento m; (*insults*) insulti mpl

abuse² [ə'bju:z] v/t abusare
di; (*treat badly*) maltrattare;
(*insult*) insultare

abusive [ə'bju:sɪv] *language*
offensivo; ***become ~*** diventare aggressivo

abysmal [ə'bɪzml] F (*very
bad*) pessimo

academic [ækə'demɪk] **1** n
docente m/f universitario,
-a **2** adj accademico; *person*
portato per lo studio; **academy** accademia f

accelerate [ək'seləreɪt] accelerare; **acceleration** accele-

razione f; **accelerator** acceleratore m

accent ['æksənt] accento m;
accentuate accentuare

accept [ək'sept] accettare;
acceptable accettabile; **acceptance** accettazione f

access ['ækses] **1** n accesso m
2 v/t accedere a; **accessible**
accessibile

accessory [ək'sesərɪ] acces-
sorio m; LAW complice m/f

accident ['æksɪdənt] incidente m; **by ~** per caso; **accidental** accidentale; **accidentally**
accidentalmente

acclimatize [ə'klaɪmətaɪz] acclimatarsi

accommodate [ə'kɒmədeɪt]
ospitare; *needs* tenere conto
di; **accommodation**, *Am*
accommodations sistemazione f

accompaniment [ə'kʌmpə-
nɪmənt] MUS accompagna-
mento m; **accompany** accompagnare

accomplice [ə'kʌmplɪs] complice m/f

accomplished [ə'kʌmplɪʃt]
dotato; **accomplishment**
of task realizzazione f; (*talent*) talento m; (*achievement*)
risultato m

accord [ə'kɔ:d] accordo m; **of
his own ~** di sua spontanea
volontà

accordance [ə'kɔ:dəns]: **in ~
with** conformemente a

according [ə'kɔ:dɪŋ]: **~ to** secondo; **accordingly** di conseguenza

accordion [əˈkɔːdɪən] fisarmonica f

account [əˈkaʊnt] *financial* conto m; *(report, description)* resoconto m; **give an ~ of** fare un resoconto di; **on no ~** per nessuna ragione; **on ~ of** a causa di; **take into ~** tenere conto di

◆ **account for** *(explain)* giustificare; *(make up)* ammontare a

accountable [əˈkaʊntəbl] responsabile; **accountant** contabile m/f; *running own business* commercialista m/f; **account number** numero m di conto; **accounts** contabilità f

accumulate [əˈkjuːmjʊleɪt] **1** *v/t* accumulare **2** *v/i* accumularsi; **accumulation** accumulazione f

accuracy [ˈækjʊrəsɪ] precisione f; **accurate** preciso; **accurately** con precisione

accusation [ækjuːˈzeɪʃn] accusa f; **accuse**: **~ s.o. of sth** accusare qn di qc; **accused** LAW accusato m, -a f; **accusing** accusatorio

accustom [əˈkʌstəm]: **get ~ed to** abituarsi

ace [eɪs] *in cards* asso m; *(in tennis: shot)* ace m inv

ache [eɪk] **1** n dolore m **2** v/i fare male

achieve [əˈtʃiːv] realizzare; *success* ottenere; **achievement of** *ambition* realizzazione f; *(thing achieved)* successo m

acid [ˈæsɪd] acido m

acknowledge [əkˈnɒlɪdʒ] riconoscere; **~ receipt of** accusare ricezione di; **acknowledg(e)ment** riconoscimento m; *(letter)* lettera f di accusata ricezione

acorn [ˈeɪkɔːn] ghianda f

acoustics [əˈkuːstɪks] acustica f

acquaint [əˈkweɪnt]: **be ~ed with** fml conoscere; **acquaintance** *person* conoscenza f

acquire [əˈkwaɪə(r)] acquisire; **acquisition** acquisizione f

acquit [əˈkwɪt] LAW assolvere; **acquittal** LAW assoluzione f

acre [ˈeɪkə(r)] acro m *(4.047m²)*

acrobat [ˈækrəbæt] acrobata m/f

across [əˈkrɒs] **1** *prep on other side of* dall'altro lato di; **walk ~ the street** attraversare la strada; **a bridge ~ the river** un ponte sul fiume; **~ Europe** all over in tutta Europa **2** *adv to other side* dall'altro lato **10 m ~** largo 10 m; **swim ~** attraversare a nuoto

act [ækt] **1** *v/i* agire; THEA recitare **2** n *(deed)* atto m; *of play* atto m; *in variety show* numero m; *(pretence)* finta f; (*law*) atto m

action ['ækʃn] azione f; **take ~** agire; **action replay** TV replay m inv

active ['æktıv] attivo; **activist** POL attivista m/f; **activity** attività f inv

actor ['æktə(r)] attore m; **actress** attrice f

actual ['æktʃʊəl] reale; *cost* effettivo; **actually** in realtà; *expressing surprise* veramente; *stressing the converse* a dire il vero

acute [ə'kju:t] acuto

ad [æd] → **advertisement**

AD [eı'di:] (:= *anno domini*) d.C. (= dopo Cristo)

adamant ['ædəmənt] categorico

adapt [ə'dæpt] **1** v/t adattare **2** v/i *of person* adattarsi; **adaptability** adattabilità f; **adaptable** adattabile; **adaptation** *of play etc* adattamento m; **adapter** *electrical* adattatore m

add [æd] **1** v/t aggiungere; MATH addizionare **2** v/i *of person* fare le somme

♦ **add on** v/t aggiungere

♦ **add up 1** v/t sommare **2** v/i fig quadrare

addict ['ædıkt] *to football, chess* maniaco m, -a f; *drug* ~ tossicomane m/f; *TV* ~ teledipendente m/f; **addicted** dipendente; **be ~ to** *drugs, alcohol* essere dedito a; **addiction** dipendenza f; **addic-**

tive: **be ~** provocare dipendenza

addition [ə'dıʃn] MATH addizione f; *to list, company etc* aggiunta f; **in ~ to** in aggiunta a; **additional** aggiuntivo; **additive** additivo m; **add-on** complemento m

address [ə'dres] **1** n indirizzo m **2** v/t *letter* indirizzare; *audience* tenere un discorso a; **address book** indirizzario m; **addressee** destinatario m, -a f

adequate ['ædıkwət] adeguato; **adequately** adeguatamente

♦ **adhere to** [æd'hıə(r)] *surface* aderire a; *rules* attenersi a

adhesive [əd'hi:sıv] adesivo m

adjacent [ə'dʒeısnt] adiacente

adjective ['ædʒıktıv] aggettivo m

adjoining [ə'dʒɔınıŋ] adiacente

adjourn [ə'dʒɜ:n] aggiornare; **adjournment** aggiornamento m

adjust [ə'dʒʌst] **1** v/t regolare **2** v/i: **~ to** adattarsi a; **adjustable** regolabile; **adjustment** regolazione f; *psychological* adattamento m

ad lib [æd'lıb] **1** adj a braccio F **2** v/i improvvisare

administer [əd'mınıstə(r)] *country* governare; **adminis-**

tration amministrazione f; (government) governo m; **administrative** amministrativo; **administrator** amministratore m, -trice f

admirable ['ædmərəbl] ammirevole

admiral ['ædmərəl] ammiraglio m

admiration [ædmə'reɪʃn] ammirazione f; **admire** ammirare; **admirer** ammiratore m, -trice f; **admiring** ammirativo; **admiringly** con ammirazione

admissible [əd'mɪsəbl] ammissibile; **admission** (confession) ammissione f; **~ free** entrata f libera; **admit** ammettere; to a place lasciare entrare; to school, club etc ammettere; to hospital ricoverare; **admittance: no ~** vietato l'accesso

adolescence [ædə'lesns] adolescenza f; **adolescent 1** n adolescente m/f **2** adj adolescenziale

adopt [ə'dɒpt] adottare; **adoption** adozione f

adorable [ə'dɔ:rəbl] adorabile; **adoration** adorazione f; **adore** adorare

adrenalin [ə'drenəlɪn] adrenalina f

adrift [ə'drɪft] alla deriva; fig sbandato

adult ['ædʌlt] **1** n adulto m, -a f **2** adj adulto; **adultery** adulterio m

advance [əd'vɑ:ns] **1** n (money) anticipo m; in science etc progresso m; MIL avanzata f; **in ~** in anticipo; **make ~s** (progress) fare progressi; sexually fare delle avances **2** v/i MIL avanzare; (make progress) fare progressi **3** v/t theory avanzare; money anticipare; knowledge, cause fare progredire; **advanced** avanzato; learner di livello avanzato

advantage [əd'vɑ:ntɪdʒ] vantaggio m; **take ~ of** opportunity approfittare di; **advantageous** vantaggioso

adventure [əd'ventʃə(r)] avventura f; **adventurous** avventuroso

adverb ['ædvɜ:b] avverbio m

adversary ['ædvəsəri] avversario m, -a f

adverse ['ædvɜ:s] avverso

advertise ['ædvətaɪz] **1** v/t job mettere un annuncio per; product reclamizzare **2** v/i for job mettere un annuncio; for product fare pubblicità; **advertisement** annuncio m; for product pubblicità f inv; **advertiser** in newspaper etc inserzionista m/f; **advertising** pubblicità f; **advertising agency** agenzia f pubblicitaria; **advertising campaign** campagna f pubblicitaria

advice [əd'vaɪs] consigli mpl; **a bit of ~** un consiglio;

advisable consigliabile; **advise** *person* consigliare a

advocate ['ædvəkeɪt] propugnare

aerial ['eərɪəl] antenna *f*; **aerial photograph** fotografia *f* aerea

aerobics [eə'rəʊbɪks] aerobica *f*

aerodynamic [eərəʊdaɪ'næmɪk] aerodinamico

aeronautical [eərəʊ'nɔːtɪkl] aeronautico

aeroplane ['eərəpleɪn] aeroplano *m*

aerosol ['eərəsɒl] spray *m inv*

aesthetic [iːs'θetɪk] estetico

affair [ə'feə(r)] (*matter*) affare *m*; (*love*) relazione *f*

affect [ə'fekt] *v/t* colpire; (*influence*) influire su; (*concern*) riguardare

affection [ə'fekʃn] affetto *m*; **affectionate** affettuoso; **affectionately** affettuosamente

affirmative [ə'fɜːmətɪv] affermativo

affluence ['æfluəns] benessere *m*; **affluent** benestante

afford [ə'fɔːd]: **be able to ~ sth** potersi permettere qc; **affordable** abbordabile

afloat [ə'fləʊt] *boat* a galla

afraid [ə'freɪd]: **be ~** avere paura (*of* di); **I'm ~** *expressing regret* sono spiacente

afresh [ə'freʃ] da capo

Africa ['æfrɪkə] Africa *f*; **African 1** *n* africano *m*, -a *f* **2** *adj*

africano; **African-American 1** *n* afroamericano *m*, -a *f* **2** *adj* afroamericano

after ['ɑːftə(r)] **1** *prep* dopo; ~ **her / me** dopo di lei / me; ~ **all** dopo tutto; ~ **that** dopo; **the day ~ tomorrow** dopodomani **2** *adv* dopo; **the day ~** il giorno dopo **3** *conj*: **after I left, I saw ...** dopo essere uscito ho visto ...; **after I left, she saw ...** dopo che io sono uscito, lei ha visto ...;

aftermath: **the ~ of war** il dopoguerra; **in the ~ of** nel periodo immediatamente successivo a; **afternoon** pomeriggio *m*; **this ~** oggi pomeriggio; **good ~** buon giorno; **after sales service** servizio *m* dopovendita; **aftershave** dopobarba *m inv*; **afterwards** dopo

again [ə'gen] di nuovo; **I never saw him** ~ non l'ho mai più visto

against [ə'genst] contro

age [eɪdʒ] **1** *n* (*also era*) età *f inv*; **she's five years of ~** ha cinque anni; **I've been waiting for ~s** F ho aspettato un secolo F **2** *v/i* invecchiare; **aged**: **a boy ~ 16** un ragazzo di 16 anni; **he was ~ 16** aveva 16 anni; **age group** fascia *f* d'età; **age limit** limite *m* d'età

agency ['eɪdʒənsɪ] agenzia *f*

agenda [ə'dʒendə] ordine *m* del giorno

agent ['eɪdʒənt] agente *m/f*

aggravate ['ægrəveɪt] aggravare; (*annoy*) seccare

aggression [ə'greʃn] aggressione *f*; **aggressive** aggressivo; **aggressively** con aggressività

aghast [ə'gɑːst] inorridito

agile ['ædʒaɪl] agile; **agility** agilità *f*

agitated ['ædʒɪteɪtɪd] agitato; **agitation** agitazione *f*; **agitator** agitatore *m*, -trice *f*

agnostic [æg'nɒstɪk] agnostico *m*, -a *f*

ago [ə'gəʊ]: 2 *days* ~ due giorni fa; *long* ~ molto tempo fa

agonize ['ægənaɪz] angosciarsi (*over* per); **agonizing** angosciante; **agony** agonia *f*; *mental* angoscia *f*

agree [ə'griː] 1 *v/i* essere d'accordo; *of figures* quadrare; (*reach agreement*) mettersi d'accordo; *I* ~ sono d'accordo 2 *v/t price* concordare; **agreeable** (*pleasant*) piacevole; **agreement** accordo *m*

agricultural [ægrɪ'kʌltʃərəl] agricolo; **agriculture** agricoltura *f*

ahead [ə'hed] davanti; (*in advance*) avanti; *be* ~ *of* essere davanti a; *plan* ~ programmare per tempo

aid [eɪd] 1 *n* aiuto *m* 2 *v/t* aiutare

aide [eɪd] assistente *m/f*

Aids [eɪdz] Aids *m*

ailing ['eɪlɪŋ] *economy* malato

ailment ['eɪlmənt] disturbo *m*

aim [eɪm] 1 *n* (*objective*) obiettivo *m* 2 *v/i in shooting* mirare; ~ *to do sth* aspirare a fare qc 3 *v/t*: *be* ~*ed at of remark etc* essere rivolto a; *of guns* essere puntato contro; **aimless** senza obiettivi; *wandering* senza meta

air [eə(r)] 1 *n* aria *f*; *by* ~ *travel* in aereo; *send mail* per via aerea; *in the open* ~ all'aperto; *on the* ~ RAD, TV in onda 2 *v/t room* arieggiare; *views* rendere noto; **airbag** airbag *m inv*; **air-conditioned** con aria condizionata; **air-conditioning** aria *f* condizionata; **aircraft** aereo *m*; **aircraft carrier** portaerei *f inv*; **air fare** tariffa *f* aerea; **air force** aeronautica *f* militare; **air hostess** hostess *f inv*; **airline** compagnia *f* aerea; **airliner** aereo *m* di linea; **airmail**: *by* ~ per via aerea; **airplane** *Am* aeroplano *m*; **airport** aeroporto *m*; **air rage** comportamento *m* di estrema irascibilità dei passeggeri di un aereo; **air terminal** terminal *m*; **air-traffic control** controllo *m* del traffico aereo; **air-traffic controller** controllore *m* di volo

aisle [aɪl] *in supermarket* corsia *f*; *in church* navata *f* laterale

ajar [ə'dʒɑː(r)]: *be* ~ essere socchiuso

alarm [əˈlɑːm] **1** *n* allarme *m* **2** *v/t* allarmare; **alarm clock** sveglia *f*; **alarming** allarmante; **alarmingly** in modo allarmante

Albania [ælˈbeɪnɪə] Albania *f*; **Albanian 1** *adj* albanese **2** *n* albanese *m/f*; *language* albanese *m*

album [ˈælbəm] album *m inv*

alcohol [ˈælkəhɒl] alcol *m*; **alcoholic 1** *n* alcolizzato *m*, -a *f* **2** *adj* alcolico

alert [əˈlɜːt] **1** *n* (*signal*) allarme *m* **2** *v/t* mettere in guardia **3** *adj* all'erta *inv*

A-level [ˈeɪlevl] *diploma di scuola media superiore in Gran Bretagna che permette di accedere all'università*

alibi [ˈælɪbaɪ] alibi *m inv*

alien [ˈeɪlɪən] **1** *n* straniero *m*, -a *f*; *from space* alieno *m*, -a *f* **2** *adj* estraneo; **alienate** alienarsi

align [əˈlaɪn] allineare

alike [əˈlaɪk] **1** *adj* simile; *be* ~ assomigliarsi **2** *adv*: *old and young* ~ vecchi e giovani allo stesso tempo

alimony [ˈælɪmənɪ] alimenti *mpl*

alive [əˈlaɪv]: *be* ~ essere vivo

all [ɔːl] **1** *adj* tutto; (*any whatever*) qualsiasi; ~ *day* tutto il giorno; *beyond* ~ *doubt* al di là di qualsiasi dubbio **2** *pron* tutto; ~ *of us* / *them* tutti noi / loro; *he ate* ~ *of it* lo ha mangiato tutto; *for*

~ *I know* per quel che ne so; ~ *at once* tutto in una volta; (*suddenly*) tutt'a un tratto; ~ *but* (*nearly*) quasi; ~ *but John agreed* (*except*) erano tutti d'accordo tranne John; ~ *the better* molto meglio; *they're not* ~ *alike* non si assomigliano affatto; *not at* ~! niente affatto!; *two* ~ SP due pari; ~ *right* ☞ **alright**

allegation [ælɪˈgeɪʃn] accusa *f*; **allege** dichiarare; **alleged** presunto; **allegedly** a quanto si suppone

allegiance [əˈliːdʒəns] fedeltà *f inv*

allergic [əˈlɜːdʒɪk] allergico (*to* a); **allergy** allergia *f*

alleviate [əˈliːvɪeɪt] alleviare

alley [ˈælɪ] vicolo *m*

alliance [əˈlaɪəns] alleanza *f*

allocate [ˈæləkeɪt] assegnare; **allocation** assegnazione *f*; (*amount*) parte *f*

allot [əˈlɒt] assegnare

allow [əˈlaʊ] permettere; (*calculate for*) calcolare; *it's not* ~*ed* è vietato

◆ **allow for** tenere conto di

allowance [əˈlaʊəns] (*money*) sussidio *m*; (*pocket money*) paghetta *f*

alloy [ˈælɔɪ] lega *m*

all-purpose multiuso *inv*; **all-round** generale; *person* eclettico; **all-time**: *be at an* ~ *low* aver raggiunto il minimo storico

ambience

◆ **allude to** [ə'lu:d] alludere a

alluring [ə'lu:rɪŋ] attraente

'all-wheel drive quattro per quattro *m inv*

ally ['ælaɪ] alleato *m*, -a *f*

almond ['ɑ:mənd] mandorla *f*

almost ['ɔ:lməʊst] quasi

alone [ə'ləʊn] solo

along [ə'lɒŋ] **1** *prep* lungo; **walk ~ the street** camminare lungo la strada **2** *adv*: **~ with** insieme con; **all ~** (*all the time*) per tutto il tempo; **alongside** di fianco a; **person** al fianco di

aloof [ə'lu:f] in disparte

aloud [ə'laʊd] ad alta voce

alphabet ['ælfəbet] alfabeto *m*; **alphabetical** alfabetico

alpine ['ælpaɪn] alpino; **Alps** Alpi *fpl*

already [ɔ:l'redɪ] già

alright [ɔ:l'raɪt]: **I'm ~** (*not hurt*) sto bene; (*have got enough*) va bene così; **is the monitor ~?** (*in working order*) funziona il monitor?; **is it ~ with you if I ...?** ti va bene se ...?; **~, you can have one!** va bene, puoi averne uno!; **that's ~** (*don't mention it*) non c'è di che; (*I don't mind*) non fa niente; **~, that's enough!** basta così!

Alsatian [æl'seɪʃn] pastore *m* tedesco

also ['ɔ:lsəʊ] anche

altar ['ɔ:ltə(r)] altare *m*

alter ['ɒltə(r)] modificare; *clothes* aggiustare; **altera-**

tion modifica *f*

alternate 1 ['ɒltəneɪt] *v/i* alternare **2** ['ɒltənət] *adj* alternato; **on ~ Mondays** un lunedì su due; **alternative 1** *n* alternativa *f* **2** *adj* alternativo; **alternatively** alternativamente

although [ɔ:l'ðəʊ] benché (+ *subj*), sebbene (+ *subj*)

altitude ['æltɪtju:d] altitudine *f*

altogether [ɔ:ltə'geðə(r)] (*completely*) completamente; (*in all*) complessivamente

altruism ['æltru:ɪzm] altruismo *m*; **altruistic** altruistico

aluminium [ælju'mɪnɪəm], *Am* **aluminum** [ə'lu:mɪnəm] alluminio *m*

always ['ɔ:lweɪz] sempre

a.m. ['eɪ'em] = **ante meridiem**) di mattina

amass [ə'mæs] accumulare

amateur ['æmətə(r)] *n* (*unskilled*) dilettante *m/f*; sp professionista *m/f*; **amateurish** *pej* dilettantesco

amaze [ə'meɪz] stupire; **amazed** stupito; **amazement** stupore *m*; **amazing** sorprendente; F (*good*) incredibile; **amazingly** incredibilmente

ambassador [æm'bæsədə(r)] ambasciatore *m*, -trice *f*

amber ['æmbə(r)] *n* ambra *f*; **at ~** giallo

ambience ['æmbɪəns] atmosfera *f*

ambiguity [æmbɪ'gjuːətɪ] ambiguità *f inv*; **ambiguous** ambiguo

ambition [æm'bɪʃn] ambizione *f*; **ambitious** ambizioso

ambivalent [æm'bɪvələnt] ambiguo

amble ['æmbl] camminare con calma

ambulance ['æmbjuləns] ambulanza *f*

ambush ['æmbʊʃ] **1** *n* agguato m **2** *v/t* tendere un agguato a

amend [ə'mend] emendare; **amendment** emendamento m; **amends: make ~** fare ammenda

amenities [ə'miːnətɪz] comodità *fpl*

America [ə'merɪkə] America *f*; **American 1** *n* americano m, -a *f* **2** *adj* americano

amicable ['æmɪkəbl] amichevole; **amicably** amichevolmente

ammunition [æmju'nɪʃn] munizioni *fpl*

amnesia [æm'niːzɪə] amnesia *f*

amnesty ['æmnəstɪ] amnistia *f*

among(st) [ə'mʌŋ(st)] tra

amoral [eɪ'mɒrəl] amorale

amount [ə'maʊnt] quantità *f inv*; (*sum of money*) importo m

◆ **amount to** ammontare a; (*be equal to*) equivalere a

amphibian [æm'fɪbɪən] anfi-

bio m

ample ['æmpl] abbondante

amplifier ['æmplɪfaɪə(r)] amplificatore m; **amplify** *sound* amplificare

amputate ['æmpjuːteɪt] amputare; **amputation** amputazione *f*

amuse [ə'mjuːz] (*make laugh etc*) divertire; (*entertain*) intrattenere; **amusement** (*merriment*) divertimento m; (*entertainment*) intrattenimento m; **amusement park** parco m giochi; **amusing** divertente

an [æn] ☞ **a**

anaemia [ə'niːmɪə] anemia *f*; **anaemic** anemico

anaesthetic [ænəs'θetɪk] anestetico m

analog ['ænəlɒg] COMPUT analogico; **analogy** analogia *f*

analyse, *Am* analyze ['ænəlaɪz] analizzare; (*psychoanalyse*) psicanalizzare; **analysis** analisi *f inv*; analyst PSYCH analista m/f; **analytical** analitico

anarchy ['ænəkɪ] anarchia *f*

ancestor ['ænsestə(r)] antenato m, -a *f*

anchor ['æŋkə(r)] **1** *n* NAUT ancora *f* **2** *v/i* NAUT gettare l'ancora; **anchorman** conduttore m; **anchorwoman** conduttrice *f*

ancient ['eɪnʃənt] antico

and [ænd] e

anemia *Am* ☞ **anaemia**

anesthetic *Am* ☞ **anaesthetic**

angel ['eɪndʒl] angelo *m*

anger ['æŋgə(r)] **1** *n* rabbia *f* **2** *v/t* fare arrabbiare

angle ['æŋgl] angolo *m*; (*position*, *fig*) angolazione *f*

angry ['æŋgrɪ] arrabbiato

animal ['ænɪml] animale *m*

animated ['ænɪmeɪtɪd] animato; **animated cartoon** cartone *m* animato; **animation** animazione *f*

animosity [ænɪ'mɒsɪtɪ] animosità *f inv*

ankle ['æŋkl] caviglia *f*

annexe, *Am* **annex** [ə'neks] *state* annettere

annihilate [ə'naɪəleɪt] annientare; **annihilation** annientamento *m*

anniversary [ænɪ'vɜːsərɪ] anniversario *m*

announce [ə'naʊns] annunciare; **announcement** annuncio *m*; *announcer* TV, RAD annunciatore *m*, -trice *f*

annoy [ə'nɔɪ] infastidire; **annoyance** (*anger*) irritazione *f*; (*nuisance*) fastidio *m*; **annoying** irritante

annual ['ænjʊəl] annuale

annul [ə'nʌl] annullare; **annulment** annullamento *m*

anonymous [ə'nɒnɪməs] anonimo

anorak ['ænəræk] giacca *f* a vento

anorexia [ænə'reksɪə] anores-sia *f*

another [ə'nʌðə(r)] **1** *adj* un altro *m*, un'altra *f* **2** *pron* un altro *m*, un'altra *f*; *one* ~ l'un l'altro; *do they know one* ~? si conoscono?

answer ['ɑːnsə(r)] **1** *n* risposta *f* **2** *v/t* rispondere a; ~ *the door* aprire la porta; **answering machine**, **answerphone** segreteria *f* telefonica

ant [ænt] formica *f*

antagonism [æn'tægənɪzm] antagonismo *m*; **antagonistic** ostile; **antagonize** contrariare

Antarctic [ænt'ɑːktɪk] Antartico *m*

antenatal [æntɪ'neɪtl]: ~ *classes* corso *m* di preparazione al parto; ~ *clinic* clinica *f* per gestanti

antenna [æn'tenə] antenna *f*

antibiotic [æntɪbaɪ'ɒtɪk] antibiotico *m*

anticipate [æn'tɪsɪpeɪt] prevedere; **anticipation** previsione *f*

anticlockwise ['æntɪklɒkwaɪz] **1** *adj* antiorario **2** *adv* in senso antiorario

antics ['æntɪks] buffonate *fpl*

antidote ['æntɪdəʊt] antidoto *m*

antifreeze ['æntɪfriːz] antigelo *m inv*

anti-globalist [æntɪ'gləʊbəlɪst] no-global *m/f inv*

antipathy [æn'tɪpəθɪ] antipatia *f*

antiquated ['æntɪkweɪtɪd] antiquato

antique [æn'tiːk] *n* pezzo *m* d'antiquariato

antiseptic [æntɪ'septɪk] **1** *adj* antisettico **2** *n* antisettico *m*

antisocial [æntɪ'səʊʃl] asociale

antivirus program [æntɪ'vaɪrəs] COMPUT programma *m* antivirus

anxiety [æŋ'zaɪətɪ] ansia *f*; **anxious** ansioso

any ['enɪ] **1** *adj* qualche; *are there ~ glasses?* ci sono dei bicchieri?; *is there ~ bread?* c'è del pane?; *is there ~ improvement?* c'è qualche miglioramento?; *there isn't ~ bread* non c'è pane; *take ~ one you like* prendi quello che vuoi **2** *pron*: *do you have ~?* ne hai?; *there aren't ~ left* non ce ne sono più; *there isn't ~ left* non ce n'è più; *~ of them could be guilty* chiunque di loro potrebbe essere colpevole **3** *adv is that ~ easier?* è un po' più facile?

anybody ['enɪbɒdɪ] qualcuno; *with negative* nessuno; *(whoever)* chiunque; *there wasn't ~ there* non c'era nessuno; *~ could do it* lo potrebbe fare chiunque

anyhow ['enɪhaʊ] comunque

anyone ['enɪwʌn] ☞ *anybody*

anything ['enɪθɪŋ] qualcosa; *with negatives* niente, nulla; *I didn't hear ~* non ho sentito niente *or* nulla; *~ but* per niente

anyway ['enɪweɪ] ☞ *anyhow*

anywhere ['enɪweə(r)] da qualche parte; *with negative* da nessuna parte; *(wherever)* dovunque; *I can't find it ~* non riesco a trovarlo da nessuna parte

apart [ə'pɑːt] *in distance* distante; *~ from (excepting)* a parte; *(in addition to)* oltre a

apartment [ə'pɑːtmənt] appartamento *m*; **apartment block** *Am* palazzo *m* (d'appartamenti)

ape [eɪp] scimmia *f*

Apennines ['æpənaɪnz] Appennini *mpl*

aperitif [ə'perɪtiːf] aperitivo *m*

apologize [ə'pɒlədʒaɪz] scusarsi *(to s.o.* con qu); **apology** scusa *f*

apostrophe [ə'pɒstrəfɪ] GRAM apostrofo *m*

app [æp] COMPUT app *f*

appalling [ə'pɔːlɪŋ] sconvolgente

apparatus [æpə'reɪtəs] apparecchio *m*

apparent [ə'pærənt] evidente; *(seeming)* apparente; **apparently** evidentemente

appeal [ə'piːl] *(charm)* attrattiva *f*; *for funds etc*, LAW appello *m*

aquarium

◆ **appeal for** fare un appello per

◆ **appeal to** (*be attractive to*) attirare

appealing [əˈpiːlɪŋ] *idea*, *offer* allettante

appear [əˈpɪə(r)] apparire; *in court* comparire; **it ~s that** ... sembra che ...; **appearance** apparizione *f*, *in court* comparizione *f*; (*look*) aspetto *m*

appendicitis [əpendɪˈsaɪtɪs] appendicite *f*; **appendix** MED, *of book etc* appendice *f*

appetite [ˈæpɪtaɪt] appetito *m*; **appetizer** *food* stuzzichino *m*; *drink* aperitivo *m*; **appetizing** approvazione *f*

applaud [əˈplɔːd] applaudire; **applause** applauso *m*; (*praise*) approvazione *f*

apple [ˈæpl] mela *f*; **apple pie** torta *f* di mele

appliance [əˈplaɪəns] apparecchio *m*; *household* elettrodomestico *m*

applicable [əˈplɪkəbl] applicabile; **applicant** candidato *m*, -a *f* application *for job etc* candidatura *f*; *for passport* domanda *f*; *for university* domanda *f* di iscrizione

apply [əˈplaɪ] 1 *v/t* applicare 2 *v/i of rule* applicarsi

◆ **apply for** *job*, *passport* fare domanda per; *university* fare domanda di iscrizione a

◆ **apply to** (*contact*) rivolgersi a; (*affect*) applicarsi a

appoint [əˈpɔɪnt] *to position* nominare; **appointment** *to position* nomina *f*; (*meeting*) appuntamento *m*

appraisal [əˈpreɪzl] valutazione *f*

appreciable [əˈpriːʃəbl] notevole; **appreciate 1** *v/t* apprezzare; (*acknowledge*) rendersi conto di **2** *v/i* FIN rivalutarsi; **appreciative** (*showing gratitude*) riconoscente; (*showing pleasure*) soddisfatto

apprehensive [æprɪˈhensɪv] apprensivo

approach [əˈprəʊtʃ] **1** *n* avvicinamento *m*; (*proposal*) contatto *m*; *to problem* approccio *m* **2** *v/t* (*get near to*) avvicinarsi a; (*contact*) contattare; *problem* abbordare; **approachable** abbordabile

appropriate [əˈprəʊprɪət] appropriato

approval [əˈpruːvl] approvazione *f*; **approve** approvare

◆ **approve of** approvare

approximate [əˈprɒksɪmət] approssimativo; **approximately** approssimativamente

apricot [ˈeɪprɪkɒt] albicocca *f*

April [ˈeɪprəl] aprile *m*

apt [æpt] *remark* appropriato; **aptitude** attitudine *f*

aqualung [ˈækwəlʌŋ] autorespiratore *m*

aquarium [əˈkweərɪəm] acquario *m*

Aquarius [ə'kweərɪəs] ASTR Acquario *m*

Arab ['ærəb] **1** *n* arabo *m*, -a *f* **2** *adj* arabo; **Arabic 1** *n* arabo *m* **2** *adj* arabo

arbitrary ['ɑ:bɪtrərɪ] arbitrario

arbitrate ['ɑ:bɪtreɪt] arbitrare; **arbitration** arbitrato *m*

arch [ɑ:tʃ] arco *m*

archaeological [ɑ:kɪə'lɒdʒɪkl] archeologico; **archaeologist** archeologo *m*, -a *f*; **archaeology** archeologia *f*

archaic [ɑ:'keɪɪk] arcaico

archbishop [ɑ:tʃ'bɪʃəp] arcivescovo *m*

archeology *Am* ☞ **archaeology**

architect ['ɑ:kɪtekt] architetto *m*; **architectural** architettonico; **architecture** architettura *f*

archives ['ɑ:kaɪvz] archivi *mpl*

Arctic ['ɑ:ktɪk] Artico *m*

ardent ['ɑ:dənt] ardente

arduous ['ɑ:djʊəs] arduo

area ['eərɪə] area *f*; (*region*) zona *f*; **area code** TELEC prefisso *m* telefonico

arena [ə'ri:nə] SP arena *f*

Argentina [ɑ:dʒən'ti:nə] Argentina *f*; **Argentinian 1** *adj* argentino **2** *n* argentino *m*, -a *f*

arguably ['ɑ:gjʊəblɪ] probabilmente; **it was ~** ... si può dire che ...; **argue** (*quarrel*) litigare; (*reason*) so-

stenere; **argument** (*quarrel*) litigio *m*; (*reasoning*) argomento *m*; **argumentative** polemico

arid ['ærɪd] *land* arido

Aries ['eəri:z] ASTR Ariete *m*

arise [ə'raɪz] *of situation* emergere

aristocracy [ærɪ'stɒkrəsɪ] aristocrazia *f*; **aristocrat** aristocratico *m*, -a *f*; **aristocratic** aristocratico

arithmetic [ə'rɪθmətɪk] aritmetica *f*

arm[1] [ɑ:m] *n* braccio *m*; *of chair* bracciolo *m*

arm[2] [ɑ:m] *v/t* armare

armaments ['ɑ:məmənts] armamenti *mpl*

armchair ['ɑ:mtʃeə(r)] poltrona *f*

armed [ɑ:md] armato; **armed forces** forze *fpl* armate; **armed robbery** rapina *f* a mano armata

armour, *Am* **armor** ['ɑ:mə(r)] armatura *f*; *metal plates* blindatura *f*

armpit ascella *f*

arms [ɑ:mz] (*weapons*) armi *fpl*

army ['ɑ:mɪ] esercito *m*

around [ə'raʊnd] **1** *prep* (*in circle, roughly*) intorno a; *room, world* attraverso; **it's ~ here** è dietro l'angolo **2** *adv* (*in the area*) qui intorno; (*encircling*) intorno; **he lives ~ here** abita da queste parti; **walk ~** andare in giro; **she has been ~** (*has travelled, is experienced*) ha girato; **he's still ~** F (*alive*) è ancora in circolazione

arouse [əˈrauz] suscitare; (*sexually*) eccitare

arrange [əˈreɪndʒ] (*put in order*) sistemare; *music* arrangiare; *meeting, party etc* organizzare; *time and place* combinare; **I've ~d to meet her** ho combinato di incontrarla; **arrangement** (*agreement*) accordo *m*; *of party, meeting* organizzazione *f*; *of furniture etc* disposizione *f*; *of music* arrangiamento *m*; **~s for** *party, meeting* preparativi *mpl*

arrears [əˈrɪəz] arretrati *mpl*

arrest [əˈrest] **1** *n* arresto *m*; **be under ~** essere in arresto **2** *v/t* arrestare

arrival [əˈraɪvl] arrivo *m*; **arrive** arrivare

◆ **arrive at** arrivare a

arrogance [ˈærəgəns] arroganza *f*; **arrogant** arrogante

arrow [ˈærəʊ] freccia *f*

arse [ɑːs] P culo *m* P

arson [ˈɑːsn] incendio *m* doloso

art [ɑːt] arte *f*

artery [ˈɑːtərɪ] arteria *f*

'art gallery galleria *f* d'arte

arthritis [ɑːˈθraɪtɪs] artrite *f*

artichoke [ˈɑːtɪtʃəʊk] carciofo *m*

article [ˈɑːtɪkl] articolo *m*

articulate [ɑːˈtɪkjʊlət] chiaro; **be ~** *of person* esprimersi bene

artificial [ɑːtɪˈfɪʃl] artificiale; (*not sincere*) finto

artillery [ɑːˈtɪlərɪ] artiglieria *f*

artist [ˈɑːtɪst] artista *m/f*; **artistic** artistico

'arts degree laurea *f* in discipline umanistiche

as [æz] **1** *conj* (*while, when*) mentre; (*because*) dato che; (*like*) come; **~ if** come se; **~ usual** come al solito **2** *adv*: **~ high ~ ...** alto come ...; **~ much ~ that?** così tanto?; **run ~ fast ~ you can** corri più veloce che puoi **3** *prep* come; **~ a child** da bambino; **~ dressed ~ a policeman** vestito da poliziotto; **work ~ a translator** essere traduttore; **~ for** quanto a; **~ Hamlet** nel ruolo di Amleto

Ascension [əˈsenʃn] REL Ascensione *f*; **ascent** *path* salita *f*; *of mountain* ascensione *f*; *fig* ascesa *f*

ash [æʃ] cenere *f*

ashamed [əˈʃeɪmd]: **be ~ of** vergognarsi di

ashore [əˈʃɔː(r)] a terra; **go ~** sbarcare

ashtray [ˈæʃtreɪ] portacenere *m*; **Ash Wednesday** mercoledì *m* inv delle Ceneri

Asia [ˈeɪʃə] Asia *f*; **Asian 1** *n* asiatico *m*, -a *f*; (*Indian, Pakistani*) indiano *m*, -a *f* **2** *adj* asiatico; (*Indian, Pakistani*) indiano; **Asian-American** americano *m*, -a *f* di origine asiatica

aside [əˈsaɪd] da parte; **~ from** a parte

ask [ɑːsk] **1** *v/t person* chiedere a; *(invite)* invitare; *question* fare; *favour* chiedere; **~ s.o. for ...** chiedere a qu ...; **~ s.o. to ...** chiedere a qu di ... **2** *v/i* chiedere

◆ **ask after** *person* chiedere di

◆ **ask for** chiedere; *person* chiedere di

◆ **ask out** chiedere da uscire a

asleep [əˈsliːp]: **he's ~** sta dormendo; **fall ~** addormentarsi

asparagus [əˈspærəgəs] asparagi *mpl*

aspect [ˈæspekt] aspetto *m*

aspirations [æspəˈreɪʃnz] aspirazioni *fpl*

aspirin [ˈæsprɪn] aspirina *f*

ass [æs] F *(idiot)* cretino *m*, -a *f*

ass² [æs] *Am* P *(bum)* culo *m* P

assassin [əˈsæsɪn] assassino *m*, -a *f*; **assassinate** assassinare; **assassination** assassinio *m*

assault [əˈsɔlt] **1** *n* assalto *m* **2** *v/t* aggredire

assemble [əˈsembl] **1** *v/t parts* assemblare **2** *v/i of people* radunarsi; **assembly** assemblea *f*; *of parts* assemblaggio *m*; **assembly line** catena *f* di montaggio

assent [əˈsent] acconsentire

assertive [əˈsɜːtɪv] *person* si-

curo di sé

assess [əˈses] valutare; **assessment** valutazione *f*

asset [ˈæset] FIN attivo *m*; *fig*: *thing* vantaggio *m*; *person* elemento *m* prezioso

assign [əˈsaɪn] *person* destinare; *thing* assegnare; **assignment** *(task)* compito *m*

assimilate [əˈsɪmɪleɪt] assimilare; *person into group* integrare

assist [əˈsɪst] assistere; **assistance** assistenza *f*; **assistant** assistente *m/f*; *in shop* commesso *m*, -a *f*; **assistant manager** vice-responsabile *m/f*; *of hotel, restaurant* vice-direttore *m*

associate 1 [əˈsəʊʃɪeɪt] *v/t* associare **2** [əˈsəʊʃɪət] *n* socio *m*, -a *f*; **association** associazione *f*

assortment [əˈsɔːtmənt] assortimento *m*

assume [əˈsjuːm] *(suppose)* supporre; **assumption** supposizione *f*

assurance [əˈʃʊərəns] assicurazione *f*; *(confidence)* sicurezza *f*; **assure** *(reassure)*: **~ s.o. of sth** assicurare qc a qu

asterisk [ˈæstərɪsk] asterisco *m*

asthma [ˈæsmə] asma *f*

astonish [əˈstɒnɪʃ] sbalordire; **astonishing** sbalorditivo; **astonishment** stupore *m*

astound [əˈstaʊnd] stupefare

astride [əˈstraɪd] a cavalcioni

di
astrology [ə'strɒlədʒi] astrologia f
astronaut ['æstrənɔːt] astronauta m/f
astronomer [ə'strɒnəmə(r)] astronomo m, -a f; **astronomical** price etc astronomico; **astronomy** astronomia f
astute [ə'stjuːt] astuto
asylum [ə'saɪləm] mental manicomio m; political asilo m
at [æt] (with places) a; **he works ~ the hospital** lavora in ospedale; **~ the baker's** dal panettiere, in panetteria; **~ Joe's** da Joe; **~ the door** alla porta; **~ 10 pounds** a 10 sterline; **~ the age of 18** all'età di 18 anni; **~ 5 o'clock** alle cinque; **~ night** di notte; **~ 150 km / h** a 150 km/h; **be good / bad ~ sth** essere / non essere bravo in qc
atheist ['eɪθiːɪst] ateo m, -a f
athlete ['æθliːt] atleta m/f; **athletic** atletico; **athletics** atletica f
Atlantic [ət'læntɪk] Atlantico m
atlas ['ætləs] atlante m
ATM [eɪtiː'em] (= **automatic teller machine**) (sportello m) Bancomat® m
atmosphere ['ætməsfɪə(r)] atmosfera f
atom ['ætəm] atomo m; **atom bomb** bomba f atomica; **atomic** atomico
♦ **atone for** [ə'təʊn] scontare

atrocious [ə'trəʊʃəs] atroce; **atrocity** atrocità f inv
attach [ə'tætʃ] attaccare; importance attribuire; document, file allegare; **attachment** to email allegato m
attack [ə'tæk] **1** n aggressione f; MIL attacco m **2** v/t aggredire; MIL attaccare
attempt [ə'tempt] **1** n tentativo m **2** v/t tentare
attend [ə'tend] partecipare a; school frequentare
♦ **attend to** (deal with) sbrigare; customer, patient assistere
attendance [ə'tendəns] partecipazione f; at school frequenza f; **attendant** in museum etc sorvegliante m/f
attention [ə'tenʃn] attenzione f; **pay ~** fare attenzione; **attentive** attento
attic ['ætɪk] soffitta f
attitude ['ætɪtjuːd] atteggiamento m
attorney [ə'tɜːni] avvocato m
attract [ə'trækt] attirare; **attraction** attrazione f; **attractive** attrattivo; person attraente
aubergine ['əʊbəʒiːn] melanzana f
auction ['ɔːkʃn] asta f
audacity [ɔː'dæsɪti] audacia f
audible ['ɔːdəbl] udibile
audience ['ɔːdiəns] pubblico m; TV telespettatori mpl; with the Pope etc udienza f
audio ['ɔːdɪəʊ] audio inv;

audiovisual audiovisivo
audit ['ɔːdɪt] **1** *n* revisione *f* contabile **2** *v/t* verificare
audition [ɔː'dɪʃn] **1** *n* audizione *f* **2** *v/i* fare un'audizione
auditor ['ɔːdɪtə(r)] revisore *m* contabile
auditorium [ɔːdɪ'tɔːrɪəm] *of theatre* sala *f*
August ['ɔːɡəst] agosto *m*
aunt [ɑːnt] zia *f*
au pair [əʊ'peə(r)] ragazza *f* alla pari
aura ['ɔːrə]: **she has an ~ of confidence** emana sicurezza
auspicious [ɔː'spɪʃəs] propizio
austere [ɔː'stɪə(r)] austero; **austerity** austerità *f inv*
Australia [ɒ'streɪlɪə] Australia *f*; **Australian 1** *adj* australiano **2** *n* australiano *m*, -a *f*
Austria ['ɒstrɪə] Austria *f*; **Austrian 1** *adj* austriaco **2** *n* austriaco *m*, -a *f*
authentic [ɔː'θentɪk] autentico; **authenticity** autenticità *f inv*
author ['ɔːθə(r)] autore *m*, autrice *f*
authoritarian [ɔːθɒrɪ'teərɪən] autoritario; **authoritative** autoritario; *information* autorevole; **authority** autorità *f inv*; (*permission*) autorizzazione *f*; **authorization** autorizzazione *f*; **authorize** autorizzare
autistic [ɔː'tɪstɪk] autistico
autobiography [ɔːtəbaɪ'ɒɡrə-

fɪ] autobiografia *f*
autocratic [ɔːtə'krætɪk] autocratico
autograph ['ɔːtəɡrɑːf] autografo *m*
automate ['ɔːtəmeɪt] automatizzare; **automatic 1** *adj* automatico **2** *n car* macchina *f* con il cambio automatico; **automatically** automaticamente; **automation** automazione *f*
automobile ['ɔːtəməbiːl] automobile *f*
autonomous [ɔː'tɒnəməs] autonomo
autopilot ['ɔːtəʊpaɪlət] pilota *m* automatico
autopsy ['ɔːtɒpsɪ] autopsia *f*
autumn ['ɔːtəm] autunno *m*
auxiliary [ɔːɡ'zɪlɪərɪ] ausiliario
available [ə'veɪləbl] disponibile
avalanche ['ævəlɑːnʃ] valanga *f*
avenue ['ævənjuː] corso *m*; *fig* strada *f*
average ['ævərɪdʒ] **1** *adj* medio; (*mediocre*) mediocre **2** *n* media *f*; **on ~** in media
◆ **average out** at risultare in media a
averse [ə'vɜːs]: **not be ~ to** non avere niente contro; **aversion** avversione *f* (**to** per)
avid ['ævɪd] avido
avocado [ævə'kɑːdəʊ] avocado *m inv*

back

avoid [əˈvɔɪd] evitare

await [əˈweɪt] attendere

awake [əˈweɪk] sveglio; **it's keeping me ~** mi impedisce di dormire

award [əˈwɔːd] **1** n (*prize*) premio m **2** v/t assegnare; *damages* riconoscere; *ceremony* ceremonia f di premiazione

aware [əˈweə(r)] conscio; **become ~ of** rendersi conto di; **awareness** consapevolezza f

away [əˈweɪ] via; SP fuori casa; **be ~ travelling, sick** etc essere via; **run ~** correre via; **look ~** guardare da un'altra parte; **it's 2 miles ~** dista 2 miglia; **away game** SP partita f fuori casa

awesome [ˈɔːsm] F (*terrific*) fantastico

awful [ˈɔːfʊl] tremendo, terribile; **awfully** F (*very*) da matti F

awkward [ˈɔːkwəd] (*clumsy*) goffo; (*difficult*) difficile; (*embarrassing*) scomodo; **feel ~** sentirsi a disagio

axe, *Am* ax [æks] **1** n scure f, accetta f **2** v/t *project, job* sopprimere

axle [ˈæksl] asse f

B

BA [biːˈeɪ] (= **Bachelor of Arts**) (*degree*) laurea f in lettere; (*person*) laureato m, -a f in lettere

baby [ˈbeɪbɪ] n bambino m, -a f; **baby-sit** v/i fare il / la baby-sitter

bachelor [ˈbætʃələ(r)] scapolo m; UNIV **~'s degree** laurea f triennale (di primo livello)

back [bæk] **1** n of *person* schiena f, of *animal, hand* dorso m; of *car, bus* parte f posteriore; of *book, house* retro m; of *clothes* rovescio m; of *drawer* fondo m; of *chair* schienale m; SP terzino m; **in the ~** (of the car) (nei sedili) di dietro; **at the ~ of the bus** in fondo all'autobus; **~ to front** al contrario **2** adj *door, steps* di dietro; *wheels, legs* posteriore; *garden* sul retro **3** adv: **please move ~** indietro, per favore; **give sth ~ to s.o.** restituire qc a qu; **she'll be ~ tomorrow** sarà di ritorno domani **4** v/t (*support*) appoggiare; *car* guidare in retromarcia; *horse* puntare su

◆ **back down** fare marcia indietro

◆ **back off** spostarsi indietro; *from danger* tirarsi indietro

◆ **back out** of *commitment* tirarsi indietro

◆ **back up 1** v/t (*support*) confermare; *claim, argument* supportare; *file* fare un backup di **2** *v/i in car* fare retromarcia

'**backache** mal *m* di schiena; **backbone** spina *f* dorsale; **backdate** retrodatare; **backdoor** porta *f* di dietro; **backer** FIN finanziatore *m*, -trice *f*; **background** sfondo *m*; *of person* background *m inv*; *of story* retroscena *mpl*; **backhand** *in tennis* rovescio *m*; **backing** *moral* appoggio *m*; MUS accompagnamento *m*; **backing group** gruppo *m* d'accompagnamento; **backlash** reazione *f* violenta; **backlog**: **~ of work** lavoro *m* arretrato; **backpack** zaino *m*; **backpacker** sacco-pelista *m/f*; **back seat** sedile *m* posteriore; **backside** F sedere *m*; **backspace (key)** (tasto di) ritorno *m*; **back streets** vicoli *mpl*; **backstroke** SP dorso *m*; **backtrack** tornare indietro; **backup** (*support*) rinforzi *mpl*; **backup** COMPUT backup *m inv*; **backup disk** COMPUT disco *m* di backup; **backward** *child* tardivo; *society* arretrato; *glance* all'indietro; **backwards** indietro; **backyard** cortile *m*

bacon ['beɪkn] pancetta *f*
bacteria [bæk'tɪərɪə] batteri *mpl*
bad [bæd] *news, manners* cat-

tivo; *weather, headache* brutto; *mistake* grave; *food* guasto; **it's not ~** non è male; **that's too ~** shame peccato!
badge [bædʒ] distintivo *m*
bad 'language parolacce *fpl*; **badly** male; *injured* gravemente; **he ~ needs ...** ha urgente bisogno di ...
badminton ['bædmɪntən] badminton *m*
bad-tempered [bæd'tempəd] irascibile
baffle ['bæfl]: **be ~d** essere perplesso
bag [bæg] borsa *f*; *plastic, paper* busta *f*
baggage ['bægɪdʒ] bagagli *mpl*; **baggage check** *Am* deposito *m* bagagli; **baggage trolley** carrello *m*
baggy ['bægɪ] senza forma
bail [beɪl] LAW cauzione *f*; **on ~** su cauzione
bait [beɪt] esca *f*
bake [beɪk] cuocere al forno; **baked potatoes** *patate cotte al forno con la buccia*; **baker** fornaio *m*, -a *f*; **bakery** panetteria *f*
balance ['bæləns] **1** *n* equilibrio *m*; (*remainder*) resto *m*; *of bank account* saldo *m* **2** *v/t* tenere in equilibrio **3** *v/i* stare in equilibrio; **balanced** (*fair*) obiettivo; *diet, personality* equilibrato; **balance sheet** bilancio *m* (di esercizio)
balcony ['bælkənɪ] balcone

m; *in theatre* prima galleria *f*

bald [bɔːld] *man* calvo; **balding** stempiato

Balkans ['bɔːlkənz]: **the** ~ i Balcani *mpl*

ball [bɔːl] palla *f*; *football* pallone *m*; **be on the** ~ essere sveglio; **play** ~ *fig* collaborare; **the** ~'s **in his court** la prossima mossa è sua

ballad ['bæləd] ballata *f*

ballerina [bælə'riːnə] ballerina *f*

ballet ['bæleɪ] *art* danza *f* classica; *dance* balletto *m*; **ballet dancer** ballerino *m* classico, ballerina *f* classica

'**ball game** F: **that's a different** ~ è un altro paio di maniche

ballistic missile [bə'lɪstɪk] missile *m* balistico

balloon [bə'luːn] *child's* palloncino *m*; *for flight* mongolfiera *f*

ballot ['bælət] **1** *n* votazione *f* **2** *v/t members* consultare tramite votazione; **ballot box** urna *f* elettorale

'**ballpark** F: **be in the right** ~ essere nell'ordine corretto di cifre; **ballpark figure** F cifra *f* approssimativa; **ballpoint** (**pen**) penna *f* a sfera

balls [bɔːlz] V palle *fpl* V

bamboo [bæm'buː] bambù *m inv*

ban [bæn] **1** *n* divieto *m* (**on** di) **2** *v/t* proibire

banal [bə'nɑːl] banale

banana [bə'nɑːnə] banana *f*

band [bænd] banda *f*; *pop* gruppo *m*; *of material* nastro *m*

bandage ['bændɪdʒ] **1** *n* benda *f* **2** *v/t* bendare

'**Band-Aid**® *Am* cerotto *m*

B&B [biːn'biː] (= **bed and breakfast**) pensione *f* familiare, bed and breakfast *m inv*

bandit ['bændɪt] brigante *m*

bandy ['bændɪ] *legs* storto

bang [bæŋ] **1** *n* colpo *m* **2** *v/t door* chiudere violentemente; (*hit*) sbattere

bangle ['bæŋgl] braccialetto *m*

bangs [bæŋz] *Am* frangia *f*

banisters ['bænɪstəz] ringhiera *fsg*

banjo ['bændʒəʊ] banjo *m inv*

bank[1] [bæŋk] *of river* riva *f*

bank[2] [bæŋk] FIN banca *f*

◆ **bank on** contare su

'**bank account** *n* conto *m* bancario; **banker** banchiere *m*; **banker's card** carta *f* assegni; **bank holiday** giorno *m* festivo; **banking** professione *f* bancaria; **bank loan** prestito *m* bancario; **bank manager** direttore *m* di banca; **bank rate** tasso *m* ufficiale di sconto; **bankroll** finanziare; **bankrupt** fallito; **go** ~ fallire; **bankruptcy** bancarotta *f*

banner ['bænə(r)] striscione *m*

banquet ['bæŋkwɪt] banchetto *m*

baptism ['bæptɪzm] battesimo *m*; **baptize** battezzare

bar¹ [bɑː(r)] *n of iron* spranga *f*; *of chocolate* tavoletta *f*; *for drinks* bar *m inv*; *(counter)* bancone *m*

bar² [bɑː(r)] *v/t* vietare l'ingresso a

barbaric [bɑː'bærɪk] barbaro

barbecue ['bɑːbɪkjuː] **1** *n* barbecue *m inv* **2** *v/t* cuocere al barbecue

barbed 'wire [bɑːbd] filo *m* spinato

barber ['bɑːbə(r)] barbiere *m*

'bar code codice *m* a barre

bare [beə(r)] *(naked)* nudo; *(room)* spoglio; **barefoot**: *be* ~ essere scalzo; **bare-headed** senza cappello; **barely** appena

bargain ['bɑːgɪn] **1** *n (deal)* patto *m*; *(good buy)* affare *m* **2** *v/i* tirare sul prezzo

barge [bɑːdʒ] NAUT chiatta *f*
◆ **barge into** piombare su

baritone ['bærɪtəʊn] *n* baritono *m*

bark¹ [bɑːk] **1** *n of dog* abbaiare *m* **2** *v/i* abbaiare

bark² [bɑːk] *of tree* corteccia *f*

'barmaid barista *f*; **barman** barista *m*

barn [bɑːn] granaio *m*

barometer [bə'rɒmɪtə(r)] *also fig* barometro *m*

barracks ['bærəks] MIL caserma *fsg*

barrel ['bærəl] *(container)* barile *m*

barren ['bærən] *land* arido

barrette [bə'ret] *Am* molletta *f*

barricade [bærɪ'keɪd] barricata *f*

barrier ['bærɪə(r)] barriera *f*

barrister ['bærɪstə(r)] avvocato *m*

'bar tender barista *m/f*

barter ['bɑːtə(r)] **1** *n* baratto *m* **2** *v/i* barattare

base [beɪs] **1** *n* base *f* **2** *v/t* basare (**on** su); **baseball** baseball *m*; *ball* palla *f* da baseball; **baseball cap** berretto *m* da baseball; **baseboard** *Am* battiscopa *m inv*; **basement** seminterrato *m*

basic ['beɪsɪk] *(rudimentary)* rudimentale; *salary* di base; *beliefs* fondamentale; **basically** essenzialmente

basin ['beɪsn] *for washing* lavandino *m*

basis ['beɪsɪs] base *f*

bask [bɑːsk] crogiolarsi

basket ['bɑːskɪt] cestino *m*; *in basketball* cesto *m*; **basketball** basket *m*, pallacanestro *f*; *ball* pallone *m* da pallacanestro

bass [beɪs] *(part)* voce *f* di basso; *(singer, guitar)* basso *m*; *(double bass)* contrabbasso *m*

bastard ['bɑːstəd] F bastardo *m*, -a *f* F

bear

bat¹ [bæt] **1** n mazza f; *for table tennis* racchetta f **2** v/i SP battere

bat² [bæt] *animal* pipistrello m

batch [bætʃ] n *of students* gruppo m; *of goods* lotto m; *of bread* infornata f

bath [bɑːθ] bagno m

bathe [beɪð] (*swim, have bath*) fare il bagno; **bathing costume** costume m da bagno

'**bathrobe** accappatoio m; **bathroom** (stanza f da) bagno m; **bath towel** asciugamano m da bagno; **bathtub** vasca f da bagno

batter ['bætə(r)] pastella f; **battered** maltrattato; *suitcase etc* malridotto

battery ['bætrɪ] pila f; MOT batteria f

battle ['bætl] **1** n *also fig* battaglia f **2** v/i *against illness etc* lottare; **battleship** corazzata f

bawl [bɔːl] (*shout*) urlare; (*weep*) strillare

bay [beɪ] (*inlet*) baia f; **bay window** bovindo m

BC [biːˈsiː] (= *before Christ*) a. C. (= avanti Cristo)

be [biː] ◇ essere; *it's me* sono io; *how much is / are …?* quant'è / quanto sono …?; *there is, there are* c'è, ci sono; *don't ~ sad* non essere triste; *how are you?* come stai?; *he's very well* sta bene; *I'm hot / cold* ho freddo / caldo; *it's hot / cold* fa

freddo / caldo; *he's seven* ha sette anni ◇ *has the postman been?* è passato il postino?; *I've never been to Japan* non sono mai stato in Giappone; *I've been here for hours* sono qui da tanto ◇ *tags: that's right, isn't it?* giusto, no?; *she's American, isn't she?* vero? ◇ *v/aux: I am thinking* sto pensando; *he's working in London* lavora a Londra ◇ *obligation: you are to do what I tell you* devi fare quello che ti dico ◇ *passive* essere; *he was killed* è stato ucciso

beach [biːtʃ] spiaggia f; **beachwear** abbigliamento m da spiaggia

beads [biːdz] perline fpl

beak [biːk] becco m

'**be-all:** *the ~ and end-all* la cosa più importante

beam [biːm] **1** n *in ceiling etc* trave f **2** v/i (*smile*) fare un sorriso radioso **3** v/t (*transmit*) trasmettere

bean [biːn] (*vegetable*) fagiolo m; *of coffee* chicco m; *be full of ~s* F essere particolarmente vivace

bear¹ [beə(r)] n *animal* orso m

bear² [beə(r)] **1** v/t *weight* portare; *costs* sostenere; (*tolerate*) sopportare; *child* dare alla luce **2** v/i: *bring pressure to ~ on* fare pressione su

bearable [ˈbeərəbl] sopportabile

beard [bɪəd] barba f

beat [biːt] **1** n of heart battito m; of music ritmo m **2** v/t of heart battere; of rain picchiettare; **~ about the bush** menar il can per l'aia **3** v/i in competition battere; (hit) picchiare; drum suonare; **~ it!** F fila!; **it ~s me** non capisco ◆ **beat up** picchiare

beaten [ˈbiːtən]: **off the ~ track** fuori mano; **beating** physical botte fpl; **beat-up** F malconcio

beautiful [ˈbjuːtɪfʊl] bello; **thanks, that's just ~!** grazie, così va bene; **beautifully** stupendamente; **beauty** bellezza f; **beauty salon**istituto m di bellezza

beaver [ˈbiːvə(r)] castoro m

because [bɪˈkɒz] perché; **~ of** a causa di

become [bɪˈkʌm] diventare; **what's ~ of her?** che ne è stato di lei?; **becoming** grazioso

bed [bed] letto m; **~ of flowers** aiuola f; **go to ~** andare a letto; **bedding** materasso m e lenzuola fpl; **bedridden** costretto a letto; **bedroom** camera f da letto; **bed-sit, bed-sitter** monolocale m; **bedtime** ora f di andare a letto

bee [biː] ape f

beech [biːtʃ] faggio m

beef [biːf] manzo m; **beefbur-**ger hamburger m inv

beep [biːp] **1** n bip m inv **2** v/i suonare

beer [bɪə(r)] birra f

beet [biːt] barbabietola f

beetle [ˈbiːtl] coleottero m

before [bɪˈfɔː(r)] **1** prep prima di **2** adv prima; **I've seen this film ~** questo film l'ho già visto **3** conj prima che (+ subj); **I saw him ~ he left** l'ho visto prima che partisse; **I saw him ~ I left** l'ho visto prima di partire; **beforehand** prima

befriend [bɪˈfrend] fare amicizia con

beg [beg] **1** v/i mendicare **2** v/t: **~ s.o. to ...** pregare qu di ...; **beggar** mendicante m/f

begin [bɪˈgɪn] cominciare; **beginner** principiante m/f; **beginning** inizio m; (origin) origine f

behalf [bɪˈhɑːf]: **on ~ of** a nome di

behave [bɪˈheɪv] comportarsi; **~ (yourself)!** comportati bene!; **behaviour**, Am **behavior** comportamento m

behind [bɪˈhaɪnd] **1** prep dietro; in order dietro a; **be ~** (responsible for) essere dietro a; (support) appoggiare **2** adv (at the back) dietro; **she had to stay ~** è dovuta rimanere; **be ~ in** match essere in svantaggio

beige [beɪʒ] beige inv

being ['bi:ɪŋ] (*existence*) esistenza *f*; (*creature*) essere *m*

belated [bɪ'leɪtɪd] in ritardo

belch [beltʃ] **1** *n* rutto *m* **2** *v/i* ruttare

Belgian ['beldʒən] **1** *adj* belga **2** *n* belga *m/f*; **Belgium** Belgio *m*

belief [bɪ'li:f] convinzione *f*; *in God* fede *f*; **believe** credere

◆ **believe in** *God, person* credere in; *ghost, person* credere a

believer [bɪ'li:və(r)] REL credente *m/f*; *I'm a great ~ in ...* credo fermamente in ...

bell [bel] *in church, school* campana *f*; *on door, bicycle* campanello *m*; **bellhop** *Am* fattorino *m* d'albergo

belligerent [bɪ'lɪdʒərənt] bellicoso

bellow ['beləʊ] urlare; *of bull* muggire

belly ['belɪ] pancia *f*

belong [bɪ'lɒŋ] *v/i*: *where does this ~?* dove va questo?; *I don't ~ here* mi sento un estraneo

◆ **belong to** appartenere a

be'longings cose *fpl*

beloved [bɪ'lʌvɪd] adorato

below [bɪ'ləʊ] **1** *prep* sotto **2** *adv* di sotto; *in text* sotto **10 degrees ~** 10 gradi sotto zero

belt [belt] cintura *f*

bench [bentʃ] *seat* panchina *f*; **benchmark** punto *m* di rife-

rimento

bend [bend] **1** *n* curva *f* **2** *v/t* piegare **3** *v/i* curvarsi; *of person* inchinarsi

◆ **bend down** chinarsi

beneath [bɪ'ni:θ] **1** *prep* sotto **2** *adv* di sotto

benefactor ['benɪfæktə(r)] benefattore *m*, -trice *f*

beneficial [benɪ'fɪʃl] vantaggioso

benefit ['benɪfɪt] **1** *n* vantaggio *m* **2** *v/t* andare a vantaggio di **3** *v/i* trarre vantaggio (*from* da)

benevolent [bɪ'nevələnt] benevolo

benign [bɪ'naɪn] benevolo; MED benigno

bequeath [bɪ'kwi:ð] *also fig* lasciare in eredità

bequest [bɪ'kwest] lascito *m*

bereaved [bɪ'ri:vd] **1** *adj* addolorato **2** *n*: *the ~* i familiari *mpl* del defunto

beret ['bereɪ] berretto *m*

berry ['berɪ] bacca *f*

berth [bɜ:θ] *on ship, train* cuccetta *f*; *for ship* ormeggio *m* **2**

beside [bɪ'saɪd] accanto a; *be ~ o.s.* essere fuori di sé; *that's ~ the point* questo non c'entra

besides [bɪ'saɪdz] **1** *adv* inoltre **2** *prep* (*apart from*) oltre a

best [best] **1** *adj* migliore **2** *adv* meglio; *it would be ~ if ...* sarebbe meglio se ...; *I like her ~* lei è quella che mi piace di più **3** *n*: *do one's*

~ fare del proprio meglio; **the** ~ il meglio; (*outstanding thing or person*) il / la migliore; **they've done the** ~ **they can** hanno fatto tutto il possibile; **make the** ~ **of** cogliere il lato buono di; **all the** ~! tanti auguri!; **best before date** scadenza *f*; **best man** *at wedding* testimone *m* dello sposo

bet [bet] **1** *n* scommessa *f* **2** *v/i* scommettere; **you** ~! ci puoi scommettere!

betray [bɪ'treɪ] tradire; **betrayal** tradimento *m*

better ['betə(r)] **1** *adj* migliore; **get** ~ migliorare **2** *adv* meglio; **you'd** ~ **ask permission** faresti meglio a chiedere il permesso; **I'd really** ~ **not** sarebbe meglio di no; **all the** ~ **for us** tanto meglio per noi; **I like her** ~ lei mi piace di più; **better off be** ~ stare meglio finanziariamente

between [bɪ'twi:n] tra

beware [bɪ'weə(r)]: ~ **of ...!** (stai) attento a ...!

bewilder [bɪ'wɪldə(r)] sconcertare; **bewildered** perplessità *f*

beyond [bɪ'jɒnd] oltre, al di là di

bias ['baɪəs] *against* pregiudizio *m*; *in favour of* preferenza *f*; **bias(s)** parziale

Bible ['baɪbl] bibbia *f*; **biblical** biblico

bicentenary [baɪsen'ti:nərɪ] bicentenario *m*

bicker ['bɪkə(r)] bisticciare

bicycle ['baɪsɪkl] bicicletta *f*

bid [bɪd] **1** *n at auction* offerta *f*; (*attempt*) tentativo *m* **2** *v/t* & *v/i at auction* offrire; **bidder** offerente *m/f*

biennial [baɪ'enɪəl] biennale

big [bɪg] **1** *adj* grande; **my** ~ **brother / sister** mio fratello / mia sorella maggiore **2** *adv*: **talk** ~ sparare grosse

bigamist ['bɪgəmɪst] bigamo *m*, -a *f*

'bighead F pallone *m* gonfiato F

bigot ['bɪgət] fanatico *m*, -a *f*

bike [baɪk] F bici *f inv* F **2** *v/i* andare in bici; **biker** motociclista *m/f*; (*courier*) corriere *m*

bikini [bɪ'ki:nɪ] bikini *m inv*

bilingual [baɪ'lɪŋgwəl] bilingue

bill [bɪl] **1** *n in hotel, restaurant* conto *m*; (*gas / electricity* ~) bolletta *f*; (*invoice*) fattura *f*; *Am: money* banconota *f*; POL disegno *m* di legge; (*poster*) avviso *m*

'billboard *Am* tabellone *m* per affissioni pubblicitarie; **billfold** *Am* portafoglio *m*

billiards ['bɪljədz] biliardo *m*

billion ['bɪljən] (*1,000,000,000*) miliardo *m*

bin [bɪn] bidone *m*; **bin lorry** camion *m* della nettezza urbana

bind [baɪnd] *also fig* legare; LAW obbligare; **binding** *agreement* vincolante

binoculars [bɪˈnɒkjʊləz] binocolo *msg*

biodegradable [baɪəʊdɪˈgreɪdəbl] biodegradabile

biographer [baɪˈɒgrəfə(r)] biografo *m*, -a *f*; **biography** biografia *f*

biological [baɪəˈlɒdʒɪkl] biologico; **biology** biologia *f*; **biotechnology** biotecnologia *f*

bird [bɜːd] uccello *m*

biro® [ˈbaɪrəʊ] biro *f*

birth [bɜːθ] *also fig* nascita *f*; (*labour*) parto *m*; **give ~ to** *child* partorire; **date of ~** data di nascita; **birth certificate** certificato *m* di nascita; **birth control** controllo *m* delle nascite; **birthday** compleanno *m*; **happy ~!** buon compleanno!; **birthplace** luogo *m* di nascita

biscuit [ˈbɪskɪt] biscotto *m*

bisexual [baɪˈseksjʊəl] bisessuale

bishop [ˈbɪʃəp] vescovo *m*

bit [bɪt] *n* (*piece*) pezzo *m*; (*part*) parte *f*; **a ~** (*a little*) un po'; **a ~ of advice** un consiglio; **~ by ~** poco a poco; **I'll be there in a ~** (*in a little while*) sarò lì tra poco

bitch [bɪtʃ] 1 *n dog* cagna *f*; F *woman* bastarda *f* F 2 *v/i* F (*complain*) lamentarsi

bite [baɪt] 1 *n* morso *m* 2 *v/t*

mordere; *one's nails* mangiarsi 3 *v/i* mordere

bitter [ˈbɪtə(r)] *taste* amaro; *person* amareggiato

black [blæk] 1 *adj* nero; *tea* senza latte 2 *n colour* nero *m*; *person* nero *m*, -a *f*
◆ **black out** (*faint*) svenire
blackberry mora *f* di rovo; **blackbird** merlo *m*; **blackboard** lavagna *f*; **black box** scatola *f* nera; **black coffee** caffè *m*; **black economy** economia *f* sommersa; **black eye** occhio *m* nero; **blacklist** lista *f* nera; **blackmail** 1 *n* ricatto *m* 2 *v/t* ricattare; **black market** mercato *m* nero; **blackness** oscurità *f*; **blackout** ELEC black-out *m inv*; MED svenimento *m*

bladder [ˈblædə(r)] vescica *f*

blade [bleɪd] *of knife* lama *f*; *of helicopter* pala *f*; *of grass* filo *m*

blame [bleɪm] 1 *n* colpa *f*; (*responsibility*) responsabilità *f* 2 *v/t*: **~ s.o. for sth** ritenere qu responsabile di qc

bland [blænd] *smile* insulso; *food* insipido

blank [blæŋk] 1 *adj* (*not written on*) bianco; *tape* vergine; *look* vuoto 2 *n* (*empty space*) spazio *m*; **blank cheque**, *Am* **blank check** assegno *m* in bianco

blanket [ˈblæŋkɪt] coperta *f*

blasphemy [ˈblæsfəmɪ] bestemmia *f*

blast [blɑːst] **1** n (*explosion*) esplosione f; (*gust*) raffica f **2** v/t far esplodere; **~!** accidenti!; **blast-off** lancio m

blatant ['bleɪtənt] palese

blaze [bleɪz] **1** n (*fire*) incendio m **2** v/i of fire ardere

blazer ['bleɪzə(r)] blazer m inv

bleach [bliːtʃ] **1** n for clothes varechina f; for hair acqua f ossigenata **2** v/t hair ossigenarsi

bleak [bliːk] countryside desolato; weather cupo; future deprimente

bleary-eyed ['blɪəraɪd]: **be ~** avere lo sguardo appannato

bleat [bliːt] v/i of sheep belare

bleed [bliːd] sanguinare; bleeding emorragia f

bleep [bliːp] **1** n blip m inv **2** v/i suonare

blemish ['blemɪʃ] on skin imperfezione f; on fruit ammaccatura f

blend [blend] **1** n miscela f **2** v/t miscelare; **blender** machine frullatore m

bless [bles] benedire; **~ you!** (in response to sneeze) salute!; **blessing** benedizione f

blind [blaɪnd] **1** adj cieco **2** n: **the ~** i ciechi **3** v/t accecare; **blind alley** vicolo m cieco; **blind date** appuntamento m al buio; **blindfold 1** n benda f **2** v/t bendare (gli occhi a); **blinding** atroce; light accecante; **blindly** a tastoni; fig ciecamente; **blind spot** in

road punto m cieco

blink [blɪŋk] of person sbattere le palpebre; of light tremolare

blister ['blɪstə(r)] vescichetta f

blizzard ['blɪzəd] bufera f di neve

bloc [blɒk] POL blocco m

block [blɒk] **1** n blocco m; in town isolato m; **~ of flats** palazzo m (d'appartamenti) **2** v/t bloccare

♦ **block out** light impedire

blockage ['blɒkɪdʒ] ingorgo m; **blockbuster** successone m; **block letters** maiuscole fpl

bloke [bləʊk] F tipo m F

blond [blɒnd] biondo; **blonde** woman bionda f

blood [blʌd] sangue m; **blood donor** donatore m, -trice f di sangue; **blood group** gruppo m sanguigno; **blood poisoning** setticemia f; **blood pressure** pressione f del sangue; **blood sample** prelievo m di sangue; **bloodshed** spargimento m di sangue; **bloodshot** iniettato di sangue; **bloodstained** macchiato di sangue; **blood test** analisi f inv del sangue; **bloodthirsty** assetato di sangue; **bloody 1** adj hands etc insanguinato; F maledetto; **~ hell!** porca miseria! F; **you're a ~ genius!** sei un geniaccio! F **2** adv: **I'm ~ tired**

sono stanco morto

bloom [bluːm] *also fig* fiorire

blossom ['blɒsəm] **1** *n* fiori *mpl* **2** *v/i also fig* fiorire

blot [blɒt] macchia *f*

◆ **blot out** *memory* cancellare; *view* nascondere

blouse [blauz] camicetta *f*

blow[1] [bləʊ] *n* colpo *m*

blow[2] [bləʊ] **1** *v/t of wind* spingere; *smoke* soffiare; **~ a whistle** fischiare; **~ one's nose** soffiarsi il naso **2** *v/i of wind, person* soffiare; *of fuse* saltare; *of tyre* scoppiare

◆ **blow out 1** *v/t candle* spegnere **2** *v/i of candle* spegnersi

◆ **blow over 1** *v/t* abbattere **2** *v/i* rovesciarsi; *of storm, argument* calmarsi

◆ **blow up 1** *v/t with explosives* far saltare; *balloon* gonfiare; *photograph* ingrandire **2** *v/i of bomb* scoppio m

'**blow-dry** asciugare col phon; **blow-out** *of tyre* scoppio m

blue [bluː] blu; *film* porno; **blue chip** sicuro; *company* di alto livello; **blues** MUS blues *m inv*; **have the ~** essere giù

bluff [blʌf] **1** *n* (*deception*) bluff *m inv* **2** *v/i* bluffare

blunder ['blʌndə(r)] **1** *n* errore *m* **2** *v/i* fare un errore

blunt [blʌnt] spuntato; *person* diretto; **bluntly** senza mezzi termini

blur [blɜː(r)] **1** *n* massa *f* indi-

stinta **2** *v/t* offuscare

◆ **blurt out** [blɜːt] spiattellare

blush [blʌʃ] **1** *n* rossore *m* **2** *v/i* arrossire; **blusher** *cosmetic* fard *m inv*

blustery ['blʌstəri] ventoso

BO [biː'əʊ] (= *body odour*) odori *mpl* corporei

board [bɔːd] **1** *n* asse *f*; *for chess* scacchiera *f*; *for notices* tabellone *m*; **~** (*of directors*) consiglio *m* (d'amministrazione); **on ~** a bordo **2** *v/t aeroplane etc* salire a bordo di **3** *v/i of passengers* salire a bordo

◆ **board up** chiudere con assi

boarder ['bɔːdə(r)] pensionante *m/f*; EDU convittore *m*, -trice *f*; **board game** gioco *m* da tavolo; **boarding card** carta *f* d'imbarco; **boarding pass** carta *f* d'imbarco; **boarding school** collegio *m*; **board meeting** riunione *f* di consiglio; **board room** sala *f* del consiglio

boast [bəʊst] vantarsi

boat [bəʊt] (*small, for leisure*) barca *f*; (*ship*) nave *f*

bodily ['bɒdɪlɪ] **1** *adj* corporale **2** *adv eject* di peso; **body** corpo *m*; *dead* cadavere *m*; **body double** controfigura *f*; **bodyguard** guardia *f* del corpo; **body language** linguaggio *m* del corpo; **bodywork** MOT carrozzeria *f*

bogus ['bəʊgəs] fasullo

boil¹ [bɔɪl] (*swelling*) foruncolo *m*

boil² [bɔɪl] **1** *v/t* far bollire **2** *v/i* bollire

◆ **boil down** to ridursi a

boiler ['bɔɪlə(r)] caldaia *f*

boisterous ['bɔɪstərəs] turbolento

bold [bəʊld] **1** *adj* (*brave*) audace **2** *n print* neretto *m*; **in ~** in neretto

bolster ['bəʊlstə(r)] *confidence* rafforzare

bolt [bəʊlt] **1** *n on door* catenaccio *m*; (*metal pin*) bullone *m* **2** *adv*: **~ upright** diritto come un fuso **3** *v/t* (*fix with bolts*) fissare con bulloni; (*close*) chiudere col catenaccio **4** *v/i* (*run off*) scappare via

bomb [bɒm] **1** *n* bomba *f* **2** *v/t* bombardare; (*blow up*) far saltare; **bombard** *also fig* bombardare; **bomb attack** attacco *m* dinamitardo; **bomber** *airplane* bombardiere *m*; *terrorist* dinamitardo *m*, -a *f*; **bomb scare** allarme-bomba *m*; **bombshell** *fig: news* bomba *f*

bond [bɒnd] **1** *n* (*tie*) legame *m*; FIN obbligazione *f* **2** *v/i* aderire

bone [bəʊn] osso *m*; *in fish* lisca *f*

bonfire ['bɒnfaɪə(r)] falò *m inv*

bonnet ['bɒnɪt] *of car* cofano *m*

bonus ['bəʊnəs] *money* gratifica *f*; (*something extra*) vantaggio *m* in più

boo [buː] **1** *n* fischio *m* **2** *v/t* & *v/i* fischiare

boob¹ [buːb] F (*mistake*) errore *m*

boob² [buːb] P (*breast*) tetta *f* P

booboo ['buːbuː] F gaffe *m inv*

book [bʊk] **1** *n* libro *m* **2** *v/t* (*reserve*) prenotare; *of policeman* multare; SP ammonire

bookcase scaffale *m*; **booked up** tutto esaurito; *person* occupatissimo; **bookie** F allibratore *m*; **booking** (*reservation*) prenotazione *f*; **booking office** biglietteria *f*; **bookkeeper** contabile *m/f*; **bookkeeping** contabilità *f*; **booklet** libretto *m*; **bookmaker** allibratore *m*; **books** (*accounts*) libri *mpl* contabili; **bookseller** libraio *m*, -a *f*; **bookshop**, *Am* **bookstore** libreria *f*

boom¹ [buːm] **1** *n* boom *m inv* **2** *v/i of business* andare a gonfie vele

boom² [buːm] *n* (*bang*) rimbombo *m*

boost [buːst] **1** *n* spinta *f* **2** *v/t sales* incrementare; *confidence* aumentare

boot [buːt] stivale *m*; (*climbing* ~) scarpone *m*; *for football* scarpetta *m*

◆ **boot up** COMPUT inizializ-

bound

zare

booth [buːð] *at market, fair* bancarella *f*; *(telephone* ~*)* cabina *f*

booze [buːz] F alcolici *mpl*; **booze-up** F bevuta *f*

border ['bɔːdə(r)] **1** *n* confine *m*; *(edge)* bordo *m* **2** *v/t country* confinare con

◆ **border on** *country* confinare con; *(almost)* rasentare

bore[1] [bɔː(r)] *v/t hole* praticare

bore[2] [bɔː(r)] **1** *n person* persona *f* noiosa **2** *v/t* annoiare

bored [bɔːd] annoiato; *I'm* ~ mi sto annoiando; **boredom** noia *f*; **boring** noioso

born [bɔːn]: *be* ~ essere nato

borrow ['bɒrəʊ] prendere in prestito

bosom ['bʊzm] *of woman* seno *m*

boss [bɒs] boss *m inv*

◆ **boss around** dare ordini a

bossy ['bɒsɪ] prepotente

botanical [bə'tænɪkl] botanico; **botany** botanica *f*

botch [bɒtʃ] fare un pasticcio con

both [bəʊθ] **1** *adj pron* entrambi, tutti *mpl* e due, tutte *fpl* e due, tutt'e due; ~ *(of the)* **brothers** *were there* tutt'e due i fratelli erano lì; ~ *of them* entrambi **2** *adv*: ~ *my mother and I* sia mia madre che io; *is it business or pleasure?* – ~ per piacere o per affari? – tutt'e due

bother ['bɒðə(r)] **1** *n* disturbo *m*; *it's no* ~ non c'è problema **2** *v/t (disturb)* disturbare; *(worry)* preoccupare **3** *v/i*: *don't* ~ *(you needn't do it)* non preoccuparti

bottle ['bɒtl] bottiglia *f*; *for baby* biberon *m*

◆ **bottle up** *feelings* reprimere

'**bottle bank** contenitore *m* per la raccolta del vetro; **bottled water** acqua *f* in bottiglia; **bottleneck** ingorgo *m*; **bottle-opener** apribottiglie *m inv*

bottom ['bɒtəm] **1** *adj* più basso **2** *n* fondo *m*; *(buttocks)* sedere *m*; *at the* ~ *of the screen* in basso sullo schermo; *at the* ~ *of the page* in fondo alla pagina

◆ **bottom out** toccare il fondo

bottom 'line *financial* risultato *m* finanziario; *the* ~ *(the real issue)* l'essenziale *m*

boulder ['bəʊldə(r)] macigno *m*

bounce [baʊns] **1** *v/t ball* far rimbalzare **2** *v/i of ball* rimbalzare; *on sofa etc* saltare; *of cheque* essere protestato; **bouncer** buttafuori *m inv*

bound[1] [baʊnd] *adj*: *be* ~ *to do sth (sure to)* dover fare per forza qc; *(obliged to)* essere obbligato a fare qc; *the train is* ~ *to be late* il treno sarà senz'altro in ritardo

bound² [baʊnd] *adj*: **be ~ for of ship** essere diretto a

bound³ [baʊnd] *n* (*jump*) balzo *m*

boundary ['baʊndərɪ] confine *m*

bouquet [bʊ'keɪ] bouquet *m inv*

bourbon ['bɜːbən] bourbon *m inv*

bout [baʊt] MED attacco *m*; *in boxing* incontro *m*

bow¹ [baʊ] **1** *n as greeting* inchino *m* **2** *v/i* inchinarsi **3** *v/t head* chinare

bow² [baʊ] *n* (*knot*) fiocco *m*; MUS archetto *m*

bow³ [baʊ] *n of ship* prua *f*

bowels ['baʊəlz] intestino *msg*

bowl¹ [baʊl] *n container* bacinella *f*; *for soup, cereal* ciotola *f*; *for cooking, salad* terrina *f*

bowl² [baʊl] **1** *n ball* boccia *f* **2** *v/i in bowling* lanciare

bowling ['baʊlɪŋ] bowling *m*; **bowling alley** pista *f* da bowling; **bowls** *nsg* (*game*) bocce *fpl*

bow 'tie (cravatta *f* a) farfalla *f*

box¹ [bɒks] *n container* scatola *f*; *on form* casella *f*

box² [bɒks] *v/i* fare pugilato

boxer ['bɒksə(r)] pugile *m*; **boxing match** in-

boxing gloves pl guantoni *mpl* da pugile; **Boxing Day** Santo Stefano; **boxing glove** guantone *m* da pugile; **boxing match** incontro *m* di pugilato

'**box number** *at post office* casella *f*; **box office** botteghino *m*

boy [bɔɪ] *child* bambino *m*; *youth* ragazzo *m*; *son* figlio *m*

boycott ['bɔɪkɒt] **1** *n* boicottaggio *m* **2** *v/t* boicottare

'**boyfriend** ragazzo *m*; **boy-scout** boy-scout *m inv*

bra [brɑː] reggiseno *m*

bracelet ['breɪslɪt] braccialetto *m*

bracket ['brækɪt] *for shelf* staffa *f*; *in text* parentesi *f inv*

brag [bræg] vantarsi

braid [breɪd] *trimming* passamaneria *f*; Am *in hair* treccia *f*

braille [breɪl] braille *m*

brain [breɪn] cervello *m*; **brainless** F deficiente; **brains** (*intelligence*) cervello *msg*; **brain surgeon** neurochirurgo *m*; **brain tumour**, Am **brain tumor** tumore *m* al cervello; **brainwash** fare il lavaggio del cervello a; **brainy** F geniale

brake [breɪk] **1** *n* freno **2** *v/i* frenare; **brake light** MOT fanalino *m* d'arresto; **brake pedal** MOT pedale *m* del freno

branch [brɑːntʃ] *of tree* ramo *m*; *of company* filiale *f*

◆ **branch out** diversificarsi

brand [brænd] **1** *n* marca *f* **2** *v/t*: **be ~ed a traitor** essere tacciato di tradimento;

brand image brand image *f inv*

brandish ['brændɪʃ] brandire

brand 'leader marca *f* leader di mercato; **brand name** marca *f*; **brand-new** nuovo di zecca

brandy ['brændɪ] brandy *m inv*

brass [brɑːs] (*alloy*) ottone *m*; **the ~** MUS gli ottoni; **brass band** fanfara *f*

brassière [brə'zɪə(r)] reggiseno *m*

brat [bræt] *pej* marmocchio *m*

brave [breɪv] coraggioso; **bravery** coraggio *m*

brawl [brɔːl] **1** *n* rissa *f* **2** *v/i* azzuffarsi

Brazil [brə'zɪl] Brasile *m*; **Brazilian 1** *adj* brasiliano **2** *n* brasiliano *m*, -a *f*

breach [briːtʃ] (*violation*) violazione *f*; *in party* rottura *f*; **breach of contract** inadempienza *f* di contratto

bread [bred] pane *m*

breadth [bredθ] larghezza *f*

'breadwinner: be the ~ mantenere la famiglia

break [breɪk] **1** *n also fig* rottura *f*; (*rest*) pausa *f*; EDU intervallo *m* **2** *v/t china, egg, bone* rompere; *rules, law* violare; *promise* non mantenere; *news* comunicare; *record* battere **3** *v/i of china, egg, toy* rompersi; *of news* diffondersi; *of storm* scoppiare

◆ **break down 1** *v/i of vehicle,*

machine avere un guasto; *of talks* arenarsi; *in tears* scoppiare in lacrime; *mentally* avere un esaurimento **2** *v/t door* buttare giù; *figures* analizzare

◆ **break even** coprire le spese

◆ **break in** (*interrupt*) interrompere; *of burglar* entrare con la forza

◆ **break off 1** *v/t* staccare; *engagement* rompere; **they've broken it off** si sono lasciati **2** *v/i* (*stop talking*) interrompersi

◆ **break up 1** *v/t into parts* scomporre; *fight* far cessare **2** *v/i of ice* spaccarsi; *of couple* separarsi; *of band, meeting* sciogliersi

breakable ['breɪkəbl] fragile; **breakage** danni *mpl*; **breakdown** *of vehicle, machine* guasto *m*; *of talks* rottura *f*; (*nervous ~*) esaurimento *m* (nervoso); *of figures* analisi *f inv*; **breakdown lorry** carro *m* attrezzi; **breakdown service** servizio *m* di soccorso stradale; **breakdown truck** carro *m* attrezzi

breakfast ['brekfəst] colazione *f*; **have ~** fare colazione

'break-in furto *m* (con scasso); **breakthrough** *in negotiations* passo *m* avanti; *of technology* scoperta *f*; **breakup** *of partnership* rottura *f*

breast [brest] seno *m*; **breast-feed** allattare; **breaststroke** nuoto *m* a rana

breath [breθ] respiro *m*; **be out of ~** essere senza fiato

breathe [briːð] respirare
◆ **breathe in** inspirare
◆ **breathe out** espirare

breathing ['briːðɪŋ] respiro *m*

breathless ['breθlɪs] senza fiato; **breathtaking** mozzafiato

breed [briːd] **1** *n* razza *f* **2** *v/t* allevare; *fig* generare **3** *v/i* of animals riprodursi; **breeding** allevamento *m*; of person educazione *f*

breeze [briːz] brezza *f*; **breezy** ventoso; *fig* brioso

brew [bruː] **1** *v/t* beer produrre **2** *v/i* of storm prepararsi; **there's trouble ~ing** ci sono guai in vista; **brewery** fabbrica *f* di birra

Brexit [ˈbreksɪt] POL, EU Brexit *f*

bribe [braɪb] **1** *n* bustarella *f* **2** *v/t* corrompere; **bribery** corruzione *f*

brick [brɪk] mattone *m*

bride [braɪd] sposa *f*; **bridegroom** sposo *m*; **bridesmaid** damigella *f* d'onore

bridge [brɪdʒ] **1** *n* ponte *m*; of ship ponte *m* di comando **2** *v/t* gap colmare
◆ **brighten up** ['braɪtn] **1** *v/t* ravvivare **2** *v/i* of weather schiarirsi; of face, person rallegrarsi

bridle ['braɪdl] briglia *f*

brief[1] [briːf] *adj* breve

brief[2] [briːf] **1** *n* (mission) missione *f* **2** *v/t*: **~ s.o. on sth** instruct dare istruzioni a qu su qc; *inform* mettere qu al corrente di qc

'**briefcase** valigetta *f*; **briefing** briefing *m* inv; **briefly** brevemente; (to sum up) in breve; **briefs** slip *m* inv

bright [braɪt] colour vivace; smile, future radioso; (sunny) luminoso; (intelligent) intelligente; **~ red** rosso vivo; **brightly** smile in modo radioso; shine, lit intensamente; coloured in modo sgargiante

brilliance ['brɪljəns] of person genialità *f*; of colour vivacità *f*; **brilliant** sunshine etc sfolgorante; (very good) eccezionale; (very intelligent) brillante

brim [brɪm] of container orlo *m*; of hat falda *f*

bring [brɪŋ] portare
◆ **bring back** (return) restituire; (re-introduce) reintrodurre; memories risvegliare
◆ **bring down** also fig abbattere; price far scendere
◆ **bring on** illness provocare
◆ **bring out** book pubblicare; new product lanciare
◆ **bring up** child allevare; subject sollevare

brink [brɪŋk] orlo *m*

brisk [brɪsk] person, tone spiccio; *walk* svelto; *trade* vivace

bristles ['brɪslz] peli *mpl*

Brit [brɪt] F britannico *m*, -a *f*;
Britain Gran Bretagna *f*;
British 1 *adj* britannico **2**
n: **the ~** i britannici

brittle ['brɪtl] fragile

broad [brɔːd] largo; *(general)*
generale; **in ~ daylight** in
pieno giorno; **broadband**
banda *f* larga; **broadcast 1**
n trasmissione *f* **2** *v/t* trasmettere; **broadcaster** giornalista *m/f* radiotelevisivo,
-a; **broad jump** *Am* salto
m in lungo; **broadly:** ~
speaking parlando in senso
lato; **broadminded** di larghe
vedute

broccoli ['brɒkəlɪ] broccoli
mpl

brochure ['brəʊʃə(r)] dépliant *m inv*, opuscolo *m*

broil [brɔɪl] *Am* fare alla griglia; **broiler** *Am on stove*
grill *m inv*

broke [brəʊk] F al verde; **broken 1** *adj* rotto; *English* sten-
tato; *marriage* fallito; **she's
from a ~ home** i suoi sono
separati; **broken-hearted**
col cuore spezzato; **broker**
mediatore *m*, -trice *f*

bronchitis [brɒŋ'kaɪtɪs] bronchite *f*

bronze [brɒnz] bronzo *m*

brooch [brəʊtʃ] spilla *f*

brothel ['brɒθl] bordello *m*

brother ['brʌðə(r)] fratello *m*;
brother-in-law cognato *m*;

brotherly fraterno

brow [braʊ] *(forehead)* fronte
f; *of hill* cima *f*

brown [braʊn] **1** *n* marrone *m*
2 *adj* marrone; *eyes, hair* castano; *(tanned)* abbronzato;
Brownie giovane esploratrice *f*; **brownie** *Am* dolcetto *m*
al cioccolato con noci;
brown sugar zucchero *m*
non raffinato

browse [braʊz] *in shop* curiosare; COMPUT navigare; ~
through a book sfogliare
un libro; **browser** COMPUT
browser *m inv*

bruise [bruːz] livido *m*; *on
fruit* ammaccatura *f*

brunette [bruː'net] brunetta *f*

brunt [brʌnt]: **bear the ~ of ...**
subire il peggio di ...

brush [brʌʃ] **1** *n* spazzola *f*;
(paint~) pennello *m*; *(tooth~)*
spazzolino *m* da denti; *(conflict)* scontro *m* **2** *v/t* spazzolare; *(touch lightly)* sfiorare
♦ **brush aside** ignorare
♦ **brush up** ripassare

brusque [bruːsk] brusco

Brussels 'sprout [brʌsls] ca-
volino *m* di Bruxelles

brutal ['bruːtl] brutale; **brutality** brutalità *f inv*; **brutally**
brutalmente; **brute** bruto *m*

bubble ['bʌbl] bolla *f*

buck[1] [bʌk] *n Am* F *(dollar)*
dollaro *m*

buck[2] [bʌk] *v/i of horse* sgrop-
pare

bucket ['bʌkɪt] secchio *m*

buckle[1] ['bʌkl] **1** *n* fibbia *f* **2** *v/t belt* allacciare

buckle[2] ['bʌkl] *v/i of wood, metal* piegarsi

bud [bʌd] BOT bocciolo *m*

buddy ['bʌdɪ] F amico *m*, -a *f*

budge [bʌdʒ] **1** *v/t* smuovere **2** *v/i* muoversi

budgerigar ['bʌdʒərɪgɑː(r)] pappagallino *m*

budget ['bʌdʒɪt] budget *m inv; of company* bilancio *m* preventivo; *of state* bilancio *m* dello Stato

buff [bʌf] appassionato *m*, -a *f*

buffalo ['bʌfələu] bufalo *m*

buffer ['bʌfə(r)] RAIL respingente *m*; COMPUT buffer *m inv; fig* cuscinetto *m*

buffet[1] ['bufeɪ] *meal* buffet *m inv*

bug [bʌg] **1** *n* (*insect*) insetto *m*; (*virus*) virus *m inv*; (*spying device*) microspia *f*; COMPUT bug *m inv* **2** *v/t room* installare microspie in; *telephone* mettere sotto controllo; F (*annoy*) seccare

buggy ['bʌgɪ] *for baby* passeggino *m*

build [bɪld] **1** *n of person* corporatura *f* **2** *v/t* costruire

◆ **build up 1** *v/t relationship* consolidare; *build up one's strength* rimettersi in forze **2** *v/i of tension, traffic* aumentare

builder ['bɪldə(r)] muratore *m; company* impresario *m* edile; **building** edificio *m*,

palazzo *m; (activity)* costruzione *f;* **building site** cantiere *m* edile; **building society** istituto *m* di credito immobiliare; **building trade** edilizia *f;* **build-up** *of traffic, pressure* aumento *m; of arms, forces* ammassamento *m; (publicity)* pubblicità *f inv;* **built-in** *wardrobe* a muro; *flash* incorporato; **built-up area** abitato *m*

bulb [bʌlb] BOT bulbo *m; (light ~)* lampadina *f*

bulge [bʌldʒ] **1** *n* rigonfiamento *m* **2** *v/i* sporgere

bulky ['bʌlkɪ] voluminoso

bull [bul] toro *m;* **bulldozer** bulldozer *m inv*

bullet ['bulɪt] proiettile *m*, pallottola *f*

bulletin ['bulɪtɪn] bollettino *m;* **bulletin board** COMPUT bulletin board *m inv; Am: on wall* bacheca *f*

'bullet-proof a prova di proiettile

'bull's-eye centro *m* del bersaglio; *hit the ~* fare centro; **bullshit** V stronzate *fpl* V

bully ['bulɪ] **1** *n* prepotente *m/f* **2** *v/t* tiranneggiare; **bullying** mobbing *m*

bum [bʌm] **1** *n* F *worthless person* mezza calzetta *f* F; (*bottom*) sedere *m; (Am: tramp)* barbone *m* **2** *v/t* F *cigarette etc* scroccare

bump [bʌmp] **1** *n (swelling)* gonfiore *m; (lump)* bernoccolo *m*; *on road* cunetta *f* **2** *v/t* battere

◆ **bump into** *table* battere contro; *(meet)* incontrare

bumper ['bʌmpə(r)] MOT paraurti *m inv*; **bumpy** *road* accidentato; *flight* movimentato

bunch [bʌntʃ] *of people* gruppo *m*; *of keys, flowers* mazzo *m*; **a ~ of grapes** un grappolo d'uva; **thanks a ~** *ironic* grazie tante!

bungalow ['bʌŋgələʊ] bungalow *m inv*

bungle ['bʌŋgl] pasticciare

bunk [bʌŋk] cuccetta *f*; **bunk beds** letti *mpl* a castello

buoy [bɔɪ] NAUT boa *f*; **buoyant** allegro; *economy* sostenuto

burden ['bɜːdn] **1** *n also fig* peso *m* **2** *v/t*: **~ s.o. with sth** *fig* opprimere qu con qc

bureau ['bjʊərəʊ] *(office)* ufficio *m*

bureaucracy [bjʊəˈrɒkrəsɪ] burocrazia *f*; **bureaucrat** burocrate *m/f*; **bureaucratic** burocratico

burger ['bɜːgə(r)] hamburger *m inv*

burglar ['bɜːglə(r)] ladro *m*; **burglar alarm** antifurto *m*; **burglarize** *Am* svaligiare; **burglary** furto *m* (con scasso); **burgle** svaligiare

burial ['berɪəl] sepoltura *f*

burn [bɜːn] **1** *n* bruciatura *f* **2** *v/t* bruciare; *of sun* scottare **3**

v/i ardere; *of house* bruciare; *of toast, get sunburnt* scottarsi, bruciarsi

◆ **burn down 1** *v/t* dare alle fiamme **2** *v/i* essere distrutto dal fuoco

burp [bɜːp] **1** *n* rutto *m* **2** *v/i* ruttare

burst [bɜːst] **1** *n in pipe* rottura *f* **2** *adj tyre* bucato **3** *v/t balloon* far scoppiare **4** *v/i of balloon, tyre* scoppiare; **~ into tears** scoppiare in lacrime; **~ out laughing** scoppiare a ridere

bury ['berɪ] seppellire; *hide* nascondere

bus [bʌs] autobus *m inv*; *(long distance)* pullman *m inv*; **bus driver** autista *m/f* di autobus

bush [bʊʃ] *plant* cespuglio *m*; *land* boscaglia *f*; **bushy** *eyebrows* irsuto

business ['bɪznɪs] *(trade)* affari *mpl*; *(company)* impresa *f*; *(work)* lavoro *m*; *(affair, matter)* faccenda *f*; *(as subject of study)* economia *f* aziendale; **on ~** per affari; **mind your own ~!** fatti gli affari tuoi!; **business card** biglietto *m* da visita (della ditta); **business class** business class *f*; **business hours** orario *msg* di apertura; **businesslike** efficiente; **businessman** uomo *m* d'affari; **business meeting** riunione *f* d'affari; **business school** istituto *m* commerciale;

business studies (*course*)
economia *f* aziendale; **business trip** viaggio *m* d'affari;
businesswoman donna *f*
d'affari

'**bus station** autostazione *f*;
bus stop fermata *f* dell'autobus

bust[1] [bʌst] *n of woman* petto
m

bust[2] [bʌst] *adj* F (*broken*)
scassato

'**bust-up** F rottura *f*; **busty**
prosperoso

busy ['bɪzɪ] **1** *adj also* TELEC
occupato; *day* intenso; *street*
animato; *shop, restaurant* affollato; **busybody** impiccione *m*, -a *f*

but [bʌt] **1** *conj* ma **2** *prep*: *all ~
him* tutti tranne lui; *the last
~ one* il penultimo; *~ for you*
se non fosse per te; *nothing
~ the best* solo il meglio

butcher ['bʊtʃə(r)] macellaio
m, -a *f*; **butcher's** macelleria
f

butt [bʌt] **1** *n of cigarette* mozzicone *m*; *Am* P (*backside*)

culo *m* P **2** *v/t* dare una testata a

butter ['bʌtə(r)] burro *m*; **buttercup** ranuncolo *m*; **butterfly** *also swimming* farfalla *f*

buttocks ['bʌtəks] natiche *fpl*

button ['bʌtn] bottone *m*; *on
machine* pulsante *m*

♦ **buy out** COM rilevare

buyer ['baɪə(r)] acquirente
m/f

buzz [bʌz] **1** *n* ronzio *m* **2** *v/i
of insect* ronzare; **buzzer** cicalino *m*

by [baɪ] *agency* da; (*near, next
to*) vicino a; (*no later than*)
entro, per; (*past*) davanti a;
(*mode of transport*) in; *~
day* di giorno; *~ bus* in autobus; *~ my watch* secondo il
mio orologio; *a book ~ ...*
un libro di ...; *~ myself / -
herself* da solo

bye(-bye) [baɪ] ciao

'**bypass** circonvallazione *f*;
MED by-pass *m inv*; **by-product** sottoprodotto *m*; **bystander** astante *m/f*

C

cab [kæb] taxi *m inv*; *of truck*
cabina *f*

cabbage ['kæbɪdʒ] cavolo *m*

'**cab driver** *esp Am* tassista
m/f

cabin ['kæbɪn] *of plane, ship*
cabina *f*; **cabin attendant**

assistente *m/f* di volo; **cabin
crew** equipaggio *m*

cabinet ['kæbɪnɪt] armadietto
m; POL Consiglio *m* dei ministri; **cabinet minister**
membro *m* del Consiglio
dei ministri

cable ['keɪbl] ELEC, *for securing* cavo *m*; ~ (*TV*) TV *f* via cavo; **cable car** funivia *f*; **cable television** televisione *f* via cavo

'cab stand *Am* stazione *f* dei taxi

cactus ['kæktəs] cactus *m inv*

cadaver [kə'dævə(r)] *Am* cadavere *m*

caddie ['kædɪ] *in golf* portamazze *m inv*

Caesarean [sɪ'zeərɪən] parto *m* cesareo

café ['kæfeɪ] caffè *m inv*, bar *m*; **cafeteria** tavola *f* calda

caffeine ['kæfiːn] caffeina *f*

cage [keɪdʒ] gabbia *f*; **cagey** evasivo

cake [keɪk] 1 *n* dolce *m*, torta *f* 2 *v/i* of mud incrostarsi

calamity [kə'læmɪtɪ] calamità *f inv*

calcium ['kælsɪəm] calcio *m*

calculate ['kælkjuleɪt] calcolare; **calculating** calcolatore; **calculation** calcolo *m*; **calculator** calcolatrice *f*

calendar ['kælɪndə(r)] calendario *m*

calf¹ [kɑːf] *young cow* vitello *m*

calf² [kɑːf] *of leg* polpaccio *m*

call [kɔːl] 1 *n* (*phone* ~) telefonata *f*; (*shout*) grido *m*; (*demand*) richiesta *f*; (*visit*) visita *f* 2 *v/t on phone*, (*summon*) chiamare; (*shout*) gridare; *meeting* convocare; **be ~ed** chiamarsi 3 *v/i on phone* chiamare; (*shout*) gridare;

(*visit*) passare

◆ **call back 1** *v/t also* TELEC richiamare 2 *v/i on phone* richiamare; (*make another visit*) ripassare

◆ **call for** (*collect*) passare a prendere; (*demand*) reclamare; (*require*) richiedere

◆ **call off** *strike* revocare; *wedding* disdire

◆ **call out** (*shout*) chiamare ad alta voce; (*summon*) chiamare

'call centre, *Am* **call center** centro *m* chiamate

caller ['kɔːlə(r)] *on phone* persona *f* che ha chiamato; (*visitor*) visitatore *m*, -trice *f*

callous ['kæləs] freddo, insensibile

calm [kɑːm] 1 *adj* calmo 2 *n* calma *f*

◆ **calm down 1** *v/t* calmare 2 *v/i* calmarsi

calmly ['kɑːmlɪ] con calma

calorie ['kælərɪ] caloria *f*

camcorder ['kæmkɔːdə(r)] videocamera *f*

camera ['kæmərə] macchina *f* fotografica; (*video* ~) videocamera *f*; (*television* ~) telecamera *f*; **cameraman** cameraman *m inv*; **camera phone** cellulare *m* con fotocamera

camouflage ['kæməflɑːʒ] 1 *n* mimetizzazione *f*; *of soldiers* tuta *f* mimetica 2 *v/t* mimetizzare

camp [kæmp] 1 *n* campo *m* 2

v/i accamparsi

campaign ['kæm'peɪn] **1** *n* campagna *f* **2** *v/i* militare

'camper-bed letto *m* da campo; **camper** *person* campeggiatore *m*, -trice *f*; *vehicle* camper *m inv*; **camping** campeggio *m*; **campsite** camping *m inv*, campeggio *m*

campus ['kæmpəs] campus *m inv*

can[1] [kæn] ◇ (*ability*) potere; **~ you hear me?** mi senti?; **I can't see** non vedo; **~ you speak French?** sai parlare il francese?; **as well as you ~** meglio che puoi ◇ (*permission*) potere; **~ I help you?** posso aiutarla?; **~ you help me?** mi può aiutare?

can[2] [kæn] *for drinks* lattina *f*; *for food* scatola *f*

Canada ['kænədə] Canada *m*; **Canadian 1** *adj* canadese **2** *n* canadese *m/f*

canal [kə'næl] (*waterway*) canale *m*

canary [kə'neərɪ] canarino *m*

cancel ['kænsl] annullare; **cancellation** annullamento *m*

cancer ['kænsə(r)] cancro *m*

Cancer ['kænsə(r)] ASTR Cancro *m*

candid ['kændɪd] franco

candidacy ['kændɪdəsɪ] candidatura *f*; **candidate** candidato *m*, -a *f*

candle ['kændl] candela *f*

candour, *Am* **candor**

['kændə(r)] franchezza *f*

candy ['kændɪ] *Am* (*sweet*) caramella *f*; (*sweets*) dolciumi *mpl*; **candy floss** zucchero *m* filato

cane [keɪn] canna *f*; *for walking* bastone *m*

canister ['kænɪstə(r)] barattolo *m*; *spray* bombola *f*

cannabis ['kænəbɪs] hashish *m*

canned [kænd] in scatola; (*recorded*) registrato

cannot ['kænɒt] ☞ **can not**

canny ['kænɪ] (*astute*) arguto

canoe [kə'nuː] canoa *f*

'can opener apriscatole *m inv*

can't [kɑːnt] = **can not**

canteen [kæn'tiːn] *in factory* mensa *f*

canvas ['kænvəs] tela *f*

canyon ['kænjən] canyon *m inv*

cap [kæp] *hat* berretto *m*; *for lens* coperchio *m*

capability [keɪpə'bɪlətɪ] *of person* capacità *f inv*; **capable** capace

capacity [kə'pæsətɪ] capacità *f inv*; *of engine* potenza *f*

capital ['kæpɪtl] *of country* capitale *f*; *capital letter* maiuscola *f*; *money* capitale *m*; **capitalism** capitalismo *m*; **capitalist 1** *adj* capitalista **2** *n* capitalista *m/f*; **capital letter** lettera *f* maiuscola; **capital punishment** pena *f* capitale

Capricorn ['kæprɪkɔːn] ASTR Capricorno *m*

capsize [kæp'saɪz] ribaltarsi

capsule ['kæpsjul] *of medicine* cachet *m inv*; (*space* ~) capsula *f*

captain ['kæptɪn] capitano *m*

caption ['kæpʃn] didascalia *f*

captivate ['kæptɪveɪt] affascinare; **captive** prigioniero; **captivity** cattività *f*; **capture**
1 *n of building, city* occupazione *f*; *of city* presa *f*; *of criminal, animal* cattura *f* **2** *v/t person, animal* catturare; *city, building* occupare; *city* prendere; *market share* conquistare

car [kɑː(r)] macchina *f*, auto *f inv*; *of train* vagone *m*; **by~** in macchina

caravan ['kærəvæn] roulotte *f inv*

'**car bomb** autobomba *f*

carbon monoxide [kɑːbən-'mɒn'ɒksaɪd] monossido *m* di carbonio

carburetor [kɑːbjʊ'reɪə(r)] carburatore *m*

carcass ['kɑːkəs] carcassa *f*

card [kɑːd] *to mark special occasion* biglietto *m*; (*post~*) cartolina *f*; (*business* ~) biglietto *m* (da visita); (*playing* ~) carta *f*; COMPUT scheda *f*; **cardboard** cartone *m*

cardiac ['kɑːdɪæk] cardiaco; **cardiac arrest** arresto *m* cardiaco

cardinal ['kɑːdɪnl] REL cardinale *m*

care [keə(r)] **1** *n of baby, pet* cure *fpl*; *of the elderly* assistenza *f*; *of the sick* cura *f*; (*worry*) preoccupazione *f*;
take ~ (*be cautious*) fare attenzione; **take** ~ (*of yourself*)! (*goodbye*) stammi bene; **take** ~ *of baby, dog* prendersi cura di; *tool, house, garden* tenere bene; (*deal with*) occuparsi di **2** *v/t* interessarsi; **I don't ~!** non mi importa
♦ **care about** interessarsi a
♦ **care for** (*look after*) prendersi cura di

career [kə'rɪə(r)] carriera *f*; (*path through life*) vita *f*

careful ['keəful] (**be**) ~ (*stai*) attento!; **carefully** con cautela; **careless** incurante; *driver, worker* sbadato; *work* fatto senza attenzione; **carelessly** senza cura; **caress** accompagnatore *m*, -trice *f*

caress [kə'res] accarezzare

'**car ferry** traghetto *m* (per le macchine)

cargo ['kɑːgəʊ] carico *m*

'**car hire** autonoleggio *m*

caricature ['kærɪkətjʊə(r)] caricatura *f*

carnation [kɑː'neɪʃn] garofano *m*

carnival ['kɑːnɪvl] carnevale *m*

'**car park** parcheggio *m*

carpenter ['kɑːpɪntə(r)] falegname *m*

carpet ['kɑːpɪt] tappeto *m*;

(fitted ~) moquette *f inv*

'car phone telefono *m* da automobile; **car rental** autonoleggio *m*

carrier ['kærɪə(r)] *(company)* compagnia *f* di trasporto; *of disease* portatore *m* sano, portatrice *f* sana

carrot ['kærət] carota *f*

carry ['kærɪ] **1** *v/t* portare; *of ship, bus etc* trasportare **2** *v/i of sound* sentirsi

◆ **carry on 1** *v/i (continue)* andare avanti, continuare **2** *v/t (conduct)* portare avanti

◆ **carry out** *survey etc* effettuare; *orders etc* eseguire

cart [kɑːt] carretto *m*; *Am: in supermarket, at airport* carrello *m*

carton ['kɑːtn] cartone *m*; *of cigarettes* stecca *f*

cartoon [kɑːˈtuːn] fumetto *m*; *on TV, film* cartone *m* animato

cartridge ['kɑːtrɪdʒ] *for gun, printer* cartuccia *f*

carve [kɑːv] *meat* tagliare; *wood* intagliare

case[1] [keɪs] *for glasses, pen* astuccio *m*; *of wine* cassa *f*; *(suitcase)* valigia *f*

case[2] [keɪs] *(instance, for police)*, MED caso *m*; LAW causa *f*; **in ~ ...** in caso; **in any ~** in ogni caso

cash [kæʃ] **1** *n* contanti *mpl*; *(money)* soldi *mpl* **2** *v/t cheque* incassare; **cash desk** cassa *f*; **cash flow** flusso *m*

di cassa; **cashier** *in shop etc* cassiere *m*, -a *f*; **cash machine**, **cashpoint** *(sportello m)* Bancomat® *m*; **cash register** cassa *f*

casino [kəˈsiːnəʊ] casinò *m inv*

casket ['kæskɪt] *Am (coffin)* bara *f*

casserole ['kæsərəʊl] *meal* stufato *m*; *container* casseruola *f*

cassette [kəˈset] cassetta *f*; **cassette recorder** registratore *m* (a cassette)

cast [kɑːst] **1** *n of play* cast *m inv*; *(mould)* stampo *m* **2** *v/t doubt, suspicion* far sorgere **(on** su); *metal* colare (in uno stampo)

cast 'iron ghisa *f*

castle ['kɑːsl] castello *m*

casual ['kæʒʊəl] *(chance)* casuale; *(offhand)* disinvolto; *remark* poco importante; *clothes* casual *inv*; **casually** *dressed* (in modo) casual; *say* con disinvoltura; **casualty** *dead person* vittima *f*; *injured* ferito *m*

cat [kæt] gatto *m*

catalogue, *Am* **catalog** ['kætəlɒg] catalogo *m*

catalyst ['kætəlɪst] catalizzatore *m*

catastrophe [kəˈtæstrəfɪ] catastrofe *f*; **catastrophic** catastrofico

catch [kætʃ] **1** *n* presa *f*; *of fish* pesca *f*; *on bag, box* chiusura *f; on door, window* fermo *m*; (*problem*) inghippo *m* **2** *v/t ball, escapee, bus, fish, illness* prendere; (*hear*) afferrare

◆ **catch on** (*become popular*) fare presa; (*understand*) afferrare

◆ **catch up** recuperare; ***catch up with s.o.*** raggiungere qu; ***catch up with sth work, studies*** mettersi in pari con qc

catching ['kætʃɪŋ] *also fig* contagioso; **catchy** *tune* orecchiabile

categoric [kætə'gɒrɪk] categorico; **category** categoria *f*

caterer ['keɪtərə(r)] ristoratore *m*, -trice *f*

caterpillar ['kætəpɪlə(r)] bruco *m*

cathedral [kə'θiːdrəl] cattedrale *f*, duomo *m*

Catholic ['kæθəlɪk] **1** *adj* cattolico **2** *n* cattolico *m*, -a *f*; **Catholicism** cattolicesimo *m*

cattle ['kætl] bestiame *m*

cauliflower ['kɒlɪflaʊə(r)] cavolfiore *m*

cause [kɔːz] **1** *n* causa *f*; (*grounds*) motivo *m* **2** *v/t* causare

caution ['kɔːʃn] **1** *n* (*carefulness*) cautela *f*, prudenza *f* **2** *v/t* (*warn*) mettere in guardia; **cautious** cauto, prudente; **cautiously** con cautela

cave [keɪv] caverna *f*, grotta *f*

caviar ['kævɪɑː(r)] caviale *m*

cavity ['kævətɪ] cavità *f inv*; *in tooth* carie *f inv*

CD [siː'diː] (= *compact disc*) CD *m inv*; **CD player** lettore *m* CD; **CD-ROM** CD-ROM *m inv*

cease [siːs] cessare; **cease-fire** cessate il fuoco *m inv*

ceiling ['siːlɪŋ] soffitto *m*; (*limit*) tetto *m*, plafond *m inv*

celeb [seleb] vip *m/f inv*

celebrate ['selɪbreɪt] festeggiare; **celebrated** acclamato; **celebration** celebrazione *f*, festeggiamento *m*; **celebrity** celebrità *f inv*

celibate ['selɪbət] *man* celibe; *woman* nubile

cell [sel] *for prisoner* cella *f*; BIO cellula *f*; *in spreadsheet* casella *f*, cella *f*

cellar ['selə(r)] cantina *f*; *of wine* collezione *f* di vini

cellist ['tʃelɪst] violoncellista *m/f*; **cello** violoncello *m*

'cell phone, cellular phone ['seljuːlə(r)] *Am* telefono *m* cellulare, cellulare *m*

cement [sɪ'ment] cemento *m*

cemetery ['semətrɪ] cimitero *m*

censor ['sensə(r)] censurare; **censorship** censura *f*

census ['sensəs] censimento *m*

cent [sent] centesimo *m*

centenary [sen'tiːnərɪ] centenario *m*

center *Am* ☞ **centre**

centigrade ['sentɪgreɪd] centigrado

centimetre, *Am* **centimeter**
['sentɪmiːtə(r)] centimetro *m*

central ['sentral] centrale;
central heating riscaldamento *m* autonomo; **cen-
tralize** accentrare; **central
locking** MOT chiusura *f* cen-
tralizzata; **central reservation** MOT banchina *f* spartitraffico

centre ['sentə(r)] **1** *n* centro *m*
2 *v/t* centrare

century ['sentʃərɪ] secolo *m*

CEO [siːiː'əʊ] (= *Chief Executive Officer*) direttore *m* generale

ceramic [sɪ'ræmɪk] ceramico

cereal ['sɪərɪəl] cereale *m*;
(*breakfast* ~) cereali *mpl*

ceremonial [serɪ'məʊnɪəl] **1**
adj da cerimonia **2** *n* cerimoniale *m*; **ceremony** cerimonia *f*

certain ['sɜːtn] (*sure, particular*) certo; **certainly** certamente; ~ *not!* certo che
no!; **certainty** certezza *f*;
it's a ~ è una cosa certa

certificate [sə'tɪfɪkət] *qualification* certificazione *f*; *official paper* certificato *m*

certify ['sɜːtɪfaɪ] dichiarare
ufficialmente

Cesarean *Am* ☞ *Caesarean*

chain [tʃeɪn] **1** *n* catena *f* **2** *v/t*:
~ *sth to sth* incatenare qc a
qc; **chain reaction** reazione
f a catena

chair [tʃeə(r)] **1** *n* sedia *f*; (*arm*
~) poltrona *f*; *at university*
cattedra *f* **2** *v/t meeting* presiedere; **chair lift** seggiovia
f; **chairman** presidente *m*;
chairmanship presidenza
f; **chairperson** presidente
m/f

chalet ['ʃæleɪ] chalet *m inv*

chalk [tʃɔːk] gesso *m*

challenge ['tʃælɪndʒ] **1** *n* sfida
f **2** *v/t* sfidare; (*call into question*) mettere alla prova;
challenger sfidante *m/f*;
challenging *job, undertaking* stimolante

chambermaid ['tʃeɪmbəmeɪd]
cameriera *f*; **Chamber of
Commerce** Camera *f* di
Commercio

champagne [ʃæm'peɪn]
champagne *m inv*

champion ['tʃæmpɪən] **1** *n* SP
campione *m*, -essa *f* **2** *v/t
cause* difendere; **championship** *event* campionato *m*; *title* titolo *m* di campione

chance [tʃɑːns] (*possibility*)
probabilità *f inv*; (*opportunity*) opportunità *f inv*; (*luck*)
caso *m*; *by* ~ per caso; *take
a* ~ correre un rischio

change [tʃeɪndʒ] **1** *n* cambiamento *m*; *small coins* moneta
f; *from purchase* resto *m*; *for
a* ~ per cambiare **2** *v/t* cambiare **3** *v/i* cambiare; (*put
on different clothes*) cambiarsi; **changeable** incostante;
weather variabile; **change-**

over passaggio *m*; *period* fase *f* di transizione; **changing room** SP spogliatoio *m*; *in shop* camerino *m*

channel ['tʃænl] *on TV, in water* canale *m*; **Channel Tunnel** tunnel *m* della Manica

chant [tʃɑːnt] **1** *n* slogan *m inv*; REL canto *m* **2** *v/i* gridare; *of demonstrators* gridare slogan; REL cantare

chaos ['keɪɒs] caos *m*; **chaotic** [keɪˈɒtɪk] caotico

chap [tʃæp] *m* F tipo *m* F

chapel ['tʃæpl] cappella *f*

chapter ['tʃæptə(r)] capitolo *m*

character ['kærɪktə(r)] carattere *m*; *(person)* tipo *m*; *in book* personaggio *m*; **characteristic 1** *n* caratteristica *f* **2** *adj* caratteristico; **characterize** caratterizzare

charge [tʃɑːdʒ] **1** *n* *(fee)* costo *m*; LAW accusa *f*; *free of ~* gratis; *be in ~* essere responsabile **2** *v/t sum of money* far pagare; *Am (put on account)* addebitare; LAW accusare; *battery* caricare **3** *v/i (attack)* attaccare; **charge account** conto *m* (spese); **charge card** carta *f* di addebito

charger ['tʃɑːdʒə(r)] *battery*, TEL caricabatteria *m*

charitable ['tʃærɪtəbl] *institution* di beneficenza; *person* caritatevole; **charity** carità *f*; *organization* associazione *f* di beneficenza

charm [tʃɑːm] **1** *n* fascino *m*; *on bracelet etc* ciondolo *m* **2** *v/t (delight)* conquistare; **charming** affascinante; *house, village* incantevole

charred [tʃɑːd] carbonizzato

chart [tʃɑːt] *n* diagramma *m*; *(map)* carta *f*

'**charter flight** volo *m* charter *inv*

chase [tʃeɪs] **1** *n* inseguimento *m* **2** *v/t* inseguire

◆ **chase away** cacciare (via)

chassis ['ʃæsɪ] *of car* telaio *m*

chat [tʃæt] **1** *n* chiacchierata *f* **2** *v/i* chiacchierare

◆ **chat up** F abbordare F

'**chatline** chat line *f inv*; **chat room** chat room *f inv*; **chat show** talk show *m inv*

chatter ['tʃætə(r)] **1** *n* parlantina *f* **2** *v/i talk* fare chiacchiere; *of teeth* battere; **chatterbox** chiacchierone *m*, -a *f*

chauffeur ['ʃəʊfə(r)] autista *m/f*

chauvinist ['ʃəʊvɪnɪst] *(male ~)* maschilista *m*

cheap [tʃiːp] economico; *(nasty)* cattivo; *(mean)* tirchio

cheat [tʃiːt] **1** *n* person imbroglione *m*, -a *f* **2** *v/t* imbrogliare **3** *v/i* imbrogliare; *in cards* barare

check¹ [tʃek] **1** *adj* shirt a quadri **2** *n* quadro *m*

check² [tʃek] *n Am* FIN assegno *m*

check³ [tʃek] **1** *n to verify sth* verifica *f* **2** *v/t & v/i* verificare

◆ **check in** registrarsi
◆ **check out 1** v/i of hotel saldare il conto **2** v/t (look into) verificare; club, restaurant etc provare
◆ **check up on** fare dei controlli su
checked ['tʃekt] material a quadri
checkered ['tʃekərd] Am material a quadri; **checkers** Am dama f
'**check-in (counter)** banco m dell'accettazione; **checking account** conto m corrente; **check-in time** check in m inv; **checklist** lista f di verifica; **checkmark** Am segno m; **check-mate** n scacco m matto; **check-out** cassa f; **check-point** posto m di blocco; **checkroom** Am for coats guardaroba m inv; **checkup** medical check up m inv; dental visita f di controllo
cheek [tʃiːk] guancia f; (impudence) sfacciataggine f; **cheeky** ['tʃiːkɪ] sfacciato
cheer [tʃɪə(r)] **1** n acclamazione f; ~**s!** (toast) salute!; ~**s!** F (thanks) grazie! **2** v/t acclamare **3** v/i fare acclamazioni
◆ **cheer up 1** v/i consolarsi; **cheer up!** su con la vita! **2** v/t tirare su
cheerful ['tʃɪəful] allegro; **cheering** acclamazioni fpl
cheerio [tʃɪərɪ'əʊ] F ciao F
'**cheerleader** ragazza f pon pon

cheese [tʃiːz] formaggio m; **cheesecake** dolce m al formaggio
chef [ʃef] chef m/f inv
chemical ['kemɪkl] **1** adj chimico **2** n sostanza f chimica; **chemist** farmacista m/f; in laboratory chimico m, -a f; **chemistry** chimica f
chemotherapy [kiːməʊ'θerəpɪ] chemioterapia f
cheque [tʃek] assegno m; **chequebook** libretto m degli assegni
cherry ['tʃerɪ] fruit ciliegia f; tree ciliegio m
chess [tʃes] scacchi mpl
chest [tʃest] of person petto m; (box) cassa f
chew [tʃuː] masticare; of dog, rats rosicchiare; **chewing gum** gomma f da masticare
chic [ʃiːk] chic inv
chick [tʃɪk] pulcino m; F (girl) ragazza f
chicken ['tʃɪkɪn] **1** n pollo m; **chickenpox** varicella f
chief [tʃiːf] **1** n principale m/f; of tribe capo m **2** adj principale; **chiefly** principalmente
child [tʃaɪld] (pl **children** ['tʃɪldrən]) also pej bambino m, -a f; **they have two children** hanno due figli; **childhood** infanzia f; **childish** pej infantile, puerile; **childlike** innocente; **childminder** baby-sitter m/f inv
children ['tʃɪldrən] pl ☞ **child**

chrysanthemum

Chile ['ʧɪlɪ] Cile m; **Chilean 1** adj cileno **2** n cileno m, -a f

chill [ʧɪl] **1** n in air freddo m; illness colpo m di freddo; **there's a ~ in the air** l'aria è fredda **2** v/t wine mettere in fresco

◆ chill out rilassarsi

chilli (pepper) ['ʧɪlɪ] peperoncino m

chilly ['ʧɪlɪ] weather, welcome freddo

chimney ['ʧɪmnɪ] camino m

chimpanzee [ʧɪmpæn'zi:] scimpanzé m inv

chin [ʧɪn] mento m

china ['ʧaɪnə] porcellana f

China ['ʧaɪnə] Cina f; **Chinese 1** adj cinese **2** n language cinese m; person cinese m/f

chip [ʧɪp] **1** n fragment scheggia f; damage scheggiatura f; in gambling fiche f inv; COMPUT chip m inv; **~s** patate fpl fritte; Am patatine fpl **2** v/t damage scheggiare

chisel ['ʧɪzl] scalpello m

chlorine ['klɔ:ri:n] cloro m

chock-full ['ʧɒkful] F strapieno

chocolate ['ʧɒkələt] cioccolato m; in box cioccolatino m; **chocolate cake** dolce m al cioccolato

choice [ʧɔɪs] **1** n scelta f; **I had no ~** non avevo scelta **2** adj (top quality) di prima scelta

choir ['kwaɪə(r)] coro m

choke [ʧəʊk] **1** n MOT starter m inv **2** v/t & v/i soffocare

cholesterol [kə'lestərɒl] colesterolo m

choose [ʧu:z] scegliere; **choosey** F selettivo

chop [ʧɒp] **1** n meat braciola f **2** v/t wood spaccare; meat, vegetables tagliare a pezzi

◆ **chop down** tree abbattere

chord [kɔ:d] MUS accordo m

chore [ʧɔ:(r)] household faccenda f domestica

choreographer [kɒrɪ'ɒgrəfə(r)] coreografo m, -a f; **choreography** coreografia f

chorus ['kɔ:rəs] singers, of song coro m

Christ [kraɪst] Cristo m; **~!** Cristo!

christen ['krɪsn] battezzare

Christian ['krɪstʃən] **1** n cristiano m, -a f **2** adj cristiano; **Christianity** cristianesimo m; **Christian name** nome m di battesimo

Christmas ['krɪsməs] Natale m; **Merry ~!** Buon Natale!; **Christmas card** biglietto m di auguri natalizi; **Christmas Day** giorno m di Natale; **Christmas Eve** vigilia f di Natale; **Christmas present** regalo m di Natale; **Christmas tree** albero m di Natale

chrome, chromium [krəʊm, 'krəʊmɪəm] cromo m

chronic ['krɒnɪk] cronico

chrysanthemum [krɪ'sænθəməm] crisantemo m

chubby ['tʃʌbɪ] paffuto

chuck [tʃʌk] F buttare

chuckle ['tʃʌkl] **1** *n* risatina *f* **2** *v/i* ridacchiare

chunk [tʃʌŋk] pezzo *m*

church [tʃɜːtʃ] chiesa *f*; **church service** funzione *f* religiosa; **churchyard** cimitero *m* (di una chiesa)

chute [ʃuːt] scivolo *m*; *for waste disposal* canale *m* di scarico

cider ['saɪdə(r)] sidro *m*

cigar [sɪ'gɑː(r)] sigaro *m*

cigarette [sɪgə'ret] sigaretta *f*; **cigarette lighter** accendino *m*

cinema ['sɪnɪmə] cinema *m inv*; **cinema goer** frequentatore *m*, -trice *f* di cinema

cinnamon ['sɪnəmən] canella *f*

circle ['sɜːkl] **1** *n* cerchio *m*; (*group*) cerchia *f* **2** *v/i* *of plane* girare in tondo; *of bird* volteggiare

circuit ['sɜːkɪt] ELEC circuito *m*; (*lap*) giro *m*; **circuit board** COMPUT circuito *m* stampato

circular ['sɜːkjʊlə(r)] **1** *n* *giving information* circolare *f* **2** *adj* circolare; **circulate 1** *v/i* circolare **2** *v/t* *memo* far circolare; **circulation** BIO circolazione *f*; *of newspaper* tiratura *f*

circumstances ['sɜːkəmstənsɪz] circostanze *fpl*; (*financial*) situazione *fsg* (eco-

nomica)

circus ['sɜːkəs] circo *m*

cistern ['sɪstən] cisterna *f*; *of WC* serbatoio *m*

citizen ['sɪtɪzn] cittadino *m*, -a *f*; **citizenship** cittadinanza *f*

city ['sɪtɪ] città *f inv*; **city centre**, *Am* **city center** centro *m* (della città); **city hall** sala *f* municipale

civic ['sɪvɪk] civico

civil ['sɪvl] civile; **civil ceremony** cerimonia *f* civile; **civil engineer** ingegnere *m* civile; **civilian 1** *n* civile *m/f* **2** *adj* *clothes* civile; **civilization** civilizzazione *f*; **civilize** civilizzare; **civil rights** diritti *mpl* civili; **civil servant** impiegato *m*, -a *f* statale; **civil service** pubblica amministrazione *f*; **civil war** guerra *f* civile

claim [kleɪm] **1** *n* (*request*) richiesta *f*; (*right*) diritto *m*; (*assertion*) affermazione *f* **2** *v/t* (*ask for as a right*) rivendicare; *damages* richiedere; (*assert*) affermare; *lost property* reclamare; **claimant** richiedente *m/f*

clairvoyant [kleə'vɔɪənt] chiaroveggente *m/f*

clam [klæm] vongola *f*

clammy ['klæmɪ] *hands* appiccicaticcio; *weather* afoso

clamp [klæmp] *fastener* morsa *f*; *for wheel* ceppo *m* (bloccaruote)

♦ **clamp down** usare il pu-

gno di ferro
◆ **clamp down on** mettere un freno a
clandestine [klæn'destɪn] clandestino
clap [klæp] (applaud) applaudire
clarification [klærɪfɪ'keɪʃn] chiarimento m; **clarify** chiarire
clarinet [klærɪ'net] clarinetto m
clarity ['klærɪtɪ] chiarezza f
clash [klæʃ] **1** n scontro m **2** v/i scontrarsi; of opinions essere in contrasto; of colours stonare; of events coincidere
clasp [klɑːsp] **1** n fastener chiusura f **2** v/t in hand stringere
class [klɑːs] **1** n (lesson) lezione f; (group of people, category) classe f **2** v/t classificare
classic ['klæsɪk] **1** adj classico **2** n classico m; **classical** classico; **classification** classificazione f; **classified** information riservato; **classified ad**(vertisement) inserzione f, annuncio m; **classify** (categorize) classificare
'**classroom** aula f; **classy** F d'alta classe
clause [klɔːz] in agreement articolo m; GRAM proposizione f
claustrophobia [klɔːstrə'fəʊbɪə] claustrofobia f
claw [klɔː] **1** n artiglio m; of lobster chela m **2** v/t (scratch)

graffiare
clay [kleɪ] argilla f
clean [kliːn] **1** adj pulito **2** adv F (completely) completamente **3** v/t pulire; teeth lavarsi; car, hands, face lavare; clothes lavare or pulire a secco
cleaner ['kliːnə(r)] male uomo m delle pulizie; female donna f delle pulizie; (dry ~) lavanderia f, tintoria f
cleanse [klenz] skin detergere; **cleanser** for skin detergente m; **cleansing cream** latte f detergente
clear [klɪə(r)] **1** adj chiaro; sky sereno; water, eyes limpido; skin uniforme; conscience pulito **2** v/t roads etc sgombe(o)rare; (acquit) scagionare; (authorize) autorizzare **3** v/i of sky schiarirsi; of mist diradarsi
◆ **clear off** F filarsela F
◆ **clear out 1** v/t cupboard sgomb(e)rare **2** v/i sparire
◆ **clear up 1** v/i (tidy up) mettere in ordine; of weather schiarirsi; of illness sparire **2** v/t (tidy) mettere in ordine; mystery risolvere
clearance ['klɪərəns] space spazio m libero; (authorization) autorizzazione f; **clearance sale** liquidazione f; **clearing** in woods radura f; **clearly** chiaramente
cleavage ['kliːvɪdʒ] décolleté m inv

clench [klentʃ] serrare

clergy ['klɜːdʒɪ] clero *m*; **clergyman** ecclesiastico *m*

clerk [klɑːk, *Am* klɜːk] impiegato *m*, -a *f*; *Am in store* commesso *m*, -a *f*

clever ['klevə(r)] intelligente; *gadget* ingegnoso

click [klɪk] **1** *n* COMPUT click *m inv* **2** *v/i of camera etc* scattare

◆ **click on** COMPUT cliccare su

client ['klaɪənt] cliente *m/f*; **clientele** clientela *f*

cliff [klɪf] scogliera *f*

climate ['klaɪmət] clima *m*; **climate change** mutazione *f* climatica

climax ['klaɪmæks] punto *m* culminante

climb [klaɪm] **1** *n up mountain* scalata *f*, arrampicata *f* **2** *v/t* salire su **3** *v/i* salire; **climber** alpinista *m/f*

clinch [klɪntʃ] *deal* concludere

cling [klɪŋ] *of clothes* essere attillato

◆ **cling to** *of child* avvinghiarsi a; *tradition* aggrapparsi a

clingy ['klɪŋɪ] *person* appiccicoso

clinic ['klɪnɪk] clinica *f*; **clinical** clinico

clip¹ [klɪp] **1** *n fastener* fermaglio *m*; *for hair* molletta *f* **2** *v/t*: ~ **sth to sth** attaccare qc a qc

clip² [klɪp] **1** *n from film* spez-

zone *f* **2** *v/t hair, grass* tagliare

clipping ['klɪpɪŋ] *from newspaper* ritaglio *m*

cloakroom ['kləʊkruːm] *for coats* guardaroba *m inv*

clock [klɒk] orologio *m*; **clock radio** radiosveglia *f*; **clockwise** in senso orario

clone [kləʊn] **1** *n clone m* **2** *v/t* clonare; **cloning** clonazione *f*

close¹ [kləʊs] **1** *adj family, friend* intimo **2** *adv* vicino; ~ **at hand** a portata di mano; ~ **by** nelle vicinanze

close² [kləʊz] *1 v/t* chiudere; *2 v/i of door, eyes* chiudersi; *of shop* chiudere

closed-circuit 'television televisione *f* a circuito chiuso; **close-knit** affiatato; **closely** *listen, watch* attentamente; *cooperate* fianco a fianco

closet ['klɒzɪt] *Am* armadio *m*

close-up ['kləʊsʌp] primo piano *m*

closing date ['kləʊzɪŋ] termine *m*

closure ['kləʊʒə(r)] chiusura *f*

clot [klɒt] **1** *n of blood* grumo *m* **2** *v/i of blood* coagularsi

cloth [klɒθ] tessuto *m*; *for cleaning* straccio *m*

clothes [kləʊðz] vestiti *mpl*; **clothes hanger** attaccapanni *m inv*; **clothes peg** molletta *f* per i panni; **clothing** abbigliamento *m*

cloud [klaud] n nuvola f
♦ cloud over rannuvolarsi
cloudless ['klaudlɪs] sereno;
cloudy nuvoloso
clout [klaut] fig (influence) impatto m
clove of 'garlic [kləuv] spicchio m d'aglio
clown [klaun] also pej pagliac-
cio m
club [klʌb] weapon clava f; in
golf mazza f; organization
club m inv
clue [kluː] indizio m
clumsiness ['klʌmzɪnɪs] gof-
faggine f; clumsy goffo,
maldestro
cluster ['klʌstə(r)] gruppo m
clutch [klʌtʃ] 1 n MOT frizione
f 2 v/t stringere
♦ clutch at cercare di afferrare
Co. (= Company) Cia (= compagnia)
c/o (= care of) presso
coach [kəutʃ] 1 n (trainer) allenatore m, -trice f; on train
vagone m; (bus) pullman m
inv 2 v/t allenare; coaching
allenamento m; coach sta-
tion stazione f di pullman
coagulate   [kəu'æɡjuleɪt]
coagularsi
coal [kəul] carbone m
coalition [kəuə'lɪʃn] coalizione f
'coalmine miniera f di carbone
coarse [kɔːs] skin, fabric ruvido; hair spesso; (vulgar)

grossolano; coarsely (vul-
garly) grossolanamente;
ground a grani grossi
coast [kəust] costa f; coastal
costiero
'coastguard   organization,
person guardia f costiera;
coastline costa f, litorale m
coat [kəut] 1 n (over~) cappotto m; of animal pelliccia f; of
paint etc mano f 2 v/t (cover)
ricoprire; coathanger attaccapanni m inv, gruccia f;
coating strato m
coax [kəuks] convincere con
le moine
cobweb ['kɒbweb] ragnatela
f
cocaine [kə'keɪn] cocaina f
cock [kɒk] chicken gallo m;
any male bird maschio m
(di uccelli); cockpit of plane
cabina f (di pilotaggio);
cockroach scarafaggio m;
cocktail cocktail m inv
cocoa ['kəukəu] drink cioccolata f calda
coconut ['kəukənʌt] cocco m;
coconut palm palma f di
cocco
code [kəud] codice m
coeducational   [kəuedju-
'keɪʃnl] misto
coerce [kəu'ɜːs] costringere
coexist [kəuɪɡ'zɪst] coesiste-
re; coexistence coesistenza
f
coffee ['kɒfɪ] caffè m inv; coffee maker caffettiera f; coffee pot caffettiera f; coffee

shop caffetteria f
coffin ['kɒfɪn] bara f
cog [kɒg] dente m
cohabit [kəʊ'hæbɪt] convivere
coherent [kəʊ'hɪərənt] coerente
coil [kɔɪl] 1 n of rope rotolo m 2 v/t: ~ (up) avvolgere
coin [kɔɪn] moneta f
coincide [kəʊɪn'saɪd] coincidere; coincidence coincidenza f
Coke® [kəʊk] Coca® f
cold [kəʊld] 1 adj freddo; I'm ~ ho freddo; it's ~ of weather fa freddo 2 n freddo m; MED raffreddore m; cold-blooded also murder a sangue freddo; person spietato; cold calling porta-a-porta m; by phone televendite fpl; coldly freddamente; coldness freddezza f; cold sore febbre f del labbro
collaborate [kə'læbəreɪt] collaborare; collaboration collaborazione f; with enemy collaborazionismo m; collaborator collaboratore m, -trice f; with enemy collaborazionista m/f
collapse [kə'læps] crollare; of person accasciarsi; collapsible pieghevole
collar ['kɒlə(r)] collo m, colletto m; of dog collare m; collar-bone clavicola f
collateral [kə'lætərəl] for loan garanzia f collaterale; collat-

eral damage danni mpl collaterali
colleague ['kɒliːg] collega m/f
collect [kə'lekt] 1 v/t person andare / venire a prendere; tickets, cleaning etc ritirare; as hobby collezionare; (gather) raccogliere 2 v/i (gather together) radunarsi 3 adv Am: call ~ telefonare a carico del destinatario; collection collezione f; in church raccolta f; of poems, stories raccolta f; collective collettivo; collector collezionista m/f
college ['kɒlɪdʒ] istituto m di studi superiori; for professional training scuola f professionale; of British university college m inv; technical college istituto m tecnico
collide [kə'laɪd] scontrarsi; collision collisione f, scontro m
colon ['kəʊlən] punctuation due punti mpl
colonel ['kɜːnl] colonnello m
colonial [kə'ləʊnɪəl] coloniale; colonize colonizzare; colony colonia f
color Am ☞ colour
colossal [kə'lɒsl] colossale
colour ['kʌlə(r)] colore m; colour-blind daltonico; coloured person di colore; colourful pieno di colori; account pittoresco
colt [kəʊlt] puledro m

column ['kɒləm] colonna f; in
newspaper rubrica f; **colum-
nist** giornalista m/f che cura
una rubrica

coma ['kəʊmə] coma m inv

comb [kəʊm] **1** n pettine m **2**
v/t pettinare; area rastrellare

combat ['kɒmbæt] **1** n combattimento m v/t combat-
tere

combination [kɒmbɪ'neɪʃn]
combinazione f

combine [kəm'baɪn] **1** v/t unire; ingredients mescolare **2**
v/i combinarsi

come [kʌm] venire; of train,
bus arrivare

◆ **come about** (happen) succedere

◆ **come across** (find) trovare

◆ **come along** (come too) venire; (turn up) presentarsi;
(progress) fare progressi

◆ **come back** ritornare

◆ **come down** venire giù; in
price, amount etc, (descend)
scendere; of rain, snow cadere

◆ **come for** (attack) assalire;
(collect) venire a prendere

◆ **come forward** farsi avanti

◆ **come from** venire da;
where do you come from?
di dove sei?

◆ **come in** entrare; of train, in
race arrivare; of tide salire

◆ **come in for** attirare; **come
in for criticism** attirare delle
critiche

◆ **come off** of handle etc stac-
carsi

◆ **come on** (progress) fare
progressi; **how's the work
coming on?** come sta ve-
nendo il lavoro?; **come on!**
dai!; in disbelief ma dai!

◆ **come out** of person, book,
sun uscire; of results, product
venir fuori; of stain venire
via

◆ **come to 1** v/t place arrivare
a; **that comes to £70** fanno
70 sterline **2** v/i (regain consciousness) rinvenire

◆ **come up** salire; of sun sorgere

◆ **come up with** new idea etc
venir fuori con

'**comeback** ritorno m; **make
a ~** tornare alla ribalta

comedian [kə'miːdɪən] comico m, -a f; pej buffone m;
comedy commedia f

comfort ['kʌmfət] **1** n comodità f inv; (consolation) conforto m **2** v/t confortare;
comfortable chair, room comodo

comic ['kɒmɪk] **1** n to read fumetto m; (comedian) comico
m, -a f **2** adj comico; **comical**
comico; **comic book** fumetto m; **comic strip** striscia f
(di fumetti)

comma ['kɒmə] virgola f

command [kə'mɑːnd] **1** n comando m **2** v/t person comandare a

commandeer [kɒmən'dɪə(r)]

appropriarsi di

commander [kə'mɑːndə(r)] comandante *m*; **commander-in-chief** comandante *m* in capo

commemorate [kə'meməreɪt] commemorare

commence [kə'mens] cominciare

commendable [kə'mendəbl] lodevole; **commendation** *for bravery* riconoscimento *m*

comment ['kɒment] **1** *n* commento *m* **2** *v/i* fare commenti; **commentary** cronaca *f*; **commentator** *on TV* telecronista *m/f*; *on radio* radiocronista *m/f*

commerce ['kɒmɜːs] commercio *m*; **commercial 1** *adj* commerciale **2** *n* (*advert*) pubblicità *f inv*; **commercial break** interruzione *f* pubblicitaria; **commercialize** *Christmas etc* commercializzare

commission [kə'mɪʃn] (*payment*, *committee*) commissione *f*; (*job*) incarico *m*

commit [kə'mɪt] *crime* commettere; *money* assegnare; **~ o.s.** impegnarsi; **commitment** impegno *m*; **committee** comitato *m*

commodity [kə'mɒdətɪ] prodotto *m*

common ['kɒmən] comune; **have sth in ~ with s.o.** avere qc in comune con qu; **com-**

monly comunemente; **common sense** buon senso *m*

commotion [kə'məʊʃn] confusione *f*

communal ['kɒmjunl] comune

communicate [kə'mjuːnɪkeɪt] comunicare; **communication** comunicazione *f*; **communications** comunicazioni *fpl*; **communicative** comunicativo

Communion [kə'mjuːnɪən] REL comunione *f*

Communism ['kɒmjʊnɪzm] comunismo *m*; **Communist 1** *adj* comunista **2** *n* comunista *m/f*

community [kə'mjuːnɪtɪ] comunità *f inv*

commute [kə'mjuːt] **1** *v/i* fare il / la pendolare **2** *v/t* LAW commutare; **commuter** pendolare *m/f*; **commuter traffic** traffico *m* dei pendolari; **commuter train** treno *m* dei pendolari

compact 1 [kəm'pækt] *adj* compatto **2** ['kɒmpækt] *n* MOT compact *m inv*

companion [kəm'pænjən] compagno *m*, -a *f*

company ['kʌmpənɪ] compagnia *f*; COM società *f inv*; **company car** auto *f inv* della ditta

comparable ['kɒmpərəbl] paragonabile; (*similar*) simile; **comparative 1** *adj* (*relative*) relativo; *study*, *method* comparato; **comparatively** relativamente; **compare 1** *v/t* paragonare (**with** a); **~d with** ... rispetto a ... **2** *v/i*: **how did he ~?** com'era rispetto agli altri?; **comparison** paragone *m*, confronto *m*

compartment [kəm'pɑ:tmənt] scomparto *m*

compass ['kʌmpəs] bussola *f*; *for geometry* compasso *m*

compassion [kəm'pæʃn] compassione *f*; **compassionate** compassionevole

compatibility [kəmpætə'bɪlɪtɪ] compatibilità *f*; **compatible** compatibile

compel [kəm'pel] costringere

compensate ['kɒmpənseɪt] **1** *v/t with money* risarcire **2** *v/i*: **~ for** compensare; **compensation** *money* risarcimento *m*; *reward* vantaggio *m*; *comfort* consolazione *f*

compete [kəm'pi:t] competere; *(take part)* gareggiare; **~ for** contendersi

competence ['kɒmpɪtəns] competenza *f*; **competent** competente

competition [kɒmpə'tɪʃn] *(contest)* concorso *m*; SP gara *f*; *(competing, competitors)* concorrenza *f*; **competitive** competitivo; *sport* agonistico; *price, offer* concorrenziale; **competitiveness** competitività *f*; **competitor** *in contest* concorrente *m/f*; **our ~s** COM la concorrenza

complacent [kəm'pleɪsənt] compiaciuto

complain [kəm'pleɪn] lamentarsi; *to shop* reclamare; **complaint** lamentela *f*; *to shop* reclamo *m*; MED disturbo *m*

complementary [kɒmplɪ'mentərɪ] complementare

complete [kəm'pli:t] **1** *(total)* completo; *(finished)* terminato **2** *v/t task, building etc* completare; *form* compilare; **completely** completamente; **completion** completamento *m*

complex ['kɒmpleks] **1** *adj* complesso **2** *n also* PSYCH complesso *m*; **complexion** *facial* carnagione *f*; **complexity** complessità *f inv*

compliance [kəm'plaɪəns] conformità *f*

complicate ['kɒmplɪkeɪt] complicare; **complicated** complicato; **complication** complicazione *f*

compliment ['kɒmplɪmənt] *n* complimento *m* **2** *v/t* fare i complimenti a; **complimentary** lusinghiero; *(free)* in omaggio

comply [kəm'plaɪ] ubbidire; **~ with** osservare; *of products, equipment* essere conforme a

component [kəm'pəʊnənt] componente *m*

compose [kəm'pəʊz] *also* MUS comporre; **composed**

(calm) calmo; **composer** MUS compositore *m*, -trice *f*; **composition** *also* MUS composizione *f*; *(essay)* tema *m*; **composure** calma *f*

compound ['kɒmpaʊnd] *n* CHEM composto *m*

comprehend [kɒmprɪ'hend] *(understand)* capire; **comprehension** comprensione *f*; **comprehensive** esauriente; **comprehensive insurance** polizza *f* casco

compress ['kɒmpres] comprimere; *information* condensare

comprise [kəm'praɪz] comprendere; *(make up)* costituire; **be ~d of** essere composto da

compromise ['kɒmprəmaɪz] **1** *n* compromesso *m* **2** *v/i* arrivare a un compromesso **3** *v/t (jeopardize)* compromettere; **~ o.s.** compromettersi

compulsion [kəm'pʌlʃn] PSYCH coazione *f*; **compulsive** *behaviour* patologico; *reading* avvincente; **compulsory** obbligatorio

computer [kəm'pjuːtə(r)] computer *m inv*; **computer game** computer game *m inv*; **computerize** computerizzare; **computer literate** che ha dimestichezza con il computer; **computer science** informatica *f*; **computer scientist** informatico *m*, -a *f*; **computing** informatica *f*

comrade ['kɒmreid] *also* POL compagno *m*, -a *f*; **comradeship** cameratismo *m*

conceal [kən'siːl] nascondere; **concealment** occultazione *f*

conceit [kən'siːt] presunzione *f*; **conceited** presuntuoso

conceivable [kən'siːvəbl] concepibile; **conceive** *of woman* concepire

concentrate ['kɒnsəntreɪt] **1** *v/i* concentrarsi **2** *v/t energies* concentrare; **concentration** concentrazione *f*

concept ['kɒnsept] concetto *m*; **conception** *of child* concepimento *m*

concern [kən'sɜːn] **1** *n (anxiety)* preoccupazione *f*; *(care)* interesse *m*; *(business)* affare *m*; *(company)* impresa *f* **2** *v/t (involve)* riguardare; *(worry)* preoccupare; **concerned** *(anxious)* preoccupato; *(caring)* interessato; *(involved)* in questione; **as far as I'm ~** per quanto mi riguarda; **concerning** riguardo a

concert ['kɒnsət] concerto *m*; **concerted** congiunto

concession [kən'seʃn] *(compromise)* concessione *f*

concise [kən'saɪs] conciso

conclude [kən'kluːd] concludere *(from* da); **conclusion** conclusione *f*; **conclusive** conclusivo

concrete ['kɒnkriːt] concreto

concussion [kən'kʌʃn] commozione f cerebrale

condemn [kən'dem] condannare; **condemnation** condanna f

condensation [kɒnden'seɪʃn] *on walls, windows* condensa f

condescend [kɒndɪ'send]: *he ~ed to speak to me* si è degnato di rivolgermi la parola; **condescending** borioso

condition [kən'dɪʃn] 1 *n* (*state, requirement*) condizione f; MED malattia f; *in/out of ~* in/fuori forma 2 *v/t* PSYCH condizionare; **conditioner** *for hair* balsamo m; *for fabric* ammorbidente m; **conditioning** PSYCH condizionamento m

condo ['kɒndəʊ] *Am* condominio m

condolences [kən'dəʊlənsɪz] condoglianze *fpl*

condom ['kɒndəm] preservativo m

condominium [kɒndə'mɪnɪəm] *Am* condominio m

condone [kən'dəʊn] *actions* scusare

conduct 1 ['kɒndʌkt] *n* (*behaviour*) condotta f 2 [kən'dʌkt] *v/t* (*carry out*), ELEC condurre; MUS dirigere; **conducted tour** visita f guidata; **conductor** MUS direttore m d'orchestra; *on bus* bigliettaio m; PHYS conduttore m

cone [kəʊn] cono m; *of pine*

tree pigna f

conference ['kɒnfərəns] congresso m; **conference room** sala f riunioni

confess [kən'fes] 1 *v/t* confessare 2 *v/i* confessare; REL confessarsi; **confession** confessione f

confide [kən'faɪd] 1 *v/t* confidare 2 *v/i* ~ *in s.o.* confidarsi con qu; **confidence** (*assurance*) sicurezza f (di sé); (*trust*) fiducia f; *in ~* in confidenza; **confident** sicuro; *person* sicuro di sé; **confidential** riservato, confidenziale; *adviser* di fiducia; **confidently** con sicurezza

confine [kən'faɪn] (*imprison*) richiudere; (*restrict*) limitare; **confined** *space* ristretto

confirm [kən'fɜːm] confermare; **confirmation** conferma f

confiscate ['kɒnfɪskeɪt] sequestrare

conflict 1 ['kɒnflɪkt] *n* conflitto m 2 [kən'flɪkt] *v/i of statements* essere in conflitto; *of dates* coincidere

conform [kən'fɔːm] conformarsi; ~ *to of products, acts etc* essere conforme a

confront [kən'frʌnt] (*face*) affrontare; ~ *s.o. with sth* mettere qu di fronte a qc; **confrontation** scontro m

confuse [kən'fjuːz] confondere; ~ *s.o. with s.o.* confondere qu con qu; **confused** confuso; **confusing** che confonde; **confusion** confusione *f*

congested [kən'dʒestɪd] congestionato; **congestion** congestione *f*

congratulate [kən'grætjuleɪt] congratularsi con; **congratulations** congratulazioni *fpl*

congregate ['kɒŋgrɪgeɪt] (*gather*) riunirsi; **congregation** REL fedeli *mpl*

congress ['kɒŋgres] (*conference*) congresso *m*; **Congress** in *USA* il Congresso; **Congressional** del Congresso; **Congressman** membro *m* del Congresso

conjecture [kən'dʒektʃə(r)] (*speculation*) congettura *f*

conjurer, conjuror ['kʌndʒərə(r)] (*magician*) prestigiatore *m*, -trice *f*

con man ['kɒnmæn] F truffatore *m*

connect [kə'nekt] (*join, link*) collegare; *to power supply* allacciare; **connected: be well~** avere conoscenze influenti; **be ~ with ...** essere collegato con; **connecting flight** coincidenza *f* (volo); **connection** (*link*) collegamento *m*; *when travelling* coincidenza *f*; (*personal contact*) conoscenza *f*; **in ~ with** a proposito di

connoisseur [kɒnə'sɜ:(r)] intenditore *m*, -trice *f*

conquer ['kɒŋkə(r)] conqui-

stare; *fear etc* vincere; **conqueror** conquistatore *m*, -trice *f*; **conquest** conquista *f*

conscience ['kɒnʃəns] coscienza *f*; **conscientious** coscienzioso; **conscientiousness** coscienziosità *f*

conscious ['kɒnʃəs] (*aware*) consapevole; (*deliberate*) conscio; MED cosciente; **consciously** consapevolmente; **consciousness** consapevolezza *f*; **lose / regain ~** perdere / riprendere conoscenza

consecutive [kən'sekjutɪv] consecutivo

consensus [kən'sensəs] consenso *m*

consent [kən'sent] **1** *n* consenso *m* **2** *v/i* acconsentire

consequence ['kɒnsɪkwəns] conseguenza *f*; **consequently** di conseguenza

conservation [kɒnsə'veɪʃn] tutela *f*; **conservationist** ambientalista *m/f*; **conservative 1** *adj* (*conventional*) conservatore; *clothes* tradizionale; *estimate* cauto; **Conservative** Br POL conservatore **2** *n* Br POL **Conservative** conservatore *m*, -trice *f*; **conserve 1** *n* (*jam*) marmellata *f* **2** *v/t* *energy* risparmiare

consider [kən'sɪdə(r)] considerare; (*show regard for*) tener conto di; (*think about*) pensare a; **considerable** considerevole; **considerably** considerevolmente; **considerate** premuroso; *be ~ of* avere riguardo per; **considerately** premurosamente; **consideration** (*thought*) considerazione *f*; (*thoughtfulness, concern*) riguardo *m*; (*factor*) fattore *m*; *take sth into ~* prendere in considerazione qc

consignment [kən'saɪnmənt] COM consegna *f*

◆ **consist of** [kən'sɪst] consistere in

consistency [kən'sɪstənsɪ] (*texture*) consistenza *f*; (*unchangingness*) coerenza *f*; **consistent** coerente

consolidate [kən'sɒlɪdeɪt] consolidare

consonant ['kɒnsənənt] GRAM consonante *f*

conspicuous [kən'spɪkjʊəs]: *be / look ~* spiccare

conspiracy [kən'spɪrəsɪ] cospirazione *f*; **conspirator** cospiratore *m*, -trice *f*; **conspire** cospirare

constant ['kɒnstənt] costante; **constantly** costantemente

constipated ['kɒnstɪpeɪtɪd] stitico; **constipation** stitichezza *f*

constituency [kən'stɪtjʊənsɪ] POL circoscrizione *f* elettorale

constitute ['kɒnstɪtjuːt] costi-

tuire; **constitution** costituzione *f*; **constitutional** POL costituzionale

constraint [kən'streɪnt] restrizione *f*

construct [kən'strʌkt] costruire; **construction** costruzione *f*; **construction industry** edilizia *f*; **construction worker** operaio *m* edile; **constructive** costruttivo

consul ['kɒnsl] console *m*; **consulate** consolato *m*

consult [kən'sʌlt] (*seek advice of*) consultare; **consultancy** (*company*) società *f inv* di consulenza; (*advice*) consulenza *f*; **consultant** consulente *m*/*f*; **consultation** consultazione *f*

consume [kən'sjuːm] consumare; **consumer** consumatore *m*, -trice *f*; **consumer confidence** fiducia *f* dei consumatori; **consumption** consumo *m*

contact ['kɒntækt] **1** *n* contatto *m*; (*person*) conoscenza *f* **2** *v/t* mettersi in contatto con; **contact lens** lente *f* a contatto

contagious [kən'teɪdʒəs] contagioso

contain [kən'teɪn] contenere; **container** contenitore *m*; COM container *m inv*; **container ship** nave *f* portacontainer

contaminate [kən'tæmɪneɪt]

contaminare; **contamination** contaminazione f

contemporary [kən'tempərərɪ] **1** adj contemporaneo **2** n coetaneo m, -a f

contempt [kən'tempt] disprezzo m; **contemptible** spregevole; **contemptuous** sprezzante

contender [kən'tendə(r)] concorrente m/f; against champion sfidante m/f; POL candidato m, -a f

content[1] ['kɒntent] n contenuto m

content[2] [kən'tent] **1** adj contento **2** v/t: ~ **o.s. with** accontentarsi di

contented [kən'tentɪd] contento; **contentment** soddisfazione f

contents ['kɒntents] of contenuto m

contest[1] ['kɒntest] n (competition) concorso m; (struggle, for power) lotta f

contest[2] [kən'test] v/t leadership etc essere in lizza per; will impugnare

contestant [kən'testənt] concorrente m/f

context ['kɒntekst] contesto m

continent ['kɒntɪnənt] continente m; **the** ~ l'Europa continentale; **continental** continentale

continual [kən'tɪnjuəl] continuo; **continually** continuamente; **continuation** segui-

to m; **continue** continuare (**doing** a fare); **continuous** ininterrotto; **continuously** ininterrottamente

contort [kən'tɔːt] contorcere

contraception [kɒntrə'sepʃn] contraccezione f; **contraceptive** anticoncezionale m, contraccettivo m

contract[1] ['kɒntrækt] n contratto m

contract[2] [kən'trækt] **1** v/i (shrink) contrarsi **2** v/t illness contrarre

contractor [kən'træktə(r)] appaltatore m, -trice f; **building** ~ ditta f di appalti (edili)

contractual [kən'træktjuəl] contrattuale

contradict [kɒntrə'dɪkt] contraddire; **contradiction** contraddizione f; **contradictory** contraddittorio

contrary[1] ['kɒntrərɪ] **1** adj contrario; ~ **to** contrariamente a **2** n: **on the** ~ al contrario

contrary[2] [kən'treərɪ]: **be** ~ (perverse) essere un bastian contrario

contrast ['kɒntrɑːst] **1** n contrasto m **2** v/t confrontare **3** v/i contrastare; **contrasting** contrastante

contravene [kɒntrə'viːn] contravvenire a

contribute [kən'trɪbjuːt] **1** v/i contribuire; to magazine collaborare (**to** con); to discus-

sion intervenire (*to* in) **2** *v/t money* contribuire con; **con-tribution**: *money* offerta *f*; *to political party, church* donazione *f*; *of time, effort* contributo *m*; *to debate* intervento *m*; *to magazine* collaborazione *f*; **contributor** *of money* finanziare *m*, -trice *f*; *to magazine* collaboratore *m*, -trice *f*

control [kən'trəʊl] **1** *n* controllo *m*; **be in ~** *of sth* tenere qc sotto controllo; **~s** *of aircraft, vehicle* comandi; **~s** (*restrictions*) restrizioni **2** *v/t* (*govern*) controllare; (*regulate*) regolare; **~ o.s.** controllarsi

controversial [kɒntrə'vɜːʃl] controverso; **controversy** polemica *f*

convalescence [kɒnvə'lesns] convalescenza *f*

convenience [kən'viːnɪəns] comodità *f inv*; **at your ~** a tuo comodo; **convenience store** negozio *m* alimentari; **convenient** comodo; **whenever it's ~** quando ti va bene

convent ['kɒnvənt] convento *m*

convention [kən'venʃn] (*tradition*) convenzione *f*; (*conference*) congresso *m*; **conventional** convenzionale; *method* tradizionale

conversation [kɒnvə'seɪʃn] conversazione *f*; **conversational** colloquiale

conversely [kən'vɜːslɪ] per contro

conversion [kən'vɜːʃn] conversione *f*; *of house* trasformazione *f*; **convert 1** *n* convertito *m*, -a *f* **2** *v/t* convertire; **convertible** *car* cabriolet *f inv*, decappottabile *f*

convey [kən'veɪ] (*transmit*) comunicare; (*carry*) trasportare; **conveyor belt** nastro *m* trasportatore

convict 1 ['kɒnvɪkt] *n* carcerato *m*, -a *f* **2** [kən'vɪkt] *v/t* LAW condannare; **conviction** LAW condanna *f*; (*belief*) convinzione *f*

convince [kən'vɪns] convincere

convoy ['kɒnvɔɪ] convoglio *m*

cook [kʊk] **1** *n* cuoco *m*, -a *f* **2** *v/t food* cucinare; *meal* preparare **3** *v/i* of *person* cucinare; *of food* cuocere; **cookbook** ricettario *m*; **cooker** cucina *f*; **cookery** cucina *f*; **cookie** Am biscotto *m*; **cooking** cucina *f*

cool [kuːl] **1** *n* F: **keep one's ~** conservare la calma **2** *adj* fresco; (*calm*) calmo; (*unfriendly*) freddo; F (*great*) grande **3** *v/i of food* raffreddarsi; *of tempers* calmarsi; *of interest* raffreddarsi **4** *v/t* F: **~ it!** calma!

◆ **cool down 1** *v/i* raffreddarsi; *of weather* rinfrescare; *fig: of tempers* calmarsi **2** *v/t food* raffreddare; *fig* calmare

cooperate [kəʊˈɒpəreɪt] cooperare; **cooperation** cooperazione f; **cooperative** (helpful) disponibile (a collaborare)

coordinate [kəʊˈɔːdɪneɪt] coordinare; **coordination** of activities coordinamento m; of body coordinazione f

cop [kɒp] F poliziotto m

cope [kəʊp] farcela; ~ **with** farcela con

copier [ˈkɒpɪə(r)] machine fotocopiatrice f

copper [ˈkɒpə(r)] metal rame m

copy [ˈkɒpɪ] **1** n copia f **2** v/t copiare

cord [kɔːd] (string) corda f; (cable) filo m; **cordless** (phone) cordless m inv

cordon [ˈkɔːdn] cordone m

cords [kɔːdz] trousers pantaloni mpl di velluto a coste

corduroy [ˈkɔːdərɔɪ] velluto m a coste

core [kɔː(r)] **1** n of fruit torsolo m; of problem nocciolo m; of organization, party cuore m **2** adj issue essenziale

cork [kɔːk] in bottle tappo m di sughero; (material) sughero m; **corkscrew** cavatappi m inv

corn [kɔːn] grain frumento m; Am (maize) granturco m

corner [ˈkɔːnə(r)] **1** n of page, room, street angolo m; of table spigolo m; in football calcio m d'angolo, corner m

inv; **in the** ~ nell'angolo; **on the** ~ of street all'angolo **2** v/t person bloccare; ~ **a market** prendersi il monopolio di un mercato **3** v/i of driver, car affrontare una curva

coronary [ˈkɒrənərɪ] **1** adj coronario **2** n infarto m

coroner [ˈkɒrənə(r)] ufficiale pubblico che indaga sui casi di morte sospetta

corporal [ˈkɔːpərəl] caporale m maggiore; **corporal punishment** punizione f corporale

corporate [ˈkɔːpərət] COM aziendale; **sense of ~ loyalty** corporativismo m; **corporation** (business) corporation f inv

corpse [kɔːps] cadavere m

correct [kəˈrekt] **1** adj giusto; **she's** ~ ha ragione **2** v/t correggere; **correction** correzione f; **correctly** giustamente

correspond [kɒrɪˈspɒnd] (match, write) corrispondere; **correspondence** corrispondenza f; **correspondent** corrispondente m/f

corridor [ˈkɒrɪdɔː(r)] corridoio m

corroborate [kəˈrɒbəreɪt] corroborare

corrosion [kəˈrəʊʒn] corrosione f

corrupt [kəˈrʌpt] **1** adj also COMPUT corrotto **2** v/t morals, *youth* traviare; (*bribe*) corrompere; **corruption** corruzione *f*

Corsica ['kɔːsɪkə] Corsica *f*; **Corsican 1** *adj* corso **2** *n* corso *m*, -a *f*

cosmetic [kɒz'metɪk] cosmetico; *surgery* estetico; *fig* di facciata; **cosmetics** cosmetici *mpl*; **cosmetic surgery** chirurgia *f* estetica

cosmopolitan [kɒzmə'pɒlɪtən] cosmopolitano

cost [kɒst] **1** *n also fig* costo *m* **2** *v/t* costare; FIN *proposal* fare il preventivo di; *how much does it ~?* quanto costa?; **cost-effective** conveniente; **cost of living** costo *m* della vita; **cost price** prezzo *m* di costo

costume ['kɒstjuːm] *for actor* costume *m*

cosy ['kəʊzɪ] (*comfortable*) gradevole; (*intimate and friendly*) intimo

cot [kɒt] *for child* lettino *m*; *Am* (*camp-bed*) letto *m* da campo

cottage ['kɒtɪdʒ] cottage *m inv*

cotton ['kɒtn] **1** *n* cotone *m* **2** *adj* di cotone; **cotton candy** *Am* zucchero *m* filato; **cotton wool** ovatta *f*

couch [kaʊtʃ] divano *m*

couchette [kuːˈʃet] cuccetta *f*

couch po'tato F teledipendente *m/f*

cough [kɒf] **1** *n* tosse *f* **2** *v/i*

tossire; *to get attention* tossicchiare; **cough medicine**, **cough syrup** sciroppo *m* per la tosse

could [kʊd]: *~ I have my key?* mi dà la chiave?; *~ you help me?* mi puoi dare una mano?; *you ~ be right* magari hai ragione; *you ~ have warned me!* avresti potuto avvisarmi!; *I ~n't say for sure* non potrei giurarci

council ['kaʊnsl] (*assembly*) consiglio *m*; (*city ~*) comune *m*; **councillor**, *Am* **councilor** consigliere *m*, -a *f* (comunale)

counsel ['kaʊnsl] **1** *n* (*advice*) consiglio *m*; (*lawyer*) avvocato *m* **2** *v/t action* consigliare; *person* offrire consulenza a; **counselling**, *Am* **counseling** terapia *f*; **counsellor**, *Am* **counselor** (*adviser*) consulente *m/f*

count [kaʊnt] **1** *n* conteggio *m* **2** *v/t & v/i* contare; *~ yourself lucky* considerati fortunato

♦ **count on** contare su

'countdown conto *m* alla rovescia

counter ['kaʊntə(r)] *in shop, café* banco *m*; *in game* segnalino *m*

'counteract neutralizzare; **counter-attack 1** *n* contrattacco *m* **2** *v/t* contrattaccare; **counterclockwise** *Am* **1** *adj* antiorario **2** *adv* in senso an-

tiorario; **counterespionage**
controspionaggio *m*; **counterfeit 1** *v/t* falsificare **2** *adj*
falso; **counterpart** *person*
omologo *m*, -a *f*; **counter-
productive** controprodu-
cente

countess ['kauntes] contessa
f

countless ['kauntlɪs] innu-
merevole

country ['kʌntrɪ] paese *m*; *as
opposed to town* campagna *f*;
countryside campagna *f*

county ['kauntɪ] contea *f*

coup [ku:] POL colpo *m* di stato, golpe *m inv*; *fig* colpo *m*

couple ['kʌpl] coppia *f*; *just a
~* solo un paio; *a ~ of* un paio
di

coupon ['ku:pɒn] buono *m*

courage ['kʌrɪdʒ] coraggio *m*;
courageous coraggioso

courgette [kuə'ʒet] zucchino
m

courier ['kurɪə(r)] (*messenger*)
corriere *m*; *with tourist party*
accompagnatore *m* turistico,
accompagnatrice *f* turistica

course [kɔ:s] *of lessons* corso
m; *of meal* portata *f*; *of ship,
plane* rotta *f*; *for golf* campo
m; *for race, skiing* pista *f*; *of ~*
(*certainly*) certo; (*naturally*)
ovviamente; *of ~ not* certo
che no; *first ~* primo *m*

court [kɔ:t] LAW corte *f*;
(*courthouse*) tribunale *m*; SP
campo *m*; **take s.o. to ~** fare
causa a qu; *out of ~* in via

amichevole; **court case** caso
m (giudiziario)

courtesy ['kɜ:təsɪ] cortesia *f*

'**courthouse** tribunale *m*, palazzo *m* di giustizia; **court-
room** aula *f* del tribunale;
courtyard cortile *m*

cousin ['kʌzn] cugino *m*, -a *f*

cover ['kʌvə(r)] **1** *n protective*
fodera *f*; *of book, magazine*
copertina *f*; (*shelter*) riparo
m; *insurance* copertura *f* **2**
v/t coprire; *distance* percorrere

◆ **cover up 1** *v/t* coprire; *fig*
insabbiare **2** *v/i*: **cover up
for s.o.** coprire qu

coverage ['kʌvərɪdʒ] *by media* copertura *f*

covert ['kʌvɜ:t] segreto

'**cover-up** insabbiamento *m*

cow [kau] mucca *f*

coward ['kauəd] vigliacco *m*,
-a *f*; **cowardice** vigliacche-
ria *f*

'**cowboy** cow-boy *m inv*

co-worker ['kəuwɜ:kə(r)] collega *m/f*

cozy *Am* → **cosy**

crab [kræb] granchio *m*

crack [kræk] **1** *n* crepa *f*;
(*joke*) battuta *f* **2** *v/t cup, glass*
incrinare; *nut* schiacciare;
code decifrare; F (*solve*) risolvere **3** *v/i* incrinarsi

◆ **crack down on** prendere
serie misure contro

cracked [krækt] *cup* incrina-
to; **cracker** *to eat* cracker *m
inv*

cradle ['kreɪdl] *for baby* culla *f*

craft[1] [krɑːft] NAUT imbarcazione *f*

craft[2] [krɑːft] *(skill)* attività *f inv* artigiana; *(trade)* mestiere *m*

'craftsman artigiano *m*

crafty ['krɑːftɪ] astuto

crag [kræg] *rock* rupe *f*

cram [kræm] *papers, food* infilare; *people* stipare

cramps [kræmps] crampo *m*

crane [kreɪn] **1** *n machine* gru *f inv* **2** *v/t*: ~ **one's neck** allungare il collo

crank [kræŋk] *person* tipo *m* strambo; **cranky** *Br (eccentric)* strampalato; *Am (bad-tempered)* irascibile

crap [kræp] P merda *f*; **don't talk ~** non dire cazzate

crash [kræʃ] **1** *n noise* fragore *m*; *accident* incidente *m*; COM crollo *m*; COMPUT crash *m inv* **2** *v/i fall noisily* fracassarsi; *of car* schiantarsi; *of two cars* scontrarsi, schiantarsi; *of plane* precipitare; *of market* crollare; COMPUT andare in crash **3** *v/t car* avere un incidente con; **crash course** corso *m* intensivo; **crash diet** dieta *f* lampo; **crash helmet** casco *m* (di protezione); **crash-land** fare un atterraggio di fortuna

crate [kreɪt] cassetta *f*

crater ['kreɪtə(r)] cratere *m*

crave [kreɪv] smaniare dalla voglia di; **craving** voglia *f*;

pej smania *f*

crawl [krɔːl] **1** *n in swimming* crawl *m* **2** *v/i on floor* andare (a) carponi; *(move slowly)* avanzare lentamente

crayon ['kreɪən] matita *f* colorata; *wax* pastello *m* a cera

craze [kreɪz] moda *f*; **crazy** pazzo

creak [kriːk] scricchiolare; **creaky** che scricchiola

cream [kriːm] **1** *n for skin* crema *f*; *for coffee, cake* panna *f*; *colour* color crema *m* **2** *adj* color panna

crease [kriːs] **1** *n* grinza *f*; *deliberate* piega *f* **2** *v/t accidentally* sgualcire

create [kriː'eɪt] creare; **creation** creazione *f*; **creative** creativo; **creator** creatore *m*, -trice *f*

creature ['kriːtʃə(r)] creatura *f*

credibility [kredə'bɪlɪtɪ] credibilità *f*; **credible** credibile

credit ['kredɪt] **1** *n* FIN credito *m*; *(honour)* merito *m* **2** *v/t amount* accreditare; **creditable** lodevole; **credit card** carta *f* di credito; **credit limit** limite *m* di credito; **creditor** creditore *m*, -trice *f*; **creditworthy** solvibile

creep [kriːp] **1** *n pej* tipo *m* odioso **2** *v/i quietly* avanzare quatto quatto; *slowly* avanzare lentamente; **creepy** F che dà i brividi

cremate [krɪ'meɪt] cremare; **cremation** cremazione *f*

crest [krest] *of hill, bird* cresta *f*

crevasse [krə'væs] voragine *f*

crevice ['krevɪs] crepa *f*

crew [kruː] *of ship, plane* equipaggio *m*; **crew cut** taglio *m* a spazzola

crib [krɪb] *Am for baby* lettino *m*

crime [kraɪm] reato *m*; *(criminality)* criminalità *f*; *(shameful act)* crimine *m*; **criminal 1** *n* delinquente *m/f* **2** *adj* LAW penale; *(shameful)* vergognoso

crimson ['krɪmzn] cremisi *inv*

cripple ['krɪpl] **1** *n* invalido *m*, -a *f* **2** *v/t person* rendere invalido; *fig* paralizzare

crisis ['kraɪsɪs] crisi *f inv*

crisp [krɪsp] *weather, lettuce, new shirt* fresco; *bacon, toast* croccante; **crisps** patatine *fpl*

criterion [kraɪ'tɪərɪən] criterio *m*

critic ['krɪtɪk] critico *m*, -a *f*; **critical** critico; **criticism** critica *f*; **criticize** criticare

Croatia [kəʊ'eɪʃə] Croazia *f*; **Croatian 1** *adj* croato **2** *n* croato *m/f*; *language* croato *m*

crockery ['krɒkərɪ] stoviglie *fpl*

crocodile ['krɒkədaɪl] coccodrillo *m*

crony ['krəʊnɪ] F amico *m*, -a *f*

crook [krʊk] truffatore *m*, -trice *f*; **crooked** *streets* tortuoso; *picture* storto; *(dishonest)* disonesto

crop [krɒp] **1** *n* raccolto *m*; *type of grain etc* coltura *f* **2** *v/t hair, photo* tagliare
♦ **crop up** saltar fuori

cross [krɒs] **1** *adj (angry)* arrabbiato **2** *n* croce *f* **3** *v/t (go across)* attraversare; ~ **o.s.** REL farsi il segno della croce **4** *v/i (go across)* attraversare; *of lines* intersecarsi
♦ **cross off**, **cross out** depennare

'crosscheck 1 *n* controllo *m* incrociato **2** *v/t* fare un controllo incrociato su; **cross-country (skiing)** sci *m* di fondo; **cross-examine** LAW interrogare in contraddittorio; **cross-eyed** strabico; **crossing** NAUT traversata *f*; **crossroads** incrocio *m*; *fig* bivio *m*; **crosswalk** *Am* passaggio *m* pedonale; **crossword (puzzle)** cruciverba *m inv*

crotch [krɒtʃ] *of person* inguine *m*; *of trousers* cavallo *m*

crouch [kraʊtʃ] accovacciarsi

crow [krəʊ] *bird* corvo *m*; **as the ~ flies** in linea d'aria

crowd [kraʊd] folla *f*; **crowded** affollato

crown [kraʊn] corona *f*; *on tooth* capsula *f*

crucial ['kruːʃl] essenziale

crucifix ['kruːsɪfɪks] crocifisso m; **crucifixion** crocifissione f; **crucify** REL crocifiggere; fig fare a pezzi

crude [kru:d] **1** adj (vulgar) volgare; (unsophisticated) rudimentale **2** n: ~ (**oil**) (petrolio m) greggio m

cruel ['kru:əl] crudele; **cruelty** crudeltà f inv

cruise [kru:z] **1** n crociera f **2** v/i of people fare una crociera; of car, plane viaggiare a velocità di crociera

crumb [krʌm] briciola f

crumble ['krʌmbl] of bread sbriciolarsi; of stonework sgretolarsi; fig: of opposition etc crollare

crumple ['krʌmpl] **1** v/t (crease) sgualcire **2** v/i (collapse) accasciarsi

crush [krʌʃ] **1** n (crowd) ressa f **2** v/t schiacciare; (crease) sgualcire

crust [krʌst] on bread crosta f

crutch [krʌtʃ] for injured person stampella f

cry [kraɪ] **1** n (call) grido m **2** v/t (call) gridare **3** v/i (weep) piangere
♦ **cry out** gridare

cryptic ['krɪptɪk] sibillino

crystal ['krɪstl] cristallo m

cube [kju:b] cubo m; **cubic** cubico

cubicle ['kju:bɪkl] cabina f

cucumber ['kju:kʌmbə(r)] cetriolo m

cuddle ['kʌdl] coccolare

cue [kju:] for actor etc imbec-

cata f; for pool stecca f

cuff [kʌf] of shirt polsino m; (blow) schiaffo m; Am (of trousers) risvolto m

culminate ['kʌlmɪneɪt]: ~ **in** culminare in; **culmination** culmine m

culprit ['kʌlprɪt] colpevole m/f

cult [kʌlt] culto m

cultivate ['kʌltɪveɪt] land coltivare; person coltivarsi; **cultivated** person colto; **cultivation** of land coltivazione f

cultural ['kʌltʃərəl] culturale; **culture** cultura f; **cultured** colto

cumulative ['kju:mjolətɪv] cumulativo

cunning ['kʌnɪŋ] **1** n astuzia f **2** adj astuto

cup [kʌp] tazza f; (trophy) coppa f

cupboard ['kʌbəd] armadio m

'**cup final** finale f di coppa

curb [kɜ:b] **1** n on powers etc freno m **2** v/t tenere a freno

cure [kjuə(r)] **1** n MED cura f **2** v/t MED guarire; by drying essiccare; by salting salare; by smoking affumicare

curiosity [kjuərɪ'ɒsɪtɪ] curiosità f inv; **curious** (inquisitive) curioso; (strange) strano

curl [kɜ:l] **1** n in hair ricciolo m; of smoke spirale f **2** v/t arricciare **3** v/i of hair arricciarsi; of leaf etc accartocciarsi
♦ **curl up** acciambellarsi

curly 348

curly ['kɜːlɪ] *hair* riccio; *tail* ~ ricciolo

currant ['kʌrənt] uva *f* passa

currency ['kʌrənsɪ] *money* valuta *f*; **foreign ~** valuta estera; **current 1** *n in sea, ELEC* corrente *f* **2** *adj* (*present*) attuale; **current ac- count** conto *m* corrente; **current affairs** attualità *f*

curry ['kʌrɪ] *dish* piatto *m* al curry; *spice* curry *m*

curse [kɜːs] **1** *n spell* maledi- zione *f*; (*swearword*) impre- cazione *f* **2** *v/t* maledire; (*swear at*) imprecare contro **3** *v/i* (*swear*) imprecare

cursor ['kɜːsə(r)] COMPUT cursore *m*

cursory ['kɜːsərɪ] di sfuggita

curt [kɜːt] brusco

curtain ['kɜːtn] tenda *f*; THEA sipario *m*

curve [kɜːv] **1** *n* curva *f* **2** *v/i* (*bend*) fare una curva

cushion ['kʊʃn] **1** *n* cuscino *m* **2** *v/t blow, fall* attutire

custody ['kʌstədɪ] *of children* custodia *f*; **in ~** LAW in deten- zione preventiva

custom ['kʌstəm] usanza *f*; COM clientela *f*; **customer** cliente *m/f*; **customer ser- vice** servizio *m* assistenza al cliente

customs ['kʌstəmz] dogana *f*; **Customs and Excise** Uf- ficio *m* Dazi e Dogana; **cus- toms officer** doganiere *m*, -a *f*

cut [kʌt] **1** *n with knife, of hair, clothes* taglio *m*; (*reduction*) riduzione *f* **2** *v/t* tagliare; (*re- duce*) ridurre; **get one's hair ~** tagliarsi i capelli

♦ **cut down 1** *v/t tree* abbatte- re **2** *v/i in smoking etc* limi- tarsi

♦ **cut off** tagliare; (*isolate*) isolare

♦ **cut up** *meat etc* sminuzzare

'cutback *in production* ridu- zione *f*; *in spending* taglio *m*

cute [kjuːt] (*pretty*) carino; (*smart, clever*) furbo

cutlery ['kʌtlərɪ] posate *fpl*

'cut-off date scadenza *f*; **cut- -price** *goods* a prezzo ridotto; *store* di articoli scontati; **cut- -throat** *competition* spietato; **cutting 1** *n from newspaper etc* ritaglio *m* **2** *adj remark* ta- gliente

CV [siːˈviː] (= *curriculum vi- tae*) curriculum vitae *m inv*

cycle ['saɪkl] **1** *n* (*bicycle*) bici- cletta *f*; *of events* ciclo *m* **2** *v/i to work* andare in bicicletta; **cycling** ciclismo *m*; **cyclist** ciclista *m/f*

cylinder ['sɪlɪndə(r)] cilindro *m*; **cylindrical** cilindrico

cynic ['sɪnɪk] cinico *m*, -a *f*; **cynical** cinico; **cynicism** ci- nismo *m*

cypress ['saɪprəs] cipresso *m*

Czech [tʃek] **1** *adj* ceco; **the ~ Republic** la Repubblica Ce- ca **2** *n person* ceco *m*, -a *f*; *language* ceco *m*

D

DA Am (= **district attorney**) procuratore *m* distrettuale
◆ **dabble in** dilettarsi di
dad [dæd] papà *m inv*
daddy ['dædɪ] papà *m inv*; **daddy longlegs** zanzarone *m*
daffodil ['dæfədɪl] trombone *m*
daft [dɑːft] stupido
dagger ['dægə(r)] pugnale *m*
daily ['deɪlɪ] **1** *n* (*paper*) quotidiano *m* **2** *adj* quotidiano
'**dairy**: ~ **products** latticini *mpl*; **food** ~ **free** senza latticini *mpl*
daisy ['deɪzɪ] margherita *f*
dam [dæm] *for water* diga *f*
damage ['dæmɪdʒ] **1** *n also fig* danno *m* **2** *v/t* danneggiare; *fig: reputation etc* compromettere; **damages** LAW risarcimento *msg*; **damaging** nocivo
damn [dæm] **1** *int* F accidenti **2** *adj* F maledetto **3** *adv* F incredibilmente; **damning** *evidence* schiacciante; *report* incriminante
damp [dæmp] umido
dance [dɑːns] **1** *n* ballo *m* **2** *v/i* ballare; *of ballerina* danzare; **dancer** (*performer*) ballerino *m*, -a *f*; **be a good** ~ ballare bene; **dancing** ballo *m*, danza *f*

dandelion ['dændɪlaɪən] dente *m* di leone
dandruff ['dændrʌf] forfora *f*
Dane [deɪn] danese *m/f*
danger ['deɪndʒə(r)] pericolo *m*; **dangerous** pericoloso
dangle ['dæŋgl] **1** *v/t* dondolare **2** *v/i* pendere
Danish ['deɪnɪʃ] **1** *adj* danese **2** *n* (*language*) danese *m*
dare [deə(r)] **1** *v/i* osare; ~ **to do sth** osare fare qc; **how** ~ **you!** come osi! **2** *v/t*: ~ **s.o. to do sth** sfidare qu a fare qc; **daring** audace
dark [dɑːk] **1** *n* buio *m*, oscurità *f* **2** *adj* room, night buio; hair, eyes, colour scuro; **dark glasses** occhiali *mpl* scuri; **darkness** oscurità *f*
darling ['dɑːlɪŋ] tesoro *m*
dart [dɑːt] **1** *n* for throwing freccetta *f* **2** *v/i* scagliarsi; **darts** game freccette *fpl*
dash [dæʃ] **1** *n* in punctuation trattino *m*; of whisky, milk goccio *m*; of salt pizzico *m* **2** *v/i* precipitarsi **3** *v/t* hopes stroncare; **dashboard** cruscotto *m*
data ['deɪtə] dati *mpl*; **database** base *f* dati; **data protection** protezione *f* dati
date[1] [deɪt] (*fruit*) dattero *m*
date[2] [deɪt] data *f*; (*meeting*) appuntamento *m*; **what's**

the ~ **today?** quanti ne abbiamo oggi?; **out of** ~ **clothes** fuori moda; *passport* scaduto; **up to** ~ aggiornato; *(fashionable)* attuale; **dated** superato

daughter ['dɔːtə(r)] figlia f; **daughter-in-law** nuora f

dawdle ['dɔːdl] ciondolare

dawn [dɔːn] alba f; *fig: of new age* albori *mpl*

day [deɪ] giorno m; *emphasizing duration* giornata f; **the** ~ **after** il giorno dopo; **the** ~ **after tomorrow** dopodomani; **the** ~ **before** il giorno prima; **the** ~ **before yesterday** l'altro ieri; **in those** ~**s** a quei tempi; **the other** ~ *(recently)* l'altro giorno; **daybreak**: **at** ~ allo spuntare del giorno; **daydream 1** n sogno m ad occhi aperti **2** v/i essere sovrappensiero; **daylight** luce f del giorno; **daytime**: **in the** ~ durante il giorno; **day return** biglietto m di andata e ritorno in giornata; **daytrip** gita f di un giorno

dazed [deɪzd] *by news* sbalordito; *by blow* stordito

dazzle ['dæzl] *of light, fig* abbagliare

dead [ded] **1** *adj* morto; *battery* scarica; *phone* muto **2** *adv* F *(very)* da matti F; ~ **beat**, ~ **tired** stanco morto **3** n: **the** ~ *(dead people)* i morti; **dead end** *street* vicolo m cieco; **dead heat** pareggio

m; **deadline** scadenza f; *for newspaper* termine m per l'invio in stampa; **deadlock** *in talks* punto m morto; **deadly** mortale

deaf [def] sordo; **deafening** assordante; **deafness** sordità f

deal [diːl] **1** n accordo m; **a great** ~ **of** un bel po' di **2** v/t *cards* distribuire

◆ **deal in** trattare; *drugs* trafficare

◆ **deal with** *(handle)* occuparsi di; *situation* gestire; *(do business with)* trattare con

dealer ['diːlə(r)] *(merchant)* commerciante m/f; *(drug* ~) spacciatore m, -trice f; **dealing** *(drug* ~) spaccio m; **dealings** *(business)* rapporti *mpl*

dear [dɪə(r)] caro; **Dear Sir** Egregio Signore

death [deθ] morte f; **death penalty** pena f di morte; **death toll** numero m delle vittime

debatable [dɪ'beɪtəbl] discutibile; **debate 1** n dibattimento m; POL dibattito m **2** v/i dibattere **3** v/t dibattere su

debit ['debɪt] **1** n addebito m **2** v/t addebitare; **debit card** bancomat m *inv*

debris ['debriː] *of plane* rottami *mpl*; *of building* macerie *fpl*

debt [det] debito m; **be in** ~

avere dei debiti; **debtor** debitore *m*, -trice *f*

debug [diːˈbʌg] COMPUT togliere gli errori da

decade [ˈdekeɪd] decennio *m*, decade *f*

decadent [ˈdekədənt] decadente

decaffeinated [diˈkæfɪneɪtɪd] decaffeinato

decay [dɪˈkeɪ] **1** *n of matter* decomposizione *f*; *of civilization* declino *m*; (*decayed matter*) marciume *m*; *in teeth* carie *f* **2** *v/i of organic matter* decomporsi; *of civilization* declinare; *of teeth* cariarsi

deceased [dɪˈsiːst]: **the ~** il defunto *m*, la defunta *f*

deceit [dɪˈsiːt] falsità *f*, disonestà *f*; **deceitful** falso, disonesto; **deceive** ingannare

December [dɪˈsembə(r)] dicembre *m*

decency [ˈdiːsənsɪ] decenza *f*; **decent** *price, proposition* corretto; *meal, sleep* decente; **a ~ guy** un uomo per bene

decentralize [diːˈsentrəlaɪz] decentralizzare

deception [dɪˈsepʃn] inganno *m*; **deceptive** ingannevole; **deceptively: it looks ~ simple** sembra semplice solo all'apparenza

decide [dɪˈsaɪd] decidere (**to do** di fare); **decided** (*definite*) deciso

decimal [ˈdesɪml] decimale *f*

decipher [dɪˈsaɪfə(r)] decifra-

re

decision [dɪˈsɪʒn] decisione *f*; **decisive** risoluto; (*crucial*) decisivo

deck [dek] *of ship* ponte *m*; *of bus* piano *m*; *of cards* mazzo *m*; **deckchair** sedia *f* a sdraio, sdraio *f inv*

declaration [dekləˈreɪʃn] dichiarazione *f*; **declare** dichiarare

decline [dɪˈklaɪn] **1** *n in number, standards* calo *m*; *in health* peggioramento *m* **2** *v/t invitation* declinare; **~ to comment** esimersi dal commentare **3** *v/i* (*refuse*) declinare; (*decrease*) diminuire; *of health* peggiorare

decode [diːˈkəʊd] decodificare

decompose [diːkəmˈpəʊz] decomporsi

décor [ˈdeɪkɔː(r)] arredamento *m*

decorate [ˈdekəreɪt] *with paint* imbiancare; *with paper* tappezzare; (*adorn*) MIL decorare; **decoration** *paint* vernice *f*; *paper* tappezzeria *f*; (*ornament*) addobbi *mpl*; MIL decorazione *f*; **decorator** (*interior ~*) imbianchino *m*

decoy [ˈdiːkɔɪ] *n* esca *f*

decrease [ˈdiːkriːs] **1** *n* diminuzione *f* **2** *v/t* ridurre **3** *v/i* ridursi

dedicate [ˈdedɪkeɪt] *book etc* dedicare; **dedicated** dedito;

dedication *in book* dedica *f*; *to cause, work* dedizione *f*

deduce [dɪ'dju:s] dedurre

deduct [dɪ'dʌkt] detrarre (**from** da); **deduction** *from salary* trattenuta *f*; *(conclusion)* deduzione *f*

deed [di:d] *(act)* azione *f*; LAW atto *m*

deep [di:p] profondo; *colour* intenso; **deepen 1** *v/t* rendere più profondo **2** *v/i* diventare più profondo; *of crisis* aggravarsi; *of mystery* infittirsi; **deep freeze** congelatore *m*

deer [dɪə(r)] cervo *m*

deface [dɪ'feɪs] vandalizzare

defamation [defə'meɪʃn] diffamazione *f*; **defamatory** diffamatorio

default [dɪ'fɔlt] COMPUT di default

defeat [dɪ'fi:t] **1** *n* sconfitta *f* **2** *v/t* sconfiggere

defect ['di:fekt] difetto *m*; **defective** difettoso

defence [dɪ'fens] difesa *f*; **defenceless** indifeso

defend [dɪ'fend] difendere; **defendant** accusato *m*, -a *f*; *in criminal case* imputato *m*, -a *f*; **defense** *Am* ☞ **defence**; **Defense Secretary** *Am* POL ministro *m* della difesa; **defensive 1** *n*: **go on the ~** mettersi sulla difensiva **2** *adj weaponry* difensivo; *person* sulla difensiva

deference ['defərəns] defe-

renza *f*

defiance [dɪ'faɪəns] sfida *f*; **defiant** provocatorio

deficiency [dɪ'fɪʃənsɪ] carenza *f*

deficit ['defɪsɪt] deficit *m inv*

define [dɪ'faɪn] definire

definite ['defɪnɪt] *date, time, answer* preciso; *improvement* netto; *(certain)* certo; **definite article** GRAM articolo *m* determinativo; **definitely** senza dubbio; *smell, hear* distintamente

definition [defɪ'nɪʃn] definizione *f*

definitive [dɪ'fɪnətɪv] *biography* più completo; *performance* migliore

defrost [di:'frɒst] *food* scongelare; *fridge* sbrinare

defuse [di:'fju:z] *bomb* disinnescare; *situation* placare

defy [dɪ'faɪ] *(disobey)* disobbedire a

degrading [dɪ'greɪdɪŋ] degradante

degree [dɪ'gri:] grado *m*; *from university* laurea *f*

dehydrated [di:haɪ'dreɪtɪd] disidratato

deign [deɪn]: **~ to ...** degnarsi di ...

dejected [dɪ'dʒektɪd] sconfortato

delay [dɪ'leɪ] **1** *n* ritardo *m* **2** *v/t* ritardare; **be ~ed** *(be late)* essere in ritardo **3** *v/i* tardare

delegate ['delɪgeɪt] **1** n delegato m, -a f **2** v/t delegare; **delegation** of task delega f; (people) delegazione f

delete [dɪ'li:t] cancellare; **delete key** COMPUT tasto m cancella; **deletion** act cancellazione f; that deleted cancellatura f

deliberate 1 [dɪ'lɪbərət] adj deliberato **2** [dɪ'lɪbəreɪt] v/i riflettere; **deliberately** deliberatamente

delicate ['delɪkət] delicato

delicatessen [delɪkə'tesn] gastronomia f

delicious [dɪ'lɪʃəs] delizioso, ottimo

delight [dɪ'laɪt] gioia f; **delighted** lieto; **delightful** molto piacevole

deliver [dɪ'lɪvə(r)] consegnare; message trasmettere; baby far nascere; speech tenere; **delivery** of goods, mail consegna f; of baby parto m; **delivery date** termine m di consegna; **delivery van** furgone m delle consegne

de luxe [də'lʌks] di lusso

demand [dɪ'mɑːnd] **1** n rivendicazione f; COM domanda f; **in ~** richiesto **2** v/t esigere; (require) richiedere; **demanding** job impegnativo; person esigente

demented [dɪ'mentɪd] demente

demo ['deməʊ] (protest) manifestazione f; of video etc dimostrazione f

democracy [dɪ'mɒkrəsɪ] democrazia f; **democrat** democratico m, -a f; **democratic** democratico

demolish [dɪ'mɒlɪʃ] demolire; **demolition** demolizione f

demonstrate ['demənstreɪt] **1** v/t (prove) dimostrare; machine fare una dimostrazione di **2** v/i politically manifestare; **demonstration** dimostrazione f; (protest) manifestazione f; (protester) manifestante m/f

demoralized [dɪ'mɒrəlaɪzd] demoralizzato; **demoralizing** demoralizzante

demote [diː'məʊt] retrocedere; MIL degradare

den [den] (study) studio m

denial [dɪ'naɪəl] negazione f

denim ['denɪm] denim m; **denims** (jeans) jeans m/m

Denmark ['denmɑːk] Danimarca f

denomination [dɪnɒmɪ'neɪʃn] of money banconota f; REL confessione f

dense [dens] fitto; **density** of population densità f inv

dent [dent] **1** n ammaccatura f **2** v/t ammaccare

dental ['dentl] treatment dentario, dentale; hospital dentistico

dented ['dentɪd] ammaccato

dentist ['dentɪst] dentista m/f; **dentures** dentiera f

Denver boot ['denvə(r)] *Am* ceppo *m* bloccaruote

deny [dɪ'naɪ] negare; *rumour* smentire

deodorant [diː'əʊdərənt] deodorante *m*

depart [dɪ'pɑːt] partire; **~ from** (*deviate from*) allontanarsi da

department [dɪ'pɑːtmənt] *of university* dipartimento *m*; *of government* ministero *m*; *of store, company* reparto *m*; **Department of State** *Am* Ministero *m* degli esteri; **department store** grande magazzino *m*

departure [dɪ'pɑːtʃə(r)] partenza *f*; (*deviation*) allontanamento *m*; **departure lounge** sala *f* partenze; **departure time** ora *f* di partenza

depend [dɪ'pend] *that* **~s** dipende; **it ~s on the weather** dipende dal tempo; **dependable** affidabile; **dependence, dependency** dipendenza *f*; **dependent 1** *n* persona *f* a carico; **a married man with ~s** un uomo sposato con famiglia a carico **2** *adj* dipendente; **~ children** figli *mpl* a carico

depict [dɪ'pɪkt] raffigurare

deplorable [dɪ'plɔːrəbl] deplorevole; **deplore** deplorare, lamentarsi di

deploy [dɪ'plɔɪ] (*use*) spiegare; (*position*) schierare

deport [dɪ'pɔːt] deportare; **deportation** deportazione *f*

deposit [dɪ'pɒzɪt] **1** *n in bank* versamento *m*, deposito *m*; *of mineral* deposito *m*; *on purchase* acconto *m*; (*against loss, damage*) cauzione *f* **2** *v/t money* versare, depositare; (*put down*) lasciare; *silt, mud* depositare; **deposit account** libretto *m* di risparmio

depot ['depəʊ] (*bus station*) rimessa *f* degli autobus; *for storage* magazzino *m*; *Am* (*train station*) stazione *f* ferroviaria

depreciate [dɪ'priːʃieɪt] FIN svalutarsi; **depreciation** FIN svalutazione *f*

depress [dɪ'pres] *person* deprimere; **depressed** depresso; **depressing** deprimente; **depression** depressione *f*

deprivation [deprɪ'veɪʃn] privazione *f*; (*lack: of sleep, food*) carenza *f*; **deprive: s.o. of sth** privare qu di qc; **deprived** socialmente svantaggiato

depth [depθ] profondità *f inv*; **in ~** (*thoroughly*) a fondo

deputy ['depjʊtɪ] vice *m/f inv*; **deputy leader** *of party* vice segretario *m*

derail [dɪ'reɪl]: **be ~ed** *of train* essere deragliato

derelict ['derəlɪkt] desolato

deride [dɪ'raɪd] deridere; **derision** derisione *f*; **derisory**

amount irrisorio

derivative [dɪ'rɪvətɪv] derivato; **derive** trarre; **be ~d from** of word derivare da

dermatologist [dɜːmə'tɒlədʒɪst] dermatologo *m*, -a *f*

derogatory [dɪ'rɒgətrɪ] peggiorativo

descend [dɪ'send] **1** *v/t* scendere; **be ~ed from** discendere da **2** *v/i* scendere; *of mood, darkness* calare; **descendant** discendente *m/f*; **descent** discesa *f*; *(ancestry)* discendenza *f*

describe [dɪ'skraɪb] descrivere; **description** descrizione *f*

desegregate [diː'segrəgeɪt] eliminare la segregazione in

desert[1] ['dezət] *n* deserto *m*

desert[2] [dɪ'zɜːt] **1** *v/t (abandon)* abbandonare **2** *v/i of soldier* disertare

deserted [dɪ'zɜːtɪd] deserto; **deserter** MIL disertore *m*; **desertion** abbandono *m*; MIL diserzione *f*

deserve [dɪ'zɜːv] meritare

design [dɪ'zaɪn] **1** *n* design *m*; *technical* progettazione *f*; *(pattern)* motivo *m* **2** *v/t house, car* progettare; *clothes* disegnare

designate ['dezɪgneɪt] *person* designare

designer [dɪ'zaɪnə(r)] designer *m/f inv*; *of building, car, ship* progettista *m/f*; **fashion ~** stilista *m/f*; **designer**

---

clothes abiti *mpl* firmati

desirable [dɪ'zaɪrəbl] desiderabile; *(advisable)* preferibile; **desire** desiderio *m*

desk [desk] scrivania *f*; *in hotel* reception *f inv*; **desk clerk** receptionist *m/f inv*; **desktop publishing** editoria *f* elettronica

desolate ['desələt] *place* desolato

despair [dɪ'speə(r)] **1** *n* disperazione *f*; **in ~** disperato **2** *v/i* disperare; **desperate** disperato; **be ~ for sth** morire dalla voglia di qc; **desperation** disperazione *f*

despicable [dɪs'pɪkəbl] deplorevole; **despise** disprezzare

despite [dɪ'spaɪt] malgrado, nonostante

dessert [dɪ'zɜːt] dolce *m*, dessert *m inv*

destination [destɪ'neɪʃn] destinazione *f*

destiny ['destɪnɪ] destino *m*

destitute ['destɪtjuːt] indigente

destroy [dɪ'strɔɪ] distruggere; **destroyer** NAUT cacciatorpediniere *m*; **destruction** distruzione *f*; **destructive** distruttivo; *child* scalmanato

detach [dɪ'tætʃ] staccare; **detached** *(objective)* distaccato; **detached house** villetta *f*; **detachment** *(objectivity)* distacco *m*

detail ['diːteɪl] dettaglio *m*; **in**

~ dettagliatamente; **detailed** dettagliato

detain [dɪ'teɪn] trattenere; **detainee** detenuto *m*, -a *f*

detect [dɪ'tekt] rilevare; *anxiety, irony* cogliere; **detection of crime** investigazione *f*; *of smoke etc* rilevamento *m*; **detective** agente *m/f* investigativo; **detector** rilevatore *m*

détente ['deɪtɒnt] POL distensione *f*

deter [dɪ'tɜː(r)] dissuadere

detergent [dɪ'tɜːdʒənt] detergente *m*

deteriorate [dɪ'tɪərɪəreɪt] deteriorarsi

determination [dɪtɜːmɪ'neɪʃn] (*resolution*) determinazione *f*; **determine** (*establish*) determinare; **determined** determinato, deciso

deterrent [dɪ'terənt] deterrente *m*

detest [dɪ'test] detestare; **detestable** detestabile

detour ['diːtʊə(r)] deviazione *f*

♦ **detract from** [dɪ'trækt] *merit, value* sminuire; *enjoyment* rovinare

devaluation [diːvæljuˈeɪʃn] svalutazione *f*; **devalue** svalutare

devastate ['devəsteɪt] *also fig* devastare

develop [dɪ'veləp] **1** *v/t film, business* sviluppare; *land, site* valorizzare; (*originate*) sco-

prire; *illness* contrarre **2** *v/i* (*grow*) svilupparsi; **~ into** diventare; **developing country** paese *m* in via di sviluppo; **development** sviluppo *m*; *of land, site* valorizzazione *f*; (*origination*) scoperta *f*

device [dɪ'vaɪs] dispositivo *m*; (*tool*) apparecchio *m*

devil ['devl] diavolo *m*

devious ['diːvɪəs] (*sly*) subdolo

devise [dɪ'vaɪz] escogitare

devoid [dɪ'vɔɪd]: **be ~ of** essere privo di

devolution [diːvə'luːʃn] POL decentramento *m*

devote [dɪ'vəʊt] dedicare; **devoted** *son etc* devoto; **devotion** *to a person* attaccamento *m*; *to one's job* dedizione *f*

devour [dɪ'vaʊə(r)] *food, book* divorare

devout [dɪ'vaʊt] devoto; **a ~ Catholic** un cattolico fervente

dew [djuː] rugiada *f*

diabetes [daɪə'biːtiːz] diabete *m*; **diabetic** diabetico *m*, -a *f*

diagnose ['daɪəgnəʊz] diagnosticare; **diagnosis** diagnosi *f inv*

diagonal [daɪ'ægənl] diagonale; **diagonally** diagonalmente

diagram ['daɪəgræm] diagramma *m*

dial ['daɪəl] **1** *n of clock, meter* quadrante *m* **2** *v/i* TELEC comporre il numero **3** v/t TELEC comporre

dialect ['daɪəlekt] dialetto m

'**dialling tone**, Am '**dial tone** segnale m di linea libera

dialogue, Am **dialog** ['daɪəlɒg] dialogo m

diameter [daɪ'æmɪtə(r)] diametro m

diamond ['daɪəmənd] diamante m; (shape) losanga f; **~s** in cards quadri mpl

diaper ['daɪəpə(r)] Am pannolino m

diaphragm ['daɪəfræm] diaframma m

diarrhoea, Am **diarrhea** [daɪə'rɪə] diarrea f

diary ['daɪərɪ] for thoughts diario m; for appointments agenda f

dice [daɪs] dado m

dictate [dɪk'teɪt] dettare; **dictator** POL dittatore m; **dictatorship** dittatura f

dictionary ['dɪkʃənrɪ] dizionario m

die [daɪ] morire

◆ **die down** of noise, fire estinguersi; of storm, excitement placarsi

◆ **die out** of custom scomparire; of species estinguersi

diesel ['diːzl] (fuel) diesel m

diet ['daɪət] **1** n dieta f **2** v/i to lose weight essere a dieta

differ ['dɪfə(r)] differire; (disagree) non essere d'accordo; **difference** differenza f; (disagreement) divergenza f; **dif-**

ferent diverso, different; **differentiate** distinguere; **~ between** things distinguere tra; people fare distinzioni tra; **differently** diversamente, differentemente

difficult ['dɪfɪkəlt] difficile; **difficulty** difficoltà f inv; **with ~** a fatica

dig [dɪg] scavare

digest [daɪ'dʒest] also fig digerire; **digestion** digestione f

digit ['dɪdʒɪt] cifra f; **digital** digitale

dignified ['dɪgnɪfaɪd] dignitoso; **dignity** dignità f

dilapidated [dɪ'læpɪdeɪtɪd] rovinato; house cadente

dilemma [dɪ'lemə] dilemma m

dilute [daɪ'luːt] diluire

dim [dɪm] **1** adj room buio; light fioco; outline indistinto; (stupid) idiota; prospects vago **2** v/i of lights abbassarsi

dime [daɪm] Am moneta da dieci centesimi

dimension [daɪ'menʃn] dimensione f

diminish [dɪ'mɪnɪʃ] diminuire

din [dɪn] baccano m

dine [daɪn] cenare

dinghy ['dɪŋgɪ] small yacht dinghy m; rubber boat gommone m

dining car ['daɪnɪŋ] RAIL vagone m ristorante; **dining room** in house sala f da pranzo; in hotel sala f ristorante

dinner ['dɪnə(r)] *in the evening* cena *f*; *at midday* pranzo *m*; *formal gathering* ricevimento *m*; **dinner jacket** smoking *m inv*; **dinner party** cena *f*

dinosaur ['daɪnəsɔː(r)] dinosauro *m*

dip [dɪp] **1** *n for food* salsa *f*; *in road* pendenza *f* **2** *v/i of road* scendere

diploma [dɪ'pləʊmə] diploma *m*

diplomacy [dɪ'pləʊməsɪ] diplomazia *f*; **diplomat** diplomatico *m*, -a *f*; **diplomatic** diplomatico

direct [daɪ'rekt] **1** *adj* diretto **2** *v/t play* mettere in scena; *film* curare la regia di; **could you please ~ me to ...?** mi può per favore indicare la strada per ...?; **direction** direzione *f*; *of film, play* regia *f*; **~s** (*instructions*), *to a place* indicazioni *fpl*; *for use* istruzioni *fpl*; **directly** (*straight*) direttamente; (*soon, immediately*) immediatamente; **director** *of company* direttore *m*, -trice *f*; *of play, film* regista *m/f*; **directory** elenco *m*; TELEC guida *f* telefonica

dirt [dɜːt] sporco *m*, sporcizia *f*; **dirty 1** *adj* sporco; (*pornographic*) sconcio **2** *v/t* sporcare

disability [dɪsə'bɪlətɪ] handicap *m inv*, invalidità *f inv*; **disabled** handicappato *m*, -a *f*; **the ~** i disabili

disadvantage [dɪsəd'vɑːntɪdʒ] svantaggio *m*; **disadvantaged** penalizzato

disagree [dɪsə'griː] *of person* non essere d'accordo

◆ **disagree with** *of person* non essere d'accordo con; *of food* fare male a

disagreeable [dɪsə'griːəbl] sgradevole; **disagreement** disaccordo *m*; (*argument*) discussione *f*

disallow [dɪsə'laʊ] *goal* annullare

disappear [dɪsə'pɪə(r)] sparire, scomparire; **disappearance** sparizione *f*, scomparsa *f*

disappoint [dɪsə'pɔɪnt] deludere; **disappointed** deluso; **disappointing** deludente; **disappointment** delusione *f*

disapproval [dɪsə'pruːvl] disapprovazione *f*; **disapprove** disapprovare; **~ of** disapprovare; **disapproving** di disapprovazione

disarm [dɪs'ɑːm] **1** *v/t* disarmare **2** *v/i* disarmarsi; **disarmament** disarmo *m*

disaster [dɪ'zɑːstə(r)] disastro *m*; **disastrous** disastroso

disband [dɪs'bænd] **1** *v/t* sciogliere **2** *v/i* sciogliersi

disbelief [dɪsbə'liːf] incredulità *f*

disc [dɪsk] disco *m*

discard [dɪ'skɑːd] sbarazzarsi di

disciplinary [dɪsɪ'plɪnərɪ] disciplinare; discipline disciplina f

'disc jockey disc jockey m/f inv

disclaim [dɪs'kleɪm] negare; responsibility declinare

disclose [dɪs'kləʊs] svelare, rivelare

disco ['dɪskəʊ] discoteca f

discomfort [dɪs'kʌmfət] disagio m; (pain) fastidio m

disconcert [dɪskən'sɜːt] sconcertare

disconnect [dɪskə'nekt] (detach) sconnettere; supply, telephones staccare

disconsolate [dɪs'kɒnsələt] sconsolato

discontent [dɪskən'tent] malcontento m; discontented scontento

discontinue [dɪskən'tɪnjuː] interrompere; be a ~d line essere fuori produzione

discotheque ['dɪskətek] discoteca f

discount ['dɪskaʊnt] sconto m

discourage [dɪs'kʌrɪdʒ] (dissuade) scoraggiare

discover [dɪs'kʌvə(r)] scoprire; discovery scoperta f

discredit [dɪs'kredɪt] screditare

discreet [dɪ'skriːt] discreto

discrepancy [dɪ'skrepənsɪ] incongruenza f

discretion [dɪ'skreʃn] discrezione f

discriminate [dɪ'skrɪmɪneɪt]: ~ against discriminare; discriminating esigente; discrimination sexual, racial etc discriminazione f

discus ['dɪskəs] SP object disco m; event lancio m del disco

discuss [dɪ'skʌs] discutere; of article trattare di; discussion discussione f

disease [dɪ'ziːz] malattia f

disembark [dɪsəm'bɑːk] sbarcare

disentangle [dɪsən'tæŋgl] districare

disfigure [dɪs'fɪgə(r)] sfigurare; fig deturpare

disgrace [dɪs'greɪs] 1 n vergogna f 2 v/t disonorare; disgraceful vergognoso

disgruntled [dɪs'grʌntld] scontento

disguise [dɪs'gaɪz] 1 n travestimento m 2 v/t voice etc camuffare; fear, anxiety dissimulare; ~ o.s. as travestirsi da

disgust [dɪs'gʌst] 1 n disgusto m 2 v/t disgustare; disgusting disgustoso

dish [dɪʃ] piatto m; for cooking recipiente m

disheartening [dɪs'hɑːtnɪŋ] demoralizzante

disheveled [dɪ'ʃevld] person, appearance arruffato; after effort scompigliato

dishonest [dɪs'ɒnɪst] disonesto; dishonesty disonestà f

dishonor *etc Am* ☞ **dishonour** *etc*

dishonor [dɪs'ɒnə(r)] disonore *m*; **dishonourable** disdicevole

'**dishwasher** *machine* lavastoviglie *f inv*; *person* lavapiatti *m/f inv*; **dishwashing liquid** *Am* detersivo *m* per i piatti

disillusion [dɪsɪ'luːʒn] disilludere; **disillusionment** disillusione *f*

disinfect [dɪsɪn'fekt] disinfettare; **disinfectant** disinfettante *m*

disinherit [dɪsɪn'herɪt] diseredare

disintegrate [dɪs'ɪntɪɡreɪt] disintegrarsi; *of marriage, building* andare in pezzi

disinterested [dɪs'ɪntərestɪd] (*unbiased*) disinteressato

disjointed [dɪs'dʒɔɪntɪd] sconnesso

disk [dɪsk] disco *m*; (*diskette*) dischetto *m*; **disk drive** COMPUT lettore *m* or drive *m inv* di dischetti; **diskette** dischetto *m*

dislike [dɪs'laɪk] **1** *n* antipatia *f* **2** *v/t*: **I ~ cats** non mi piacciono i gatti

dislocate ['dɪsləkeɪt] lussare

disloyal [dɪs'lɔɪəl] sleale; **disloyalty** slealtà *f*

dismal ['dɪzməl] *weather, news* deprimente; *person* (*sad*), *failure* triste; *person* (*negative*) ombroso

dismantle [dɪs'mæntl] smontare; *organization* demolire

dismay [dɪs'meɪ] costernazione *f*

dismiss [dɪs'mɪs] *employee* licenziare; *suggestion* scartare; *idea* accantonare; **dismissal** *of employee* licenziamento *m*

disobedience [dɪsə'biːdɪəns] disobbidienza *f*; **disobedient** disobbidiente; **disobey** disobbedire a

disorder [dɪs'ɔːdə(r)] (*untidiness*) disordine *m*; (*unrest*) disordini *mpl*; MED disturbo *m*

disorganized [dɪs'ɔːɡənaɪzd] disorganizzato

disoriented [dɪs'ɔːrɪəntɪd], **disorientated** [dɪs'ɔːrɪənteɪtɪd] disorientato

disown [dɪs'əʊn] disconoscere

disparaging [dɪ'spærɪdʒɪŋ] dispregiativo

disparity [dɪ'spærətɪ] disparità *f inv*

dispassionate [dɪ'spæʃənət] spassionato

dispatch [dɪ'spætʃ] (*send*) spedire

disperse [dɪ'spɜːs] *of crowd* disperdersi; *of mist* dissiparsi

display [dɪ'spleɪ] **1** *n* esposizione *f*, mostra *f*; *in shop window* articoli *mpl* in esposizione; COMPUT visualizzazione *f* **2** *v/t emotion* manifestare; *at exhibition* esporre;

(for sale) esporre in vendita; COMPUT visualizzare

displease [dɪs'pliːz] contrariare; **displeasure** disappunto *m*

disposable [dɪ'spəʊzəbl] usa e getta *inv*; **disposable income** reddito *m* disponibile; **disposal** eliminazione *f*; *of waste* smaltimento *m*; **put sth at s.o.'s** ~ mettere qc a disposizione di qu

◆ **dispose of** [dɪ'spəʊz] *(get rid of)* sbarazzarsi di

disposed [dɪ'spəʊzd]: **be ~ to do sth** *(willing)* essere disposto a fare qc; **be well ~ towards** essere ben disposto verso

disprove [dɪs'pruːv] smentire

dispute [dɪ'spjuːt] **1** *n* controversia *f*; *industrial* contestazione *f* **2** *v/t* contestare; *(fight over)* contendersi

disqualification [dɪskwɒlɪfɪ'keɪʃn] squalifica *f*; **disqualify** squalificare

disregard [dɪsrə'gɑːd] **1** *n* mancanza *f* di considerazione **2** *v/t* ignorare

disreputable [dɪs'repjʊtəbl] depravato; *area* malfamato

disrespect [dɪsrə'spekt] mancanza *f* di rispetto; **disrespectful** irriverente

disrupt [dɪs'rʌpt] *train service* creare disagi a; *meeting, class* disturbare; **disruption** of *train service* disagio *m*; *of meeting, class* disturbo *m*

dissatisfaction [dɪssætɪs'fækʃn] insoddisfazione *f*; **dissatisfied** insoddisfatto

dissident ['dɪsɪdənt] dissidente *m/f*

dissimilar [dɪs'sɪmɪlə(r)] dissimile

dissolute ['dɪsəluːt] *adj* dissoluto

dissolve [dɪ'zɒlv] **1** *v/t* *substance* sciogliere **2** *v/i* *of substance* sciogliersi

distance ['dɪstəns] distanza *f*; **in the** ~ in lontananza; **distant** lontano

distaste [dɪs'teɪst] avversione *f*; **distasteful** spiacevole

distinct [dɪ'stɪŋkt] *(clear)* netto; *(different)* distinto; **distinction** *(differentiation)* distinzione *f*; **hotel of** ~ hotel d'eccezione; **distinctive** caratteristico; **distinctly** *(decidedly)* decisamente

distinguish [dɪ'stɪŋwɪʃ] *(see)* distinguere; **between X and Y** distinguere tra X e Y; **distinguished** *(famous)* insigne; *(dignified)* decisamente

distort [dɪ'stɔːt] distorcere

distract [dɪ'strækt] *person* distrarre; *attention* distogliere

distraught [dɪ'strɔːt] affranto

distress [dɪ'stres] **1** *n* sofferenza *f* **2** *v/t* *(upset)* angosciare; **distressing** sconvolgente

distribute [dɪ'strɪbjuːt] distribuire; **distribution** distribuzione f; **distributor** COM distributore m

district ['dɪstrɪkt] quartiere m; **district attorney** Am procuratore m distrettuale

distrust [dɪs'trʌst] diffidenza f

disturb [dɪ'stɜːb] disturbare; **disturbance** (*interruption*) fastidio m; **~s** (*civil unrest*) disordini mpl; **disturbed** turbato; *psychologically* malato di mente; **disturbing** inquietante

disused [dɪs'juːzd] inutilizzato

ditch [dɪtʃ] **1** n fosso m **2** v/t F *boyfriend* scaricare F; F *car* sbarazzarsi di

dive [daɪv] **1** n tuffo m; *underwater* immersione f; *of plane* picchiata f; F *bar* etc bettola f F **2** v/i tuffarsi; *underwater* fare immersione; *of submarine* immergersi; *of plane* scendere in picchiata; **dive off board** tuffatore m, -trice f; *underwater* sub m/f inv, sommozzatore m, -trice f

diverge [daɪ'vɜːdʒ] divergere

diversification [daɪvɜːsɪfɪ'keɪʃn] COM diversificazione f; **diversify** COM diversificare; **diversion** *for traffic* deviazione f; *to distract attention* diversivo m; **diversity** varietà f inv

divert [daɪ'vɜːt] *traffic* deviare; *attention* sviare

divide [dɪ'vaɪd] dividere

dividend ['dɪvɪdend] FIN dividendo m

divine [dɪ'vaɪn] REL, F divino

diving ['daɪvɪŋ] *from board* tuffi mpl; *underwater* immersione f; **diving board** trampolino m

division [dɪ'vɪʒn] divisione f; *of company* sezione f

divorce [dɪ'vɔːs] **1** n divorzio m **2** v/t divorziare da **3** v/i divorziare; **divorced** divorziato; **divorcee** divorziato m, -a f

divulge [daɪ'vʌldʒ] divulgare

DIY [diːaɪ'waɪ] (= *do it yourself*) fai da te m inv, bricolage m

dizziness ['dɪzɪnəs] giramento m di testa, vertigini fpl; **dizzy** stordito; **I feel ~** mi gira la testa

DJ [diː'dʒeɪ] (= *disc jockey*) dj m/f inv; (= *dinner jacket*) smoking m inv

DNA [diːen'eɪ] (= *deoxyribonucleic acid*) DNA m inv (= acido m deossiribonucleico)

do [duː] **1** v/t fare; *one's hair* farsi; *100mph* etc andare a; **~ the ironing / cooking** stirare / cucinare; **have one's hair done** farsi fare i capelli **2** v/i (*be suitable, enough*) andare bene; **that will ~!** basta così!; **~ well** (*do a good job*) essere bravo; (*be in good health*) stare bene; *of busi-*

ness andare bene; **well done!** bravo!; **how ~ you ~?** molto piacere

◆ **do away with** abolire

◆ **do up** (*renovate*) restaurare; (*fasten*) allacciare

◆ **do with: I could do with ...** mi ci vorrebbe ...

◆ **do without 1** v/i farne a meno **2** v/t far a meno di

docile ['dəʊsaɪl] docile

dock[1] [dɒk] **1** *n* NAUT bacino *m* **2** v/i *of ship* entrare in porto; *of spaceship* agganciarsi

dock[2] [dɒk] LAW banco *m* degli imputati

doctor ['dɒktə(r)] MED dottore *m*, -essa *f*; **doctorate** dottorato *m*

doctrine ['dɒktrɪn] dottrina *f*

document ['dɒkjumənt] documento *m*; **documentary** documentario *m*; **documentation** documentazione *f*

dodge [dɒdʒ] *blow* schivare; *person, issue* evitare; *question* aggirare

dog [dɒg] **1** *n* cane *m* **2** v/t *of bad luck* perseguitare

dogged ['dɒgɪd] accanito

dogma ['dɒgmə] dogma *m*; **dogmatic** dogmatico

'dog-tired F stravolto

do-it-yourself [du:ɪtjə'self] fai da te *m*

doldrums ['dɒldrəmz]: **be in the ~** *of economy* essere in stallo; *of person* essere giù di corda

doll [dɒl] *toy*, F *woman* bambola *f*

dollar ['dɒlə(r)] dollaro *m*

Dolomites ['dɒləmaɪts] Dolomiti *mpl*

dolphin ['dɒlfɪn] delfino *m*

dome [dəʊm] *of building* cupola *f*

domestic [də'mestɪk] domestico; *news, policy* interno; **domestic flight** volo *m* nazionale

dominant ['dɒmɪnənt] dominante; *member* principale; **dominate** dominare; **domination** dominio *m*; **domineering** autoritario

donate [dəʊ'neɪt] donare; **donation** donazione *f*

donkey ['dɒŋkɪ] asino *m*

donor ['dəʊnə(r)] donatore *m*, -trice *f*

donut ['dəʊnʌt] *Am* bombolone *m*, krapfen *m inv*

doodle ['du:dl] scarabocchiare

doom [du:m] (*fate*) destino *f*; (*ruin*) rovina *f*; **doomed** *project* condannato al fallimento

door [dɔ:(r)] porta *f*; *of car* portiera *f*; **doorbell** campanello *m*; **doorman** usciere *m*; **doorway** vano *m* della porta

dope [dəʊp] (*drugs*) droga *f* leggera; F (*idiot*) cretino *m*, -a *f*

dormant ['dɔ:mənt]: **~ volcano** vulcano *m* inattivo

dormitory ['dɔ:mɪtrɪ] dormitorio *m*; *Am* casa *f* dello studente

dose [dəʊs] dose *f*

dot [dɒt] puntino *m*; *in email address* punto *m*

double ['dʌbl] **1** *n amount* doppio; (*person*) sosia *m inv*; *of film star* controfigura *f* **2** *adj* doppio **3** *adv*: **~ the amount** il doppio della quantità **4** *v/t & v/i* raddoppiare; **double-bass** contrabbasso *m*; **double bed** letto *m* matrimoniale; **doublecheck** ricontrollare; **double-click** cliccare due volte (**on** su); **doublecross** fare il doppio gioco con; **double glazing** doppi vetri *mpl*; **double park** parcheggiare in doppia fila; **double room** camera *f* doppia; **with double bed** camera *f* matrimoniale; **doubles** *in tennis* doppio *msg*

doubt [daʊt] **1** *n* dubbio *m*; **be in ~** essere in dubbio; **no ~** (*probably*) senz'altro **2** *v/t* dubitare di; **doubtful** *look* dubbio; **be ~** *of person* essere dubbioso; **doubtless** senza dubbio

dough [dəʊ] impasto *m*; **doughnut** bombolone *m*, krapfen *m inv*

dove [dʌv] colomba *f*; *fig* pacifista *m/f*

down [daʊn] **1** *adv* (*downwards*) giù; **~ there** laggiù; **£200 ~** *as deposit* un acconto

di £200; **~ south** a sud; **be ~** *of price, rate* essere diminuito; (*not working*) non funzionare; F (*depressed*) essere giù **2** *prep* giù da; (*along*) lungo; **walk ~ a street** percorrere una strada; **down-and-out** senza tetto *m/f inv*; **downhill** in discesa; **go ~** *fig* peggiorare; **downhill skiing** discesa *f* libera; **download** COMPUT **1** *v/t* scaricare **2** *n* scaricamento *m*; **downmarket** di fascia medio-bassa; **down payment** deposito *m*, acconto *m*; **downplay** minimizzare; **downpour** acquazzone *m*; **downright 1** *adj*: **it's a ~ lie** è una bugia bella e buona; **he's a ~ idiot** è un perfetto idiota **2** *adv dangerous etc* assolutamente; **downscale** *Am* di fascia medio-bassa; **downside** (*disadvantage*) contropartita *f*; **downsize** *company* ridimensionare; **the ~d version of** *car* la versione ridotta; **downstairs** al piano di sotto; **downtown** in centro; **downwards** verso il basso

doze [dəʊz] fare un sonnellino

♦ **doze off** assopirsi

dozen ['dʌzn] dozzina *f*

drab [dræb] *adj* scialbo

draft [drɑːft] *n of document* bozza *f*; *Am* MIL leva *f*; *Am* ☞ **draught 2** *v/t document* fare una bozza di; *Am* MIL arruolare; **draft dodger** _Am_ MIL renitente _m_ alla leva

drag [dræg] **1** _v/t (pull)_ trascinare; _(search)_ dragare **2** _v/i of time_ non passare mai; _of show, film_ trascinarsi

drain [dreɪn] **1** _n (pipe)_ tubo _m_ di scarico; _under street_ tombino _m_ **2** _v/t water_ fare colare; _oil_ fare uscire; _vegetables_ scolare; _land_ drenare; _glass, tank_ svuotare; _(exhaust: person)_ svuotare; **drainage** _(drains)_ fognatura _f_; _of water from soil_ drenaggio _m_; **drainpipe** tubo _m_ di scarico

drama ['drɑːmə] arte _f_ drammatica; _(excitement)_ dramma _m_; _(play: on TV)_ sceneggiato _m_; **dramatic** drammatico; _(exciting)_ sorprendente; _gesture_ teatrale; **dramatist** drammaturgo _m_, -a _f_; **dramatize** _story_ adattare; _fig_ drammatizzare

drapes [dreɪps] _Am_ tende _fpl_

drastic ['dræstɪk] drastico

draught [drɑːft] _of air_ corrente _f_ (d'aria); **~ (beer)** birra _f_ alla spina; **draught beer** birra _f_ alla spina; **draughts** _game_ dama _f_; **draughtsman** disegnatore _m_ industriale; _of plan_ disegnatore _m_, -trice _f_; **draughty** pieno di correnti d'aria

draw [drɔː] **1** _n in game_ pareggio _m_; _in lottery_ estrazione _f_; _(attraction)_ attrazione _f_ **2** _v/t picture_ disegnare; _curtain, ti-_

rare; _in lottery, gun, knife_ estrarre; _(attract)_ attirare; _(lead)_ tirare; _from bank account_ ritirare **3** _v/i of game_ pareggiare

◆ **draw back 1** _v/i (recoil)_ tirarsi indietro **2** _v/t hand_ ritirare; _curtains_ aprire

◆ **draw out** _wallet etc_ estrarre; _money from bank_ ritirare

◆ **draw up 1** _v/t document_ redigere; _chair_ accostare **2** _v/i of vehicle_ fermarsi

'drawback inconveniente _m_

drawer [drɔː(r)] _of desk etc_ cassetto _m_

drawing ['drɔːɪŋ] disegno _m_; **drawing pin** puntina _f_

drawl [drɔːl] pronuncia _f_ strascicata

dread [dred] aver il terrore di; **dreadful** terribile; **dreadfully** _F_ _(extremely)_ terribilmente; _behave_ malissimo

dream [driːm] **1** _n_ sogno _m_ **2** _v/i_ sognare; **I ~t about you** ti ho sognato

◆ **dream up** sognare

dreary ['drɪərɪ] deprimente; _(boring)_ noioso

dredge [dredʒ] _canal_ dragare

◆ **dredge up** _fig_ scovare

dregs [dregz] _of coffee_ fondi _mpl_; **the ~ of society** la feccia della società

dress [dres] **1** _n for woman_ vestito _m_; _(clothing)_ abbigliamento _m_ **2** _v/t person_ vestire; _wound_ medicare; _salad_ condire; **get ~ed** vestirsi **3** _v/i ve-_

stirsi

◆ **dress up** vestirsi elegante; (*wear a disguise*) travestirsi

'**dress circle** prima galleria *f*; **dresser** *in kitchen* credenza *f*; **dressing** *for salad* condimento *m*; *for wound* medicazione *f*; **dressing gown** vestaglia *f*; **dress rehearsal** prova *f* generale

dribble ['drɪbl] *of person* sbavare; *of water* gocciolare; SP dribblare

dried [draɪd] *fruit etc* essicato

drier ['draɪr] ☞ **dryer**

drift [drɪft] *of snow* accumularsi; *of ship* andare alla deriva; (*go off course*) uscire dalla rotta; *of person* vagabondare

◆ **drift apart** *of couple* allontanarsi (l'uno dall'altro)

drifter ['drɪftə(r)] vagabondo *m*, -a *f*

drill [drɪl] **1** *n* (*tool*) trapano *m*; (*exercise*), MIL esercitazione *f* **2** *v/t* tunnel scavare; **~ a hole** fare un foro col trapano **3** *v/i for oil* trivellare; MIL addestrarsi

drily ['draɪlɪ] *remark* ironicamente

drink [drɪŋk] **1** *n* bevanda *f*; **non-alcoholic ~** bibita *f* (analcolica); **a ~ of ...** un bicchiere di ... **2** *v/t* & *v/i* bere

◆ **drink up 1** *v/i* (*finish drink*) finire il bicchiere **2** *v/t* (*drink completely*) finire di bere

drinkable ['drɪŋkəbl] potabi-

le; **drinker** bevitore *m*, -trice *f*; **drinking water** acqua *f* potabile

drip [drɪp] **1** *n* goccia *f*; MED flebo *f inv* **2** *v/i* gocciolare

drive [draɪv] **1** *n* outing giro *m* in macchina; (*driveway*) viale *m*; (*energy*) grinta *f*; COMPUT lettore *m*; (*campaign*) campagna *f* **2** *v/t vehicle* guidare; (*take in car*) portare (in macchina); TECH azionare **3** *v/i* guidare; **I ~ to work** vado al lavoro in macchina

◆ **drive in** *nail* piantare

drivel ['drɪvl] sciocchezze *fpl*

driver ['draɪvə(r)] guidatore *m*, -trice *f*, conducente *m/f*; *of train* macchinista *m/f*; COMPUT driver *m inv*; **driver's license** Am patente *f* (di guida); **driveway** viale *m*; **driving 1** *n* guida *f* **2** *adj rain* violento; **driving lesson** lezione *f* di guida; **driving licence** patente *f* (di guida); **driving school** scuola *f* guida; **driving test** esame *m* di guida

drizzle ['drɪzl] *n* pioggerella *f* **2** *v/i* piovigginare

drop [drɒp] **1** *n* *of rain* goccia *f*; *in price, temperature* calo *m* **2** *v/t* far cadere; *from plane* sganciare; *person from car* lasciare; *person from team* scartare; (*stop seeing*) smettere di frequentare; *charges, demand etc* abbandonare; (*give up*) lasciare perdere **3**

v/i cadere; *(decline)* calare
◆ **drop in** passare
◆ **drop off 1** *v/t person, goods* lasciare **2** *v/i (fall asleep)* addormentarsi; *(decline)* calare
◆ **drop out** *from competition, school* ritirarsi

drought [draut] siccità *f inv*
drown [draun] annegare
drowsy ['drauzɪ] sonnolento
drug [drʌg] **1** *n* droga *f*; **be on ~s** drogarsi **2** *v/t* drogare; **drug addict** tossicodipendente *m/f*; **drug dealer** spacciatore *m*, -trice *f* (di droga); **druggist** *Am* farmacista *m/f*; **drugstore** *Am* negozio-bar che vende articoli vari, inclusi medicinali; **drug trafficking** traffico *m* di droga

drum [drʌm] MUS tamburo *m*; *(container)* bidone *m*; **~s** *in pop music* batteria *f*; **drummer** batterista *m/f*; *in brass band* percussionista *m/f*; **drumstick** MUS bacchetta *f*

drunk [drʌŋk] **1** *n* ubriacone *m*, -a *f* **2** *adj* ubriaco; **get ~** ubriacarsi; **drunk driving** guida *f* in stato di ebbrezza
dry [draɪ] **1** *adj* secco *2* *v/t & v/i* asciugare; **dry-clean** pulire *or* lavare a secco; **dry cleaner** tintoria *f*; **dryer** *machine* asciugatrice *f*

dual ['dju:əl] doppio; **dual carriageway** carreggiata *f* a due corsie
dub [dʌb] *movie* doppiare

dubious ['dju:bɪəs] equivoco; *(having doubts)* dubbioso
duchess ['dʌtʃɪs] duchessa *f*
duck [dʌk] **1** *n* anatra *f* **2** *v/i* piegarsi
dud [dʌd] F *(false bill)* falso *m*
due [dju:] dovuto; *the rent is* **~ tomorrow** domani scade la rata dell'affitto
duke [dju:k] duca *m*
dull [dʌl] *weather* grigio; *sound, pain* sordo; *(boring)* noioso
duly ['dju:lɪ] *(as expected)* come previsto; *(properly)* debitamente
dumb [dʌm] *(mute)* muto; *Am* F *(stupid)* stupido
dummy ['dʌmɪ] *for clothes* manichino *m*; *for baby* succhiotto *m*
dump [dʌmp] **1** *n for rubbish* discarica *f*; *(unpleasant place)* postaccio *m* **2** *v/t (deposit)* lasciare; *(dispose of)* scaricare; *waste* sbarazzarsi di
dune [dju:n] duna *f*
duplex (apartment) ['du:pleks] appartamento *m* su due piani
duplicate ['dju:plɪkət] duplicato *m*
durable ['djuərəbl] *material* resistente
during ['djuərɪŋ] durante
dusk [dʌsk] crepuscolo *m*
dust [dʌst] **1** *n* polvere *f* **2** *v/t* spolverare; **dustbin** bidone *m* della spazzatura; **duster**

straccio *m* (per spolverare); **dustpan** paletta *f*; **dusty** *table* impolverato; *road* polveroso

Dutch [dʌtʃ] **1** *adj* olandese **2** *n language* olandese *m*; **the ~** gli Olandesi

duty ['djuːtɪ] dovere *m*; *on goods* tassa *f* doganale, dazio *m*; **be on ~** essere di servizio; **duty free** duty free *inv*

DVD [diːviː'diː] (= *digital versatile disk*) DVD *m inv*

dwarf [dwɔːf] **1** *n* nano *m*, -a *f*

2 *v/t* fare scomparire

dwindle ['dwɪndl] diminuire

dye [daɪ] **1** *n* tintura *f*; *for food* colorante *m* **2** *v/t* colorare, tingere

dying ['daɪɪŋ] morente; *tradition* in via di disparizione

dynamic [daɪˈnæmɪk] dinamico; **dynamism** dinamismo *m*

dynasty ['dɪnəstɪ] dinastia *f*

dyslexic [dɪsˈleksɪk] **1** *adj* dislessico **2** *n* dislessico *m*, -a *f*

E

each [iːtʃ] **1** *adj* ogni **2** *adv* ciascuno; **they're £1.50 ~** costano £1,50 ciascuno **3** *pron* ciascuno *m*, -a *f*, ognuno *m*, -a *f*; **~ other** l'un l'altro *m*, l'una l'altra *f*; **we know ~ other** ci conosciamo

eager ['iːgə(r)] entusiasta; **be ~ to do sth** essere ansioso di fare qc; **eagerly** ansiosamente; **eagerness** smania *f*

eagle ['iːgl] aquila *f*; **eagle-eyed**: **be ~ eyed** avere l'occhio di falco

ear[1] [ɪə(r)] orecchio *m*

ear[2] [ɪə(r)] *of corn* spiga *f*

earache mal di orecchi

early ['ɜːlɪ] **1** *adj* (*not late*) primo; *arrival* anticipato; (*farther back in time*) antico; **~ October** inizio ottobre; **at an ~ age** in giovane età; **let's**

have an ~ supper ceniamo presto **2** *adv* (*not late*) presto; (*ahead of time*) in anticipo; **early bird** (*early riser*) persona *f* mattiniera

earmark ['ɪəmɑːk] riservare

earn [ɜːn] guadagnare; *interest* fruttare; *holiday, respect etc* guadagnarsi

earnest ['ɜːnɪst] serio

earnings ['ɜːnɪŋz] guadagno *m*

'earphones cuffie *fpl* (d'ascolto); **earring** orecchino *m*; **earshot**: **within ~ a** portata d'orecchio; **out of ~** fuori dalla portata d'orecchio

earth [ɜːθ] **1** *n also* ELEC terra *f* **2** *v/t* ELEC mettere a terra; **earthenware** terracotta *f*; **earthly** terreno; **it's no ~**

use ... F è perfettamente inutile ...;**earthquake** terremoto *m*

ease [i:z] **1** *n* facilità *f*; **feel at ~** sentirsi a proprio agio **2** *v/t* (*relieve*) alleviare; **it will ~ my mind** mi darà sollievo **3** *v/i of pain* alleviarsi

◆ **ease off 1** *v/t* (*remove*) togliere con cautela **2** *v/i of pain, rain* diminuire

easel ['i:zl] cavalletto *m*

easily ['i:zɪlɪ] facilmente; (*by far*) di gran lunga

east [i:st] **1** *n* est *m* **2** *adj* orientale **3** *adv travel* a est; **~ of** a est di

Easter ['i:stə(r)] Pasqua *f*; **Easter Day** il giorno *or* la domenica *or* la Pasqua; **Easter egg** uovo *m* di Pasqua

easterly ['i:stəlɪ]: **~ wind** vento *m* dell'est; **in an ~ direction** verso est

Easter 'Monday lunedì *m inv* di Pasqua, Pasquetta *f*

eastern ['i:stən] orientale

Easter 'Sunday il giorno *or* la domenica di Pasqua

eastward ['i:stwəd] verso est

easy ['i:zɪ] facile; (*relaxed*) tranquillo; **easy chair** poltrona *f*; **easy-going**: **he's very ~** gli va bene quasi tutto

eat [i:t] mangiare

◆ **eat out** mangiare fuori

eatable ['i:təbl] commestibile; *lunch, dish* mangiabile

eavesdrop ['i:vzdrɒp]: **~ on s.o.** origliare qu

ebb [eb] *of tide* rifluire

e-bike ['i:baɪk] bici *f* elettrica

e-book ['i:bʊk] e-book *m inv*, libro *m* elettronico; **e-business** e-commerce *m*, commercio *m* elettronico

eccentric [ɪk'sentrɪk] **1** *adj* eccentrico **2** *n* eccentrico *m*, -a *f*; **eccentricity** eccentricità *f inv*

echo ['ekəʊ] **1** *n* eco *f* **2** *v/i* risuonare **3** *v/t words* ripetere; *views* condividere

eclipse [ɪ'klɪps] **1** *n* eclissi *f inv* **2** *v/t fig* eclissare

ecofriendly ['i:kəʊfrendlɪ] ecologico

ecological [i:kə'lɒdʒɪkl] ecologico; **ecologically** ecologicamente; **ecologically friendly** ecologico; **ecologist** ecologista *m/f*; **ecology** ecologia *f*

economic [i:kə'nɒmɪk] economico; **economical** (*cheap*) economico; (*thrifty*) parsimonioso; **economics** *nsg* economia *f*; *financial aspects* aspetti *mpl* economici; **economist** economista *m/f*; **economize** risparmiare, fare economia

◆ **economize on** risparmiare su

economy [ɪ'kɒnəmɪ] economia *f*; **economy class** classe *f* economica

ecosystem ['i:kəʊsɪstm] ecosistema *m*; **ecotourism** agriturismo *m*

ecstasy ['ekstəsɪ] estasi *f inv*;
ecstatic in estasi
eczema ['eksmə] eczema *m*
edge [edʒ] **1** *n of knife* filo *m*;
of table, seat, lawn bordo *m*;
of road ciglio *m*; *of cliff* orlo
m; **on ~** teso **2** *v/i (move
slowly)* muoversi con cautela; **edgeways: I couldn't
get a word in ~** non sono riuscito a piazzare una parola;
edgy teso
edible ['edɪbl] commestibile
edit ['edɪt] *text* rivedere; *prepare for publication* curare;
newspaper dirigere; *TV program, film* montare; COM-
PUT editare; **edition** edizione *f*; **editor** *of text* revisore
m; *of publication* curatore
m, -trice *f*; *of newspaper* direttore *m*, -trice; *of TV program* responsabile *m/f* del
montaggio; *of film* tecnico
m del montaggio; *of film*
editorial 1 *adj* editoriale; **the ~ staff**
la redazione **2** *n* editoriale *m*
educate ['edjʊkeɪt] *child*
istruire; *consumers* educare;
he was ~d at ... ha studiato
a ...; **educated** istruito; **education** istruzione *f*; **the ~
system** la pubblica istruzione; **educational** didattico;
(*informative*) istruttivo
eerie ['ɪərɪ] inquietante
effect [ɪ'fekt] effetto *m*; **effective** efficace; (*striking*) d'effetto
effeminate [ɪ'femɪnət] effe-

minato
efficiency [ɪ'fɪʃənsɪ] efficienza *f*; *of machine* rendimento
m; **efficient** efficiente; *machine* ad alto rendimento; **ef-
ficiently** con efficienza
effort ['efət] sforzo *m*; **effort-
less** facile
e.g. [iː'dʒiː] ad *or* per esempio
egg [eg] uovo *m*; **eggcup** portauovo *m inv*; **egghead** F in-
tellettualoide *m/f*; **eggplant**
Am melanzana *f*
ego ['iːgəʊ] ego *m*; **egocentric** egocentrico; **egoism**
egoismo *m*; **egoist** egoista
m/f
eiderdown ['aɪdədaʊn] (*quilt*)
piumino *m*
eight [eɪt] otto *f*; **eighteen** diciotto; **eighteenth** diciottesimo; **eighth** ottavo; **eighth
note** Am MUS croma *f*;
eightieth ottantesimo;
eighty ottanta
either ['aɪðə(r)] **1** *adj* l'uno o
l'altro; (*both*) entrambi *pl* **2**
pron l'uno o l'altro *m*,
l'una o l'altra *f* **3** *adv* nemmeno, neppure; **I won't go
~** non vado nemmeno *or*
neppure io **4** *conj*: **~ my
mother or my sister** mia
madre o mia sorella; **he
doesn't like ~ wine or beer**
non gli piacciono né il vino,
né la birra
eject [ɪ'dʒekt] **1** *v/t* espellere **2**
v/i from plane eiettarsi
♦ **eke out** [iːk] usare con par-

simonia; *grant etc* arrotondare; *eke out a living* tirare avanti

el [el] *Am* ferrovia *f* sopraelevata

elaborate 1 [ɪˈlæbərət] *adj* elaborato 2 [ɪˈlæbəreɪt] *v/i* fornire particolari

elapse [ɪˈlæps] trascorrere

elastic [ɪˈlæstɪk] 1 *adj* elastico 2 *n* elastico *m*; **elasticated** elasticizzato; **elastic band** elastico *m*

Elastoplast® [ɪˈlæstəplɑːst] cerotto *m*

elated [ɪˈleɪtɪd] esultante; **elation** esultanza *f*

elbow [ˈelbəʊ] gomito *m*

elder [ˈeldə(r)] 1 *adj* maggiore 2 *n* maggiore *m/f*; **elderly** 1 *adj* anziano; 2 *npl* **the ~** gli anziani; **eldest** 1 *adj* maggiore 2 *n* maggiore *m/f*

elect [ɪˈlekt] eleggere; **elected** eletto; **election** elezione *f*; **election campaign** campagna *f* elettorale; **election day** giorno *m* delle elezioni; **electorate** elettorato *m*

electric [ɪˈlektrɪk] *also fig* elettrico; **electrical** elettrico; **electric chair** sedia *f* elettrica; **electrician** elettricista *m/f*; **electricity** elettricità *f*; **electrify** elettrificare; *fig* elettrizzare

electrocute [ɪˈlektrəkjuːt] fulminare

electron [ɪˈlektrɒn] elettrone *m*; **electronic** elettronico;

electronics elettronica *f*

elegance [ˈelɪɡəns] eleganza *f*; **elegant** elegante

element [ˈelɪmənt] elemento *m*; **elementary** elementare; **elementary school** *Am* scuola *f* elementare

elephant [ˈelɪfənt] elefante *m*

elevate [ˈelɪveɪt] elevare; **elevated railroad** *Am* ferrovia *f* sopraelevata; **elevation** (*altitude*) altitudine *f*; **elevator** *Am* ascensore *m*

eleven [ɪˈlevn] undici; **eleventh** undicesimo

eligible [ˈelɪdʒəbl]: **be ~ to do sth** avere il diritto di fare qc

eliminate [ɪˈlɪmɪneɪt] eliminare; **elimination** eliminazione *f*

elite [eɪˈliːt] 1 *n* elite *f inv* 2 *adj* elitario

eloquence [ˈeləkwəns] eloquenza *f*; **eloquent** eloquente

else [els]: *anything ~* qualcos'altro; *nothing ~* nient'altro; *nobody ~* nessun altro; *everyone ~ is going* tutti gli altri vanno; *someone ~* qualcun altro; *something ~* qualcos'altro; *let's go somewhere ~* andiamo da qualche altra parte; *or ~* altrimenti; *elsewhere* altrove

elude [ɪˈluːd] sfuggire a; **elusive** *person* difficile da trovare; *quality* raro

emaciated [ɪˈmeɪsɪeɪtɪd] emaciato

e-mail ['iːmeɪl] **1** n e-mail m inv **2** v/t person mandare un e-mail a; text mandare per e-mail; **e-mail address** indirizzo m e-mail

emancipation [ɪmænsɪ'peɪʃn] emancipazione f

embalm [ɪm'bɑːm] imbalsamare

embankment [ɪm'bæŋkmənt] of river argine m; RAIL massicciata f

embargo [em'bɑːgəʊ] embargo m inv

embark [ɪm'bɑːk] imbarcarsi

embarrass [ɪm'bærəs] imbarazzare; **embarrassed** imbarazzato; **embarrassing** imbarazzante; **embarrassment** imbarazzo m

embassy ['embəsɪ] ambasciata f

embezzle [ɪm'bezl] appropriarsi indebitamente di; **embezzlement** appropriazione f indebita

emblem ['embləm] emblema f

embodiment [ɪm'bɒdɪmənt] incarnazione f; **embody** incarnare

embrace [ɪm'breɪs] **1** n abbraccio m **2** v/t (hug, include) abbracciare **3** v/i of two people abbracciarsi

embroider [ɪm'brɔɪdə(r)] ricamare; fig ricamare su

embroidery [ɪm'brɔɪdərɪ] ricamo m

embryo ['embrɪəʊ] embrione m; **embryonic** fig embrionale

emerald ['emərəld] smeraldo m; colour verde m smeraldo

emerge [ɪ'mɜːdʒ] (appear) emergere; **it has ~d that ...** è emerso che ...

emergency [ɪ'mɜːdʒənsɪ] emergenza f; **emergency exit** uscita f di sicurezza; **emergency landing** atterraggio m di fortuna; **emergency services** servizi mpl di soccorso

emigrant ['emɪgrənt] emigrante m/f; **emigrate** emigrare; **emigration** emigrazione f

Eminence ['emɪnəns]: REL **His ~** Sua Eminenza; **eminent** eminente

emission [ɪ'mɪʃn] of gases emanazione f; **emit** heat, gases emanare; light, smoke emettere; smell esalare

emotion [ɪ'məʊʃn] emozione f; **emotional** problems, development emozionale; (causing emotion) commovente; (showing emotion) commosso

emperor ['empərə(r)] imperatore m

emphasis ['emfəsɪs] enfasi f; on word rilievo m; **emphasize** enfatizzare; word dare rilievo a; **emphatic** enfatico

empire ['empaɪə(r)] impero m

employ [ɪm'plɔɪ] dare lavoro a; (take on) assumere; (use) impiegare; **employee** dipendente m/f; **employer** datore *m*, -trice *f* di lavoro; **employment** occupazione *f*; *(work)* impiego *m*

emptiness ['emptinis] vuoto *m*; **empty 1** *adj* vuoto **2** *v/t* vuotare **3** *v/i of room, street* svuotarsi

emulate ['emjuleit] emulare

enable [i'neibl] *person* permettere a; *thing* permettere

enchanting [in'ʧɑ:ntiŋ] incantevole

encircle [in'sɜ:kl] circondare

enclose [in'kləuz] *in letter* allegare; *area* recintare; **enclosure** *with letter* allegato *m*

encore ['ɒŋkɔ:(r)] bis *m inv*

encounter [in'kauntə(r)] **1** *n* incontro *m* **2** *v/t* incontrare

encourage [in'kʌriʤ] incoraggiare; **encouragement** incoraggiamento *m*; **encouraging** incoraggiante

encyclopedia [insaiklə'pi:diə] enciclopedia *f*

end [end] **1** *n (conclusion, purpose)* fine *m*; *(extremity)* estremità *f inv*; **in the ~** alla fine **2** *v/t* terminare **3** *v/i* finire

◆ **end up** finire

endanger [in'deinʤə(r)] mettere in pericolo; **endangered species** specie *f* in via d'estinzione

endeavour, *Am* **endeavor** [in'devə(r)] **1** *n* tentativo *m* **2** *v/t* tentare

endemic [in'demik] endemico

ending ['endiŋ] finale *m*; GRAM desinenza *f*; **endless** interminabile

endorse [en'dɔ:s] *candidacy* appoggiare; *product* fare pubblicità a; **endorsement** *of candidacy* appoggio *m*; *of product* pubblicità *f*

end 'product prodotto *m* finale

endurance [in'djurəns] resistenza *f*; **endure 1** *v/t* sopportare **2** *v/i (last)* resistere; **enduring** durevole

end-'user utente *m* finale

enemy ['enəmi] nemico *m*, -a *f*

energetic [enə'ʤetik] energico; **energy** energia *f*; **energy supply** rifornimento *m* di energia elettrica

enforce [in'fɔ:s] far rispettare

engage [in'geiʤ] **1** *v/t (hire)* ingaggiare **2** *v/i* TECH ingranare; **engaged** *to be married* fidanzato; **get ~** fidanzarsi; TELEC *(appointment)* impegno *m*; *to be married* fidanzamento *m*; MIL scontro *m*; **engagement ring** anello *m* di fidanzamento

engine ['enʤin] motore *m*; **engineering** ingegneria *f*; **engineer** ingegnere *m*; *for sound, software* tecnico *m*; NAUT macchinista *m*

England ['ingland] Inghilterra *f*; **English 1** *adj* inglese **2** *n (language)* inglese *m*, *the* ~ gli inglesi; **English Channel** Manica *f*; **Englishman** inglese *m*; **Englishwoman** inglese *f*

engrave [ɪnˈgreɪv] incidere; **engraving** *(drawing)* stampa *f*; *(design)* incisione *f*

engrossed [ɪnˈgrəʊst]: ~ *in* assorto in

engulf [ɪnˈgʌlf] avvolgere

enhance [ɪnˈhɑːns] accrescere; *performance, reputation* migliorare

enigma [ɪˈnɪgmə] enigma *m*

enjoy [ɪnˈdʒɔɪ]: *did you* ~ *the film?* ti è piaciuto il film?; *I* ~ *reading* mi piace leggere; ~ *(your meal)!* buon appetito!; ~ *o.s.* divertirsi; **enjoyable** piacevole; **enjoyment** piacere *m*, divertimento *m*

enlarge [ɪnˈlɑːdʒ] ingrandire; **enlargement** ingrandimento *m*

enlighten [ɪnˈlaɪtn] illuminare

enlist [ɪnˈlɪst] MIL arruolarsi

enmity [ˈenmətɪ] inimicizia *f*

enormous [ɪˈnɔːməs] enorme; **enormously** enormemente

enough [ɪˈnʌf] **1** *adj* sufficiente, abbastanza *inv* **2** *pron* abbastanza; *will £50 be* ~? saranno sufficienti £50?; *that's* ~! basta! **3** *adv* abbastanza; *strangely* ~ per quanto strano

enquire [ɪnˈkwaɪə(r)] chiedere informazioni, informarsi

enrol, *Am* **enroll** [ɪnˈrəʊl] iscriversi

en suite (bathroom) [ˈɒnswiːt] bagno *m* in camera

ensure [ɪnˈʃʊə(r)] assicurare

entail [ɪnˈteɪl] comportare

entangle [ɪnˈtæŋgl] *in rope* impigliare

enter [ˈentə(r)] **1** *v/t room, house* entrare in; *competition* iscriversi a; COMPUT inserire **2** *v/i* entrare; *in competition* iscriversi **3** *n* COMPUT invio *m*

enterprise [ˈentəpraɪz] *(initiative)* intraprendenza *f*; *(venture)* impresa *f*; **enterprising** intraprendente

entertain [entəˈteɪn] *(amuse)* intrattenere; *(consider: idea)* considerare; **entertainer** artista *m/f*; **entertaining** divertente; **entertainment** divertimento *m*

enthusiasm [ɪnˈθjuːzɪæzm] entusiasmo *m*; **enthusiast** appassionato *m*, -a *f*; **enthusiastic** entusiasta; **enthusiastically** con entusiasmo

entire [ɪnˈtaɪə(r)] intero; **entirely** interamente

entitle [ɪnˈtaɪtl] dare il diritto a; *be* ~*d to do sth* avere il diritto di fare qc

entrance [ˈentrəns] entrata *f*, ingresso *m*; THEA entrata *f* in scena

entranced [ɪnˈtrɑːnst] incantato

'entrance exam(ination)

erosion

esame *m* di ammissione

entrant ['entrənt] concorrente *m/f*

entrepreneur [ɒntrəprə'nɜ:] imprenditore *m*, -trice *f*; **entrepreneurial** imprenditoriale

entrust [ɪn'trʌst] affidare

entry ['entrɪ] (*way in*) entrata *f*; *in diary* annotazione *f*; *in accounts, dictionary* voce *f*; **entryphone** citofono *m*

envelop [ɪn'veləp] avviluppare

envelope ['envələʊp] busta *f*

enviable ['envɪəbl] invidiabile; **envious** invidioso; **be ~ of s.o.** essere invidioso di qu

environment [ɪn'vaɪərənmənt] ambiente *m*; **environmental** ambientale; **environmentalist** ambientalista *m/f*; **environmentally friendly** ecologico; **environmental protection** tutela *f* dell'ambiente; **environs** dintorni *mpl*

envoy ['envɔɪ] inviato *m*, -a *f*

envy ['envɪ] **1** *n* invidia *f* **2** *v/t*: **~ s.o. sth** invidiare qc a qu

epic ['epɪk] **1** *n* epopea *f* **2** *adj journey* mitico

epicentre, *Am* **epicenter** ['episentr] epicentro *m*

epidemic [epɪ'demɪk] epidemia *f*

episode ['episəʊd] episodio *m*

epitaph ['epɪtɑ:f] epitaffio *m*

epoch ['i:pɒk] epoca *f*

equal ['i:kwl] **1** *adj* uguale **2** *n*: **be the ~ of** essere equivalente a; **treat s.o. as his ~** trattare qualcuno alla pari **3** *v/t* (*be as good as*) uguagliare; **equality** uguaglianza *f*, parità *f*; **equalize 1** *v/t* uniformare **2** *v/i* SP pareggiare; **equalizer** SP gol *m* inv del pareggio; **equally** ugualmente; **equal rights** parità *f* di diritti

equation [ɪ'kweɪʒn] MATH equazione *f*

equator [ɪ'kweɪtə(r)] equatore *m*

equip [ɪ'kwɪp] equipaggiare; **equipment** equipaggiamento *m*; *electrical, electronic* apparecchiature *fpl*

equity ['ekwətɪ] FIN capitale *m* azionario

equivalent [ɪ'kwɪvələnt] **1** *adj* equivalente **2** *n* equivalente *m*

era ['ɪərə] era *f*

eradicate [ɪ'rædɪkeɪt] sradicare

erase [ɪ'reɪz] cancellare; **eraser** gomma *f* (da cancellare)

e-reader ['i:ri:dər] lettore *m* di e-book

erect [ɪ'rekt] **1** *adj* eretto **2** *v/t* erigere; **erection** erezione *f*

ergonomic [ɜ:gəʊ'nɒmɪk] ergonomico

erode [ɪ'rəʊd] erodere; *fig* intaccare; **erosion** erosione *f*; *fig* diminuzione *f* erotic [ɪˈrɒtɪk] erotico

errand [ˈerənd] commissione f

erratic [ɪˈrætɪk] irregolare

error [ˈerə(r)] errore m; error message COMPUT messaggio m di errore

erupt [ɪˈrʌpt] of volcano eruttare; of violence esplodere; of person dare in escandescenze; eruption of volcano eruzione f; of violence esplosione f

escalate [ˈeskəleɪt] of costs aumentare; of war intensificarsi; escalation escalation f inv; escalator scala f mobile

escape [ɪˈskeɪp] 1 n of prisoner, animal, gas fuga f 2 v/i of prisoner, animal scappare, fuggire; of gas fuoriuscire

escort 1 [ˈeskɔːt] n accompagnatore m, -trice f; (guard) scorta f 2 [ɪˈskɔːt] v/t socially accompagnare; act as guard to scortare

especially [ɪˈspeʃlɪ] specialmente

espionage [ˈespɪənɑːʒ] spionaggio m

espresso (coffee) [esˈpresəʊ] espresso m

essay [ˈeseɪ] saggio m; in school tema m

essential [ɪˈsenʃl] essenziale

establish [ɪˈstæblɪʃ] company fondare; (create, determine) stabilire; establishment firm azienda f; restaurant lo-

cale m

estate [ɪˈsteɪt] land tenuta f; of dead person patrimonio m; estate agent agente m/f immobiliare; estate car giardiniera f

esthetic Am ☞ aesthetic

estimate [ˈestɪmət] 1 n stima f, valutazione f; COM preventivo m 2 v/t stimare

estuary [ˈestjʊərɪ] estuario m

etc [etˈsetrə] (= et cetera) ecc. (= eccetera)

eternal [ɪˈtɜːnl] eterno; eternity eternità f inv

ethical [ˈeθɪkl] etico; ethics etica f

ethnic [ˈeθnɪk] etnico; ethnic minority minoranza f etnica

e-ticket [ˈiːtɪkɪt] biglietto m acquistato su Internet

EU [iːˈjuː] (= European Union) UE f (= Unione europea)

euphemism [ˈjuːfəmɪzm] eufemismo m

euro [ˈjʊərəʊ] euro m inv; Euro MP eurodeputato m, -a f

Europe [ˈjʊərəp] Europa f; European 1 adj europeo 2 n europeo m, -a f; European Parliament Parlamento m europeo; European Union Unione f europea

euthanasia [juːθəˈneɪzɪə] eutanasia f

evacuate [ɪˈvækjʊeɪt] evacuare

evade [ɪˈveɪd] eludere; taxes evadere

exceed

evaluate [ɪ'væljʊeɪt] valutare; **evaluation** valutazione f

evaporate [ɪ'væpəreɪt] evaporare; *of confidence* svanire; **evaporation** evaporazione f

evasion [ɪ'veɪʒn] elusione f; *of taxes* evasione f; **evasive** evasivo

eve [iːv] vigilia f

even ['iːvn] **1** adj (regular) omogeneo; *breathing* regolare; *surface* piano; (number) pari inv; *players, game* alla pari; **get ~ with ...** farla pagare a ... **2** adv persino; **~ bigger** ancora più grande; **not ~** nemmeno, neppure; **~ so** nonostante questo; **~ if** anche se **3** v/t: **~ the score** pareggiare

evening ['iːvnɪŋ] sera f; **in the ~** di sera; **this ~** stasera; **good ~** buona sera; **evening class** corso m serale; **evening dress** *for woman* vestito m da sera; *for man* abito m scuro

evenly ['iːvnlɪ] (regularly) in modo omogeneo; *breathe* regolarmente

event [ɪ'vent] evento m, avvenimento m; SP prova f; **eventful** movimentato

eventually [ɪ'ventjʊəlɪ] finalmente, alla fine

ever ['evə(r)] mai; **have you ~ been to ...?** sei mai stato in ...?; **for ~** per sempre; **as ~** come sempre; **~ since he**

left da quando è partito; **everlasting** eterno

every ['evrɪ] ogni; **~ other day** un giorno sì, uno no; **~ now and then** ogni tanto; **everybody** tutti; **everyday** di tutti i giorni; **everyone** tutti pl; **everything** tutto; **everywhere** dovunque, dappertutto; (wherever) dovunque

evict [ɪ'vɪkt] sfrattare

evidence ['evɪdəns] prova f; **give ~** testimoniare; **evident** evidente; **evidently** evidentemente

evil ['iːvl] **1** adj cattivo **2** n male m

evolution [iːvə'luːʃn] evoluzione f; **evolve** evolvere

ex [eks] F *wife / husband* ex m/f inv F

exact [ɪg'zækt] esatto; **exacting** *task* impegnativo; *employer* esigente; *standards* rigido; **exactly** esattamente

exaggerate [ɪg'zædʒəreɪt] esagerare; **exaggeration** esagerazione f

exam [ɪg'zæm] esame m; **examination** esame m; *of patient* visita f; **examine** esaminare; *patient* visitare

example [ɪg'zɑːmpl] esempio m; *for* ~ ad *or* per esempio

excavate ['ekskəveɪt] (dig) scavare; *of archaeologist* riportare alla luce; **excavation** scavo m

exceed [ɪk'siːd] (be more than) eccedere, superare;

(*go beyond*) oltrepassare, superare; **exceedingly** estremamente

excel [ɪk'sel] **1** v/i eccellere; **~ at** eccellere in **2** v/t: **~ o.s.** superare se stesso; **excellence** eccellenza f; **excellent** eccellente

except [ɪk'sept] eccetto; **~ for** fatta eccezione per; **exceptional** eccezionale; **exceptionally** (*extremely*) eccezionalmente; **exception** eccezione f

excerpt ['eksɜːpt] estratto m

excess [ɪk'ses] **1** n eccesso m **2** adj in eccesso; **excess baggage** eccedenza f di bagaglio; **excessive** eccessivo

exchange [ɪks'tʃeɪndʒ] **1** n scambio m **2** v/t cambiare (**for** con); **exchange rate** FIN tasso m di cambio

Exchequer [ɪks'tʃekə(r)] tesoro m

excite [ɪk'saɪt] (*make enthusiastic*) eccitare; **excited** eccitato; **get ~** eccitarsi; **excitement** eccitazione f; **exciting** eccitante, emozionante

exclaim [ɪk'skleɪm] esclamare; **exclamation** esclamazione f; **exclamation mark**, Am **exclamation point** punto m esclamativo

exclude [ɪk'skluːd] escludere; **excluding** ad esclusione di; **exclusive** esclusivo

excuse 1 [ɪk'skjuːs] n scusa f **2** [ɪk'skjuːz] v/t scusare; **~ me**

to get attention, interrupting scusami; *to get past* permesso

ex-di'rectory: *be* **~** non comparire sull'elenco telefonico

execute ['eksɪkjuːt] *criminal* giustiziare; *plan* attuare; **execution** *of criminal* esecuzione f; *of plan* attuazione f; **executive** dirigente m/f

exempt [ɪg'zempt]: *be* **~ from** essere esente da

exercise ['eksəsaɪz] **1** n esercizio m; MIL esercitazione f **2** v/t *muscle* fare esercizio con; *dog* far fare esercizio a; *caution* adoperare **3** v/i fare esercizio; **exercise bike** cyclette f inv; **exercise book** EDU quaderno m di esercizi

exhale [eks'heɪl] esalare

exhaust [ɪg'zɔːst] **1** n *fumes* gas *mpl* di scarico; *pipe* tubo m di scappamento **2** v/t (*tire*) estenuare; (*use up*) esaurire; **exhausted** (*tired*) esausto; **exhausting** estenuante; **exhaustion** spossatezza f; **exhaustive** esauriente; **exhaust pipe** tubo m di scappamento

exhibit [ɪg'zɪbɪt] **1** n *in exhibition* oggetto m esposto; LAW prova f **2** v/t *of artist* esporre; (*give evidence of*) manifestare; **exhibition** esposizione f; *of bad behaviour* manifestazione f; *of skill* dimostrazione f

exhilarating [ɪg'zɪləreɪtɪŋ] emozionante

exile ['eksaɪl] **1** n esilio m; person esiliato m, -a f **2** v/t esiliare

exist [ɪg'zɪst] esistere; ~ **on** vivere di; **existence** esistenza
f; **in** ~ esistente; **existing** attuale

exit ['eksɪt] **1** n uscita f **2** v/i
COMPUT uscire

exonerate [ɪg'zɒnəreɪt] scagionare

exorbitant [ɪg'zɔːbɪtənt] esorbitante

exotic [ɪg'zɒtɪk] esotico

expand [ɪk'spænd] **1** v/t
espandere **2** v/i espandersi;
of metal dilatarsi; **expanse**
distesa f; **expansion** espansione f; of metal dilatazione f

expect [ɪk'spekt] **1** v/t aspettare; (suppose, demand)
aspettarsi **2** v/i: **be** ~ing
aspettare un bambino; **I** ~
so immagino di sì; **expectant mother** donna f in stato
interessante; **expectation**
aspettativa f

expedition [ekspɪ'dɪʃn] spedizione f

expel [ɪk'spel] espellere

expendable [ɪk'spendəbl]
person sacrificabile

expenditure [ɪk'spendɪtʃə(r)]
spesa f

expense [ɪk'spens] spesa f;
expenses spese fpl; **expensive** caro

experience [ɪk'spɪərɪəns] **1**
n esperienza f **2** v/t pain, pleasure provare; difficulty incon-

trare; **experienced** con
esperienza

experiment [ɪk'sperɪmənt] **1**
n sperimento m **2** v/i fare
esperimenti; **experimental**
sperimentale

expert ['ekspɜːt] **1** adj esperto
2 n esperto m, -a f; **expertise**
competenza f

expiration date [ɪkspɪ'reɪʃn]
Am data f di scadenza; **expire** scadere; **expiry** scadenza f; **expiry date** data f di
scadenza

explain [ɪk'spleɪn] spiegare;
explanation spiegazione f;
explanatory esplicativo

explicit [ɪk'splɪsɪt] instructions esplicito; **explicitly**
state, forbid esplicitamente

explode [ɪk'spləʊd] **1** v/i of
bomb esplodere **2** v/t bomb
fare esplodere

exploit[1] ['eksplɔɪt] n exploit
m inv

exploit[2] [ɪk'splɔɪt] v/t person,
resources sfruttare

exploitation [eksplɔɪ'teɪʃn]
sfruttamento m

exploration [eksplə'reɪʃn]
esplorazione f; **exploratory**
surgery esplorativo; **explore**
country, possibility etc esplorare; **explorer** esploratore
m, -trice f

explosion [ɪk'spləʊʒn] also in
population esplosione f; **explosive** esplosivo m

export ['ekspɔːt] **1** n esportazione f; item prodotto m di esportazione **2** v/t goods, COMPUT esportare; **exporter** esportatore m, -trice f

expose [ɪk'spəʊz] (uncover) scoprire; scandal, person denunciare; **exposure** esposizione f; to cold weather esposizione f prolungata al freddo; of dishonest behaviour denuncia f; PHOT posa f

express [ɪk'spres] **1** adj (fast, explicit) espresso **2** n (train) espresso m **3** v/t esprimere; **expression** espressione f; **expressive** espressivo; **expressly** espressamente; **expressway** autostrada f

expulsion [ɪk'spʌlʃn] espulsione f

extend [ɪk'stend] **1** v/t estendere; house, repertoire ampliare; runway prolungare; contract, visa prorogare **2** v/i of garden etc estendersi; **extension** to house annesso m; of contract, visa proroga f; TELEC interno m; **extension cable** prolunga f; **extensive** ampio; extent ampiezza f; **to a certain ~** fino a un certo punto

exterior [ɪk'stɪərɪə(r)] **1** adj esterno **2** n of building esterno m; of person aspetto m esteriore

exterminate [ɪk'stɜːmɪnət] sterminare

external [ɪk'stɜːnl] (outside) esterno

extinct [ɪk'stɪŋkt] species

estinto; **extinction** of species estinzione f; **extinguish** spegnere; **extinguisher** estintore m

extortion [ɪk'stɔːʃn] estorsione f

extra ['ekstrə] **1** n extra m inv **2** adj in più; **be ~** (cost more) essere a parte **3** adv particolarmente

extract[1] ['ekstrækt] n estratto m

extract[2] [ɪk'strækt] v/t estrarre; information estorcere

extraction [ɪk'strækʃn] estrazione f

extradite ['ekstrədaɪt] estradare; **extradition** estradizione f

extramarital [ekstrə'mærɪtl] extraconiugale

extraordinary [ɪk'strɔːdɪnərɪ] straordinario

extra 'time SP tempi mpl supplementari

extravagance [ɪk'strævəgəns] stravaganza f; **extravagant** with money stravagante

extreme [ɪk'striːm] **1** n estremo m **2** adj estremo; **extremely** estremamente; **extremist** estremista m/f

extrovert ['ekstrəvɜːt] estroverso m, -a f

exuberant [ɪg'zjuːbərənt] esuberante

eye [aɪ] **1** n occhio m **2** v/t scrutare; **eyeball** bulbo m oculare; **eyebrow** sopracciglio m; **eyecatching** appariscente; **eyeglasses** Am occhiali mpl; **eyelid** palpebra f; **eyeliner** eyeliner m inv; **eyeshadow** ombretto m;

eyesight vista f; **eyesore** pugno m in un occhio; **eyewitness** testimone m/f oculare

F

fabric ['fæbrɪk] tessuto m
fabulous ['fæbjʊləs] fantastico
façade [fə'sɑːd] facciata f
face [feɪs] **1** n viso m, faccia f; ~ **to** ~ faccia a faccia; **lose** ~ perdere la faccia **2** v/t person, sea etc essere di fronte a; facts affrontare
◆ **face up to** affrontare
'**facecloth** guanto m di spugna; **facelift** lifting m inv del viso; **facial** pulizia f del viso
facilitate [fə'sɪlɪteɪt] facilitare; **facilities** strutture fpl
fact [fækt] fatto m; **in** ~, **as a matter of** ~ in realtà
faction ['fækʃn] fazione f
factor ['fæktə(r)] fattore m
factory ['fæktərɪ] fabbrica f
faculty ['fækəltɪ] facoltà f inv
fad [fæd] mania f passeggera
fade [feɪd] v/i of colours sbiadire; of light smorzarsi; of memories svanire; **faded** colour, jeans sbiadito
fag [fæg] F cigarette sigaretta f; Am pej homosexual finocchio m
fail [feɪl] **1** v/i fallire **2** v/t test essere bocciato a; **he never**

~**s to write** non manca mai di scrivere **2** n: **without** ~ con certezza; **failing** difetto m; **failure** fallimento m
faint [feɪnt] **1** adj vago **2** v/i svenire; **faintly** vagamente
fair[1] [feə(r)] (fun ~) luna park m inv; COM fiera f
fair[2] [feə(r)] **1** adj hair biondo; complexion chiaro; (just) giusto **2** adv: ~ **enough** e va bene
fairly ['feəlɪ] treat giustamente; (quite) piuttosto; **fairness** of treatment giustizia f
fairy ['feərɪ] fata; **fairy tale** fiaba f, favola f
faith [feɪθ] fede f; **faithful** fedele
fake [feɪk] **1** n falso m **2** adj falso **3** v/t (forge) falsificare; (feign) simulare
fall[1] [fɔːl] n Am autunno m
fall[2] [fɔːl] **1** v/i of person, night cadere; of prices, temperature calare; **2** v/i ill ammalarsi **2** n of person, government caduta f; in price, temperature calo m
◆ **fall back on** ricorrere a
◆ **fall behind** with work rimanere indietro
◆ **fall for** (fall in love with) in-

namorarsi di; (be deceived by) abboccare a
◆ **fall through** of plans andare a monte

fallible ['fæləbl] fallibile

falling star ['fɔːlɪŋ] stella f cadente

false [fɔːls] falso; **false start** in race falsa partenza f; **false teeth** dentiera f; **falsify** falsificare

fame [feɪm] fama f

familiar [fə'mɪljə(r)] familiare; (intimate) intimo; **be ~ with sth** conoscere bene qc; **familiarity** with subject etc buona conoscenza f (**with** di); **familiarize**: **~ o.s. with ...** familiarizzarsi con ...

family ['fæməlɪ] famiglia f; **family doctor** medico m di famiglia; **family name** cognome m; **family planning** pianificazione f familiare; **family planning clinic** consultorio m per la pianificazione familiare; **family tree** albero m genealogico

famine ['fæmɪn] fame f

famous ['feɪməs] famoso; **be ~ for ...** essere noto per ...

fan[1] [fæn] n (supporter) fan m/f

fan[2] [fæn] **1** n for cooling: electric ventilatore m; handheld ventaglio m **2** v/t: **~ o.s.** farsi aria

fanatical [fə'nætɪkl] fanatico; **fanaticism** fanatismo m

'fan belt MOT cinghia f della ventola

fancy ['fænsɪ] **1** adj design stravagante **2** n: **as the ~ takes you** quanto ti va; **take a ~ to s.o.** prendere a benvolere qu **3** v/t F avere voglia di; **he fancies you** gli piaci; **fancy dress** costume m

fantasize ['fæntəsaɪz] fantasticare; **fantastic** (very good) fantastico; (very big) enorme; **fantasy** fantasia f

far [fɑː(r)] lontano; (much) molto; **~ away** lontano; **how ~ is it to ...?** quanto dista ...?; **as ~ as the corner** fino all'angolo; **as ~ as I know** per quanto ne so; **you've gone too ~** in behaviour sei andato troppo oltre; **so ~ so good** fin qui tutto bene

farce [fɑːs] farsa f

fare [feə(r)] n for travel tariffa f

Far 'East Estremo Oriente m

farewell [feə'wel] addio m

farfetched [fɑː'fetʃt] inverosimile

farm [fɑːm] fattoria f
◆ **farm out** dare in appalto

farmer ['fɑːmə(r)] agricoltore m, -trice f; **farmhouse** cascina f; **farming** agricoltura f; **farmworker** bracciante m/f; **farmyard** cortile m di una cascina

far-'off lontano; **farsighted** previdente; optically presbi-

fear

te

fart [fɑːt] **1** *n* F scoreggia *f* F, peto *m* **2** *v/i* F scoreggiare F, petare

farther ['fɑːðə(r)] più lontano; **farthest** più lontano

fascinate ['fæsɪneɪt] affascinare; **fascinating** affascinante; **fascination** *with subject* fascino *m*

fascism ['fæʃɪzm] fascismo *m*; **fascist 1** *n* fascista *m/f* **2** *adj* fascista

fashion ['fæʃn] moda *f*; (*manner*) maniera *f*, modo *m*; **in ~** alla moda; **out of ~** fuori moda; **fashionable** alla moda; **fashionably** alla moda; **fashion-conscious** fanatico della moda; **fashion designer** stilista *m/f*; **fashion show** sfilata *f* di moda

fast¹ [fɑːst] **1** *adj* veloce, rapido; **be ~** *of clock* essere avanti **2** *adv* velocemente, veloce; **~ asleep** profondamente addormentato

fast² [fɑːst] *n not eating* digiuno *m*

fasten ['fɑːsn] **1** *v/t* chiudere; *dress, seat-belt* allacciare; **~ sth onto sth** attaccare qc a qc **2** *v/i of dress etc* allacciarsi; **fastener** chiusura *f*

'fast food fast food *m*; **fast forward 1** *n on video etc* riavvolgimento *m* rapido **2** *v/i* riavvolgere rapidamente; **fast lane** *on road* corsia *f* di sorpasso; **in the ~** *fig: of life* a

cento all'ora; **fast train** rapido *m*

fat [fæt] **1** *adj* grasso **2** *n* grasso *m*

fatal ['feɪtl] fatale

fatality [fə'tælətɪ] vittima *f*; **fatally**: **~ injured** ferito a morte

fate [feɪt] fato *m*

'fat free privo di grassi

father ['fɑːðə(r)] padre *m*; **Father Christmas** Babbo *m* Natale; **fatherhood** paternità *f*; **father-in-law** suocero *m*; **fatherly** paterno

fatigue [fə'tiːg] stanchezza *f*

fatten ['fætn] *animal* ingrassare; **fatty 1** *adj* grasso **2** *n* F *person* ciccione *m*, -a *f*

faucet ['fɔːsɪt] *Am* rubinetto *m*

fault [fɔːlt] *n* (*defect*) difetto *m*; **it's your / my ~** è colpa tua / mia; **find ~ with** criticare; **faultless** impeccabile; **faulty** difettoso

favor *etc Am* → **favour** *etc*

favour ['feɪvə(r)] **1** *n* favore *m*; **do s.o. a ~** fare un favore a qu; **in ~ of ...** a favore di ... **2** *v/t* (*prefer*) preferire, prediligere; **favourable** favorevole; **favourite 1** *n* prediletto *m*, -a *f*; *food* piatto *m* preferito; *in race, competition* favorito *m*, -a *f* **2** *adj* preferito; **favouritism** favoritismo *m*

fax [fæks] **1** *n* fax *m inv* **2** *v/t* *document* inviare per fax

fear [fɪə(r)] **1** *n* paura *f* **2** *v/t*

avere paura di; **fearless** intrepido; **fearlessly** intrepidamente

feasibility study [fiːzə'bɪlətɪ] studio *m* di fattibilità; **feasible** fattibile

feast [fiːst] banchetto *m*

feat [fiːt] prodezza *f*

feather ['feðə(r)] piuma *f*

feature ['fiːtʃə(r)] **1** *n* of face tratto *m*; of city, building, style caratteristica *f*; in newspaper servizio *m*; film lungometraggio *m*; **make a ~ of** ... mettere l'accento su ... **2** *v/t* of film avere come protagonista; **feature film** lungometraggio *m*

February ['februərɪ] febbraio *m*

federal ['fedərəl] federale; **federation** federazione *f*

fed 'up F: **be ~ with** ... essere stufo di ... F

fee [fiː] tariffa *f*; of lawyer, doctor etc onorario *m*

feeble ['fiːbl] debole

feed [fiːd] nutrire; family mantenere; baby dare da mangiare a; **feedback** riscontro *m*, feedback *m*

feel [fiːl] **1** *v/t* (touch) toccare; (sense) sentire; pain, pleasure sentire; (think) pensare **2** *v/i* sentirsi; **it ~s like silk** sembra seta; **I ~ tired** mi sento stanco; **how are you ~ing today?** come ti senti oggi?; **do you ~ like a drink?** hai voglia di bere qualcosa?; **I**

don't ~ like it non ne ho voglia

◆ **feel up to** sentirsi in grado di

feeler ['fiːlə(r)] of insect antenna *f*; **feeling** sentimento *m*; (emotion) sensazione *f*; (sensation) sensibilità *f*

feet [fiːt] *pl* ☞ **foot**

fellow 'citizen concittadino *m*, -a *f*

felony ['felənɪ] delitto *m*

felt [felt] feltro *m*; **felt tip, felt-tip(ped) pen** pennarello *m*

female ['fiːmeɪl] **1** femmina *f*; typical of women femminile **2** *n* femmina *f*; F (woman) donna *f*

feminine ['femɪnɪn] **1** adj femminile **2** *n* GRAM femminile *m*; **feminism** femminismo *m*; **feminist 1** *n* femminista *f* **2** adj femminista

fence [fens] *n* recinto *m*; **sit on the ~** non prendere partito

fender ['fendə(r)] Am parafango *m*

fermentation [fɜːmen'teɪʃn] fermentazione *f*

ferocious [fə'rəʊʃəs] feroce

ferry ['ferɪ] traghetto *m*

fertile ['fɜːtaɪl] fertile; **fertility** [fɜː'tɪlətɪ] fertilità *f*; of woman fecondare; **fertilizer** for soil fertilizzante *m*

fervent ['fɜːvənt] fervente

fester ['festə(r)] of wound fare infezione

festival ['festɪvl] festival *m*

inv; **festive** festivo; **the ~ season** le festività; **festivities** festeggiamenti *mpl*

fetal ['fi:tl] fetale

fetch [fetʃ] andare / venire a prendere; *thing* prendere; *price* rendere

fetus ['fi:təs] feto *m*

feud [fju:d] **1** *n* faida *f* **2** *v/i* litigare

fever ['fi:və(r)] febbre *f*; **feverish** *also* **fig** febbrile

few [fju:] **1** *adj* pochi; **a ~ people** alcune persone, qualche persona; **a ~ books** alcuni libri, qualche libro; **quite a ~**, **a good ~** (*a lot*) parecchi **2** *pron* (*not many*) pochi; **a ~** (*some*) alcuni; **quite a ~**, **a good ~** (*a lot*) parecchi; **fewer** meno (than di)

fiancé [fɪ'ɒnseɪ] fidanzato *m*; **fiancée** fidanzata *f*

fiasco [fɪ'æskəʊ] fiasco *m*

fiber *Am* ➔ **fibre**

fibre ['faɪbə(r)] fibra *f*; **fibre optics** tecnologia *f* delle fibre ottiche; **fibreglass** fibra *f* di vetro

fickle ['fɪkl] incostante

fiction ['fɪkʃn] narrativa *f*; (*made-up story*) storia *f*; **fictional** immaginario; **fictitious** fittizio

fiddle ['fɪdl] **1** *n* F (*violin*) violino *m*; **it's a ~** F (*cheat*) è una fregatura F **2** *v/i*: **~ with ...** giocherellare con ...; **~ around with ...** trafficare con ... **3** *v/t accounts* truccare

fidget ['fɪdʒɪt] agitarsi; **fidgety** in agitazione

field [fi:ld] campo *m*; (*competitors in race*) formazione *f*; **fielder** SP esterno *m*

fierce [fɪəs] *animal* feroce; *storm* violento; **fiercely** ferocemente

fiery ['faɪərɪ] focoso

fifteen [fɪf'ti:n] quindici; **fifteenth** quindicesimo; **fifth** quinto; **fiftieth** cinquantesimo; **fifty** cinquanta; **fifty-fifty** metà e metà

fig [fɪg] fico *m*

fight [faɪt] **1** *n* lotta *f*; *in war* combattimento *m*; (*argument*) litigio *m*; *in boxing* incontro *m* **2** *v/t* combattere; *injustice, fire* lottare contro; *in boxing* battersi contro **3** *v/i in war* combattere; *of drunks, schoolkids* azzuffarsi; (*argue*) litigare; **fighter** combattente *m/f*; *aeroplane* caccia *m inv*; (*boxer*) pugile *m*; **she's a ~** è combattiva; **fighting** risse *fpl*; MIL lotta *f*

figurative ['fɪgjərətɪv] *use of word* figurato; *art* figurativo

figure ['fɪgə(r)] *n* (*digit*) cifra *f*; *of person* linea *f*; (*form, shape*) figura *f*

◆ **figure on** F (*plan*) contare (di)

◆ **figure out** (*understand*) capire; *calculation* calcolare

file[1] [faɪl] **1** *n for papers* raccoglitore *m*; *contents* dossier *m inv*; COMPUT file *m inv*; **on ~**

in archivio **2** *v/t documents* schedare

file² [faɪl] *n for wood, finger-nails* lima *f*

filing cabinet ['faɪlɪŋ], *Am* **file cabinet** schedario *m*

fill [fɪl] riempire; *tooth* otturare

◆ **fill in** *form* compilare; *hole* riempire; **fill s.o. in** mettere al corrente qu

◆ **fill out 1** *v/t form* compilare **2** *v/i (get fatter)* arrotondarsi

fillet ['fɪlɪt] filetto *m*

filling ['fɪlɪŋ] **1** *n in sandwich* ripieno *m; in tooth* otturazione *f* **2** *adj food* pesante; **filling station** stazione *f* di rifornimento

film [fɪlm] **1** *n for camera* pellicola *f; at cinema* film *m inv* **2** *v/t* filmare; *scene* girare; **film-maker** regista *m/f;* **film star** stella *f* del cinema

filter ['fɪltə(r)] **1** *n* filtro *m* **2** *v/t* filtrare

filth [fɪlθ] sporcizia *f;* **filthy** sporco; *language etc* volgare

final ['faɪnl] **1** *adj* finale **2** *n SP* finale *m;* **finale** finale *m;* **finalist** finalista *m/f;* **finalize** mettere a punto; **finally** infine; *(at last)* finalmente

finance ['faɪnæns] **1** *n* finanza *f* **2** *v/t* finanziare; **financial** finanziario; **financially** finanziariamente; **financial year** anno *m* fiscale; **financier** finanziatore *m,* -trice *f*

find [faɪnd] trovare

◆ **find out** scoprire

findings ['faɪndɪŋz] *of report* conclusioni *fpl*

fine¹ [faɪn] *day, weather, city* bello; *wine, performance* buono; *distinction, line* sottile; **how's that? – that's ~** com'è? – va benissimo; **that's ~ by me** a me sta bene

fine² [faɪn] **1** *n penalty* multa *f* **2** *v/t* multare

finger ['fɪŋɡə(r)] **1** *n* dito *m* **2** *v/t* passare le dita su; **fingernail** unghia *f;* **fingerprint** impronta *f* digitale

finicky ['fɪnɪkɪ] *person* pignolo; *design* complicato

finish ['fɪnɪʃ] **1** *v/t* finire; **~ doing sth** finire di fare qc **2** *v/i* finire **3** *n of product* finitura *f*

◆ **finish up** *food* finire; **he finished up liking London** Londra ha finito per piacergli

◆ **finish with** *boyfriend etc* lasciare

'finishing line traguardo *m*

Finland ['fɪnlənd] Finlandia *f;* **Finn** finlandese *m/f;* **Finnish 1** *adj* finlandese, finnico **2** *n language* finlandese *m*

fir [fɜ:(r)] abete *m*

fire ['faɪə(r)] **1** *n* fuoco *m;* *(blaze)* incendio *m; bonfire, campfire* falò *m inv; be on ~* essere in fiamme; *catch ~* prendere fuoco; *set sth on ~, set fire to sth* dare fuoco a qc **2** *v/i (shoot)* sparare **3** *v/t F (dismiss)* licenziare; **fire alarm** allarme *m* antincendio; **firearm** arma *f* da fuoco; **fire brigade** vigili *mpl* del fuoco; **firecracker** petardo *m*; **fire department** *Am* vigili *mpl* del fuoco; **fire engine** autopompa *f*; **fire escape** scala *f* antincendio; **fire extinguisher** estintore *m*; **fire fighter** pompiere *m*; **fireman** pompiere *m*; **fireplace** camino *m*; **fire station** caserma *f* dei pompieri; **fire truck** autopompa *f*; **fireworks** fuochi *mpl* d'artificio

firm¹ [fɜːm] *adj* grip, handshake energico; muscles sodo; voice, parents deciso; decision risoluto; date, offer definitivo; control rigido; foundations solido; believer convinto

firm² [fɜːm] *n* COM azienda *f*

first [fɜːst] **1** *adj* primo **2** *n* primo *m*, -a *f* **3** *adv* arrive, finish per primo; (beforehand) prima; **~ of all** (for one reason) innanzitutto; **at ~** in un primo tempo, al principio; **first aid** pronto soccorso *m*; **first class 1** *adj* di prima classe **2** *adv* travel in prima classe; **first floor** primo piano *m*; piano *m* terra; **First Lady** First Lady *f inv*; **firstly** in primo luogo; **first name** nome *m* di battesimo; **first night** prima serata *f*; **first-rate** di prima qualità

fiscal ['fɪskl] fiscale; **fiscal year** *Am* anno *m* fiscale

fish [fɪʃ] **1** *n* pesce *m* **2** *v/i* pescare; **fisherman** pescatore *m*; **fish finger** bastoncino *m* di pesce; **fishing** pesca *f*; **fishing boat** peschereccio *m*; **fishing rod** canna *f* da pesca; **fishmonger** pescivendolo *m*; **fish stick** *Am* bastoncino *m* di pesce; **fishy** F (suspicious) sospetto

fist [fɪst] pugno *m*

fit¹ [fɪt] *n* MED attacco *m*; **a ~ of jealousy** un accesso di gelosia

fit² [fɪt] *adj* physically in forma; morally adatto; **keep ~** tenersi in forma

fit³ [fɪt] **1** *v/t* of clothes andare bene a; (attach) installare **2** *v/i* of clothes andare bene; of piece of furniture etc starci

fitness ['fɪtnɪs] physical forma *f*; **fitting** appropriato; **fittings** equipaggiamento *msg*

five [faɪv] cinque

fix [fɪks] **1** *n* (solution) soluzione *f* **2** *v/t* (attach, arrange) fissare; (repair) aggiustare; lunch preparare; dishonestly: match etc manipolare; **fixed** in position fisso; timescale, exchange rate stabilito

fizzy ['fɪzɪ] drink gassato

flab [flæb] on body ciccia *f*; **flabby** muscles flaccido

flag¹ [flæg] *n* bandiera *f*

flag² [flæg] *v/i* (tire) soccombere

'flagpole asta *f*

flagrant ['fleıgrənt] flagrante

flair [fleə(r)] (*talent*) talento *m*; (*style*) stile *m*

flake [fleık] *n of snow* fiocco *m*; *of paint, plaster* scaglia *f*

flamboyant [flæm'bɔıənt] *personality* esuberante; **flamboyantly** in modo vistoso

flame [fleım] *n* fiamma *f*; **go up in ~s** incendiarsi

flammable ['flæməbl] infiammabile

flank [flæŋk] **1** *n* fianco *m* **2** *v/t*: **be ~ed by** essere affiancato da

flannel ['flænl] guanto *m* di spugna

flap [flæp] **1** *n of envelope, pocket* falda *f*; *of table* ribalta *f*; **be in a ~** F essere in fibrillazione F **2** *v/t wings* sbattere **3** *v/i of flag etc* sventolare

♦ flare up [fler] *of violence, illness* esplodere; *of fire* divampare

flash [flæʃ] **1** *n of light* lampo *m*; PHOT flash *m inv*; **in a ~** F in un istante; **~ of lightning** lampo *m* **2** *v/i of light* lampeggiare **3** *v/t*: **~ one's headlights** lampeggiare; **flashback** *in film* flashback *m inv*; **flashlight** pila *f*; PHOT flash *m inv*; **flashy** *pej* appariscente

flask [flɑːsk] (*vacuum* ~) termos *m inv*

flat¹ [flæt] **1** *adj* piatto; *beer* sgassato; *battery, tyre* a terra;

shoes basso; ***A / B*** ~ MUS la / si bemolle; ***and that's*** ~ F punto e basta F **2** *adv* MUS sotto tonalità; **~ out** *work, run* a tutto gas **3** *n* gomma *f* a terra

flat² [flæt] *n* (*apartment*) appartamento *m*

flatly ['flætlı] *refuse, deny* risolutamente; **flatmate** compagno *m*, -a *f* di appartamento; **flat rate** tariffa *f* forfettaria; **flatten** *land, road* livellare; *by bombing, demolition* radere al suolo

flatter ['flætə(r)] adulare; **flatterer** adulatore *m*, -trice *f*; **flattering** *comments* lusinghiero; **Jane's dress is very** ~ il vestito di Jane le dona molto; **flattery** adulazione *f*

flavor *Am* ☞ **flavour**

flavour ['fleıvə(r)] **1** *n* gusto *m* **2** *v/t food* insaporire; **flavouring** aroma *m*

flaw [flɔː] difetto *m*; **flawless** perfetto

flea [fliː] pulce *f*

flee [fliː] scappare

fleet [fliːt] NAUT flotta *f*; *of taxis, trucks* parco *m* macchine

fleeting ['fliːtıŋ] *visit etc* di sfuggita

flesh [fleʃ] carne *f*; *of fruit* polpa *f*

flex [fleks] **1** *v/t muscles* flettere **2** *n* ELEC cavo *m*; **flex(i)time** orario *m* flessibile;

flexibility flessibilità *f*; **flexible** flessibile

flicker ['flɪkə(r)] *of light* tremolare

flier ['flaɪə(r)] *(circular)* volantino *m*

flight [flaɪt] volo *m*; *(fleeing)* fuga *f*; **~ (of stairs)** rampa *f* (di scale); **flight attendant** assistente *m/f* di volo; **flight deck** *in plane* cabina *f* di pilotaggio; *of aircraft carrier* ponte *m* di decollo; **flight number** numero *m* di volo; **flight path** rotta *f* (di volo); **flight recorder** registratore *m* di volo; **flight time** *departure* orario *m* di volo; *duration* durata *f* di volo; **flighty** volubile

flimsy ['flɪmzɪ] *furniture* leggero; *dress, material* sottile; *excuse* debole

flinch [flɪntʃ] sobbalzare

flipper ['flɪpə(r)] *for swimming* pinna *f*

flirt [flɜːt] **1** *v/i* flirtare **2** *n* flirt *m inv*; **flirtatious** civettuolo

float [fləʊt] galleggiare; FIN fluttuare

flock [flɒk] **1** *n* *of sheep* gregge *m* **2** *v/i* accorrere in massa

flood [flʌd] **1** *n* inondazione *f* **2** *v/t of river* inondare; **flooding** inondazione *f*; **floodlight** riflettore *m*; **flood waters** acque *fpl* di inondazione

floor [flɔː(r)] pavimento *m*; *(story)* piano *m*; **floorboard**

asse *f* del pavimento; **floorlamp** *Am* lampada *f* a stelo

flop [flɒp] **1** *v/i* crollare; F *(fail)* fare fiasco **2** *n* F *(failure)* fiasco *m*; **floppy (disk)** floppy *m inv*, **floppy disk** *m inv*

Florence ['flɒrəns] Firenze *f*; **Florentine 1** *adj* fiorentino **2** *n* fiorentino *m*, -a *f*

florist ['flɒrɪst] fiorista *m/f*

flour ['flaʊə(r)] farina *f*

flourish ['flʌrɪʃ] fiorire; *of business, civilization* prosperare; **flourishing** *business, trade* prospero

flow [fləʊ] **1** *v/i of river, traffic, current* scorrere; *of work* procedere **2** *n of river, ideas* flusso *m*; **flowchart** diagramma *m* (di flusso)

flower ['flaʊə(r)] **1** *n* fiore *m* **2** *v/i* fiorire; **flowerpot** vaso *m* per fiori

flu [fluː] influenza *f*

fluctuate ['flʌktjʊeɪt] oscillare; **fluctuation** oscillazione *f*

fluency ['fluːənsɪ] *in a language* scioltezza *f*; **fluent** fluente; *he speaks ~ Spanish* parla correntemente lo spagnolo; **fluently** *speak, write* correntemente

fluid ['fluːɪd] fluido *m*

flunk [flʌŋk] *Am* F essere bocciato a

flush [flʌʃ] **1** *v/t toilet* tirare l'acqua di **2** *v/i (go red)* diventare rosso **3** *adj (level)* a filo; **~ with ...** a filo con ...

flute [fluːt] MUS flauto *m* traverso

flutter ['flʌtə(r)] *of wings* sbattere; *of flag* sventolare; *of heart* battere forte

fly¹ [flaɪ] *n insect* mosca *f*

fly² [flaɪ] *n on trousers* patta *f*

fly³ [flaɪ] **1** *v/t* volare; *of flag* sventolare; *(rush)* precipitarsi; ~ **into a rage** perdere le staffe **2** *v/t aeroplane* pilotare; *airline* volare con; *(transport by air)* spedire per via aerea

◆ **fly away** *of bird, plane* volare via

◆ **fly back** *(travel back)* ritornare (in aereo)

◆ **fly past** *of time* volare

flying ['flaɪɪŋ] volare *m*; **flyover** MOT cavalcavia *m inv*

foam [fəʊm] *on liquid* schiuma *f*; **foam rubber** gommapiuma**®** *f*

focus ['fəʊkəs] *of attention* centro *m*; PHOT fuoco *m*; **be in ~ / be out of ~** PHOT essere a fuoco / non essere a fuoco

◆ **focus on** *issue* focalizzare l'attenzione su; PHOT mettere a fuoco

fodder ['fɒdə(r)] foraggio *m*

fog [fɒg] nebbia *f*; **foggy** nebbioso

foil¹ [fɔɪl] *n* carta *f* stagnola

foil² [fɔɪl] *v/t (thwart)* sventare

fold [fəʊld] **1** *v/t paper etc* piegare; ~ **one's arms** incrociare le braccia **2** *v/i of business*

chiudere i battenti **3** *n in cloth etc* piega *f*

◆ **fold up** *v/t chairs etc* chiudere; *clothes* piegare **2** *v/i of chair, table* chiudere

folder ['fəʊldə(r)] *for documents* cartellina *f*; COMPUT *directory f inv*; **folding** pieghevole

foliage ['fəʊlɪɪdʒ] fogliame *m*

folk [fəʊk] *(people)* gente *f*; **my ~** *(family)* i miei parenti; **come in, ~s** F entrate, gente F; **folk music** musica *f* folk; **folk singer** cantante *m/f* folk; **folk song** canzone *f* popolare

◆ **follow up** *inquiry* dare seguito a

follow ['fɒləʊ] **1** *v/t (also understand)* seguire **2** *v/i* seguire; *logically* quadrare; **as ~s** quanto segue

follower ['fɒləʊə(r)] *of politician etc* seguace *m/f*; *of football team* tifoso *m*, -a *f*; **following 1** *adj* seguente **2** *n people* seguito *m*; **the ~** quanto segue

fond [fɒnd] *(loving)* affezionato; *memory* caro; **he is ~ of travel** gli piace viaggiare; **I'm very ~ of him** gli voglio molto

fondle ['fɒndl] accarezzare

fondness ['fɒndnɪs] *for person* affetto *m*; *for wine, food* gusto *m*

font [fɒnt] *for printing* carattere *m*; *in church* fonte *f* battesimale

food [fuːd] cibo m; **Italian ~** la cucina italiana; **there's no ~ in the house** non c'è niente da mangiare in casa; **foodie** buongustaio m, -a f; **food poisoning** intossicazione f alimentare

fool [fuːl] **1** n pazzo m, -a f; **make a ~ of o.s.** rendersi ridicolo **2** v/t ingannare; **foolhardy** temerario; **foolish** sciocco; **foolproof** a prova di idiota

foot [fut] (pl **feet** [fiːt]) also measurement piede m; **on ~** a piedi; **at the ~ of the page** a piè di pagina; **put one's ~ in it** F fare una gaffe; **footage** pellicola f cinematografica; **football** (soccer) calcio m; American football m americano; (ball) pallone m da calcio; for American football pallone m da football americano; **footballer** calciatore m, -trice f; **football pitch** campo m da calcio; **football player** soccer calciatore m, -trice f; American style giocatore m di football americano; **foothills** colline fpl pedemontane; **footnote** nota f a piè di pagina; **footpath** sentiero m; **footprint** impronta f di piede; **footstep** passo m

for [fɔː(r)] per; **a train ~ ...** un treno per ...; **what is this ~?** a cosa serve?; **what ~?** a che

scopo?, perché?; **~ three days** per tre giorni; **I am ~ the idea** sono a favore dell'idea; **how much did you sell it ~?** a quanto l'hai venduto?

forbid [fə'bɪd] vietare, proibire (**to do** di fare); **forbidden** vietato, proibito; **smoking ~** vietato fumare; **parking ~** divieto di sosta; **forbidding** ostile

force [fɔːs] **1** n forza f; **come into ~** of law etc entrare in vigore; **the ~s** MIL le forze armate **2** v/t door, lock forzare; **~ s.o. to do sth** forzare or costringere qu a fare qc; **forced** forzato f/a; **forced landing** atterraggio m d'emergenza; **forceful** argument, speaker convincente; character energico

forceps ['fɔːseps] MED forcipe f

forcibly ['fɔːsəblɪ] restrain con la forza

foreboding [fə'bəʊdɪŋ] presentimento m; **forecast 1** n previsione f **2** v/t prevedere; **forefathers** antenati mpl; **forefinger** indice m; **foregone: that's a ~ conclusion** è una conclusione scontata; **foreground** primo piano m; **forehand** in tennis diritto m; **forehead** fronte f

foreign ['fɒrən] straniero; trade, policy estero; **foreign affairs** affari mpl esteri; **foreign body** corpo m estraneo; **foreign currency** valuta *f* estera; **foreigner** straniero *m*, -a *f*; **foreign exchange** cambio *m* valutario; **Foreign Office** Ministero *m* degli esteri; **Foreign Secretary** *in UK* ministro *m* degli esteri

'**foreman** caposquadra *m*; **foremost** 1 *adv* (*uppermost*) soprattutto 2 *adj* (*leading*) principale

forensic '**medicine** [fǝ'rensɪk] medicina *f* legale; **forensic scientist** medico *m* legale

'**forerunner** precursore *m*; **foresee** prevedere; **foresight** lungimiranza *f*

forest ['fɒrɪst] foresta *f*; **forestry** scienze *fpl* forestali

fore'tell predire

forever [fǝ'revǝ(r)] per sempre

foreword ['fɔːwɜːd] prefazione *f*

forfeit ['fɔːfɪt] *right, privilege etc* perdere

forge [fɔːdʒ] (*counterfeit*) contraffare; *signature* falsificare; **forgery** (*banknote*) falsificazione *f*; (*document*) falso *m*

forget [fǝ'get] dimenticare; **forgetful** smemorato

forgive [fǝ'gɪv] perdonare; **forgiveness** perdono *m*

fork [fɔːk] *for eating* forchetta *f*; *for gardening* forca *f*; *in road* biforcazione *f*; **forklift truck** muletto *m*

form [fɔːm] **1** *n* (*shape*) forma

f; (*document*) modulo *m*; *in school* classe *f*; **be on / off** ~ essere in / fuori forma **2** *v/t in clay etc* modellare; *friendship* creare; *opinion* formarsi; *past tense etc* formare; (*constitute*) costituire **3** *v/i* (*take shape, develop*) formarsi; **formal** formale; **formality** formalità *f inv*; **formally** formalmente

format ['fɔːmæt] **1** *v/t diskette* formattare; *document* impaginare **2** *n* (*size: of magazine etc*) formato *m*; (*makeup: of programme*) formula *f*

formation [fɔː'meɪʃn] formazione *f*

former ['fɔːmǝ(r)] *wife, president* ex *inv*; *statement, arrangement* precedente; **the** ~ quest'ultimo; **formerly** precedentemente

formidable ['fɔːmɪdǝbl] imponente

formula ['fɔːmjʊlǝ] formula *f*

fort [fɔːt] MIL forte *m*

forthcoming ['fɔːθkʌmɪŋ] (*future*) prossimo; *personality* comunicativo

'**forthright** schietto

fortieth ['fɔːtɪɪθ] quarantesimo, -a

fortnight ['fɔːtnaɪt] due settimane

fortress ['fɔːtrɪs] MIL fortezza *f*

fortunate ['fɔːtʃʊnǝt] fortunato; **fortunately** fortunatamente; **fortune** sorte *f*; (*lot*

of money) fortuna *f*; **tell
s.o.'s ~** predire il futuro a
qu; **fortune-teller** chiromante *m/f*

forty ['fɔːtɪ] quaranta

Forum ['fɔːrəm] *Roman* foro
m

forward ['fɔːwəd] **1** *adv* avanti
2 *adj pej: person* diretto **3** *n*
SP attaccante *m* **4** *v/t letter*
inoltrare; **forwarding agent**
COM spedizioniere *m*; **for-
ward-looking** progressista

fossil ['fɒsl] fossile *m*

foster ['fɒstə(r)] *child* avere in
affidamento; *attitude, belief*
incoraggiare; **foster parents**
genitori *mpl* con affidamento

foul [faʊl] **1** *n* SP fallo *m* **2** *adj
smell* pessimo; *weather* orri-
bile **3** *v/t* SP fare un fallo contro

found [faʊnd] *school etc* fondare; **foundation** *of theory
etc* fondamenta *fpl*; (*organization*) fondazione *f*; **make-
-up** fondotinta *m*; **foundations** *of building* fondamenta *fpl*; **founder** fondatore *m*,
-trice *f*

fountain ['faʊntɪn] fontana *f*

four [fɔː(r)] quattro; **four-star
hotel etc** a quattro stelle;
fourteen quattordici; **fourteenth** quattordicesimo;
fourth quarto; **four-wheel
drive** MOT quattro per quattro *m inv*

fox [fɒks] **1** *n* volpe *f* **2** *v/t* (*puz-*

zle) mettere in difficoltà

foyer ['fɔɪeɪ] atrio *m*

fraction ['frækʃn] frazione *f*;
fractionally lievemente

fracture ['fræktʃə(r)] **1** *n* frattura *f* **2** *v/t* fratturare

fragile ['frædʒaɪl] fragile

fragment ['frægmənt] frammento *m*

fragrance ['freɪgrəns] fra-
granza,*f*; **fragrant** profuma-
to

frail [freɪl] gracile

frame [freɪm] **1** *n of picture,
window* cornice *f*; *of glasses*
montatura *f*; *of bicycle* telaio
m; **~ of mind** stato m d'animo **2** *v/t picture* incorniciare;
F *person* incastrare F;
framework struttura *f*

France [frɑːns] Francia *f*

franchise ['fræntʃaɪz] *for business* concessione *f*

frank [fræŋk] franco; **frankly**
francamente; **frankness**
franchezza *f*

frantic ['fræntɪk] *attempt* frenetico; (*worried*) agitatissi-
mo

fraternal [frə'tɜːnl] fraterno

fraud [frɔːd] frode *f*; *person*
impostore *m*, -trice *f*; **fraud-
ulent** fraudolento

frayed [freɪd] *cuffs* liso

freak [friːk] **1** *n unusual event*
fenomeno *m* anomalo; *two-
-headed person etc* scherzo
m di natura; F *strange person*
tipo *m*, -a *f* strambo, -a;
movie ~ F (*fanatic*) fanatico

m, -a f del cinema **2** *adj* wind, storm violento

freckle ['frekl] lentiggine f

free [fri:] **1** *adj* libero; (*no cost*) gratuito; **for** ~ *travel, get sth* gratis **2** *v/t prisoners* liberare; **freedom** libertà f; **free enterprise** liberalismo m economico; **freefone number** numero m verde; **free kick** *in soccer* calcio m di punizione; **freelance** free lance *inv*; **freely** *admit* apertamente; **free sample** campione m gratuito; **free speech** libertà f di espressione; **freeway** Am autostrada f

freeze [fri:z] **1** *v/t* gelare; *wages, account* congelare; *video* bloccare **2** *v/i of water* gelare; **freeze-dried** liofilizzato; **freezer** freezer m *inv*, congelatore m; **freezing 1** *adj* gelato; **it's** ~ (**cold**) *of weather* si gela; *of water* è gelata; **I'm** ~ sono congelato **2** n: **10 below** ~ 10 gradi sotto zero

freight [freɪt] carico m; *costs* trasporto m; **freighter** *ship* nave f da carico; *plane* aereo f da carico

French [frentʃ] **1** *adj* francese **2** n (*language*) francese m; **the** ~ i francesi; **French fries** patate fpl fritte; **Frenchman** francese m; **French windows** vetrata f; **Frenchwoman** francese f

frenzied ['frenzɪd] *attack, activity* frenetico; *mob* impaz-

zito; **frenzy** frenesia f

frequency ['fri:kwənsɪ] frequenza f

frequent[1] ['fri:kwənt] *adj* frequente

frequent[2] [frɪ'kwent] *v/t bar etc* frequentare

frequently ['fri:kwəntlɪ] frequentemente

fresh [freʃ] fresco; *start* nuovo; Am (*impertinent*) sfacciato; **fresh air** aria f fresca

◆ **freshen up** ['freʃn] **1** *v/i* rinfrescarsi **2** *v/t room, paintwork* rinfrescare

freshly ['freʃlɪ] appena; **freshman** studente m del primo anno, matricola f; **freshwater** d'acqua dolce

friction ['frɪkʃn] PHYS frizione f; *between people* attrito m

Friday ['fraɪdeɪ] venerdì m *inv*

fridge [frɪdʒ] frigo m

fried egg [fraɪd] uovo m fritto

friend [frend] amico m, -a f; **make** ~**s** fare amicizia; **friendliness** amichevolezza f; **friendly 1** *adj* amichevole; (*easy to use*) facile da usare; **be** ~ **with s.o.** (*be friends*) essere amico di qu **2** n SP amichevole f; **friendship** amicizia f

fries [fraɪz] patate fpl fritte

fright [fraɪt] paura f; **frighten** spaventare; **be** ~**ed** (**of**) aver paura (di); **frightening** spaventoso

frill [frɪl] *on dress etc* volant m *inv*; ~**s** (*fancy extras*) fronzoli *mpl*

fringe [frɪndʒ] frangia *f*; *(edge)* margini *mpl*; **fringe benefits** benefici *mpl* accessori

frisk [frɪsk] frugare F

♦ **fritter away** [ˈfrɪtə(r)] *time, fortune* sprecare

frivolity [frɪˈvɒlətɪ] frivolezza *f*; **frivolous** frivolo F

frizzy [ˈfrɪzɪ] *hair* crespo

frog [frɒg] rana *f*; **frogman** sommozzatore *m*

from [frɒm] ◇ *in time* da; **~ 9 to 5 (o'clock)** dalle 9 alle 5; **~ today** on da oggi in poi ◇ *in space* da; **~ here to there** da qui a lì ◇ *origin* di; **a letter ~ Jo** una lettera di Jo; **I am ~ Liverpool** sono di Liverpool ◇ *(because of)* di; **tired ~ the journey** stanco del viaggio; **it's ~ overeating** è a causa del troppo mangiare

front [frʌnt] **1** *n of building* lato *m* principale; *of car, statue* davanti *m inv*; *of book* copertina *f*; *(cover organization)* facciata *f*; MIL, *of weather* fronte *m*; **in ~** davanti; **in ~ of** davanti a **2** *adj wheel, seat* anteriore **3** *v/t TV programme* presentare; **front door** porta *f* principale

frontier [ˈfrʌntɪə(r)] *also fig* frontiera *f*

'front line MIL fronte *m*; **front page** *of newspaper* prima pagina *f*; **front-wheel drive** trazione *f* anteriore

frost [frɒst] brina *f*; **frostbite**

congelamento *m*; **frosting** *Am on cake* glassatura *f*; **frosty** *also fig* gelido

froth [frɒθ] spuma *f*

frown [fraʊn] **1** *n* cipiglio *m* **2** *v/i* aggrottare le sopracciglia

frozen [ˈfrəʊzn] gelido; *food* surgelato; **I'm ~** F sono congelato F

fruit [fruːt] frutto *m*; *collective* frutta *f*; **fruitful** *discussions etc* fruttuoso; **fruit juice** succo *m* di frutta; **fruit machine** slot machine *f inv*; **fruit salad** macedonia *f*

frustrate [frʌˈstreɪt] *person* frustrare; *plans* scombussolare; **frustrating** frustrante; **frustration** frustrazione *f*; **sexual ~** insoddisfazione *f* sessuale

fry [fraɪ] friggere; **frying pan** padella *f*

fuck [fʌk] V scopare V; **~ !** cazzo! V

fuel [ˈfjuːəl] **1** *n* carburante *m* **2** *v/t fig* alimentare

fugitive [ˈfjuːdʒətɪv] *n* fuggiasco *m*, -a *f*

fulfil, *Am* **fulfill** [fʊlˈfɪl] *dreams* realizzare; *contract* eseguire; *requirements* corrispondere a; **feel ~led** in job, life sentirsi insoddisfatto; **fulfilment**, *Am* **fulfillment** *of contract* esecuzione *f*; *of dreams* realizzazione *f*; *moral, spiritual* soddisfazione *f*

full [fʊl] pieno **(of** di**)**; *account* esauriente; *life* intenso; **~ up**

hotel, with food pieno; **in ~** write per intero; **pay in ~** saldare il conto; **full moon** luna *f* piena; **full stop** punto *m* fermo; **full-time** a tempo pieno; **fully** *booked, recovered* completamente; *understand, explain* perfettamente; *describe* ampiamente

fumble ['fʌmbl] *catch* farsi sfuggire

fumes [fjuːmz] esalazioni *fpl*

fun [fʌn] **1** *n* divertimento *m*; **it was great ~** era molto divertente; **have ~!** divertiti!; **for ~** per divertirsi; *(joking)* per scherzo; **make ~ of** prendere in giro **2** *adj* F divertente

function ['fʌŋkʃn] **1** *n* (*purpose*) funzione *f*; *(reception etc)* cerimonia *f* **2** *v/i* funzionare; **~ as** servire da; **functional** funzionale

fund [fʌnd] **1** *n* fondo *m* **2** *v/t project etc* finanziare

fundamental [fʌndə'mentl] fondamentale; **fundamentalist** fondamentalista *m/f*; **fundamentally** fondamentalmente

funding ['fʌndɪŋ] *money* fondi *mpl*

funeral ['fjuːnərəl] funerale *m*; **funeral home**, **funeral parlour** obitorio *m*

fungus ['fʌŋgəs] fungo *m*

funicular ('railway') [fjuː'nɪkjʊlə(r)] funicolare *f*

funnily ['fʌnɪlɪ] *(oddly)* stra-

namente; *(comically)* in modo divertente; **~ enough** per quanto strano; **funny** *(comical)* divertente; *(odd)* strano

fur [fɜː(r)] pelliccia *f*; *on animal* pelo *m*

furious ['fjʊərɪəs] *(angry)* furioso; *(intense)* spaventoso

furnace ['fɜːnɪs] fornace *f*

furnish ['fɜːnɪʃ] *room* arredare; *(supply)* fornire; **furniture** mobili *mpl*; **a piece of ~** un mobile

further ['fɜːðə(r)] **1** *adj (additional)* ulteriore; *(more distant)* più lontano; **have you anything ~ to say?** ha qualcosa da aggiungere? **2** *adv walk, drive* oltre; **~, I want to say ...** inoltre, volevo dire ...; **two miles ~** *(on)* due miglia più avanti **3** *v/t cause etc* favorire; **furthermore** inoltre; **furthest 1** *adj* più lontano **2** *adv*: **this is the ~ north** è il punto più a nord

furtive ['fɜːtɪv] *glance* furtivo

fury ['fjʊərɪ] furia *f*

fuse [fjuːz] ELEC **1** *n* fusibile *m* **2** *v/t* bruciarsi **3** *v/t* bruciare; **fusebox** scatola *f* dei fusibili

fusion ['fjuːʒn] fusione *f*

fuss [fʌs] agitazione *f*; *about film, event* scalpore *m*; **make a ~ complain** fare storie; **make a ~ of** be very attentive *to* colmare qu di attenzioni; **fussy** *person* difficile; *design* *etc* complicato; **be a ~ eater** essere schizzinoso nel mangiare

futile ['fjuːtaɪl] futile; **futility** futilità *f*

future ['fjuːtʃə(r)] **1** *n* futuro *m* **2** *adj* futuro; **futuristic** futuristico

fuzzy ['fʌzɪ] *hair* crespo; (*out of focus*) sfuocato

G

gadget ['gædʒɪt] congegno *m*

gag [gæg] **1** *n* bavaglio *m*; (*joke*) battuta *f* **2** *v/t person* imbavagliare; *the press* azzittire

gain [geɪn] (*acquire*) acquisire, acquistare; **~ 10 pounds** aumentare di 10 libbre

gala ['gɑːlə] *concert etc* serata *f* di gala

galaxy ['gæləksɪ] galassia *f*

gale [geɪl] bufera *f*

gallery ['gælərɪ] galleria *f*

gallon ['gælən] gallone *m*; (*0,546l, in USA 0,785l,*)

gallop ['gæləp] galoppare

gamble ['gæmbl] giocare (d'azzardo); **gambler** giocatore *m*, -trice *f* (d'azzardo); **gambling** gioco *m* (d'azzardo)

game [geɪm] gioco *m*; (*match, in tennis*) partita *f*

gang [gæŋ] banda *f*; **gangster** malvivente *m*, gangster *m inv*; **gangway** passaggio *m*; *for ship* passerella *f*

gap [gæp] *in wall, for parking* buco *m*; *in conversation* vuoto *m*; *in time* intervallo *m*; *in story, education* lacuna *f*; *be-*

tween personalities scarto *m*

gape [geɪp] *of person* rimanere a bocca aperta; **gaping** *hole* spalancato

'gap year *anno tra la fine del liceo e l'inizio dell'università dedicato ad altre attività*

garage ['gærɪdʒ] *for parking* garage *m inv*; *for repairs* officina *f*; *for petrol* stazione *f* di servizio

garbage ['gɑːbɪdʒ] rifiuti *mpl*; (*fig: nonsense*) idiozie *fpl*; **garbage can** bidone *m* della spazzatura; **garbage truck** *Am* camion *m* della nettezza urbana

garbled ['gɑːbld] *message* ingarbugliato

garden ['gɑːdn] giardino *m*; *for vegetables* orto *m*; **gardening** giardinaggio *m*

garish ['geərɪʃ] sgargiante

garlic ['gɑːlɪk] aglio *m*

garment ['gɑːmənt] *fml* capo *m* d'abbigliamento

garnish ['gɑːnɪʃ] guarnire

gas [gæs] gas *m inv*; *Am* (*gasoline*) benzina *f*

gash [gæʃ] taglio *m*

gasket ['gæskɪt] guarnizione f

gasoline ['gæsəliːn] Am benzina f

gasp [gɑːsp] **1** n sussulto m **2** v/i rimanere senza fiato; ~ **for breath** essere senza fiato

'gas pedal Am acceleratore m; **gas pump** Am pompa f della benzina; **gas station** Am stazione f di rifornimento; **gas stove** cucina f a gas

gate [geɪt] cancello m; of city, castle, at airport porta f; **gateway** ingresso m; fig via f d'accesso

gather ['gæðə(r)] **1** v/t facts raccogliere; ~ **speed** acquistare velocità **2** v/i (understand) dedurre; **gathering** (group of people) raduno m

gaudy ['gɔːdɪ] pacchiano

gauge [geɪdʒ] **1** n indicatore m **2** v/t pressure misurare; opinion valutare

gaunt [gɔːnt] smunto

gawky ['gɔːkɪ] impacciato

gawp [gɔːp] F fissare come un ebete F

gay [geɪ] gay inv; **gay marriage** matrimonio m gay

gaze [geɪz] **1** n sguardo m **2** v/i fissare

gear [gɪə(r)] (equipment) equipaggiamento m; in vehicles marcia f; **gearbox** MOT scatola f del cambio; **gear lever**, **gear shift** MOT leva f del cambio

geese [giːs] pl ☞ **goose**

gel [dʒel] for hair, shower gel m inv

gem [dʒem] gemma f; fig: book etc capolavoro m; person perla f rara

Gemini ['dʒemɪnaɪ] ASTR Gemelli mpl

gender ['dʒendə(r)] genere m

gene [dʒiːn] gene m

general ['dʒenrəl] **1** n MIL generale m **2** adj generale; **generalization** generalizzazione f; **generalize** generalizzare; **generally** generalmente; ~ **speaking** in generale

generate ['dʒenəreɪt] generare; in linguistics formare; **generation** generazione f; **generator** ELEC generatore m

generosity [dʒenə'rɒsɪtɪ] generosità f; **generous** generoso

genetic [dʒɪ'netɪk] genetico; **genetically** geneticamente; ~ **modified** transgenico; **genetic engineering** ingegneria f genetica; **genetic fingerprint** esame m del DNA; **genetics** genetica f

genial ['dʒiːnɪəl] gioviale

genitals ['dʒenɪtlz] genitali mpl

genius ['dʒiːnɪəs] genio m

Genoa ['dʒenəʊə] Genova f

genocide ['dʒenəsaɪd] genocidio m

gentle ['dʒentl] delicato; breeze, slope dolce; **gentle-**

man signore *m*; *he's a real ~* è un vero gentleman; **gentleness** delicatezza *f*; *of breeze, slope* dolcezza *f*; **gently** delicatamente; *blow, slope* dolcemente

gents [dʒents] *toilet* bagno *m* degli uomini

genuine ['dʒenjʊɪn] autentico; (*sincere*) sincero; **genuinely** sinceramente

geographical [dʒɪə'græfɪkl] geografico; **geography** geografia *f*

geological [dʒɪə'lɒdʒɪkl] geologico; **geologist** geologo *m*, -a *f*; **geology** geologia *f*

geometric, **geometrical** [dʒɪə'metrɪk(l)] geometrico; **geometry** geometria *f*

geriatric [dʒerɪ'ætrɪk] **1** *adj* geriatrico **2** *n* anziano *m*, -a *f*

germ [dʒɜːm] *also fig* germe *m*

German ['dʒɜːmən] **1** *adj* tedesco **2** *n person* tedesco *m*, -a *f*; *language* tedesco *m*; **German measles** rosolia *f*; **German shepherd** pastore *m* tedesco; **Germany** Germania *f*

gesture ['dʒestʃə(r)] *also fig* gesto *m*

get [get] prendere; (*fetch*) andare a prendere; (*receive: letter*) ricevere; (*receive: knowledge, respect etc*) ottenere; (*become*) diventare; (*understand*) afferrare; *~ sth done causative* farsi fare qc; *~*

s.o. to do sth far fare qc a qu; *I'll ~ him to do it* glielo faccio fare; *~ to do sth have opportunity* avere occasione di fare qc; *~ one's hair cut* tagliarsi i capelli; *~ sth ready* preparare qc; *~ going* (*leave*) andare via; *have got* avere; *I have got to study* devo studiare

◆ **get at** (*criticize*) prendersela con; (*imply, mean*) volere arrivare a

◆ **get back 1** *v/i* (*return*) ritornare; *I'll get back to you on that* ti faccio sapere **2** *v/t* (*obtain again*) recuperare

◆ **get by** (*pass*) passare; *financially* tirare avanti

◆ **get down 1** *v/i from ladder etc* scendere; (*duck etc*) abbassarsi **2** *v/t* (*depress*) buttare giù

◆ **get in 1** *v/i of train, plane* arrivare; (*come home*) arrivare a casa; *to car* salire; *how did they get in?* of thieves, mice etc come sono entrati? **2** *v/t to suitcase etc* far entrare

◆ **get into** *house* entrare in; *car* salire in

◆ **get off 1** *v/i from bus etc* scendere; (*finish work*) finire; (*not be punished*) cavarsela **2** *v/t* (*remove*) togliere; *clothes* togliersi

◆ **get off with** F *sexually* rimorchiare F; *get off with a small fine* cavarsela con una piccola multa

◆ **get on 1** v/i to bike, bus, train salire; (be friendly) andare d'accordo; (advance: of time) farsi tardi; (become old) invecchiare; (make progress) procedere; **he's getting on well at school** se la sta cavando bene a scuola **2** v/t: **get on the bus** salire sull'autobus

◆ **get out 1** v/i of car etc scendere; of prison uscire; **get out!** fuori!; **let's get out of here** usciamo da qui **2** v/t nail, something jammed tirare fuori; stain mandare via; gun, pen tirare fuori

◆ **get over** fence, disappointment etc superare; lover etc dimenticare

◆ **get through** on telephone prendere la linea; (make self understood) farsi capire

◆ **get up 1** v/i of person, wind alzarsi **2** v/t (climb: hill) salire su

'**getaway car** macchina f per la fuga; **get-together** ritrovo m

ghastly ['gɑ:stlɪ] orrendo

ghetto ['getəʊ] ghetto m

ghost [gəʊst] fantasma m, spettro m; **ghostly** spettrale

ghoul [gu:l] persona f morbosa

giant ['dʒaɪənt] **1** n gigante m **2** adj gigante

gibberish ['dʒɪbərɪʃ] F bestialità fpl F

gibe [dʒaɪb] frecciatina f

giddiness ['gɪdɪnɪs] giramenti mpl di testa; **giddy**: **I feel ~** mi gira la testa

gift [gɪft] regalo m; (talent) dono m; **gifted** dotato; **gift token**, **gift voucher** buono m d'acquisto; **giftwrap**: **~ sth** fare un pacco regalo

gig [gɪg] F concerto m

gigabyte ['gɪgəbaɪt] COMPUT gigabyte m inv

gigantic [dʒaɪˈgæntɪk] gigante

giggle ['gɪgl] **1** v/i ridacchiare **2** n risatina f

gimmick ['gɪmɪk] trovata f

gin [dʒɪn] gin m inv; **~ and tonic** gin and tonic m inv

ginger ['dʒɪndʒə(r)] **1** n spice zenzero m **2** adj hair rosso carota; cat rosso

gipsy ['dʒɪpsɪ] zingaro m, -a f

giraffe [dʒɪˈrɑ:f] giraffa f

girder ['gɜ:də(r)] n trave f

girl [gɜ:l] ragazza f; **girlfriend** of boy ragazza f; of girl amica f; **girl guide** giovane esploratrice f; **girlish** tipicamente femminile

gist [dʒɪst] sostanza f

give [gɪv] dare; present fare; (supply: electricity etc) fornire; talk, groan fare; party dare; pain, appetite far venire

◆ **give away** as present regalare; (betray) tradire

◆ **give back** restituire

◆ **give in 1** v/i (surrender) arrendersi **2** v/t (hand in) consegnare

◆ **give onto** (*open onto*) dare su

◆ **give out 1** *v/t* leaflets etc distribuire **2** *v/i of supplies, strength* esaurirsi

◆ **give up 1** *v/t* smoking etc rinunciare a; **give o.s. up to the police** consegnarsi alla polizia **2** *v/i* (*cease habit*) smettere; (*stop making effort*) lasciar perdere

◆ **give way** of bridge etc cedere; MOT dare la precedenza

give-and-'take concessioni *fpl* reciproche

gizmo ['gizməʊ] *Am* aggeggio *m*

glad [glæd] contento; **gladly** volentieri

glamor ['glæmə(r)] *Am* ☞ **glamour; glamorize** esaltare; **glamorous** affascinante; **glamour** fascino *m*

glance [glɑːns] **1** *n* sguardo *m*; **at first ~** a prima vista **2** *v/i* dare un'occhiata *or* uno sguardo

gland [glænd] ghiandola *f*

glare [gleə(r)] **1** *n* of sun, lights luce *f* abbagliante **2** *v/i* of sun, lights splendere di luce abbagliante

◆ **glare at** guardare di storto

glaring ['gleərɪŋ] mistake lampante

glass [glɑːs] material vetro *m*; for drink bicchiere *m*; **glasses** occhiali *mpl*

glazed [gleɪzd] expression assente

gleam [gliːm] **1** *n* luccichio *m* **2** *v/i* luccicare

glee [gliː] allegria *f*; **gleeful** allegro

glib [glɪb] poco convincente; **glibly** in modo poco convincente

glide [glaɪd] of skier, boat scivolare; of bird, plane planare; **glider** aliante *m*; **gliding** SP volo *m* planato

glimpse [glɪmps] **1** *n* occhiata *f*; **catch a ~ of** intravedere **2** *v/t* intravedere

glint [glɪnt] **1** *n* luccichio *m* **2** *v/i* of light, eyes luccicare

glisten ['glɪsn] scintillare

glitter ['glɪtə(r)] brillare

gloat [gləʊt] gongolare

◆ **gloat over** compiacersi di

global ['gləʊbl] (*worldwide*) mondiale; without exceptions globale; **globalization** globalizzazione *f*; **globalize** globalizzare; **global warming** effetto *m* serra; **globe** globo *m*; model of earth mappamondo *m*

gloom [gluːm] (*darkness*) penombra *f*; mood tristezza *f*; **gloomy** room buio; mood, person triste; day grigio

glorious ['glɔːrɪəs] weather, day splendido; victory glorioso; **glory** gloria *f*; (*beauty*) splendore *m*

gloss [glɒs] (*shine*) vernice *f*; **glossary** glossario *m*; **gloss paint** vernice *f* lucida;

glossy 1 adj paper patinato **2** n magazine rivista f su carta patinata

glove [glʌv] guanto m; **glove compartment** cruscotto m

glow [gləʊ] **1** n of light, fire bagliore m; in cheeks colorito m vivo; of candle luce f fioca **2** v/i of light brillare; **her cheeks ~ed** è diventata rossa; **glowing** description entusiastico

glucose ['gluːkəʊs] glucosio m

glue [gluː] **1** n colla f **2** v/t: ~ **sth to sth** incollare qc a qc

glum [glʌm] triste

glut [glʌt] eccesso m

glutton ['glʌtən] ghiottone m, -a f

gnaw [nɔː] bone rosicchiare

go [gəʊ] **1** n (try) tentativo m; **it's my ~** tocca a me; **have a ~ at sth** (try) fare un tentativo in qc; **be on the ~** essere indaffarato; **in one ~** drink, write etc tutto in una volta **2** v/i andare; (leave: of train, plane) partire; (leave: of people) andare via; (work, function) funzionare; (become) diventare; (come out: of stain etc) andare via; (cease: of pain etc) sparire; (match: of colours etc) stare bene insieme; **let's ~!** andiamo!; **how's the work ~ing?** come va il lavoro?; **be all gone** (finished) essere finito; **to ~** Am food da asporto

◆ **go along with** suggestion concordare con

◆ **go away** of person, pain andare via; of rain smettere

◆ **go back** (return) ritornare; (date back) rimontare; **go back to sleep** tornare a dormire

◆ **go by** of car, people, time passare

◆ **go down** scendere; of sun, ship tramontare; of ship affondare; of swelling diminuire

◆ **go in** to room, house entrare; of sun andare via; (fit: of part etc) andare

◆ **go off** v/i (leave) andarsene; of bomb esplodere; of gun sparare; of alarm scattare; of light spegnersi; of milk etc andare a male **2** v/t (stop liking) stufarsi di

◆ **go on** (continue) andare avanti; (happen) succedere

◆ **go out** of person uscire; of light, fire spegnersi

◆ **go out with** romantically uscire con

◆ **go over** (check) esaminare

◆ **go through** hard times passare; (check) controllare; (read through) leggere

◆ **go under** (sink) affondare; of company fallire

◆ **go up** salire

◆ **go without 1** v/t food etc fare a meno di **2** v/i farne a meno

'go-ahead 1 n via libera m;

get the ~ avere il via libera **2** *adj* (*enterprising, dynamic*) intraprendente

goal [gəʊl] (*sport: target*) rete *f*; (*sport: points*) gol *m inv*; (*objective*) obiettivo *m*; **goalie F** portiere *m*; **goalkeeper** portiere *m*; **goal kick** rimessa *f*; **goalpost** palo *m*

goat [gəʊt] capra *f*

gobble ['gɒbl] tranguiare

gobbledygook ['gɒbldɪguːk] F linguaggio *m* incomprensibile

'**go-between** mediatore *m*, -trice *f*

god [gɒd] dio *m*; **thank God!** grazie a Dio!; **godchild** figlioccio *m*, -a *f*; **goddess** dea *f*; **godfather** *also in mafia* padrino *m*; **godmother** madrina *f*

gofer ['gəʊfə(r)] F galoppino *m*, -a *f* F

goggles ['gɒglz] occhialini *mpl*

goings-on [gəʊɪŋz'ɒn] vicende *fpl*

gold [gəʊld] **1** *n* oro *m* **2** *adj* d'oro; **golden** dorato; **golden wedding** (*anniversary*) nozze *fpl* d'oro; **goldfish** pesce *m* rosso; **gold mine** *fig* miniera *f* d'oro; **golf** [gɒlf] golf *m*; **golf ball** palla *f* da golf; **golf club** *organization* club *m inv* di golf; *stick* mazza *f* da golf; **golf course** campo *m* di golf; **golfer** giocatore *m*, -trice

di golf

gondola ['gɒndələ] gondola *f*; **gondolier** gondoliere *m*

good [gʊd] **1** *adj* buono; *weather, film* bello; *actor, child* bravo; **a ~ many** un bel po (di); **be ~ at** essere bravo in; **be ~ for s.o.** fare bene a qu; **be ~ for sth** andare bene per qu; **~! **bene!; *it's* **~ to see you** è bello vederti **2** *n* bene *m*; **it did him no ~** non gli ha fatto bene; **goodbye** arrivederci; **say ~ to s.o.** salutare qu; **good-for--nothing** buono *m*, -a *f* a nulla; **Good Friday** venerdì *m inv* santo; **good-humoured,** *Am* **good-humored** di buon umore; **good-looking** attraente; **good-natured** di buon cuore; **goodness** bontà *f*; **thank ~!** grazie al cielo; **goods** COM merce *fsg*; **goodwill** buona volontà *f*

goof [gu:f] F fare una gaffe

goose [gu:s] (*pl* **geese** [gi:s]) oca *f*; **gooseberry** uva *f* spina; **goose bumps** pelle *f* d'oca

gorgeous ['gɔːdʒəs] stupendo; *smell* ottimo

gorilla [gə'rɪlə] gorilla *m*

Gospel ['gɒspl] vangelo *m*

gossip ['gɒsɪp] **1** *n* pettegolezzo *m*; *person* pettegolo *m*, -a *f* **2** *v/i* spettegolare; **gossip column** cronaca *f* rosa

gourmet ['gʊəmeɪ] *n* bungustaio *m*, -a *f*

govern ['gʌvn] governare;
government governo *m*;
governor governatore *m*

gown [gaʊn] *long dress* abito
m lungo; *wedding dress* abito
m da sposa; *of academic,
judge* toga *f*; *of surgeon* camice *m*

grab [græb] afferrare; **~ some
sleep** farsi una dormita

grace [greɪs] *of dancer etc* grazia *f*; *before meals* preghiera *f*
(prima di un pasto); **graceful** aggraziato; **gracious** *person* cortese; *style* elegante

grade [greɪd] **1** *n (quality)*
qualità *f inv*; EDU voto *m* **2**
v/t classificare; **grade crossing** *Am* passaggio *m* a livello; **grade school** *Am* scuola
f elementare

gradient ['greɪdɪənt] pendenza *f*

gradual ['grædʒʊəl] graduale;
gradually gradualmente

graduate ['grædʒʊət] **1** *n* laureato *m*, -a *f* **2** *v/i from university* laurearsi; **graduation**
laurea *f*; *ceremony* cerimonia
f di laurea

graffiti [grə'fiːtiː] graffiti *mpl*

graft [grɑːft] **1** *n* BOT innesto
m; MED trapianto *m*; F *(hard
work)* duro lavoro *m*; *Am* F
corruzione *f* **2** *v/t* BOT innestare; MED trapiantare

grain [greɪn] cereali *mpl*; *seed*
granello *m*; *of rice, wheat*
chicco *m*; *in wood* venatura *f*

gram [græm] grammo *m*

grammar ['græmə(r)] grammatica *f*; **grammar school**
liceo *m*; **grammatical** grammaticale

grand [grænd] **1** *adj* grandioso; F *(very good)* eccezionale
2 *n* F *(£1000)* mille sterline
fpl; **grandchild** nipote *m/f*;
granddaughter nipote *f*;
grandeur grandiosità *f*;
grandfather nonno *m*;
grand jury *Am* gran giurì
m; **grandmother** nonna *f*;
grandparents nonni *mpl*;
grand piano pianoforte *m*
a coda; **grandson** nipote *m*

granite ['grænɪt] granito *m*

granny ['grænɪ] F nonna *f*

grant [grɑːnt] **1** *n money* sussidio *m*; *for university* borsa *f*
di studio **2** *v/t* issa assegnare;
permission concedere; *wish*
esaudire; **take sth for ~ed**
dare qc per scontato; **he
takes his wife for ~ed** considera quello che fa sua moglie come dovuto

granule ['grænjuːl] granello
m

grape [greɪp] acino *m* d'uva;
~s uva *fsg*; **grapefruit** pompelmo *m*; **grapefruit juice**
succo *m* di pompelmo

graph [grɑːf] grafico *m*;
graphic 1 *adj* grafico; *(vivid)*
vivido **2** *n* COMPUT grafico
m; **~s** grafica *f*

♦ **grapple with** ['græpl] attacker lottare con; *problem*

etc essere alle prese con

grasp [grɑ:sp] **1** *n physical* presa *f*; *mental* comprensione *f* **2** *v/t physically, mentally* afferrare

grass [grɑ:s] erba *f*; **grasshopper** cavalletta *f*; **grass roots** *people* massa *f* popolare; **grassy** erboso

grate¹ [greɪt] *n* metal grata *f*

grate² [greɪt] **1** *v/t in cooking* grattugiare **2** *v/i of sounds* stridere

grateful ['greɪtful] grato (*to* a); **gratefully** con gratitudine

gratify ['grætɪfaɪ] soddisfare

grating ['greɪtɪŋ] **1** *n* grata *f* **2** *adj sound, voice* stridente

gratitude ['grætɪtjuːd] gratitudine *f*

grave¹ [greɪv] *n* tomba *f*

grave² [greɪv] *adj* grave

gravel ['grævl] ghiaia *f*

'gravestone lapide *f*; **graveyard** cimitero *m*

gravity ['grævətɪ] PHYS forza *f* di gravità

gravy ['greɪvɪ] sugo *m* della carne

gray *Am* ☞ **grey**

graze¹ [greɪz] *v/i of cow, horse* brucare

graze² [greɪz] **1** *v/t arm etc* graffiare **2** *n* graffio *m*

grease [gri:s] grasso *m*; **greasy** *food, hair* grasso; *hands, plate* unto

great [greɪt] grande; F (*very good*) fantastico; **Great Bri-**tain Gran Bretagna *f*; **greatly** molto; **greatness** grandezza *f*

Greece [gri:s] Grecia *f*

greed [gri:d] avidità *f*; *for food* ingordigia *f*; **greedily** con avidità; *eat* con ingordigia; **greedy** avido; *for food* ingordo

Greek [gri:k] **1** *n* greco *m*, -a *f*; *language* greco *m* **2** *adj* greco

green [gri:n] verde; *environmentally* ecologico; **the Greens** POL i verdi; **green beans** fagiolini *mpl*; **green belt** *zona f verde tutt'intorno ad una città*; **green card** *driving insurance* carta *f* verde; *Am* (*work permit*) permesso *m* di lavoro; **greenhouse** serra *f*; **greenhouse effect** effetto *m* serra; **greens** verdura *f*

greet [gri:t] salutare; **greeting** saluto *m*

grenade [grɪ'neɪd] granata *f*

grey [greɪ] grigio; *hair* bianco; **grey-haired** con i capelli bianchi; **greyhound** levriero *m*

grid [grɪd] grata *f*; *on map* reticolato *m*; **gridiron** *Am* SP campo *m* da calcio; **gridlock** *in traffic* ingorgo *m*

grief [gri:f] dolore *m*; **grief-stricken** addolorato; **grievance** rimostranza *f*; **grieve** essere addolorato (*for* per)

grill [grɪl] **1** *n for cooking* grill *m inv*; *metal frame* griglia *f*;

dish grigliata *f*; *on window* grata *f* **2** *v/t food* fare alla griglia; (*interrogate*) mettere sotto torchio

grille [grɪl] grata *f*

grim [grɪm] cupo; *determination* accanito

grimace ['grɪməs] smorfia *f*

grime [graɪm] sporcizia *f*; **grimy** sudicio

grin [grɪn] **1** *n* sorriso *m* **2** *v/i* sorridere

grind [graɪnd] *coffee, meat* macinare; **~ one's teeth** digrignare i denti

grip [grɪp] **1** *n on rope etc* presa *f* **2** *v/t* afferrare; *of brakes* fare presa su; **be ~ped by sth** *by panic* essere preso da qc; **gripping** avvincente

gristle ['grɪsl] cartilagine *f*

grit [grɪt] **1** *n* (*dirt*) granelli *mpl*; *for roads* sabbia *f* **2** *v/t*: **~ one's teeth** stringere i denti; **gritty** F *book, film etc* realistico

groan [grəʊn] **1** *n* gemito *m* **2** *v/i* gemere

grocer ['grəʊsə(r)] droghiere *m*; **at the ~'s** (*shop*) dal droghiere; **groceries** generi *mpl* alimentari; **grocery store** *Am* drogheria *f*

groggy ['grɒgɪ] F intontito

groin [grɔɪn] ANAT inguine *m*

groom [gru:m] **1** *n for bride* sposo *m*; *for horse* stalliere *m* **2** *v/t horse* strigliare; (*train, prepare*) preparare; **well ~ed** *in appearance* ben curato

groove [gru:v] scanalatura *f*

grope [grəʊp] **1** *v/i in the dark* brancolare **2** *v/t sexually* palpeggiare

gross [grəʊs] (*coarse, vulgar*) volgare; *exaggeration* madornale; FIN lordo

grotty ['grɒtɪ] F *street, flat* squallido; **I feel ~** sto da schifo F

ground [graʊnd] **1** *n* suolo *m*; (*area, for sport*) terreno *m*; (*reason*) motivo *m*, ragione *f*; *Am* ELEC terra *f*; **on the ~** per terra; **on the ~s of** a causa di; *Am* ELEC mettere a terra; **ground floor** pianoterra *m inv*; **grounding** *in subject* basi *fpl*; **groundless** infondato; **ground meat** *Am* carne *f* tritata; **groundwork** lavoro *m* di preparazione

group [gru:p] **1** *n* gruppo *m* **2** *v/t* raggruppare; **groupie** *ragazza che segue un gruppo o cantante rock in tutti i concerti*

grouse [graʊs] F lamentela *f* **2** *v/i* brontolare

grovel ['grɒvl] *fig* umiliarsi

grow [grəʊ] **1** *v/i* crescere; *of number* aumentare; *of business* svilupparsi; **~ old / tired** invecchiare / stancarsi; **~ into sth** diventare qc **2** *v/t flowers* coltivare

◆ **grow up** *of person* crescere; *of city* svilupparsi

growl [graʊl] **1** *n* grugnito *m* **2** *v/i* ringhiare

'grown-up 1 *n* adulto *m*, -a **2** *adj* adulto

growth [grəʊθ] *of person* crescita *f*; *of company* sviluppo *m*; (*increase*) aumento *m*; MED tumore *m*

grudge [grʌdʒ] **1** *n* rancore *m*; **bear s.o. a ~** portare rancore a qu **2** *v/t:* **~ s.o. sth** invidiare qc a qu; **grudging** riluttante; **grudgingly** a malincuore

gruelling, *Am* **grueling** ['gruːəlɪŋ] estenuante

gruff [grʌf] burbero

grumble ['grʌmbl] brontolare; **grumbler** brontolone *m*, -a *f*

grunt [grʌnt] **1** *n* grugnito *m* **2** *v/i* grugnire

guarantee [gærən'tiː] **1** *n* garanzia *f*; **~ period** periodo *m* di garanzia **2** *v/t* garantire; **guarantor** garante *m*

guard [gɑːd] **1** *n* guardia *m*; **be on one's ~ against** stare in guardia contro **2** *v/t* fare la guardia a; **guard dog** cane *m* da guardia; **guarded** *reply* cauto; **guardian** LAW tutore *m*, -trice *f*

guerrilla [gəˈrɪlə] guerrigliero *m*, -a *f*; **guerrilla warfare** guerriglia *f*

guess [ges] **1** *n* supposizione *f* **2** *v/t the answer* indovinare; **I ~ so** suppongo di sì **3** *v/i* indovinare; **guesswork** congettura *f*

guest [gest] ospite *m/f*; **guesthouse** pensione *f*;

guestroom camera *f* degli ospiti

guidance ['gaɪdəns] consigli *mpl*; **guide 1** *n person, book* guida *f* **2** *v/t* guidare; **guidebook** guida *f* turistica; **guided missile** missile *m* guidato; **guide dog** cane *m* per ciechi; **guided tour** visita *f* guidata; **guidelines** direttive *fpl*

guilt [gɪlt] colpa *f*; LAW colpevolezza *f*; **guilty** *also* LAW colpevole; **have a ~ conscience** avere la coscienza sporca

guinea pig ['gɪnɪpɪg] porcellino *m* d'india; *for experiments, fig* cavia *f*

guitar [gɪˈtɑː(r)] chitarra *f*; **guitarist** chitarrista *m/f*

gulf [gʌlf] golfo *m*; *fig* divario *m*

gull [gʌl] *bird* gabbiano *m*

gullet ['gʌlɪt] ANAT esofago *m*

gullible ['gʌlɪbl] credulone

gulp [gʌlp] **1** *n of water* sorso *m*; *of air* boccata *f* **2** *v/i in surprise* deglutire

◆ **gulp down** *drink* ingoiare; *food* trangugiare

gum¹ [gʌm] *in mouth* gengiva *f*

gum² [gʌm] (*glue*) colla *f*; (*chewing gum*) gomma *f*

gun [gʌn] *pistol, revolver, rifle* arma *f* da fuoco; (*cannon*) cannone *m*

◆ **gun down** sparare a morte

'gunfire spari *mpl*; **gunman**

uomo *m* armato; *robber* rapinatore *m*; **gunshot** sparo *m*; **gunshot wound** ferita *f* da arma da fuoco

gurgle ['gɜːgl] *of baby, drain* gorgogliare

guru ['guru] *fig* guru *m inv*

gush [gʌʃ] *of liquid* sgorgare

gust [gʌst] raffica *f*

gusto ['gʌstəʊ]: **with** ~ con slancio

gusty ['gʌstɪ] *of weather* ventoso; ~ **wind** vento a raffiche

gut [gʌt] **1** *n* intestino *m*; F *(stomach)* pancia *f* **2** *v/t* (*destroy*) sventrare; **guts** F *(courage)* fegato *m* F; **gutsy**

F *person* che ha fegato; F *thing to do* che richiede fegato

gutter ['gʌtə(r)] *on pavement* canaletto *m* di scolo; *on roof* grondaia *f*

guy [gaɪ] F tipo *m* F; **hey, you** ~**s** ei, gente

guzzle ['gʌzl] ingozzarsi di

gym [dʒɪm] palestra *f*; *activity* ginnastica *f*; **gymnast** ginnasta *m/f*; **gymnastics** ginnastica *f*

gynaecologist [gaɪnɪ'kɒlədʒɪst] ginecologo *m*, -a *f*; **gynaecology**, *Am* **gynecology** ginecologia *f*

gypsy ['dʒɪpsɪ] zingaro *m*, -a *f*

H

habit ['hæbɪt] abitudine *f*

habitable ['hæbɪtəbl] abitabile; **habitat** habitat *m inv*

habitual [hə'bɪtjʊəl] solito; *smoker, drinker* incallito

hacker ['hækə(r)] COMPUT hacker *m/f inv*

hackneyed ['hæknɪd] trito

haemorrhage ['hemərɪdʒ] **1** *n* emorragia *f* **2** *v/i* avere un'emorragia

haggard ['hægəd] tirato

haggle ['hægl] contrattare

hail [heɪl] grandine *f*

hair [heə(r)] capelli *mpl*; *single* capello *m*; *on body, of animal* pelo *m*; **hairbrush** spazzola *f* per capelli; **haircut** taglio *m*

di capelli; **hairdo** pettinatura *f*; **hairdresser** parrucchiere *m*, -a *f*; **at the** ~**'s** dal parrucchiere; **hairdryer** fon *m inv*; **hairpin** forcina *f*; **hairpin bend** tornante *m*; **hair-raising** terrificante; **hair remover** crema *f* depilatoria; **hair-splitting** pedanteria *f*; **hairstyle** acconciatura *f*; **hairstylist** parrucchiere *m*, -a *f*; **hairy** *arm, animal* peloso; F *(frightening)* preoccupante

half [hɑːf] **1** *n* metà *f inv*, mezzo *m*; ~ **past ten** le dieci e mezza; ~ **an hour** mezz'ora **2** *adj* mezzo **3** *adv* a metà;

half-hearted poco convinto; **half time** SP intervallo *m*; **halfway 1** *adj* stage, point intermedio **2** *adv also fig* a metà strada; ~ **finished** fatto a metà

hall [hɔːl] *large room* sala *f*; *hallway in house* ingresso *m*

Hallowe'en [hæləʊˈiːn] vigilia *f* d'Ognissanti

halo [ˈheɪləʊ] aureola *f*

halt [hɔːlt] **1** *v/i* fermarsi **2** *v/t* fermare

halve [hɑːv] dimezzare

ham [hæm] prosciutto *m*; **hamburger** hamburger *m inv*

hammer [ˈhæmə(r)] **1** *n* martello *m* **2** *v/i* martellare; ~ **at the door** picchiare alla porta

hammock [ˈhæmək] amaca *f*

hamper[1] [ˈhæmpə(r)] *n for food* cestino *m*

hamper[2] [ˈhæmpə(r)] *v/t (obstruct)* ostacolare

hamster [ˈhæmstə(r)] criceto *m*

hand [hænd] *n* mano *m*; *of clock* lancetta *f*; *(worker)* operaio *m*; **at** ~, **to** ~ a portata di mano; **by** ~ a mano; **on the one** ~ ..., **on the other** ~ ... da un lato ..., dall'altro ...; **in** ~ *(being done)* in corso; **on your right** ~ sulla tua destra; **change** ~**s** cambiare di mano; **give s.o. a** ~ dare una mano a qu

◆ **hand down** passare

◆ **hand out** distribuire

◆ **hand over** consegnare; *child to parent etc* dare

handbag borsetta *f*; **hand baggage** bagaglio *m* a mano; **handbrake** freno *m* a mano; **handcuff** ammanettare; **handcuffs** manette *fpl*; **handheld** COMPUT palmare *m*, PDA *m inv*

handicap [ˈhændɪkæp] handicap *m inv*; **handicapped** handicappato

handkerchief [ˈhæŋkəʧɪf] fazzoletto *m*

handle [ˈhændl] **1** *n* maniglia *f* **2** *v/t goods* maneggiare; *case, deal* trattare; *difficult person* prendere; **let me~ this** lascia fare a me; **handlebars** manubrio *msg*

hand luggage bagaglio *m* a mano; **handmade** fatto a mano; **hands-free** vivavoce *m inv*; **handshake** stretta *f* di mano; **hands-off** *approach* teorico; **he has a~ style of management** non partecipa direttamente agli aspetti pratici della gestione

handsome [ˈhænsəm] bello

hands-'on *experience* pratico; **he has a~ style of management** partecipa direttamente agli aspetti pratici della gestione

handwriting calligrafia *f*; **handwritten** scritto a mano; **handy** *tool, device* pratico; **it's~ for the shops** è comodo per i negozi

hang [hæŋ] **1** *v/t picture* appendere; *person* impiccare **2** *v/i of dress, hair* cadere **3** *n*: **get the ~ of F** capire

◆ **hang on** (*wait*) aspettare

◆ **hang up** TELEC riattaccare

hangar ['hæŋə(r)] hangar *m inv*

hanger ['hæŋə(r)] *for clothes* gruccia *f*

hang glider ['hæŋglaɪdə(r)] deltaplano *m*; **hang gliding** deltaplano *m*; **hangover** postumi *mpl* della sbornia

hankie, hanky ['hæŋkɪ] F fazzoletto *m*

haphazard [hæp'hæzəd] a casaccio

happen ['hæpn] succedere

happily ['hæpɪlɪ] allegramente; (*gladly*) volentieri; (*luckily*) per fortuna; **happiness** felicità *f*; **happy** felice; **happy-go-lucky** spensierato

harass [hə'ræs] tormentare; *sexually* molestare; **harassed** stressato; **harassment** persecuzione *f*; **sexual ~** molestie *fpl* sessuali

harbour, *Am* **harbor** ['hɑːbə(r)] **1** *n* porto *m* **2** *v/t criminal* dar rifugio a; *grudge* covare

hard [hɑːd] **1** *adj* duro; (*difficult*) difficile; *facts, evidence* concreto; *drug* pesante; **~ of hearing** duro d'orecchio **2** *adv work* con impegno; *rain, pull, push* forte; **try ~**

impegnarsi; **hardback** libro *m* con copertina rigida; **hard-boiled** *egg* sodo; **hard copy** copia *f* stampata; **hard core** *pornography* pornografia *f* hard-core; **hard currency** valuta *f* forte; **hard disk** disco *m* rigido, hard disk *m inv*; **harden 1** *v/t* indurire **2** *v/i of glue* indurirsi; *of attitude* irrigidirsi; **hard hat** casco *m*; (*construction worker*) muratore *m*; **hardheaded** pratico; **hardhearted** dal cuore duro; **hard line** linea *f* dura; **hardliner** sostenitore *m*, -trice *f* della linea dura

hardly ['hɑːdlɪ] a malapena; **~ ever** quasi mai; **you can ~ expect him to …** non puoi certo aspettarti che lui …

hardness ['hɑːdnɪs] durezza *f*; (*difficulty*) difficoltà *f*; **hardship** difficoltà *fpl* economiche; **hard up** al verde; **hardware** ferramenta *fpl*; COMPUT hardware *m*; **hardware store** negozio *m* di ferramenta; **hard-working** che lavora duro; **hardy** resistente

harm [hɑːm] **1** *n* danno *m* **2** *v/t* danneggiare; **harmful** dannoso; **harmless** innocuo

harmonious [hɑː'məʊnɪəs] armonioso; **harmonize** armonizzare; **harmony** armonia *f*

harp [hɑːp] arpa *f*

harsh [hɑːʃ] *criticism, words*

duro; *colour, light* troppo forte; **harshly** duramente

harvest ['hɑːvɪst] raccolto *m*

hashtag ['hæʃtæg] COMPUT hashtag *m*, cancelletto *m*

haste [heɪst] fretta *f*; **hastily** in fretta; **hasty** frettoloso

hat [hæt] cappello *m*

hatch [hætʃ] *for serving food* passavivande *m inv*; *on ship* boccaporto *m*

◆ **hatch out** *of eggs* schiudersi

hatchet ['hætʃɪt] ascia *f*; **bury the ~** seppellire l'ascia di guerra

hate [heɪt] **1** *n* odio *m* **2** *v/t* odiare; **hatred** odio *m*

haughty ['hɔːtɪ] altezzoso

haul [hɔːl] **1** *n of fish* pescata *f* **2** *v/t (pull)* trascinare; **haulage** autotrasporto *m*

haunch [hɔːntʃ] anca *f*

haunt [hɔːnt] **1** *v/t:* **this place is ~ed** qui c'è un fantasma / ci sono i fantasmi **2** *n* ritrovo *m*

have [hæv] **1** *v/t* ◇ avere; *breakfast, shower* fare; **I'll ~ a coffee** prendo un caffè; **~ lunch / dinner** pranzare / cenare ◇ *must:* **~ (got) to** dovere; **I ~ (got) to go** devo andare ◇ *causative:* **I had the printer fixed** ho fatto riparare la stampante **2** *v/aux* avere; *with verbs of motion* essere; **~ you seen her?** l'hai vista? / **I ~ come** sono venuto

◆ **have on** *(wear)* portare, indossare; *do you have anything on tonight? (have planned)* hai programmi per stasera?

haven ['heɪvn] *fig* oasi *f inv*

hawk [hɔːk] *also fig* falco *m*

hay [heɪ] fieno *m*; **hay fever** raffreddore *m* da fieno

hazard ['hæzəd] *n* rischio *m*; **hazard lights** MOT luci *fpl* di emergenza; **hazardous** rischioso

haze [heɪz] foschia *f*

hazelnut ['heɪzlnʌt] nocciola *f*

hazy ['heɪzɪ] *view* indistinto; *memories* vago

he [hiː] lui; **~'s French** è francese; **there ~ is** eccolo

head [hed] **1** *n* testa *f*; *of (boss, leader)* capo *m*; *of primary school* direttore *m*, -trice *f*; *of secondary school* preside *m/f*; *on beer* schiuma *f*; **~s or tails?** testa o croce?; **at the ~ of the list** in cima alla lista *f*; *of (lead)* essere a capo di; *ball* colpire di testa

◆ **head for** *place* dirigersi verso; *(be destined for)* andare incontro a

'headache mal *m* di testa; **headband** fascia *f* per i capelli; **header** *in soccer* colpo *m* di testa; *in document* intestazione *f*; **headhunter** COM cacciatore *m* di teste; **heading** *in list* titolo *m*; **headlamp** fanale *m*; **headline** *in* *newspaper* titolo *m*; **make the ~s** fare titolo; headmaster *in primary school* direttore *m*; *in secondary school* preside *m*; **headmistress** *in primary school* direttrice *f*; *in secondary school* preside *f*; **head office** *of company* sede *f* centrale; **head-on 1** *adv crash* frontalmente **2** *adj crash* frontale; **headphones** cuffie *fpl*; **headquarters** sede *fsg*; MIL quartiere *msg* generale; **headrest** poggiatesta *m inv*; **headroom** *for vehicle under bridge* altezza *f* utile; *in car* altezza *f* dell'abitacolo; **headscarf** foulard *m inv*; **headstrong** testardo; **head waiter** capocameriere *m*; **heady** *wine* es inebriante

heal [hiːl] guarire

health [helθ] salute *f*; *(public ~)* sanità *f*; **your ~!** (alla) salute!; **health care** assistenza *f* sanitaria; **health food** alimenti *mpl* naturali; **health food store** negozio *m* di alimenti naturali; **health insurance** assicurazione *f* contro le malattie; **health resort** stazione *f* termale; **healthy** *also fig* sano

heap [hiːp] *n* mucchio *m*

hear [hɪə(r)] sentire

◆ **hear from** *(have news from)* avere notizie di

hearing ['hɪərɪŋ] udito *m*; LAW udienza *f*; **be within / out of**

~ essere / non essere a portata di voce; **hearing aid** apparecchio *m* acustico

hearse [hɜːs] carro *m* funebre

heart [hɑːt] cuore *m*; *of problem etc* nocciolo *m*; **know sth by ~** sapere qc a memoria; **heart attack** infarto *m*; **heartbreaking** straziante; **heartbroken** affranto; **heartburn** bruciore *m* di stomaco; **heart failure** infarto *m*

hearth [hɑːθ] focolare *m*

heartless ['hɑːtlɪs] spietato; **heart throb** F idolo *m*; **hearty** *appetite* robusto; *meal* sostanzioso; *person* gioviale

heat [hiːt] calore *m*; *(hot weather)* caldo *m*

◆ **heat up** riscaldare

heated ['hiːtɪd] *pool* riscaldato; *discussion* animato; **heater** *radiator* termosifone *m*; *electric, gas* stufa *f*; *in car* riscaldamento *m*; **heating** riscaldamento *m*; **heatproof, heat-resistant** termoresistente; **heatwave** ondata *f* di caldo

heave [hiːv] *(lift)* sollevare

heaven ['hevn] paradiso *m*; **good ~s!** santo cielo!; **heavenly** F divino

heavy ['hevɪ] pesante; *cold, rain, accent* forte; *traffic* intenso; *food* pesante; *smoker* accanito; *drinker* forte; *loss, casualties* ingente; **heavy-duty** resistente; **heavy-**

weight SP di pesi massimi

hectic ['hektɪk] frenetico

hedge [hedʒ] siepe f; **hedgehog** riccio m

heel [hiːl] of foot tallone m,
calcagno m; of shoe tacco
m; **heel bar** calzoleria f
istantanea

hefty ['heftɪ] massiccio

height [haɪt] altezza f; of aeroplane altitudine f; **at the ~
of summer** nel pieno dell'e-
state; **heighten** effect, tension aumentare

heir [eə(r)] erede m; **heiress**
ereditiera f

helicopter ['helɪkɒptə(r)] elicottero m

hell [hel] inferno m; **what the
~ are you doing** F che diavolo fai? F; **go to..!** F va' all'inferno! F

hello [hə'ləʊ] informal ciao;
more formal buongiorno;
buona sera; TELEC pronto;
say ~ to s.o. salutare qu

helmet ['helmɪt] of motorcyclist casco m; of soldier elmetto m

help [help] 1 n aiuto m 2 v/t
aiutare; **~ o.s.** to food servir-
si; **I can't ~ it** non ci posso far
niente; **helper** aiutante m/f;
helpful person di aiuto; advice utile; **he was very ~**
mi è stato di grande aiuto;
helping of food porzione f;
helpless (unable to cope) indifeso; (powerless) impotente; **helplessness** impotenza

f; **help menu** COMPUT menu
m inv della guida in linea

hem [hem] of dress etc orlo m

hemisphere   ['hemɪsfɪə(r)]
emisfero m

'hemline orlo m

hemorrhage Am ☞ **haemor-
rhage**

hen [hen] gallina f

'hen party equivalente al femminile della festa d'addio al
celibato

hepatitis [hepə'taɪtɪs] epatite
f

her [hɜː(r)] 1 adj il suo m, la
sua f; i suoi mpl, le sue fpl;
~ sister / brother sua sorella / suo fratello 2 pron direct
object la; indirect object le; after prep lei; **I know ~** la conosco; **I gave ~ the keys** le ho
dato le chiavi; **this is for ~**
questo è per lei; **who? - ~**
chi? - lei

herb [hɜːb] for medicines erba
f medicinale; for flavouring
erba f aromatica; **herb(al)
tea** tisana f

herd [hɜːd] mandria f

here [hɪə(r)] qui, qua; **~'s to
you!** as toast salute!; **~ you
are** giving sth ecco qui

hereditary [hɪ'redɪtərɪ] ereditario; **heredity** ereditarietà f
inv; **heritage** patrimonio m

hernia ['hɜːnɪə] MED ernia f

hero ['hɪərəʊ] eroe m; **heroic**
eroico; **heroically** eroica-
mente

heroin ['herəʊɪn] eroina f

heroine ['herəʊɪn] eroina f

heroism ['herəʊɪzm] eroismo m

herpes ['hɜːpiːz] MED herpes m

hers [hɜːz] il suo m, la sua f, i suoi mpl, le sue fpl; *a friend of ~* un suo amico

herself [hɜː'self] *reflexive* si; *emphatic* se stessa; *after prep* sé, se stessa; *she hurt ~* si è fatta male

hesitant ['hezɪtənt] esitante; **hesitantly** con esitazione; **hesitate** esitare; **hesitation** esitazione f

heterosexual [hetərəʊ'seksjʊəl] eterosessuale

hi [haɪ] ciao

hibernate ['haɪbəneɪt] andare in letargo

hiccup ['hɪkʌp] singhiozzo m; *(minor problem)* intoppo m

hidden ['hɪdn] nascosto

hide[1] ['haɪd] **1** *v/t* nascondere **2** *v/i* nascondersi

hide[2] [haɪd] n *of animal* pelle f

hide-and-'seek nascondino m; **hideaway** rifugio m

hideous ['hɪdɪəs] orrendo; *crime* atroce

hiding ['haɪdɪŋ] *(beating)* batosta f; **hiding place** nascondiglio m

hierarchy ['haɪərɑːkɪ] gerarchia f

high [haɪ] **1** *adj* alto; *wind, speed* forte; *quality, hopes* buono; *(on drugs)* fatto **F 2** *n in statistics* livello m record **3** *adv* in alto; **highbrow** intellettuale; **highchair** seggiolone m; **highclass** di (prima) classe; **High Court** Corte f Suprema; **high-frequency** ad alta frequenza; **high-grade** di buona qualità; **high-handed** autoritario; **high-heeled** col tacco alto; **high jump** salto m in alto; **high-level** ad alto livello; **highlight 1** n *(main event)* clou m *inv*; *in hair* colpo m di sole **2** *v/t with pen* evidenziare; COMPUT selezionare; **highlighter** evidenziatore m; **highly** *desirable, likely* molto; *paid* profumatamente; *think ~ of s.o.* stimare molto qu; **highly strung** nervoso; **high performance** *drill, battery* ad alto rendimento; **high-pitched** acuto; **high point** clou m *inv*; **high-powered** *engine* potente; *intellectual* di prestigio; **high-pressure** TECH ad alta pressione; *salesman* aggressivo; **high pressure** *weather* area di bassa pressione f; **high school** scuola f superiore; **high street** via f principale; **high tech 1** *n* high-tech m **2** *adj* high tech; **highway** Am autostrada f

hijack ['haɪdʒæk] **1** *v/t* dirottare **2** *n* dirottamento m; **hijacker** dirottatore m, -trice f

hike[1] [haɪk] **1** *n* camminata f **2** *v/i* fare camminate

hike² [haɪk] *n in prices* aumento *m*

hiker ['haɪkə(r)] escursionista *m/f*; **hiking** escursionismo *m*

hilarious [hɪ'leərɪəs] divertentissimo

hill [hɪl] collina *f*; *(slope)* altura *f*; **hillside** pendio *m*; **hilltop** cima *f* della collina; **hilly** collinoso

hilt [hɪlt] impugnatura *f*

him [hɪm] *direct object* lo; *indirect object* gli; *after prep* lui; **I know ~** lo conosco; **I gave ~ the keys** gli ho dato le chiavi; **this is for ~** questo è per lui; **who? – ~** chi? – lui

himself [hɪm'self] se stesso; *after prep* sé, se stesso; **he hurt ~** si è fatto male

hinder ['hɪndə(r)] intralciare; **hindrance** intralcio *m*

hinge [hɪndʒ] cardine *m*

hint [hɪnt] *(clue)* accenno *m*; *(piece of advice)* consiglio *m*; *(implied suggestion)* allusione *f*; *of red, sadness etc* punta *f*

hip [hɪp] fianco *m*; **hip pocket** tasca *f* posteriore

hippopotamus [hɪpə'pɒtəməs] ippopotamo *m*

hire ['haɪə(r)] *room, hall* affittare; *workers, staff* assumere; *conjuror etc* ingaggiare; *hire car* macchina *f* a noleggio; **hire purchase** acquisto *m* rateale

his [hɪz] **1** *adj* il suo *m*, la sua *f*, i suoi *mpl*, le sue *fpl*; **~ sis-**

ter / **brother** sua sorella / suo fratello **2** *pron* il suo *m*, la sua *f*, i suoi *mpl*, le sue *fpl*; **a friend of ~** un suo amico

hiss [hɪs] sibilare

historian [hɪ'stɔːrɪən] storico *m*, -a *f*; **historic** storico; **historical** storico; **history** storia *f*

hit [hɪt] **1** *v/t* colpire; *(collide with)* sbattere contro; **I ~ my knee** ho battuto il ginocchio; **it suddenly ~ me** *(realized)* improvvisamente ho realizzato **2** *n (blow)* colpo *m*; *(success)* successo *m*; *on website* visita *f*
♦ **hit out at** *(criticize)* attaccare

hitch [hɪtʃ] **1** *n (problem)* contrattempo *m* **2** *v/t:* **~ sth to sth** legare qc a qc; **~ a lift** chiedere un passaggio **3** *v/i (hitchhike)* fare l'autostop; **hitchhike** fare l'autostop; **hitchhiker** autostoppista *m/f*; **hitchhiking** autostop *m*

HIV [eɪtʃaɪ'viː] *(= human immunodeficiency virus)* HIV *m*

hive [haɪv] *for bees* alveare *m*

HIV-'positive sieropositivo

hoard [hɔːd] **1** *n* provvista *f*;

hilt

historian

hi-'tech [hɪ] **1** *n* high-tech **2** *adj* high tech

'hitlist libro *m* nero; **hitman** sicario *m*; **hit-or-miss:** *on a* **~ basis** affidandosi al caso; **hit squad** commando *m*

of money gruzzolo *m* **2** *v/t* accumulare; **hoarding** tabellone *m* per affissioni pubblicitarie

hoarse ['hɔːs] rauco

hoax [həʊks] scherzo *m*; *malicious* falso allarme *m*

hobble ['hɒbl] zoppicare

hobby ['hɒbɪ] hobby *m inv*

hobo ['həʊbəʊ] *Am* barbone *m*, -a *f*

hockey ['hɒkɪ] hockey *m* (su prato); *Am* hockey *m* sul ghiaccio

hog [hɒg] *esp Am* maiale *m*

hoist [hɔɪst] **1** *n* montacarichi *m* inv **2** *v/t* (*lift*) sollevare; *flag* issare

hold [həʊld] **1** *v/t in hand* tenere; (*support, keep in place*) reggere; *passport etc* avere; *prisoner, suspect* trattenere; (*contain*) contenere; *job, post* occupare; *~ hands* tenersi per mano; *~ one's breath* trattenere il fiato; *~ that ...* (*believe, maintain*) sostenere che ...; *~ the line* TELEC resti in linea **2** *n in ship, plane* stiva *f*; *catch* ~ *of sth* afferrare qc; *lose one's* ~ *on sth* *on rope etc* perdere la presa su qc

◆ **hold back 1** *v/t crowds* contenere; *facts* nascondere **2** *v/i* (*hesitate*) esitare

◆ **hold out 1** *v/t hand* tendere; *prospect* offrire **2** *v/i of supplies* durare; (*survive*) resistere

◆ **hold up** *hand* alzare; *bank etc* rapinare; (*make late*) trattenere

holder ['həʊldə(r)] (*container*) contenitore *m*; *of passport* titolare *m*; *of ticket* possessore *m*; *of record* detentore *m*, -trice *f*; **holding company** holding *f inv*; **holdup** (*robbery*) rapina *f*; (*delay*) ritardo *m*

hole [həʊl] buco *m*

holiday ['hɒlɪdeɪ] vacanza *f*; *public* giorno *m* festivo; (*day off*) giorno *m* di ferie; *go on* ~ andare in vacanza

Holland ['hɒlənd] Olanda *f*

hollow ['hɒləʊ] cavo, vuoto; *cheeks* infossato

holocaust ['hɒləkɔːst] olocausto *m*

hologram ['hɒləgræm] ologramma *m*

holster ['həʊlstə(r)] fondina *f*

holy ['həʊlɪ] santo; **Holy Spirit** Spirito *m* Santo; **Holy Week** settimana *f* santa

home [həʊm] **1** *n* casa *f*; (*native country*) patria *f*; *for old people* casa *f* di riposo; *for children* istituto *m*; *at* ~ a casa; SP in casa; *make yourself at* ~ fai come a casa tua; *work from* ~ lavorare da casa **2** *adv* andare a casa; *go* ~ andare a casa; *is she* ~ *yet?* è tornata?; *home address* indirizzo *m* di casa; *home banking* home-banking *m*; *homecoming* ritorno *m*; *home*

computer computer *m inv* (per casa); **home game** incontro *m*; **homeless** senza tetto; **the ~** i senzacasa; **homeloving** casalingo; **homely** semplice; (*welcoming*) accogliente; **homemade** fatto in casa, casalingo; **home match** incontro *m* casalingo; **Home Office** Ministero *m* degli Interni; **home page** home page *f*; **Home Secretary** Ministro *m* degli Interni; **homesick**: **be ~** avere nostalgia di casa; **home town** città *f* natale; **homeward** verso casa; **homework** EDU compiti *mpl* a casa

homicide ['hɒmɪsaɪd] *crime* omicidio *m*; *Am: police department* (squadra *f*) omicidi *f*

homophobia [hɒmə'fəʊbɪə] omofobia *f*

homosexual [hɒmə'seksjʊəl] **1** *adj* omosessuale **2** *n* omosessuale *m/f*

honest ['ɒnɪst] onesto; **honestly** onestamente; **~!** ma insomma!; **honesty** onestà *f*

honey ['hʌnɪ] miele *m*; F (*darling*) tesoro *m*; **honeymoon** luna *f* di miele

honk [hɒŋk] *horn* suonare

honor *Am* ☞ **honour**

honour ['ɒnə(r)] **1** *n* onore *m* **2** *v/t* onorare; **honourable** onorevole

hood [hʊd] *over head* cappuc-cio *m*; *over cooker* cappa *f*; MOT *on convertible* capote *f inv*; *Am* MOT cofano *m*

hoodlum ['huːdləm] gangster *m inv*

hook [hʊk] gancio *m*; *for fishing* amo *m*; **off the ~** TELEC staccato; **hooked**: **be ~ on s.o. / sth** essere fanatico di qu / qc; **be ~ on sth** *on drugs* essere assuefatto a qc; **hooker** F prostituta *f*; *in rugby* tallonatore *m*

hooligan ['huːlɪgən] teppista *m/f*; **hooliganism** teppismo *m*

hoot [huːt] **1** *v/t* *horn* suonare **2** *v/i* *of car* suonare il clacson; *of owl* gufare

hop [hɒp] saltare

hope [həʊp] **1** *n* speranza *f* **2** *v/i* sperare; **~ for sth** augurarsi qc; **I ~ so** spero di sì **3** *v/t*: **~ that …** sperare che; **hopeful** ottimista; (*promising*) promettente; **hopefully** *say, wait* con ottimismo; (*I / we hope*) si spera; **hopeless** *position, prospect* senza speranza; (*useless: person*) negato F

horizon [hə'raɪzn] orizzonte *m*; **horizontal** orizzontale

hormone ['hɔːməʊn] ormone *m*

horn [hɔːn] *of animal* corno *m*; MOT clacson *m inv*

hornet ['hɔːnɪt] calabrone *m*

horny ['hɔːnɪ] *Am* F *sexually* arrapato P

horrible ['hɒrɪbl] orribile; **horrify** inorridire; *I was horrified* ero scioccato; **horrifying** *experience* terrificante; *idea, prices* allucinante; **horror** orrore *m*; **the ~s of war** le atrocità della guerra

horse [hɔːs] cavallo *m*; **horse race** corsa *f* di cavalli; **horseshoe** ferro *m* di cavallo

horticulture ['hɔːtɪkʌltʃə(r)] orticoltura *f*

hose [həʊz] tubo *m* di gomma

hospitable [hɒ'spɪtəbl] ospitale

hospital ['hɒspɪtl] ospedale *m*; **hospitality** ospitalità *f*

host [həʊst] *at party, reception* padrone *m* di casa; *of TV programme* presentatore *m*, -trice *f*

hostage ['hɒstɪdʒ] ostaggio *m*; **be taken ~** essere preso in ostaggio; **hostage taker** sequestratore *m*

hostel ['hɒstl] *for students* pensionato *m*; *(youth ~)* ostello *m* (della gioventù)

hostess ['həʊstɪs] *at party, reception* padrona *f* di casa; *on aeroplane* hostess *f inv*

hostile ['hɒstaɪl] ostile; **hostility** ostilità *f inv*

hot [hɒt] *weather, water* caldo; *(spicy)* piccante; F *(good)* bravo (**at sth** in qc); *it's ~* fa caldo; *I'm ~* ho caldo; **hot dog** hot dog *m inv*

hotel [həʊ'tel] albergo *m*

hour ['aʊə(r)] ora *f*

house 1 [haʊs] *n* casa *f*; POL camera *f*; THEA sala *f*; **at your ~** a casa tua, da te **2** [haʊz] *v/t* alloggiare; **housebreaking** furto *m* con scasso; **household** famiglia *f*; **household name** nome *m* conosciuto; **housekeeper** governante *f*; **House of Representatives** la camera *f* dei rappresentanti; **housewarming (party)** festa *per* inaugurare la nuova casa; **housewife** casalinga *f*; **housework** lavori *mpl* domestici; **housing** alloggi *mpl*; TECH alloggiamento *m*

hovel ['hɒvl] tugurio *m*

hover ['hɒvə(r)] librarsi

how [haʊ] come; **~ are you?** come stai?; **~ about ...?** che ne dici di ...?; **~ much?** quanto?; **~ much is it?** of *cost* quant'è?; **~ many?** quanti?; **~ odd / lovely!** che strano / bello!; **however** comunque; **~ big they are** per quanto grandi siano

howl [haʊl] *of dog* ululare; *of person in pain* urlare; **~ with laughter** sbellicarsi dalle risate; **howler** *mistake* strafalcione *m*

hub [hʌb] *of wheel* mozzo *m*; **hubcap** coprimozzo *m*

◆ **huddle together** ['hʌdl] stringersi l'un l'altro

hug [hʌɡ] **1** *v/t* abbracciare **2** *n* abbraccio *m* huge [hjuːdʒ] enorme

hull [hʌl] scafo *m*

hum [hʌm] canticchiare; *of machine* ronzare

human ['hjuːmən] **1** *n* essere *m* umano **2** *adj* umano; human being essere *m* umano

humane [hjuː'meɪn] umano

humanitarian [hjuːmænɪ-'teərɪən] umanitario

humanity [hjuː'mænətɪ] umanità *f*; human race genere *m* umano; human resources risorse *fpl* umane

humble ['hʌmbl] umile; *house* modesto

humdrum ['hʌmdrʌm] monotono

humid ['hjuːmɪd] umido; humidifier umidificatore *m*; humidity umidità *f*

humiliate [hjuː'mɪlɪeɪt] umiliare; humiliating umiliante; humiliation umiliazione *f*; humility umiltà *f*

humor *Am* ☞ **humour**

humorous ['hjuːmərəs] *person* spiritoso; *story* umoristico; **humour** umorismo *m*; *(mood)* umore *m*; *sense of ~* senso del'umorismo

hunch [hʌntʃ] *(idea)* impressione *f*; *of detective* intuizione *f*

hundred ['hʌndrəd] cento *m*; *a ~ ...* cento ...; hundredth centesimo

Hungarian [hʌŋ'geərɪən] **1** *adj* ungherese **2** *n person* ungherese *m/f*; *language* ung-

gherese *m*; **Hungary** Ungheria *f*

hunger ['hʌŋgə(r)] fame *f*

hung-'over: *feel ~* avere i postumi della sbornia

hungry ['hʌŋgrɪ] affamato; *I'm ~* ho fame

hunk [hʌŋk] *n* tocco *m*; F *(man)* fusto *m* F

hunt [hʌnt] **1** *n for animals* caccia *f*; *for job, house, missing child* ricerca *f* **2** *v/t animal* cacciare; hunter cacciatore *m*, -trice *f*; hunting caccia *f*

hurdle ['hɜːdl] *also fig* ostacolo *m*

hurl [hɜːl] scagliare

hurray [hʊ'reɪ] urrà!

hurricane ['hʌrɪkən] uragano *m*

hurried ['hʌrɪd] frettoloso; **hurry 1** *n* fretta *f*; *be in a ~* avere fretta **2** *v/i* sbrigarsi

♦ **hurry up 1** *v/i* sbrigarsi; *hurry up!* sbrigati! **2** *v/t* fare fretta a

hurt [hɜːt] **1** *v/i* far male; *does it ~?* ti fa male? **2** *v/t physically* far male a; *emotionally* ferire

husband ['hʌzbənd] marito *m*

hush [hʌʃ] silenzio *m*

♦ **hush up** *scandal etc* mettere a tacere

husky ['hʌskɪ] *voice* roco

hut [hʌt] capanno *m*

hybrid ['haɪbrɪd] ibrido *m*

hydrant ['haɪdrənt] idrante *m*

hydraulic [har'drɔːlɪk] idraulico
hydroelectric [haɪdrəʊ'lek-
trɪk] idroelettrico
hydrogen ['haɪdrədʒən] idro-
geno *m*
hygiene ['haɪdʒiːn] igiene *f*;
hygienic igienico
hymn [hɪm] inno *m* (sacro)
hype [haɪp] pubblicità *f*
hyperactive [haɪpər'æktɪv]
iperattivo; **hypermarket**
ipermercato *m*; **hypersensitive** ipersensibile; **hypertext**
COMPUT ipertesto *m*
hyphen ['haɪfn] trattino *m*
hypnosis [hɪp'nəʊsɪs] ipnosi

f; **hypnotize** ipnotizzare
hypocrisy [hɪ'pɒkrəsɪ] ipocrisia *f*; **hypocrite** ipocrita *m/f*;
hypocritical ipocrita
hypothermia [haɪpəʊ'θɜːmɪə]
ipotermia *f*
hypothesis [haɪ'pɒθəsɪs] ipotesi *f inv*; **hypothetical** ipotetico
hysterectomy [hɪstə'rektə-
mɪ] isterectomia *f*
hysteria [hɪ'stɪərɪə] isteria *f*;
hysterical isterico; F (*very
funny*) buffissimo; **become**
~ avere una crisi isterica;
hysterics *laughter* attacco
m di risa; MED crisi *f* isterica

I

I [aɪ] io; ~ **am English** sono inglese; *here* ~ *am* eccomi
ice [aɪs] ghiaccio *m*; **iceberg**
iceberg *m inv*; **icebox** Am
frigo *m*; **ice cream** gelato
m; **ice cube** cubetto *m* di
ghiaccio; **iced** *drink* ghiacciato; *cake* glassato; **ice
hockey** hockey *m* sul ghiaccio; **ice lolly** ghiacciolo *m*;
ice rink pista *f* di pattinaggio; **ice skate** pattinare
(sul ghiaccio); **ice skating**
pattinaggio *m* (sul ghiaccio)
icicle ['aɪsɪkl] ghiacciolo *m*
icing ['aɪsɪŋ] glassa *f*
icon ['aɪkɒn] *cultural* mito *m*;
COMPUT icona *f*
icy ['aɪsɪ] *road, surface* ghiac-

ciato; *welcome* glaciale
ID [aɪ'diː] (= *identity*): *have
you got any* ~ *on you?* ha
un documento d'identità?
idea [aɪ'dɪə] idea *f*; *good* ~*!*
ottima idea!; *I have no* ~
non ne ho la minima idea;
ideal ideale; **idealistic** *person* idealista; *views* idealisti-
co
identical [aɪ'dentɪkl] identico;
~ *twins* gemelli *mpl* monozi-
gotici; **identification** identifi-
cazione *f*, riconoscimento
m; *papers etc* documento
m di riconoscimento *or* d'identità; **identify** (*recognize*)
identificare, riconoscere;
(*point out*) individuare;

identity identità f *inv*; ~ *card* carta f d'identità

ideological [aɪdɪə'lɒdʒɪkl] ideologico; ideology ideologia f

idiomatic [ɪdɪə'mætɪk] naturale

idiot ['ɪdɪət] idiota m/f; idiotic idiota

idle ['aɪdl] **1** *adj person* disoccupato; *threat* vuoto; *machinery* inattivo **2** *v/i of engine* girare al minimo

idol ['aɪdl] idolo m; idolize idolatrare

idyllic [ɪ'dɪlɪk] idilli(a)co

if [ɪf] se

ignite [ɪg'naɪt] dar fuoco a; ignition *in car* accensione f; ~ *key* chiave f dell'accensione

ignorance ['ɪgnərəns] ignoranza f; ignorant (*rude*) cafone; *be* ~ *of sth* ignorare qc; ignore ignorare

ill [ɪl] ammalato; *fall* ~, *be taken* ~ ammalarsi; *feel* ~ sentirsi male

illegal [ɪ'liːgl] illegale

illegible [ɪ'ledʒəbl] illeggibile

illegitimate [ɪlɪ'dʒɪtɪmət] *child* illegittimo

illicit [ɪ'lɪsɪt] *copy*, *imports* illegale; *pleasure*, *relationship* illecito

illiterate [ɪ'lɪtərət] analfabeta

illness ['ɪlnɪs] malattia f

illogical [ɪ'lɒdʒɪkl] illogico

ill'treat maltrattare

illuminating [ɪ'luːmɪneɪtɪŋ] *remarks etc* chiarificatore

illusion [ɪ'luːʒn] illusione f

illustrate ['ɪləstreɪt] illustrare; illustration illustrazione f; *with examples* esemplificazione f; illustrator illustratore m, -trice f

image ['ɪmɪdʒ] immagine f; (*exact likeness*) ritratto; image-conscious attento all'immagine

imaginary [ɪ'mædʒɪnərɪ] immaginario; imagination immaginazione f, fantasia f; imaginative fantasioso; imagine immaginare; *you're imagining things* è frutto della tua immaginazione

IMF [aɪem'ef] (= *International Monetary Fund*) FMI m (= Fondo m Monetario Internazionale)

imitate ['ɪmɪteɪt] imitare; imitation imitazione f

immaculate [ɪ'mækjʊlət] immacolato

immature [ɪmə'tʃʊə(r)] immaturo

immediate [ɪ'miːdɪət] immediato; *the* ~ *family* i familiari più stretti; immediately immediatamente; ~ *after the bank* subito dopo la banca

immense [ɪ'mens] immenso

immerse [ɪ'mɜːs] immergere

immigrant [ɪ'mɪgrənt] immigrato m, -a f; immigrate immigrare; immigration immigrazione f

imminent ['ɪmɪnənt] imminente

immobilize [ɪˈməʊbɪlaɪz] im-mobilizzare; **immobilizer** *on car* immobilizzatore *m*

immoderate [ɪˈmɒdərət] smoderato

immoral [ɪˈmɒrəl] immorale; **immorality** immoralità *f inv*

immortal [ɪˈmɔːtl] immortale; **immortality** immortalità *f*

immune [ɪˈmjuːn] *to illness, infection* immune; *from ruling, requirement* esente; **immune system** MED sistema *m* immunitario; **immunity** immunità *f inv*; *from ruling* esenzione *f*

impact [ˈɪmpækt] *of meteorite, vehicle* urto *m*; *of new manager etc* impatto *m*; *(effect)* effetto *m*

impair [ɪmˈpeə(r)] danneggiare

impartial [ɪmˈpɑːʃl] imparziale

impassable [ɪmˈpɑːsəbl] *road* impraticabile

impassioned [ɪmˈpæʃnd] *speech, plea* appassionato

impatience [ɪmˈpeɪʃəns] impazienza *f*; **impatient** impaziente; **impatiently** con impazienza

impeach [ɪmˈpiːtʃ] *President* mettere in stato d'accusa

impeccable [ɪmˈpekəbl] impeccabile

impede [ɪmˈpiːd] ostacolare; **impediment** *in speech* difetto *m*

impending [ɪmˈpendɪŋ] im-minente

imperative [ɪmˈperətɪv] **1** *adj* essenziale **2** *n* GRAM imperativo *m*

imperfect [ɪmˈpɜːfekt] **1** *adj* imperfetto **2** *n* GRAM imperfetto *m*

impersonal [ɪmˈpɜːsənl] impersonale; **impersonate** *as a joke* imitare; *illegally* fingersi

impertinence [ɪmˈpɜːtɪnəns] impertinenza *f*; **impertinent** impertinente

impervious [ɪmˈpɜːvɪəs]: **~ to** indifferente a

impetuous [ɪmˈpetjʊəs] impetuoso

impetus [ˈɪmpɪtəs] *of campaign etc* impeto *m*

implement [ˈɪmplɪmənt] **1** *n* utensile *m* **2** *v/t* implementare

implicate [ˈɪmplɪkeɪt] implicare; **implication** conseguenza *f* possibile; **by ~** implicitamente

implicit [ɪmˈplɪsɪt] implicito; *trust* assoluto

implore [ɪmˈplɔː(r)] implorare

imply [ɪmˈplaɪ] implicare; *(suggest)* insinuare

impolite [ɪmpəˈlaɪt] maleducato

import [ˈɪmpɔːt] **1** *n* importazione *f*; *item* articolo *m* d'importazione **2** *v/t* importare

importance [ɪmˈpɔːtəns] importanza *f*; **important** importante

inborn

importer [ɪm'pɔːtə(r)] importatore *m*, -trice *f*

impose [ɪm'pəʊz] *tax* imporre; ~ **o.s. on s.o.** disturbare qu; **imposing** imponente

impossibility [ɪmpɒsɪ'bɪlɪtɪ] impossibilità *f inv*; **impossible** impossibile

impotence [ɪm'pres] impotenza *f*; **impotent** impotente

impractical [ɪm'præktɪkəl] *person* senza senso pratico; *suggestion* poco pratico

impress [ɪm'pres] fare colpo su; **be ~ed by s.o.** / **sth** essere colpito da qu / qc; **impression** impressione *f*; (*impersonation*) imitazione *f*; **impressionable** impressionabile; **impressive** notevole

imprint [ɪmprɪnt] *of credit card* impressione *f*

imprison [ɪm'prɪzn] incarcerare; **imprisonment** carcerazione *f*

improbable [ɪm'prɒbəbəl] improbabile

improve [ɪm'pruːv] migliorare; **improvement** miglioramento *m*

improvise ['ɪmprəvaɪz] improvvisare

impudent ['ɪmpjʊdənt] impudente

impulse ['ɪmpʌls] impulso *m*; **do sth on an ~** fare qc d'impulso; **impulsive** impulsivo

in [ɪn] **1** *prep* ◇ *place*: ~ **Milan** a Milano; ~ **the street** per strada; ~ **the box** nella scato-

la; **wounded ~ the leg** ferito alla gamba ◇ *time*: ~ **1999** nel 1999; ~ **two hours** *from now* tra due ore; *over period of* in due ore; ~ **the morning** la mattina; ~ **the summer** d'estate; ~ **September** a *or* in settembre ◇ *manner*: ~ **English** in inglese; ~ **a loud voice** a voce alta; ~ **yellow** di giallo ◇ (*while*): ~ **crossing the road** mentre attraversava la strada ◇: **one ~ ten** uno su dieci **2** *adv*: **be ~** *at home* essere a casa; *in the building etc* esserci; *arrived: of train* essere arrivato; *in its position* essere dentro; **is she ~?** c'è?; ~ **here** / **there** qui / lì (dentro) **3** *adj* (*fashionable, popular*) in, di moda

inability [ɪnə'bɪlɪtɪ] incapacità *f inv*

inaccurate [ɪn'ækjʊrət] inaccurato

inactive [ɪn'æktɪv] inattivo

inadequate [ɪn'ædɪkwət] inadeguato

inadvisable [ɪnəd'vaɪzəbl] sconsigliabile

inanimate [ɪn'ænɪmət] inanimato

inappropriate [ɪnə'prəʊprɪət] inappropriato

inaudible [ɪn'ɔːdɪbl] impercettibile

inaugural [ɪ'nɔːgjʊrəl] *speech* inaugurale; **inaugurate** inaugurare

inborn ['ɪnbɔːn] innato

Inc. [ıŋk] (= *incorporated*) Inc.

incalculable [ın'kælkjʊləbl] incalcolabile

incapable [ın'keıpəbl] incapace (*of doing* di fare)

incense ['ınsens] *in church* incenso *m*

incentive [ın'sentıv] incentivo *m*

incessant [ın'sesnt] incessante; **incessantly** incessantemente

incest ['ınsest] incesto *m*

inch [ıntʃ] pollice *m*

incident ['ınsıdənt] incidente *m*; **incidental** casuale; **~ expenses** spese accessorie; **incidentally** a proposito

incision [ın'sıʒn] incisione *f*; **incisive** acuto

incite [ın'saıt] incitare; **~ s.o. to do sth** istigare qu a fare qc

inclination [ınklı'neıʃn] inclinazione *f*

inclose, inclosure ☞ **enclose, enclosure**

include [ın'kluːd] includere, comprendere; **including** compreso, incluso; **inclusive 1** *adj price* tutto compreso **2** *prep:* **~ of VAT** IVA compresa **3** *adv:* **from Monday to Thursday** ~ dal lunedì al giovedì compreso

incoherent [ınkəʊ'hıərnt] incoerente

income ['ınkəm] reddito *m*; **income tax** imposta *f* sul reddito

incoming ['ınkʌmıŋ] *adj flight, phonecall, mail* in arrivo; *tide* montante; *president* entrante

incomparable [ın'kɒmprəbl] incomparabile

incompatibility [ınkəmpætı'bılıtı] incompatibilità *f inv*; **incompatible** incompatibile

incompetence [ın'kɒmpıtəns] incompetenza *f*; **incompetent** incompetente

incomplete [ınkəm'pliːt] incompleto

incomprehensible [ınkɒmprı'hensıbl] incomprensibile

inconceivable [ınkən'siːvəbl] inconcepibile

inconsiderate [ınkən'sıdərət] poco gentile

inconsistent [ınkən'sıstənt] incoerente

inconsolable [ınkən'səʊləbl] *adj* inconsolabile

inconspicuous [ınkən'spıkjʊəs] poco visibile; **make o.s. ~** passare inosservato

inconvenience [ınkən'viːnıəns] inconveniente *m*; **inconvenient** scomodo; *time* poco opportuno

incorporate [ın'kɔːpəreıt] includere

incorrect [ınkə'rekt] *answer* errato; *behaviour* scorretto; **am I ~ in thinking …?** sbaglio a pensare che …?

increase 1 [ın'kriːs] *v/t e v/i* aumentare **2** ['ınkriːs] *n* au-

mento *m*; **on the~** in aumento; **increasing** crescente; **increasingly** sempre più
incredible [ɪnˈkredɪbl] incredibile
incur [ɪnˈkɜː(r)] *costs* affrontare; *debts* contrarre; *s.o.'s anger* esporsi a
incurable [ɪnˈkjʊərəbl] incurabile
indecent [ɪnˈdiːsnt] indecente
indecisive [ɪndɪˈsaɪsɪv] indeciso; **indecisiveness** indecisione *f*
indeed [ɪnˈdiːd] (*in fact*) in effetti; (*yes, agreeing*) esatto; **very much ~** moltissimo
indefinable [ɪndɪˈfaɪnəbl] indefinibile
indefinite [ɪnˈdefɪnɪt] indeterminato; **~ article** GRAM articolo *m* indeterminativo; **indefinitely** a tempo indeterminato
indelicate [ɪnˈdelɪkət] indelicato
independence [ɪndɪˈpendəns] indipendenza *f*; **Independence Day** *in USA* festa *f* dell'indipendenza americana (*4 luglio*); **independent** indipendente; **independently** indipendentemente; **~ of** indipendentemente da
indescribable [ɪndɪˈskraɪbəbl] indescrivibile
index [ˈɪndeks] indice *m*
India [ˈɪndɪə] India *f*; **Indian 1** *adj* indiano **2** *n person* india-

no *m*, -a *f*; *American* indiano *m*, -a *f* d'america
indicate [ˈɪndɪkeɪt] **1** *v/t* indicare **2** *v/i when driving* segnalare (il cambiamento di direzione); **indication** indicazione *f*; **indicator** MOT freccia *f*
indict [ɪnˈdaɪt] incriminare
indifference [ɪnˈdɪfrəns] indifferenza *f*; **indifferent** indifferente; (*mediocre*) mediocre
indigestion [ɪndɪˈdʒestʃn] indigestione *f*
indignant [ɪnˈdɪgnənt] indignato; **indignation** indignazione *f*
indirect [ɪndɪˈrekt] indiretto; **indirectly** indirettamente
indiscreet [ɪndɪˈskriːt] indiscreto
indiscriminate [ɪndɪˈskrɪmɪnət] indiscriminato
indispensable [ɪndɪˈspensəbl] indispensabile
indisposed [ɪndɪˈspəʊzd] (*not well*) indisposto
indisputable [ɪndɪˈspjuːtəbl] indiscutibile
indistinct [ɪndɪˈstɪŋkt] indistinto
indistinguishable [ɪndɪˈstɪŋgwɪʃəbl] indistinguibile
individual [ɪndɪˈvɪdjuəl] **1** *n* individuo *m* **2** *adj* (*separate*) singolo; (*personal*) individuale; **individually** individualmente
indoctrinate [ɪnˈdɒktrɪneɪt]

indottrinare

Indonesia [ɪndə'niːʒə] Indonesia f; **Indonesian 1** adj indonesiano **2** n person indonesiano m, -a f

indoor ['ɪndɔː(r)] activities, games al coperto; arena, pool coperto; **indoors** in building all'interno; at home in casa

indorse ☞ **endorse**

indulgent [ɪn'dʌldʒənt] indulgente

industrial [ɪn'dʌstrɪəl] industriale; **industrial dispute** vertenza f sindacale; **industrialist** industriale m; **industrious** diligente; **industry** industria f

ineffective [ɪnɪ'fektɪv] inefficace

inefficient [ɪnɪ'fɪʃənt] inefficiente

inept [ɪ'nept] inetto

inequality [ɪnɪ'kwɒlɪtɪ] disuguaglianza f

inescapable [ɪnɪ'skeɪpəbl] inevitabile

inevitable [ɪn'evɪtəbl] inevitabile; **inevitably** inevitabilmente

inexcusable [ɪnɪk'skjuːzəbl] imperdonabile

inexhaustible [ɪnɪg'zɔːstəbl] supply inesauribile

inexpensive [ɪnɪk'spensɪv] poco costoso, economico

inexperienced [ɪnɪk'spɪərɪənst] inesperto

inexplicable [ɪnɪk'splɪkəbl] inspiegabile

infallible [ɪn'fælɪbl] infallibile

infamous ['ɪnfəməs] famigerato

infancy ['ɪnfənsɪ] of person infanzia f; of state, institution stadio m iniziale; **infant** bambino m piccolo, bambina f piccola; **infantile** pej infantile

infantry ['ɪnfəntrɪ] fanteria f

infatuated [ɪn'fætʃueɪtɪd]: **be ~ with s.o.** essere infatuato di qu

infect [ɪn'fekt] of person contagiare; food, water contaminare; **become ~ed** of wound infettarsi; of person contagiarsi; **infection** infezione f; **infectious** disease infettivo, contagioso; laughter contagioso

infer [ɪn'fɜː(r)]: **~ sth from sth** dedurre qc da qc

inferior [ɪn'fɪərɪə(r)] inferiore; **inferiority** inferiorità f; **inferiority complex** complesso m d'inferiorità

infertile [ɪn'fɜːtaɪl] sterile; **infertility** sterilità f

infidelity [ɪnfɪ'delɪtɪ] infedeltà f inv

infinite ['ɪnfɪnət] infinito; **infinitive** infinito m

infinity [ɪn'fɪnətɪ] infinito m

inflammable [ɪn'flæməbl] infiammabile; **inflammation** MED infiammazione f

inflatable [ɪn'fleɪtəbl] dinghy gonfiabile; **inflate** tyre, dinghy gonfiare; economy infla-

zionare; **inflation** inflazione
f; **inflationary** inflazionisti-
co
inflexible [ɪn'fleksɪbl] inflessibile
inflict [ɪn'flɪkt]: ~ *sth on s.o.*
punishment infliggere qc a
qu; *suffering* procurare qc a
qu
'in-flight: ~ *entertainment* intrattenimento a bordo
influence ['ɪnfluəns] **1** *n* influenza f **2** *v/t s.o.'s thinking*
esercitare un'influenza su;
decision influenzare; **influential** *writer, film-maker* autorevole; *she knows ~ people* conosce gente influente
inform [ɪn'fɔ:m] **1** *v/t* informare **2** *v/i*: ~ *on s.o.* denunciare
qu
informal [ɪn'fɔ:məl] informale; **informality** informalità f
informant [ɪn'fɔ:mənt] informatore m, -trice f; **information** informazione f; *a bit of*
~ un'informazione; **information science** informatica f;
information technology informatica f; **informative** *article etc* istruttivo; *he wasn't
very* ~ non è stato di grande
aiuto; **informer** informatore
m, -trice f
infra-red [ɪnfrə'red] infrarosso; **infrastructure** ['ɪnfrə-
strʌktʃə(r)] infrastruttura f
infrequent [ɪn'fri:kwənt] raro
infuriate [ɪn'fjʊərɪeɪt] far infuriare; **infuriating** esaspe-

rante
ingenious [ɪn'dʒi:nɪəs] ingegnoso
ingot ['ɪŋgət] lingotto m
ingratitude [ɪn'grætɪtju:d] ingratitudine f
ingredient [ɪn'gri:dɪənt] *for
cooking* ingrediente m; *for
success* elemento m
inhabit [ɪn'hæbɪt] abitare; **inhabitant** abitante m/f
inhale [ɪn'heɪl] **1** *v/t* inalare **2**
v/i when smoking aspirare;
inhaler MED aerosol m
inherit [ɪn'herɪt] ereditare; **inheritance** eredità f *inv*
inhibited [ɪn'hɪbɪtɪd] inibito;
inhibition inibizione f
inhospitable [ɪnhɒ'spɪtəbl]
inospitale
'in-house 1 *adj* aziendale **2**
adv work all'interno dell'a-
zienda
inhuman [ɪn'hju:mən] disumano
initial [ɪ'nɪʃl] **1** *adj* iniziale **2** *n*
iniziale f **3** *v/t* (*write initials
on*) siglare (con le iniziali);
initially inizialmente; **initi-
ate** avviare; **initiation** avviamento m; **initiative** iniziativa f; *do sth on one's own*
~ fare qc di propria iniziativa; *take the* ~ prendere l'iniziativa
inject [ɪn'dʒekt] iniettare;
capital investire; **injection**
iniezione f; *of capital* investimento m
injure ['ɪndʒə(r)] ferire; **in-**

jured 1 *adj leg* ferito; *feelings offeso* 2 *npl* feriti *mpl*; **injury** ferita *f*

injustice [ɪnˈdʒʌstɪs] ingiustizia *f*

ink [ɪŋk] inchiostro *m*; **inkjet (printer)** stampante *f* a getto d'inchiostro

inland [ˈɪnlənd] *areas* dell'interno; *mail* nazionale; **Inland Revenue** fisco *m*

in-laws [ˈɪnlɔːz] *famiglia della moglie / del marito*; (*wife's / husband's parents*) suoceri *mpl*

inmate [ˈɪnmeɪt] *of prison* detenuto *m*, -a *f*; *of mental hospital* ricoverato *m*, -a *f*

inn [ɪn] locanda *f*

innate [ɪˈneɪt] innato

inner [ˈɪnə(r)] interno; **inner city** centro in degrado di una zona urbana; ~ **decay** degrado del centro urbano

innocence [ˈɪnəsəns] innocenza *f*; **innocent** innocente

innocuous [ɪˈnɒkjuəs] innocuo

innovation [ɪnəˈveɪʃn] innovazione *f*; **innovative** innovativo; **innovator** innovatore *m*, -trice *f*

inoculate [ɪˈnɒkjuleɪt] vaccinare; **inoculation** vaccinazione *f*

inoffensive [ɪnəˈfensɪv] inoffensivo

'in-patient degente *m/f*

input [ˈɪnput] 1 *n* contributo *m*; COMPUT input *m inv* 2 *v/t into project* contribuire con; COMPUT inserire

inquest [ˈɪnkwest] inchiesta *f* giudiziaria

inquire [ɪnˈkwaɪə(r)] domandare; ~ **into sth** svolgere indagini su qc; **inquiry** richiesta *f* di informazioni; (*public* ~) indagine *f*

inquisitive [ɪnˈkwɪzətɪv] curioso

insane [ɪnˈseɪn] pazzo

insanitary [ɪnˈsænɪtrɪ] antigienico

insanity [ɪnˈsænɪtɪ] infermità *f* mentale

inscription [ɪnˈskrɪpʃn] iscrizione *f*

insect [ˈɪnsekt] insetto *m*; **insecticide** insetticida *m*

insecure [ɪnsɪˈkjuə(r)] insicuro; **insecurity** insicurezza *f*

insensitive [ɪnˈsensɪtɪv] insensibile

insert 1 [ˈɪnsɜːt] *n in magazine etc* inserto *m* 2 [ɪnˈsɜːt] *v/t* inserire

inside [ɪnˈsaɪd] 1 *n* interno *m*; *of road* destra *f*, sinistra *f*; ~ **out** a rovescio; **turn sth out** rivoltare qc; **know sth** ~ **out** sapere qc a menadito 2 *prep* dentro; ~ **of 2 hours** in meno di due ore 3 *adv stay, go* dentro 4 *adj* interno; ~ **information** informazioni riservate; ~ **lane** SP corsia *f* interna; *on road* corsia *f* di marcia

inside 'pocket tasca *f* interna; **insider: an ~ from the Department** un impiegato del Ministero; **insider trading** FIN insider trading m; **insides** pancia fsg; *intestines* budella fpl

insignificant [ɪnsɪɡˈnɪfɪkənt] insignificante

insincere [ɪnsɪnˈsɪə(r)] falso; **insincerity** falsità f

insinuate [ɪnˈsɪnjʊeɪt] (*imply*) insinuare

insist [ɪnˈsɪst] insistere; *please keep it, I ~* tienilo, ci tengo!

◆ **insist on** esigere; *insist on doing sth* insistere per fare qc

insistent [ɪnˈsɪstənt] insistente

insolent [ˈɪnsələnt] insolente

insoluble [ɪnˈsɒljʊbl] *problem* insolubile; *substance* insolubile

insolvent [ɪnˈsɒlvənt] insolvente

insomnia [ɪnˈsɒmnɪə] insonnia f

inspect [ɪnˈspekt] *work, tickets, baggage* controllare; *factory, school* ispezionare; **inspection** *of work, tickets, baggage* controllo m; *of factory, school* ispezione f; **inspector** *in factory* ispettore m, -trice f; *on buses* controllore m; *of police* ispettore m

inspiration [ɪnspəˈreɪʃn] ispirazione f; (*very good idea*) lampo m di genio; **inspire**

respect etc suscitare; *be ~d by s.o. / sth* essere ispirato da qu / qc

instability [ɪnstəˈbɪlɪtɪ] instabilità f inv

install [ɪnˈstɔːl] installare; **installation** installazione f; *military ~* struttura f militare; **instalment**, Am **installment** *of story, TV drama etc* puntata f; (*payment*) rata f; **installment plan** Am acquisto m rateale

instance [ˈɪnstəns] (*example*) esempio m; *for ~* per esempio

instant [ˈɪnstənt] **1** *adj* immediato **2** n istante m; *in an ~* in un attimo; **instantaneous** immediato; **instant coffee** caffè m inv istantaneo *or* solubile; **instantly** istantaneamente

instead [ɪnˈsted] invece; *~ of* invece di

instinct [ˈɪnstɪŋkt] istinto m; **instinctive** istintivo

institute [ˈɪnstɪtjuːt] **1** n istituto m **2** v/t *new law* introdurre; *enquiry* avviare; **institution** istituto m; *sth traditional* istituzione f; (*setting up*) avviamento m

instruct [ɪnˈstrʌkt] (*order*) dare istruzioni a; (*teach*) istruire; **instruction** istruzione f; *~s for use* istruzioni per l'uso; **instructive** istruttivo; **instructor** istruttore m, -trice f

instrument ['ɪnstrʊmənt] strumento *m*

insubordinate [ɪnsəˈbɔːdɪnət] insubordinato

insufficient [ɪnsəˈfɪʃnt] insufficiente

insulate ['ɪnsjʊleɪt] ELEC isolare; *against cold* isolare termicamente; **insulation** ELEC isolamento *m*; *against cold* isolamento *m* termico

insulin ['ɪnsjʊlɪn] insulina *f*

insult 1 ['ɪnsʌlt] *n* insulto *m* **2** [ɪnˈsʌlt] *v/t* insultare

insurance [ɪnˈʃʊərəns] assicurazione *f*; **insurance company** compagnia *f* di assicurazioni; **insurance policy** polizza *f* di assicurazione; **insurance premium** premio *m* assicurativo; **insure** assicurare

insurmountable [ɪnsəˈmaʊntəbl] insormontabile

intact [ɪnˈtækt] intatto

integrate ['ɪntɪgreɪt] integrare; **integrity** integrità *f*

intellect ['ɪntəlekt] intelletto *m*; **intellectual 1** *adj* intellettuale **2** *n* intellettuale *m/f*

intelligence [ɪnˈtelɪdʒəns] intelligenza *f*; (*information*) informazioni *fpl*; **intelligent** intelligente

intelligible [ɪnˈtelɪdʒəbl] intelligibile

intend [ɪnˈtend]: **~ to do sth** (*do on purpose*) volere fare qc; (*plan to do*) avere intenzione di fare qc

intense [ɪnˈtens] intenso; *concentration* profondo; *personality* serio; **intensify 1** *v/t effect, pressure* intensificare **2** *v/i of pain* acuirsi; *of fighting* intensificarsi; **intensity** intensità *f inv*; **intensive** intensivo; **intensive care (unit)** MED (reparto *m* di) terapia *f* intensiva

intention [ɪnˈtenʃn] intenzione *f*; **intentional** intenzionale; **intentionally** intenzionalmente

interaction [ɪntərˈækʃn] interazione *f*; **interactive** interattivo

intercept [ɪntəˈsept] intercettare

interchange ['ɪntətʃeɪndʒ] MOT interscambio *m*; **interchangeable** interscambiabile

intercom ['ɪntəkɒm] citofono *m*

intercourse ['ɪntəkɔːs] *sexual* rapporto *m* sessuale

interdependent [ɪntədɪˈpendənt] interdipendente

interest ['ɪntrəst] **1** *n* interesse *m*; *money paid / received* interessi *mpl*; **take an ~ in sth** interessarsi di qc **2** *v/t* interessare; **interested** interessato; **be ~ in sth** interessarsi di qc; **interesting** interessante; **interest rate** FIN tasso *m* d'interesse

interface ['ɪntəfeɪs] **1** *n* interfaccia *f* **2** *v/i* interfacciarsi

interfere [ɪntə'fɪə(r)] interferire; **interference** interferenza f; *on radio* interferenze fpl

interior [ɪn'tɪərɪə(r)] **1** adj interno **2** n of house interno m; of country entroterra m; **interior decorator** arredatore m, -trice f; **interior design** architettura f d'interni; **interior designer** architetto m d'interni

interlude ['ɪntəlu:d] at theatre, concert intervallo m; (period) parentesi f inv

intermediary [ɪntə'mi:dɪərɪ] intermediario m, -a f; **intermediate** intermedio

intermission [ɪntə'mɪʃn] in theatre, cinema intervallo m

internal [ɪn'tɜ:nl] interno; **internally**: *he's bleeding ~* ha un'emorragia interna; *not to be taken ~* per uso esterno; **Internal Revenue (Service)** Am fisco m

international [ɪntə'næʃnl] **1** adj internazionale **2** n match partita f internazionale; player giocatore m, -trice f della nazionale; **internationally** a livello internazionale

Internet ['ɪntənet] Internet m; **on the ~** su Internet; **~ service provider** provider m inv di servizi Internet

interpret [ɪn'tɜ:prɪt] **1** v/t tradurre; piece of music, comment etc interpretare **2** v/i fare da interprete; **interpretation** traduzione f; of piece of music, meaning interpretazione f; **interpreter** interprete m/f

interrogate [ɪn'terəgeɪt] interrogare; **interrogation** interrogatorio m; **interrogator** interrogante m/f

interrupt [ɪntə'rʌpt] interrompere; **interruption** interruzione f

intersect [ɪntə'sekt] **1** v/t intersecare **2** v/i intersecarsi; **intersection** of roads incrocio m

interstate ['ɪntəsteɪt] Am autostrada f interstatale

interval ['ɪntəvl] intervallo m; **sunny ~s** schiarite fpl

intervene [ɪntə'vi:n] of person, police etc intervenire; of time trascorrere; **intervention** intervento m

interview ['ɪntəvju:] **1** n on TV, in paper intervista f; for job intervista f d'assunzione, colloquio m di lavoro **2** v/t on TV, for paper intervistare; for job sottoporre a intervista; **interviewer** on TV, for paper intervistatore m, -trice f; (for job) persona che conduce un'intervista d'assunzione

intimate ['ɪntɪmət] intimo; *be ~ with s.o. sexually* avere rapporti intimi con qu

intimidate [ɪn'tɪmɪdeɪt] intimidire; **intimidation** intimidazione f

into ['ɪntu] in; **be ~ sth** F (*like*) amare qc; (*be involved with*) interessarsi di qc; **be ~ drugs** fare uso di droga; **when you're ~ the job** quando sei pratico del lavoro

intolerable [ɪn'tɒlərəbl] intollerabile; **intolerant** intollerante

intoxicated [ɪn'tɒksɪkeɪtɪd] ubriaco

intravenous [ɪntrə'viːnəs] endovenoso

intricate ['ɪntrɪkət] complicato

intrigue 1 ['ɪntriːg] n intrigo m **2** [ɪn'triːg] v/t intrigare; **I would be ~d to know ...** m'interesserebbe molto sapere ...; **intriguing** intrigante

introduce [ɪntrə'djuːs] person presentare; new technique etc introdurre; **may I ~ ...?** permette che le presenti ...; **introduction** to person presentazione f; to new food, sport etc approccio m; in book, of new technique introduzione f

introvert ['ɪntrəvɜːt] introverso m, -a f

intrude [ɪn'truːd] importunare; **intruder** intruso m, -a f; **intrusion** intrusione f

intuition [ɪntjuː'ɪʃn] intuito m

invade [ɪn'veɪd] invadere

invalid[1] ['ɪnvælɪd] adj non valido

invalid[2] ['ɪnvəlɪd] n MED invalido m, -a f

invalidate [ɪn'vælɪdeɪt] invalidare

invaluable [ɪn'væljʊbl] prezioso

invariably [ɪn'veɪrɪəbl] (always) invariabilmente

invasion [ɪn'veɪʒn] invasione f

invent [ɪn'vent] inventare; **invention** invenzione f; **inventive** fantasioso; **inventor** inventore m, -trice f

inventory ['ɪnvəntrɪ] inventario m

invert [ɪn'vɜːt] invertire; **inverted commas** virgolette fpl

invest [ɪn'vest] investire

investigate [ɪn'vestɪgeɪt] indagare su; **investigation** indagine f; **investigative journalism** giornalismo m investigativo

investment [ɪn'vestmənt] investimento m; **investor** investitore m, -trice f

invigorating [ɪn'vɪgəreɪtɪŋ] climate tonificante

invincible [ɪn'vɪnsəbl] invincibile

invisible [ɪn'vɪzɪbl] invisibile

invitation [ɪnvɪ'teɪʃn] invito m; **invite** invitare

invoice ['ɪnvɔɪs] **1** n fattura f **2** v/t customer fatturare

involuntary [ɪn'vɒləntrɪ] involontario

involve [ɪn'vɒlv] hard work, expense comportare; (con-

cern) riguardare; **what does it ~?** che cosa comporta?; **get ~d with sth** entrare a far parte di qc; **get ~d with s.o.** *emotionally, romantically* legarsi a qu; **involved** (*complex*) complesso; **involvement** *in a project etc* partecipazione *f*; *in crime, accident* coinvolgimento *m*

invulnerable [ɪn'vʌlnərəbl] invulnerabile

inward ['ɪnwəd] **1** *adj feeling, thoughts* intimo **2** *adv* verso l'interno; **inwardly** dentro di sé

IQ [ar'kju:] (= *intelligence quotient*) quoziente *m* d'intelligenza

Iran [ɪ'rɑːn] Iran *m*; **Iranian 1** *adj* iraniano **2** *n* iraniano *m*, -a *f*

Iraq [ɪ'ræːk] Iraq *m*; **Iraqi 1** *adj* iracheno **2** *n* iracheno *m*, -a *f*

Ireland ['aɪələnd] Irlanda *f*; **Irish** irlandese; **Irishman** irlandese *m*; **Irishwoman** irlandese *f*

iron ['aɪən] **1** *n* ferro *m*; *for clothes* ferro *m* da stiro **2** *v/t shirts etc* stirare

'ironing board asse *m* da stiro

irony ['aɪərənɪ] ironia *f*

irrational [ɪ'ræʃənl] irrazionale

irreconcilable [ɪrekən'saɪləbl] inconciliabile

irregular [ɪ'regjʊlə(r)] irrego-

lare

irrelevant [ɪ'reləvənt] non pertinente

irreplaceable [ɪrɪ'pleɪsəbl] insostituibile

irrepressible [ɪrɪ'presəbl] *sense of humour* incontenibile; *person* che non si lascia abbattere

irresistible [ɪrɪ'zɪstəbl] irresistibile

irresponsible [ɪrɪ'spɒnsəbl] irresponsabile

irreverent [ɪ'revərənt] irriverente

irrevocable [ɪ'revəkəbl] irrevocabile

irrigate ['ɪrɪgeɪt] irrigare; **irrigation** irrigazione *f*

irritable ['ɪrɪtəbl] irritabile; **irritate** irritare; **irritating** irritante; **irritation** irritazione *f*

Islam ['ɪzlɑːm] Islam *m*; **Islamic** islamico

island ['aɪlənd] isola *f*; **islander** isolano *m*, -a *f*

isolate ['aɪsəleɪt] isolare; **isolated** isolato; **isolation** isolamento *m*; **in ~** *taken etc* da solo

ISP [aɪes'piː] (= *Internet service provider*) provider *m inv* di servizi Internet

Israel ['ɪzreɪl] Israele *m*; **Israeli 1** *adj* israeliano **2** *n person* israeliano *m*, -a *f*

issue ['ɪʃuː] **1** *n* (*matter*) questione *f*; (*result*) risultato *m*; *of magazine* numero *m*; **take ~ with s.o. / sth** prendere

posizione contro qu / qc **2**
v/t passports rilasciare; *supplies* distribuire; *coins* emettere; *warning* dare

IT [aɪˈtiː] (= *information technology*) IT *f*

it [ɪt] ◇ *as subject: what colour is ~?* – *~ is red* di che
colore è? – è rosso; *~'s rain-
ing* piove; *~'s me / him* sono
io / è lui; *~'s Charlie here*
TELEC sono Charlie; *that's
~! (that's right)* proprio così!;
(finished) finito! ◇ *as object*
lo *m*, la *f*; *I broke~* l'ho rotto,
-a

Italian [ɪˈtæljən] **1** *adj* italiano
2 *n person* italiano *m*, -a *f*;
language italiano *m*

italic [ɪˈtælɪk] in corsivo

Italy [ˈɪtəlɪ] Italia *f*

itch [ɪtʃ] **1** *n* prurito *m* **2** *v/i*
prudere

item [ˈaɪtəm] *on agenda* punto
m (all'ordine del giorno); *on
shopping list* articolo *m*; *in
accounts* voce *f*; *news* ~ notizia *f*; **itemize** *invoice* detta-
gliare

itinerary [aɪˈtɪnərərɪ] itinerario *m*

its [ɪts] il suo *m*, la sua *f*, i suoi
mpl, le sue *fpl*

it's [ɪts] ☞ *it is, it has*

itself [ɪtˈself] *reflexive* si;
emphatic di per sé; *by ~
(alone)* da solo; *(automatically)* da sé

J

jab [dʒæb] conficcare

jack [dʒæk] MOT cric *m inv; in
cards* fante *m*

jacket [ˈdʒækɪt] *n* giacca *f; of
book* copertina *f*

jackpot [ˈdʒækpɒt] montepremi *m;
hit the ~* vincere il primo
premio; *fig* fare un terno al
lotto

jagged [ˈdʒægɪd] frastagliato

jail [dʒeɪl] prigione *f*

jam¹ [dʒæm] *for bread* marmellata *f*

jam² [dʒæm] **1** *n* MOT ingorgo
m; be in a ~ F *(difficulty)* essere in difficoltà **2** *v/t (ram)*
ficcare; *(cause to stick)* bloc-

care; *be ~med of roads* essere congestionato; *of door,
window* essere bloccato **3**
v/i (stick) bloccarsi

janitor [ˈdʒænɪtə(r)] custode
m

January [ˈdʒænjʊərɪ] gennaio
m

Japan [dʒəˈpæn] Giappone
m; **Japanese 1** *adj* giapponese **2** *n person* giapponese *m/f; language* giapponese *m*

jar [dʒɑː(r)] *container* barattolo *m*

jargon [ˈdʒɑːgən] gergo *m*

javelin [ˈdʒævlɪn] giavellotto
m

jaw [dʒɔː] mascella *m*

jaywalker ['dʒeɪwɔːkə(r)] pedone *m* indisciplinato

jazz [dʒæz] jazz *m*

jealous ['dʒeləs] geloso; **jealousy** gelosia *f*

jeans [dʒiːnz] jeans *mpl*

jeep [dʒiːp] jeep *f inv*

jeer [dʒɪə(r)] **1** *n* scherno *m* **2** *v/i* schernire; **~ at** schernire

Jello® ['dʒeləʊ] *Am* gelatina *f*

jelly ['dʒelɪ] *Br* gelatina *f*; *Am* marmellata *f*; **jellyfish** medusa *f*

jeopardize ['dʒepədaɪz] mettere in pericolo

jerk[1] [dʒɜːk] **1** *n* scossone *m* **2** *v/t* dare uno strattone

jerk[2] [dʒɜːk] *n* F idiota *m/f*; **jerky** ['dʒɜːkɪ] *movement* a scatti

Jesus ['dʒiːzəs] Gesù *m*

jet [dʒet] **1** *n of water* zampillo *m*; (*nozzle*) becco *m*; *airplane* jet *m inv* **2** *v/i travel* volare; **jetlag** jet-lag *m*

jettison ['dʒetɪsn] gettare; *fig* abbandonare

jetty ['dʒetɪ] molo *m*

Jew [dʒuː] ebreo *m*, -a *f*

jewel ['dʒuːəl] gioiello *m*; *fig: person* perla *f*; **jeweller**, *Am* **jeweler** gioielliere *m*

Jewish ['dʒuːɪʃ] ebraico; *people* ebreo

jigsaw (**puzzle**) ['dʒɪgsɔː] puzzle *m inv*

jilt [dʒɪlt] piantare F

jingle ['dʒɪŋgl] **1** *n song* jingle *m inv* **2** *v/i of keys, coins* tin-

tinnare

jinx [dʒɪŋks] *person* iettatore *m*, -trice *f*; **there's a ~ on this project** questo progetto è iellato

jittery ['dʒɪtərɪ] F nervoso

job [dʒɒb] (*employment*) lavoro *m*; (*task*) compito *m*; **it's a good ~ you ...** meno male che tu ...; **job description** elenco *m* delle mansioni; **jobless** disoccupato

jockey ['dʒɒkɪ] fantino *m*

jog [dʒɒg] **1** *n corsa f*; **go for a ~** andare a fare footing **2** *v/i as exercise* fare footing **3** *v/t elbow etc* urtare; **~ s.o.'s memory** rinfrescare la memoria a qu; **jogger** *person* persona *f* che fa footing; *Am shoe* scarpa *f* da ginnastica; *jogging* footing *m*; **go ~** fare footing

john [dʒɒn] *Am* F gabinetto *m*

join [dʒɔɪn] **1** *n giuntura f* **2** *v/i of roads, rivers* unirsi; (*become a member*) iscriversi **3** *v/t* (*connect*) unire; *person* unirsi a; *club* iscriversi a; (*go to work for*) entrare in; *of road* congiungersi a

♦ **join in** partecipare

joint [dʒɔɪnt] **1** *n* ANAT articolazione *f*; *in woodwork* giunto *m*; *of meat* arrosto *m*; *of cannabis* spinello *m* **2** *adj* (*shared*) comune; **joint account** conto *m* comune; **joint venture** joint venture *f inv*

joke [dʒəʊk] **1** n story barzelletta f; (practical ~) scherzo m **2** v/i (pretend) scherzare; **joker** in cards jolly m inv; F burlone m, -a f; **jokingly** scherzosamente

jostle ['dʒɒsl] spintonare

journal ['dʒɜːnl] magazine rivista f; diary diario m; **journalism** giornalismo m; **journalist** giornalista m/f

journey ['dʒɜːnɪ] viaggio m

joy [dʒɔɪ] gioia f

jubilant ['dʒuːbɪlənt] esultante; **jubilation** giubilo m

judge [dʒʌdʒ] **1** n giudice m **2** v/t giudicare; competition fare da giudice a **3** v/i giudicare; **judg(e)ment** giudizio m; **an error of ~** un errore di valutazione; **Judg(e)ment Day** il giorno m del giudizio

judicial [dʒuː'dɪʃl] giudiziario

jug [dʒʌg] brocca f

juggle [dʒʌgl] fare giochi di destrezza con; fig: conflicting demands destreggiarsi fra; figures manipolare; **juggler** giocoliere m

juice [dʒuːs] succo m; juicy succoso; news, gossip piccante

July [dʒʊ'laɪ] luglio m

jumbo (jet) ['dʒʌmbəʊ] jumbo m (jet); **jumbo-sized** gigante

jump [dʒʌmp] **1** n salto m; (increase) impennata f **2** v/i jump; (increase) aumentare rapidamente, avere un'im-

pennata; in surprise sobbalzare; ~ **to conclusions** arrivare a conclusioni affrettate **3** v/t fence etc saltare; F (attack) aggredire; ~ **the queue** non rispettare la fila; ~ **the lights** passare col rosso

♦ **jump at** opportunity prendere al balzo

jumper ['dʒʌmpə(r)] Br pullover m inv; Am dress scamiciato m; **jumpy** nervoso

junction ['dʒʌŋkʃn] of roads incrocio m

June [dʒuːn] giugno m

jungle ['dʒʌŋgl] giungla f

junior ['dʒuːnɪə(r)] **1** adj (subordinate) subalterno; (younger) giovane **2** n in rank subalterno m, -a f; **she is ten years my ~** ha dieci anni meno di me; junior high Am scuola per ragazzi dai 12 ai 15 anni

junk [dʒʌŋk] robaccia f; **junk food** alimenti mpl poco sani, porcherie fpl; **junkie** F tossico m, -a f F; **junk mail** posta f spazzatura

jurisdiction [dʒʊərɪs'dɪkʃn] LAW giurisdizione f

juror ['dʒʊərə(r)] giurato m, -a f; **jury** giuria f

just [dʒʌst] **1** adj giusto **2** adv (barely) appena; (exactly) proprio; (only) solo; **I've ~ seen her** l'ho appena vista; ~ **about** (almost) quasi; **I was ~ about to leave when** ... stavo proprio per andarmene quando ...; **~ now** (*a few moments ago*) proprio ora; (*at the moment*) al momento; **~ you wait!** aspetta un po'!; **~ be quiet!** fai silenzio!; **~ as rich** altrettanto ricco

justice ['dʒʌstɪs] giustizia *f*; **justifiable** [dʒʌstɪ'faɪəbl] giustificabile; **justifiably** a ra-

gione; **justification** giustificazione *f*; **justify** *also text* giustificare

justly ['dʒʌstlɪ] giustamente

♦ jut out [dʒʌt] sporgere

juvenile ['dʒuːvənaɪl] **1** *adj* minorile; *pej* puerile **2** *n fml* minore *m/f*; **juvenile delinquent** delinquente *m/f* minorile

K

k [keɪ] (= *kilobyte*) k (= kilobyte *m inv*); (= *thousand*) mille

kangaroo [kæŋgə'ruː] canguro *m*

keel [kiːl] NAUT chiglia *f*

keen [kiːn] *person* entusiasta; *interest, competition* vivo; **be ~ on sth** essere appassionato di qc; **be ~ to do sth** aver molta voglia di fare qc

keep [kiːp] **1** *v/t* tenere; (*not lose*) mantenere; (*detain*) trattenere; *family* mantenere; *animals* allevare; **~ a promise** mantenere una promessa; **~ s.o. company** tenere compagnia a qu; **~ s.o. waiting** far aspettare qu; **~ sth to o.s.** (*not tell*) tenere qc per sé; **~ sth from s.o.** nascondere qc a qu; **~ s.o. from doing sth** impedire a qu di fare qc; **~ trying!** continua a provare! **2** *v/i* (*remain*) rimanere; *of food, milk*

conservarsi; **~ left** tenere la sinistra; **~ straight on** vai sempre dritto; **~ still** stare fermo

♦ keep away 1 *v/i* stare alla larga; *keep away from ...* stai alla larga da ... **2** *v/t* tenere lontano; **keep s.o. away from sth** tenere qu lontano da qc

♦ keep back (*hold in check*) trattenere; *information* nascondere

♦ keep down *voice* abbassare; *costs, inflation* contenere; *food* trattenere

♦ keep off 1 *v/t* (*avoid*) evitare; **keep off the grass** non calpestare l'erba **2** *v/i*: **if the rain keeps off** se non piove

♦ keep on 1 *v/i* continuare; **keep on doing sth** continuare a fare qc **2** *v/t employee, coat* tenere

♦ keep out 1 *v/t the cold* proteggere da; *person* escludere **2** *v/i of room* non entrare (*of* in); *of argument etc* non immischiarsi (*of* in); **keep out** *as sign* vietato l'ingresso

◆ keep to *path, rules* seguire; **keep to the point** non divagare

◆ keep up **1** *v/i when running etc* tener dietro **2** *v/t dare*, *payments* stare dietro a; *bridge, pants* reggere

◆ keep up with stare al passo con; (*stay in touch with*) mantenere i rapporti con

keeping ['ki:pɪŋ]: **be in ~ with** essere in armonia con; **keepsake** ricordo *m*

kennel ['kenl] canile *m*; **kennels** canile *m*

kerb [kɜ:b] orlo *m* del marciapiede

ketchup ['ketʃʌp] ketchup *m inv*

kettle ['ketl] bollitore *m*

key [ki:] **1** *n to door, drawer*, MUS chiave *f*; *on keyboard* tasto *m* **2** *adj* (*vital*) chiave **3** *v/t* COMPUT battere

◆ key in *data* immettere

'keyboard COMPUT, MUS tastiera *f*; **keyboarder** COMPUT, MUS tastierista *m/f*; **keycard** tessera *f* magnetica; **keyed-up** agitato; **keyhole** buco *m* della serratura; **keyring** portachiavi *m inv*; **keyword** parola *f* chiave

khaki ['kɑ:kɪ] cachi *inv*

kick [kɪk] **1** *n* calcio *m*; (*just*

for **~s** F (solo) per il gusto di farlo **2** *v/t dare* un calcio a; F *habit* liberarsi da **3** *v/i* dare calci; SP calciare; *of horse* scalciare

◆ kick around (*treat harshly*) maltrattare; F (*discuss*) discutere di; **kick a ball around** giocare a pallone

◆ kick off *of player* dare il calcio d'inizio; F (*start*) iniziare;

◆ kick out buttar fuori

'kickback F (*bribe*) tangente *f*; **kickoff** SP calcio *m* d'inizio

kid [kɪd] **1** *n* F (*child*) bambino *m*, -a *f*; F (*young person*) ragazzo *m*, -a *f*; **→ brother** fratello minore **2** *v/t* F prendere in giro **3** *v/i* F scherzare

kidnap ['kɪdnæp] rapire, sequestrare; **kidnapper** rapitore *m*, -trice *f*; **kidnapping** rapimento *m*, sequestro *m* (di persona)

kidney ['kɪdnɪ] ANAT rene *m*; *in cooking* rognone *m*

kill [kɪl] uccidere; *plant, time* ammazzare; **be ~ed in an accident** morire in un incidente; **~ o.s.** suicidarsi; **killer** (*murderer*) assassino *m*, -a *f*; (*hired* **~**) killer *m/f inv*; **killing** omicidio *m*; **make a ~** F (*lots of money*) fare un pacco di soldi F

kiln [kɪln] fornace *f*

kilo ['ki:ləʊ] chilo *m*; **kilobyte**

kilobyte *m inv*; **kilogram** chilogrammo *m*; **kilometre**, *Am* **kilometer** chilometro *m*

kind¹ [kaɪnd] *adj* gentile

kind² [kaɪnd] *n* (*sort*) tipo *m*; (*make, brand*) marca *f*; **nothing of the ~!** niente affatto!; **~ of sad / strange** F un po' triste / strano

kind-hearted [kaɪnd'hɑːtɪd] di buon cuore; **kindly** gentile; **kindness** gentilezza *f*

king [kɪŋ] re *m inv*; **kingdom** regno *m*

kinky ['kɪŋkɪ] F particolare F

kiosk ['kiːɒsk] edicola *f*

kiss [kɪs] **1** *n* bacio *m* **2** *v/t* baciare **3** *v/i* baciarsi

kit [kɪt] kit *m inv*; (*equipment*) attrezzatura *f*

kitchen ['kɪtʃɪn] cucina *f*

kite [kaɪt] aquilone *m*

kitten ['kɪtn] gattino *m*

kitty ['kɪtɪ] *money* cassa *f* comune

knack [næk] capacità *f*; **there's a ~ to it** bisogna saperlo fare

knee [niː] ginocchio *m*; **kneecap** rotula *f*

kneel [niːl] inginocchiarsi

'knee-length al ginocchio

knife [naɪf] **1** *n* coltello *m* **2** *v/t* accoltellare

knight [naɪt] *n* cavaliere *m*

knit [nɪt] **1** *v/t* fare a maglia **2** *v/i* lavorare a maglia; **knitwear** maglieria *f*

knob [nɒb] *on door* pomello *m*; *of butter* noce *f*

knock [nɒk] **1** *n on door* colpo *m*; (*blow*) botta *f* **2** *v/t* (*hit*) colpire; *head, knee* battere; F (*criticize*) criticare **3** *v/i at the door* bussare (**at** a); **I ~ed my head** ho battuto la testa

◆ **knock down** *of car* investire; *object, building etc* buttar giù; F (*reduce the price of*) scontare

◆ **knock out** (*make unconscious*) mettere K.O. F; *power lines etc* mettere fuori uso; (*eliminate*) eliminare

◆ **knock over** far cadere; *of car* investire

'knockout *in boxing* K.O. *m inv*

knot [nɒt] **1** *n* nodo *m* **2** *v/t* annodare

know [nəʊ] **1** *v/t* sapere; *person, place* conoscere; (*recognize*) riconoscere **2** *v/i* sapere; **I don't ~** non so **3** *n*: **be in the ~** F essere beninformato; **know-all** F sapientone *m*, -a *f*; **knowhow** F know-how *m*; **knowing** d'intesa; **knowingly** (*wittingly*) deliberatamente; *smile etc* con aria d'intesa; **know-it-all** *Am* F sapientone *m*, -a *f*; **knowledge** conoscenza *f*; **to the best of my ~** per quanto ne sappia

knuckle ['nʌkl] nocca *f*

Koran [kəˈrɑːn] Corano *m*

Korea [kəˈriːə] Corea f; **Korean 1** *adj* coreano **2** *n* coreano *m*, -a f; *language* coreano *m*

kosher [ˈkəʊʃə(r)] REL kasher; F a posto
kudos [ˈkjuːdɒs] gloria f

L

lab [læb] laboratorio *m*
label [ˈleɪbl] **1** *n* etichetta f **2** *v/t baggage* mettere l'etichetta su
labor *Am* ☞ **labour**
laboratory [ləˈbɒrətrɪ] laboratorio *m*
laborious [ləˈbɔːrɪəs] laborioso
'labor union *Am* sindacato *m*
labour [ˈleɪbə(r)] lavoro *m*; *in pregnancy* travaglio *m*; **be in ~** avere le doglie fpl; **laboured** *style, speech* pesante; **labourer** manovale *m*
lace [leɪs] *material* pizzo *m*; *for shoe* laccio *m*
lack [læk] **1** *n* mancanza f **2** *v/t* mancare di **3** *v/i:* **be ~ing** mancare
lacquer [ˈlækə(r)] lacca f
lactose [ˈlæktəʊs] lattosio *m*
ladder [ˈlædə(r)] scala f (a pioli); *in tights* sfilatura f
ladies room [ˈleɪdiːz] bagno *m* per donne
lady [ˈleɪdɪ] signora f; **ladybird**, *Am* **ladybug** coccinella f; **ladylike** da signora; **she's not very ~** non è certo una signora
lager [ˈlɑːgə(r)] birra f (bionda)

laidback [leɪdˈbæk] rilassato
lake [leɪk] lago *m*
lamb [læm] agnello *m*
lame [leɪm] *person* zoppo; *excuse* zoppicante
laminated [ˈlæmɪneɪtɪd] *surface* laminato; *paper* plastificato
lamp [læmp] lampada f; **lamppost** lampione *m*; **lampshade** paralume *m*
land [lænd] **1** *n* terra f; *(shore)* terra f; *(country)* paese *m*; **by~** via di terra; **on ~** sulla terraferma **2** *v/t aeroplane* far atterrare; *job* accaparrarsi **3** *v/i* of aeroplane atterrare; *of ball, sth thrown* cadere; *landing* of aeroplane atterraggio *m*; *top of staircase* pianerottolo *m*; **landing strip** pista f d'atterraggio; **landlady** of bar proprietaria f; of rented room padrona f di casa; **landlord** of bar proprietario *m*; of rented room padrone *m* di casa; **landmark** punto *m* di riferimento; fig teatro f miliare; **land owner** proprietario *m*, -a f terriero, -a; **landscape 1** *n* paesaggio *m* **2** *adv print* landscape, orizzontale;

landslide frana *f*; **landslide victory** vittoria *f* schiacciante

lane [leɪn] *in country* viottolo *m*; *(alley)* vicolo *m*; MOT corsia *f*

language ['læŋgwɪdʒ] lingua *f*; *(speech, style)* linguaggio *m*; **language lab** laboratorio *m* linguistico

lap[1] [læp] *of track* giro *m* (di pista)

lap[2] [læp] *of water* sciabordio *m*

lap[3] [læp] *of person* grembo *m*

lapel [lə'pel] bavero *m*

lapse [læps] **1** *(mistake, slip)* mancanza *f*; *of time* intervallo *m*; **~ of memory** vuoto *m* di memoria **2** *v/i* scadere; **~ into** cadere in

laptop COMPUT laptop *m inv*

larceny ['lɑːsənɪ] furto *m*

larder ['lɑːdə(r)] dispensa *f*

large [lɑːdʒ] grande; **at~** in libertà; **largely** *(mainly)* in gran parte

laryngitis [lærɪn'dʒaɪtɪs] laringite *f*

laser ['leɪzə(r)] laser *m inv*; **laser printer** stampante *f* laser

lash[1] [læʃ] *with whip* frustare

lash[2] [læʃ] *(eyelash)* ciglio *m*

last[1] [lɑːst] **1** *adj in series* ultimo; *(preceding)* precedente; **~ night** ieri sera; **~ year** l'anno scorso **2** *adv* **he finished ~** ha finito per ultimo; **when I saw him** l'ultima volta che

l'ho visto; **at ~** finalmente

last[2] [lɑːst] *v/i* durare

lasting ['lɑːstɪŋ] duraturo; **lastly** per finire

late [leɪt] **1** *adj (behind time)* in ritardo; *in day* tardi; **it's getting ~** si sta facendo tardi; **the ~ 19th century** il tardo XIX secolo **2** *adv* tardi; **lately** recentemente; **later** più tardi; **see you ~!** a più tardi; **~ on** più tardi; **latest 1** *adj*: **~ ultimo**, più recente **2** *n*: **at the ~** al più tardi

Latin ['lætɪn] **1** *adj* latino **2** *n* latino *m*; **Latin America** America *f* Latina; **Latin American 1** *n* latino-americano *m*, -a *f* **2** *adj* latino-americano

latitude ['lætɪtjuːd] latitudine *f*; *(freedom to act)* libertà *f* d'azione

latter ['lætə(r)]: **the ~** quest'ultimo

laugh [lɑːf] **1** *n* risata *f*; **it was a ~** F ci siamo divertiti **2** *v/i* ridere

◆ **laugh at** ridere di

laughter ['lɑːftə(r)] risata *f*

launch [lɔːntʃ] **1** *n boat* lancia *f*; *of rocket, product* lancio *m*; *of ship* varo *m* **2** *v/t rocket, product* lanciare; *ship* varare

launder ['lɔːndə(r)] lavare e stirare; **~ money** riciclare denaro sporco; **laundrette** lavanderia *f* automatica; **laundromat**® *Am* lavanderia *f* automatica; **laundry**

place lavanderia *f; clothes* bucato *m*

lavatory ['lævətri] gabinetto *m*

lavish ['lævɪʃ] *meal* lauto; *reception, lifestyle* sontuoso

law [lɔː] legge *f; criminal / civil ~* diritto *m* penale / civile; *against the ~* contro la legge; *forbidden by ~* vietato dalla legge; **law-abiding** che rispetta la legge; **law court** tribunale *m*; **lawful** legale; **lawless** senza legge

lawn [lɔːn] prato *m* (all'inglese); **lawn mower** tagliaerba *m inv*

'lawsuit azione *f* legale; **lawyer** avvocato *m*

lax [læks] permissivo

laxative ['læksətɪv] lassativo *m*

lay [leɪ] (*put down*) posare; *eggs* deporre; **V** (*sexually*) scopare **V**

♦ **lay off** *workers* licenziare; *temporarily* mettere in cassa integrazione

♦ **lay out** *objects* disporre; *page* impaginare

layer ['leɪə(r)] strato *m*

'layman laico *m*

'lay-out *of page* impaginazione *f; of garden, room* disposizione *f*

lazy ['leɪzɪ] *person* pigro; *day* passato a oziare

lb (= *pound*) libbra *f*

lead¹ [liːd] **1** *v/t procession, race* essere in testa a; *compa-*

ny, team essere a capo di; (*guide, take*) condurre **2** *v/i in race, competition* essere in testa; (*provide leadership*) dirigere; *a street ~ing off the square* una strada che parte dalla piazza; *a street ~ing into the square* una strada che sbocca sulla piazza **3** *n in race* posizione *f* di testa; *be in the ~* essere in testa; *take the ~* passare in testa

lead² [liːd] *for dog* guinzaglio *m*

lead³ [led] *substance* piombo *m*

leaded ['ledɪd] *petrol* con piombo

leader ['liːdə(r)] capo *m; in race, on market* leader *m/f inv; in newspaper* editoriale *m*; **leadership** *of party etc* direzione *f*, leadership *f; ~ contest* lotta *f* per la direzione

lead-free ['ledfriː] *petrol* senza piombo

leading ['liːdɪŋ] *runner* in testa; *company, product* leader *inv;* **leading-edge** *company, technology* all'avanguardia

leaf [liːf] foglia *f*

♦ **leaf through** sfogliare

leaflet ['liːflət] dépliant *m inv*

league [liːg] lega *f;* SP campionato *m*

leak [liːk] **1** *n of water* perdita *f; of gas* fuga *f; there's been a ~ of information* c'è è stata una fuga di notizie **2** *v/i of pipe* perdere; *of boat far acqua*

lean[1] [li:n] **1** *v/i be at an angle* pendere; **~ against sth** appoggiarsi a qc **2** *v/t* appoggiare

lean[2] [li:n] *adj meat* magro

leap [li:p] **1** *n* salto *m* **2** *v/i* saltare; **leap year** anno *m* bisestile

learn [lɜ:n] imparare; (*hear*) apprendere; **learner** principiante *m/f*; **learning** (*knowledge*) sapere *m*; *act* apprendimento *m*

lease [li:s] **1** *n* (contratto *m* di) affitto *m* **2** *v/t flat, equipment* affittare

◆ **lease out** dare in affitto

leash [li:ʃ] *for dog* guinzaglio *m*

least [li:st] **1** *adj* (*slightest*) minimo **2** *adv* meno **3** *n* minimo *m*; **not in the ~ surpised** per niente sorpreso; **at ~** almeno

leather ['leðə(r)] **1** *n* pelle *f*, cuoio *m* **2** *adj* di pelle, di cuoio

leave [li:v] **1** *n* (*holiday*) congedo *m*; MIL licenza *f* **2** *v/t* lasciare; *room, house, office* uscire da; *station, airport* partire da; (*forget*) dimenticare; **~ school** finire gli studi; **s.o. / sth alone** lasciare stare qu / qc; **be left** rimanere **3** *v/i of person, plane, bus* partire

◆ **leave behind** *intentionally* lasciare; (*forget*) dimenticare

◆ **leave out** omettere; (*not put away*) lasciare in giro; **leave me out of this** non mi immischiare in questa faccenda

'**leaving party** festa *f* d'addio

lecture ['lektʃə(r)] **1** *n* lezione *f* **2** *v/i at university* insegnare; **lecture hall** aula *f* magna; **lecturer** professore *m*, -essa universitario, -a

ledge [ledʒ] *of window* davanzale *m*; *on rock face* sporgenza *f*; **ledger** COM libro *m* mastro

left[1] [left] **1** *adj* sinistro; POL di sinistra **2** *n* sinistra *f*; *on / to the* ~ a sinistra **3** *adv* a sinistra; **left-hand** sinistro; **left-handed** mancino; **left luggage (office)** deposito *m* bagagli; **left-overs** *food* avanzi *mpl*; **left-wing** POL di sinistra

leg [leg] *of person, table* gamba *f*; *of animal* zampa *f*; *of turkey, chicken* coscia *f*; *of lamb* cosciotto *m*; **pull s.o.'s** ~ prendere in giro qu

legal ['li:gl] legale; **legal adviser** consulente *m/f* legale; **legality** legalità *f inv*; **legalize** legalizzare

legend ['ledʒənd] leggenda *f*; **legendary** leggendario

legible ['ledʒɪbl] leggibile

legislate ['ledʒɪsleɪt] legiferare; **legislation** legislazione *f*;

legislative legislativo; **legislature** POL legislatura *f*

legitimate [lɪ'dʒɪtɪmət] legittimo

'leg room spazio *m* per le gambe

leisure ['leʒə(r)] svago *m*; **at your** ~ con comodo; **leisurely** tranquillo

lemon ['lemən] limone *m*; **lemonade** fizzy gazzosa *f*; *made from lemon juice* limonata *f*

lend [lend] prestare; ~ *s.o.* **sth** prestare qc a qu

length [leŋθ] lunghezza *f*; *piece: of material* taglio *m*; **at** ~ *explain* a lungo; *(eventually)* alla fine; **lengthen** allungare; **lengthy** lungo

lenient ['liːnɪənt] indulgente

lens [lenz] *of camera* obiettivo *m*; *of spectacles* lente *f*; *of eye* cristallino *m*

Lent [lent] REL Quaresima *f*

Leo ['liːəʊ] ASTR Leone *m*

leopard ['lepəd] leopardo *m*

leotard ['liːətɑːd] body *m inv*

lesbian ['lezbɪən] **1** *n* lesbica *f* **2** *adj* di / per lesbiche

less [les] *(di)* meno; ~ **interesting** meno interessante; ~ **than £200** meno di £200; **lessen** diminuire

lesson ['lesn] lezione *f*

let [let] *(allow)* lasciare; *(rent)* affittare; ~ *s.o.* **do sth** lasciar fare qc a qu; ~ **me go!** lasciami andare!; ~**'s go / stay** andiamo / restiamo; ~ **alone** tanto meno; ~ **go of sth** *of rope, handle* mollare qc

◆ **let down** *hair* sciogliersi; *blinds* abbassare; *(disappoint)* deludere; *dress, trousers* allungare

◆ **let in** *to house* far entrare

◆ **let out** *from room* far uscire; *jacket etc* allargare; *groan, yell* emettere

◆ **let up** *(stop)* smettere

lethal ['liːθl] mortale

lethargic [lɪ'θɑːdʒɪk] fiacco; **lethargy** fiacchezza *f*

letter ['letə(r)] lettera *f*; **letterbox** *on street* buca *f* delle lettere; *in door* cassetta *f* della posta; **letterhead** *heading* intestatura *f*; *(headed paper)* carta *f* intestata

lettuce ['letɪs] lattuga *f*

leukemia [luː'kiːmɪə] leucemia *f*

level ['levl] **1** *adj surface* piano; *in competition, scores* pari; **draw** ~ **with** *s.o.* *in match* pareggiare **2** *n* livello *m*; **on the** ~ F *(honest)* onesto; **level crossing** passaggio *m* a livello; **level-headed** posato

lever ['liːvə(r), *Am* 'levər] **1** *n* leva *f* **2** *v/t:* ~ **sth open** aprire qc facendo leva; **leverage** forza *f*; *(influence)* influenza *f*

levy ['levɪ] *taxes* imporre

liability [laɪə'bɪlətɪ] *(responsibility)* responsabilità *f inv*; **liable** responsabile; **it's** ~ **to**

break (*likely*) è probabile
che si rompa

◆ **liaise with** [lɪ'eɪz] tenere i
contatti con

liaison [lɪ'eɪzɒn] (*contacts*)
contatti *mpl*

liar ['laɪə(r)] bugiardo *m*, -a *f*

libel ['laɪbl] **1** *n* diffamazione *f*
2 *v/t* diffamare

liberal ['lɪbrəl] (*broad-mind-
ed*), POL liberale; *portion
etc* abbondante

liberate ['lɪbəreɪt] liberare;
liberated emancipato; **liberation** liberazione *f*; **liberty**
libertà *f inv*; **at ~** *of prisoner
etc* in libertà; **be at ~ to do
sth** poter fare qc

Libra ['liːbrə] ASTR Bilancia *f*

librarian [laɪ'breərɪən] bibliotecario *m*, -a *f*; **library** biblioteca *f*

Libya ['lɪbɪə] Libia *f*; **Libyan 1**
adj libico **2** *n person* libico *m*,
-a *f*

lice [laɪs] *pl* ↘ **louse**

licence ['laɪsns] (*driving ~*)
patente *f*; (*road tax ~*) bollo
m (auto); *for TV* canone *m*
(televisivo); *for imports* ↘ ex-
ports licenza *f*; *for dog* tassa *f*

license ['laɪsns] **1** *v/t* (*issue ~
to*) rilasciare la licenza a;
the car isn't ~d la macchina
non ha il bollo **2** *n Am* ↘ **licence**; **license number** *Am*
numero *m* di targa; **license
plate** *Am* targa *f*

lick [lɪk] **1** *n* leccata *f* **2** *v/t* leccare; **~ one's lips** leccarsi i

baffi

lid [lɪd] coperchio *m*

lie¹ [laɪ] **1** *n* bugia *f*; **tell ~s** dire bugie **2** *v/i* mentire

lie² [laɪ] *v/i of person* sdraiarsi;
of object stare; (*be situated*)
trovarsi

◆ **lie down** sdraiarsi

lieutenant [lef'tenənt, *Am* lu-
'tenənt] tenente *m*

life [laɪf] vita *f*; *of machine* durata *f*; *of battery* autonomia
f; **that's ~!** così è la vita!; **life
belt** salvagente *m inv*; **lifeboat** lancia *f* di salvataggio;
life expectancy aspettativa *f*
di vita; **lifeguard** bagnino *m*,
-a *f*; **life imprisonment** ergastolo *m*; **life insurance** assicurazione *f* sulla vita; **life
jacket** giubbotto *m* di salvataggio; **lifeless** senza vita;
lifelike fedele; **lifelong** di
vecchia data; **lifesized** a
grandezza naturale; **life-
-threatening** mortale; **lifetime**: **in my ~** in vita mia

lift [lɪft] **1** *v/t* sollevare **2** *v/i of
fog* diradarsi **3** *n in building*
ascensore *m*; *in car* passaggio *m*; **give s.o. a ~** dare
un passaggio a qu; **lift-off**
of rocket decollo *m*

ligament ['lɪgəmənt] legamento *m*

light¹ [laɪt] **1** *n* luce *f*; **have
you got a ~?** hai da accende-
re? **2** *v/t* accendere; (*illuminate*) illuminare **3** *adj not
dark* chiaro

◆ **light up 1** v/t (*illuminate*) illuminare **2** v/i (*start to smoke*) accendersi una sigaretta

light² [laɪt] **1** adj not heavy leggero **2** adv: *travel* ~ viaggiare leggero

'**light bulb** lampadina f

lighten¹ ['laɪtn] colour schiarire

lighten² ['laɪtn] load alleggerire

lighter ['laɪtə(r)] for cigarettes accendino m; **light-headed** stordito; **lighting** illuminazione f; **lightness** leggerezza f; **lightning** fulmine m; **lightweight** in boxing peso m leggero; **light year** anno m luce

like¹ [laɪk] **1** prep come; ~ *this* / *that* così; *what is she* ~? in looks, character com'è?; *it's not* ~ *him* not his character non è da lui; *look* ~ *s.o.* assomigliare a qu **2** conj (*as*) come; ~ *I said* come ho già detto

like² [laɪk] v/t: *I* ~ *it* / *her* mi piace; *I would* ~ ... vorrei ...; *I would* ~ *to* ... vorrei ...; *would you* ~ ...? ti va ...?; *would you* ~ *to* ...? ti va di ...?; *he* ~*s swimming* gli piace nuotare; *if you* ~ se vuoi

likeable ['laɪkəbl] simpatico; **likelihood** probabilità f; **likely** probabile; *not* ~! difficile!; **likeness** (*resemblance*) somiglianza f; **likewise** al-

trettanto; **liking** predilizione f; *take a* ~ *to s.o.* prendere qu in simpatia

lily ['lɪlɪ] giglio m

limb [lɪm] arto m

lime¹ [laɪm] fruit limetta f

lime² [laɪm] substance calce f

limit ['lɪmɪt] **1** n limite m; *that's the* ~! F è il colmo! **2** v/t limitare; **limitation** limite m; **limited company** società f inv a responsabilità limitata

limousine ['lɪməziːn] limousine f inv

limp¹ [lɪmp] adj floscio

limp² [lɪmp] **1** n: *he has a* ~ zoppica **2** v/i zoppicare

line¹ [laɪn] n linea f; of people, trees fila f; of text riga f; of business settore m; *the* ~ *is busy* è occupato; *hold the* ~ rimanga in linea; *draw the* ~ *at sth* non tollerare qc; ~ *of inquiry* pista f; ~ *of reasoning* filo m del ragionamento; *stand in* ~ Am fare la fila; *in* ~ *with* ... (*conforming with*) in linea con ...

line² [laɪn] v/t foderare

linear ['lɪnɪə(r)] lineare

linen ['lɪnɪn] material lino m; sheets etc biancheria f

liner ['laɪnə(r)] ship transatlantico m

linesman ['laɪnzmən] SP guardalinee m inv

linger ['lɪŋgə(r)] of person attardarsi; of smell, pain persistere

lingerie ['lænʒərɪ] lingerie *f*

linguist ['lɪŋgwɪst] linguista *m/f*; *person good at languages* poliglotta *m/f*; **linguistic** linguistico

lining ['laɪnɪŋ] *of clothes* fodera *f*; *of brakes* guarnizione *f*

link [lɪŋk] **1** *n* legame *m*; *in chain* anello *m* **2** *v/t* collegare

lion ['laɪən] leone *m*

lip [lɪp] labbro *m*; **~s** labbra

liposuction ['lɪpəʊsʌkʃən] liposuzione *f*

'**lipread** leggere le labbra; **lipstick** rossetto *m*

liqueur [lɪ'kjʊə(r)] liquore *m*

liquid ['lɪkwɪd] **1** *n* liquido *m* **2** *adj* liquido; **liquidate** liquidare; **liquidation** liquidazione *f*; *go into* **~** andare in liquidazione; **liquidity** FIN liquidità *f*; **liquidize** frullare; **liquidizer** frullatore *m*

liquor ['lɪkə(r)] superalcolici *mpl*; **liquor store** *Am* negozio *m* di alcolici

lisp [lɪsp] **1** *n* lisca *f* **2** *v/i* parlare con la lisca

list [lɪst] **1** *n* elenco *m*, lista *f* **2** *v/t* elencare

listen ['lɪsn] ascoltare

◆ **listen to** ascoltare

listener ['lɪsnə(r)] *to radio* ascoltatore *m*, -trice *f*; *he's a good* **~** sa ascoltare

listless ['lɪstlɪs] apatico

liter *Am* ☞ **litre**

literal ['lɪtərəl] letterale; **literally** letteralmente

literary ['lɪtərərɪ] letterario; **literature** letteratura *f*; (*leaflets*) opuscoli *mpl*

litre ['liːtə(r)] litro *m*

litter ['lɪtə(r)] rifiuti *mpl*; *of animal* cucciolata *f*; **litter bin** bidone *m* dei rifiuti

little ['lɪtl] **1** *adj* piccolo **2** *n*: *the* **~** il poco che so; *a* **~** un po'; *a* **~** *wine* un po' di vino **3** *adv*: **~** *by* **~** poco a poco; *a* **~** *bigger* un po' più grande

live[1] [lɪv] *v/i* (*reside*) abitare; (*be alive*) vivere

◆ **live up**: *live it up* fare la bella vita

◆ **live up to** essere all'altezza di

live[2] [laɪv] **1** *adj broadcast* dal vivo; *ammunition* carico **2** *adv broadcast* in diretta; *record* dal vivo

livelihood ['laɪvlɪhʊd] mezzi *mpl* di sostentamento; *earn one's* **~** guadagnarsi da vivere; **liveliness** vivacità *f*; **lively** vivace

liver ['lɪvə(r)] fegato *m*

livestream ['laɪvstriːm] diretta *f* streaming

livestock ['laɪvstɒk] bestiame *m*

livid ['lɪvɪd] (*angry*) furibondo

living ['lɪvɪŋ] **1** *adj* in vita **2** *n*: *earn one's* **~** guadagnarsi da vivere; *what do you do for a* **~**? che lavoro fai?; **living room** salotto *m*, soggiorno *m*

lizard ['lɪzəd] lucertola f

load [ləʊd] 1 n carico m; ~s of
F un sacco di 2 v/t caricare

loaf [ləʊf]: a ~ of bread una
pagnotta

◆ loaf around F oziare

loafer ['ləʊfə(r)] shoe mocassino m

loan [ləʊn] 1 n prestito m; on
~ in prestito 2 v/t: ~ s.o. sth
prestare qc a qu

loathe [ləʊð] detestare; loathing disgusto m

lobby ['lɒbɪ] in hotel, theatre
atrio m; POL lobby f inv

lobe [ləʊb] of ear lobo m

lobster ['lɒbstə(r)] aragosta f

local ['ləʊkl] 1 adj people, bar
del posto; produce locale 2 n
persona f del posto; local
call TELEC telefonata f urbana; local elections elezioni
fpl amministrative; local
government amministrazione f locale

locality località f inv; localize
localizzare; locally live,
work nella zona; local time
ora f locale

locate [ləʊ'keɪt] new factory
etc situare; identify position
of localizzare; be ~d essere
situato; location (siting) ubicazione f; identifying position
of localizzazione f; on ~ film
in esterni

lock¹ [lɒk] of hair ciocca f

lock² [lɒk] 1 n on door serratura f 2 v/t door chiudere a
chiave

◆ lock up in prison mettere
dentro

locker ['lɒkə(r)] armadietto
m; locker room spogliatoio
m

locust ['ləʊkəst] locusta f

lodge [lɒdʒ] 1 v/t complaint
presentare 2 v/i of bullet conficcarsi

lofty ['lɒftɪ] peak alto; ideals
nobile

log [lɒg] wood ceppo m; written record giornale m

◆ log in fare il log in

◆ log off disconnettersi
(from da)

◆ log on fare il log on, connettersi (to a)

◆ log out fare il log out

log 'cabin casetta f di legno

logic ['lɒdʒɪk] logica f; logical
logico; logically a rigor di
logica; arrange in modo logico

logistics [lə'dʒɪstɪks] npl logistica f

logo ['ləʊgəʊ] logo m inv

loiter ['lɔɪtə(r)] gironzolare

lollipop ['lɒlɪpɒp] lecca lecca
m inv

London ['lʌndən] Londra f

loneliness ['ləʊnlɪnɪs] solitudine f; lonely person solo;
place isolato; loner persona
f solitaria

long¹ [lɒŋ] 1 adj lungo; it's a ~
way è lontano 2 adv: don't
be ~ torna presto 5 weeks
is too ~ 5 settimane è troppo; will it take ~? ci vorrà

tanto?; *that was ~ ago* è stato tanto tempo fa; *~ before then* molto prima di allora; *before ~* prima di; *we can't wait any ~er* non possiamo attendere oltre; *he no ~er works here* non lavora più qui; *so ~ as* (*provided*) sempre che; *so ~!* arrivederci!

long² [lɒŋ] *v/i*: *~ for sth* desiderare ardentemente qc; *be ~ing to do sth* desiderare ardentemente fare qc; **long-distance** *phonecall* interurbano; *race* di fondo; *flight* intercontinentale; **longevity** longevità *f*; **longing** desiderio *m*; **longitude** longitudine *f*; **long jump** salto *m* in lungo; **long-range** *missile* a lunga gittata; *forecast* a lungo termine; **long-sleeved** a maniche lunghe; **long-standing** di vecchia data; **long-term** *plans, investment* a lunga scadenza; *relationship* stabile; **long wave** RAD onde *fpl* lunghe

loo [luː] F gabinetto *m*

look [lʊk] **1** *n* (*appearance*) aspetto *m*; (*glance*) sguardo *m*; **have a ~ at sth** *examine* dare un'occhiata a qc; *can I have a ~?* *in shop etc* posso dare un'occhiata?; *~s* (*beauty*) bellezza *f* **2** *v/i* guardare; (*search*) cercare; (*seem*) sembrare

◆ **look after** badare a

◆ **look ahead** *fig* pensare al futuro

◆ **look around** *in shop etc* dare un'occhiata in giro; (*look back*) guardarsi indietro

◆ **look at** guardare; (*consider*) considerare

◆ **look back** guardare indietro

◆ **look down on** disprezzare

◆ **look for** cercare

◆ **look forward to**: *I'm looking forward to the holidays* non vedo l'ora che arrivino le vacanze

◆ **look into** (*investigate*) esaminare

◆ **look onto** *garden, street* dare su

◆ **look out** *of window etc* guardare fuori; (*pay attention*) fare attenzione; *look out!* attento!

◆ **look over** *house, translation* esaminare

◆ **look through** *magazine, notes* scorrere

◆ **look to** (*rely on*) contare su

◆ **look up 1** *v/i from paper etc* sollevare lo sguardo; (*improve*) migliorare **2** *v/t word, phone number* cercare; (*visit*) andare a trovare

◆ **look up to** (*respect*) avere rispetto per

'lookout *person* sentinella *f*; *be on the ~ for accommodation etc* cercare di trovare; *new staff etc* essere alla ricerca di

loop [luːp] cappio *m*; **loophole** *in law etc* scappatoia *f*

loose [luːs] *wire, button* allentato; *clothes* ampio; *tooth* che tentenna; *morals* dissoluto; *wording* vago; **~ change** spiccioli *mpl*; **loosely** *tied* senza stringere; *worded* vagamente; **loosen** allentare

loot [luːt] **1** *n* bottino *m* **2** *v/i* saccheggiare; **looter** saccheggiatore *m*, -trice *f*

lop-sided [lɒpˈsaɪdɪd] sbilenco

Lord [lɔːd] *(God)* Signore *m*; **the (House of) ~s** la camera dei Lord

lorry [ˈlɒrɪ] camion *m inv*; **lorry driver** camionista *m*

lose [luːz] **1** *v/t object* perdere **2** *v/i* SP perdere; *of clock* andare indietro; **I'm lost** mi sono perso; **get lost!** F sparisci!; **loser** *in contest* perdente *m/f*; F *in life* sfigato *m*, -a *f* F

loss [lɒs] perdita *f*; **make a ~** subire una perdita; **be at a ~** essere perplesso

lost [lɒst] perso; **lost property office**, *Am* **lost and found** ufficio *m* oggetti smarriti

lot [lɒt]: **a ~ (of)**, **~s (of)** molto; **~s of ice creams** molti gelati; **the ~** tutto

lotion [ˈləʊʃn] lozione *f*

lottery [ˈlɒtərɪ] lotteria *f*

loud [laʊd] *music, voice, noise*

forte; *colour* sgargiante; **loudspeaker** altoparlante *m*; *for stereo* cassa *f* dello stereo

lounge [laʊndʒ] *in house* soggiorno *m*; *in hotel* salone *m*; *at airport* sala *f* partenze

louse [laʊs] *(pl lice* [laɪs]) pidocchio *m*; **lousy** F schifoso F

lout [laʊt] teppista *m/f*

lovable [ˈlʌvəbl] adorabile; **love 1** *n* amore *m*; *in tennis* zero *m*; **be in ~** essere innamorato; **fall in ~** innamorarsi; **make ~** fare l'amore (**to** con) **2** *v/t* amare; **~ doing sth** amare fare qc; **love affair** relazione *f*; **lovely** *face, colour, holiday* bello; *meal, smell* buono; **we had a ~ time** siamo stati benissimo; **lover** amante *m/f*; **loving** affettuoso; **lovingly** amorosamente

low [ləʊ] **1** *adj* basso; *quality* scarso; **be feeling ~** sentirsi giù; **be on petrol** avere poca benzina **2** *n in weather* depressione *f*; *in sales, statistics* minimo *m*; **lowbrow** di scarso spessore culturale; **low-calorie** ipocalorico; **low-cut** *dress* scollato; **lower** *boat, sth to the ground* calare; *flag, hemline* ammainare; *pressure, price* abbassare; **low-fat** a basso contenuto lipidico; **lowkey** discreto

loyal [ˈlɔɪəl] leale; **loyally** leal

mente; **loyalty** lealtà *f inv*
lozenge ['lɒzɪndʒ] rombo *m*;
tablet pastiglia *f*
Ltd (= *limited*) s.r.l. (= società
a responsabilità limitata)
lubricant ['luːbrɪkənt] lubrificante *m*; **lubricate** lubrificare; **lubrication** lubrificazio-
ne *f*
lucid ['luːsɪd] (*clear*) chiaro;
(*sane*) lucido
luck [lʌk] fortuna *f*; **bad ~**
sfortuna; **hard ~!** che sfortuna!; **good ~** fortuna *f*; **good
~!** buona fortuna!; **luckily**
fortunatamente; **lucky** fortunato; **you were~** hai avuto
fortuna; **that's ~!** che fortuna!
lucrative ['luːkrətɪv] redditizio
ludicrous ['luːdɪkrəs] ridicolo
lug [lʌg] F trascinare
luggage ['lʌgɪdʒ] bagagli *mpl*
lukewarm ['luːkwɔːm] tiepido
lull [lʌl] *in fighting* momento
m di calma; *in conversation*
pausa *f*
lumber ['lʌmbə(r)] (*timber*)
legname *m*
luminous ['luːmɪnəs] luminoso

lump [lʌmp] *of sugar* zolletta
f; (*swelling*) nodulo *m*; **lump
sum** pagamento *m* unico;
lumpy *sauce* grumoso; *mattress* pieno di buchi
lunacy ['luːnəsɪ] pazzia *f*
lunar ['luːnə(r)] lunare
lunatic ['luːnətɪk] pazzo *m*, -a
f
lunch [lʌntʃ] pranzo *m*; **have~**
pranzare; **lunch box** cestino
m del pranzo; **lunch break**
pausa *f* pranzo; **lunch hour**
pausa *f* pranzo; **lunchtime**
ora *f* di pranzo
lung [lʌŋ] polmone *m*
lurch [lɜːtʃ] barcollare
lure [luə(r)] **1** *n* attrattiva *f* **2**
v/t attirare
lurid ['luərɪd] *colour* sgargiante; *details* scandaloso
lurk [lɜːk] *of person* appostar-
si; *of doubt* persistere
lush [lʌʃ] *vegetation* lussureg-
giante
lust [lʌst] libidine *f*
luxurious [lʌg'ʒuərɪəs] lussuoso; **luxuriously** lussuosa-
mente; **luxury 1** *n* lusso *m* **2**
adj di lusso
lynch [lɪntʃ] linciare
lyrics ['lɪrɪks] parole *fpl*, testi
mpl

M

MA [em'eɪ] (= *Master of Arts*)
master *m inv*

ma'am [mæm] *Am* signora *f*

machine [mə'ʃiːn] macchina
f; **machine gun** mitragliatrice *f*; **machinery** macchinario *m*

machismo [mə'kɪzməʊ] machismo *m*

macho ['mætʃəʊ] macho *m*

macro ['mækrəʊ] COMPUT
macro *f*

mad [mæd] pazzo *m*; F (*angry*)
furioso; **be ~ about** F (*keen
on*) andar matto per; **drive
s.o. ~** far impazzire qu;
madden (*infuriate*) esasperare; **maddening** esasperante

made-to-measure su misura

'madhouse *fig* manicomio *m*;
madly come un matto; **~ in
love** pazzamente innamorato; **madman** pazzo *m*; **madness** pazzia *f*

Madonna [mə'dɒnə] Madonna *f*

Mafia ['mæfɪə] Mafia *f*

magazine [mægə'ziːn] *printed*
rivista *f*

Magi ['meɪdʒaɪ] REL Re Magi
mpl

magic ['mædʒɪk] **1** *n* magia *f*;
tricks giochi *mpl* di prestigio
2 *adj* magico; **magical** magico; **magician** *performer* mago *m*, -a *f*; **magic spell** in-

cantesimo *m*

magnanimous [mæg'næn-
ɪməs] magnanimo

magnet ['mægnɪt] calamita *f*,
magnete *m*; **magnetic** cala-
mitato; *also fig* magnetico;
magnetism *of person* ma-
gnetismo *m*

magnificence [mæg'nɪfɪsəns]
magnificenza *f*; **magnificent**
magnifico

magnify ['mægnɪfaɪ] ingrandire; *difficulties* ingigantire;
magnifying glass lente *f*
d'ingrandimento

magnitude ['mægnɪtjuːd] *of
problem* portata *f*

maid [meɪd] *servant* domestica *f*; *in hotel* cameriera *f*

maiden name ['meɪdn] nome
m da ragazza; **maiden voyage** viaggio *m* inaugurale

mail [meɪl] **1** *n* posta *f* **2** *v/t letter* spedire; *person* spedire a;
mailbox *Am* buca *f* delle lettere; *of house* cassetta *f* delle
lettere; COMPUT (*not Am*)
casella *f* postale; **mailing list**
mailing list *m inv*; **mailman**
Am postino *m*; **mail-order
firm** ditta *f* di vendita per
corrispondenza; **mailshot**
mailing *m inv*

maim [meɪm] mutilare

main [meɪn] principale; **main
course** piatto *m* principale;

mainframe mainframe *m*
inv; mainland terraferma *f*,
continente *m*; on the ~ sul
continente; mainly principalmente; main road strada
f principale; main street corso *m*

maintain [meɪnˈteɪn] *pace,
speed, relationship* mantenere; *innocence, guilt* sostenere;
~ that sostenere che; maintenance *of machine, house*
manutenzione *f*; *money* alimenti *mpl*; *of law and order*
mantenimento *m*

majestic [məˈdʒestɪk] mae-
stoso

major [ˈmeɪdʒə(r)] 1 *adj* (*significant*) importante, principale; in C ~ MUS in Do maggiore 2 *n* MIL maggiore *m*

◆ major in *Am* specializzarsi
in

majority [məˈdʒɒrətɪ] *also*
POL maggioranza *f*; be in
the ~ essere in maggioranza

make [meɪk] 1 *n* (*brand*) marca *f* 2 *v/t* *brand*; *decision* prendere; (*earn*) guadagnare;
MATH fare; ~ it catch bus,
train, come, succeed farcela;
what time do you ~ it?
che ore fai?; ~ believe far
finta; ~ do with arrangiarsi
con; what do you ~ of it? cosa ne pensi?; ~ s.o. do sth
(*force to*) far fare qc a qu;
(*cause to*) spingere qu a fare
qc; ~ s.o. happy far felice
qu, rendere felice qu

◆ make off with (*steal*) svignarsela con

◆ make out *list* fare; *cheque*
compilare; (*see*) distinguere;
(*imply*) far capire

◆ make up 1 *v/i* *of woman,
actor* truccarsi; *after quarrel*
fare la pace 2 *v/t* *story, excuse*
inventare; *face* truccare;
(*constitute*) costituire; be
made up of essere composto
da; make it up *after quarrel*
fare la pace

◆ make up for compensare
'make-believe finta *f*

maker [ˈmeɪkə(r)] *manufacturer* fabbricante *m/f*; makeshift improvvisato; make-
-up (*cosmetics*) trucco *m*

maladjusted [mæləˈdʒʌstɪd]
disadattato

male [meɪl] 1 *adj* maschile; *animal* maschio 2 *n* *man* uomo
m; *animal, bird* maschio *m*;
male chauvinism maschili-
smo *m*; male chauvinist
pig maschilista *m*

malevolent [məˈlevələnt] ma-
levolo

malfunction [mælˈfʌŋkʃn] 1 *n*
cattivo *m* funzionamento 2
v/i funzionare male

malice [ˈmælɪs] cattiveria *f*,
malvagità *f*; malicious cattivo, malvagio

malignant [məˈlɪgnənt] *tumour* maligno

mall [mæl] (*shopping* ~) centro
m commerciale

malnutrition [mælnjuˈtrɪʃn]

denutrizione f

maltreat [mæl'tri:t] maltrattare; **maltreatment** maltrattamento m

mammal ['mæml] mammifero m

man [mæn] **1** n (pl **men** [men]) uomo m; humanity umanità f; in draughts pedina f **2** v/t telephones, front desk essere di servizio a; it was ~ned by a crew of three aveva un equipaggio di tre persone

manage ['mænɪdʒ] **1** v/t business, money gestire; can you ~ the suitcase? ce la fai a portare la valigia?; ~ to ... riuscire a ... **2** v/i cope, financially tirare avanti; (financially); can you ~? ce la fai?; **manageable** suitcase etc maneggevole; hair docile; able to be done fattibile; **management** (managing) gestione f; (managers) direzione f; **management consultant** consulente m/f di gestione aziendale; **manager** manager m/f inv, direttore m, -trice f; **managerial** manageriale; **managing director** direttore m generale

mandate ['mændeɪt] (authority, task) mandato m; **mandatory** obbligatorio

maneuver Am ☞ **manoeuvre**

mangle ['mæŋgl] (crush) stritolare

manhandle ['mænhændl] per-

son malmenare; object caricare

manhood ['mænhʊd] maturity età f adulta; (virility) virilità f; **manhunt** caccia f all'uomo

mania ['meɪnɪə] (craze) mania f; **maniac** F pazzo m, -a f

manicure ['mænɪkjʊə(r)] manicure f inv

manifest ['mænɪfest] **1** adj palese **2** v/t manifestare

manipulate [mə'nɪpjʊleɪt] manipolare; **manipulation** manipolazione f; **manipulative** manipolatore

man'kind umanità f; **manly** virile; **man-made** sintetico

manner ['mænə(r)] of doing sth maniera f, modo m; (attitude) modo m di fare; **manners**: good / bad ~ buone / cattive maniere fpl; **have no** ~ essere maleducato

manoeuvre [mə'nu:və(r)] **1** n manovra f **2** v/t manovrare

'manpower manodopera f, personale m; **manslaughter** omicidio m colposo

manual ['mænjʊəl] **1** adj manuale **2** n manuale m; **manually** manualmente

manufacture [mænjʊ-'fæktʃə(r)] **1** n manifattura f **2** v/t equipment fabbricare; **manufacturer** fabbricante m/f; **manufacturing** industry manifatturiero

manure [mə'njʊə(r)] letame

m

manuscript ['mænjuskrɪpt]
manoscritto *m*; *typed* dattiloscritto *m*

many ['menɪ] **1** *adj* molti; ~
times molte volte; *not* ~
people / taxis poche persone / pochi taxi; *too* ~ *problems / beers* troppi problemi / troppe birre **2** *pron*
molti *m*, molte *f*; *a great* ~,
a good ~ moltissimi; *how*
~ *do you need?* quanti te
ne servono? *as* ~ *as 200*
ben 200

map [mæp] cartina *f*; (*street* ~)
pianta *f*, piantina *f*

maple ['meɪpl] acero *m*

mar [maː(r)] guastare

marathon ['mærəθɒn] *race*
maratona *f*

marble ['maːbl] *material* marmo *m*

March [maːtʃ] marzo *m*

march [maːtʃ] **1** *n* marcia *f*;
(*demonstration*) dimostrazione *f*, manifestazione *f* **2** *v/i*
marciare; *in protest* dimostrare, manifestare; **march**-
er dimostrante *m/f*, manifestante *m/f*

Mardi Gras ['maːdɪgraː] *Am*
martedì *m* grasso

margin ['maːdʒɪn] *of page*
margine *m*; COM margine
m di guadagno; *by a narrow*
~ di stretta misura; **marginal**
(*slight*) leggero; **marginally**
(*slightly*) leggermente

marihuana, **marijuana**

[mærɪ'hwaːnə] marijuana *f*

marina [məˈriːnə] porticciolo
m

marine [məˈriːn] **1** *adj* marino
2 *n* MIL marina *f* militare

marital ['mærɪtl] coniugale;
marital status stato *m* civile

maritime ['mærɪtaɪm] marittimo

mark [maːk] **1** *n* (*stain*) macchia *f*; (*sign, token*) segno
m; (*trace*) EDU voto *m* **2** *v/t*
(*stain*) macchiare; EDU correggere; (*indicate*) indicare;
(*commemorate*) celebrare **3**
v/i of fabric macchiarsi;
marked (*definite*) spiccato;
marker (*highlighter*) evidenziatore *m*

market ['maːkɪt] **1** *n* mercato
m **2** *v/t* vendere; **marketable**
commercializzabile; **market**
economy economia *f* di
mercato; **marketing** marketing *m*; **market leader** leader
m inv del mercato; **market**-
place *in town* piazza *f* del
mercato; *for commodities*
piazza *f*, mercato *m*; **market**
research ricerca *f* di mercato; **market share** quota *f* di
mercato

'mark-up ricarico *m*

marmalade ['maːməleɪd]
marmellata *f* d'arance

marriage ['mærɪdʒ] matrimonio *m*; *event* nozze *fpl*; **marr**-
iage certificate certificato
m di matrimonio; **married**
sposato; *be* ~ *to ...* essere

sposato con ...; **married life** vita f coniugale; **marry** sposare; *of priest* unire in matrimonio; **get married** sposarsi

marsh [mɑːʃ] palude f

marshal ['mɑːʃl] *official* membro m del servizio d'ordine

martial arts [mɑːʃl'ɑːts] arti *fpl* marziali; **martial law** legge f marziale

martyr ['mɑːtə(r)] martire *m/f*

marvel ['mɑːvl] meraviglia f; **marvellous**, *Am* **marvelous** meraviglioso

Marxism ['mɑːksɪzm] marxismo m; **Marxist 1** *adj* marxista **2** *n* marxista *m/f*

mascara [mæ'skɑːrə] mascara *m inv*

mascot ['mæskət] mascotte f *inv*

masculine ['mæskjʊlɪn] maschile; **masculinity** (*virility*) virilità f

mash [mæʃ] passare, schiacciare; **mashed potatoes** purè m di patate

mask [mɑːsk] **1** n maschera f **2** *v/t feelings* mascherare

masochism ['mæsəkɪzm] masochismo m; **masochist** ['mæsəkɪst] masochista *m/f*

mass¹ [mæs] **1** *n great amount* massa f; **.es of** F un sacco di F **2** *v/i* radunarsi

mass² [mæs] REL messa f

massacre ['mæsəkə(r)] **1** n *also fig* massacro m **2** *v/t also fig* massacrare

massage ['mæsɑːʒ] **1** n massaggio m **2** *v/t* massaggiare; *figures* manipolare

massive ['mæsɪv] enorme; *heart attack* grave

mass 'media mass media *mpl*; **mass-produce** produrre in serie; **mass production** produzione f in serie; **mass transit** *Am* i trasporti pubblici

mast [mɑːst] *of ship* albero m; *for radio signal* palo m dell'antenna

master ['mɑːstə(r)] **1** n *of dog* padrone m; *of ship* capitano m **2** *v/t skill, language* avere completa padronanza di; *situation* dominare; **master bedroom** camera f da letto principale; **master key** passe-partout *m inv*; **masterly** magistrale; **mastermind 1** n *fig* cervello m **2** *v/t* ideare; **masterpiece** capolavoro m; **master's (degree)** *m inv*; laurea f magistrale; **mastery** padronanza f

mat [mæt] *for floor* tappetino m; *for table* tovaglietta f all'americana

match¹ [mætʃ] n *for cigarette* fiammifero m; *made of wax* cerino m

match² [mætʃ] **1** n (*competition*) partita f; **be no ~ for s.o.** non poter competere con qu **2** *v/t (be the same as)* abbinare; (*equal*) uguagliare **3** *v/i of colours, pat-*

terns intonarsi

matching ['mætʃɪŋ] abbinato

mate [meɪt] **1** *n of animal* compagno *m*, -a *f*; NAUT secondo *m*; F *friend* amico *m*, -a *f* **2** *v/i* accoppiarsi

material [mə'tɪərɪəl] **1** *n fabric* stoffa *f*, tessuto *m*; *substance* materia *f*; **~s** occorrente *m* **2** *adj* materiale; **materialism** materialismo *m*; **materialist** materialista *m/f*; **materialistic** materialistico; **materialize** materializzarsi

maternal [mə'tɜːnl] materno; **maternity** maternità *f*; **maternity leave** congedo *m* per maternità; **maternity ward** reparto *m* maternità

math [mæθ] *Am* **↔ maths**; **mathematical** matematico; **mathematician** matematico *m*, -a *f*; **mathematics** matematica *f*; **maths** matematica *f*

matinée ['mætɪneɪ] matinée *f inv*

matriarch ['meɪtrɪɑːk] matriarca *f*

matrimony ['mætrɪmənɪ] matrimonio *m*

matt [mæt] opaco

matter ['mætə(r)] **1** *n (affair)* questione *f*, faccenda *f*; PHYS materia *f*; *as a ~ of fact* a dir la verità; *what's the ~?* cosa c'è?; *no ~ what she says* qualsiasi cosa dica **2** *v/i* importare; *it doesn't ~* non importa; **matter-of-fact**

distaccato

mattress ['mætrɪs] materasso *m*

mature [mə'tjuə(r)] **1** *adj* maturo **2** *v/i of person, insurance policy etc* maturare; *of wine* invecchiare; **maturity** maturità *f*

maximize ['mæksɪmaɪz] massimizzare; **maximum 1** *adj* massimo **2** *n* massimo *m*

May [meɪ] maggio *m*

may [meɪ] ◊ *(possibility)*: *it ~ rain* potrebbe piovere, può darsi che piova; *it ~ not happen* può darsi che non succeda ◊ *(permission)*: *~ I help?* posso aiutare?

maybe ['meɪbɪ] forse

mayonnaise [meɪə'neɪz] maionese *f*

mayor ['meə(r)] sindaco *m*

maze [meɪz] *also fig* dedalo *m*, labirinto *m*

MB (= **megabyte**) MB *m* (= megabyte *m inv*)

MBA [embi:'eɪ] (= **master of business administration**) master in amministrazione aziendale

MD [em'di:] (= **Doctor of Medicine**) dottore in medicina

me [mi:] mi; *after prep, stressed* me; *she knows ~* mi conosce; *she spoke to ~* mi ha parlato; *it's ~* sono io; *who? - ~?* chi? - io?

meadow ['medəu] prato *m*

meagre, *Am* **meager** ['mi:gə(r)] scarso

meal [miːl] pranzo *m*, pasto *m*;
enjoy your ~! buon appeti-
to!

mean¹ [miːn] *adj with money*
avaro; (*nasty*) cattivo

mean² [miːn] **1** *v/t* (*signify*) significare, voler dire; *do you
~ it?* dici sul serio?; *~ to do
sth* avere l'intenzione di fare qc; *be ~t for* essere destinato a; *of remark* essere diretto a **2** *v/i*: *~ well* avere
buone intenzioni

meaning [ˈmiːnɪŋ] *of word* significato *m*; **meaningful**
(*comprehensible*) comprensibile; (*constructive*) costruttivo; *glance* eloquente; **mean-
ingless** *sentence etc* senza
senso; *gesture* vuoto

means [miːnz] *financial* mezzi
mpl; (*nsg: way*) modo *m*; *~ of
transport* mezzo *m* di trasporto; *by all* ~ (*certainly*)
certamente; *by no* ~ *rich*
lungi dall'essere ricco; *by* ~
of per mezzo di

meantime [ˈmiːntaɪm] intanto

measles [ˈmiːzlz] morbillo *m*

measure [ˈmeʒə(r)] **1** *n* (*step*)
misura *f* **2** *v/t* prendere le misure di **3** *v/i* misurare
♦ **measure up to** dimostrarsi all'altezza di

measurement [ˈmeʒəmənt]
action misurazione *f*; (*dimension*) misura *f*; **measuring
tape** metro *m* a nastro

meat [miːt] carne *f*; **meatball**

polpetta *f*

mechanic [mɪˈkænɪk] meccanico *m*; **mechanical** *also fig*
meccanico; **mechanical engineer** ingegnere *m* meccanico; **mechanically** *also fig*
meccanicamente; **mecha-
nism** meccanismo *m*; **mech-
anize** meccanizzare

medal [ˈmedl] medaglia *f*;
medallist, *Am* **medalist** vincitore *m*,-trice *f* di una medaglia

meddle [ˈmedl] (*interfere*) immischiarsi; *~ with* (*tinker*)
mettere le mani in

media [ˈmiːdɪə]: *the* ~ i mass
media *mpl*; **media** *coverage*: *it was given a lot of
~* gli è stato dato molto spazio in TV e sui giornali

mediaeval → **medieval**

median strip [miːdɪənˈstrɪp]
Am banchina *f* spartitraffico

'media studies scienze *fpl*
delle comunicazioni

mediate [ˈmiːdɪeɪt] fare da
mediatore *m*, -trice *f*; **mediation** mediazione *f*; **mediator** mediatore *m*, -trice *f*

medical [ˈmedɪkl] **1** *adj* medico **2** *n* visita *f* medica; **medi-
cated** medicato; **medica-
tion** medicina *f*; **medicinal**
medicinale; **medicine** *m*, -trice *f*
cina *f*

medieval [medrˈiːvl] medievale

mediocre [miːdɪˈəʊkə(r)] mediocre; **mediocrity** medio-

crità f

meditate ['medɪteɪt] *meditare*; **meditation** *meditazione* f

Mediterranean [medɪtə'reɪnɪən] **1** *adj mediterraneo* **2** *n*: **the ~** il Mar Mediterraneo; *area* i paesi mediterranei

medium ['miːdɪəm] **1** *adj (average)* medio; *steak* cotto al punto giusto **2** *n in size* media f; *(vehicle)* strumento m; *(spiritualist)* medium m/f *inv*; **medium-sized** di grandezza media; **medium wave** RAD onde fpl medie

medley ['medlɪ] *(assortment)* misto m

meet [miːt] **1** *v/t* incontrare; *(get to know)* conoscere; *(collect)* andare *or* venire a prendere; *in competition* affrontare; *of eyes* incrociare; *(satisfy)* soddisfare; **I'll ~ you there** ci vediamo lì **2** *v/i* incontrarsi; *in competition* affrontarsi; *of eyes* incrociarsi; *of committee etc* riunirsi; **have you two met?** *(do you know each other?)* vi conoscete? **3** *n* SP raduno m sportivo

◆ **meet with** *person* avere un incontro con; *opposition, approval etc* incontrare; **it met with success / failure** ha avuto successo / è fallito

meeting ['miːtɪŋ] incontro m; *of committee, in business* riu-

nione f; **he's in a ~** è in riunione

megabyte ['megəbaɪt] COMPUT megabyte m *inv*

mellow ['meləʊ] **1** *adj maturo* **2** *v/i of person* addolcirsi

melodious [mɪ'ləʊdɪəs] melodioso

melodramatic [melədrə'mætɪk] melodrammatico

melody ['melədɪ] melodia f

melon ['melən] melone m

melt [melt] **1** *v/i* sciogliersi **2** *v/t* sciogliere; **melting pot** *fig* crogiolo m di culture

member ['membə(r)] *of family* componente m/f; *of club* socio m; *of organization* membro m; **Member of Congress** membro m del Congresso; **Member of Parliament** membro m del Parlamento, deputato m; **membership** iscrizione f; *number of members* numero m dei soci

membrane ['membreɪn] membrana f

memento [me'mentəʊ] souvenir m *inv*

memo ['meməʊ] circolare f

memoirs ['memwɑːz] memorie fpl

memorable ['memərəbl] memorabile

memorial [mɪ'mɔːrɪəl] **1** *adj* commemorativo **2** *n also fig* memorial m *inv*

memorize ['meməraɪz] memorizzare; **memory** *(recol-*

lection) ricordo *m*; *power of recollection* memoria *f*; COMPUT memoria *f*; **memory stick** memory stick *f inv*

men [men] *pl* ☞ **man**

menace ['menɪs] **1** *n* (*threat*) minaccia *f*; *person* pericolo *m* pubblico; (*nuisance*) peste *f* **2** *v/t* minacciare; **menacing** minaccioso

mend [mend] riparare

menial ['miːnɪəl] umile

menopause ['menəpɔːz] menopausa *f*

'men's room bagno *m* (degli uomini)

menstruate ['menstrʊeɪt] avere le mestruazioni; **menstruation** mestruazione *f*

mental ['mentl] mentale; *F* (*crazy*) pazzo; **mental hospital** ospedale *m* psichiatrico; **mental illness** malattia *f* mentale; **mentality** mentalità *f inv*; **mentally** inwardly mentalmente; *calculate etc* a mente; **mentally ill** malato di mente

mention ['menʃn] **1** *n* cenno *m* **2** *v/t* accennare a; *don't* ~ *it* (*you're welcome*) non c'è di che

mentor ['mentɔː(r)] guida *f* spirituale

menu ['menjuː] *also* COMPUT menu *m inv*

mercenary ['mɜːsɪnərɪ] **1** *adj* mercenario **2** *n* MIL mercenario *m*

merchandise ['mɜːtʃəndaɪz]

merce *f*

merchant ['mɜːtʃənt] commerciante *m*/*f*; **merchant bank** banca *f* d'affari

merciful ['mɜːsɪfʊl] misericordioso; **mercifully** (*thankfully*) per fortuna; **merciless** spietato; **mercy** misericordia *f*; *be at s.o.'s* ~ essere alla mercé di qu

mere [mɪə(r)] semplice; **merely** soltanto

merge [mɜːdʒ] *of two lines etc* unirsi; *of companies* fondersi; **merger** COM fusione *f*

merit ['merɪt] **1** *n* (*worth*) merito *m*; (*advantage*) vantaggio *m* **2** *v/t* meritare

mesh [meʃ] *in net* maglia *f*

mess [mes] (*untidiness*) disordine *m*; (*trouble*) pasticcio *m*; *be a* ~ *of room, desk, hair* essere in disordine; *of situation, s.o.'s life* essere un pasticcio

message ['mesɪdʒ] *also fig* messaggio *m*

messenger ['mesɪndʒə(r)] (*courier*) fattorino *m*, -a *f*

messy ['mesɪ] *room* in disordine; *person* disordinato; *job* sporco; *divorce, situation* antipatico

metabolism [mətæˈbəlɪzm] metabolismo *m*

metal ['metl] **1** *adj in or* di metallo **2** *n* metallo *m*; **metallic** metallico

metaphor ['metəfə(r)] metafora *f*

meteor ['miːtɪə(r)] meteora f;
meteoric fig fulmineo; **meteorite** meteorite m or f

meteorological [miːtɪərə'lɒdʒɪkl] meteorologico; **meteorologist** meteorologo m, -a f; **meteorology** meteorologia f

meter[1] ['miːtə(r)] for gas etc contatore m; (parking ~) parchimetro m

meter[2] Am ☞ **metre**

method ['meθəd] metodo m; **methodical** metodico

meticulous [mɪ'tɪkjʊləs] meticoloso

metre ['miːtə(r)] metro m

metropolis [mɪ'trɒpəlɪs] metropoli f inv; **metropolitan** metropolitano

mew [mjuː] ☞ **miaow**

Mexican ['meksɪkən] **1** adj messicano **2** n messicano m, -a f; **Mexico** Messico m

miaow [mɪaʊ] **1** n miao m **2** v/i miagolare

mice [maɪs] pl ☞ **mouse**

'**microchip** microchip m inv; **microclimate** microclima m; **microcosm** microcosmo m; **microorganism** microrganismo m; **microphone** microfono m; **microprocessor** microprocessore m; **microscope** microscopio m; **microscopic** microscopico; **microwave** oven forno m a microonde

midday [mɪd'deɪ] mezzogiorno m

middle ['mɪdl] **1** adj di mezzo **2** n mezzo m; **in the ~ of** of floor, room nel centro di, in mezzo a; of period of time a metà di; **be in the ~ of doing sth** stare facendo qc; **middle-aged** di mezz'età; **Middle Ages** Medioevo m; **middle class** borghese; **middle class(es)** la borghesia f; **Middle East** Medio Oriente m; **middleman** intermediario m; **middle name** secondo nome m; **middleweight** boxer peso m medio

midfielder [mɪd'fiːldə(r)] centrocampista m

midnight ['mɪdnaɪt] mezzanotte f; **midsummer** piena estate f; **midweek** a metà settimana; **Midwest** regione f medio-occidentale degli USA; **midwife** ostetrica f; **midwinter** pieno inverno m

might[1] [maɪt] I ~ **be late** potrei far tardi; **it ~ rain** magari piove; **you ~ have told me!** potevi dirmelo!

might[2] [maɪt] (power) forze fpl

mighty ['maɪtɪ] **1** adj potente **2** adv F (extremely) molto

migraine ['miːɡreɪn] emicrania f

migrant worker ['maɪɡrənt] emigrante m/f; **migrate** emigrare; of birds migrare; **migration** emigrazione f; of birds migrazione f

mike [maɪk] F microfono *m*

Milan [mɪˈlæn] Milano *f*

mild [maɪld] *weather* mite; *cheese*, *person* dolce; *curry* poco piccante; *punishment*, *sedative* leggero; *mildly* gentilmente; *(slightly)* moderatamente; **to put it ∼** a dir poco; **mildness** *of weather* mitezza *f*; *of person*, *voice* dolcezza *f*

mile [maɪl] miglio *m*; **∼s better** F molto meglio; **mileage** chilometraggio *m*; **mileometer** contachilometri *m*; **milestone** *also fig* pietra *f* miliare

militant [ˈmɪlɪtənt] **1** *adj* militante **2** *n* militante *m/f*

military [ˈmɪlɪtrɪ] **1** *adj* militare **2** *n*: **the ∼** l'esercito *m*; **military service** servizio *m* militare

militia [mɪˈlɪʃə] milizia *f*

milk [mɪlk] **1** *n* latte *m* **2** *v/t* mungere; **milk chocolate** cioccolato *m* al latte; **milkman** lattaio *m*; **milkshake** frappé *m inv*

mill [mɪl] *for grain* mulino *m*; *for textiles* fabbrica *f*

millennium [mɪˈlenɪəm] millennio *m*

milligram [ˈmɪlɪɡræm] milligrammo *m*

millimetre, *Am* **millimeter** [ˈmɪlɪmiːtə(r)] millimetro *m*

million [ˈmɪljən] milione *m*; **millionaire** miliardario *m*, -a *f*

mime [maɪm] mimare

mimic [ˈmɪmɪk] **1** *n* imitatore *m*, -trice *f* **2** *v/t* imitare

mince [mɪns] *meat* carne *f* tritata

mind [maɪnd] **1** *n* mente *f*; **it's all in your ∼** è solo la tua immaginazione; **be out of one's ∼** essere matto; **keep sth in ∼** tenere presente qc; **change one's ∼** cambiare idea; **it didn't enter my ∼** non mi è passato per la testa; **make up one's ∼** decidersi; **have sth on one's ∼** essere preoccupato per qc; **keep one's ∼ on sth** concentrarsi su qc; **speak one's ∼** dire quello che si pensa **2** *v/t* *(look after)* tenere d'occhio; *children* badare a; *(heed)* fare attenzione a; **I don't ∼ what we do** non importa cosa facciamo; **do you ∼ if I smoke?** le dispiace se fumo?; **∼ the step!** attento al gradino!; **∼ your own business!** fatti gli affari tuoi! **3** *v/i*: **∼!** *(be careful)* attenzione!; **never ∼!** non farci caso!; **I don't ∼** è uguale *o* indifferente; **mind-boggling** incredibile; **mindless** *violence* insensato

mine¹ [maɪn] *pron* il mio *m*, la mia *f*; i miei *mpl*, le mie *fpl*; **a cousin of ∼** un mio cugino

mine² [maɪn] *n for coal etc* miniera *f*

mine³ [maɪn] **1** *n explosive* mina *f* **2** *v/t* minare '**minefield** *also fig* campo *m* minato; **miner** minatore *m*

mineral ['mɪnərəl] minerale *m*; **mineral water** acqua *f* minerale

'**minesweeper** NAUT dragamine *m inv*

mingle ['mɪŋgl] *of sounds* mischiarsi; *at party* mescolarsi

mini ['mɪnɪ] *skirt* mini *f inv*

miniature ['mɪnɪtʃə(r)] in miniatura

minimal ['mɪnɪməl] minimo; **minimalism** minimalismo *m*; **minimize** minimizzare; **minimum 1** *adj* minimo **2** *n* minimo *m*; **minimum wage** salario *m* minimo garantito

mining ['maɪnɪŋ] industria *f* mineraria

'**miniskirt** minigonna *f*

minister ['mɪnɪstə(r)] POL ministro *m*; REL pastore *m*; **ministerial** ministeriale; **Minister of Defence** ministro *m* della difesa; **ministry** POL ministero *m*

mink [mɪŋk] visone *m*

minor ['maɪnə(r)] **1** *adj* piccolo; **in D ~** MUS in Re minore **2** *n* LAW minorenne *m/f*; **minority** minoranza *f*

mint [mɪnt] *herb* menta *f*; *chocolate* cioccolato *m* alla menta; *sweet* mentina *f*

minus ['maɪnəs] **1** *n* (*~ sign*) meno *m* **2** *prep* meno; **~ 10 degrees** 10 gradi sotto zero

minuscule ['mɪnəskjuːl] minuscolo

minute[1] ['mɪnɪt] *n of time* minuto *m*; **in a ~** (*soon*) in un attimo; **just a ~** un attimo

minute[2] [maɪ'njuːt] *adj* (*tiny*) piccolissimo; (*detailed*) minuzioso; **in ~ detail** minuziosamente

minute hand ['mɪnɪt] lancetta *f* dei minuti

minutely [maɪ'njuːtlɪ] (*in detail*) minuziosamente; (*very slightly*) appena

minutes ['mɪnɪts] *of meeting* verbale *m*

miracle ['mɪrəkl] miracolo *m*; **miraculous** miracoloso; **miraculously** miracolosamente

mirror ['mɪrə(r)] **1** *n* specchio *m*; MOT specchietto *m* **2** *v/t* riflettere

misanthropist [mɪ'zænθrə-pɪst] misantropo *m*

misbehave [mɪsbə'heɪv] comportarsi male; **misbehaviour**, *Am* **misbehavior** comportamento *m* scorretto

miscalculate [mɪs'kælkjulleɪt] calcolare male; **miscalculation** errore *m* di calcolo

miscarriage ['mɪskærɪdʒ] MED aborto *m* spontaneo; **~ of justice** errore *m* giudiziario

miscellaneous [mɪsə'leɪnɪəs] eterogeneo

mischief ['mɪstʃɪf] (*naughtiness*) birichinate *fpl*; **mischievous** (*naughty*) birichino; (*malicious*) perfido

misconception [mɪskən-'sepʃn] idea *f* sbagliata

misconduct [mɪs'kɒndʌkt] reato *m* professionale

misconstrue [mɪskən'struː] interpretare male

misdemeanour, *Am* misdemeanor [mɪsdɪ'miːnə(r)] infrazione *f*

miser [maɪzə(r)] avaro *m*, -a *f*

miserable ['mɪzrəbl] (*unhappy*) infelice; *weather*, *performance* deprimente

miserly ['maɪzəlɪ] *person* avaro; *amount* misero

misery ['mɪzərɪ] (*unhappiness*) tristezza *f*; (*wretchedness*) miseria *f*

misfire [mɪs'faɪə(r)] *of scheme* far cilecca; *of engine* perdere colpi

misfit ['mɪsfɪt] *in society* disadattato *m*, -a *f*

misfortune [mɪs'fɔːtʃən] sfortuna *f*

misgivings [mɪs'gɪvɪŋz] dubbi *mpl*

misguided [mɪs'gaɪdɪd] *attempts, theory* sbagliato

mishandle [mɪs'hændl] *situation* gestire male

misinform [mɪsɪn'fɔːm] informare male

misinterpret [mɪsɪn'tɜːprɪt] interpretare male; **misinterpretation** interpretazione *f* errata

misjudge [mɪs'dʒʌdʒ] giudicare male

mislay [mɪs'leɪ] smarrire

mislead [mɪs'liːd] trarre in inganno; **misleading** fuorviante

mismanage [mɪs'mænɪdʒ] gestire male; **mismanagement** cattiva gestione *f*

misprint ['mɪsprɪnt] refuso *m*

mispronounce [mɪs-prə'naʊns] pronunciare male; **mispronunciation** errore *m* di pronuncia

misread [mɪs'riːd] *word, figures* leggere male; *situation* interpretare male

misrepresent [mɪsreprɪ'zent] *facts, truth* travisare

miss¹ [mɪs]: *Miss Smith* signorina Smith; *~!* signorina!

miss² [mɪs] **1** *n*: **give the meeting a ~** non andare alla riunione **2** *v/t* (*not hit*) mancare; *emotionally* sentire la mancanza di; *bus, train, plane* perdere; (*not be present at*) mancare a; *I ~ you* mi manchi **3** *v/i* fallire

misshapen [mɪs'ʃeɪpən] deforme

missile ['mɪsaɪl] (*rocket*) missile *m*

missing ['mɪsɪŋ] scomparso; **be ~** *of person, plane* essere disperso; *there's a piece ~* manca un pezzo

mission ['mɪʃn] (*task, people*) missione *f*

misspell [mɪs'spel] scrivere male

mist [mɪst] foschia *f*

mistake [mɪ'steɪk] **1** *n* errore *m*, sbaglio *m*; **make a ~** fare un errore, sbagliarsi; **by ~** per errore **2** *v/t* sbagliare; **~ sth for sth** scambiare qc per qc; mistaken sbagliato; **be ~** sbagliarsi

mister ['mɪstə(r)] *☞* **Mr**

mistress ['mɪstrɪs] *lover* amante *f*; *of dog* padrona *f*

mistrust [mɪs'trʌst] **1** *n* diffidenza *f* **2** *v/t* diffidare di

misty ['mɪstɪ] *weather* nebbioso; *eyes* velato

misunderstand [mɪsʌndə-'stænd] fraintendere; misunderstanding *mistake* malinteso *m*, equivoco *m*; *argument* dissapore *m*

misuse **1** [mɪs'juːs] *n* uso *m* improprio **2** [mɪs'juːz] *v/t* usare impropriamente

mitigating circumstances ['mɪtɪgeɪtɪŋ] circostanze *fpl* attenuanti

mitt [mɪt] *in baseball* guantone *m*; mitten muffola *f*

mix [mɪks] **1** *n* (*mixture*) mescolanza *f*; *in cooking*: *ready to use* preparato *m* **2** *v/t* mescolare **3** *v/i socially* socializzare

◆ **mix up** confondere; **mix sth up with sth** scambiare qc per qc; **be mixed up** *emotionally* avere disturbi emotivi; *of figures, papers* essere in disordine; **be mixed up in** essere coinvolto in

mixed [mɪkst] misto; *reac-*

tions, reviews contrastante; **I've got ~ feelings** sono combattuto; mixer *for food* mixer *m inv*; *drink* bibita da mischiare a un superalcolico; mixture miscuglio *m*; *medicine* sciroppo *m*; mix-up confusione *f*

moan [məʊn] **1** *n of pain* lamento *m*, gemito *m*; (*complaint*) lamentela *f* **2** *v/i in pain* lamentarsi, gemere; (*complain*) lamentarsi

mob [mɒb] **1** *n* folla *f* **2** *v/t* prendere d'assalto

mobile ['məʊbaɪl] **1** *adj that can be moved* mobile; **she's less ~ now** non si può muovere tanto, ora **2** *n for decoration* mobile *m inv*; *phone* telefonino *m*; mobile home casamobile *f*; mobile phone telefono *m* cellulare; mobility mobilità *f*

mobster ['mɒbstə(r)] gangster *m inv*

mock [mɒk] **1** *adj exam, election* simulato **2** *v/t* deridere; mockery (*derision*) scherno *m*; (*travesty*) farsa *f*

mode [məʊd] *form* mezzo *m*; COMPUT modalità *f inv*

model ['mɒdl] **1** *adj employee, husband* modello; *boat, plane* in miniatura **2** *n* (*miniature*) modellino *m*; (*pattern*) modello *m*; (*fashion ~*) indossatrice *f*; **male ~** indossatore *m* **3** *v/t* indossare **4** *v/i for designer* fare l'indossatore /

-trice; *for artist* posare
modem ['məʊdem] modem *m*
inv
moderate 1 ['mɒdərət] *adj*
moderato **2** ['mɒdərət] *n*
POL moderato *m*, -a *f* **3**
['mɒdəreɪt] *v/t* moderare;
moderately abbastanza;
moderation (*restraint*) moderazione *f*
modern ['mɒdn] moderno;
modernization modernizza-
zione *f*; **modernize 1** *v/t*
modernizzare **2** *v/i* moder-
nizzarsi
modest ['mɒdɪst] modesto;
modesty modestia *f*
modification [mɒdɪfɪ'keɪʃn]
modifica *f*; **modify** modificare
module ['mɒdju:l] modulo *m*
moist [mɔɪst] umido;
moisten inumidire; **mois-
ture** umidità *f*; **moisturizer**
for skin idratante *m*
molasses [mə'læsɪz] melassa
f
mold *etc Am* ➝ **mould** *etc*
molecule [mə'lekjʊlə(r)] molecola *f*
molest [mə'lest] *child, woman*
molestare
mollycoddle ['mɒlɪkɒdl] F
coccolare
molten ['məʊltən] fuso
mom [mɒm] F mamma *f*
moment ['məʊmənt] attimo
m, istante *m*; **at the ~** al momento; **for the ~** per il momento; **momentarily** (*for a*

moment) per un momento;
Am (*in a moment*) da un momento all'altro; **momentary**
momentaneo; **momentous**
importante
momentum [mə'mentəm] impeto *m*
monarch ['mɒnək] monarca
m
monastery ['mɒnəstrɪ] monastero *m*; **monastic** mona-
stico
Monday ['mʌndeɪ] lunedì *m*
inv
monetary ['mʌnɪtrɪ] monetario
money ['mʌnɪ] denaro *m*, soldi *mpl*; **money belt** marsu-
pio *m*; **money market** mercato *m* monetario; **money
order** vaglia *m*
mongrel ['mʌŋgrəl] cane *m*
bastardo
monitor ['mɒnɪtə(r)] **1** *n* COM-
PUT monitor *m inv* **2** *v/t* osservare
monk [mʌŋk] frate *m*, monaco *m*
monkey ['mʌŋkɪ] scimmia *f*; F
(*child*) diavoletto *m*; **monkey wrench** chiave *f* a rullino
monologue, *Am* **monolog**
['mɒnəlɒg] monologo *m*
monopolize [mə'nɒpəlaɪz] *also fig* monopolizzare; **monopoly** monopolio *m*
monotonous [mə'nɒtənəs]
monotono; **monotony** monotonia *f*

monster ['mɒnstə(r)] mostro m; monstrosity obbrobio m

month [mʌnθ] mese m; monthly 1 adj mensile 2 adv mensilmente 3 n magazine mensile m

monument ['mɒnjumənt] monumento m

mood [muːd] (frame of mind) umore m; (bad ~) malumore m; of meeting, country clima m; be in a good / bad ~ essere di cattivo / buon umore; moody lunatico; (bad-tempered) di cattivo umore

moon [muːn] luna f; moonlight 1 n chiaro m di luna 2 v/i F lavorare in nero; moonlit night di luna piena

moor [mʊə(r)] boat ormeggiare

moose [muːs] alce m

mop [mɒp] 1 n for floor mocio® m; for dishes spazzolino per i piatti 2 v/t floor lavare; eyes, face asciugare

♦ mop up raccogliere; MIL eliminare

moped ['məʊped] motorino m

moral ['mɒrəl] 1 adj morale; person di saldi principi morali 2 n of story morale f; ~s principi mpl morali

morale [məˈrɑːl] morale m

morality [məˈrælətɪ] moralità f inv

morbid ['mɔːbɪd] morboso

more [mɔː(r)] 1 adj più, altro; some ~ tea? dell'altro tè?; a few ~ sandwiches qualche altro tramezzino; for ~ information per maggiori informazioni; ~ and ~ students / time sempre più studenti / tempo; there's no ~ ... non c'è più ... 2 adv più; with verbs di più; ~ important più importante; ~ and ~ sempre più; ~ or less più o meno; once ~ ancora una volta; ~ than 100 oltre 100; I don't live there any~ non abito più lì 3 pron: do you want some ~? ne vuoi ancora?, ne vuoi dell'altro; a little ~ un altro po'; moreover inoltre

morgue [mɔːg] obitorio m

morning ['mɔːnɪŋ] mattino m, mattina f; in the ~ di mattina; (tomorrow) domattina; this ~ stamattina; tomorrow ~ domani mattina; good ~ buongiorno

moron ['mɔːrɒn] F idiota m/f

morphine ['mɔːfiːn] morfina f

mortal ['mɔːtl] 1 adj mortale 2 n mortale m/f; mortality mortalità f

mortar ['mɔːtə(r)] MIL mortaio m cement malta f

mortgage ['mɔːɡɪdʒ] 1 n mutuo m ipotecario 2 v/t ipotecare

mortuary ['mɔːtjʊərɪ] camera f mortuaria

mosaic [məʊˈzeɪɪk] mosaico m

Moscow ['mɒskəʊ] Mosca f

Moslem ☞ Muslim

mosque [mɒsk] moschea f

mosquito [mɒsˈkiːtəʊ] zanzara f

moss [mɒs] muschio m

most [məʊst] **1** adj la maggior parte di; ~ **Saturdays** quasi tutti i sabati **2** adv (very) estremamente; **the ~ beautiful** il più bello; **the one I like ~** quello che mi piace di più; **~ of all** soprattutto **3** pron la maggior parte (**of** di); **at (the)** ~ al massimo; **make the ~ of** approfittare (al massimo) di; **mostly** per lo più

MOT [eməʊˈtiː] revisione annuale obbligatoria dei veicoli

motel [məʊˈtel] motel m inv

moth [mɒθ] falena f; (clothes ~) tarma f

mother [ˈmʌðə(r)] **1** n madre f **2** v/t fare da mamma a; **motherhood** maternità f; **Mothering Sunday**, **Mother's Day**; **mother-in-law** suocera f; **motherly** materno; **Mother's Day** Festa f della mamma; **mother tongue** madrelingua f

motif [məʊˈtiːf] motivo m

motion [ˈməʊʃn] (movement) moto m; (proposal) mozione f; **motionless** immobile

motivate [ˈməʊtɪveɪt] person motivare; **motivation** motivazione f; **motive** motivo m

motor [ˈməʊtə(r)] motore m, F car macchina f; **motorbike** moto f; **motorboat** motoscafo m; **motorcycle** motoci-

cletta f; **motorcyclist** motociclista m/f; **motor home** casamobile f; **motorist** automobilista m/f; **motor mechanic** meccanico m; **motor racing** automobilismo m; **motor vehicle** autoveicolo m; **motorway** autostrada f

mould¹ [məʊld] n on food muffa f

mould² [məʊld] **1** n stampo m **2** v/t also fig plasmare

mouldy [ˈməʊldɪ] food ammuffito

mound [maʊnd] (hillock) collinetta f; (pile) mucchio m; Am: in baseball pedana f del lanciatore

mount [maʊnt] **1** n (horse) cavalcatura f; **Mount McKinlay** il Monte McKinlay **2** v/t steps salire; horse montare a; bicycle montare in; campaign organizzare; jewel montare **3** v/i (increase) aumentare

♦ **mount up** accumularsi

mountain [ˈmaʊntɪn] montagna f; **mountain bike** mountain bike f inv; **mountaineer** alpinista m/f; **mountaineering** alpinismo m; **mountainous** montuoso

mourn [mɔːn] **1** v/t piangere **2** v/i: ~ **for** piangere la morte di; **mourner** persona che partecipa a un corteo funebre; **mournful** triste; **mourning** lutto m; **be in ~** essere in lutto; **wear** ~ portare il lutto

mouse [maʊs] (*pl* **mice** [maɪs]) topo *m*; COMPUT mouse *m inv*; **mouse mat**, **mouse pad** COMPUT tappetino *m* del mouse

moustache [məˈstɑː(r)] baffi *mpl*

mouth [maʊθ] bocca *f*; *of river* foce *f*; **mouthful** *of food* boccone *m*; *of drink* sorsata *f*; **mouthorgan** armonica *f* a bocca; **mouthpiece** *of instrument* bocchino *m*; (*spokesperson*) portavoce *m/f*; **mouthwash** collutorio *m*; **mouthwatering** che fa venire l'acquolina

move [muːv] **1** *n* (*step, action, in game*) mossa *f*; *change of house* trasloco *m*; **get a ~ on!** F spicciati! **2** *v/t object* spostare, muovere; (*transfer*) trasferire; *emotionally* commuovere; ~ **house** traslocare **3** *v/i* muoversi, spostarsi; (*transfer*) trasferirsi

◆ **move around** *in room* muoversi; *from place to place* spostarsi

◆ **move in** trasferirsi

movement [ˈmuːvmənt] movimento *m*; **movers** *Am* firm ditta *f* di traslochi

movie [ˈmuːvɪ] film *m inv*; **go to a ~/the ~s** andare al cinema; **moviegoer** frequentatore *m*, -trice *f* di cinema; **movie theater** *Am* cinema *m inv*

moving [ˈmuːvɪŋ] *which can move* mobile; *emotionally* commovente

mow [məʊ] *grass* tagliare, falciare; **mower** tosaerba *m inv*

MP [emˈpiː] (= ***Member of Parliament***) deputato *m*; (= ***Military Policeman***) polizia *f* militare

mph [empiːˈeɪtʃ] (= ***miles per hour***) miglia orarie

Mr [ˈmɪstə(r)] signor

Mrs [ˈmɪsɪz] signora

Ms [mɪz] signora *appellativo usato sia per donne sposate che nubili*

much [mʌtʃ] **1** *adj* molto; **so ~ money** tanti soldi; **how ~ sugar?** quanto zucchero?; **as ~ ... as ...** tanto ... quanto ... **2** *adv* molto; **very ~** moltissimo; **too ~** troppo; **as ~ as ...** tanto quanto ... **3** *pron* molto; **nothing ~** niente di particolare

mud [mʌd] fango *m*

muddle [ˈmʌdl] **1** *n* disordine *m*; **I'm in a ~** sono confuso **2** *v/t* confondere

muddy [ˈmʌdɪ] fangoso; *hands, boots* sporco di fango

muesli [ˈmuːzlɪ] müsli *m*

muffin [ˈmʌfɪn] pasticcino *m*

muffle [ˈmʌfl] *sound* attutire; *voice* camuffare; **muffler** *Am* MOT marmitta *f*

mug[1] [mʌg] *n for tea, coffee* tazzone *m*; F (*face*) faccia *f*

mug[2] [mʌg] *v/t attack* aggredire

mugger ['mʌgə(r)] aggressore *m*; **mugging** aggressione *f*; **muggy** afoso

mule [mjuːl] *animal* mulo *m*; *Am* (*slipper*) mule *f inv*

multicultural [mʌltɪ'kʌltʃərəl] multiculturale

multilateral [mʌltɪ'lætərəl] POL multilaterale

multimedia [mʌltɪ'miːdɪə] **1** *adj* multimediale **2** *n* multimedialità **1**

multinational [mʌltɪ'næʃnl] **1** *adj* multinazionale **2** *n* COM multinazionale *f*

multiple ['mʌltɪpl] multiplo; **multiple sclerosis** sclerosi *f* multipla

multiplex (cinema) ['mʌltɪpleks] cinema *m inv* multisale

multiplication [mʌltɪplɪ-'keɪʃn] moltiplicazione *f*; **multiply** **1** *v/t* moltiplicare **2** *v/i* moltiplicarsi

multi-storey (car park) [mʌltɪ'stɔːrɪ] parcheggio *m* a più piani

mum [mʌm] mamma *f*

mumble ['mʌmbl] **1** *n* borbottio *m* **2** *v/t & v/i* borbottare

mummy ['mʌmɪ] mamma *f*

mumps [mʌmps] orecchioni *mpl*

munch [mʌntʃ] sgranocchiare

municipal [mjuː'nɪsɪpl] municipale

mural ['mjʊərəl] murale *m*

murder ['mɜːdə(r)] **1** *n* omicidio *m* **2** *v/t* uccidere; *song* ro-

vinare; **murderer** omicida *m/f*

murky ['mɜːkɪ] *also fig* torbido

murmur ['mɜːmə(r)] **1** *n* mormorio *m* **2** *v/t* mormorare

muscle ['mʌsl] muscolo *m*; **muscular** *pain, strain* muscolare; *person* muscoloso

museum [mjuː'zɪəm] museo *m*

mushroom ['mʌʃrʊm] **1** *n* fungo *m* **2** *v/i* crescere rapidamente

music ['mjuːzɪk] musica *f*; *in written form* spartito *m*; **musical 1** *adj* musicale; *person* portato per la musica; *voice* melodioso **2** *n* musical *m inv*; **musical instrument** strumento *m* musicale; **musician** musicista *m/f*

Muslim ['mʊzlɪm] **1** *adj* islamico **2** *n* musulmano *m*, -a *f*

mussel ['mʌsl] cozza *f*

must [mʌst] ◇ (*necessity*): **I ~ be on time** devo arrivare in orario; **I ~n't be late** non devo far tardi ◇ (*probability*): **it ~ be about 6 o'clock** devono essere circa le sei

mustache *Am* ☞ **moustache**

mustard ['mʌstəd] senape *f*

musty ['mʌstɪ] *smell* di stantio; *room* che sa di stantio

mutilate ['mjuːtɪleɪt] mutilare

mutiny ['mjuːtɪnɪ] **1** *n* ammutinamento *m* **2** *v/i* ammutinarsi

mutter ['mʌtə(r)] farfugliare

mutual ['mju:tjʊəl] *admiration* reciproco; *friend* in comune

muzzle ['mʌzl] **1** *n of animal* muso *m*; *for dog* museruola *f* **2** *v/t*: **~ the press** imbavagliare la stampa

my [maɪ] il mio *m*, la mia *f*, i miei *mpl*, le mie *fpl*; **~ sister / brother** mia sorella / mio fratello

myself [maɪ'self] mi; *emphatic* io stesso; *after prep* me stesso; **I've hurt ~** mi sono fatto male

mysterious [mɪ'stɪərɪəs] misterioso; **mysteriously** misteriosamente; **mystery** mistero *m*; **mystify** lasciare perplesso

myth [mɪθ] *also fig* mito *m*; **mythical** mitico

N

nag [næg] **1** *v/i of person* brontolare di continuo **2** *v/t* assillare; **nagging** *person* brontolone; *doubt*, *pain* assillante

nail [neɪl] *for wood* chiodo *m*; *on finger*, *toe* unghia *f*; **nail clippers** *npl* tagliaunghie *m inv*; **nail file** limetta *f* per unghie; **nail polish** smalto *m* per unghie; **nail polish remover** solvente *m* per unghie

naive [naɪ'iːv] ingenuo

naked ['neɪkɪd] nudo

name [neɪm] **1** *n* nome *m*; **what's your ~?** come ti chiami? **2** *v/t* chiamare; **namely** cioè; **namesake** omonimo *m*, -a *f*

nanny ['nænɪ] bambinaia *f*

nap [næp] sonnellino *m*; **have a ~** farsi un sonnellino

napkin ['næpkɪn] (*table ~*) tovagliolo *m*; (*sanitary ~*) assorbente *m*

Naples ['neɪpəlz] Napoli *f*

nappy ['næpɪ] pannolino *m*

narcotic [nɑː'kɒtɪk] narcotico *m*

narrate [nə'reɪt] raccontare, narrare; **narrative 1** *n story* racconto **2** *adj poem*, *style* narrativo; **narrator** narratore *m*, -trice *f*

narrow ['nærəʊ] stretto; *views*, *mind* ristretto; *victory* di stretta misura; **narrowly** *win* di stretta misura; **~ escape sth** scampare a qc per un pelo F; **narrow-minded** di idee ristrette

nasty ['nɑːstɪ] *person*, *remark*, *smell*, *weather* cattivo; *cut*, *wound*, *disease* brutto

nation ['neɪʃn] nazione *f*; **national 1** *adj* nazionale **2** *n* cittadino *m*, -a *f*; **national anthem** inno *m* nazionale; **national debt** debito *m* pubblico; **nationalism** nazionalismo *m*; **nationality** nazionalità *f* inv; **nationalize** *industry etc* nazionalizzare

native ['neɪtɪv] **1** *adj* indigeno; ~ **language** madrelingua *f* **2** *n* (*tribesman*) indigeno *m*, -a *f*; **she's a ~ of New York** è originaria di New York; **Native American** indiano *m*, -a *f* d'america; **native speaker**: **English** ~ persona *f* di madrelingua inglese

NATO ['neɪtəʊ] (= **North Atlantic Treaty Organization**) NATO *f*

natural ['næt∫rəl] naturale; **naturalist** naturalista *m/f*; **naturalize**: **become** ~**d** naturalizzarsi; **naturally** (*of course*) naturalmente; (*behave, speak* con naturalezza; (*by nature*) per natura; **nature** natura *f*; **nature reserve** riserva *f* naturale

naughty ['nɔːtɪ] cattivo; *photograph, word etc* spinto

nausea ['nɔːzɪə] nausea *f*; **nauseate** (*fig: disgust*) disgustare; **nauseating** *smell, taste* nauseante; *person* disgustoso; **nauseous**: **feel** ~ avere la nausea

nautical ['nɔːtɪkl] nautico

naval ['neɪvl] navale; *officer, uniform* della marina

navel ['neɪvl] ombelico *m*

navigate ['nævɪgeɪt] *also* COMPUT navigare; *in car* fare da navigatore / -trice; **navigation** navigazione *f*; **navi-**

gator *on ship, in aeroplane* ufficiale *m* di rotta; *in car* navigatore *m*, -trice *f*

navy ['neɪvɪ] marina *f* militare; **navy blue 1** *n* blu *m inv* scuro **2** *adj* blu scuro

near [nɪə(r)] **1** *adv* vicino **2** *prep* vicino a; **do you go ~ the bank?** va dalle parti della banca? **3** *adj* vicino; **in the ~ future** nel prossimo futuro; **nearby** *live* vicino; **nearly** quasi; **near-sighted** miope

neat [niːt] *room, desk, person* ordinato; *whisky* liscio; *solution* efficace; F (*terrific*) fantastico

necessarily ['nesəsərɪlɪ] necessariamente; **necessary** necessario; **it is ~ to ...** è necessario ..., bisogna ...; **necessity** necessità *f inv*

neck [nek] collo *m*; **necklace** collana *f*; **neckline** *of dress* scollo *m*; **necktie** cravatta *f*

née [neɪ] nata

need [niːd] **1** *n* bisogno *m*; **if ~ be** se necessario; **be in ~** (*be needy*) essere bisognoso; **be in ~ of sth** aver bisogno di qc; **you don't ~ to wait** non c'è bisogno che aspetti; **I ~ to talk to you** ti devo parlare

needle ['niːdl] *for sewing, on dial* ago *m*; **needlework** cucito *m*

needy ['niːdɪ] bisognoso

negative ['negətɪv] negativo

neglect [nɪ'glekt] **1** *n* trascuratezza *f* **2** *v/t* trascurare; **ne-**

glected *gardens, author* trascurato

negligence ['neglɪdʒəns] negligenza *f*; **negligent** negligente; **negligible** *quantity* trascurabile

negotiable [nɪ'gəʊʃəbl] negoziabile; **negotiate 1** *v/i* trattare **2** *v/t deal, settlement* negoziare; *obstacles* superare; *bend in road* affrontare; **negotiation** negoziato *m*; **negotiator** negoziatore *m*, -trice *f*

neighbor *etc Am* ☞ **neighbour** *etc*

neighbour ['neɪbə(r)] vicino *m*, -a *f*; **neighbourhood** *in town* quartiere *m*; **in the ~ of** *fig* intorno a; **neighbouring** *house, state* confinante; **neighbourly** amichevole

neither ['naɪðə(r)] **1** *adj*: ~ **player** nessuno dei due giocatori **2** *pron* nessuno *m* dei due, nessuna *f* delle due **3** *adv*: ~ **... nor ...** né ... né ... **4** *conj* neanche; ~ **do I** neanch'io

neon light ['niːɒn] luce *f* al neon

nephew ['nevjuː] nipote *m* (di zii)

nerve [nɜːv] nervo *m*; (*courage*) coraggio *m*; (*impudence*) faccia *f* tosta; **get on s.o.'s ~s** dare sui nervi a qu; **nerve-racking** snervante; **nervous** nervoso; **be ~ about doing sth** essere ansioso all'idea di fare qc; **nervous breakdown** esaurimento *m* nervoso; **nervousness** nervosismo *m*; **nervous wreck**: **be a ~** avere i nervi a pezzi

nest [nest] nido *m*

net[1] [net] *n for fishing* retino *m*; *for tennis* rete *f*; COMPUT Internet *f*; **on the ~** su Internet

net[2] [net] *adj* COM netto

nettle ['netl] ortica *f*

network *of contacts, cells,* COMPUT rete *f*; **social ~** rete *f* sociale; **networking** *mettere in* rete *f* di contatti professionali in situazioni informali

neurologist [njʊə'rɒlədʒɪst] neurologo *m*, -a *f*

neurosis [njʊə'rəʊsɪs] nevrosi *f inv*

neurotic nevrotico

neuter ['njuːtə(r)] *animal* sterilizzare

neutral ['njuːtrəl] **1** *adj country* neutrale; *colour* neutro **2** *n gear* folle *m*; **neutrality** neutralità *f*; **neutralize** neutralizzare

never ['nevə(r)] mai; ~*! in disbelief* ma va'!; **you're ~ going to believe this** non ci crederesti mai; **nevertheless** comunque, tuttavia

new [njuː] nuovo; **that's nothing ~** non è una novità; **newborn** neonato; **newcomer** nuovo arrivato *m*, nuova arrivata *f*; **newly** (*recently*) recentemente; **newly weds** sposini *mpl*

news [njuːz] notizia *f*; *on TV, radio* notiziario *m*; novità *f inv*; **any ~?** ci sono novità?; **that's ~ to me** mi giunge nuovo; **newsagent** giornalaio *m*; **newscast** telegiornale *m*; **newscaster** giornalista *m/f* televisivo, -a; **news flash** notizia *f* flash; **newspaper** giornale *m*; **newsreader** giornalista *m/f* radiotelevisivo, -a; **news report** notiziario *m*; **newsstand** edicola *f*; **newsvendor** edicolante *m/f*

New 'Year anno *m* nuovo; **Happy New Year!** buon anno!; **New Year's Day** capodanno *m*; **New Year's Eve** San Silvestro *m*

next [nekst] **1** *adj in time* prossimo; *in space* vicino; **the ~ month** il mese dopo; **who's ~?** a chi tocca? **2** *adv* dopo; **~ to** (*beside*) accanto a; (*in comparison with*) a paragone di; **next door 1** *adj: ~ neighbour* vicino *m*, -a *f* di casa **2** *adv* live nella casa accanto; **next of kin** parente *m/f* prossimo

nibble ['nɪbl] mordicchiare

nice [naɪs] *person* carino, gentile; *day, weather, party* bello; *meal, food* buono; **that's very ~ of you** molto gentile da parte tua!; **nicely** *written, presented* bene

niche [niːʃ] nicchia *f*

nick [nɪk] *cut* taglietto *m*; **in the ~ of time** appena in tempo

nickel ['nɪkl] *material* nichel *m*; *Am coin* moneta *f* da 5 centesimi di dollaro

'nickname soprannome *m*

niece [niːs] nipote *f* (di zii)

night [naɪt] notte *f*; (*evening*) sera *f*; **at ~** di notte / di sera; **last ~** ieri notte / ieri sera; **stay the ~** rimanere a dormire; **work ~s** fare il turno di notte; **good ~** buona notte; **nightcap** (*drink*) bicchierino bevuto prima di andare a letto; **nightclub** night(-club) *m inv*; **nightdress** camicia *f* da notte; **night flight** volo *m* notturno; **nightlife** vita *f* notturna; **nightly** ogni sera; *late at night* ogni notte; **nightmare** *also fig* incubo *m*; **night porter** portiere *m*, -a; **night school** scuola *f* serale; **night shift** turno *m* di notte; **nightshirt** camicia *f* da notte (*da uomo*); **nightspot** locale *m* notturno; **nighttime**: **at ~** di notte, la notte

nimble ['nɪmbl] agile

nine [naɪn] nove; **nineteen** diciannove; **nineteenth** diciannovesimo; **ninetieth** novantesimo; **ninety** novanta; **ninth** nono

nip [nɪp] (*pinch*) pizzico *m*; (*bite*) morso *m*

nipple ['nɪpl] capezzolo *m*

nitrogen ['naɪtrədʒn] azoto *m*

no [nəʊ] **1** *adv* no **2** *adj* nessuno; **there's ~ coffee left** non c'è più caffè; **I have ~ money** non ho soldi; **~ smoking** vietato fumare

noble ['nəʊbl] nobile

nobody ['nəʊbɑːdɪ] nessuno; **~ knows** nessuno lo sa; **there was ~ at home** non c'era nessuno in casa

no-brainer [nəʊ'breɪnə(r)] **F** cretinata *f*; **a real ~ of a decision** una decisione semplicissima

nod [nɒd] **1** *n* cenno *m* del capo **2** *v/i* fare un cenno col capo; **~ in agreement** annuire
◆ **nod off** (*fall asleep*) appisolarsi

noise [nɔɪz] (*sound*) rumore *m*; *loud, unpleasant* chiasso *m*; *noisy* rumoroso; *children, party* chiassoso; **don't be so ~** non fate tanto rumore

nominal ['nɒmɪnl] *amount* simbolico

nominate ['nɒmɪneɪt] (*appoint*) designare; **nomination** (*appointing*) nomina *f*; *person proposed* candidato *m*, -a *f*; **nominee** candidato *m*, -a *f*

nonalco'holic analcolico

nonchalant ['nɒnʃələnt] noncurante

noncommissioned 'officer ['nɒnkəmɪʃnd] sottufficiale *m*

noncommittal [nɒnkə'mɪtl] *person, response* evasivo

nondescript ['nɒndɪskrɪpt] ordinario

none [nʌn] nessuno *m*, -a *f*; **there are ~ left** non ne sono rimasti; **there is ~ left** non ne è rimasto, non è rimasto niente

nonentity [nɒn'entətɪ] nullità *f inv*

nonetheless [nʌnðə'les] nondimeno

none'xistent inesistente

non'fiction opere *fpl* non di narrativa

noninter'ference, noninter'vention non intervento *m*

no-'nonsense *approach* pragmatico

non'payment mancato pagamento *m*

nonpol'luting non inquinante

non'resident *in country* non residente *m/f*; (*in hotel*) persona chi non è cliente di un albergo

nonre'turnable a fondo perduto

nonsense ['nɒnsəns] sciocchezze *fpl*; **don't talk ~** non dire sciocchezze

non'smoker non fumatore *m*, -trice *f*

non'standard fuori standard, non di serie; *use of a word* che fa eccezione

non'stick *pans* antiaderente

non'stop 1 *adj flight, train* diretto; *chatter* continuo **2** *adv* fly, *travel* senza scalo; *chatter*, *argue* di continuo

non'union non appartenente al sindacato

non'violence non violenza *f*; **nonviolent** non violento

noodles ['nuːdlz] spaghetti *mpl* cinesi

noon [nuːn] mezzogiorno *m*

'no-one → **nobody**

noose [nuːs] cappio *m*

nor [nɔː(r)] né; **~ do I** neanch'io, neanche a me

norm [nɔːm] norma *f*; **normal** normale; **normality** normalità *f*; **normally** (*usually*) di solito; *in a normal way* normalmente

north [nɔːθ] **1** *n* nord *m* **2** *adj* settentrionale, nord *inv* **3** *adv* travel verso nord; **~ of** a nord di; **North America** America *f* del Nord; **North American 1** *n* nordamericano *m*, -a *f* **2** *adj* nordamericano; **northeast** nordest *m*; **northerly** *wind* settentrionale; *direction* nord *inv*; **northern** settentrionale; **northerner** settentrionale *m/f*; **North Korea** Corea *f* del Nord; **North Korean 1** *adj* nordcoreano **2** *n* nordcoreano *m*, -a *f*; **North Pole** polo *m* nord; **northward** *travel* verso nord; **northwest** nordovest *m*

Norway ['nɔːweɪ] Norvegia *f*; **Norwegian 1** *adj* norvegese

2 *n* person norvegese *m/f*; *language* norvegese *m*

nose [nəʊz] naso *m*; **right under my ~!** proprio sotto il naso!

♦ **nose around** F curiosare

nostalgia [nɒ'stældʒɪə] nostalgia *f*; **nostalgic** nostalgico

nostril ['nɒstrəl] narice *f*

nosy ['nəʊzɪ] F curioso

not [nɒt] non; *I hope ~* spero di no; *I don't know* non so; *he didn't help* non ha aiutato; **~ me** io no

notable ['nəʊtəbl] notevole

notch [nɒtʃ] tacca *f*

note [nəʊt] MUS, *comment on text* nota *f*; *short letter* biglietto *m*; *memo to self* appunto *m*; *money* banconota *f*; **take ~s** prendere appunti; **take ~ of sth** prendere nota di qc; **notebook** taccuino *m*; COMPUT notebook *m inv*; **noted** noto; **notepad** bloc-notes *m inv*; **notepaper** carta *f* da lettere

nothing ['nʌθɪŋ] niente; **~ but** nient'altro che; **~ much** niente di speciale; **for ~** (*for free*) gratis; (*for no reason*) per un nonnulla

notice ['nəʊtɪs] **1** *n* on notice board, in street avviso *m*; (*advance warning*) preavviso *m*; *in newspaper* annuncio *m*; *to leave job* preavviso *m*; *to leave house* disdetta *f*; **at short ~** con un breve preavviso; *until further ~* fino a nuovo avviso; *hand in one's ~ to employer* presentare le dimissioni; *take no ~ of s.o.* / *sth* non fare caso a qu / qc **2** v/t notare; **notice board** bacheca *f*; **noticeable** sensibile

notify ['nəʊtɪfaɪ] informare

notion ['nəʊʃn] idea *f*

notorious [nəʊ'tɔ:rɪəs] famigerato

nought [nɔ:t] zero *m*

noun [naʊn] nome *m*, sostantivo *m*

nourishing ['nʌrɪʃɪŋ] nutriente; **nourishment** nutrimento *m*

novel ['nɒvl] romanzo *m*; **novelist** romanziere *m*, -a *f*

novelty ['nɒvltɪ] novità *f inv*

November [nəʊ'vembə(r)] novembre *m*

novice ['nɒvɪs] principiante *m/f*

now [naʊ] ora, adesso; *~ and again*, *~ and then* ogni tanto; *by ~* ormai; *from ~ on* d'ora in poi; *right ~* subito; *just ~* (proprio) adesso; *~*, *~!* su, su!; **nowadays** oggigiorno

nowhere ['nəʊweə(r)] da nessuna parte; *it's ~ near finished* è ben lontano dall'essere terminato

nuclear ['nju:klɪə(r)] nucleare; **nuclear energy** energia *f* nucleare; **nuclear physics** fisica *f* nucleare; **nuclear**

power energia *f* nucleare; POL potenza *f* nucleare; **nuclear power station** centrale *f* nucleare; **nuclear reactor** reattore *m* nucleare; **nuclear waste** scorie *fpl* radioattive; **nuclear weapon** arma *f* nucleare

nude [nju:d] **1** *adj* nudo **2** *n painting* nudo *m*; *in the ~* nudo

nudge [nʌdʒ] dare un colpetto di gomito a; *parked car* spostare leggermente

nudist ['nju:dɪst] nudista *m/f*

nuisance ['nju:sns] seccatura *f*; *make a ~* / *o.s.* dare fastidio

null and 'void [nʌl] nullo

numb [nʌm] intirizzito; *emotionally* impietrito

number ['nʌmbə(r)] **1** *n* numero *m*; *(quantity)* quantità *f inv* **2** v/t *put a number on* numerare; **number plate** *of vehicle* targa *f*

numeral ['nju:mərəl] numero *m*

numerate ['nju:mərət] *adj*: *be ~* avere buone basi in matematica; *of children* saper contare

numerous ['nju:mərəs] numeroso

nun [nʌn] suora *f*

nurse [nɜ:s] infermiere *m*, -a *f*; **nursery school** asilo *m*; *in house* stanza *f* dei bambini; *for plants* vivaio *m*; **nursery rhyme** filastrocca *f*;

nursery school scuola *f* materna; **nursing** professione *f* d'infermiere; **nursing home** *for old people* casa *f* di riposo

nut [nʌt] noce *f*; *for bolt* dado *m*; **nutcrackers** schiaccianoci *m inv*

nutrient ['njuːtrɪənt] sostanza *f* nutritiva; **nutrition** alimen-

tazione *f*; **nutritious** nutriente

nuts [nʌts] F (*crazy*) svitato; **be ∼ about s.o.** essere pazzo di qu

'nutshell: *in a ∼* in poche parole

nutty ['nʌtɪ] *taste* di noce; F (*crazy*) pazzo

O

oak [əʊk] *tree* quercia *f*; *wood* rovere *m*

oar [ɔː(r)] remo *m*

oasis [əʊ'eɪsɪs] *also fig* oasi *f inv*

oath [əʊθ] LAW giuramento *m*; (*swearword*) imprecazione *f*

'oatmeal farina *f* d'avena

obedience [ə'biːdɪəns] ubbidienza *f*; **obedient** ubbidiente; **obediently** docilmente

obese [əʊ'biːs] obeso; **obesity** obesità *f*

obey [ə'beɪ] *parents* ubbidire a; *law* osservare

obituary [ə'bɪtjʊərɪ] necrologio *m*

object¹ ['ɒbdʒɪkt] *n* (*thing*) oggetto *m*; (*aim*) scopo *m*; GRAM complemento *m*

object² [əb'dʒekt] *v/i* avere da obiettare

objection [əb'dʒekʃn] obiezione *f*; **objectionable** (*unpleasant*) antipatico; **objective 1** *adj* obiettivo **2** *n* obiet-

tivo *m*; **objectively** obiettivamente; **objectivity** obiettività *f*

obligation [ɒblɪ'geɪʃn] obbligo *m*; **obligatory** obbligatorio; **obliging** servizievole

oblique [ə'bliːk] **1** *adj reference* indiretto **2** *n in punctuation* barra *f*

obliterate [ə'blɪtəreɪt] *city* annientare; *memory* cancellare

oblivion [ə'blɪvɪən] oblio *m*; *fall into ∼* cadere in oblio

oblong ['ɒblɒŋ] **1** *adj* rettangolare **2** *n* rettangolo *m*

obnoxious [əb'nɒkʃəs] offensivo; *smell* sgradevole; *person* odioso; *dog, child* insopportabile

obscene [əb'siːn] osceno; *salary, poverty* vergognoso; **obscenity** oscenità *f inv*

obscure [əb'skjʊə(r)] oscuro; **obscurity** oscurità *f inv*

observant [əb'zɜːvnt] osservante; **observation** osservazione *f*; **observatory** osservatorio m; **observe** osservare; **observer** osservatore m, -trice f

obsess [əbˈses]: **be ~ed with** essere fissato con; **obsession** fissazione f; **obsessive** ossessivo

obsolete [ˈɒbsəliːt] model obsoleto; word disusato

obstacle [ˈɒbstəkl] also fig ostacolo

obstetrician [ɒbstəˈtrɪʃn] ostetrico m, -a f; **obstetrics** ostetricia f

obstinacy [ˈɒbstɪnəsɪ] ostinazione f; **obstinate** ostinato

obstruct [əbˈstrʌkt] road ostruire; investigation, police ostacolare; **obstruction** on road etc ostruzione f; **obstructive** behaviour, tactics ostruzionista

obtain [əbˈteɪn] ottenere; **obtainable** products reperibile

obtuse [əbˈtjuːs] fig ottuso

obvious [ˈɒbvɪəs] ovvio, evidente; **obviously** ovviamente, evidentemente

occasion [əˈkeɪʒn] occasione f; **occasional** sporadico; **I like the ~ whisky** bevo un whisky ogni tanto; **occasionally** ogni tanto

occupant [ˈɒkjupənt] of vehicle occupante m/f; of building abitante m/f; **occupation** (job) professione f; of country occupazione f; **occupy** occupare

occur [əˈkɜː(r)] accadere; it

~red to me that ... mi è venuto in mente che ...; **occurrence** evento m

ocean [ˈəʊʃn] oceano m

o'clock [əˈklɒk]: **at five ~** alle cinque; **it's one ~** è l'una; **it's three ~** sono le tre

October [ɒkˈtəubə(r)] ottobre m

octopus [ˈɒktəpəs] polpo m

odd [ɒd] (strange) strano; (not even) dispari; **the ~ one out** l'eccezione f; **50 ~** 50 e rotti; **oddball** F persona f stramba; **odds and ends** objects cianfrusaglie fpl; things to do cose fpl; **odds-on**: **the ~ favourite** il favorito; **it's ~ that ...** è praticamente scontato che ...

odometer [əʊˈdɒmətə(r)] Am contachilometri m

odour, Am **odor** [ˈəʊdə(r)] odore m

of [ɒv] di; **the name ~ the street / hotel** il nome della strada / dell'albergo; **it's made ~ steel** è di acciaio; **die ~ cancer** morire di cancro; **a friend ~ mine** un mio amico; **very nice ~ him** molto gentile da parte sua

off [ɒf] **1** prep: **a lane ~ the main road** not far from un sentiero poco lontano dalla strada principale; **leading off** un sentiero che parte dalla strada principale; **£20 ~ the price** 20 sterline di sconto **2** adv: **be ~ of light,**

TV etc essere spento; *of gas, tap* essere chiuso; *(cancelled)* essere annullato; *of food* essere finito; **she was ~ today** *not at work* oggi non era al lavoro; **we're ~ tomorrow** *leaving* partiamo domani; **take a day ~** prendere un giorno libero; **it's 3 miles ~** dista 3 miglia; **it's a long way ~** è molto lontano **3** *adj food* andato a male; **~ switch** interruttore *m* di spegnimento

offence [əˈfens] LAW reato *m*; **take ~ at sth** offendersi per qc; **offend** *(insult)* offendere; **offender** LAW delinquente *m/f*; **offense** *Am → offence*; **offensive 1** *adj behaviour, remark,* offensivo; *smell* sgradevole **2** *n* (MIL: *attack)* offensiva *f*

offer [ˈɒfə(r)] **1** *n* offerta *f* **2** *v/t* offrire; **~ s.o. sth** offrire qc a qu

off'hand *attitude* disinvolto

office [ˈɒfɪs] ufficio *m*; *(position)* carica *f*; **office hours** orario *m* d'ufficio; **officer** MIL ufficiale *m*; *in police* agente *m/f*; **official 1** *adj* ufficiale **2** *n* funzionario *m*, -a *f*; **officially** ufficialmente; **officious** invadente

'off-licence negozio *m* di alcolici

'off-line disconnesso, off-line *inv*; **go ~** disconnettersi

'off-peak *rates* ridotto; **~ elec-**tricity elettricità *f* a tariffa ridotta

'off-season bassa stagione *f*

'offset *losses* compensare

'offshore *drilling rig, investment* off-shore *inv*

'offside LAW *etc* destro; *on the left* sinistro **2** *adv* SP in fuorigioco

'offspring figli *mpl*; *of animal* piccoli *mpl*

off-the-'record ufficioso

often [ˈɒfn] spesso; **how ~ do you go there?** ogni quanto tempo ci vai?

oil [ɔɪl] **1** *n* olio *m*; *petroleum* petrolio *m*; *for central heating* nafta *f* **2** *v/t* oliare; **oil change** cambio *m* dell'olio; **oil company** compagnia *f* petrolifera; **oilfield** giacimento *m* petrolifero; **oil painting** quadro *m* a olio; **oil refinery** raffineria *f* di petrolio; **oil rig** piattaforma *f* petrolifera; **oil slick** chiazza *f* di petrolio; **oil tanker** petroliera *f*; **oil well** pozzo *m* petrolifero; **oily** unto

ointment [ˈɔɪntmənt] pomata *f*

ok [əʊˈkeɪ]: **can I ~?** posso? - va bene!; **is it ~ with you if ...?** ti va bene se ...?; **does that look ~?** ti sembra che vada bene?; **that's ~ by me** per me va bene; **are you ~?** *well, not hurt* stai bene?; **he's ~** *(is a good guy)* è in gamba

old [əʊld] vecchio; (*previous*) precedente; **how ~ is he?** quanti anni ha?; **old age** vecchiaia *f*; **old-age pensioner** pensionato *m*, -a *f*; **old-fashioned** antiquato

olive ['ɒlɪv] oliva *f*; **olive oil** olio *m* d'oliva

Olympic 'Games [ə'lɪmpɪk] Olimpiadi *fpl*, giochi *mpl* olimpici

omelette, *Am***omelet** ['ɒmlɪt] frittata *f*

ominous ['ɒmɪnəs] sinistro

omission [ə'mɪʃn] omissione *f*; **on purpose** esclusione *f*; **omit** omettere; **on purpose** escludere; **~ to do sth** tralasciare di fare qc

on [ɒn] **1** *prep* su; **~ the table** sul tavolo; **~ the bus** in autobus; **~ TV** alla TV; **~ Sunday** domenica; **~ Sundays** di domenica; **~ the 1st of June** il primo (di) giugno; **I'm ~ antibiotics** sto prendendo antibiotici; **this is ~ me** (*I'm paying*) offro io; **have you any money ~ you?** hai dei soldi con te?; **~ his arrival** al suo arrivo; **~ hearing this** al sentire queste parole **2** *adj*: **be ~** of light, TV etc essere acceso; of gas, tap essere aperto; of machine essere in funzione; of handbrake essere inserito; **it's ~ after the news** of programme è dopo il notiziario; **the meeting is ~ scheduled**

to happen la riunione si fa; **with his jacket ~** con la giacca; **what's ~ tonight?** on TV etc cosa c'è stasera?; **I've got something ~ tonight** *planned* stasera ho un impegno; **you're ~** *I accept your offer etc* d'accordo; **that's not ~** (*not allowed, not fair*) non è giusto; **~ you go** (*go ahead*) fai pure; **talk ~** continuare a parlare; **and so ~** e così via; **~ and ~** talk etc senza sosta **3** *adj*: **the ~ switch** l'interruttore *m* d'accensione

once [wʌns] **1** *adv* (*one time*) una volta; (*formerly*) un tempo; **~ again, ~ more** ancora una volta; **at ~** (*immediately*) subito; **all at ~** (*suddenly*) improvvisamente; (*all*) **at ~** (*together*) contemporaneamente; **~ upon a time there was ...** c'era una volta ... **2** *conj* non appena; **~ you have finished** non appena hai finito

one [wʌn] **1** *number* uno *m* **2** *adj* uno, -a; **~ day** un giorno **3** *pron* uno *m*, -a *f*; **which ~?** quale?; **that ~** quello *m*, -a *f*; **this ~** questo *m*, -a *f*; **~ by ~** *enter, deal with* uno alla volta; **~ another** l'un l'altro, a vicenda; **what can ~ say?** cosa si può dire?; **the little ~s** i piccoli; **one-off 1** *n* fatto *m* eccezionale; *person* persona *f* eccezionale **2** *adj* unico; **one-parent family** famiglia *f* monogenitore; **oneself** si; *after prep* se stesso *m*, -a *f*, sé; **cut ~** tagliarsi; **do sth ~** fare qc da sé; **one-way street** strada *f* a senso unico; **one-way ticket** biglietto *m* di sola andata

onion ['ʌnjən] cipolla *f*

'on-line connesso, on-line *inv*; **go ~** connettersi; **on-line banking** telebanking *m*; **on-line shopping** shopping *m* in Rete

onlooker ['ɒnlʊkə(r)] astante *m*

only ['əʊnlɪ] **1** *adv* solo; **not ~ X but also Y** non solo X ma anche Y; **~ just** a malapena **2** *adj* unico; **~ son** unico figlio maschio

'onset inizio *m*

'onside SP non in fuorigioco

on-the-job 'training training *m inv* sul lavoro

onto ['ɒntuː]: **put sth ~ sth** mettere qc sopra qc

onwards ['ɒnwədz] in avanti; **from ... ~** da ... in poi

opaque [əʊ'peɪk] *glass* opaco

open ['əʊpən] **1** *adj* aperto; **in the ~ air** all'aria aperta **2** *v/t* aprire **3** *v/i of door, shop* aprirsi; *of flower* sbocciare; **open-air** *meeting, concert* all'aperto; *pool* scoperto; **open day** giornata *f* di apertura al pubblico; **open-ended** *contract etc* aperto; **opening** *in wall etc* apertura *f*; *of film, novel etc* inizio *m*; *(job*

going) posto *m* vacante; **openly** *(honestly, frankly)* apertamente; **open-minded** aperto; **open ticket** biglietto *m* aperto

opera ['ɒprə] lirica *f*, opera *f*; **opera house** teatro *m* dell'opera; **opera singer** cantante lirico *m*, -a *f*

operate ['ɒpəreɪt] **1** *v/i of company* operare; *of airline, bus service* essere in servizio; *of machine* funzionare; MED operare, intervenire **2** *v/t machine* far funzionare

♦ **operate on** MED operare

'operating room *Am* MED sala *f* operatoria; **operating system** COMPUT sistema *m* operativo; **operation** operazione *f*; MED intervento *m* (chirurgico), operazione *f*; *of machine* funzionamento *m*; **have an ~** MED subire un intervento (chirurgico); **operator** TELEC centralinista *m/f*; *of machine* operatore *m*, -trice *f*; *(tour ~)* operatore *m* turistico

opinion [ə'pɪnjən] opinione *f*, parere *m*; **in my ~** a mio parere; **opinion poll** sondaggio *m* d'opinione

opponent [ə'pəʊnənt] avversario *m*, -a *f*

opportunist [ɒpə'tjuːnɪst] opportunista *m/f*; **opportunity** opportunità *f inv*

oppose [ə'pəʊz] opporsi a; **be ~d to ...** essere contrario a

...; **as** ~**d to** ... piuttosto che ...

opposite ['ɒpəzɪt] **1** adj direction opposto; meaning, views contrario; house di fronte; **the** ~ **side of the road** l'altro lato della strada **2** n contrario m; **opposite number** omologo m

opposition [ɒpə'zɪʃn] opposizione f

oppress [ə'pres] people opprimere; **oppressive** rule oppressivo; weather opprimente

optical illusion ['ɒptɪkl] illusione f ottica

optician [ɒp'tɪʃn] dispensing ottico m, -a f; ophthalmic optometrista m/f

optimism ['ɒptɪmɪzm] ottimismo m; **optimist** ottimista m/f; **optimistic** view ottimistico; person ottimista; **optimistically** ottimisticamente

optimum ['ɒptɪməm] **1** adj ottimale **2** n optimum m inv

option ['ɒpʃn] possibilità f inv, opzione f; **he had no other** ~ non ha avuto scelta; **optional** facoltativo

or [ɔː(r)] o; **he can't hear** ~ **see** non può né sentire né vedere; ~ **else!** o guai a te!

oral ['ɔːrəl] orale

orange ['ɒrɪndʒ] **1** adj colour arancione **2** n fruit arancia f; colour arancione m; **orange juice** succo m d'arancia

orator ['ɒrətə(r)] oratore m, -trice f

orbit ['ɔːbɪt] **1** n of earth orbita f **2** v/t the earth orbitare intorno a

orchard ['ɔːtʃəd] frutteto m

orchestra ['ɔːkɪstrə] orchestra f

orchid ['ɔːkɪd] orchidea f

ordain [ɔː'deɪn] priest ordinare

ordeal [ɔː'diːl] esperienza f traumatizzante

order ['ɔːdə(r)] **1** n ordine m; for goods, in restaurant ordinazione f; **in** ~ **to do sth** così da fare qc; **out of** ~ (not functioning) fuori servizio; (not in sequence) fuori posto **2** v/t ordinare; ~ **s.o. to do sth** ordinare a qu di fare qc **3** v/i ordinare

orderly ['ɔːdəlɪ] **1** adj room, mind ordinato; crowd disciplinato **2** n in hospital inserviente m/f

ordinarily [ɔːdɪ'neərɪlɪ] (as a rule) normalmente; **ordinary** normale; pej ordinario

ore [ɔː(r)] minerale m grezzo

organ ['ɔːgən] ANAT, MUS organo m; **organic** food, fertilizer biologico; **organically grown** biologicamente; **organism** organismo m

organization [ɔːgənaɪ'zeɪʃn] organizzazione f; **organize** organizzare; **organized** person organizzatore m, -trice f

orgasm ['ɔːgæzm] orgasmo m

orient ['ɔːrɪənt] *Am* orientare;
Oriental 1 *adj* orientale 2 *n* orientale *m/f*; orientate orientare

origin ['ɒrɪdʒɪn] origine *f*;
original 1 *adj* originale 2 *n painting etc* originale *m*; originality originalità *f*; originally (*at first*) in origine; ~ he comes from France è di origini francesi; originate 1 *v/t scheme*, *idea* dare origine a 2 *v/i of idea*, *belief* avere origine

ornamental [ɔːnə'mentl] ornamentale

ornate [ɔː'neɪt] *style* ornato

orphan ['ɔːfn] orfano *m*, -a *f*

orthodox ['ɔːθədɒks] *also fig* ortodosso

orthopedic [ɔːθə'piːdɪk] ortopedico

ostensibly [ɒ'stensəblɪ] apparentemente

ostentatious [ɒsten'teɪʃəs] ostentato

ostracize ['ɒstrəsaɪz] ostracizzare

other ['ʌðə(r)] 1 *adj* altro; the ~ day l'altro giorno; every ~ day a giorni alterni; every ~ person una persona su due 2 *n* l'altro *m*, -a *f*; the ~s gli altri; otherwise altrimenti; (*differently*) diversamente

ought [ɔːt] I / you ~ to know dovrei / dovresti saperlo; you ~ to have done it avresti dovuto farlo

ounce [auns] oncia *f*

our [auə(r)] il nostro *m*, la nostra *f*, i nostri *mpl*, le nostre *fpl*; ~ brother / sister nostro fratello / nostra sorella; ours il nostro *m*, la nostra *f*, i nostri *mpl*, le nostre *fpl*; ourselves ci; *emphatic* noi stessi / noi stesse; *after prep* noi

oust [aust] *from office* esautorare

out [aut]: be ~ of light, fire essere spento; *of flower* essere sbocciato; *of sun* splendere; not at home, not in building essere fuori; *of calculations* essere sbagliato; (*be published*) essere uscito; *of secret* essere svelato; no longer in competition essere eliminato; (*no longer in fashion*) essere out; he's ~ in the garden è in giardino; (*get*) ~! fuori!; that's ~! (*out of the question*) è fuori discussione!; he's ~ to win fully intends to è deciso a vincere

outboard 'motor motore *m* fuoribordo

'outbreak scoppio *m*

'outcast emarginato *m*, -a *f*

'outcome risultato *m*

'outcry protesta *f*

out'dated sorpassato

out'do superare

'outdoor toilet, activities, life all'aperto; pool scoperto; outdoors all'aperto

outer ['autə(r)] wall etc

esterno

'outfit (*clothes*) completo *m*; (*company, organization*) organizzazione *f*

'outgoing flight, mail in partenza; *personality* estroverso

out'grow habits, interests perdere

outing ['autɪŋ] (*trip*) gita *f*

out'last durare più di

'outlet of pipe scarico *m*; *for sales* punto *m* di vendita; *Am* ELEC presa *f* (di corrente)

'outline 1 *n of person, building etc* profilo *m*; *of plan, novel* abbozzo *m* **2** *v/t* plans etc abbozzare

out'live sopravvivere a

'outlook (*prospects*) prospettiva *f*

out'number superare numericamente

out of ◇ *motion* fuori; *fall ~ the window* cadere fuori dalla finestra; *of plan, position* da; *20 miles ~ Newcastle* 20 miglia da Newcastle ◇ *cause* per; *~ jealousy* per gelosia ◇ (*without*) senza; *we're ~ petrol* siamo senza benzina ◇ *from a group* su *5 ~ 10* 5 su 10

out-of-'date *passport* scaduto; *values* superato

'output 1 *n of factory* produzione *f*; COMPUT output *m inv* **2** *v/t* (*produce*) produrre

'outrage 1 *n feeling* sdegno *m*; *act* atrocità *f inv* **2** *v/t* indi-

gnare; **outrageous** *acts* scioccante; *prices* scandaloso

out'right 1 *adj winner* assoluto **2** *adv* win nettamente; *kill* sul colpo

'outset: *at / from the ~* all' / dall'inizio

out'shine eclissare

'outside 1 *adj* esterno **2** *adv sit, go* fuori **3** *prep* fuori da; (*apart from*) al di fuori da **4** *n of building*, case etc esterno *m*; *at the ~* al massimo; **outsider** estraneo *m*, -a *f*; *in election, race* outsider *m inv*

'outsize *clothing* di taglia forte

'outskirts periferia *f*

out'smart ☞ **outwit**

'outsource dare in appalto a terzi

out'standing eccezionale; FIN da saldare

outstretched ['autstretʃt] *hands* teso

outward ['autwəd] *appearance* esteriore; *~ journey* viaggio *m* d'andata; **outwardly** esteriormente

out'weigh contare più di

out'wit riuscire a gabbare

oval ['əuvl] ovale

oven ['ʌvn] forno *m*

over ['əuvə(r)] **1** *prep* (*above*) sopra, su; (*across*) dall'altra parte di; (*more than*) oltre; (*during*) nel corso di; *travel all ~ Brazil* girare tutto il Brasile; *you find them* *all ~ Brazil* si trovano dappertutto in Brasile; **we're the worst** il peggio è passato; **~ and above** oltre a **2** *adv:* **be ~** *(finished)* essere finito; *(left)* essere rimasto; **~ to you** *(your turn)* tocca a te; **~here** / **there** qui / lì; *it hurts all* ~ mi fa male dappertutto; **painted white all ~** tutto dipinto di bianco; **I've told you ~ and ~ again** te l'ho detto mille volte; **do sth ~ again** rifare qc

'**overall** *length* totale; **overalls** tuta *f* da lavoro

over'**awe** intimidire

over'**balance** perdere l'equilibrio

over'**bearing** autoritario

'**overcast** *sky* coperto *m*

over'**charge** *customer* far pagare più del dovuto a

'**overcoat** cappotto *m*

over'**come** *difficulties* superare; **be ~ by emotion** essere sopraffatto dall'emozione

over'**crowded** sovraffollato

over'**do** *(exaggerate)* esagerare; *in cooking* stracuocere; **overdone** *meat* stracotto

'**overdose** overdose *f inv*

'**overdraft** scoperto *m* (di conto); **have an ~** avere il conto scoperto; **overdraw: be £800 ~n** essere (allo) scoperto di 800 sterline

over'**dressed** troppo elegante

'**overdrive** MOT overdrive *m*

inv

over'**estimate** sovrastimare

over'**expose** sovraesporre

'**overflow**[1] *n pipe* troppopieno *m*

over'**flow**[2] *v/i of water* traboccare; *of river* straripare

'**overhead** *lights, cables* in alto, aereo; *railway* sopraelevato; **overheads** FIN costi *mpl* di gestione

over'**hear** sentire per caso

over'**heated** *room, engine* surriscaldato

over'**joyed** [əʊvəˈdʒɔɪd] felicissimo

'**overland** via terra

'**overlap** *(partly cover)* sovrapporsi; *(partly coincide)* coincidere

over'**load** sovraccaricare

over'**look** *of tall building etc* dominare, dare su; *deliberately* chiudere un occhio su; *accidentally* non notare

'**overly** [ˈəʊvəlɪ] troppo; **not ~ ...** non particolarmente ...

'**overnight** *travel* di notte; *stay* per la notte; *fig change etc* da un giorno all'altro

'**overpass** cavalcavia *m inv*

over'**power** *physically* sopraffare

over'**priced** [əʊvəˈpraɪst] troppo caro

over'**rated** [əʊvəˈreɪtɪd] sopravvalutato

over'**ride** *decision etc* annulla-

re; (*be more important than*)
prevalere su; **overriding**
decision principale

over'rule *decision* annullare

over'seas all'estero

over'see sorvegliare

over'shadow *fig* eclissare

'oversight svista *f*

oversimplifi'cation semplificazione *f* eccessiva

over'sleep non svegliarsi in tempo

over'state esagerare; **over-statement** esagerazione *f*

over'take *in work, development* superare; MOT sorpassare

over'throw[1] *v/t government* rovesciare

'overthrow[2] *n of government* rovesciamento *m*

'overtime 1 *n* straordinario *m* **2** *adv*: **work ~** fare lo straordinario

over'turn 1 *v/t vehicle, object* ribaltare; *government* rovesciare **2** *v/i of vehicle* ribaltar-

si

'overview visione *f* d'insieme

overwhelming [əʊvə'welmɪŋ] *feeling* profondo; *majority* schiacciante

over'work 1 *n* lavoro *m* eccessivo **2** *v/i* lavorare troppo

owe [əʊ] dovere (**s.o.** *a* qu);
owing to a causa di

owl [aʊl] gufo *m*

own[1] [əʊn] *v/t* possedere

own[2] [əʊn] **1** *adj* proprio; **my ~ car** la mia macchina; **my very ~ mother** proprio mia madre **2** *pron*: **a car of my ~** un'auto tutta mia; **on my / his ~** da solo

♦ **own up** confessare

owner ['əʊnə(r)] proprietario *m*, -a *f*; **ownership** proprietà *f*

oxygen ['ɒksɪdʒən] ossigeno *m*

oyster ['ɔɪstə(r)] ostrica *f*

ozone ['əʊzəʊn] ozono *m*;
ozone layer fascia *f* or strato *m* d'ozono

P

PA [piː'eɪ] (= **personal assistant**) assistente personale

pace [peɪs] (*step*) passo *m*;
(*speed*) ritmo *m*; **pacemaker** MED pacemaker *m inv*; SP battistrada *m inv*

Pacific [pə'sɪfɪk]: **the ~ (Ocean)** il Pacifico

pacifier ['pæsɪfaɪə(r)] *Am for*

baby succhiotto *m*; **pacifism** pacifismo *m*; **pacifist** pacifista *m/f*; **pacify** placare

pack [pæk] **1** *n* (*back~*) zaino *m*; *of cereal, food* confezione *f*; *of cigarettes* pacchetto *m*; *of peas etc* confezione *f*; *of cards* mazzo *m* **2** *v/t bag* fare; *item of clothing etc* mettere in valigia; *goods* imballare; *groceries* imbustare **3** *v/i* fare la valigia / le valigie; **package 1** *n* (*parcel*) pacco *m*; *of offers etc* pacchetto *m* **2** *v/t* confezionare; **packaging** *also fig* confezione *f*; **packed** (*crowded*) affollato; **packet** confezione *f*; *of cigarettes, crisps* pacchetto *m*

pact [pækt] patto *m*

pad¹ [pæd] **1** *n piece of cloth etc* tampone *m*; *for writing* blocchetto *m* **2** *v/t with material* imbottire; *speech, report* farcire

pad² [pæd] *v/i* (*move quietly*) camminare a passi felpati

padding ['pædɪŋ] *material* imbottitura *f*; *in speech etc* riempitivo *m*

paddle ['pædl] **1** *n for canoe* pagaia *f* **2** *v/i in canoe* pagaiare

paddock ['pædək] paddock *m inv*

padlock ['pædlɒk] lucchetto *m*

page¹ [peɪdʒ] *n of book etc* pagina *f*

page² [peɪdʒ] *v/t* (*call*) chiamare con l'altoparlante

pager ['peɪdʒə(r)] cercapersone *m inv*

paid em'ployment occupazione *f* rimunerata

pain [peɪn] dolore *m*; **be in ~** soffrire; **a ~ in the neck** F una rottura *f* di scatole; **painful** (*distressing*) doloro-

so; (*laborious*) difficile; **painfully** (*extremely*, *acutely*) estremamente; **painkiller** analgesico *m*; **painstaking** accurato

paint [peɪnt] **1** *n for wall, car* vernice *f*; *for artist* colore *m* **2** *v/t wall etc* pitturare; *picture* dipingere; **paintbrush** pennello *m*; **painter** *decorator* imbianchino *m*; *artist* pittore *m*, -trice *f*; **painting** *activity* pittura *f*; (*picture*) quadro *m*; **paintwork** vernice *f*

pair [peə(r)] *of objects* paio *m*; *of animals, people* coppia *f*; **a ~ of shoes** un paio di scarpe

pajamas *Am* ☞ **pyjamas**

Pakistan [pɑːkɪˈstɑːn] Pakistan *m*; **Pakistani 1** *n* pakistano *m*, -a *f* **2** *adj* pakistano

pal [pæl] F (*friend*) amico *m*, -a *f*

palace ['pælɪs] palazzo *m* signorile

palate ['pælət] palato *m*

palatial [pəˈleɪʃl] sfarzoso

pale [peɪl] pallido

Palestine ['pæləstaɪn] Palestina *f*; **Palestinian 1** *n* palestinese *m/f* **2** *adj* palestinese

pallet ['pælɪt] pallet *m inv*

pallor ['pælə(r)] pallore *m*

palm [pɑːm] *of hand* palma *f*; **palm tree** palma *f*

paltry ['pɔːltrɪ] irrisorio

pamper ['pæmpə(r)] viziare

pamphlet ['pæmflɪt] volantino *m*

pan [pæn] *for cooking* pentola

f; *for frying* padella f; **pancake** crêpe f *inv*

pandemonium [pændɪˈməʊnɪəm] pandemonio m

pane [peɪn]: ~ **(of glass)** vetro m

panel [ˈpænl] pannello m; *of experts* gruppo m; *of judges* giuria f; **panelling**, *Am* **paneling** rivestimento m a pannelli

panic [ˈpænɪk] **1** n panico m **2** v/i: **don't** ~ non farti prendere dal panico; **panic-stricken** in preda al panico

panorama [pænəˈrɑːmə] panorama m; **panoramic** panoramico

pant [pænt] ansimare

panties [ˈpæntɪz] mutandine fpl

pantihose ☞ **pantyhose**

pants [pænts] pantaloni mpl

pantyhose [ˈpæntɪhəʊz] collant mpl

papal [ˈpeɪpəl] pontificio

paper [ˈpeɪpə(r)] **1** n *material* carta f; *(news~)* giornale m; *(wall~)* carta f da parati; *academic* relazione f; *(examination* ~*)* esame m; ~**s** *(identity* ~*s, documents)* documenti mpl **2** v/t carta f *v/t room, walls* tappezzare; **paperback** tascabile m; **paper clip** graffetta f; **paperwork** disbrigo delle pratiche

parachute [ˈpærəʃuːt] **1** n paracadute m *inv* **2** v/i paracadutarsi **3** v/t *troops, supplies*

paracadutare

parade [pəˈreɪd] **1** n *(procession)* sfilata f **2** v/i sfilare

paradise [ˈpærədaɪs] paradiso m

paradox [ˈpærədɒks] paradosso m; **paradoxical** paradossale; **paradoxically** paradossalmente

paragraph [ˈpærəgrɑːf] paragrafo m

parallel [ˈpærəlel] **1** n *(in geometry)* parallela f; GEOG, fig parallelo m; **do two things in** ~ fare due cose in parallelo **2** adj *also fig* parallelo **3** v/t *(match)* uguagliare

paralysis [pəˈræləsɪs] *also fig* paralisi f *inv*; **paralyze** *also fig* paralizzare

paramedic [pærəˈmedɪk] paramedico m, -a f

parameter [pəˈræmɪtə(r)] parametro m

paramilitary [pærəˈmɪlɪtrɪ] **1** adj paramilitare **2** n *appartenente ad un'organizzazione paramilitare*

paranoia [pærəˈnɔɪə] paranoia f; **paranoid** paranoide

paraphrase [ˈpærəfreɪz] parafrasare

parasite [ˈpærəsaɪt] *also fig* parassita m

parasol [ˈpærəsɒl] parasole m

paratrooper [ˈpærətruːpə(r)] MIL paracadutista m

parcel [ˈpɑːsl] pacco m

pardon [ˈpɑːdn] **1** n LAW grazia *f*; **I beg your ~?** (*what did you say*) prego?; **I beg your ~** (*I'm sorry*) scusi **2** *v/t* scusare; LAW graziare

parent ['peərənt] genitore *m*; **parental** dei genitori; **parent company** società *f* inv madre; **parent-teacher association** *organizzazione composta da genitori e insegnanti*

parish ['pærɪʃ] parrocchia *f*

park[1] [pɑːk] *n* parco *m*

park[2] [pɑːk] *v/t & v/i* MOT parcheggiare

parking ['pɑːkɪŋ] MOT parcheggio *m*; **no ~** sosta *f* vietata; **parking brake** *Am* freno *m* a mano; **parking garage** *Am* parcheggio *m* coperto; **parking lot** *Am* parcheggio *m*; **parking meter** parchimetro *m*; **parking ticket** multa *f* per sosta vietata

parliament ['pɑːləmənt] parlamento *m*

parole [pə'rəʊl] **1** *n* libertà *f* vigilata **2** *v/t* concedere la libertà vigilata a

parrot ['pærət] pappagallo *m*

part [pɑːt] **1** *n* parte *f*; *of machine* pezzo *m*; *Am*: *in hair* riga *f*; **take ~ in** prendere parte in **2** *adv* (*partly*) in parte **3** *v/i* separarsi **4** *v/t*: **~ one's hair** farsi la riga; **partial** (*incomplete*) parziale; **be ~ to** avere un debole per; **partially** parzialmente

participant [pɑː'tɪsɪpənt] partecipante *m/f*; **participate** partecipare (*in a*); **participation** partecipazione *f*

particular [pə'tɪkjʊlə(r)] (*specific*) particolare; (*fussy*) pignolo; **in ~** in particolare; **particularly** particolarmente

parting ['pɑːtɪŋ] *of people* separazione *f*; *in hair* riga *f*

partition [pɑː'tɪʃn] (*screen*) tramezzo *m*; (*of country*) suddivisione *f*

partly ['pɑːtlɪ] in parte

partner ['pɑːtnə(r)] COM socio *m*, -a *f*; *in relationship* partner *m/f* inv; *in particular activity* compagno *m*, -a *f*; **partnership** COM società *f* inv; *in particular activity* sodalizio *m*

'part-time part-time

party ['pɑːtɪ] **1** *n* (*celebration*) festa *f*; POL partito *m*; (*group*) gruppo *m* **2** *v/i* F far baldoria; **party-pooper** F guastafeste *m/f* inv

pass [pɑːs] **1** *n* for entry passi *m* inv; SP passaggio *m*; *in mountains* passo *m*; **make a ~ at** fare avances a **2** *v/t* (*hand*) passare; (*go past*) passare davanti a; (*overtake*) sorpassare; (*go beyond*) superare; (*approve*) approvare; SP passare; **~ an exam** superare un esame; **~ sentence** LAW emanare la sentenza; **~ the time** passare il tempo **3** *v/i* passare; *in exam* essere promosso

◆ **pass away** *euph* spegnersi

◆ **pass on 1** *v/t information, book, savings* passare (**to** a) **2** *v/i* (*euph*: *die*) mancare

◆ **pass out** (*faint*) svenire

◆ **pass up** *opportunity* lasciarsi sfuggire

passable ['paːsəbl] *road* transitabile; (*acceptable*) passabile

passage ['pæsɪdʒ] (*corridor*) passaggio *m*; *from book* passo *m*; **the ~ of time** il passare del tempo

passenger ['pæsɪndʒə(r)] passeggero *m*, -a *f*

passer-by [pɑːsə'baɪ] passante *m/f*

passion ['pæʃn] passione *f*; **passionate** appassionato

passive ['pæsɪv] **1** *adj* passivo **2** GRAM passivo *m*; **passive smoking** fumo *m* passivo

'passport passaporto *m*; **passport control** controllo *m* passaporti; **password** parola *f* d'ordine; COMPUT password *f inv*

past [pɑːst] **1** *adj* (*former*) precedente; **in the ~ few days** nei giorni scorsi **2** *n* passato *m*; **in the ~** nel passato **3** *prep* in *position* oltre; **it's half ~ two** sono le due e mezza; **it's ~ seven o'clock** sono le sette passate **4** *adv*: **run ~** passare di corsa

pasta ['pæstə] pasta *f*

paste [peɪst] **1** *n* (*adhesive*) colla *f* **2** *v/t* (*stick*) incollare

pastime ['pɑːstaɪm] passatempo *m*

pastry ['peɪstrɪ] *for pie* pasta *f* (sfoglia); (*small cake*) pasticcino *m*

'past tense GRAM passato *m*

pasty ['peɪstɪ] *complexion* smorto

pat [pæt] **1** *n* colpetto *m*; *affectionate* buffetto *m* **2** *v/t* dare un colpetto a; *affectionately* dare un buffetto a

patch [pætʃ] **1** *n* *on clothing* pezza *f*; (*period of time*) periodo *m*; (*area*) zona *f*; **go through a bad ~** attraversare un brutto periodo; **be not a ~ on** *fig* non essere niente a paragone di *v/t clothing* rattoppare

◆ **patch up** (*repair*) riparare alla meglio; *quarrel* risolvere

patchy ['pætʃɪ] *quality* irregolare; *work* discontinuo, disuguale

patent ['peɪtnt] **1** *adj* palese **2** *n for invention* brevetto *m* **3** *v/t invention* brevettare

paternal [pə'tɜːnl] paterno; **paternalism** paternalismo *m*; **paternalistic** paternalistico; **paternity** paternità *f inv*; **paternity leave** congedo *m* di paternità

path [pɑːθ] sentiero *m*; *fig* strada *f*

pathetic [pə'θetɪk] patetico; F (*very bad*) penoso

pathological [pæθəˈlɒdʒɪkl]
patologico

patience [ˈpeɪʃns] pazienza *f*;
card game solitario *m*; **patient 1** *n* paziente *m/f* **2** *adj*
paziente; **be ~!** abbi pazienza!; **patiently** pazientemen-
te

patio [ˈpætɪəʊ] terrazza *f*

patriot [ˈpeɪtrɪət] patriota
m/f; **patriotic** patriottico;
patriotism patriottismo *m*

patrol [pəˈtrəʊl] **1** *n* pattuglia *f*
2 *v/t* sbarre, border pattuglia-
re; **patrol car** autopattuglia
f; **patrolman** agente *m/f* di
pattuglia; **patrol wagon**
Am furgone *m* cellulare

patron [ˈpeɪtrən] *of artist* pa-
trocinatore *m*, -trice *f*; *of
charity* patrono *m*, -essa *f*;
of shop, cinema cliente *m/f*;
patronize *person* trattare
con condiscendenza; **pa-
tronizing** condiscendente;
patron saint patrono *m*, -a *f*

pattern [ˈpætn] *on fabric* motivo *m*, disegno *m*; *for sewing*
(carta) modello *m*; *in behaviour, events* schema *m*

paunch [pɔːntʃ] pancia *f*

pause [pɔːz] **1** *n* pausa *f* **2** *v/i*
fermarsi **3** *v/t* *tape* fermare

pave [peɪv] pavimentare; ~
the way for *fig* aprire la strada a; **pavement** *Br* marciapiede *m*; *Am* manto *m* stradale

paw [pɔː] **1** *n of animal, F*
(*hand*) zampa *f* **2** *v/t* F palpa-

re

pawn [pɔːn] *in chess* pedone
m; *fig* pedina *f*

pay [peɪ] **1** *n* paga *f* **2** *v/t* pagare; ~ **s.o. a compliment** fare
un complimento a qu **3** *v/i*
pagare; (*be profitable*) rendere; *it doesn't ~ to ...* non
conviene ...; ~ *for purchase*
pagare

◆ **pay back** *person* restituire i
soldi a; *loan* restituire; (*get
revenge on*) farla pagare a

◆ **pay off 1** *v/t* *debt* estinguere; *workers* liquidare; *corrupt
official* comprare **2** *v/i* (*be
profitable*) dare frutti

◆ **pay up** pagare

payable [ˈpeɪəbl] pagabile;
pay cheque, *Am* **pay check**
assegno *m* paga; **payday**
giorno *m* di paga; **payee** be-
neficiario *m*, -a *f*; **payment**
pagamento *m*; **pay phone**
telefono *m* pubblico

PC [piːˈsiː] (= **personal computer**) PC *m inv*; (= **politically correct**) politicamente
corretto; (= **police consta-
ble**) agente *m/f* di polizia

PDA [piːdiːˈeɪ] (= **personal
digital assistant**) PDA *m
inv*

pea [piː] pisello *m*

peace [piːs] pace *f*; **peaceful**
tranquillo; *demonstration* pacifico; **peacefully** tranquillamente; *demonstrate* pacifi-
camente

peach [piːtʃ] pesca *f*; *tree* pesco *m*

peak [piːk] **1** *n* vetta *f*; *fig* apice *m* **2** *v/i* raggiungere il livello massimo; **peak hours** ore *fpl* di punta

peanut ['piːnʌt] arachide *f*; **get paid ~s** F essere pagati una miseria F; **peanut butter** burro *m* d'arachidi

pear [peə(r)] pera *f*; *tree* pero *m*

pearl [pɜːl] perla *f*

pebble ['pebl] ciottolo *m*

pecan ['piːkən] noce *f* pecan

peck [pek] **1** *n* (*bite*) beccata *f*; (*kiss*) bacetto *m* **2** *v/t* (*bite*) beccare; (*kiss*) dare un bacetto a

peculiar [pɪ'kjuːliə(r)] (*strange*) strano; **~ to** (*special*) caratteristico di; **peculiarity** (*strangeness*) stranezza *f*; (*special feature*) caratteristica *f*

pedal ['pedl] **1** *n of bike* pedale *m* **2** *v/i* pedalare; (*cycle*) andare in bicicletta

pedantic [pɪ'dæntɪk] pedante

peddle ['pedl] *drugs* spacciare

pedestrian [pɪ'destrɪən] pedone *m*; **pedestrian crossing** passaggio *m* pedonale; **pedestrian precinct** zona *f* pedonale

pediatric [piːdɪ'ætrɪk] pediatrico; **pediatrician** pediatra *m/f*; **pediatrics** pediatria *f*

pedicure ['pedɪkjʊə(r)] pedicure *f inv*

pedigree ['pedɪgriː] **1** *n* pedi-

gree *m inv* **2** *adj* di razza pura

pee [piː] F fare pipì F

peek [piːk] **1** *n* sbirciata *f* **2** *v/i* sbirciare F

peel [piːl] **1** *n* buccia *f*; *of citrus fruit* scorza *f* **2** *v/t fruit, vegetables* sbucciare **3** *v/i of nose, shoulders* spellarsi; *of paint* scrostarsi

peep [piːp] ☞ **peek**; **peep-hole** spioncino *m*

peer[1] [pɪə(r)] *n* (*equal*) pari *m/f inv*

peer[2] [pɪə(r)] *v/i* guardare; **~ at** scrutare

peg [peg] *for coat* attaccapanni *m inv*; *for tent* picchetto *m*; **off the ~** prêt-à-porter

pejorative [pɪ'dʒɒrətɪv] peggiorativo

pellet ['pelɪt] pallina *f*; (*bullet*) pallino *m*

pen[1] [pen] penna *f*

pen[2] [pen] (*enclosure*) recinto *m*

pen[3] [pen] *Am* ☞ **penitentiary**

penalize ['piːnəlaɪz] penalizzare

penalty ['penltɪ] ammenda *f*; *in soccer* rigore *m*; *in rugby* punizione *f*; **take the ~** battere il rigore / la punizione; **penalty area** SP area *f* di rigore; **penalty clause** LAW penale *f*; **penalty kick** *in soccer* calcio *m* di rigore; *in rugby* calcio *m* di punizione; **penalty shoot-out** rigori *mpl*; **penalty spot** dischetto *m* di rigore

pencil ['pensil] matita *f*; **pencil sharpener** temperamatite *m inv*

pendant ['pendənt] *necklace* pendaglio *m*

penetrate ['penitreit] penetrare in; **penetration** penetrazione *f*

penguin ['peŋgwin] pinguino *m*

penicillin [peni'silin] penicillina *f*

peninsula [pə'ninsjulə] penisola *f*

penis ['piːnis] pene *m*

penitence ['penitəns] penitenza *f*; **penitentiary** *Am* prigione *f*

'pen name pseudonimo *m*

pennant ['penənt] gagliardetto *m*

penniless ['penilis] al verde

'pen pal amico *m*, -a *f* di penna

pension ['penʃn] pensione *f*
◆ **pension off** mandare in pensione

'pension scheme schema *m* pensionistico

pensive ['pensiv] pensieroso

Pentagon ['pentəgɒn]: **the ~** il Pentagono

pentathlon [pen'tæθlən] pentathlon *m inv*

penthouse ['penthaus] attico *m*

pent-up ['pentʌp] represso

penultimate [pe'nʌltimət] penultimo

people ['piːpl] gente *f*, persone *fpl*; (*nsg: race, tribe*) popolazione *f*; **the ~** (*the citizens*) il popolo; **the American ~** gli americani; **~ say ...** si dice che ...

pepper ['pepə(r)] *spice* pepe *m*; *vegetable* peperone *m*; **peppermint** *sweet* mentina *f*; *flavouring* menta *f*

per [pɜː(r)] **a 100 km ~ hour** 100 km all'ora; **£50 ~ night** 50 sterline a notte; **~ annum** all'anno

perceive [pə'siːv] percepire; (*view, interpret*) interpretare

percent [pə'sent] per cento; **percentage** percentuale *f*

perceptible [pə'septəbl] percettibile; **perceptibly** percettibilmente; **perception** percezione *f*; (*insightfulness*) sensibilità *f*; **perceptive** perspicace

percolate ['pɜːkəleit] *of coffee* filtrare; **percolator** caffettiera *f* a filtro

perfect 1 ['pɜːfikt] *adj* perfetto **2** ['pɜːfikt] *n* GRAM passato *m* prossimo **3** [pə'fekt] *v/t* perfezionare; **perfection** perfezione *f*; **perfectionist** perfezionista *m/f*; **perfectly** perfettamente

perforated ['pɜːfəreitid] *line* perforato

perform [pə'fɔːm] **1** *v/t* (*carry out*) eseguire; *of actors* interpretare **2** *v/i* *of actor, musi-*

cian, dancer esibirsi; *the car
~s well* la macchina dà otti-
me prestazioni; **performance** *by actor* interpretazione *f*; *by musician* esecuzione
f; *(show)* spettacolo *m*; *of
employee, company etc* rendimento *m*; *of machine* prestazioni *fpl*; **performer** artista *m/f*

perfume ['pɜːfjuːm] profumo
m

perfunctory [pə'fʌŋktərɪ] superficiale

perhaps [pə'hæps] forse

peril ['perəl] pericolo *m*

perimeter [pə'rɪmɪtə(r)] peri-
metro *m*

period ['pɪərɪəd] *time* periodo
m; *(menstruation)* mestruazioni *fpl*; *Am punctuation
mark* punto *m* fermo; *I don't
want to, ~!* *Am* non voglio,
punto e basta!; **periodic** periodico; **periodical** periodico *m*

peripheral [pə'rɪfərəl] **1** *adj
not crucial* marginale **2** *n*
COMPUT periferica *f*; **periphery** periferia *f*

perish ['perɪʃ] *of rubber* deteriorarsi; *of person* perire;
perishable *food* deteriorabile

perjure ['pɜːdʒə(r)]: *~ o.s.*
spergiurare; **perjury** falso
giuramento *m*

perk [pɜːk] *of job* vantaggio *m*

perm [pɜːm] **1** *n* permanente *f*
2 *v/t*: *have one's hair ~ed*

farsi fare la permanente;
permanent permanente;
job, address fisso; **perma-
nently** permanentemente

permeate ['pɜːmɪeɪt] perme-
are

permissible [pə'mɪsəbl] permesso, ammissibile; **permission** permesso *m*; **permis-
sive** permissivo

permit 1 ['pɜːmɪt] *n* permesso
m **2** [pə'mɪt] *v/t* permettere
(*s.o. to do* a qu di fare)

perpendicular [pɜːpən'dɪk-
jʊlə(r)] perpendicolare

perpetual [pər'petʃʊəl] perenne; **perpetually** perenne-
mente

perplex [pə'pleks] lasciare
perplesso; **perplexity** perplessità *f inv*

persecute ['pɜːsɪkjuːt] perseguitare; **persecution** persecuzione *f*; **persecutor** perse-
cutore *m*, -trice *f*

perseverance [pɜːsɪ'vɪərəns]
perseveranza *f*; **persevere**
perseverare

persist [pə'sɪst] persistere;
persistent *person, questions*
insistente; *rain, unemployment etc* continuo; **persis-
tently** *(continually)* continuamente

person ['pɜːsn] persona *f*; *in ~*
di persona; **personal** personale; **personal computer**
personal computer *m inv*;
personality personalità *f
inv*; **personally** personal-

mente; **don't take it ~** non offendersi; **personal organizer** agenda *f* elettronica; **personal stereo Walkman®** *m inv*; **personify** *of person* personificare

personnel [pɜːsə'nel] *employees* personale *m*; *department* ufficio *m* del personale

perspective [pə'spektɪv] *in art* prospettiva *f*; **get sth into ~** vedere qc nella giusta prospettiva

perspiration [pɜːspɪ'reɪʃn] traspirazione *f*; **perspire** sudare

persuade [pə'sweɪd] persuadere; **~ s.o. to do sth** persuadere qu a fare qc; **persuasion** persuasione *f*; **persuasive** persuasivo

perturb [pə'tɜːb] inquietare; **perturbing** inquietante

pervasive [pə'veɪsɪv] *influence, ideas* diffuso

perversion [pə'vɜːʃn] *sexual* perversione *f*; **pervert** *sexual* pervertito *m*, -a *f*

pessimism ['pesɪmɪzm] pessimismo *m*; **pessimist** pessimista *m/f*; **pessimistic** *view* pessimistico; *person* pessimista

pest [pest] animale / insetto *m* nocivo; *F person* peste *f*

pester ['pestə(r)] assillare; **~ s.o. to do sth** assillare qu perché faccia qc

pesticide ['pestɪsaɪd] pesticida *m*

pet [pet] **1** *n animal* animale *m* domestico; (*favourite*) favorito *m*, -a *f* **2** *adj* preferito **3** *v/t animal* accarezzare **4** *v/i of couple* pomiciare F

petite [pə'tiːt] minuta

petition [pə'tɪʃn] petizione *f*

petrify ['petrɪfaɪ] terrorizzare

petrochemical [petrəʊ'kemɪkl] petrolchimico

petrol ['petrl] benzina *f*

petroleum [pɪ'trəʊlɪəm] petrolio *m*

'petrol pump pompa *f* della benzina; **petrol station** stazione *f* di rifornimento

petting ['petɪŋ] petting *m*

petty ['petɪ] *person, behaviour* meschino; *details* insignificante; **petty cash** piccola cassa *f*

pew [pjuː] banco *m* (di chiesa)

pharmaceutical [fɑːmə'sjuːtɪkl] farmaceutico; **pharmaceuticals** farmaceutici *mpl*

pharmacist ['fɑːməsɪst] farmacista *m/f*; **pharmacy** *shop* farmacia *f*

phase [feɪz] fase *f*
♦ **phase in** introdurre gradualmente
♦ **phase out** eliminare gradualmente

PhD [piːeɪtʃ'diː] (= *Doctor of Philosophy*) dottorato *m* di ricerca

phenomenal [fɪ'nɒmɪnl] fenomenale; **phenomenon** fenomeno *m*

philanthropic [fɪlən'θrɒpɪk]
filantropico; philanthropist
filantropo m, -a f; philanthropy filantropia f

Philippines ['fɪlɪpiːnz]: the ~
le Filippine fpl

philosopher [fɪ'lɒsəfə(r)] filosofo m, -a f; philosophical
filosofico; philosophy filosofia f

phobia ['fəubɪə] fobia f
phon(e)y ['fəunɪ] F falso
phone [fəun] 1 n telefono m;
be on the ~ be talking essere
al telefono 2 v/t telefonare a
3 v/i telefonare; phone book
guida f telefonica, elenco telefonico m; phone booth
telefono f; phone call
telefonata f; phone card
scheda f telefonica; phone
number numero m di telefono

photo ['fəutəu] foto f; photocopier fotocopiatrice f;
photocopy 1 n fotocopia f 2
v/t fotocopiare; photogenic fotogenico; photograph 1
n fotografia f 2 v/t fotografare; photographer fotografo
m, -a f; photography fotografia f

phrase [freɪz] 1 n frase f 2 v/t
esprimere

physical ['fɪzɪkl] 1 adj fisico 2
n MED visita f medica; physically fisicamente

physician [fɪ'zɪʃn] medico m
physicist ['fɪzɪsɪst] fisico m,
-a f; physics fisica f

physiotherapist [fɪzɪəu'θerapɪst] fisioterapeuta m/f;
physiotherapy fisioterapia f
physique [fɪ'ziːk] fisico m
pianist ['pɪənɪst] pianista m/f;
piano piano m
pick [pɪk] (choose) scegliere;
flowers, fruit raccogliere; ~
one's nose mettersi le dita
nel naso
♦ pick up 1 v/t prendere;
phone sollevare; baby prendere in braccio; from ground
raccogliere; (collect) andare / venire a prendere; information raccogliere; in car far
salire; man, woman rimorchiare F; language, skill imparare; habit, illness prendere; (buy) trovare 2 v/i (improve) migliorare
picket ['pɪkɪt] 1 n of strikers
picchetto m 2 v/t picchettare
'pickpocket borseggiatore m,
-trice f; pick-up (truck) Am
furgone m (aperto), pick up
m inv; picky F difficile (da
accontentare)
picnic ['pɪknɪk] 1 n picnic m
inv 2 v/i fare un picnic
picture ['pɪktʃə(r)] 1 n photo
foto f; painting quadro m; illustration figura f; film film
m inv; put / keep s.o. in
the ~ mettere / tenere al
corrente qu 2 v/t immaginare; pictures cinema m; picturesque pittoresco
pie [paɪ] sweet torta f; savoury
pasticcio m

piece [piːs] pezzo *m*; *a ~ of pie / bread* una fetta di torta / pane; *a ~ of advice* un consiglio; *take to ~s* smontare

◆ **piece together** *broken plate* rimettere insieme; *evidence* ricostruire

piecemeal ['piːsmiːl] poco alla volta

pier [pɪə(r)] *at seaside* pontile *m*

pierce [pɪəs] (*penetrate*) trapassare; *ears* farsi i buchi in; **piercing** *noise* lacerante; *eyes* penetrante; *wind* pungente

pig [pɪg] *also fig* maiale *m*

pigeon ['pɪdʒɪn] piccione *m*; **pigeonhole** casella *f*

pigheaded [pɪg'hedɪd] testardo; **pigsty** *also fig* porcile *m*

pile [paɪl] mucchio *m*; F *a ~ of work* un sacco di lavoro F

◆ **pile up** *v/i of work, bills* accumularsi **2** *v/t* ammucchiare

pile-up ['paɪlʌp] MOT tamponamento *m* a catena

pilfering ['pɪlfərɪŋ] piccoli furti *mpl*

pilgrim ['pɪlgrɪm] pellegrino *m*, -a *f*

pill [pɪl] pastiglia *f*; *be on the ~* prendere la pillola

pillar ['pɪlə(r)] colonna *f*; **pillarbox** buca *f* delle lettere

pillow ['pɪləʊ] guanciale *m*; **pillowcase, pillowslip** federa *f*

pilot ['paɪlət] **1** *n of plane* pilota *m/f* **2** *v/t plane* pilotare

pimp [pɪmp] ruffiano *m*

pimple ['pɪmpl] brufolo *m*

PIN [pɪn] (= *personal identification number*) numero *m* di codice segreto

pin [pɪn] **1** *n for sewing* spillo *m*; *in bowling* birillo *m*; (*badge*) spilla *f*; ELEC spinotto *m* **2** *v/t* (*hold down*) immobilizzare; (*attach*) attaccare; *on lapel* appuntare

◆ **pin up** *notice* appuntare

pinafore dress ['pɪnəfɔːr] scamiciato *m*

pincers ['pɪnsəz] *tool* tenaglie *fpl*; *of crab* chele *fpl*

pinch [pɪntʃ] **1** *n* pizzico *m* **2** *v/t* pizzicare **3** *v/i of shoes* stringere

pine [paɪn] pino *m*; *~ furniture* mobili *mpl* di pino; **pineapple** ananas *m inv*

pink [pɪŋk] rosa *inv*

pinnacle ['pɪnəkl] *fig* apice *m*

pinpoint indicare con esattezza; **pins and needles** formicolio *m*

pint [paɪnt] pinta *f*

pin-up (girl) pin-up *f inv*

pioneer [paɪə'nɪə(r)] **1** *n fig* pioniere *m*, -a *f* **2** *v/t* essere il / la pioniere di; **pioneering** *work* pionieristico

pious ['paɪəs] pio

pip [pɪp] *of fruit* seme *m*

pipe [paɪp] **1** *n* tubo *m*; *for smoking* pipa *f* **2** *v/t* trasportare con condutture; **pipe-**

line conduttura *f*; **in the ~** *fig* in arrivo

pirate ['paɪərət] **1** *n* pirata *m* **2** *v/t software* piratare

Pisces ['paɪsi:z] ASTR Pesci *m/f inv*

piss [pɪs] **1** *v/i P* (*urinate*) pisciare P **2** *n* (*urine*) piscio *m* P; **take the ~out of s.o.** P prendere qu per il culo P ◆ **piss off** P **1** *v/i* sparire; **piss off!** levati dalle palle! P **2** *v/t*: **it pisses me off** mi fa incazzare

pissed [pɪst] P (*drunk*) sbronzo F; *Am* (*annoyed*) seccato

pistol ['pɪstl] pistola *f*

piston ['pɪstən] pistone *m*

pit [pɪt] *n* (*hole*) buca *f*; (*coal mine*) miniera *f*

pitch¹ [pɪtʃ] *n* MUS intonazione *f*

pitch² [pɪtʃ] *v/t tent* piantare; *ball* lanciare

pitcher¹ ['pɪtʃə(r)] *in baseball* lanciatore *m*

pitcher² ['pɪtʃə(r)] *container* brocca *f*

pitfall ['pɪtfɔːl] tranello *m*

pitiful ['pɪtɪful] *sight* pietoso; *excuse, attempt* penoso; **pitiless** spietato

pittance ['pɪtns] miseria *f*

pity ['pɪtɪ] **1** *n* pietà *f*; **it's a ~ that** è un peccato che; **what a ~!** che peccato!; **take ~ on** avere pietà di **2** *v/t person* avere pietà di

pizza ['piːtsə] pizza *f*

placard ['plækɑːd] cartello *m*

place [pleɪs] **1** *n* posto *m*; *flat, house* casa *f*; **at my / his ~** a casa mia / sua; **in ~ of** invece di; **feel out of ~** sentirsi fuori posto; **take ~** aver luogo; **in the first ~** (*firstly*) in primo luogo **2** *v/t* (*put*) piazzare; **I can't quite ~ you** non mi ricordo dove ci siamo conosciuti; **~ an order** fare un'ordinazione

placid ['plæsɪd] placido

plagiarism ['pleɪdʒərɪzm] plagio *m*; **plagiarize** plagiare

plague [pleɪg] **1** *n* peste *f* **2** *v/t* (*bother*) tormentare

plain¹ [pleɪn] *n* pianura *f*

plain² [pleɪn] **1** *adj* (*clear, obvious*) chiaro; *not fancy* semplice; *not pretty* scialbo; *not patterned* in tinta unita; (*blunt*) franco; **~ chocolate** cioccolato *m* fondente **2** *adv* semplicemente; **plainly** (*clearly*) chiaramente; (*bluntly*) francamente; (*simply*) semplicemente; **plain-spoken** franco

plaintive ['pleɪntɪv] lamentoso

plait [plæt] treccia *f*

plan [plæn] **1** *n* (*project, intention*) piano *m*; (*drawing*) progetto *m* **2** *v/t* (*prepare*) organizzare; (*design*) progettare; **~ to do** avere in programma di **3** *v/i* pianificare

plane¹ [pleɪn] (*aeroplane*) aereo *m*

plane² [pleɪn] *tool* pialla f

planet ['plænɪt] pianeta m

plank [plæŋk] *of wood* asse f; *fig: of policy* punto m

planning ['plænɪŋ] pianificazione f

plant¹ [plɑːnt] **1** n pianta f **2** v/t piantare

plant² [plɑːnt] (*factory*) stabilimento m; (*equipment*) impianto m

plantation [plæn'teɪʃn] piantagione f

plaque [plæk] *on wall, teeth* placca f

plaster ['plɑːstə(r)] **1** n *on wall* intonaco m; *sticking* cerotto m **2** v/t *wall* intonacare

plastic ['plæstɪk] **1** n plastica f **2** adj di plastica; **plastic money** carte fpl di credito; **plastic surgeon** chirurgo m plastico; **plastic surgery** chirurgia f plastica

plate [pleɪt] *for food* piatto m; *sheet of metal* lastra f

plateau ['plætəʊ] altopiano m

platform ['plætfɔːm] (*stage*) palco m; *of railway station* binario m; *fig: political* piattaforma f

platinum ['plætɪnəm] **1** n platino m **2** adj di platino

platonic [plə'tɒnɪk] platonico

platoon [plə'tuːn] *of soldiers* plotone m

plausible ['plɔːzəbl] plausibile

play [pleɪ] **1** n gioco m; *in theatre, on TV* commedia f **2** v/i *of children, SP* giocare; *of musician* suonare **3** v/t MUS suonare; *game* giocare a; *opponent* giocare contro; (*perform: Macbeth etc*) rappresentare; *particular role* interpretare; **~ a joke on** fare uno scherzo a

◆ **play around** F (*be unfaithful*): **his wife's been playing around** sua moglie lo ha tradito

◆ **play down** minimizzare

◆ **play up** *of machine* fare noie; *of child* fare i capricci; *of tooth, bad back etc* fare male

player ['pleɪə(r)] SP giocatore m, -trice f; *musician* musicista m/f; *actor* attore m, -trice f; **playful** *punch, mood* scherzoso; **puppy** giocherellone; **playground** *in school* cortile m per la ricreazione; *in park* parco m giochi; **playing card** carta f da gioco; **playwright** commediografo m, -a f

plaza ['plɑːzə] *for shopping* centro m commerciale

plc [piːel'siː] (= **public limited company**) società f inv a responsabilità limitata quotata in borsa

plea [pliː] appello m

plead [pliːd]: **~ guilty / not guilty** dichiararsi colpevole / innocente; **~ with** supplicare

pleasant ['pleznt] piacevole

please [pli:z] **1** *adv* per favore; *more tea? – yes*, ~ ancora tè? – sì, grazie; ~ *do* fai pure, prego **2** *v/t* far piacere a; ~ *yourself* fai come ti pare; *pleased* contento; ~ *to meet you* piacere!; *pleasing* piacevole; *pleasure* (*happiness, satisfaction*) contentezza *f*; (*as opposed to work*) piacere *m*; (*delight*) gioia *f*; *it's a* ~ (*you're welcome*) è un piacere; *with* ~ con vero piacere

pleat [pli:t] *in skirt* piega *f*

pledge [pledʒ] **1** *n* (*promise*) promessa *f* **2** *v/t* (*promise*) promettere

plentiful ['plentɪfʊl] abbondante; *plenty* abbondanza *f*; ~ *of* molto; *that's* ~ basta così; *there's* ~ *for everyone* ce n'è per tutti

pliable ['plaɪəbl] flessibile

pliers ['plaɪəz] pinze *fpl*

plight [plaɪt] situazione *f* critica

plod [plɒd] *walk* trascinarsi

plook [plu:k] brufolo *m*

plot¹ [plɒt] *n land* appezzamento *m*

plot² [plɒt] **1** *n* (*conspiracy*) complotto *m*; *of novel* trama *f* **2** *v/t* & *v/i* complottare

plotter ['plɒtə(r)] cospiratore *m*, -trice *f*; COMPUT plotter *m inv*

plough, *Am* **plow** [plaʊ] **1** *n* aratro *m* **2** *v/t* & *v/i* arare

◆ **plough back** *profits* reinvestire

pluck [plʌk] *eyebrows* pinzare; *chicken* spennare

plug [plʌg] **1** *n for sink, bath* tappo *m*; *electrical* spina *f*; (*spark* ~) candela *f*; *for new book etc* pubblicità *f inv* **2** *v/t hole* tappare; *new book etc* fare pubblicità a

◆ **plug in** attaccare (alla presa)

plumage ['plu:mɪdʒ] piumaggio *m*

plumber ['plʌmə(r)] idraulico *m*; *plumbing pipes* impianto *m* idraulico

plummet ['plʌmɪt] *of aeroplane* precipitare; *of share prices* crollare

plump [plʌmp] *person, chicken* in carne; *hands, feet, face* paffuto

plunge [plʌndʒ] **1** *n* caduta *f*; *in prices* crollo *m*; *take the* ~ fare il gran passo **2** *v/i* precipitare; *of prices* crollare **3** *v/t knife* conficcare; *plunging neckline* profondo

plural ['plʊərəl] plurale *m*

plus [plʌs] **1** *prep* più **2** *adj*: *£500* ~ oltre 500 sterline **3** *n symbol* più *m inv*; (*advantage*) vantaggio *m* **4** *conj* (*moreover, in addition*) per di più

plush [plʌʃ] di lusso

plywood ['plaɪwʊd] compensato *m*

PM [pi:'em] (= *Prime Minister*) primo ministro *m*

p.m. [pi:'em] (= *post meridi-*

em): *at* 2 ~ alle 2 del pomeriggio; *at* **10.30** ~ alle 10.30 di sera

pneumonia [njuːˈməʊnɪə] polmonite *f*

poach¹ [pəʊtʃ] *cook* bollire; *egg* fare in camicia

poach² [pəʊtʃ] *game* cacciare di frodo; *fish* pescare di frodo

poached egg [pəʊtʃtˈeg] uovo *m* in camicia

P.O. Box [piːˈəʊbɒks] casella *f* postale

pocket [ˈpɒkɪt] **1** *n* tasca *f* **2** *adj* (*miniature*) in miniatura **3** *v/t* intascare; **pocket book** *Am* (*wallet*) portafoglio *m*; (*purse*) borsetta *f*; **pocket calculator** calcolatrice *f* tascabile

podium [ˈpəʊdɪəm] podio *m*

poem [ˈpəʊɪm] poesia *f*; **poet** poeta *m*, -essa *f*; **poetic** poetico; **poetic justice** giustizia *f* divina; **poetry** poesia *f*

poignant [ˈpɔɪnjənt] commovente

point [pɔɪnt] **1** *n of pencil, knife* punta *f*; *in competition* punto *m*; (*purpose*) senso *m*; (*moment*) punto *m*; *in argument, discussion* punto *m*; *in decimals* virgola *f*; *that's beside the* ~ non c'entra; *be on the* ~ *of* stare per; *get to the* ~ venire al dunque; *that's a* ~ questo, in effetti, è vero; *the* ~ *is ...* il fatto è che ...; *there's*

no ~ *in waiting* non ha senso aspettare **2** *v/i* indicare **3** *v/t gun* puntare (*at* contro)

◆ **point out** *sights, advantages* indicare

◆ **point to** *with finger* additare; (*fig: indicate*) far presupporre

pointed [ˈpɔɪntɪd] *remark* significativo; **pointer** *for teacher* bacchetta *f*; (*hint*) consiglio *m*; (*sign, indication*) indizio *m*; **pointless** inutile; **point of view** punto *m* di vista

poise [pɔɪz] padronanza *f* di sé; **poised** *person* posato

poison [ˈpɔɪzn] **1** *n* veleno *m* **2** *v/t* avvelenare; **poisonous** velenoso

poke [pəʊk] **1** *n* colpetto *m* **2** *v/t* (*prod*) dare un colpetto a; (*stick*) ficcare

◆ **poke around** F curiosare

poker [ˈpəʊkə(r)] *card game* poker *m*

Poland [ˈpəʊlənd] Polonia *f*

polar [ˈpəʊlə(r)] polare

Pole [pəʊl] polacco *m*, -a *f*

pole¹ [pəʊl] *of wood, metal* paletto *m*

pole² [pəʊl] *of earth* polo *m*; **polevault** salto *m* con l'asta

police [pəˈliːs] polizia *f*; **police car** auto *f* della polizia; **policeman** poliziotto *m*; **police state** stato *m* di polizia; **police station** commissariato *m* di polizia; **policewoman** donna *f* poliziotto

policy[1] ['pɒlɪsɪ] politica *f*

policy[2] ['pɒlɪsɪ] (*insurance ∼*) polizza *f*

polio ['pəʊlɪəʊ] polio *f*

Polish ['pəʊlɪʃ] **1** *adj* polacco **2** *n language* polacco *m*

polish ['pɒlɪʃ] **1** *n product* lucido *m*; (*nail ∼*) smalto *m* **2** *v/t* lucidare; *speech* rifinire; **polished** *performance* impeccabile

polite [pə'laɪt] cortese; **politely** cortesemente; **politeness** cortesia *f*

political [pə'lɪtɪkl] politico; **politically correct** politicamente corretto; **politician** uomo *m* politico, donna *f* politica; **politics** politica *f*

poll [pəʊl] **1** *n* (*survey*) sondaggio *m*; **go to the ∼s** (*vote*) andare alle urne **2** *v/t people* fare un sondaggio tra; *votes* guadagnare

pollen ['pɒlən] polline *m*

'polling station seggio *m* elettorale

pollster ['pɒlstə(r)] esperto *m*, -a *f* di sondaggi

pollutant [pə'luːtənt] sostanza *f* inquinante; **pollute** inquinare; **pollution** inquinamento *m*

'polo shirt polo *f inv*

polyester [pɒlɪ'estə(r)] poliestere *m*

polystyrene [pɒlɪ'staɪriːn] polistirolo *m*

polyunsaturated [pɒlɪʌn'sætʃəreɪtɪd] polinsa-

turo

pompous ['pɒmpəs] pomposo

pond [pɒnd] stagno *m*

pontiff ['pɒntɪf] pontefice *m*

pony ['pəʊnɪ] pony *m inv*; **ponytail** coda *f* (di cavallo)

poo(h) [puː] F (*faeces*) popò *f inv*

poodle ['puːdl] barboncino *m*

pool[1] [puːl] *n* (*swimming ∼*) piscina *f*; *of water, blood* pozza *f*

pool[2] [puːl] *game* biliardo *m*

pool[3] [puːl] **1** *n common fund* cassa *f* comune **2** *v/t resources* mettere insieme

'pool hall sala *f* da biliardo; **pool table** tavolo *m* da biliardo

poop [puːp] *Am* F (*faeces*) popò *f inv*

pooped [puːpt] F stanco morto

poor [pʊə(r)] **1** *adj* povero; *not good* misero; **be in ∼ health** essere in cattiva salute **2** *n*: **the ∼** i poveri; **poorly 1** *adv* male **2** *adj* (*unwell*) indisposto

pop[1] [pɒp] **1** *n noise* schiocco *m* **2** *v/i of balloon etc* scoppiare **3** *v/t cork* stappare; *balloon* far scoppiare

pop[2] [pɒp] **1** *n* MUS pop *m* **2** *adj* pop *inv*

pop[3] [pɒp] *Am* F papà *m inv*

◆ **pop out** F (*go out for a short time*) fare un salto fuori

◆ **pop up** F (*appear suddenly*)

saltare fuori

'popcorn popcorn *m*

pope [pəʊp] papa *m*

Popsicle® ['pɒpsɪkl] *Am* ghiacciolo *m*

popular ['pɒpjʊlə(r)] popolare; *belief, support* diffuso; **popularity** popolarità *f*

populate ['pɒpjʊleɪt] popolare; **population** popolazione *f*

porch [pɔːtʃ] porticato *m*; *Am*: *outside house* veranda *f*

◆ **pore over** studiare attentamente

pork [pɔːk] maiale *m*

porn [pɔːn] F porno *m* F; **pornographic** pornografico; **pornography** pornografia *f*

port¹ [pɔːt] *n* (*harbour, drink*) porto *m*

port² [pɔːt] *adj* (*left-hand*) babordo

portable ['pɔːtəbl] **1** *adj* portatile **2** *n* portatile *m*

porter ['pɔːtə(r)] portiere *m*

porthole ['pɔːthəʊl] NAUT oblò *m inv*

portion ['pɔːʃn] parte *f*; *of food* porzione *f*

portrait ['pɔːtreɪt] **1** *n* ritratto *m* **2** *adv* *print* verticale; **portray** *of artist* ritrarre; *of actor* interpretare; *of author* descrivere

Portugal ['pɔːtjʊgl] Portogallo *m*; **Portuguese 1** *adj* portoghese **2** *n* *person* portoghese *m/f*; *language* portoghese *m*

pose [pəʊz] **1** *n* (*pretence*) posa *f* **2** *v/i for artist* posare; **~ as** farsi passare per **3** *v/t* *problem, threat* creare

posh [pɒʃ] F elegante; *pej* snob

position [pə'zɪʃn] **1** *n* posizione *f*; *what would you do in my ~?* cosa faresti al mio posto? **2** *v/t* sistemare, piazzare

positive ['pɒzɪtɪv] positivo; *be ~* (*sure*) essere certo; **positively** (*downright*) decisamente; (*definitely*) assolutamente; *think* in modo positivo

possess [pə'zes] possedere; **possession** (*ownership*) possesso *m*; *thing owned* bene *m*; *~s* averi *mpl*; **possessive** *also* GRAM possessivo

possibility [pɒsə'bɪlətɪ] possibilità *f inv*; **possible** possibile; *the best ~ ...* la miglior ... possibile; **possibly** (*perhaps*) forse; *that can't ~ be right* non è possibile che sia giusto

post¹ [pəʊst] **1** *n* *of wood, metal* palo *m* **2** *v/t* *notice* affiggere; *profits* annunciare; *keep s.o. ~ed* tenere informato qu

post² [pəʊst] **1** *n* (*place of duty*) posto *m* **2** *v/t* *soldier, employee* assegnare; *guards* piazzare

post³ [pəʊst] **1** *n* (*mail*) posta *f* **2** *v/t letter* spedire (per posta); (*put in the mail*) imbucare

postage ['pəʊstɪdʒ] affrancatura *f*; **postage stamp** *fml* francobollo *m*;**postal** postale;**postbox** buca *f* delle lettere; **postcard** cartolina *f*; **postcode** codice *m* di avviamento postale; **postdate** postdatare

poster ['pəʊstə(r)] manifesto *m*; *for decoration* poster *m inv*

postgraduate ['pəʊstgrædjʊt] **1** *n* studente *m* / studentessa *f* di un corso post-universitario **2** *adj* post-universitario

posthumous ['pɒstjʊməs] postumo

posting ['pəʊstɪŋ] *(assignment)* incarico *m*

'postman postino *m*; **postmark** timbro *m* postale

postmortem [pəʊst'mɔːtəm] autopsia *f*

'post office ufficio *m* postale

postpone [pəʊst'pəʊn] rinviare;**postponement** rinvio *m*

pot[1] [pɒt] *for cooking* pentola *f*; *for coffee* caffettiera *f*; *for tea* teiera *f*; *for plant* vaso *m*

pot[2] [pɒt] F *(marijuana)* erba *f* F

potato [pə'teɪtəʊ] patata *f*; **potato crisps**, *Am* **potato chips** patatine *fpl*

potent ['pəʊtənt] potente

potential [pə'tenʃl] **1** *adj* potenziale **2** *n* potenziale *m*;

potentially *adv* potenzialmente

pothole ['pɒthəʊl] *in road* buca *f*

potter ['pɒtə(r)] vasaio *m*, -a *f*; **pottery** ceramica *f*; *items* vasellame *m*; *place* laboratorio *m* di ceramica

potty ['pɒtɪ] *for baby* vasino *m*

pouch [paʊtʃ] *(bag)* borsa *f*

poultry ['pəʊltrɪ] *birds* volatili *mpl*; *meat* pollame *m*

pound[1] [paʊnd] *n weight* libbra *f*; FIN sterlina *f*

pound[2] [paʊnd] *n for strays* canile *m* municipale; *for cars* deposito *m* auto

pound[3] [paʊnd] *v/i of heart* battere forte; **~ on** *(hammer on)* picchiare su

♦ **pour out** *liquid* versare; *troubles* sfogarsi raccontando

pout [paʊt] fare il broncio

poverty ['pɒvətɪ] povertà *f*

powder ['paʊdə(r)] **1** *n* polvere *f*; *for face* cipria *f* **2** *v/t*: **~ one's face** incipriarsi la cipria

power ['paʊə(r)] **1** *n (strength)* forza *f*; *of engine* potenza *f*; *(authority)* potere *m*; *(energy)* energia *f*; *(electricity)* elettricità *f*; **in ~** POL al potere **2** *v/t*: **~ed by atomic energy** a propulsione atomica;**power cut** interruzione *f* di corrente; **power failure** guasto *m* alla linea elettrica; **powerful** potente; **powerless** impotente; **be ~ to ...** non poter far niente per ...; **power line** linea f elettrica; **power outage** Am interruzione f di corrente; **power station** centrale f elettrica; **power steering** servosterzo m

PR [piː'ɑː(r)] (= **public relations**) relazioni fpl pubbliche

practical ['præktɪkl] pratico; **practically** behave, think in modo pratico; (almost) praticamente

practice ['præktɪs] 1 n pratica f; (training) esercizio m; (rehearsal) prove fpl; (custom) consuetudine f; **in ~** (in reality) in pratica; **be out of ~** essere fuori allenamento 2 v/t & v/i Am ☞ **practise**

practise ['præktɪs] 1 v/t esercitarsi in; law, medicine esercitare 2 v/i esercitarsi

pragmatic [præg'mætɪk] pragmatico

prairie ['preərɪ] prateria f

praise [preɪz] 1 n lode f 2 v/t lodare; **praiseworthy** lodevole

prawn [prɔːn] gamberetto m

pray [preɪ] pregare; **prayer** preghiera f

preach [priːtʃ] predicare; **preacher** predicatore m, -trice f

precarious [prɪ'keərɪəs] precario

precaution [prɪ'kɔːʃn] precauzione f; **precautionary** measure di precauzione

precede [prɪ'siːd] precedere; **precedent** precedente m; **preceding** precedente

precious ['preʃəs] prezioso

precise [prɪ'saɪs] preciso; **precisely** precisamente; **precision** precisione f

precocious [prɪ'kəʊʃəs] child precoce

preconceived [priːkən'siːvd] idea preconcetto

precondition [prɪkən'dɪʃn] condizione f indispensabile

predator ['predətə(r)] animal predatore m, -trice f; **predatory** rapace

predecessor ['priːdɪsesə(r)] predecessore m

predicament [prɪ'dɪkəmənt] situazione f difficile

predict [prɪ'dɪkt] predire; **predictable** prevedibile; **prediction** predizione f

predominant [prɪ'dɒmɪnənt] predominante; **predominantly** prevalentemente

prefabricated [priː'fæbrɪkeɪtɪd] prefabbricato

preface ['prefɪs] prefazione f

prefer [prɪ'fɜː(r)] preferire (**to** a); **preferable** preferibile; **preferably** preferibilmente; **preference** preferenza f; **preferential** preferenziale

pregnancy ['pregnənsɪ] gravidanza f; **pregnant** incinta; **get ~** restare incinta

prehistoric [priːhɪsˈtɒrɪk] preistorico

prejudice ['predʒʊdɪs] **1** *n* pregiudizio *m* **2** *v/t person* influenzare; *chances* pregiudicare; **prejudiced** prevenuto

preliminary [prɪ'lɪmɪnərɪ] preliminare

premarital [priː'mærɪtl] prematrimoniale

premature ['premətjʊə(r)] prematuro

premeditated [priː'medɪteɪtɪd] premeditato

premier ['premɪə(r)] (*Prime Minister*) premier *m inv*

première ['premɪə(r)] première *f inv*, prima *f*

premises ['premɪsɪz] locali *mpl*

premium ['priːmɪəm] *in insurance* premio *m*

prenatal [priː'neɪtl] prenatale

preoccupied [prɪ'ɒkjʊpaɪd] preoccupato

preparation [prepə'reɪʃn] preparazione *f*; **in~ for** in vista di; **~s** preparativi *mpl*; **prepare** **1** *v/t* preparare; **be ~d to do sth** (*willing*) essere preparato a fare qc; **be ~d for sth** (*be expecting*) essere preparato per qc **2** *v/i* prepararsi

preposition [prepə'zɪʃn] preposizione *f*

preposterous [prɪ'pɒstərəs] ridicolo

prerequisite [priː'rekwɪzɪt] condizione *f* indispensabile

prescribe [prɪ'skraɪb] *of doctor* prescrivere; **prescription** MED ricetta *f* medica

presence ['prezns] presenza *f*; **in the ~ of** in presenza di

present[1] ['preznt] **1** *adj* (*current*) attuale; **be~** essere **2** *n*: **the~** *also* GRAM il presente; **at~** al momento

present[2] ['preznt] *n* (*gift*) regalo *m*

present[3] [prɪ'zent] *v/t award* consegnare; *bouquet* offrire; *programme* presentare; **~ s.o. with sth, ~ sth to s.o.** offrire qc a qu

presentation [prezn'teɪʃn] presentazione *f*; **present-day** di oggi; **presenter** presentatore *m*, -trice *f*; **presently** (*at the moment*) attualmente; (*soon*) tra breve

preservative [prɪ'zɜːvətɪv] conservante *m*; **preserve 1** *n* (*domain*) dominio *m* **2** *v/t standards*, *peace etc* mantenere; *wood etc* proteggere; *food* conservare

preside [prɪ'zaɪd] *at meeting* presiedere; **presidency** presidenza *f*; **president** presidente *m*; **presidential** presidenziale

press [pres] **1** *n*: **the~** la stampa **2** *v/t button* premere; (*urge*) far pressione su; (*squeeze*) stringere; *clothes* stirare; *grapes*, *olives* spremere **3** *v/i*: **~ for** fare pressioni per ottenere; **press con-**

ference conferenza *f* stampa; **pressing** urgente; **press-up** flessione *f* sulle braccia

pressure ['preʃə(r)] **1** *n* pressione *f* **2** *v/t* fare delle pressioni su

prestige [pre'sti:ʒ] prestigio *m*; **prestigious** prestigioso *m*

presumably [prɪ'zju:məblɪ] presumibilmente; **presume** presumere; **presumption** *of innocence, guilt* presunzione *f*

presuppose [pri:sə'pəʊs] presupporre

pre-tax ['pri:tæks] al lordo d'imposta

pretence [prɪ'tens] finta *f*; **pretend 1** *v/t* fingere **2** *v/i* fare finta; **pretense** *Am* ☞ **pretence**; **pretentious** pretenzioso

pretext ['pri:tekst] pretesto *m*

pretty ['prɪtɪ] **1** *adj* carino **2** *adv* (*quite*) piuttosto

prevail [prɪ'veɪl] (*triumph*) prevalere; **prevailing** prevalente

prevent [prɪ'vent] prevenire; **~ s.o. (from) doing sth** impedire a qu di fare qc; **prevention** prevenzione *f*; **preventive** preventivo

preview ['pri:vju:] *of film, exhibition* anteprima *f*

previous ['pri:vɪəs] precedente; **~ to** prima di; **previously** precedentemente

prey [preɪ] preda *f*

price [praɪs] **1** *n* prezzo *m* **2** *v/t* COM fissare il prezzo di; **priceless** di valore inestimabile; **price war** guerra *f* dei prezzi; **pricey** F caro

prick[1] [prɪk] **1** *n pain* puntura *f* **2** *v/t* (*jab*) pungere

prick[2] [prɪk] *n* V (*penis*) cazzo *m* V; *person* testa *f* di cazzo V

prickle ['prɪkl] *on plant* spina *f*; **prickly** *plant* spinoso; *beard* ispido; (*irritable*) permaloso

pride [praɪd] **1** *n in person, achievement* orgoglio *m*; (*self-respect*) amor *m* proprio **2** *v/t*: **~ o.s. on** vantarsi di

priest [pri:st] prete *m*

primarily [praɪ'meərɪlɪ] principalmente; **primary 1** *adj* principale **2** *n Am* POL (*elezione f*) primaria *f*; **primary school** scuola *f* elementare

prime 'minister primo ministro *m*

primitive ['prɪmɪtɪv] primitivo

prince [prɪns] principe *m*; **princess** principessa *f*

principal ['prɪnsəpl] **1** *adj* principale **2** *n of school* preside *m/f*; **principally** principalmente

principle ['prɪnsəpl] principio *m*; **on ~** per principio; **in ~** in linea di principio

print [prɪnt] **1** *n in book etc* caratteri *mpl*; *photograph* stampa *f*; *mark* impronta *f*; **out of ~** esaurito **2** *v/t* stampare; (*use block capitals*) scrivere in stampatello; **printer** *person* tipografo *m*; *machine* stampante *f*; **printout** stampato *m*

prior ['praɪə(r)] **1** *adj* precedente **2** *prep*: **~ to** prima di

prioritize [praɪ'ɒrətaɪz] (*put in order of priority*) classificare in ordine d'importanza; (*give priority to*) dare precedenza a; **priority** priorità *f inv*; **have ~** avere la precedenza

prison ['prɪzn] prigione *f*; **prisoner** prigioniero *m*, -a *f*; **take s.o. ~** fare prigioniero qu; **prisoner of war** prigioniero *m* di guerra

privacy ['prɪvəsɪ] privacy *f*; **private 1** *adj* privato *m* **2** *n* MIL soldato *m* semplice; **in ~** in privato; **privately** (*in private*) in privato; (*inwardly*) dentro di sé; **~ owned** privato; **private sector** settore *m* privato; **privatize** privatizzare

privilege ['prɪvɪlɪdʒ] privilegio *m*; (*honour*) onore *m*; **privileged** privilegiato; (*honoured*) onorato

prize [praɪz] **1** *n* premio *m* **2** *v/t* dare molto valore a; **prizewinner** vincitore *m*, -trice *f*; **prizewinning** vincente

pro[1] [prəʊ] *n*: **the ~s and cons** i pro e i contro

pro[2] [prəʊ] *☞* **professional**

pro[3] [prəʊ] *prep*: **be ~ ...** (*in favour of*) essere a favore di ...

probability [prɒbə'bɪlətɪ] probabilità *f inv*; **probable** probabile; **probably** probabilmente

probation [prə'beɪʃn] *in job* periodo *m* di prova; LAW libertà *f* vigilata; **on ~** *in job* in prova

probe [prəʊb] **1** *n* (*investigation*) indagine *f*; *scientific* sonda *f* **2** *v/t* esplorare; (*investigate*) investigare

problem ['prɒbləm] problema *m*; **no ~** non c'è problema

procedure [prə'siːdʒə(r)] procedura *f*

proceed [prə'siːd] *of people* proseguire; *of work etc* procedere; **proceedings** (*events*) avvenimenti *mpl*; **proceeds** ricavato *m*

process ['prəʊses] **1** *n* processo *m* **2** *v/t food, raw materials* trattare; *data* elaborare; *application etc* sbrigare; **~ed cheese** formaggio *m* fuso; **procession** processione *f*; **processor** processore *m*

prod [prɒd] **1** *n* colpetto *m* **2** *v/t* dare un colpetto a

prodigy ['prɒdɪdʒɪ]: (*infant*) **~** bambino *m*, -a *f* prodigio

produce[1] ['prɒdjuːs] *n* prodotti *mpl*

produce[2] [prə'djuːs] *v/t* produrre; (*bring about*) dare origine a; (*bring out*) tirar fuori; *play* mettere in scena

producer [prə'dju:sə(r)] produttore *m*, -trice *f*; *of play* regista *m/f*; **product** prodotto *m*; (*result*) risultato *m*; **production** produzione *f*; *of play* regia *f*; **a new ~ of ...** una nuova messa in scena di ...; **productive** produttivo; **productivity** produttività *f*

profess [prə'fes] dichiarare; **profession** professione *f*; **professional 1** *adj* professionale; *advice, help* di un esperto; *piece of work* da professionista; **turn ~** passare al professionismo 2 *n* professionista *m/f*; **professionally** *play sport* a livello professionistico; (*well, skilfully*) in modo professionale **professor** [prə'fesə(r)] professore *m* (universitario)

proficiency [prə'fɪʃnsɪ] competenza *f*; **proficient** competente

profile ['prəufaɪl] profilo *m*

profit ['prɒfɪt] **1** *n* profitto *m* 2 *v/i*: **~ from** trarre profitto da; **profitability** redditività *f*; **profitable** redditizio

profound [prə'faund] profondo

prognosis [prɒg'nəusɪs] prognosi *f inv*

programme, *Am and Br* COMPUT **program** ['prəuɡræm] **1** *n* programma *m* 2 *v/t* programmare; **programmer** COMPUT programmato-

re *m*, -trice *f*

progress 1 ['prəuɡres] *n* progresso *m*; **in ~** in corso 2 [prə'ɡres] *v/i* (*advance in time*) procedere; (*move on*) avanzare; (*make progress*) fare progressi; **progressive** (*enlightened*) progressista; *which progresses* progressivo; **progressively** progressivamente

prohibit [prə'hɪbɪt] proibire; **prohibitive** *prices* proibitivo

project[1] ['prɒdʒekt] *n* (*plan*) piano *m*; (*undertaking*) progetto *m*; EDU ricerca *f*

project[2] [prə'dʒekt] **1** *v/t figures, sales* fare una proiezione di; *film* proiettare **2** *v/i* (*stick out*) sporgere in fuori

projection [prə'dʒekʃn] (*forecast*) proiezione *f*; **projector** *for slides* proiettore *m*

prologue, *Am* **prolog** ['prəulɒɡ] prologo *m*

prolong [prə'lɒŋ] prolungare

prominent ['prɒmɪnənt] *nose, chin* sporgente; (*significant*) prominente

promiscuity [prɒmɪ'skju:ətɪ] promiscuità *f*; **promiscuous** promiscuo

promise ['prɒmɪs] **1** *n* promessa *f* 2 *v/t & v/i* promettere; **promising** promettente

promote [prə'məut] promuovere; **promoter** *of event* promoter *m/f inv*; **promotion** promozione *f*; **get ~ in job** essere promosso

prompt [prɒmpt] **1** *adj* (*on time*) puntuale; (*speedy*) tempestivo **2** *adv*: **at two o'clock ~** alle due in punto **3** *v/t* (*cause*) causare; *actor* dare l'imbeccata a; **promptly** (*on time*) puntualmente; (*immediately*) prontamente

prone [prəʊn]: **be ~ to** essere soggetto a

pronoun ['prəʊnaʊn] pronome *m*

pronounce [prə'naʊns] pronunciare; (*declare*) dichiarare

pronto ['prɒntəʊ] F immediatamente

pronunciation [prənʌnsɪ'eɪʃn] pronuncia *f*

proof [pruːf] prova *f*; *of book* bozza *f*

prop [prɒp] **1** *v/t* appoggiare **2** *n* THEA materiale *m* di scena
♦ prop up *also fig* sostenere

propaganda [prɒpə'gændə] propaganda *f*

propel [prə'pel] spingere; *of engine, fuel* azionare; **propeller** elica *f*

proper ['prɒpə(r)] (*real*) vero e proprio; (*correct*) giusto; (*fitting*) appropriato; **properly** (*correctly*) correttamente; (*fittingly*) in modo appropriato

property ['prɒpətɪ] proprietà *f inv*; **property developer** impresario *m* edile

proportion [prə'pɔːʃn] proporzione *f*; **proportional**

proporzionale; **proportional representation** POL rappresentanza *f* proporzionale

proposal [prə'pəʊzl] proposta *f*; **propose 1** *v/t* (*suggest*) proporre; **~ to do sth** (*plan*) proporsi di fare qc **2** *v/i make offer of marriage* fare una proposta di matrimonio; **proposition 1** *n* proposta *f* **2** *v/t woman* fare proposte sessuali a

proprietor [prə'praɪətə(r)] proprietario *m*, -a *f*

prose [prəʊz] prosa *f*

prosecute ['prɒsɪkjuːt] LAW intentare azione legale contro; *of lawyer* sostenere l'accusa contro; **prosecution** LAW azione *f* giudiziaria; (*lawyers*) accusa *f*

prospect ['prɒspekt] (*chance, likelihood*) probabilità *f inv*; *thought of something in the future* prospettiva *f*; **~s** prospettive *fpl*; **prospective** potenziale

prosper ['prɒspə(r)] prosperare; **prosperity** prosperità *f*; **prosperous** prospero

prostitute ['prɒstɪtjuːt] prostituta *f*; **male ~** prostituto *m*; **prostitution** prostituzione *f*

protect [prə'tekt] proteggere; **protection** protezione *f*; **protective** protettivo; **protector** protettore *m*, -trice *f*

protein ['prəʊtiːn] proteina *f*

protest 1 ['prəʊtest] *n* prote-

sta *f* **2** [prə'test] *v/t* protestare **3** [prə'test] *v/i* protestare; POL manifestare, protestare
Protestant ['prɒtɪstənt] **1** *n* protestante *m/f* **2** *adj* protestante
protester [prə'testə(r)] dimostrante *m/f*, manifestante *m/f*
prototype ['prəʊtətaɪp] prototipo *m*
protrude [prə'tru:d] sporgere; **protruding** sporgente
proud [praʊd] orgoglioso, fiero; **be ~ of** essere fiero di; **proudly** con orgoglio
prove [pru:v] dimostrare
proverb ['prɒvɜ:b] proverbio *m*
provide [prə'vaɪd] *money, food* fornire; *opportunity* offrire; **~ s.o. with sth** fornire qu di qc; **~d that** (*on condition that*) a condizione che
province ['prɒvɪns] provincia *f*; **provincial** *also pej* provinciale
provision [prə'vɪʒn] (*supply*) fornitura *f*; *of law, contract* disposizione *f*; **provisional** provvisorio
provocation [prɒvə'keɪʃn] provocazione *f*; **provocative** provocatorio; *sexually* provocante; **provoke** (*cause*) causare; (*annoy*) provocare
prowl [praʊl] aggirarsi; **prowler** tipo *m* sospetto
proximity [prɒk'sɪmətɪ] prossimità *f*

proxy ['prɒksɪ] (*authority*) procura *f*; *person* procuratore *m*, -trice *f*, mandatario *m*, -a *f*
prudence ['pru:dns] prudenza *f*; **prudent** prudente
prudish ['pru:dɪʃ] che si scandalizza facilmente
pry [praɪ] essere indiscreto
PS [pi:'es] (= *postscript*) P.S. (= posto *scriptum m*)
pseudonym ['sju:dənɪm] pseudonimo *m*
psychiatric [saɪkɪ'ætrɪk] psichiatrico; **psychiatrist** psichiatra *m/f*; **psychiatry** psichiatria *f*
psychoanalysis [saɪkəʊən'æləsɪs] psicanalisi *f*; **psychoanalyst** psicanalista *m/f*; **psychoanalyze** psicanalizzare
psychological [saɪkə'lɒdʒɪkl] psicologico; **psychologically** psicologicamente; **psychologist** psicologo *m*, -a *f*; **psychology** psicologia *f*
psychopath ['saɪkəpæθ] psicopatico *m*, -a *f*
psychosomatic [saɪkəʊsə'mætɪk] psicosomatico
pub [pʌb] pub *m* inv
pubic hair [pju:bɪk'heə(r)] peli *mpl* del pube
public ['pʌblɪk] **1** *adj* pubblico **2** *n*: **the ~** il pubblico; **in ~** in pubblico; **public transport** mezzi *mpl* pubblici
publication [pʌblɪ'keɪʃn]

pubblicazione f

public 'holiday giorno m festivo

publicity [pʌb'lɪsətɪ] pubblicità f; **publicize** make known far sapere in giro; COM reclamizzare

publicly ['pʌblɪklɪ] pubblicamente

'public school Br scuola f privata; Am scuola pubblica

publish ['pʌblɪʃ] pubblicare; **publisher** editore m; **publishing** editoria f; **publishing company** casa f editrice

pudding ['pudɪŋ] dish budino m; part of meal dolce m

puddle ['pʌdl] n pozzanghera f

puff [pʌf] **1** n of wind, smoke soffio m **2** v/i (pant) ansimare; **puffy** eyes, face gonfio

puke [pjuːk] F vomitare

pull [pol] **1** n on rope tirata f; F (appeal) attrattiva f; F (influence) influenza f **2** v/t (drag) tirare; tooth togliere; ~ **a muscle** farsi uno strappo muscolare **3** v/i tirare

◆ **pull ahead** in race, competition portarsi in testa

◆ **pull down** (lower) tirar giù; (demolish) demolire

◆ **pull in** of bus, train arrivare

◆ **pull out** v/t tirar fuori; troops (far) ritirare **2** v/i of agreement, competition, MIL ritirarsi; of ship partire

◆ **pull over** of driver accostarsi

◆ **pull through** from an illness farcela F

◆ **pull up 1** v/t (raise) tirar su; plant, weeds strappare **2** v/i of car etc fermarsi

pulley ['pulɪ] puleggia f

pulsate [pʌl'seɪt] of heart, blood pulsare; of rhythm vibrare

pulse [pʌls] polso m

pulverize ['pʌlvəraɪz] polverizzare

pump [pʌmp] **1** n pompa f **2** v/t pompare

pumpkin ['pʌmpkɪn] zucca f

pun [pʌn] gioco m di parole

punch [pʌntʃ] **1** n blow pugno m; implement punzonatrice f **2** v/t with fist dare un pugno a; hole perforare; ticket forare

punctual ['pʌŋktjʊəl] puntuale; **punctuality** puntualità f

punctuation ['pʌŋktjʊ'eɪʃn] punteggiatura f

puncture ['pʌŋktʃə(r)] **1** n foratura f **2** v/t forare

punish ['pʌnɪʃ] punire; **punishing** pace, schedule estenuante; **punishment** punizione f

puny ['pjuːnɪ] person gracile

pup [pʌp] cucciolo m

pupil[1] ['pjuːpl] of eye pupilla f

pupil[2] ['pjuːpl] (student) allievo m, -a f

puppet ['pʌpɪt] burattino m; with strings marionetta f

puppy ['pʌpɪ] cucciolo m

purchase[1] ['pɜːtʃəs] **1** *n* acquisto *m* **2** *v/t* acquistare

purchase[2] ['pɜːtʃəs] *n* (*grip*) presa *f*

purchaser ['pɜːtʃəsə(r)] acquirente *m/f*

pure [pjʊə(r)] puro; **~ new wool** pura lana *f* vergine; **purely** puramente

purge [pɜːdʒ] **1** *n* *of political party* epurazione *f* **2** *v/t* epurare

purify ['pjʊərɪfaɪ] purificare

puritan ['pjʊərɪtən] puritano *m*, -a *f*

purity ['pjʊərɪtɪ] purezza *f*

purple ['pɜːpl] viola *inv*

purpose ['pɜːpəs] (*aim*, *object*) scopo *m*; **on ~** di proposito; **purposely** di proposito

purr [pɜː(r)] *of cat* far le fusa

purse [pɜːs] *for money* borsellino *m*; *Am* handbag borsetta *f*

pursue [pə'sjuː] *person* inseguire; *career* intraprendere; *course of action* proseguire; **pursuer** inseguitore *m*, -trice *f*; **pursuit** (*chase*) inseguimento *m*; *of happiness etc* ricerca *f*; *activity* occupazione *f*

push [pʊʃ] **1** *n* (*shove*) spinta *f* **2** *v/t* (*shove*) spingere; *button* premere; (*pressurize*) fare pressioni su; F *drugs* spacciare; **be ~ed for** F essere a corto di **3** *v/i* spingere

◆ **push on** (*continue*) continuare

'pushchair passeggino *m*; **pusher** F *of drugs* spacciatore *m*, -trice *f*; **push-up** flessione *f* sulle braccia; **pushy** F troppo intraprendente

puss, pussy (cat) [pʊs, 'pʊsɪ (kæt)] F micio *m*, -a *f*

put [pʊt] mettere; *question* porre; **~ the cost at** stimare il costo intorno a

◆ **put across** *ideas etc* trasmettere

◆ **put aside** mettere da parte

◆ **put away** *in cupboard etc* mettere via; *in institution* rinchiudere; (*consume*) far fuori; *money* mettere da parte; *animal* abbattere

◆ **put back** (*replace*) rimettere a posto

◆ **put down** mettere giù; *deposit* versare; *rebellion* reprimere; *animal* abbattere; (*belittle*) sminuire; *in writing* scrivere; **put X down to Y** (*attribute*) attribuire X a Y

◆ **put forward** *idea etc* avanzare

◆ **put in** inserire; *overtime* fare; *time*, *effort* dedicare; *request*, *claim* presentare

◆ **put off** *light*, *TV* spegnere; (*postpone*) rimandare; (*deter*) scoraggiare; (*repel*) disgustare

◆ **put on** *light*, *TV* accendere; *music* mettere su; *jacket*, *shoes*, *glasses* mettersi; *make-up* mettere; (*perform*) mettere in scena; (*assume*) affetta-

re; **she's just putting it on**
sta solo fingendo
◆ **put out** *hand* allungare; *fire*
light spegnere
◆ **put together** (*assemble*)
montare; (*organize*) organizzare
◆ **put up** *hand* alzare; *person*
ospitare; (*erect*) costruire;
prices aumentare; *poster* affiggere; *money* fornire; **put**
up for sale mettere in vendita

◆ **put up with** sopportare
putty ['pʌtɪ] mastice *m*
puzzle ['pʌzl] **1** *n* (*mystery*)
mistero *m*; *game* rebus *m*
inv; *jigsaw* puzzle *m inv* **2**
v/t lasciar perplesso; **puz-**
zling inspiegabile
PVC [pi:vi:'si:] (= **polyvinyl**
chloride) PVC *m* (= polivinilcloruro *m*)
pyjamas [pə'dʒɑːməz] pigiama *m*
pylon ['paɪlən] pilone *m*

Q

quack [kwæk] *of duck* fare
qua qua
quadrangle ['kwɒdræŋgl] *figure* quadrilatero *m*; *courtyard* cortile *m*
quadruped ['kwɒdruped]
quadrupede *m*
quail [kweɪl] *pretty* perdersi d'animo
quaint [kweɪnt] *pretty* pittoresco; *eccentric*: *ideas etc* curioso
quake [kweɪk] **1** *n* (*earthquake*) terremoto *m* **2** *v/i also*
fig tremare
qualification [kwɒlɪfɪ'keɪʃn]
from university etc titolo *m*
di studio; *qualified*: *doctor,*
engineer etc abilitato; (*restricted*) con riserva; **qualify**
1 *v/t of degree, course etc* abilitare; *remark etc* precisare **2**
v/i (*get certificate etc*) ottene-

re la qualifica (**as** di); *in*
competition qualificarsi
quality ['kwɒlɪtɪ] qualità *f*
inv; **quality control** controllo *m* (di) qualità; **quality**
time tempo *m* di qualità
qualm [kwɑːm]: **have no ~s**
about ... non aver scrupoli
a ...
quandary ['kwɒndərɪ] dilemma *m*; **be in a ~** avere un dilemma
quantify ['kwɒntɪfaɪ] quantificare
quantity ['kwɒntətɪ] quantità
f inv
quarantine ['kwɒrəntiːn]
quarantena *f*
quarrel ['kwɒrəl] **1** *n* litigio *m*
2 *v/i* litigare
quarry[1] ['kwɒrɪ] *in hunt* preda
f
quarry[2] ['kwɒrɪ] *for mining*

cava f

quart [kwɔːt] quarto m di gallone (*Br 1,136 l, Am 0,946 l*)

quarter ['kwɔːtə(r)] quarto m; *part of town* quartiere m; **a ~ of an hour** un quarto d'ora; **(a) ~ to 5** le cinque meno un quarto; **(a) ~ past 5** le cinque e un quarto; **quarter-final** partita f dei quarti mpl di finale; **quarter-finalist** concorrente m/f dei quarti di finale; **quarterly 1** adj trimestrale **2** adv trimestralmente; **quarters** MIL quartiere mpl; **quartet** MUS quartetto m

quartz [kwɔːts] quarzo m

quash [kwɔʃ] *rebellion* reprimere; *court decision* annullare

quaver ['kweɪvə(r)] **1** n *in voice* tremolio m; MUS croma f **2** v/i *of voice* tremolare

quay [kiː] banchina f

queasy ['kwiːzɪ] nauseato

queen [kwiːn] regina f

queer [kwɪə(r)] (*peculiar*) strano

quell [kwel] soffocare

quench [kwentʃ] *also fig* spegnere

query ['kwɪərɪ] **1** n interrogativo m **2** v/t *express doubt about* contestare; *check* controllare

quest [kwest] ricerca f

question ['kwestʃn] **1** n domanda f; *matter* questione f; **it's a ~ of money** è questione di soldi; **that's out**

of the ~ è fuori discussione **2** v/t *person* interrogare; (*doubt*) dubitare di; **questionable** discutibile; (*dubious*) dubbio; **questioning 1** adj *look, tone* interrogativo **2** n interrogatorio m; **question mark** punto m interrogativo; **questionnaire** questionario m

queue [kjuː] **1** n coda f, fila f **2** v/i fare la fila *or* la coda

quibble ['kwɪbl] cavillare

quick [kwɪk] *person* svelto; *reply, change* veloce; **be ~!** fai presto!, fai in fretta!; **let's have a ~ drink** beviamo qualcosina?; **quickly** rapidamente, in fretta; **quick-witted** sveglio

quid [kwɪd] F sterlina f; **50 ~** 50 sterline

quiet ['kwaɪət] *voice, music* basso; *engine* silenzioso; *street, life, town* tranquillo; **keep ~ about sth** tenere segreto qc; **~!** silenzio!; **quietly** *not loudly* silenziosamente; (*without fuss*) semplicemente; (*peacefully*) tranquillamente; **quietness** *of night, street* tranquillità f, calma f; *of voice* dolcezza f

quilt [kwɪlt] *on bed* piumino m

quinine ['kwɪniːn] chinino m

quip [kwɪp] **1** n battuta f (di spirito) **2** v/i scherzare

quirk [kwɜːk] bizzarria f; **quirky** bizzarro

quit [kwɪt] **1** *v/t job* mollare F **2** *v/i* (*leave job*) licenziarsi; COMPUT uscire

quite [kwaɪt] (*fairly*) abbastanza; (*completely*) completamente; *is that right? – not* ~ giusto? - non esattamente; ~*!* esatto!; ~ *a lot drink, change* parecchio; ~ *a lot better* molto meglio; ~ *a few* un bel po'; *it was ~ a surprise* è stata una bella sorpresa

quiver ['kwɪvə(r)] tremare

quiz [kwɪz] **1** *n* quiz *m inv* **2** *v/t* interrogare

quota ['kwəʊtə] quota *f*

quotation [kwəʊ'teɪʃn] *from author* citazione *f*; *price* preventivo *m*; quotation marks virgolette *fpl*; **quote 1** *n from author* citazione *f*; *price* preventivo *m*; (*quotation mark*) virgoletta *f*; *in* ~*s* tra virgolette **2** *v/t text* citare; *price* stimare

R

rabbit ['ræbɪt] coniglio *m*

rabble ['ræbl] marmaglia *f*; rabble-rouser agitatore *m*, -trice *f*

rabies ['reɪbiːz] rabbia *f*, idrofobia *f*

raccoon [rə'kuːn] procione *m*

race[1] [reɪs] *n of people* razza *f*

race[2] [reɪs] **1** *n* SP gara *f*; *the* ~*s* (*horse races*) le corse **2** *v/i* (*run fast*) correre **3** *v/t*: *I'll* ~ *you* facciamo una gara 'racecourse ippodromo *m*; racehorse cavallo *m* da corsa; race riot scontri *mpl* razziali; racetrack pista *f*; *for horses* ippodromo *m*

racial ['reɪʃl] razziale

racing ['reɪsɪŋ] corse *fpl*; racing car auto *f inv* da corsa; racing driver pilota *m* automobilistico

racism ['reɪsɪzm] razzismo *m*;

racist 1 *n* razzista *m/f* **2** *adj* razzista

rack [ræk] **1** *n for parking bikes* rastrelliera *f*; *for bags on train* portabagagli *m inv*; *for CDs* porta-CD *m inv* **2** *v/t*: ~ *one's brains* scervellarsi

racket[1] ['rækɪt] SP racchetta *f*

racket[2] ['rækɪt] (*noise*) baccano *m*; *criminal activity* racket *m inv*

radar ['reɪdɑː(r)] radar *m inv*

radiance ['reɪdɪəns] splendore *m*; radiant *smile* splendente; *appearance* raggiante; radiate *of heat, light* diffondersi; radiation PHYS radiazione *f*; radiator *in room* termosifone *m*; *in car* radiatore *m*

radical ['rædɪkl] **1** *adj* radicale **2** *n* radicale *m/f*; radicalism

POL radicalismo *m*; **radically** radicalmente

radio ['reɪdɪəʊ] radio *f inv*; **on the ~** alla radio; **radioactive** radioattivo; **radioactivity** radioattività *f*; **radio alarm** radiosveglia *f*; **radiographer** radiologo *m*, -a *f*; **radiography** radiografia *f*; **radio station** stazione *f* radiofonica, radio *f inv*

radius ['reɪdɪəs] raggio *m*

raft [rɑːft] zattera *f*

rafter ['rɑːftə(r)] travicello *m*

rag [ræg] *for cleaning etc* straccio *m*

rage [reɪdʒ] **1** *n* rabbia *f*, collera *f*; **be all the ~** F essere di moda **2** *v/i of person* infierire; *of storm* infuriare

ragged ['rægɪd] stracciato

raid [reɪd] **1** *n* raid *m inv* 2 *v/t of police, robbers* fare un raid in; *fridge, orchard* fare razzia in; **raider** *on bank etc* rapinatore *m*, -trice *f*

rail [reɪl] *on track* rotaia *f*; (*hand~*) corrimano *m*; (*barrier*) parapetto *m*; **towel ~** portasciugamano *m inv*; **by ~** in treno; **railings** *around park etc* inferriata *f*; **railroad** *Am* ferrovia *f*; **railway** ferrovia *f*; **railway station** stazione *f* ferroviaria

rain [reɪn] **1** *n* pioggia *f*; **in the ~** sotto la pioggia **2** *v/i* piovere; **it's ~ing** sta piovendo; **rainbow** arcobaleno *m*; **raincheck**: **can I take a ~**

on that? *Am* F posso riservarmi di farlo in seguito?; **raincoat** impermeabile *m*; **raindrop** goccia *f* di pioggia; **rainfall** piovosità *f*; **rain forest** foresta *f* pluviale; **rainproof** *fabric* impermeabile; **rainstorm** temporale *m*; **rainy** *day* di pioggia; *weather* piovoso; **it's ~** piove molto

raise [reɪz] **1** *n in salary* aumento *m* **2** *v/t shelf, question* sollevare; *offer* aumentare; *children* allevare; *money* raccogliere

raisin ['reɪzn] uva *f* passa

rake [reɪk] *for garden* rastrello *m*

rally ['rælɪ] *meeting* raduno *m*; MOT rally *m inv*; *in tennis* scambio *m*

RAM [ræm] COMPUT (= *random access memory*) RAM *f inv*

ram [ræm] **1** *n* montone *m* **2** *v/t ship, car* sbattere contro

ramble ['ræmbl] **1** *n walk* escursione *f* **2** *v/i walk* fare passeggiate; *in speaking* divagare; *talk incoherently* vaneggiare; **rambling** *speech* sconnesso

ramp [ræmp] rampa *f*; *for raising vehicle* ponte *m* idraulico

rampant ['ræmpənt] *inflation* dilagante

rampart ['ræmpɔːt] bastione *m*

ramshackle ['ræmʃækl] sgangherato

ranch [rɑːntʃ] ranch *m inv*; rancher *(owner)* proprietario *m* di un ranch; ranchhand lavoratore *m*, -trice *f* di un ranch

rancid ['rænsɪd] rancido

rancour, *Am* rancor ['ræŋkə(r)] rancore *m*

R&D [ɑːrən'diː] (= *research and development*) ricerca *f* e sviluppo *m*

random ['rændəm] **1** *adj* casuale; **~ sample** campione *m* casuale **2** *n*: **at ~** a caso

randy ['rændɪ] F arrapato

range [reɪndʒ] **1** *n of products* gamma *f*; *of missile, gun* gittata *f*; *of salary* scala *f*; *of voice* estensione *f*; *of mountains* catena *f*; **at close ~** a distanza ravvicinata **2** *v/i*: **~ from X to Y** variare da X a Y; **ranger** *Am* guardia *f* forestale

rank [ræŋk] **1** *n* MIL grado *m*; *in society* rango *m*; **the ~s** MIL la truppa **2** *v/t* classificare

♦ **rank among** classificarsi tra

ransack ['rænsæk] saccheggiare

ransom ['rænsəm] riscatto *m*; **ransom money** ((soldi *mpl* del) riscatto *m*

rap [ræp] **1** *n at door etc* colpo *m*; MUS rap *m* **2** *v/t table etc* battere

rape[1] [reɪp] **1** *n* stupro *m* **2** *v/t* violentare

rape[2] [reɪp] *n* BOT colza *f*

rapid ['ræpɪd] rapido; rapidity rapidità *f*; rapidly rapidamente; rapids rapide *fpl*

rapist ['reɪpɪst] violentatore *m*

rare [reə(r)] raro; *steak* al sangue; rarely raramente; rarity rarità *f inv*

rascal ['rɑːskl] birbante *m/f*

rash[1] [ræʃ] *n* MED orticaria *f*

rash[2] [ræʃ] *adj action* avventato

rashly ['ræʃlɪ] avventatamente

raspberry ['rɑːzbərɪ] lampone *m*

rat [ræt] ratto *m*

rate [reɪt] *of exchange* tasso *m*; *of pay, pricing* tariffa *f*; *(speed)* ritmo *m*; **at this ~** *(at this speed, carrying on like this)* di questo passo; **at any ~** in ogni modo

rather ['rɑːðə(r)] piuttosto; **I would ~ stay here** preferirei stare qui

ratification [rætɪfɪ'keɪʃn] ratifica *f*; ratify ratificare

ratings ['reɪtɪŋz] indice *m* d'ascolto

ratio ['reɪʃɪəʊ] proporzione *f*

ration ['ræʃn] **1** *n* razione *f* **2** *v/t supplies* razionare

rational ['ræʃənl] razionale; rationality razionalità *f*; rationalization razionalizzazione *f*; rationalize razionalizzare; rationally razionalmente rattle ['rætl] 1 n noise rumore m; toy sonaglio m 2 v/t scuotere 3 v/i far rumore; rattlesnake serpente m a sonagli

raucous ['rɔːkəs] sguaiato

rave [reɪv] 1 v/i delirare; ~ about sth be very enthusiastic entusiasmarsi per qc 2 n party rave m inv

ravenous ['rævənəs] famelico

'rave review recensione f entusiastica

ravine [rə'viːn] burrone m

ravishing ['rævɪʃɪŋ] incantevole

raw [rɔː] meat, vegetable crudo; sugar, iron grezzo; raw materials materia f prima

ray [reɪ] raggio m

razor ['reɪzə(r)] rasoio m; razor blade lametta f da barba

re [riː] COM con riferimento a

reach [riːtʃ] 1 n: within ~ vicino (of a); within arm's reach a portata (di mano); out of ~ non a portata (of di); keep out of ~ of children tenere lontano dalla portata dei bambini 2 v/t city arrivare a; decision, agreement raggiungere; can you ~ it? ci arrivi?

react [rɪ'ækt] reagire; reaction reazione f; reactionary 1 n POL reazionario m, -a f 2 adj POL reazionario; reactor nuclear reattore m

read [riːd] leggere

♦ read out aloud leggere a

voce alta

♦ read up on documentarsi su

readable ['riːdəbl] leggibile; reader person lettore m, -trice f

readily ['redɪlɪ] (willingly) volentieri; (easily) facilmente

reading ['riːdɪŋ] also from meter lettura f

readjust [riːə'dʒʌst] 1 v/t regolare 2 v/i to conditions riadattarsi

ready ['redɪ] pronto; get (o.s.) ~ prepararsi; get sth ~ preparare qc; ready cash contanti mpl; ready-made stew etc precotto; solution bell'e pronto; ready-to-wear confezionato

real [riːl] vero; real estate proprietà fpl immobiliari; real estate agent agente m/f immobiliare; realism realismo m; realist realista m/f; realistic realistico; realistically realisticamente; reality realtà f inv; reality show TV reality show m inv; realize rendersi conto di, realizzare; FIN realizzare; I ~ now that ... ora capisco che ...; really veramente; ~? davvero?; not ~ (not much) non proprio; real-time COMPUT in tempo reale; real time COMPUT tempo reale

realtor ['riːltə(r)] Am agente m/f immobiliare; realty Am

proprietà *fpl* immobiliari
reappear [riːəˈpɪə(r)] riapparire; **reappearance** ricomparsa *f*
rear [rɪə(r)] **1** *n of building* retro *m*; *of train* parte *f* posteriore **2** *adj* posteriore
rearm [riːˈɑːm] **1** *v/t* riarmare **2** *v/i* riarmarsi
rearrange [riːəˈreɪnʒ] *furniture* spostare; *schedule, meetings* cambiare
rear-view 'mirror specchietto *m* retrovisore
reason [ˈriːzn] **1** *n faculty* ragione *f*; (*cause*) motivo *m*; **listen to ~** ascoltare ragione **2** *v/i*: **~ with s.o.** far ragionare con qu; **reasonable** *person, price* ragionevole; *weather, health* discreto; **a ~ number of people** un discreto numero di persone; **reasonably** *act, behave* ragionevolmente; (*quite*) abbastanza; **reasoning** ragionamento *m*
reassure [riːəˈʃʊə(r)] rassicurare; **reassuring** rassicurante
rebate [ˈriːbeɪt] *money back* rimborso *m*
rebel 1 [ˈrebl] *n* ribelle *m/f* **2** [rɪˈbel] *v/i* ribellarsi; **rebellion** ribellione *f*; **rebellious** ribelle; **rebelliousness** spirito *m* di ribellione
rebound [rɪˈbaʊnd] *of ball etc* rimbalzare
rebuild [ˈriːbɪld] ricostruire

recall [rɪˈkɔːl] richiamare; (*remember*) ricordare
recap [ˈriːkæp] F ricapitolare
recapture [riːˈkæptʃə(r)] *criminal* ricatturare; *town* riconquistare
recede [rɪˈsiːd] *of flood waters* abbassarsi; **receding** *forehead, chin* sfuggente; **have a ~ hairline** essere stempiato
receipt [rɪˈsiːt] *for purchase* ricevuta *f*, scontrino *m*; **~s** FIN introiti *mpl*; **receive** ricevere; **receiver** TELEC ricevitore *m*; *for radio* apparecchio *m* ricevente; **receivership**: **be in ~** essere in amministrazione controllata
recent [ˈriːsnt] recente; **recently** recentemente
reception [rɪˈsepʃn] *recep-tion f inv; formal party* ricevimento *m*; (*welcome*) accoglienza *f*; *on radio, mobile* ricezione *f*; **reception desk** banco *m* della reception; **receptionist** receptionist *m/f inv*; **receptive**: **be ~ to sth** essere ricettivo verso qc
recess [ˈriːses] *in wall etc* rientranza *f*; *of parliament* vacanza *f*; *Am* EDU intervallo *m*; **recession** *economic* recessione *f*
recharge [riːˈtʃɑːdʒ] *battery* ricaricare
recipe [ˈresəpɪ] ricetta *f*
recipient [rɪˈsɪpɪənt] destinatario *m*, -a *f*
reciprocal [rɪˈsɪprəkl] reci-

proco

recite [rɪ'saɪt] *poem* recitare; *details, facts* enumerare

reckless ['reklɪs] spericolato; **recklessly** in modo spericolato; *spend* avventatamente

reckon ['rekən] (*think, consider*) pensare

◆ **reckon on** contare su

reclaim [rɪ'kleɪm] *land* bonificare; *lost property* recuperare

recline [rɪ'klaɪn] sdraiarsi; **recliner chair** poltrona *f* reclinabile

recluse [rɪ'kluːs] eremita *m/f*

recognition [rekəg'nɪʃn] *of state, s.o.'s achievements* riconoscimento *m*; **recognizable** riconoscibile; **recognize** riconoscere

recoil [rɪ'kɔɪl] indietreggiare

recollect [rekə'lekt] rammentare; **recollection** ricordo *m*

recommend [rekə'mend] consigliare; **recommendation** consiglio *m*

recompense ['rekəmpens] ricompensa *f*; LAW risarcimento *m*

reconcile ['rekənsaɪl] *people, differences* riconciliare; *facts* conciliare; **~ o.s. to** ... rassegnarsi a ...; **reconciliation** *of people, differences* riconciliazione *f*; *of facts* conciliazione *f*

recondition [riːkən'dɪʃn] ricondizionare

reconnaissance [rɪ'kɒnɪsns] MIL ricognizione *f*

reconsider [riːkən'sɪdə(r)] **1** *v/t offer* riconsiderare **2** *v/i* ripensare

reconstruct [riːkən'strʌkt] *city, crime, life* ricostruire

record[1] ['rekɔːd] *n* MUS disco *m*; SP etc record *m* inv, primato *m*; *written document etc* nota *f*; *in database* record *m* inv; **~s** archivio *m*; **say sth off the ~** dire qc ufficiosamente; **have a criminal ~** avere precedenti penali

record[2] [rɪ'kɔːd] *v/t electronically* registrare; *in writing* annotare

'record-breaking da record;

recorder [rɪ'kɔːdə(r)] MUS flauto *m* dolce

'record holder primatista *m/f*

recording [rɪ'kɔːdɪŋ] registrazione *f*; **recording studio** sala *f* di registrazione

'record player giradischi *m* inv

re-count ['riːkaʊnt] **1** *n of votes* nuovo conteggio *m* **2** *v/t* (*count again*) ricontare

recount [rɪ'kaʊnt] (*tell*) raccontare

recoup [rɪ'kuːp] *financial losses* rifarsi di

recover [rɪ'kʌvə(r)] **1** *v/t stolen goods* recuperare **2** *v/i from illness* rimettersi; *of business* riprendersi; **recovery** *of stolen goods* recupero *m*; *from illness* guarigione *f*

recreation [rekrɪ'eɪʃn] ricreazione *f*; **recreational** *done* *for pleasure* ricreativo

recruit [rɪˈkruːt] **1** n MIL recluta f; *to company* neoassunto m, -a f **2** v/t *new staff* assumere; *members* arruolare; **recruitment** assunzione f; MIL, POL reclutamento m

rectangle [ˈrektæŋgl] rettangolo m; **rectangular** rettangolare

rectify [ˈrektɪfaɪ] rettificare

recuperate [rɪˈkjuːpəreɪt] ricuperare

recur [rɪˈkɜː(r)] *of error, event* ripetersi; *of symptoms* ripresentarsi; **recurrent** ricorrente

recyclable [riːˈsaɪkləbl] riciclabile; **recycle** riciclare; **recycling** riciclo m

red [red] rosso; **in the ~** FIN in rosso; **Red Cross** Croce f Rossa

redecorate [riːˈdekəreɪt] ritinteggiare; *change wallpaper* ritappezzare

redeem [rɪˈdiːm] *debt* estinguere; *sinners* redimere; **redeeming feature** aspetto m positivo

redevelop [riːdɪˈveləp] *part of town* risanare

red-handed [redˈhændɪd]: **catch s.o. ~** cogliere qu in flagrante; **redhead** rosso m, -a f; **red light** *at traffic lights* rosso m; **red light district** quartiere m a luci rosse; **red meat** carni fpl rosse; **redneck** *Am* F reazionario

m, -a f; **red tape** F burocrazia f

reduce [rɪˈdjuːs] ridurre; **reduction** riduzione f

redundancy [rɪˈdʌndənsɪ] *at work* licenziamento m; **redundant** (*unnecessary*) superfluo; **be made ~** *at work* essere licenziato

reef [riːf] *in sea* scogliera f; **reef knot** nodo m piano

reek [riːk] puzzare (**of** di)

reel [riːl] *of film* rullino m; *of thread* rocchetto m; *of tape* bobina f; *of fishing line* mulinello m

re-e'lect rieleggere; **re-election** rielezione f

re-'entry *of spacecraft* rientro m

ref [ref] F arbitro m

♦ **refer to** [rɪˈfɜː(r)] riferirsi a; *dictionary etc* consultare

referee [refəˈriː] SP arbitro m; *for job* referenza f; **reference** (*allusion*) allusione f; *for job* referenza f; (~ *number*) (numero m di) riferimento m; **reference book** opera f di consultazione; **reference number** numero m di riferimento

referendum [refəˈrendəm] referendum m *inv*

refill [ˈriːfɪl] riempire

refine [rɪˈfaɪn] raffinare; **refinement** *to process, machine* miglioramento m; **refinery** raffineria f

reflect [rɪˈflekt] **1** v/t *light* riflettere; **be ~ed in** riflettersi in **2** v/i (think) riflettere; re‐**flection** in water, glass etc riflesso m; (consideration) riflessione f; **on ~** dopo aver riflettuto

reflex ['ri:fleks] in body riflesso m

reform [rɪ'fɔ:m] **1** n riforma f **2** v/t riformare; **reformer** riformatore m, -trice f

refrain [rɪ'freɪn] fml: **please ~ from smoking** si prega di non fumare

refresh [rɪ'freʃ] person ristorare; **feel ~ed** sentirsi ristorato; **refreshing** drink rinfrescante; experience piacevole; **refreshments** rinfreschi mpl

refrigerate [rɪ'frɪdʒəreɪt] v/t **keep ~d** conservare in frigo; **refrigerator** frigorifero m

refuel [ri:'fju:əl] **1** v/t aeroplane rifornire di carburante **2** v/i of aeroplane, car far rifornimento

refuge ['refju:dʒ] rifugio m; **take ~** from storm ecc ripararsi; **refugee** rifugiato m, -a f, profugo m, -a f

refund ['ri:fʌnd] n rimborso m **2** [rɪ'fʌnd] v/t rimborsare

refusal [rɪ'fju:zl] rifiuto m

refuse[1] [rɪ'fju:z] rifiutare; **~ to do sth** rifiutare di fare qc

refuse[2] ['refju:s] n rifiuti mpl

regain [rɪ'geɪn] control, lost territory, the lead riconquistare

regard [rɪ'gɑ:d] **1** n: **have great ~ for s.o.** avere molta stima di qu; **with ~ to** riguardo a; (kind) **~s** cordiali saluti; **with no ~ for** senza alcun riguardo per **2** v/t: **~ as** considerare come qc; **regarding** riguardo a; **regardless** lo stesso; **~ of** senza tener conto di

regime [reɪ'ʒi:m] (government) regime m

regiment ['redʒɪmənt] reggimento m

region ['ri:dʒən] regione f; **in the ~ of** intorno a; **regional** regionale

register ['redʒɪstə(r)] **1** n registro m **2** v/t birth, death: by individual denunciare; by authorities registrare; vehicle iscrivere; letter assicurare; emotion mostrare **3** v/i at university iscriversi; **registered letter** (lettera f) assicurata f; **registration** at university iscrizione f; **registration number** MOT numero m di targa; **registry office** ufficio m di stato civile

regret [rɪ'gret] **1** v/t rammaricarsi di; missed opportunity rimpiangere **2** n rammarico m; **regretful** di rammarico, regretfully purtroppo; **regrettable** deplorevole; regrettably purtroppo

regular ['regjʊlə(r)] **1** adj regolare; (ordinary) normale **2** n at bar etc cliente m/f abituale; **regularity** regolarità f *inv*; **regularly** regolarmente

regulate ['regjuleɪt] regolare;

regulation (*rule*) regolamento *m*; *control* controllo *m*

rehabilitate [riːhə'bɪlɪteɪt] *ex--criminal* riabilitare; *disabled person* rieducare

rehearsal [rɪ'hɜːsl] prova *f*; **rehearse** provare

reign [reɪn] **1** *n* regno *m* **2** *v/i* regnare

reimburse [riːɪm'bɜːs] rimborsare

reinforce [riːɪn'fɔːs] rinforzare; **reinforced concrete** cemento *m* armato; **reinforcements** MIL rinforzi *mpl*

reinstate [riːɪn'steɪt] reintegrare

reiterate [riː'ɪtəreɪt] *fml* ripetere

reject [rɪ'dʒekt] respingere; **rejection** rifiuto *m*

relapse ['riːlæps] MED ricaduta *f*

relate [rɪ'leɪt] **1** *v/t story* raccontare **2** *v/i*: **~ to ...** be connected with riferirsi a ...; **he doesn't ~ to people** non sa stabilire un rapporto con gli altri; **related** by family imparentato; *events, ideas etc* collegato; **relation** in family parente *m/f*; (*connection*) rapporto *m*; **business ~s** rapporti d'affari; **relationship** rapporto *m*; **relative 1** *n* parente *m/f* **2** *adj* relativo; **relatively** relativa-

mente

relax [rɪ'læks] **1** *v/i* rilassarsi; **~!** rilassati! **2** *v/t* rilassare; **relaxation** relax *m inv*; *of rules etc* rilassamento *m*; **relaxed** rilassato; **relaxing** rilassante

relay [riː'leɪ] **1** *v/t* trasmettere **2** *n*: **~ (race** (corsa *f* a) staffetta *f*

release [rɪ'liːs] **1** *n from prison* rilascio *m*; *of CD etc* uscita *f*; *of software* versione *f* **2** *v/t prisoner* rilasciare; *hand-brake* togliere; *film, record* far uscire; *information* rendere noto

relegate ['relɪgeɪt] relegare; **be ~d** SP essere retrocesso; **relegation** SP retrocessione *f*

relent [rɪ'lent] cedere; **relentless** incessante, implacabile

relevance ['reləvəns] pertinenza *f*

relevant ['reləvənt] pertinente

reliability [rɪlaɪə'bɪlətɪ] affidabilità *f*; **reliable** affidabile; **reliance** dipendenza *f* (**on** da); **reliant**: **be ~ on** dipendere da

relic ['relɪk] reliquia *f*

relief [rɪ'liːf] sollievo *m*; **relieve** *pressure, pain* alleviare; (*take over from*) dare il cambio a; **be ~d** *at news etc* essere sollevato

religion [rɪ'lɪdʒən] religione *f*; **religious** religioso; **religiously** religiosamente

relinquish [rɪ'lɪŋkwɪʃ] rinunciare a

relish ['relɪʃ] **1** *n sauce* salsa *f*; *(enjoyment)* gusto *m* **2** *v/t idea, prospect* gradire

relive [riː'lɪv] rivivere

relocate [riːlə'keɪt] *of business, employee* trasferirsi

reluctance [rɪ'lʌktəns] riluttanza *f*; **reluctant** riluttante; **be~ to do** essere restio a fare qc; **reluctantly** a malincuore

◆ **rely on** [rɪ'laɪ] contare su; **rely on s.o. to do sth** contare su qu perché faccia qc

remain [rɪ'meɪn] rimanere; **remainder** *also* MATH resto *m*; **remaining** restante; **remains** *of body* resti *mpl*

remake ['riːmeɪk] *of film* remake *m inv*

remand [rɪ'mɑːnd] **1** *v/t:* **~ s.o. in custody** ordinare la custodia cautelare di qu **2** *n:* **be on ~** essere in attesa di giudizio

remark [rɪ'mɑːk] **1** *n* commento *m* **2** *v/t* osservare; **remarkable** notevole; **remarkably** notevolmente

remarry [riː'mærɪ] risposarsi

remedy ['remədɪ] rimedio *m*

remember [rɪ'membə(r)] **1** *v/t* ricordare **2** *v/i* ricordare, ricordarsi

remind [rɪ'maɪnd]: **~ s.o. of s.o. / sth** ricordare qu / qc a qu; **~ s.o. to do sth** ricordare a qu di fare qc; **reminder** promemoria *m*; COM *for*

payment sollecito *m*

reminisce [remɪ'nɪs] rievocare il passato

remission [rɪ'mɪʃn] REL MED remissione *f*

remnant ['remnənt] resto *m*; *of fabric* scampolo *m*

remorse [rɪ'mɔːs] rimorso *m*; **remorseless** spietato

remote [rɪ'məʊt] *village* isolato; *possibility* remoto; *(aloof)* distante; *ancestor* lontano; **remote control** *for TV* telecomando *m*; **remotely** *related, connected* lontanamente; **just ~ possible** vagamente possibile

removable [rɪ'muːvəbl] staccabile; **removal** rimozione *f*; *from home* trasloco *m*; **removal firm** ditta *f* di traslochi; **remove** togliere; MED asportare; *doubt, suspicion* eliminare

remuneration [rɪmjuːnə-'reɪʃn] rimunerazione *f*

Renaissance [rɪ'neɪsəns] Rinascimento *m*

rename [riː'neɪm] ribattezzare; *file* rinominare

rendez-vous ['rɒndeɪvuː] *(meeting)* incontro *m*

renew [rɪ'njuː] *contract* rinnovare; **feel ~ed** sentirsi rinato; **renewal** *of contract etc* rinnovo *m*

renounce [rɪ'naʊns] rinunciare a

renovate ['renəveɪt] ristrutturare; **renovation** ristrutturazione f

rent [rent] **1** n affitto m; **for ~**
affittasi **2** v/t apartment affittare; car, equipment, noleggiare; (**~ out**) affittare; **rental**
for apartment affitto m; for
car noleggio m; for TV,
phone canone m; **rental car**
macchina f a noleggio;
rent-free gratis

reopen [riː'əʊpn] riaprire

reorganization [riːɔːgənaɪ-
'zeɪʃn] riorganizzazione f;
reorganize riorganizzare

repaint [riː'peɪnt] ridipingere

repair [rɪ'peə(r)] **1** v/t riparare
2 n: **in a bad state of ~** in cattivo stato; **~s** riparazioni fpl;
repairman tecnico m

repatriate [riː'pætrɪeɪt] rimpatriare; **repatriation** rimpatrio m

repay [riː'peɪ] money restituire; person ripagare; **repayment** pagamento m

repeal [rɪ'piːl] law abrogare

repeat [rɪ'piːt] **1** v/t ripetere **2**
n programme replica f; **repeatedly** ripetutamente

repel [rɪ'pel] invaders, attack
respingere; (disgust) ripugnare; **repellent 1** n (insect
~) insettifugo m **2** adj ripugnante

repercussions [riːpə'kʌʃnz]
ripercussioni fpl

repertoire ['repətwɑː(r)] repertorio m

repetition [repɪ'tɪʃn] ripetizione f; **repetitive** ripetitivo

replace [rɪ'pleɪs] (put back)
mettere a posto; (take the
place of) sostituire; **replacement** person sostituto m, -a
f; act sostituzione f; **replacement part** pezzo m di ricambio

replay ['riːpleɪ] **1** n recording
replay m inv; match spareggio m **2** v/t match ripiocare

replenish [rɪ'plenɪʃ] container
riempire; supplies rifornire

replica ['replɪkə] copia f

reply [rɪ'plaɪ] **1** n risposta f **2**
v/t & v/i rispondere

report [rɪ'pɔːt] **1** n (account)
resoconto m; by journalist
servizio m; EDU pagella f **2**
v/t facts fare un servizio su;
to authorities denunciare **3**
v/i of journalist fare un reportage; (present o.s.) presentarsi

♦ **report to** in business rendere conto a

reporter [rɪ'pɔːtə(r)] giornalista m/f

repossess [riːpə'zes] COM riprendere possesso di

represent [reprɪ'zent] rappresentare; **representative
1** n rappresentante m/f **2**
adj (typical) rappresentativo

repress [rɪ'pres] reprimere;
repression POL repressione
f; **repressive** POL repressivo

reprieve [rɪ'priːv] **1** n LAW sospensione f della pena capitale; fig proroga f **2** v/t prisoner sospendere l'esecuzio-

ne di
reprimand ['reprimɑːnd] ammonire
reprint ['riːprɪnt] **1** n ristampa f **2** v/t ristampare
reprisal [rɪ'praɪzl] rappresaglia f; **take ~s** fare delle rappresaglie
reproach [rɪ'prəʊtʃ] **1** n rimprovero m; **be beyond ~** essere irreprensibile **2** v/t rimproverare; **reproachful** di rimprovero
reproduce [riːprə'djuːs] **1** v/t riprodurre **2** v/i riprodursi; **reproduction** riproduzione f; **reproductive** riproduttivo
reptile ['reptaɪl] rettile m
republic [rɪ'pʌblɪk] repubblica f; **republican 1** n repubblicano m, -a f **2** adj repubblicano
repulsive [rɪ'pʌlsɪv] ripugnante
reputable ['repjʊtəbl] rispettabile; **reputation** reputazione f; **reputedly** a quanto si dice
request [rɪ'kwest] **1** n richiesta f; **on ~** su richiesta **2** v/t richiedere
require [rɪ'kwaɪə(r)] (need) aver bisogno di; **it ~s great care** richiede molta cura; **as ~d by law** come prescritto dalla legge; **required** (necessary) necessario; **requirement** (need) esigenza f; (condition) requisito m
requisition [rekwɪ'zɪʃn] re-

quisire
reroute [riː'ruːt] aeroplane etc deviare
rerun ['riːrʌn] **1** n of programme replica f **2** v/t of programme replicare
reschedule [riː'ʃedjuːl] stabilire di nuovo
rescue ['reskjuː] **1** n salvataggio m; **come to s.o.'s ~** andare in aiuto a qu **2** v/t salvare
research [rɪ'sɜːtʃ] ricerca f; **research and development** ricerca f e sviluppo m; **research assistant** assistente ricercatore m, -trice f; **researcher** ricercatore m, -trice f
resemblance [rɪ'zembləns] somiglianza f; **resemble** (as)somigliare a
resent [rɪ'zent] risentirsi per; **resentful** pieno di risentimento; **resentfully** con risentimento; **resentment** risentimento m
reservation [rezə'veɪʃn] of room, table prenotazione f; mental, special area riserva f; **I have a ~** in hotel, restaurant ho prenotato; **reserve 1** n (store) riserva f; (aloofness) riserbo m; SP riserva f; **~s** FIN riserve fpl; **keep sth in ~** tenere qc di riserva **2** v/t seat, table prenotare; judgment riservarsi; **reserved** person, manner riservato; table, seat prenotato

restful

reservoir ['rezəvwɑː(r)] *for water* bacino *m* idrico

residence ['rezɪdəns] *fml: house etc* residenza *f*; (*stay*) permanenza *f*; residence permit permesso *m* di residenza; resident residente *m/f*; residential residenziale

residue ['rezɪdjuː] residuo *m*

resign [rɪ'zaɪn] 1 *v/t position* dimettersi da; 2 *v/i from job* dimettersi; resignation *from job* dimissioni *fpl; mental* rassegnazione *f*

resilient [rɪ'zɪlɪənt] *personality* che ha molte risorse; *material* resistente

resist [rɪ'zɪst] 1 *v/t* resistere a 2 *v/i* resistere; resistance resistenza *f*; resistant *material* resistente

resolute ['rezəluːt] risoluto; resolution (*decision*) risoluzione *f*; *made at New Year etc* proposito *m*; (*determination*) risolutezza *f*; *of problem* soluzione *f*; *of image* risoluzione *f*

resort [rɪ'zɔːt] *place* località *f inv; holiday* ~ luogo *m* di villeggiatura; ski ~ stazione *f* sciistica; as a last ~ come ultima risorsa

♦ resort to far ricorso a

♦ resound with [rɪ'zaʊnd] risuonare di

resounding [rɪ'zaʊndɪŋ] *success, victory* clamoroso

resource [rɪ'sɔːs] risorsa *f*; fi-

nancial ~s mezzi *mpl* economici; leave s.o. to his own ~s lasciare qu in balia di se stesso; resourceful pieno di risorse

respect [rɪ'spekt] 1 *n* rispetto *m*; with ~ to riguardo a; in this / that ~ quanto a questo; in many ~s sotto molti aspetti; pay one's last ~s to s.o. rendere omaggio a qu 2 *v/t* rispettare; respectability rispettabilità *f*; respectable rispettabile; respectful rispettoso; respectively rispettivamente

respiration [respɪ'reɪʃn] respirazione *f*; respirator MED respiratore *m*

respite ['respaɪt] tregua *f*; without ~ senza tregua

respond [rɪ'spɒnd] rispondere; response risposta *f*

responsibility [rɪspɒnsɪ'bɪlɪtɪ] responsabilità *f inv*; responsible responsabile (for) di; *job, position* di responsabilità

rest¹ [rest] 1 *n* riposo *m*; set s.o.'s mind at ~ tranquillizzare qu 2 *v/i* riposare; ~ on ... (*be based on*) basarsi su ...; (*lean against*) poggiare su ... 3 *v/t* (*lean, balance*) appoggiare

rest² [rest]: the ~ il resto *m*

restaurant ['restrɒnt] ristorante *m*

restful ['restful] riposante;

rest home casa *f* di riposo; **restless** irrequieto; **have a ~ night** passare una notte agitata; **restlessly** nervosamente

restoration [restə'reɪʃn] restauro *m*; **restore** *building etc* restaurare; *(bring back)* restituire

restrain [rɪ'streɪn] *dog, troops* frenare; *emotions* reprimere; **~ o.s.** trattenersi; **restraint** *(self-control)* autocontrollo *m*

restrict [rɪ'strɪkt] limitare; **restricted** *view* limitato; **restriction** restrizione *f*

'rest room *Am* gabinetto *m*

result [rɪ'zʌlt] risultato *m*; **as a ~ of this** in conseguenza di ciò

♦ **result from** risultare da, derivare da

♦ **result in** dare luogo a

résumé ['rezumeɪ] *Am* curriculum vitae *m inv*

resume [rɪ'zju:m] riprendere

resumption [rɪ'zʌmpʃn] ripresa *f*

resurface [ri:'sɜ:fɪs] **1** *v/t roads* asfaltare **2** *v/i (reappear)* riaffiorare

Resurrection [rezə'rekʃn] REL resurrezione *f*

retail ['ri:teɪl] **1** *adv* al dettaglio **2** *v/i:* **~ at** essere in vendita a; **retailer** dettagliante *m/f*; **retail price** prezzo *m* al dettaglio

retain [rɪ'teɪn] conservare; re-

tainer FIN onorario *m*

retaliate [rɪ'tælɪeɪt] vendicarsi; **retaliation** rappresaglia *f*

rethink [ri:'θɪŋk] riconsiderare

reticence ['retɪsns] riservatezza *f*; **reticent** riservato

retire [rɪ'taɪə(r)] *from work* andare in pensione; **retired** in pensione; **retirement** pensione *f*; *act* pensionamento *m*; **retirement age** età *f inv* pensionabile; **retiring** riservato

retort [rɪ'tɔːt] **1** *n* replica *f* **2** *v/t* replicare

retract [rɪ'trækt] *claws* ritrarre; *undercarriage* far rientrare; *statement* ritrattare

re-'train riqualificarsi

retreat [rɪ'triːt] **1** *v/i* ritirarsi **2** *n* MIL ritirata *f*; *place* rifugio *m*

retrieve [rɪ'triːv] recuperare; **retriever** *dog* cane *m* da riporto

retroactive [retrəʊ'æktɪv] retroattivo; **retroactively** retroattivamente

retrograde ['retrəgreɪd] retrogrado

retrospective [retrə'spekt ɪv] retrospettiva *f*

return [rɪ'tɜːn] **1** *n* ritorno *m*; *(giving back)* restituzione *f*; COMPUT (tasto *m*) invio *m*; *in tennis* risposta *f* al servizio; (**~ ticket**) andata e ritorno *m inv*; **by ~ (of post)** a stretto giro di posta; **~s**

(*profit*) rendimento *m*; **many happy ~s (of the day)** cento di questi giorni; **in ~ for** in cambio di **2** *v/t* (*give back*) restituire; (*put back*) rimettere; *favour, invitation* ricambiare **3** *v/i* (*go back, come back*) ritornare; *of symptoms, doubts etc* ricomparire; **return flight** volo *m* di ritorno; **return ticket** biglietto *m* (di) andata e ritorno

reunification [riːjuːnɪfɪ'keɪ-ʃn] riunificazione *f*

reunion [riː'juːnɪən] riunione *f*; **reunite** riunire

reusable [riː'juːzəbl] riutilizzabile; **reuse** riutilizzare

◆ **rev up** [rev] *engine* far andare su di giri

revaluation [riːvæljʊ'eɪʃn] rivalutazione *f*

reveal [rɪ'viːl] (*make visible*) mostrare; (*make known*) rivelare; **revealing** *remark* rivelatore; *dress* scollato; **revelation** rivelazione *f*

revenge [rɪ'vendʒ] vendetta *f*; **take one's ~** vendicarsi

revenue ['revənjuː] reddito *m*

reverberate [rɪ'vɜːbəreɪt] *of sound* rimbombare

revere [rɪ'vɪə(r)] riverire; **reverence** rispetto *m*; Reverend REL reverendo *m*; **reverent** riverente

reverse [rɪ'vɜːs] **1** *adj sequence* opposto; **in ~ order** in ordine inverso **2** *n* (*opposite*) contrario *m*; (*back*) ro-

vescio *m*; MOT retromarcia *f* **3** *v/t sequence* invertire; **~ the charges** TELEC telefonare a carico del destinatario **4** *v/i* MOT fare marcia indietro

review [rɪ'vjuː] **1** *n of book, film* recensione *f*; *of troops* rivista *f*; *of situation etc* revisione *f* **2** *v/t book, film* recensire; *troops* passare in rivista; *situation etc* riesaminare; **reviewer** *of book, film* critico *m*, -a *f*

revise [rɪ'vaɪz] **1** *v/t opinion, text* rivedere; EDU ripassare **2** *v/i* EDU ripassare; **revision** *of opinion, text* revisione *f*; *for exam* ripasso *m*

revival [rɪ'vaɪvl] *of custom, style etc* revival *m inv*; *of patient* ripresa *f*; **revive 1** *v/t custom, style etc* riportare alla moda; *patient* rianimare **2** *v/i of business etc* riprendersi

revoke [rɪ'vəʊk] *licence* revocare

revolt [rɪ'vəʊlt] **1** *n* rivolta *f* **2** *v/i* ribellarsi; **revolting** schifoso; **revolution** rivoluzione *f*; **revolutionary 1** *n* POL rivoluzionario *m*, -a *f* **2** *adj* rivoluzionario; **revolutionize** rivoluzionare

revolve [rɪ'vɒlv] ruotare; **revolver** revolver *m inv*

revulsion [rɪ'vʌlʃn] ribrezzo *m*

reward [rɪ'wɔːd] **1** *n financial* ricompensa *f*; *benefit derived* vantaggio *m* **2** *v/t financially* ricompensare; **rewarding** *experience* gratificante

rewind [riː'waɪnd] *film, tape* riavvolgere

rewrite [riː'raɪt] riscrivere

rhetoric ['retərɪk] retorica *f*

rheumatism ['ruːmətɪzm] reumatismo *m*

rhinoceros [raɪ'nɒsərəs] rinoceronte *m*

rhubarb ['ruːbɑːb] rabarbaro *m*

rhyme [raɪm] **1** *n* rima *f* **2** *v/i* rimare; **~ with** fare rima con

rhythm ['rɪðm] ritmo *m*

rib [rɪb] ANAT costola *f*

ribbon ['rɪbən] nastro *m*

rice [raɪs] riso *m*

rich [rɪtʃ] **1** *adj* ricco; *food* pesante **2** *n*: **the ~** i ricchi *mpl*; **richly** *deserved* pienamente

ricochet ['rɪkəʃeɪ] rimbalzare

rid [rɪd]: **get ~ of** sbarazzarsi di; **riddance**: **good ~!** che liberazione!

ride [raɪd] **1** *n on horse* cavalcata *f*; *in vehicle* giro *m*; *(journey)* viaggio *m*; **do you want a ~ into town?** vuoi uno strappo in città? **2** *v/t*: **~ a horse** andare a cavallo; **~ a bike** andare in bicicletta **3** *v/i on horse* andare a cavallo; *on bike* andare; *in vehicle* viaggiare; **rider** *on horse* cavallerizzo *m*, -a *f*; *on bike* ciclista *m/f*

ridge [rɪdʒ] *raised strip* sporgenza *f*; *of mountain* cresta

f; *of roof* punta *f*

ridicule ['rɪdɪkjuːl] **1** *n* ridicolo *m* **2** *v/t* ridicolizzare; **ridiculous** ridicolo; **ridiculously** incredibilmente

riding ['raɪdɪŋ] *on horseback* equitazione *f*

rifle ['raɪfl] fucile *m*

rift [rɪft] *in earth* crepa *f*; *in party etc* spaccatura *f*

rig [rɪg] **1** *n* (*oil* ~) piattaforma *f* petrolifera **2** *v/t elections* manipolare

right [raɪt] **1** *adj (correct)* esatto; *(proper, just)* giusto; *(suitable)* adatto; *not left* destro; **be ~** *of answer* essere esatto; *of person* avere ragione; *of clock* essere giusto; **put things ~** sistemare le cose **2** *adv (directly)* proprio; *(correctly)* bene; *(completely)* completamente; *not left* a destra; **~ now** *(immediately)* subito; *(at the moment)* adesso **3** *n civil, legal etc* diritto *m*; *not left*, POL destra *f*; **on the ~** a destra; **turn to the ~**, **take a ~** girare a destra; **be in the ~** avere ragione; **know ~ from wrong** saper distinguere il bene dal male; **right-angle** angolo *m* retto; **rightful** *owner etc* legittimo; **right-hand drive** MOT guida *f* a destra; *car* auto *f inv* con guida a destra; **righthanded**: **be ~** usare la (mano) destra; **righthand man** braccio *m* destro; **right of way** *in traffic* (diritto *m* di) precedenza *f*; *across land* diritto *m* di accesso; **right wing** POL destra *f*; SP esterno *m* destro; **right -wing** POL di destra; **right winger** POL persona *f* di destra; **right-wing extremism** POL estremismo *m* di destra

rigid ['rɪdʒɪd] *material, principles* rigido; *attitude* inflessibile

rigor *Am* ☞ **rigour**

rigorous ['rɪgərəs] rigoroso; **rigorously** *check* rigorosamente; *rigour* rigore *m*

rile [raɪl] F irritare

rim [rɪm] *of wheel* cerchione *m*; *of cup* orlo *m*; *of spectacles* montatura *f*

ring¹ [rɪŋ] (*circle*) cerchio *m*; *on finger* anello *m*; *in boxing* ring *m inv*, quadrato *m*; *at circus* pista *f*

ring² [rɪŋ] **1** *n of bell* trillo *m*; *of voice* suono *m* **2** *v/t bell* suonare; TELEC chiamare **3** *v/i of bell* suonare

'ringleader capobanda *m inv*; **ring-pull** linguetta *f*

rink [rɪŋk] pista *f* di pattinaggio su ghiaccio

rinse [rɪns] **1** *n for hair colour* cachet *m inv* **2** *v/t* sciacquare

riot ['raɪət] **1** *n* sommossa *f* **2** *v/i* causare disordini; **rioter** dimostrante *m/f*; **riot police** reparti *mpl* (di polizia) antisommossa

rip [rɪp] **1** *n in cloth etc* strappo *m* **2** *v/t cloth etc* strappare

♦ **rip off** F *customers* fregare F

ripe [raɪp] *fruit* maturo; **ripen** *of fruit* maturare; **ripeness** *of fruit* maturazione *f*

'rip-off F fregatura *f*

ripple ['rɪpl] *on water* increspatura *f*

rise [raɪz] **1** *v/i from chair etc* alzarsi; *of sun* sorgere; *of price, temperature* aumentare; *of water level* salire **2** *n aumento m*; **give~ to** dare origine a; **riser:** *be an early / be a late ~* essere mattiniero / alzarsi sempre tardi

risk [rɪsk] **1** *n* rischio *m*; **take a ~** correre un rischio **2** *v/t* rischiare; **risky** rischioso

ritual ['rɪtjʊəl] **1** *n* rituale *m* **2** *adj* rituale

rival ['raɪvl] **1** *n* rivale *m/f*; *in business* concorrente *m/f* **2** *v/t* competere con; **rivalry** rivalità *f inv*

river ['rɪvə(r)] fiume *m*; **riverbank** sponda *f* del fiume; **riverbed** letto *m* del fiume; **riverside 1** *adj* sul fiume **2** *n* riva *f* del fiume

riveting ['rɪvɪtɪŋ] avvincente

Riviera [rɪvɪ'eərə]: *the Italian ~* la riviera (ligure)

road [rəʊd] strada *f*; *it's just down the ~* è qui vicino; **roadblock** posto *m* di blocco; **road hog** pirata *m* della strada; **road holding** *of vehicle* tenuta *f* di strada; **road**

map carta *f* automobilistica; **road rage** comportamento di estrema aggressività da parte di automobilisti; **road safety** sicurezza *f* sulle strade; **roadsign** cartello *m* stradale; **roadway** carreggiata *f*; **road works** *npl* lavori *mpl* stradali; **roadworthy** in buono stato di marcia

roam [rəʊm] vagabondare

roar [rɔː(r)] **1** *n* of engine rombo *m* 2 *vi* of lion ruggito *m*; of traffic fragore *m* 2 *vi* of engine rombare; of lion ruggire; of person gridare; **~ with laughter** ridere fragorosamente

roast [rəʊst] **1** *n* beef etc arrosto *m* **2** *v/t* arrostire; coffee beans, peanuts tostare **3** *vii* of food arrostirsi; in hot room, climate scoppiare di caldo; **roast beef** arrosto *m* di manzo; **roast pork** arrosto *m* di maiale

rob [rɒb] person, bank rapinare; **robber** rapinatore *m*, -trice *f*; **robbery** rapina *f*

robe [rəʊb] of judge toga *f*; of priest tonaca *f*; Am (dressing gown) vestaglia *f*

robin ['rɒbɪn] pettirosso *m*

robot ['rəʊbɒt] robot *m inv*

robust [rəʊ'bʌst] robusto

rock [rɒk] **1** *n* roccia *f*; MUS rock *m*; **on the ~s** drink con ghiaccio; marriage in crisi **2** *v/t* baby cullare; cradle far dondolare; (surprise) scon-

volgere **3** *v/i* on chair dondolarsi; **rock and roll** rock and roll *m*; **rock band** gruppo *m* rock; **rock-bottom** prices bassissimo; **rock bottom**: **reach ~** toccare il fondo; **rock climber** rocciatore *m*, -trice *f*; **rock climbing** roccia *f*

rocket ['rɒkɪt] **1** *n* razzo *m* **2** *v/i* of prices etc salire alle stelle

rocking chair ['rɒkɪŋ] sedia *f* a dondolo; **rocking horse** cavallo *m* a dondolo

'rock star rockstar *f*

rocky ['rɒkɪ] shore roccioso; (shaky) instabile

rod [rɒd] sbarra *f*; for fishing canna *f*

rodent ['rəʊdnt] roditore *m*

rogue [rəʊg] briccone *m*, -a *f*

role [rəʊl] ruolo *m*; **role model** modello *m* di comportamento

roll [rəʊl] **1** *n* of bread panino *m*; of film rullino *m*; (list, register) lista *f* **2** *v/i* of ball etc rotolare; of boat dondolare

♦ **roll over 1** *v/i* rigirarsi **2** *v/t* person, object girare; loan, agreement rinnovare

'roll call appello *m*; **roller** for hair bigodino *m*; **roller blade**® roller blade *m inv*; **roller coaster** montagne *fpl* russe; **roller skate** pattino *m* a rotelle

ROM [rɒm] COMPUT (= read only memory) ROM *f inv*

Roman ['rəʊmən] **1** adj romano **2** n Romano m, -a f; **Roman Catholic 1** n REL cattolico m, -a f **2** adj cattolico

romance [rə'mæns] (affair) storia f d'amore; novel romanzo m rosa; film film m inv d'amore; **romantic** romantico

Rome [rəʊm] Roma f

roof [ruːf] tetto m; **roof box** MOT box portabagagli m inv; **roof rack** MOT portabagagli m inv

rookie ['rʊkɪ] Am F pivello m

room [ruːm] stanza f; (bedroom) camera f (da letto); (space) posto m; **room clerk** Am receptionist m/f inv; **room mate** Am compagno m, -a f di stanza; in apartment compagno m, -a f di appartamento; **room service** servizio m in camera; **room temperature** temperatura f ambiente; **roomy** house, car etc spazioso; clothes ampio

root [ruːt] radice f

rope [rəʊp] corda f, fune f

rosary ['rəʊzərɪ] REL rosario m

rose [rəʊz] BOT rosa f

roster ['rɒstə(r)] turni mpl; actual document tabella f dei turni

rostrum ['rɒstrəm] podio m

rosy ['rəʊzɪ] roseo

rot [rɒt] **1** n marciume m **2** v/i marcire

rotate [rəʊ'teɪt] **1** v/i of blades,

earth ruotare **2** v/t girare; crops avvicendare; rotazione f; **in** ~ a turno

rotten ['rɒtn] food, wood etc marcio; F (very bad) schifoso F

rough [rʌf] **1** adj hands, skin, surface ruvido; ground accidentato; (coarse) rozzo; (violent) violento; crossing movimentato; seas grosso; (approximate) approssimativo; **~ draft** abbozzo m **2** adv: **sleep ~** dormire all'addiaccio **3** n in golf erba f alta; **roughage** in food fibre fpl; **roughly** (approximately) circa; (harshly) bruscamente; **~ speaking** grosso modo

roulette [ruː'let] roulette f inv

round [raʊnd] **1** adj rotondo n of postman, doctor gir of toast fetta f; of drink m; of competition gir in boxing match r inv **3** n corner gir & prep ☞ **aroun**

◆ **round up** figu re; suspects, c nare

roundabout adj indire tatoria interne **trip** t (di) ro men zione rudime

gliare; *emotions* risvegliare; rousing entusiasmante

route [ruːt] *of car* itinerario *m*; *of plane, ship* rotta *f*; *of bus* percorso *m*

routine [ruːˈtiːn] **1** *adj* abituale **2** *n* routine *f*; *as a matter of* ~ d'abitudine

row¹ [rəʊ] *n (line)* fila *f*; *5 days in a* ~ 5 giorni di fila

row² [rəʊ] *v/t boat* remare

row³ [raʊ] *n (quarrel)* litigio *m*; *(noise)* baccano *m*

'rowboat *Am* barca *f* a remi

rowdy [ˈraʊdɪ] turbolento

'rowing boat barca *f* a remi

royal [ˈrɔɪəl] reale; **royalty** *(royal persons)* reali *mpl*; *on book, recording* royalty *f inv*

rub [rʌb] sfregare, strofinare

rubber [ˈrʌbə(r)] **1** *n* gomma *f* **2** *adj* di gomma; **rubber band** elastico *m*

rubbish [ˈrʌbɪʃ] immondizia *f*; *(poor quality)* porcheria *f*; *(nonsense)* sciocchezza *f*; **rubbish bin** pattumiera *f*

ᴉbble [ˈrʌbl] macerie *fpl*

ᴉby [ˈruːbɪ] *jewel* rubino *m*

ᴉcksack [ˈrʌksæk] zaino *m*

ᴉder [ˈrʌdə(r)] timone *m*

ᴉdy [ˈrʌdɪ] *complexion* ru- ᴉondo

[ruːd] maleducato; *lan- ᴉ* volgare; *it's* ~ *to* ... è ᴉva educazione ...; *(impolitely)* scortese- ᴉrudeness* maleduca-

ᴉtary [ruːdɪˈmentərɪ]

rudimentale; **rudiments** rudimenti *mpl*

rueful [ˈruːful] rassegnato; **ruefully** con aria rassegnata

ruffian [ˈrʌfɪən] delinquente *m/f*

ruffle [ˈrʌfl] **1** *n (on dress)* gala *f* **2** *v/t hair* scompigliare; *person* turbare; *get* ~*d* agitarsi

rug [rʌg] tappeto *m*; *(blanket)* coperta *f* (da viaggio)

rugby [ˈrʌgbɪ] rugby *m*; **rugby league** rugby *m* a tredici; **rugby player** giocatore *m* di rugby; **rugby union** rugby *m* a quindici

rugged [ˈrʌgɪd] *coastline* frastagliato; *face, features* marcato

ruin [ˈruːɪn] **1** *n* rovina *f* **2** *v/t* rovinare

rule [ruːl] *n of club, game* regola *f*; *(authority)* dominio *m*; *for measuring* metro *m* (a stecche). **2** *v/t country* governare; *the judge* ~*d that* ... il giudice ha stabilito che ... **3** *v/i of monarch* regnare

♦ **rule out** escludere

ruler [ˈruːlə(r)] *for measuring* righello *m*; *of state* capo *m*; **ruling 1** *n* decisione *f* **2** *adj party* di governo

rum [rʌm] *drink* rum *m inv*

rumble [ˈrʌmbl] *of stomach* brontolare; *of thunder* rimbombare

rumour, *Am* **rumor** [ˈruː-

mə(r)] **1** *n* voce *f* **2** *v/t*: **it is
~ed that ...** corre voce che
...

rump [rʌmp] *of animal* groppa
f

rumple [ˈrʌmpl] *clothes, paper*
spiegazzare

ˈrumpsteak bistecca *f* di girello

run [rʌn] **1** *n on foot* corsa *f*;
Am in tights sfilatura *f*; **go
for a ~** andare a correre;
go for a ~ in the car andare
a fare un giro in macchina;
make a ~ for it scappare; **a
criminal on the ~** un evaso,
un'evasa; **in the short-/in
the long ~** sulle prime / alla
lunga; **a ~ on the dollar** una
forte richiesta di dollari **2** *v/i
of person, animal* correre; *of
river* scorrere; *of trains, buses*
viaggiare; *of paint, makeup*
sbavare; *of nose* colare; *of
play* tenere il cartellone; *of
software* girare; *of engine,
machine* funzionare; **~ for
President** *in election* candidarsi alla presidenza **3** *v/t*
correre; *(take part in: race)*
partecipare a; *business, hotel,
project etc* gestire; *software*
lanciare; *car* usare; *risk* correre; **can I ~ you to the station?** ti porto alla stazione?
◆ **run across** *(meet)* imbattersi in
◆ **run away** scappare
◆ **run down 1** *v/t (knock
down)* investire; *(criticize)*

parlare male di; *stocks* ridurre **2** *v/i of battery* scaricarsi
◆ **run into** *(meet)* imbattersi
in; *difficulties* trovare
◆ **run off 1** *v/i* scappare **2** *v/t
(print off)* stampare
◆ **run out** *of contract, time*
scadere; *of supplies* esaurirsi
◆ **run out of** *patience* perdere; *supplies* rimanere senza;
I ran out of petrol ho finito
la benzina
◆ **run over 1** *v/t (knock
down)* investire; *details* rivedere **2**
v/i of water etc traboccare
◆ **run up** *debts, bill* accumulare

ˈrunaway ragazzo *m*, -a *f*
scappato di casa; **run-down**
person debilitato; *area, building* fatiscente

rung [rʌŋ] *of ladder* piolo *m*

runner [ˈrʌnə(r)] *athlete* velocista *m/f*; **runner beans** fagiolini *mpl*; **runner-up** secondo *m*, -a *f* classificato
(-a); **running 1** *n* SP corsa
f; *of business* gestione *f* **2**
adj: **for two days ~** per due
giorni di seguito; **running
water** acqua *f* corrente; **run-
ny** *substance* liquido; *nose*
che cola; **run-up** SP rincorsa
f; **in the ~ to** nel periodo che
precede; **runway** pista *f*

rupture [ˈrʌptʃə(r)] **1** *n* rottura
f; MED lacerazione *f*; *(hernia)*
ernia *f* **2** *v/i of pipe etc* scoppiare

rural [ˈrʊərəl] rurale

ruse [ruːz] stratagemma *m*

rush [rʌʃ] **1** *n* corsa *f*; **do sth in a** ~ fare qc di corsa; **be in a** ~ andare di fretta **2** *v/t person* mettere fretta a; *meal* mangiare in fretta; ~ **s.o. to hospital** portare qu di corsa all'ospedale **3** *v/i* affrettarsi; **rush hour** ora *f* di punta

Russia ['rʌʃə] Russia *f*; **Russian 1** *adj* russo **2** *n* russo *m*, -a *f*; *language* russo *m*

rust [rʌst] **1** *n* ruggine *f* **2** *v/i* arrugginirsi; **rust-proof** a prova di ruggine

rusty ['rʌstɪ] *also fig* arrugginito

rut [rʌt] *in road* solco *m*; **be in a** ~ *fig* essersi fossilizzato

ruthless ['ruːθlɪs] spietato; **ruthlessly** spietatamente; **ruthlessness** spietatezza *f*

rye [raɪ] segale *f*; **rye bread** pane *m* di segale

S

sabotage ['sæbətɑːʒ] **1** *n* sabotaggio *m* **2** *v/t* sabotare; **saboteur** sabotatore *m*, -trice *f*

sachet ['sæʃeɪ] bustina *f*

sack [sæk] **1** *n bag* sacco *m* **2** *v/t* F licenziare

sacred ['seɪkrɪd] sacro

sacrifice ['sækrɪfaɪs] **1** *n also fig* sacrificio *m* **2** *v/t* sacrificare

sacrilege ['sækrɪlɪdʒ] sacrilegio *m*

sad [sæd] triste; *state of affairs* deplorevole

saddle ['sædl] **1** *n* sella *f* **2** *v/t horse* sellare; ~ **s.o. with sth** *fig* affibbiare qc a qu

sadism ['seɪdɪzm] sadismo *m*; **sadist** sadista *m/f*; **sadistic** sadistico

sadly ['sædlɪ] tristemente; (*regrettably*) purtroppo; **sadness** tristezza *f*

safe [seɪf] **1** *adj not dangerous* sicuro; *not in danger* al sicuro; *driver* prudente **2** *n* cassaforte *f*; **safeguard 1** *n* protezione *f*, salvaguardia *f*; *as a* ~ **against** per proteggersi contro **2** *v/t* proteggere; **safely** arrive, complete test etc senza problemi; *drive* prudentemente; *assume* tranquillamente; **safety** sicurezza *f*; **safety pin** spilla *f* di sicurezza

sag [sæg] *of ceiling* incurvarsi; *of rope* allentarsi

saga ['sɑːgə] saga *f*

sage [seɪdʒ] *herb* salvia *f*

Sagittarius [sædʒɪ'teərɪəs] ASTR Sagittario *m*

sail [seɪl] **1** *n of boat* vela *f*; *trip* veleggiata *f*; **go for a** ~ fare un giro in barca (a vela) **2** *v/t yacht* pilotare **3** *v/i* fare vela; (*depart*) salpare; **sail-**

board 1 *n* windsurf *m inv* 2
v/i fare windsurf; **sailboard-
ing** windsurf *m*; **sailboat**
Am barca *f* a vela; **sailing**
SP vela *f*; **sailing boat** barca
f a vela; **sailor** marinaio *m*
saint [seɪnt] santo *m*, -a *f*
sake [seɪk]: **for my ~** per il
mio bene; **for the ~ of** per
salad ['sæləd] insalata *f*; **salad dressing** condimento *m*
per l'insalata
salary ['sælərɪ] stipendio *m*
sale [seɪl] vendita *f*; *at reduced
prices* svendita *f*, saldi *mpl*;
for ~ sign in vendita; **be on
~** essere in vendita; **sales department** reparto *m* vendite;
sales clerk *Am in store* commesso *m*, -a *f*; **sales figures**
fatturato *m*; **salesman** venditore *m*; **sales manager** direttore *m*, -trice *f* delle vendite; **saleswoman** venditri-
ce *f*
salient ['seɪlɪənt] saliente
saliva [sə'laɪvə] saliva *f*
salmon ['sæmən] salmone *m*
saloon [sə'luːn] (*bar*) bar *m
inv*; MOT berlina *f*
salt [sɒlt] sale *m*; **salty** salato
salute [sə'luːt] 1 *n* MIL saluto
m 2 *v/t* & *v/i* salutare
salvage ['sælvɪdʒ] *from wreck*
ricuperare
salvation [sæl'veɪʃn] salvezza
f
same [seɪm] 1 *adj* stesso 2
pron stesso; **the ~** lo stesso,
la stessa; *Happy New Year*

– the ~ to you Buon anno!
– grazie e altrettanto!; *it's
all the ~ to me* per me è
uguale 3 *adv*: **the ~** allo stesso modo; *look* / *sound the ~*
sembrare uguale
sample ['sɑːmpl] campione *m*
sanction ['sæŋkʃn] 1 *n* (*approval*) approvazione *f*; (*penalty*) sanzione *f* 2 *v/t* (*approve*) sancire
sanctity ['sæŋktətɪ] santità *f*
sand [sænd] 1 *n* sabbia *f* 2 *v/t
with sandpaper* smerigliare
sandal ['sændl] sandalo *m*
'**sandbag** sacchetto *m* di sabbia; **sand dune** duna *f*;
sander *tool* smerigliatrice
f; **sandpaper** 1 *n* carta *f* sme-
rigliata 2 *v/t* smerigliare
sandwich ['sænwɪdʒ] tramezzino *m*
sandy ['sændɪ] *beach* sabbioso; *full of sand* pieno di sabbia; *hair* rossiccio
sane [seɪn] sano di mente
sanitarium [sænɪ'teərɪəm] casa
f di cura
sanitary ['sænɪtərɪ] *conditions*
igienico; *installations* sanitario; **sanitary towel** assorbente *m* (igienico); **sanita-
tion** impianti *mpl* igienici;
(*removal of waste*) fognature
fpl
sanity ['sænɪtɪ] sanità *f* mentale
Santa Claus ['sæntəklɔːz]
Babbo *m* Natale
sap [sæp] 1 *n in tree* linfa *f* 2 *v/t*

s.o.'s energy indebolire

sapphire ['sæfaɪə(r)] zaffiro m

sarcasm ['sɑːkæzm] sarcasmo m; sarcastic sarcastico; sarcastically sarcasticamente

sardine [sɑːˈdiːn] sardina f

Sardinia [sɑːˈdɪnɪə] Sardegna f; Sardinian 1 adj sardo 2 n sardo m, -a f

sardonic [sɑːˈdɒnɪk] sardonico

Satan ['seɪtn] Satana m

satellite ['sætəlaɪt] satellite m; satellite dish antenna f parabolica; satellite TV TV f inv satellitare

satin ['sætɪn] satin m

satire ['sætaɪə(r)] satira f; satirical satirico; satirize satireggiare

satisfaction [sætɪsˈfækʃn] soddisfazione f; satisfactory soddisfacente; just good enough sufficiente; satisfy soddisfare; requirement rispondere a; I am satisfied that ... (convinced) sono convinto che ...

Saturday ['sætədeɪ] sabato m

sauce [sɔːs] salsa f, sugo m; saucepan pentola f; saucer piattino m

Saudi Arabia [saʊdɪəˈreɪbɪə] Arabia f Saudita; Saudi Arabian 1 adj saudita 2 n person saudita m/f

sauna ['sɔːnə] sauna f

sausage ['sɒsɪdʒ] salsiccia f

savage ['sævɪdʒ] 1 adj animal selvaggio; criticism feroce 2 n selvaggio m, -a f; savagery ferocia f

save [seɪv] 1 v/t (rescue) salvare; money, time, effort risparmiare; (collect) raccogliere; COMPUT salvare; goal parare 2 v/i (put money aside) risparmiare; SP parare 3 n SP parata f; saver person risparmiatore m, -trice f; savings risparmi mpl; savings account libretto m di risparmio; savings and loan Am istituto m di credito immobiliare; savings bank cassa f di risparmio

saviour, Am savior ['seɪvjə(r)] REL salvatore m

savor etc Am ☞ savour etc

savour ['seɪvə(r)] assaporare; savoury not sweet salato (non dolce)

saw [sɔː] 1 n tool sega f 2 v/t segare; sawdust segatura f

saxophone ['sæksəfəʊn] sassofono m

say [seɪ] dire; that is to ~ sarebbe a dire; saying detto m

scab [skæb] on skin crosta f

scaffolding ['skæfəldɪŋ] impalcature fpl

scald [skɔːld] scottare; ~ o.s. scottarsi

scale¹ [skeɪl] on fish scaglia f

scale² [skeɪl] 1 n of map, MUS scala f; of project portata f 2 v/t cliffs etc scalare

scales [skeɪlz] for weighing

bilancia *fsg*

scallop ['skɒləp] capasanta *f*

scalp [skælp] cuoio *m* capelluto

scalpel ['skælpl] bisturi *m*

scam [skæm] F truffa *f*

scampi ['skæmpɪ] gamberoni *mpl* in pastella fritti

scan [skæn] **1** *v/t horizon* scrutare; *page* scorrere; *foetus* fare l'ecografia di; *brain* fare la TAC di; COMPUT scannerizzare **2** *n* (*brain* ~) TAC *f inv*; *of foetus* ecografia *f*

◆ **scan in** COMPUT scannerizzare

scandal ['skændl] scandalo *m*; **scandalize** scandalizzare; **scandalous** scandaloso

scanner ['skænə(r)] scanner *m inv*

scanty ['skæntɪ] *clothes* succinto

scapegoat ['skeɪpɡəʊt] capro *m* espiatorio

scar [skɑː(r)] **1** *n* cicatrice *f* **2** *v/t face* lasciare cicatrici su; *fig* segnare

scarce [skeəs] *in short supply* scarso; **scarcely** appena; **there was** ~ **anything left** non rimaneva quasi più niente; **scarcity** scarsità *f inv*

scare [skeə(r)] **1** *v/t* spaventare; **be** ~**d of** avere paura di **2** *n* (*panic, alarm*) panico *m*; **scaremonger** allarmista *m/f*

scarf [skɑːf] *around neck*

sciarpa *f*; *over head* foulard *m inv*

scarlet ['skɑːlət] scarlatto

scary ['skeərɪ] che fa paura

scathing ['skeɪðɪŋ] caustico

scatter ['skætə(r)] **1** *v/t leaflets, seeds* spargere; *crowd* disperdere **2** *v/i of people* disperdersi; **scatterbrained** sventato; **scattered** *family, villages* sparpagliato; ~ **showers** precipitazioni sparse

scavenge ['skævɪndʒ] frugare tra i rifiuti; **scavenger** animale *m* necrofago; *person* persona *f* che fruga tra i rifiuti

scenario [sɪ'nɑːrɪəʊ] scenario *m*

scene [siːn] scena *f*; (*argument*) scenata *f*; **make a** ~ fare una scenata; ~**s** THEA scenografia *f*; **behind the** ~**s** dietro le quinte; **scenery** paesaggio *m*; THEA scenario *m*

scent [sent] profumo *m*; *of animal* odore *m*

sceptic ['skeptɪk] scettico *m*, -a *f*; **sceptical** scettico; **scepticism** scetticismo *m*

schedule ['ʃedjuːl] **1** *n of events, work* programma *m*; *for trains* orario *m*; **be on** ~ *of work, of train* etc essere in orario; **be behind** ~ *of work, of train* etc essere in ritardo **2** *v/t put on schedule* programmare; **scheduled flight** volo *m* di linea

scheme [skiːm] **1** *n* (*plan*) pia-

no *m*; (*plot*) complotto *m* **2**
v/i (*plot*) complottare, tramare; **scheming** intrigante

schizophrenia [skɪtsə'fri:-
nɪə] schizofrenia *f*; **schizo-
phrenic 1** *n* schizofrenico
m, -a *f* **2** *adj* schizofrenico

scholar ['skɒlə(r)] studioso
m, -a *f*; **scholarly** dotto;
scholarship (*scholarly
work*) erudizione *f*; (*financial award*) borsa *f* di studio

school [sku:l] scuola *f*; *Am*
(*university*) università *f*; **
school bag** cartella *f*;
schoolboy scolaro *m*;
schoolchildren scolari
mpl; **school days** tempi
mpl della scuola; **schoolgirl**
scolara *f*; **schoolteacher** insegnante *m/f*

science ['saɪəns] scienza *f*;
science fiction fantascienza
f; **scientific** scientifico; **scientist** scienziato *m*, -a *f*

scissors ['sɪzəz] forbici *fpl*

scoff¹ [skɒf] *v/t food* sbafare

scoff² [skɒf] *v/i* (*mock*) canzonare

scold [skəʊld] sgridare

scoop [sku:p] *for grain, flour*
paletta *f*; *for ice cream* cucchiaio *m* dosatore; *of ice
cream* pallina *f*; (*story*) scoop
m inv

scooter ['sku:tə(r)] *with motor* scooter *m inv*; *child's* monopattino *m*

scope [skəʊp] portata *f*; (*freedom, opportunity*) possibilità

f

scorch [skɔ:tʃ] bruciare;
scorching torrido

score [skɔ:(r)] **1** *n SP* punteggio *m*; (*written music*) spartito *m*; *of film etc* colonna *f* sonora; **what's the ~?** *SP* a
quanto sono / siamo? **2** *v/t
goal, point* segnare; (*cut*) incidere **3** *v/i* segnare; (*keep
the score*) tenere il punteggio; **scoreboard** segnapunti
m inv; **scorer** *of goal, point*
marcatore *m*, -trice *f*

scorn [skɔ:n] **1** *n* disprezzo *m*
2 *v/t idea* disprezzare; **scornful** sprezzante; **scornfully**
sprezzantemente

Scorpio ['skɔ:pɪəʊ] ASTR
Scorpione *m*

Scot [skɒt] scozzese *m/f*;
Scotch (*whisky*) scotch *m
inv*; **Scotch tape®** *Am*
scotch® *m*; **Scotland** Scozia
f; **Scotsman** scozzese *m*;
Scotswoman scozzese *f*;
Scottish scozzese

scoundrel ['skaʊndrəl] birbante *m/f*

scour ['skaʊə(r)] (*search*) setacciare

scowl [skaʊl] **1** *n* sguardo *m*
torvo **2** *v/i* guardare storto

scramble ['skræmbl] **1** *n*
(*rush*) corsa *f* **2** *v/t message*
rendere indecifrabile **3** *v/i*:
he ~d to his feet si rialzò
in fretta; **scrambled eggs**
uova *fpl* strapazzate

scrap [skræp] **1** *n metal* rottame *m*; (*fight*) zuffa *f*; (*little bit*) briciolo *m* **2** *v/t* plan, project abbandonare

scrape [skreɪp] **1** *n* on paintwork graffio *m* **2** *v/t* paintwork, arm etc graffiare; **~ a living** sbarcare il lunario

'scrap metal rottami *mpl*

scrappy ['skræpɪ] F, writing senza capo né coda

scratch [skrætʃ] **1** *n* mark graffio *m*; **start from ~** ricominciare da zero; **not up to ~** non all'altezza **2** *v/t* (*mark*) graffiare; because of itch grattare **3** *v/i* of cat, nails graffiare

scrawl [skrɔːl] **1** *n* scarabocchio *m* **2** *v/t* scarabocchiare

scrawny ['skrɔːnɪ] scheletrico

scream [skriːm] **1** *n* urlo *m* **2** *v/i* urlare

screech [skriːtʃ] **1** *n* of tyres stridio *m*; (*scream*) strillo *m* **2** *v/i* of tyres stridere; (*scream*) strillare

screen [skriːn] **1** *n* in room, hospital paravento *m*; of smoke cortina *f*; cinema, COMPUT, of television schermo *m* **2** *v/t* (*protect, hide*) riparare; film proiettare; for security reasons vagliare; **screenplay** sceneggiatura *f*; **screen saver** COMPUT salvaschermo *m inv*; **screen test** for movie provino *m*

screw [skruː] **1** *n* vite *f* (metallica) **2** *v/t* avvitare (**to** a); V scopare V; F (*cheat*) fregare

F; **screwdriver** cacciavite *m*; **screwed up** F psychologically complessato; **screw top** on bottle tappo *m* a vite; **screwy** F svitato

scribble ['skrɪbl] **1** *n* scarabocchio *m* **2** *v/t* & *v/i* (*write quickly*) scarabocchiare

script [skrɪpt] for film, play copione *m*; (*form of writing*) scrittura *f*; **scripture: the (Holy) Scriptures** le Sacre Scritture *fpl*; **scriptwriter** sceneggiatore *m*, -trice *f*

◆ **scroll down** COMPUT far scorrere il testo in avanti

◆ **scroll up** COMPUT far scorrere il testo indietro

scrounge [skraʊndʒ] scroccare; **scrounger** scroccone *m*, -a *f*

scrub [skrʌb] floors, hands sfregare (con spazzola)

scrum [skrʌm] in rugby mischia *f*

scruples ['skruːplz] scrupoli *mpl*; **scrupulous** scrupoloso; **scrupulously** (*meticulously*) scrupolosamente

scrutinize ['skruːtɪnaɪz] text esaminare attentamente; face scrutare; **scrutiny** attento esame *m*

scuba diving ['skuːbə] immersione *f* subacquea

scuffle ['skʌfl] tafferuglio *m*

sculptor ['skʌlptə(r)] scultore *m*, -trice *f*; **sculpture** scultura *f* scum [skʌm] *on liquid* schiuma *f*; (*pej: people*) feccia *f*

sea [siː] mare *m*; **by the ~** al mare; seabird uccello *m* marino; seafood frutti *mpl* di mare; seafront lungomare *m inv*; seagull gabbiano *m*

seal[1] *n animal* foca *f*

seal[2] [siːl] **1** *n on document* sigillo *m*; TECH chiusura *f* ermetica **2** *v/t container* chiudere ermeticamente

'sea level: **above / below ~** sopra / sotto il livello del mare

seam [siːm] *on garment* cucitura *f*; *of ore* filone *m*

'seaman [siːmən] marinaio *m*; sea-port porto *m* marittimo

search [sɜːtʃ] **1** *n for s.o. / sth* ricerca *f*; *of person, building* perquisizione *f* **2** *v/t person, building, baggage* perquisire; *area* perlustrare

◆ search for cercare

searching [sɜːtʃɪŋ] *look* penetrante; searchlight riflettore *m*

'seashore riva *f* (del mare); seasick: **be ~** avere il mal di mare; **get ~** soffrire il mal di mare; seaside: **at the ~** al mare; **~ resort** località *f inv* balneare

season [siːzn] stagione *f*; **in / out of ~** in / fuori stagione; seasonal stagionale; seasoned *wood* stagionato; *traveller, campaigner etc* esperto; seasoning condimento *m*; season ticket abbonamento *m*

seat [siːt] **1** *n* posto *m*; *of trousers* fondo *m*; POL seggio *m*; **please take a ~** si accomodi **2** *v/t* (*have seating for*) avere posti a sedere per; seat belt cintura *f* di sicurezza

'sea urchin riccio *m* di mare; seaweed alga *f*

secluded [sɪ'kluːdɪd] appartato

second [sekənd] **1** *n of time* secondo *m*; **just a ~** un attimo **2** *adj* secondo **3** *adv* come in secondo **4** *v/t motion* appoggiare; secondary secondario; second floor secondo piano *m*; *Am* primo piano *m*; second hand *on clock* lancetta *f* dei secondi; second-hand di seconda mano; secondly in secondo luogo; second-rate di second'ordine; second thoughts: *I've had ~ thoughts* ci ho ripensato

secrecy [siːkrəsɪ] segretezza *f*; secret **1** *n* segreto *m* **2** *adj* segreto; secret agent agente *m* segreto

secretarial [sekrə'teəriəl] *tasks, job* di segretaria; secretary segretario *m*, -a *f*; POL ministro *m*; Secretary of State *in USA* Segretario *m* di Stato

secretive [siːkrətɪv] riservato; secretly segretamente;

secret service servizio *m* segreto

sect [sekt] setta *f*

section ['sekʃn] sezione *f*

sector ['sektə(r)] settore *m*

secular ['sekjulə(r)] laico

secure [sɪ'kjuə(r)] **1** *adj self etc* saldo *feeling* sicuro; *job* stabile **2** *v/t shelf etc* assicurare; *s.o.'s help, finances* assicurarsi; **securities market** FIN mercato *m* dei titoli; **security** sicurezza *f*; *in relationship* stabilità *f*; *for investment* garanzia *f*; **security alert** stato *m* di allarme; **security-conscious** attento alla sicurezza; **security forces** forze *fpl* di sicurezza; **security guard** guardia *f* giurata; **security risk** minaccia *f* per la sicurezza

sedan [sɪ'dæn] *Am* MOT berlina *f*

sedate [sɪ'deɪt] *patient* somministrare sedativi a; **sedation**: **be under ~** essere sotto l'effetto di sedativi; **sedative** sedativo *m*

sedentary ['sedəntərɪ] *job* sedentario

sediment ['sedɪmənt] sedimento *m*

seduce [sɪ'djuːs] sedurre; **seduction** seduzione *f*; **seductive** *smile, look* seducente; *offer* allettante

see [siː] vedere; (*understand*) capire; **I'll ~ you to the door** t'accompagno alla porta; **~**

you! F ciao! F

◆ **see off** *at airport etc* salutare; (*chase away*) scacciare

seed [siːd] *single* seme *m*; *collective* semi *mpl*; *in tennis* testa *f* di serie; **seedy** *bar, district* squallido

seeing (that) ['siːɪŋ] visto che

'seeing eye dog® *Am* cane *m* per ciechi

seek [siːk] cercare

seem [siːm] sembrare; **seemingly** apparentemente

seesaw ['siːsɔː] altalena *f* (a bilico)

'see-through trasparente

segment ['segmənt] segmento *m*; *of orange* spicchio *m*

segregate ['segrɪgeɪt] separare; **segregation** segregazione *f*

seismology [saɪz'mɒlədʒɪ] sismologia *f*

seize [siːz] *s.o., s.o.'s arm* afferrare; *power* prendere; *opportunity* cogliere; *of police etc* sequestrare

◆ **seize up** *of engine* grippare

seizure ['siːʒə(r)] MED attacco *m*; *of drugs etc* sequestro *m*

seldom ['seldəm] raramente

select [sɪ'lekt] **1** *v/t* selezionare **2** *adj* (*exclusive*) scelto; **selection** scelta *f*; *that / those chosen* selezione *f*; **selective** selettivo

self [self] io *m*; **self-assurance** sicurezza *f* di sé; **self--assured** sicuro di sé; **self-**

-catering apartment appartamento *m* indipendente con cucina; **self-centred,** *Am* **self-centered** egocentrico; **self-confessed** dichiarato; **self-confidence** fiducia *f* in se stessi; **self-confident** sicuro di sé; **self-conscious** insicuro; *smile* imbarazzato; *feel* ~ sentirsi a disagio; **self-consciousness** disagio *m*; **self-control** autocontrollo *m*; **self-defence,** *Am* **self-defense** *personal* legittima difesa *f*; *of state* autodifesa *f*; **self-doubt** dubbi *mpl* personali; **self-employed** autonomo; **self-evident** evidente; **self-government** autogoverno *m*

selfie ['selfi] selfie *m*
self-interest interesse *m* personale
selfish egoista; **selfless** *person* altruista; *attitude* altruistico; **self-made man** selfmade man *m* *inv*; **self-pity** autocommiserazione *f*; **self-portrait** autoritratto *m*; **self-reliant** indipendente; **self-respect** dignità *f*; **self-satisfied** *pej* soddisfatto di sé; **self-service** self-service; **self-service** *restaurant* self-service *m* *inv*; **self-taught** autodidatta
sell [sel] **1** *v/t* vendere **2** *v/i* of *products* vendere; **sell-by date** data *f* di scadenza; *be past its* ~ essere scaduto;

seller venditore *m*, -trice *f*; **selling** COM vendita *f*; **selling point** COM punto *m* forte (che fa vendere il prodotto)
Sellotape® ['seləteɪp] scotch® *m*
semester [sɪ'mestə(r)] semestre *m*
semi ['semi, *Am* 'semaɪ] *Br* villa *f* bifamiliare; *Am* *truck* autoarticolato *m*; **semicircle** semicerchio *m*; **semi-colon** punto e virgola *m*; **semiconductor** ELEC semiconduttore *m*; **semidetached (house)** villa *f* bifamiliare; **semifinal** semifinale *f*; **semifinalist** semifinalista *m/f*
seminar ['semɪnɑː(r)] seminario *m*
semi'skilled parzialmente qualificato
senate ['senət] senato *m*; **senator** senatore *m*, -trice *f*
send [send] mandare (*to* a)
♦ **send back** mandare indietro
♦ **send for** *doctor, help* (mandare a) chiamare
♦ **send off** *letter, fax etc* spedire; *footballer* espellere
♦ **send up** (*mock*) prendere in giro
sender ['sendə(r)] *of letter* mittente *m/f*
senile ['siːnaɪl] *pej* rimbambito; **senility** *pej* rimbambimento *m*
senior ['siːnɪə(r)] (*older*) più

anziano; *in rank* di grado superiore; **senior citizen** anziano *m*, -a *f*; **seniority** *in job* anzianità *f*

sensation [sen'seɪʃn] *(feeling)* sensazione *f*; *(surprise event)* scalpore *m*; **be a ~** essere sensazionale; **sensational** sensazionale

sense [sens] **1** *n (meaning)* significato *m*; *(purpose, point, sight, smell etc)* senso *m*; *(common sense)* buonsenso *m*; *(feeling)* sensazione *f*; *come to one's ~s* tornare in sé; *it doesn't make ~* non ha senso; *there's no ~ in trying* non ha senso provare **2** *v/t* sentire; **senseless** *(pointless)* assurdo

sensible ['sensəbl] *person, decision* assennato; *advice* sensato; *clothes, shoes* pratico; **sensibly** assennatamente

sensitive ['sensɪtɪv] sensibile; **sensitivity** sensibilità *f inv*

sensor ['sensə(r)] sensore *m*

sensual ['sensjʊəl] sensuale; **sensuality** sensualità *f*

sensuous ['sensjʊəs] sensuale

sentence ['sentəns] **1** *n* GRAM frase *m*; LAW condanna *f* **2** *v/t* LAW condannare

sentiment ['sentɪmənt] *(sentimentality)* sentimentalismo *m*; *(opinion)* opinione *f*; **sentimental** sentimentale; **sentimentality** sentimentalismo

m

sentry ['sentrɪ] sentinella *f*

separate 1 ['sepərət] *adj* separato **2** ['sepəreɪt] *v/t* separare *(from)* da) **3** ['sepəreɪt] *v/i of couple* separarsi; **separated** *couple* separato; **separately** separatamente; **separation** separazione *f*

September [sep'tembə(r)] settembre *m*

septic ['septɪk] infetto; *go ~ of wound* infettarsi

sequel ['siːkwəl] seguito *m*

sequence ['siːkwəns] sequenza *f*; *in ~* di seguito

Serbia ['sɜːbɪə] Serbia *f*; **Serbian 1** *adj* serbo **2** *n* serbo *m*, -a *f*; *language* serbo *m*

serene [sɪ'riːn] sereno

sergeant ['sɑːdʒənt] sergente *m*

serial ['sɪərɪəl] serial *m inv*; **serialize** *novel on TV* trasmettere a puntate; **serial killer** serial killer *m/f inv*; **serial number** *of product* numero *m* di serie

series ['sɪəriːz] serie *f inv*

serious ['sɪərɪəs] *illness, situation* grave; *person, company* serio; *I'm ~* dico sul serio; **seriously** *injured* gravemente; *(extremely)* estremamente; *take s.o. ~* prendere sul serio qu; **seriousness** *of situation, illness etc* gravità *f*; *of person* serietà *f*

sermon ['sɜːmən] predica *f*

servant ['sɜːvənt] domestico

m, -a *f*

serve [sɜːv] **1** *n* *in tennis* servizio *m* **2** *v/t* *food, customer, one's country* servire; **it ~s you right** ti sta bene **3** *v/i* servire; *as politician etc* prestare servizio; **server** COMPUT server *m inv*; *in tennis* battitore *m* **1** *also n in tennis* servizio *m*; **service** **1** *n also in tennis* servizio *m*; *for machine* manutenzione *f*; *for vehicle* revisione *f*; **~s** servizi; **the ~s** MIL le forze armate **2** *v/t* *vehicle* revisionare; *machine* fare la manutenzione di; **service charge** servizio *m*; **serviceman** MIL militare *m*; **service provider** COMPUT fornitore *m* di servizi; **service sector** settore *m* terziario; **service station** stazione *f* di servizio; **serving** *of food* porzione *f*

session ['seʃn] *of parliament* sessione *f*; *with consultant etc* seduta *f*

set [set] **1** *n of tools* set *m inv*; *of dishes, knives* servizio *m*; *of books* raccolta *f*; *of people* cerchia *f*; MATH insieme *m*; (THEA: *scenery*) scenografia *f*; *where a film is made, in tennis* set *m inv* **2** *v/t* (*place*) mettere; *film, novel etc* ambientare; *date, time, limit* fissare; *alarm clock* mettere; *broken limb* ingessare; *jewel* montare; **~ the table** apparecchiare (la tavola); **~ a task for s.o.** assegnare un compito a qu **3**

v/i of sun tramontare; *of glue* indurirsi **4** *adj ideas* rigido; (*ready*) pronto; **be very ~ in one's ways** essere abitudinario; **~ meal** menù *m inv* fisso

◆ **set off 1** *v/i on journey* partire **2** *v/t explosion* causare; *alarm* far scattare

◆ **set out 1** *v/i on journey* partire **2** *v/t ideas, goods* esporre; **set out to do sth** (*intend*) proporsi di fare qc

◆ **set up 1** *v/t company* fondare; *system* mettere in opera; *equipment, machine* piazzare; F (*frame*) incastrare F **2** *v/i in business* mettersi in affari

'**setback** contrattempo *m*
settee [se'tiː] divano *m*
setting ['setɪŋ] *of novel etc* ambientazione *f*; *of house* posizione *f*

settle ['setl] **1** *v/i of bird, dust, beer* posarsi; *of building* assestarsi; *to live* stabilirsi **2** *v/t dispute* comporre; *issue, uncertainty* risolvere; *debts, bill* saldare; *nerves, stomach* calmare; **that ~s it!** è deciso!

◆ **settle down** (*stop being noisy*) calmarsi; (*stop wild living*) mettere la testa a posto; *in an area* stabilirsi

◆ **settle for** (*accept*) accontentarsi di

◆ **settle up** (*pay*) regolare i conti; *in hotel etc* pagare il conto

settled ['setld] *weather* stabile; **settlement** *of dispute* composizione *f*; (*payment*) pagamento *m*; **settler** *in new country* colonizzatore *m*, -trice *f*

'**set-up** (*structure*) organizzazione *f*; (*relationship*) relazione *f*; F (*frameup*) montatura *f*

seven ['sevn] sette; **seventeen** diciassette; **seventeenth** diciassettesimo; **seventh** settimo; **seventieth** settantesimo; **seventy** settanta

sever ['sevə(r)] *arm, cable etc* recidere; *relations* troncare

several ['sevrl] **1** *adj* parecchi **2** *pron* parecchi *m*, -ie *f*

severe [sɪ'vɪə(r)] *illness* grave; *penalty, teacher, face* severo; *winter, weather* rigido; **severely** *punish* severamente; *speak* duramente; *injured, disrupted* gravemente; **severity** *of illness* gravità *f*; *of look etc* durezza *f*; *of penalty* severità *f*; *of winter* rigidità *f*

sew [səʊ] cucire

sewage ['su:ɪdʒ] acque *fpl* di scolo; **sewer** fogna *f*

sewing ['səʊɪŋ] cucito m

sex [seks] sesso *m*; **have ~ with** avere rapporti sessuali con; **sexist 1** *adj* sessista **2** *n* sessista *m/f*; **sexual** sessuale; **sexual intercourse** rapporti *mpl* sessuali; **sexuality** sessualità *f*; **sexually** ses-

sualmente; **sexually transmitted disease** malattia *f* venerea; **sexy** sexy *inv*

shabbily ['ʃæbɪlɪ] *dressed* in modo trasandato; *treat* in modo meschino; **shabby** *coat etc* trasandato; *treatment* meschino

shack [ʃæk] baracca *f*

shade [ʃeɪd] **1** *n for lamp* paralume *m*; *of colour* tonalità *f inv*; **in the ~** all'ombra **2** *v/t from sun, light* riparare

shadow ['ʃædəʊ] ombra *f*

shady ['ʃeɪdɪ] *spot* all'ombra; *character* losco

shaft [ʃɑːft] *of axle* albero *m*; *of mine* pozzo *m*

shake [ʃeɪk] **1** *n*: **give sth a good ~** dare una scrollata a qc **2** *v/t* scuotere; *emotionally* sconvolgere; **~ one's head** *in refusal* scuotere la testa; **~ hands with s.o.** stringere la mano a qu **3** *v/i of hands, voice, building* tremare; **shaken** *emotionally* scosso; **shake-up** rimpasto *m*; **shaky** *table etc* traballante; *after illness, shock* debole; *grasp of sth, grammar etc* incerto; *voice, hand* tremante

shall [ʃæl] ◇ *future*: **I ~ do my best** farò del mio meglio ◇ *suggesting*: **~ we go now?** andiamo?

shallow ['ʃæləʊ] *water* poco profondo; *person* superficiale shambles ['ʃæmblz] casino *m* F

shame [ʃeɪm] **1** *n* vergogna *f*; *what a ~!* che peccato!; *~ on you!* vergognati! **2** *v/t family etc* svergognare; **shameful** vergognoso; **shameless** svergognato

shampoo [ʃæm'puː] shampoo *m inv*

shape [ʃeɪp] **1** *n* forma *f* **2** *v/t clay* dar forma a; *character* forgiare; *the future* determinare; **shapeless** *dress etc* informe; **shapely** *figure* ben fatto

share [ʃeə(r)] **1** *n* parte *f*; FIN azione *f* **2** *v/t* dividere; *s.o.'s feelings* condividere **3** *v/i* dividere; **shareholder** azionista *m/f*

shark [ʃɑːk] squalo *m*

sharp [ʃɑːp] **1** *adj knife* affilato; *mind, pain* acuto; *taste* aspro **2** *adv* MUS in diesis; *at 3 o'clock ~* alle 3 precise; **sharpen** *knife* affilare; *skills* raffinare; **sharp practice** pratiche *fpl* poco oneste

shatter ['ʃætə(r)] **1** *v/t glass* frantumare; *illusions* distruggere **2** *v/i* of glass frantumarsi; **shattered** F (*exhausted*) esausto; (*very upset*) sconvolto; **shattering** *news, experience* sconvolgente

shave [ʃeɪv] **1** *v/t* radere **2** *v/i* farsi la barba **3** *n*: *have a ~* farsi la barba; *that was a close ~* ce l'abbiamo fatta

per un pelo; **shaven** *head* rasato; **shaver** *electric* rasoio *m*

shawl [ʃɔːl] scialle *m*

she [ʃiː] lei; *~ has three children* ha tre figli; *there ~ is* eccola

shears [ʃɪəz] *for gardening* cesoie *fpl*; *for sewing* forbici *fpl*

sheath [ʃiːθ] *for knife* guaina *f*; *contraceptive* preservativo *m*

shed¹ [ʃed] *v/t blood* spargere; *tears* versare; *leaves* perdere

shed² [ʃed] *n* baracca *f*

sheep [ʃiːp] pecora *f*; **sheepdog** cane *m* pastore; **sheepish** imbarazzato

sheer [ʃɪə(r)] *madness, luxury* puro; *cliffs* ripido

sheet [ʃiːt] *for bed* lenzuolo *m*; *of paper* foglio *m*; *of metal, glass* lastra *f*

shelf [ʃelf] mensola *f*; **shelves** scaffale *msg*, ripiani *mpl*

shell [ʃel] **1** *n* of mussel etc conchiglia *f*; of egg guscio *m*; of tortoise corazza *f*; MIL granata *f* **2** *v/t peas* sbucciare; MIL bombardare; **shellfire** bombardamento *m*; **shellfish** crostacei *mpl*

shelter ['ʃeltə(r)] **1** *n* (*refuge*) riparo *m*; (*construction*) rifugio *m* **2** *v/i* ripararsi **3** *v/t* (*protect*) proteggere; **sheltered** *place* riparato; *lead a ~ life* vivere nella bambagia

shelve [ʃelv] *fig plans* accantonare

shepherd ['ʃepəd] pastore *m*

sherry ['ʃerɪ] sherry *m inv*

shield [ʃiːld] **1** *n* scudo *m; sports trophy* scudetto *m;* TECH schermo *m* di protezione *f; Am badge of policeman* distintivo *m* **2** *v/t (protect)* proteggere

shift [ʃɪft] **1** *n (change)* cambiamento *m; period of work* turno *m* **2** *v/t (move)* spostare; *stains etc* togliere **3** *v/i (move)* spostarsi; *of wind* cambiare direzione; **shift key** COMPUT tasto *m* shift; **shifty** *pej* losco

shimmer ['ʃɪmə(r)] luccicare

shin [ʃɪn] stinco *m*

shine [ʃaɪn] **1** *v/i* splendere; *fig: of student etc* brillare **2** *n on shoes etc* lucentezza *f*

shingle ['ʃɪŋgl] *on beach* ciottoli *mpl*

shiny ['ʃaɪnɪ] lucido

ship [ʃɪp] **1** *n* nave *f* **2** *v/t (send)* spedire; *(send by sea)* spedire via mare **3** *v/i of new product* essere spedito; **shipment** carico *m;* **shipowner** armatore *m;* **shipping** *(sea traffic)* navigazione *f; (sending)* trasporto *m;* **shipping company** compagnia *f* di navigazione; **shipshape** in perfetto ordine; **shipwreck 1** *n* naufragio *m* **2** *v/t:* **be ~ed** naufragare; **shipyard** cantiere *m* navale

shirker ['ʃɜːkə(r)] scansafatiche *m/f inv*

shirt [ʃɜːt] camicia *f*

shit [ʃɪt] **1** *n* P merda *f* P; *bad quality goods, work* stronzata *f* P **2** *v/i* cagare P **3** *int* merda P; **shitty** F di merda P

shiver ['ʃɪvə(r)] rabbrividire

shock [ʃɒk] **1** *n* shock *m inv;* ELEC scossa *f;* **be in ~** MED essere in stato di shock **2** *v/t* scioccare; **shock absorber** MOT ammortizzatore *m;* **shocking** scandaloso; F *(very bad)* allucinante F

shoddy ['ʃɒdɪ] *goods* scadente; *behaviour* meschino

shoe [ʃuː] scarpa *f;* **shoe-lace** laccio *m* di scarpa; **shoemaker** calzolaio *m;* **shoe mender** calzolaio *m;* **shoeshop**, *Am* **shoestore** negozio *m* di scarpe

shoot [ʃuːt] **1** *n* BOT germoglio *m* **2** *v/t* sparare; *film* girare; **~ s.o. in the leg** colpire qu alla gamba

◆ **shoot down** *plane* abbattere

◆ **shoot up** *of prices* salire alle stelle; *of children* crescere molto; *of new buildings etc* spuntare

shooting star ['ʃuːtɪŋ] stella *f* cadente

shop [ʃɒp] **1** *n* negozio *m;* **talk ~** parlare di lavoro **2** *v/i* fare acquisti; **go ~ping** andare a fare spese; **shop assistant** commesso *m,* -a *f;* **shopkeeper** negoziante *m/f;*

shoplifter taccheggiatore *m*, -trice *f*;shoplifting taccheggio *m*; shopper acquirente *m*/*f*; shopping *items* spesa *f*; go ~ andare a fare spese; do one's ~ fare la spesa; shopping bag borsa *f* per la spesa; shopping list lista *f* della spesa;shopping mall centro *m* commerciale; shop window vetrina *f*

shore [ʃɔː(r)] riva *f*; on ~ *not at sea* a terra

short [ʃɔːt] **1** *adj* corto; *in height* basso; *in time* breve; be ~ of essere a corto di **2** *adv*: cut ~ interrompere; go ~ of fare a meno di; in ~ in breve; shortage mancanza *f*; shortcoming difetto *m*; shortcut scorciatoia *f*; shorten **1** *v/t* accorciare **2** *v/i* accorciarsi; shortfall deficit *m inv*; in hours *etc* mancanza *f*; shortlist *of candidates* rosa *f* dei candidati; short-lived di breve durata; shortly (*soon*) tra breve; ~ before / after poco prima / dopo;shortness *of visit* brevità *f*; *in height* bassa statura *f*; shorts calzoncini *mpl*; shortsighted *also fig* miope; short-sleeved a maniche corte; short-staffed a corto di personale; short-tempered irascibile; short-term a breve termine; short wave RAD onde *fpl* corte

shot [ʃɒt] *from gun* sparo *m*; (*photograph*) foto *f*; (*injection*) puntura *f*; like a ~ *accept, run off* come un razzo; shotgun fucile *m* da caccia

should [ʃʊd]: what ~ I do? cosa devo fare?; you ~n't do that non dovresti farlo; you ~ have heard him! avresti dovuto sentirlo!

shoulder ['ʃəʊldə(r)] ANAT spalla *f*

shout [ʃaʊt] **1** *n* grido *m*, urlo *m* **2** *v/t & v/i* gridare, urlare; shouting urla *fpl*

shove [ʃʌv] **1** *n* spinta *f* **2** *v/t & v/i* spingere

shovel [ʃʌvl] **1** *n* pala *f* **2** *v/t* spalare

show [ʃəʊ] **1** *n* THEA, TV spettacolo *m*; (*display*) manifestazione *f*; on ~ *at an exhibition* esposto; it's all done for ~ *pej* è tutta una scena **2** *v/t passport etc* mostrare; *interest, emotion* dimostrare; *at exhibition* esporre; *film* proiettare **3** *v/i* (*be visible*) vedersi; does it ~? si vede?; what's ~ing at the cinema? cosa danno al cinema?

◆ show in far entrare

◆ show off **1** *v/t skills* mettere in risalto **2** *v/i pej* mettersi in mostra

◆ show up **1** *v/t shortcomings etc* far risaltare **2** *v/i* F (*arrive, turn up*) farsi vedere F; (*be visible*) notarsi

'show business il mondo dello spettacolo; showcase

vetrinetta f; *fig* vetrina f; **showdown** regolamento m di conti

shower ['ʃaʊə(r)] **1** n *of rain* acquazzone m; *to wash* doccia f; **take a ~** fare una doccia **2** v/i fare la doccia; **shower-proof** impermeabile

'showjumping concorso m ippico; **show-off** *pej* esibizionista m/f; **showroom** show-room m *inv*; **showy** appariscente

shred [ʃred] **1** n *of paper* strisciolina f; *of cloth* brandello m; *of evidence etc* briciolo m **2** v/t *paper* stracciare; *in cooking* sminuzzare; **shredder** **for** *documents* distruttore m di documenti

shrewd [ʃruːd] scaltro; *investment* oculato; **shrewdness** oculatezza f

shriek [ʃriːk] **1** n strillo m **2** v/i strillare

shrill [ʃrɪl] stridulo

shrimp [ʃrɪmp] gamberetto m

shrine [ʃraɪn] santuario m

shrink[1] [ʃrɪŋk] v/i *of material* restringersi; *of support etc* diminuire

shrink[2] [ʃrɪŋk] n F *(psychiatrist)* strizzacervelli m/f *inv*

'shrink-wrapping *process* cellofanatura f; *material* cellophane® m

shrivel ['ʃrɪvl] avvizzire

Shrove Tuesday [ʃrəʊv] martedì m grasso

shrub [ʃrʌb] arbusto m;

shrubbery arboreto m

shrug [ʃrʌg]: **~ one's shoulders** alzare le spalle

shudder ['ʃʌdə(r)] **1** n *of fear, disgust* brivido m; *of earth etc* tremore m **2** v/i *with fear, disgust* rabbrividire; *of earth, building* tremare; **I ~ to think** non oso immaginare

shuffle ['ʃʌfl] **1** v/t *cards* mescolare **2** v/i *in walking* strascicare i piedi

shun [ʃʌn] evitare

shut [ʃʌt] **1** v/t chiudere **2** v/i *of door, box* chiudersi; *of shop, bank* chiudere; **they were ~** era chiuso

◆ **shut down** v/t *business* chiudere; *computer* spegnere **2** v/i *of business* chiudere i battenti; *of computer* spegnersi

◆ **shut up** v/i F *(be quiet)* star zitto; **shut up!** zitto!

shutter ['ʃʌtə(r)] *on window* battente m; PHOT otturatore m

'shuttlebus bus m *inv* navetta

shy [ʃaɪ] timido; **shyness** timidezza f

Sicilian [sɪ'sɪlɪən] **1** *adj* siciliano **2** n siciliano m, -a f; **Sicily** Sicilia f

sick [sɪk] malato; *sense of humour* crudele; **I feel ~** *about* **to vomit** ho la nausea; **be ~** *(vomit)* vomitare; **be ~ of** *(fed up with)* essere stufo di

sicken ['sɪkn] **1** v/t *(disgust)* disgustare; Am *(make ill)* fare ammalare **2** v/i: *be ~ing for sth* covare qc; **sickening** disgustoso; **sick leave**: *be on ~* essere in (congedo per) malattia; **sickness** malattia f; (*vomiting*) nausea f

side [saɪd] *of box, house* lato m; *of person, mountain* fianco m; *of page, record* facciata f; SP squadra f; *take ~s* (*favour one side*) prendere posizione; *I'm on your ~* sono dalla tua (parte); *~ by ~* fianco a fianco; *at the ~ of the road* sul ciglio della strada; *on the small ~* piuttosto piccolo; **sideboard** *furniture* credenza f; **side effect** effetto m collaterale; **sideline 1** n attività f inv collaterale **2** v/t: *feel ~d* sentirsi sminuito; **sidestep** scansare; *fig* schivare; **side street** via f laterale; **sidewalk** *Am* marciapiede m; **sideways** di lato

siege [siːdʒ] assedio m; *lay ~ to* assediare

sieve [sɪv] setaccio m

sift [sɪft] setacciare

sigh [saɪ] **1** n sospiro m **2** v/i sospirare

sight [saɪt] vista f; *~s of city* luoghi mpl da visitare; *catch ~ of* intravedere; *know by ~* conoscere di vista; *be in ~ of* essere visibile da; *out of ~* non visibile; *lose ~ of main objective* perdere di vista; **sightseeing** visita f turistica; *go ~* fare un giro turisti-

co; **sightseer** turista m/f

sign [saɪn] **1** n (*indication*) segno m; (*road ~*) segnale m; *outside shop* insegna f **2** v/t & v/i *document* firmare

signal ['sɪgnl] **1** n segnale m **2** v/i *of driver* segnalare

signatory ['sɪgnətrɪ] firmatario m, -a f

signature ['sɪgnətʃə(r)] firma f

significance [sɪg'nɪfɪkəns] importanza f; (*meaning*) significato m; **significant** *event etc* significativo; (*quite large*) notevole; **significantly** *larger, more expensive* notevolmente

signify ['sɪgnɪfaɪ] significare

'sign language linguaggio m dei segni; **signpost** cartello m stradale

silence ['saɪləns] **1** n silenzio m **2** v/t mettere a tacere; **silencer** MOT marmitta f; **silent** silenzioso; *film* muto; *stay ~ not comment* tacere

silhouette [sɪluː'et] sagoma f

silicon ['sɪlɪkən] silicio m

silicone ['sɪlɪkəʊn] silicone m

silk [sɪlk] **1** n seta f **2** adj *shirt etc* di seta; **silky** setoso

silliness ['sɪlɪnɪs] stupidità f; **silly** stupido

silo ['saɪləʊ] silo m

silver ['sɪlvə(r)] **1** n argento m; *objects* argenteria f **2** adj *ring* d'argento; *colour* argentato; **silverware** argenteria f

similar ['sɪmɪlə(r)] simile (*to*

a); **similarity** rassomiglianza *f*; **similarly** allo stesso modo

simple ['sɪmpl] semplice; *person* sempliciotto; **simple-minded** *pej* sempliciotto; **simplicity** semplicità *f*; **simplify** semplificare; **simplistic** semplicistico; **simply** (*absolutely*) assolutamente; *in a simple way* semplicemente

simultaneous [sɪml'teɪnɪəs] simultaneo; **simultaneously** simultaneamente

sin [sɪn] **1** *n* peccato *m* **2** *v/i* peccare

since [sɪns] **1** *prep* da; **~** *last week* dalla scorsa settimana **2** *adv* da allora; *I haven't seen him* **~** non lo vedo da allora **3** *conj in expressions of time* da quando; (*seeing that*) visto che

sincere [sɪn'sɪə(r)] sincero; **sincerely** con sincerità; *hope* sinceramente; *Yours* **~** Distinti saluti; **sincerity** sincerità *f*

sinful ['sɪnfʊl] peccaminoso

sing [sɪŋ] cantare

singe [sɪndʒ] bruciacchiare

singer ['sɪŋə(r)] cantante *m/f*

single ['sɪŋgl] **1** *adj* (*sole*) solo; (*not double*) singolo; *bed, sheet* a una piazza; (*not married*) single; *with reference to Europe* unico; *there wasn't a* **~** *...* non c'era nemmeno un ...; *in* **~** *file* in fila indiana **2** *n* MUS singolo *m*; (**~** *room*) (camera *f*) singola *f*; *ticket*

biglietto *m* di sola andata; *person* single *m/f inv*; **~** *s in tennis* singolo; **single-handed** da solo; **single-minded** determinato; **single mother** ragazza *f* madre; **single parent** genitore *m* single; **single parent family** famiglia *f* monoparentale; **single room** (camera *f*) singola *f*

singular ['sɪŋgjʊlə(r)] GRAM **1** *adj* singolare **2** *n* singolare *m*

sinister ['sɪnɪstə(r)] sinistro

sink [sɪŋk] **1** *n* lavandino *m* **2** *v/i of ship* affondare; *of object* andare a fondo; *of sun* calare; *of interest rates etc* scendere **3** *v/t ship* (far) affondare; *funds* investire

◆ **sink in** *of liquid* penetrare; *it still hasn't really sunk in of realization* ancora non mi rendo conto

sinner ['sɪnə(r)] peccatore *m*, -trice *f*

sinusitis [saɪnə'saɪtɪs] MED sinusite *f*

sip [sɪp] **1** *n* sorso *m* **2** *v/t* sorseggiare

sir [sɜː(r)] signore *m*; *Sir Charles* Sir Charles

siren ['saɪrən] sirena *f*

sirloin ['sɜːlɔɪn] controfiletto *m*

sister ['sɪstə(r)] sorella *f*; *in hospital* (infermiera *f*) caposala *f*; **sister-in-law** cognata *f*

sit [sɪt] **1** *v/i* sedere; (*sit down*)

sedersi **2** *v/t exam* dare
♦ **sit down** sedersi

sitcom ['sɪtkɒm] sitcom *f inv*

site [saɪt] **1** *n* luogo *m* **2** *v/t*
new offices etc situare

sitting ['sɪtɪŋ] *of committee,*
court sessione *f*; *for artist se-*
duta f; *for meals* turno *m*; **sit-**
ting room salotto *m*

situated ['sɪtjʊeɪtɪd] situato;
be ~ trovarsi; **situation** situazione *f*; *of building etc* posizione *f*

six [sɪks] sei; **sixteen** sedici;
sixteenth: sedicesimo; **sixth**
sesto; **sixtieth** sessantesimo;
sixty sessanta

size [saɪz] dimensioni *fpl*; *of*
clothes taglia *f*, misura *f*; *of*
shoes numero *m*; **sizeable**
considerevole

skate [skeɪt] **1** *n* pattino *m* **2**
v/i pattinare; **skateboard**
skateboard *m inv*; **skate-**
boarding skateboard *m*;
skater pattinatore *m*, -trice
f; **skating** pattinaggio *m*;
skating rink pista *f* di pattinaggio

skeleton ['skelɪtn] scheletro
m

skeptic *Am* ☞ **sceptic**

sketch [sketʃ] **1** *n* abbozzo *m*,
THEA sketch *m inv* **2** *v/t* abbozzare; **sketchy** *knowledge*
etc lacunoso

ski [skiː] **1** *n* sci *m inv* **2** *v/i* sciare

skid [skɪd] **1** *n* sbandata *f* **2** *v/i*
sbandare

skier ['skiːə(r)] sciatore *m*,
-trice *f*; **skiing** sci *m*; **go ~**
andare a sciare; **ski instruc-**
tor maestro *m*, -a *f* di sci

skilful, *Am* **skillful** ['skɪlful]
abile; **skilfully**, *Am* **skillfully**
abilmente

'ski lift impianto *m* di risalita

skill [skɪl] abilità *f inv*; **what**
~s do you have? quali capacità possiede?; **skilled** abile;
skillful *Am* ☞ **skilful**

skim [skɪm] *surface* sfiorare;
milk scremare

skimpy ['skɪmpɪ] *account etc*
scarso; *dress* succinto

skin [skɪn] **1** *n of* pelle *f*; *of*
fruit buccia *f* **2** *v/t* scoiare;
skin diving immersioni *fpl*
subacquee

skinny ['skɪnɪ] magro; **skin-**
tight aderente

skip [skɪp] **1** *n little jump* salto
m **2** *v/i* saltellare; *with skip-*
ping rope saltare **3** *v/t* (*omit*)
saltare

'ski pole racchetta *f* da sci

skipper ['skɪpə(r)] NAUT skipper *m inv*; *of team* capitano
m

'ski resort stazione *f* sciistica

skirt [skɜːt] gonna *f*; **skirting**
board battiscopa *m inv*

'ski run pista *f* da sci; **ski tow**
sciovia *f*

skull [skʌl] cranio *m*

skunk [skʌŋk] moffetta *f*

sky [skaɪ] cielo *m*; **skylight** lu-
cernario *m*; **skyline** profilo
m (contro il cielo); **sky-**

scraper grattacielo *m*

slab [slæb] *of stone* lastra *f; of cake etc* fetta *f*

slack [slæk] *rope* allentato; *person, work* negligente; *period* lento; **slacken** *rope* allentare; *pace* rallentare; **slacks** pantaloni *mpl* casual

◆ **slag off** [slæg] **P** parlare male di

slam [slæm] *door* sbattere

slander ['slɑːndə(r)] **1** *n* diffamazione *f* **2** *v/t* diffamare; **slanderous** diffamatorio

slang [slæŋ] slang *m inv; of a specific group* gergo *m*

slant [slɑːnt] **1** *v/i* pendere **2** *n* pendenza *f; given to a story* angolazione *f;* **slanting** *roof* spiovente

slap [slæp] **1** *n* blow schiaffo *m* **2** *v/t* schiaffeggiare; **slapdash** *work* frettoloso; *person* pressapochista; **slap-up meal** F pranzo *m* coi fiocchi

slash [slæʃ] **1** *n cut* taglio *m; in punctuation* barra *f* **2** *v/t skin, painting* squarciare; *prices* abbattere

slaughter ['slɔːtə(r)] **1** *n of animals* macellazione *f; of people, troops* massacro *m* **2** *v/t animals* macellare; *people, troops* massacrare; **slaughterhouse** mattatoio *m*

slave [sleɪv] schiavo *m, -a f*

slay [sleɪ] ammazzare; **slaying** Am *(murder)* omicidio *m*

sleaze [sliːz] POL corruzione *f;* **sleazy** *bar, characters* sordido

sleep [sliːp] **1** *n* sonno *m;* **go to** ~ addormentarsi; **I couldn't get to** ~ non sono riuscito a dormire **2** *v/i* dormire

◆ **sleep in** *(have a long lie)* dormire fino a tardi

◆ **sleep on** *proposal, decision* dormire su; **sleep on it** dormirci su

◆ **sleep with** *(have sex with)* andare a letto con

sleeping bag ['sliːpɪŋ] sacco *m* a pelo; **sleeping car** RAIL vagone *m* letto; **sleeping pill** sonnifero *m;* **sleepless night** in bianco; **sleep walker** sonnambulo *m, -a f;* **sleep walking** sonnambulismo *m;* **sleepy** *child* assonnato; *town* addormentato; **I'm** ~ ho sonno

sleet [sliːt] nevischio *m*

sleeve [sliːv] *of jacket etc* manica *f;* **sleeveless** senza maniche

sleight of 'hand [slaɪt] gioco *m* di prestigio

slender ['slendə(r)] snello; *chance, margin* piccolo

slice [slaɪs] **1** *n also fig* fetta *f* **2** *v/t loaf etc* affettare

slick [slɪk] **1** *adj performance* brillante; *(pej: cunning)* scaltro **2** *n of oil* chiazza *f* di petrolio

slide [slaɪd] **1** *n for kids* scivolo *m;* PHOT diapositiva *f* **2** *v/i* scivolare; *of exchange rate etc* calare 3 v/t far scivolare

slight [slaɪt] **1** adj person, figure gracile; (small) leggero; **no, not in the ~est** no, per nulla **2** n (insult) offesa f; **slightly** leggermente

slim [slɪm] **1** adj slanciato; chance scarso **2** v/i dimagrire; **I'm ~ming** sono a dieta

slime [slaɪm] melma f; **slimy** liquid melmoso; person viscido

sling [slɪŋ] **1** n for arm fascia f a tracolla **2** v/t (throw) lanciare

slip [slɪp] **1** n (mistake) errore m **2** v/i on ice etc scivolare; of quality etc peggiorare; **he ~ped out of the room** è sgattaiolato fuori dalla stanza **3** v/t (put) far scivolare; **it ~ped my mind** mi è passato di mente

♦ **slip up** (make a mistake) sbagliarsi

slipped 'disc [slɪpt] ernia f del disco

slipper ['slɪpə(r)] pantofola f

slippery ['slɪpərɪ] scivoloso

'slip road rampa f di accesso; **slip-up** (mistake) errore m

slit [slɪt] **1** n (tear) strappo m; (hole) fessura f; in skirt spacco m **2** v/t envelope, packet aprire (tagliando); throat tagliare

sliver ['slɪvə(r)] scheggia f

slob [slɒb] pej sudicione m, -a f

slog [slɒg] faticata f

slogan ['sləʊgən] slogan m inv

slop [slɒp] rovesciare, versare

slope [sləʊp] **1** n in pendenza f; of mountain pendio m **2** v/i essere inclinato; **the road ~s down to the sea** la strada scende fino al mare

sloppy ['slɒpɪ] work, editing trascurato; in dressing sciatto; (too sentimental) sdolcinato

slot [slɒt] fessura f; in schedule spazio m; **slot machine** for vending distributore m automatico; for gambling slot-machine f inv

Slovak ['sləʊvæk] **1** adj slovacco **2** n slovacco m, -a f; language slovacco m; **Slovakia** Slovacchia f

Slovene ['sləʊviːn] **1** adj sloveno **2** n sloveno m, -a f; language sloveno m; **Slovenia** Slovenia f

slovenly ['slʌvnlɪ] sciatto

slow [sləʊ] lento; **be ~** of clock essere indietro

♦ **slow down** rallentare

'slowcoach F lumaca f F; **slowdown** in production rallentamento m; **slowly** lentamente; **slow motion: in ~** al rallentatore; **slowness** lentezza f

sluggish ['slʌgɪʃ] lento

slum [slʌm] slum m inv

slump [slʌmp] **1** n in trade crollo m **2** v/i economically crollare; of person accasciarsi

slur [slɜː(r)] **1** n calunnia f **2** v/t words biascicare

slush [slʌʃ] fanghiglia f; (pej: sentimental stuff) smancerie fpl; **slush fund** fondi mpl neri

slut [slʌt] pej sgualdrina f

sly [slaɪ] scaltro

smack [smæk] **1** n on the bottom sculacciata f; in the face schiaffo m **2** v/t child picchiare; bottom sculacciare

small [smɔːl] **1** adj piccolo **2** n: **the ~ of the back** le reni; **small change** spiccioli mpl; **small hours**: **the ~** le ore fpl piccole; **small talk** conversazione f di circostanza

smart¹ [smɑːt] adj (elegant) elegante; (intelligent) intelligente; pace svelto; **get ~ with** fare il furbo con F

smart² [smɑːt] v/i (hurt) bruciare

'smart card smart card f inv; **smartly** dressed elegantemente; **smartphone** ['smɑːtfəʊn] smartphone m

smash [smæʃ] **1** n noise fracasso m; (car crash) scontro m; in tennis schiacciata f **2** v/t break spaccare; hit hard sbattere; **~ sth to pieces** mandare in frantumi qc **3** v/i break frantumarsi

smattering ['smætərɪŋ] of a language infarinatura f

smear [smɪə(r)] **1** n of ink etc macchia f; MED striscio m; on character calunnia f **2** v/t character calunniare

smell [smel] **1** n odore m; **sense of ~** olfatto m, odorato m **2** v/t sentire odore di; test by smelling sentire **3** v/i unpleasantly puzzare; (sniff) odorare; **what does it ~ of?** che odore ha?; **you ~ of beer** puzzi di birra; **smelly** puzzolente

smile [smaɪl] **1** n sorriso m **2** v/i sorridere

smirk [smɜːk] sorriso m compiaciuto

smoke [sməʊk] **1** n fumo m; **have a ~** fumare **2** v/t cigarettes etc fumare; bacon affumicare **3** v/i fumare; **smoke-free** totalmente non smoking; **smoker** fumatore m, -trice f; smoking fumo m; **no ~** vietato fumare; **smoky** room, air pieno di fumo

smolder Am ☞ **smoulder**

smooth [smuːð] **1** adj surface, skin, sea liscio; sea calmo; transition senza problemi; pej: person mellifluo **2** v/t hair lisciare; **smoothly** without problems senza problemi

smother ['smʌðə(r)] flames, person soffocare

smoulder ['sməʊldə(r)] covare sotto la cenere

smudge [smʌdʒ] **1** n sbavatura f **2** v/t sbavare

smug [smʌg] compiaciuto

smuggle ['smʌgl] contrabbandare; **smuggler** contrabbandiere *m*, -a *f*; **smuggling** contrabbando *m*

smutty ['smʌtɪ] *joke* sconcio

snack [snæk] spuntino *m*

snag [snæg] (*problem*) problema *m*

snail [sneɪl] chiocciola *f*, *in cooking* lumaca *f*; **snail mail** F posta *f* lumaca

snake [sneɪk] serpente *m*

snap [snæp] **1** *n sound* botto *m*; PHOT foto *f* **2** *v/t break* spezzare; (*say sharply*) dire bruscamente **3** *v/i break* spezzarsi **4** *adj decision* immediato; **snappy** *person*, *mood* irritabile; F (*quick*) rapido; (*elegant*) elegante; **snapshot** istantanea *f*

snarl [snɑːl] **1** *n of dog* ringhio *m* **2** *v/i* ringhiare

snatch [snætʃ] afferrare; (*steal*) scippare; (*kidnap*) rapire

snazzy ['snæzɪ] F chic *inv*

sneakers ['sniːkəz] *Am* scarpe *fpl* da ginnastica

sneaky ['sniːkɪ] F (*crafty*) scaltro

sneer [snɪə(r)] **1** *n* sogghigno *m* **2** *v/i* sogghignare

sneeze [sniːz] **1** *n* starnuto *m* **2** *v/i* starnutire

snicker ['snɪkə(r)] ridacchiare

sniff [snɪf] **1** *v/i to clear nose* tirare su col naso; *of dog* fiutare **2** *v/t smell* annusare

sniper ['snaɪpə(r)] cecchino *m*

snivel ['snɪvl] *pej* frignare

snob [snɒb] snob *m/f inv*; **snobbery** snobismo *m*; **snobbish** snob *inv*

◆ **snoop around** [snuːp] ficcanasare

snooty ['snuːtɪ] snob *inv*

snooze [snuːz] **1** *n* sonnellino *m*; **have a ~** fare un sonnellino **2** *v/i* sonnecchiare

snore [snɔː(r)] russare; **snoring** russare *m*

snorkel ['snɔːkl] boccaglio *m*

snort [snɔːt] sbuffare

snow [snəʊ] **1** *n* neve *f* **2** *v/i* nevicare

◆ **snow under**: **be snowed under with ...** essere sommerso di ...

'**snowball** palla *f* di neve; **snow chains** *npl* MOT catene *fpl* da neve; **snowdrift** cumulo *m* di neve; **snowflake** fiocco *m* di neve; **snowman** pupazzo *m* di neve; **snowplough**, *Am* **snowplow** spazzaneve *m inv*; **snowstorm** tormenta *f*; **snowy** *weather* nevoso; *roofs, hills* innevato

snub [snʌb] **1** *n* affronto *m* **2** *v/t* snobbare; **snub-nosed** col naso all'insù

snug [snʌg] al calduccio; (*tight-fitting*) attillato

so [səʊ] **1** *adv* così; **~ hot** così caldo; **not ~** much non così tanto; **~ much easier** molto più facile; **I miss you ~** mi

manchi tanto; **~ am / do I**
anch'io; **and ~ on** e così
via **2** *pron*: **I hope ~** spero
di sì; **I don't think ~** non credo, credo di no **50 or ~** circa
50 **3** *conj (for that reason)* così; *(in order that)* così che;
(that) I could come too così
che potessi venire anch'io; **~
what?** F e allora?

soak [səʊk] *(steep)* mettere a
bagno; *of water* inzuppare;
soaked fradicio; **soaking
(wet)** bagnato fradicio

soap [səʊp] *for washing* sapone *m*; **soap (opera)** soap
(opera) *f* inv, telenovela *f*;
soapy *water* saponato

soar [sɔ:(r)] *of rocket etc* in-
nalzarsi; *of prices* aumentare
vertiginosamente

sob [sɒb] **1** *n* singhiozzo *m* **2**
v/i singhiozzare

sober [ˈsəʊbə(r)] sobrio; *(serious)* serio

◆ **sober up** smaltire la sbornia

so-'called cosiddetto
soccer [ˈsɒkə(r)] calcio *m*
sociable [ˈsəʊʃəbl] socievole
social [ˈsəʊʃl] sociale; **social
democrat** socialdemocrati-
co *m*, -a *f*; **socialism** socialismo *m*; **socialist 1** *adj* socialista **2** *n* socialista *m/f*; **socialize** socializzare; **social
life** vita *f* sociale; **social science** scienza *f* sociale; **social security** sussidio *m* della previdenza sociale; **social**

work assistenza *f* sociale;
social worker assistente
m/f sociale

society [səˈsaɪətɪ] società *f*
inv; *(organization)* associazione *f*

sociologist [səʊsɪˈɒlədʒɪst]
sociologo *m*, -a *f*; **sociology**
sociologia *f*

sock[1] [sɒk] *n* calzino *m*

sock[2] [sɒk] *v/t* F *(punch)* dare
un pugno a

socket [ˈsɒkɪt] *for light bulb*
portalampada *m* inv; *in wall*
presa *f* (di corrente); *of eye*
orbita *f*

soda [ˈsəʊdə] *(~ water)* seltz
m inv; *Am* bibita *f* analcolica

sofa [ˈsəʊfə] divano *m*

soft [sɒft] *pillow* soffice; *chair,
skin* morbido; *light, colour*
tenue; *music* soft inv; *voice*
sommesso; *(lenient)* indulgente; **soft drink** bibita *f*;
soft drug droga *f* leggera;
soften *butter etc* ammorbidire; *position* attenuare; *impact, blow* attutire; **softly**
speak sommessamente;
software software *m*

soggy [ˈsɒgɪ] molle e pesante
soil [sɔɪl] **1** *n (earth)* terra *f* **2**
v/t sporcare

solar energy [ˈsəʊlə(r)] energia *f* solare; **solar panel** pannello *m* solare

soldier [ˈsəʊldʒə(r)] soldato
m

sole[1] [səʊl] *n of foot* pianta *f*
(del piede); *of shoe* suola *f*

sole² [səʊl] *adj* unico; (*exclusive*) esclusivo

solely ['səʊlɪ] solamente

solemn ['sɒləm] solenne; **solemnity** solennità *f inv*; **solemnly** solennemente

solicit [sə'lɪsɪt] *of prostitute* adescare; **solicitor** avvocato *m*

solid ['sɒlɪd] (*hard*) solido; (*without holes*) compatto; *gold, silver* massiccio; (*sturdy*) robusto; *evidence* concreto; *support* forte; **solidarity** solidarietà *f*

solitaire ['sɒlɪteə(r)] *card game* solitario *m*

solitary ['sɒlɪtərɪ] *life, activity* solitario; (*single*) solo; **solitude** solitudine *f*

solo ['səʊləʊ] **1** *n* MUS assolo *m* **2** *adj* performance solista; **soloist** solista *m/f*

soluble ['sɒljʊbl] *substance* solubile; *problem* risolvibile; **solution** soluzione *f*

solve [sɒlv] risolvere; **solvent** *financially* solvibile

sombre, *Am* **somber** ['sɒmbə(r)] (*dark*) scuro; (*serious*) tetro

some [sʌm] **1** *adj* (*amount*) un po' di, del; (*number*) delle *f*, ~ **people say that** ... alcuni dicono che ... **2** *pron* (*amount*) un po'; (*number*) alcuni *m*, -e *f*; **would you like** ~? ne vuoi un po'?; ~ **of the students** alcuni studenti; **somebody**

qualcuno; **someday** un giorno; **somehow** (*by one means or another*) in qualche modo; (*for some unknown reason*) per qualche motivo; **someone** ☞ **somebody**; **someplace** ☞ **somewhere**

somersault ['sʌməsɔːlt] **1** *n* capriola *f* **2** *v/i* fare una capriola

something qualcosa; **sometime** (*one of these days*) uno di questi giorni; ~ **last year** l'anno scorso; **sometimes** a volte; **somewhat** piuttosto; **somewhere 1** *adv* da qualche parte **2** *pron* un posto; *let's go* ~ *quiet* andiamo in un posto tranquillo

son [sʌn] figlio *m*

song [sɒŋ] canzone *f*; *of birds* canto *m*

son-in-law genero *m*; **son of a bitch** V figlio *m* di puttana P

soon [suːn] presto; **as** ~ **as** non appena; **as** ~ **as possible** prima possibile; ~**er or later** presto o tardi; **the** ~**er the better** prima è, meglio è; *how* ~ *can you be ready?* fra quanto sei pronto?

soothe [suːð] calmare

sophisticated [sə'fɪstɪkeɪtɪd] sofisticato; **sophistication** *of person* raffinatezza *f*; *of machine* complessità *f*

sophomore ['sɒfəmɔːr] *Am* studente *m/f* del secondo anno

soprano [sə'prɑːnəʊ] soprano *m/f*

sordid ['sɔːdɪd] sordido

sore [sɔː(r)] **1** *adj* (*painful*) dolorante; *is it* ~? fa male? **2** *n* piaga *f*; **sore throat** mal *m* di gola

sorrow ['sɒrəʊ] dispiacere *m*, dolore *m*

sorry ['sɒrɪ] *day, sight* triste; (*I'm*) ~*!* apologizing scusa!; *polite form* scusi!; *I'm* ~ *regretting* mi dispiace; *I feel* ~ *for her* mi dispiace per lei

sort [sɔːt] **1** *n* tipo *m*; ~ *of* ... F un po' ...; *is it finished?* - ~ *of* F è terminato? - quasi **2** *v/t* separare; COMPUT ordinare

SOS [esəʊ'es] SOS *m inv*

so-'so F così così

soul [səʊl] anima *f*; *the poor* ~ il poverino, la poverina

sound[1] [saʊnd] **1** *adj* (*sensible*) valido; (*healthy*) sano; *sleep* profondo; *structure* solido **2** *adv*: *be* ~ *asleep* dormire profondamente

sound[2] [saʊnd] **1** *n* suono *m*; (*noise*) rumore *m* **2** *v/i*: *that* ~*s interesting* sembra interessante

'soundbite slogan *m inv*; **soundly** *sleep* profondamente; *beaten* duramente; **soundproof** insonorizzato; **soundtrack** colonna *f* sonora

soup [suːp] minestra *f*

sour ['saʊə(r)] *apple, orange* aspro; *milk, expression, comment* acido

source [sɔːs] fonte *f*; *of river* sorgente *f*

south [saʊθ] **1** *adj* meridionale, del sud **2** *n* sud *m* **3** *adv* *travel* verso sud; ~ *of* a sud di; **South Africa** Repubblica *f* Sudafricana; **South African 1** *adj* sudafricano **2** *n* sudafricano *m*, -a *f*; **South America** Sudamerica *m*; **South American 1** *adj* sudamericano **2** *n* sudamericano *m*, -a *f*; **southeast 1** *n* sud-est *m* **2** *adj* sud-orientale **3** *adv* verso sud-est; **southeastern** sud-orientale; **southerly** meridionale; **southern** del sud; **southerner** abitante *m/f* del sud; **southernmost** più a sud; **South Pole** polo *m* sud; **southwards** verso sud; **southwest 1** *n* sud-ovest *m* **2** *adj* sud-occidentale **3** *adv* verso sud-ovest; **southwestern** sud-occidentale

souvenir [suːvə'nɪə(r)] souvenir *m inv*

sovereign ['sɒvrɪn] *state* sovrano; **sovereignty** *of state* sovranità *f*

sow[1] [saʊ] *n pig* scrofa *f*

sow[2] [səʊ] *v/t seeds* seminare

soya ['sɔɪə], *US* **soy** [sɔɪ] soia *f*; **soy**(**a**) **milk** latte *m* di soia; **soya sauce** salsa *f* di soia

spa [spɑː] *resort m* spa; (*hotel*)

hotel *m* spa

space [speɪs] spazio *m; in car park* posto *m;* **space-bar** COMPUT barra *f* spaziatrice; **spacecraft** veicolo *m* spaziale; **spaceship** astronave *f;* **space shuttle** shuttle *m inv;* **space station** stazione *f* spaziale; **spacious** spazioso

spade [speɪd] *for digging* vanga *f;* **~s** *in card game* picche *mpl*

spaghetti [spəˈgetɪ] spaghetti *mpl*

Spain [speɪn] Spagna *f*

spam [spæm] spam *f*

span [spæn] coprire; *of bridge* attraversare

Spaniard [ˈspænjəd] spagnolo *m*, -a *f;* **Spanish 1** *adj* spagnolo **2** *n language* spagnolo *m*

spanner [ˈspænə(r)] chiave *f* inglese

spare [speə(r)] **1** *v/t* (*do without*) fare a meno di; **can you ~ £50?** mi puoi prestare 50 sterline?; **can you ~ the time?** hai tempo?; **have money / time to ~** avere soldi / tempo d'avanzo **2** *adj* in più **3** *n* ricambio *m;* **spare part** pezzo *m* di ricambio; **spare ribs** costine *fpl* di maiale; **spare room** stanza *f* degli ospiti; **spare time** tempo *m* libero; **spare wheel** MOT ruota *f* di scorta; **sparing:** **be ~ with** andarci piano con; **sparingly** con modera-

zione

spark [spɑːk] scintilla *f*

sparkle [ˈspɑːkl] brillare; **sparkling wine** vino *m* frizzante

'spark plug candela *f*

sparrow [ˈspærəʊ] passero *m*

sparse [spɑːs] *vegetation* rado; **sparsely:** **~ populated** scarsamente popolato

spartan [ˈspɑːtn] spartano

spasmodic [spæzˈmɒdɪk] irregolare

spate [speɪt] *fig* ondata *f*

spatial [ˈspeɪʃl] spaziale

speak [spiːk] **1** *v/i* parlare; **...ing** TELEC sono io **2** *v/t for foreign language* parlare; *the truth* dire

♦ **speak up** (*speak louder*) parlare ad alta voce

speaker [ˈspiːkə(r)] oratore *m*, -trice *f; of sound system* cassa *f;* **Italian ~** italofono *m*, -a *f;* **speaker phone** telefono *m* con vivavoce

spear [spɪə(r)] lancia *f*

special [ˈspeʃl] speciale; (*particular*) particolare; **special effects** effetti *mpl* speciali; **specialist** specialista *m/f;* **speciality** specialità *f inv;* **specialize** specializzarsi (*in* in); **specially** ☞ **especially**; **specialty** specialità *f inv*

species [ˈspiːʃiːz] specie *f inv*

specific [spəˈsɪfɪk] specifico; **specifically** specificamente; **specifications** *of machine etc* caratteristiche *fpl* tecniche; **specify** specificare

specimen ['spesɪmən] campione *m*

spectacle ['spektəkl] (*impressive sight*) spettacolo *m*; (**a pair of**) **~s** (un paio di) occhiali *mpl*; **spectacular** spettacolare

spectator [spek'teɪtə(r)] spettatore *m*, -trice *f*

spectrum ['spektrəm] *fig* gamma *f*

speculate ['spekjuleɪt] fare congetture (**on** su); FIN speculare; **speculation** congetture *fpl*, FIN speculazione *f*; **speculator** FIN speculatore *m*, -trice *f*

speech [spiːtʃ] discorso *m*; *in play* monologo *m*; (*ability to speak*) parola *f*; (*way of speaking*) linguaggio *m*; **speechless** *with shock, surprise* senza parole

speed [spiːd] **1** *n* velocità *f inv*; (*quickness*) rapidità *f inv* **2** *v/i* (*go quickly*) andare a tutta velocità; (*drive too quickly*) superare il limite di velocità

◆ **speed up 1** *v/i* andare più veloce **2** *v/t* accelerare

'**speedboat** motoscafo *m*; **speed bump** dosso *m* di rallentamento; **speedily** rapidamente; **speeding** *when driving* eccesso *m* di velocità; **speed limit** limite *m* di velocità; **speedometer** tachimetro *m*; **speedy** rapido

spell[1] [spel] **1** *v/t*: **how do you ~ ...?** come si scrive ...?; **could you ~ that please?** me lo può dettare lettera per lettera? **2** *v/i* sapere come si scrivono le parole

spell[2] [spel] *n* (*period of time*) periodo *m*

'**spellchecker** COMPUT correttore *m* ortografico; **spelling** ortografia *f*

spend [spend] *money* spendere; *time* passare; **spendthrift** *pej* spendaccione *m*, -a *f*

sperm [spɜːm] spermatozoo *m*; (*semen*) sperma *m*

sphere [sfɪə(r)] *also fig* sfera *f*

spice [spaɪs] (*seasoning*) spezia *f*; **spicy** *food* piccante

spider ['spaɪdə(r)] ragno *m*; **spider's web** ragnatela *f*

spike [spaɪk] *on railings* spunzone *m*; *on plant* spina *f*; *on animal* aculeo *m*; *on running shoes* chiodo *m*

spill [spɪl] **1** *v/t* versare **2** *v/i* versarsi **3** *n* *of oil etc* fuoriuscita *f*

spin[1] [spɪn] **1** *n* giro *m*; *on ball* effetto *m* **2** *v/t* far girare; *ball* imprimere l'effetto a **3** *v/i* *of wheel* girare

spin[2] [spɪn] *v/t* *wool, cotton* filare; *web* tessere

spinach ['spɪnɪdʒ] spinaci *mpl*

spinal ['spaɪnl] spinale; **spinal column** colonna *f* vertebrale, spina *f* dorsale; **spinal cord** midollo *m* spinale

'spin doctor esperto che ha il compito di presentare ai media le decisioni di un partito o personaggio politico sotto la luce migliore

spine [spaɪn] of person, animal spina f dorsale; of book dorso m; on plant, hedgehog spina f; **spineless** (cowardly) smidollato

'spin-off applicazione f secondaria

spinster ['spɪnstə(r)] zitella f

spiny ['spaɪnɪ] spinoso

spiral ['spaɪrəl] **1** n spirale f **2** v/i (rise quickly) salire vertiginosamente; **spiral staircase** scala f a chiocciola

spire ['spaɪə(r)] spira f, guglia f

spirit ['spɪrɪt] spirito m; **spirited** debate animato; defence energico; performance brioso; **spirits** (morale) morale msg; **be in good / poor** ~ essere su / giù di morale; **spiritual** spirituale

spit [spɪt] of person sputare

spite [spaɪt] dispetto m; **in** ~ **of** malgrado; **spiteful** dispettoso; **spitefully** dispettosamente

spitting image ['spɪtɪŋ]: **be the** ~ **of s.o.** essere il ritratto sputato di qu

splash [splæʃ] **1** n (noise) tonfo m; (small amount of liquid) schizzo m; of colour macchia f **2** v/t person schizzare; water, mud spruzzare **3** v/i schizza-

re; of waves infrangersi

'splashdown ammaraggio m

splendid ['splendɪd] magnifico; **splendour**, Am **splendor** magnificenza f

splint [splɪnt] MED stecca f

splinter ['splɪntə(r)] **1** n scheggia f **2** v/i scheggiarsi

split [splɪt] **1** n in leather strappo m; in wood crepa f; (disagreement) spaccatura f; (division, share) divisione f **2** v/t leather strappare; wood, logs spaccare; (cause disagreement in) spaccare; (divide) dividere **3** v/i of leather strapparsi; of wood spaccarsi; (disagree) spaccarsi

♦ **split up** of couple separarsi

splitting ['splɪtɪŋ]: ~ **headache** feroce mal m inv di testa

spoil [spɔɪl] child viziare; surprise, party rovinare; **spoilsport** F guastafeste m/f; **spoilt** child viziato; **be** ~ **for choice** avere (solo) l'imbarazzo della scelta

spoke [spəʊk] of wheel raggio m

spokesperson ['spəʊkspɜːsən] portavoce m/f

sponge [spʌndʒ] spugna f; **sponger** F scroccone m, -a f

sponsor ['spɒnsə(r)] **1** n for immigration etc garante m/f inv; of TV programme, sports event, for fundraising sponsor m inv **2** v/t for immigra-

tion, *membership* garantire per; *TV programme, sports event* sponsorizzare; **sponsorship** sponsorizzazione *f*

spontaneous [spɒn'teɪnɪəs] spontaneo; **spontaneously** spontaneamente

spool [spuːl] bobina *f*

spoon [spuːn] cucchiaio *m*; **spoonful** cucchiaio *f*

sporadic [spə'rædɪk] sporadico

sport [spɔːt] sport *m inv*; **sporting** sportivo; **sports jacket** giacca *f* sportiva; **sports car** auto *f inv* sportiva; **sportsman** sportivo *m*; **sportswear** abbigliamento *m* sportivo; **sportswoman** sportiva *f*; **sporty** sportivo

spot¹ [spɒt] *n* (*pimple*) brufolo *m*; *caused by measles etc* foruncolo *m*; *part of pattern* pois *m inv*

spot² [spɒt] *n* (*place*) posticino *m*; **on the ~** (*in the place in question*) sul posto; (*immediately*) immediatamente

spot³ [spɒt] *v/t* (*notice*) notare; (*identify*) trovare

'spot check controllo *m* casuale; **spotless** pulitissimo; **spotlight** faretto *m*; **spotty** *with pimples* brufoloso

spouse [spaʊs] *fml* coniuge *m/f*

spout [spaʊt] **1** *n* beccuccio *m* **2** *v/i of liquid* sgorgare **3** *v/t* F: **~ nonsense** ciarlare

sprain [spreɪn] **1** *n* slogatura *f*

2 *v/t* slogarsi

sprawl [sprɔːl] *n of city* estendersi; **send s.o. ~ing** *of punch* mandare qu a gambe all'aria; **sprawling** *city* tentacolare

spray [spreɪ] **1** *n of sea water* spruzzi *mpl*; *for hair* lacca *f*; (*container*) spray *m inv* **2** *v/t* spruzzare; **spraygun** pistola *f* a spruzzo

spread [spred] **1** *n of disease, religion etc* diffusione *f*; F *big meal* banchetto *m* **2** *v/t* (*lay*) stendere; *butter, jam* spalmare; *news, rumour, disease* diffondere; *arms, legs* allargare **3** *v/i* diffondersi; **spreadsheet** COMPUT spreadsheet *m inv*

sprightly ['spraɪtlɪ] arzillo

spring¹ *n* [sprɪŋ] *season* primavera *f*

spring² [sprɪŋ] *n device* molla *f*

spring³ [sprɪŋ] **1** *n* (*jump*) balzo *m*; (*stream*) sorgente *f* **2** *v/i* (*jump*) balzare; **~ from** derivare da

'springboard trampolino *m*; **spring onion** cipollotto *m*; **springtime** primavera *f*

sprinkle ['sprɪŋkl] spruzzare; **~ sth with** cospargere qc di; **sprinkler** *for garden* irrigatore *m*; *in ceiling* sprinkler *m inv*

sprint [sprɪnt] **1** *n*: scatto *m*; **the 100 metres ~** i cento metri piani **2** *v/i* fare uno scatto;

sprinter SP velocista *m/f*

spud [spʌd] F patata *f*

spy [spaɪ] **1** *n* spia *f* **2** *v/i* fare la spia **3** *v/t* (*see*) scorgere

♦ **spy on** spiare

squabble ['skwɒbl] **1** *n* bisticcio *m* **2** *v/i* bisticciare

squalid ['skwɒlɪd] squallido; *fig* squallido

squalor ['skwɒlə(r)] squallore *m*

squander ['skwɒndə(r)] *money* dilapidare

square [skweə(r)] **1** *adj in shape* quadrato; ~ **mile** miglio quadrato **2** *n shape* quadrato *m*; *in town* piazza *f*; *in board game* casella *f*; MATH quadrato *m*; **we're back to ~ one** siamo punto e a capo; **square root** radice *f* quadrata

squash[1] [skwɒʃ] *n vegetable* zucca *f*

squash[2] [skwɒʃ] *n game* squash *m*

squash[3] [skwɒʃ] *v/t* (*crush*) schiacciare

squat [skwɒt] **1** *adj in shape* tozzo **2** *v/i* (*sit*) accovacciarsi; *illegally* occupare abusivamente

squeak [skwi:k] **1** *n of mouse* squittio *m*; *of hinge* cigolio *m* **2** *v/i of mouse* squittire; *of hinge* cigolare; *of shoes* scricchiolare; **squeaky** *hinge* cigolante; *shoes* scricchiolante; *voice* stridulo; **squeaky clean** F pulito

squeal [skwi:l] **1** *n of pain, laughter* strillo *m*; *of brakes*

stridore *m* **2** *v/i* strillare; *of brakes* stridere

squeamish ['skwi:mɪʃ]: **be** ~ avere lo stomaco delicato

squeeze [skwi:z] **1** *n of hand, shoulder* stretta *f* **2** *v/t hand* stringere; *orange, lemon* spremere; *sponge* strizzare

squid [skwɪd] calamaro *m*

squint [skwɪnt] strabismo *m*

squirm [skw3:m] (*wriggle*) contorcersi; ~ (**with embarrassment**) morire di vergogna

squirrel ['skwɪrəl] scoiattolo *m*

squirt [skw3:t] *v/t* spruzzare **2** *n* F *pej* microbo *m* F

St *abbr* (= *saint*) S. (= santo *m*, santa *f*); (= *street*) v. (= via *f*)

stab [stæb] accoltellare

stability [stə'bɪlɪtɪ] stabilità *f*; **stabilize** **1** *v/t* stabilizzare **2** *v/i* stabilizzarsi; **stable**[1] *adj* stabile; *person* stabile; **stable**[2] *n for horses* stalla *f*; *establishment* scuderia *f*

stack [stæk] **1** *n* (*pile*) pila *f*; **~s of** F un sacco di F **2** *v/t* mettere in pila

stadium ['steɪdɪəm] stadio *m*

staff [stɑ:f] (*employees*) personale *msg*; (*teachers*) corpo *m* insegnante; **staffroom** *in school* sala *f* professori

stage[1] [steɪdʒ] *n in life, project etc* fase *f*; *of journey* tappa *f*

stage[2] [steɪdʒ] **1** *n* THEA palcoscenico *m* **2** *v/t play* mettere in scena; *demonstration* organizzare

stagger ['stægə(r)] **1** v/i barcollare **2** v/t (amaze) sbalordire; holidays, breaks etc scaglionare; **staggering** sbalorditivo

stagnant ['stægnənt] also fig stagnante; **stagnate** of person, mind vegetare

'**stag party** (festa f di) addio m al celibato

stain [stein] **1** n (dirty mark) macchia f; for wood mordente m **2** v/t (dirty) macchiare; wood dare il mordente a **3** v/i of wine etc macchiare; of fabric macchiarsi; **stained-glass window** vetrata f colorata; **stainless steel** acciaio m inossidabile

stair [steə(r)] scalino m; **the ~s** le scale; **staircase** scala f

stake [steik] **1** n of wood paletto m; when gambling puntata f; (investment) partecipazione f; **be at ~** essere in gioco **2** v/t tree puntellare; money puntare

stale [steil] bread raffermo; air viziato; fig: news vecchio; **stalemate** in chess stallo m; fig punto m morto

stalk¹ [stɔːk] n of fruit picciolo m; of plant gambo m

stalk² [stɔːk] v/t animal seguire; person perseguitare (con telefonate, lettere ecc)

stall¹ [stɔːl] n at market bancarella f; for cow, horse box m inv

stall² [stɔːl] **1** v/i of vehicle fermarsi; (play for time) temporeggiare **2** v/t engine far spegnere; people trattenere

stalls [stɔːlz] platea f

stalwart ['stɔːlwət] supporter fedele

stamina ['stæminə] resistenza f

stammer ['stæmə(r)] **1** n balbuzie f **2** v/i balbettare

stamp¹ [stæmp] **1** n for letter francobollo m; (date ~ etc) timbro m **2** v/t letter affrancare; document, passport timbrare; **~ed addressed envelope** busta f affrancata per la risposta

stamp² [stæmp] v/t: **~ one's feet** pestare i piedi

stance [stɑːns] (position) presa f di posizione

stand [stænd] **1** n at exhibition stand m inv; (witness ~) banco m dei testimoni; (support, base) base f; **take the ~** LAW testimoniare **2** v/i (be situated: of person) stare; of object, building trovarsi; as opposed to sit stare in piedi; (rise) alzarsi in piedi **3** v/t (tolerate) sopportare; (put) mettere; **you don't ~ a chance** non hai alcuna probabilità; **~ s.o. a drink** offrire da bere a qu

◆ **stand by 1** v/i (not take action) stare a guardare; (be ready) tenersi pronto **2** v/t person stare al fianco di; de-

cision mantenere

◆ **stand down** (*withdraw*) ritirarsi

◆ **stand for** (*tolerate*) tollerare; (*mean*) significare; *freedom etc* rappresentare

◆ **stand out** spiccare; *of person, building* distinguersi

◆ **stand up 1** *v/i* alzarsi in piedi **2** *v/t* F *on date* dare buca a F

◆ **stand up for** difendere

◆ **stand up to** far fronte a

standard ['stændəd] **1** *adj* (*usual*) comune; *model* standard *inv* **2** *n* (*level*) livello *m*; (*expectation*) aspettativa *f*; TECH standard *m inv*; *be up to ~* essere di buona qualità; **standardize** standardizzare; **standard of living** tenore *m* di vita

'**standby** *ticket* biglietto *m* stand-by; **on** *~ at airport* in lista d'attesa; **on** *~ of troops etc* pronto; **standing** in *society etc* posizione *f*; (*repute*) reputazione *f*; *of long ~* di lunga durata; **standoffish** scostante; **standpoint** punto *m* di vista; **standstill**: *be at a ~* essere fermo; *bring to a ~* fermare

staple¹ ['steɪpl] *n* (*foodstuff*) alimento *m* base

staple² ['steɪpl] **1** *n* (*fastener*) graffa *f* **2** *v/t* pinzare

stapler ['steɪplə(r)] pinzatrice *f*

star [stɑː(r)] **1** *n in sky* stella *f*;

fig star *f inv* **2** *v/t*: *a film ~ring Julia Roberts* un film interpretato da Julia Roberts; **starboard** a tribordo

stare [steə(r)] fissare; *~ at* fissare

stark [stɑːk] **1** *adj landscape* desolato; *colour scheme* austero; *reminder, contrast etc* brusco **2** *adv*: *~ naked* completamente nudo

starling ['stɑːlɪŋ] storno *m*

starry ['stɑːrɪ] *night* stellato

start [stɑːt] **1** *n* inizio *m*; *get off to a good ~* cominciare bene **2** *v/i* iniziare, cominciare; *of engine, car* partire; *~ing from tomorrow* a partire da domani **3** *v/t* cominciare; *engine, car* mettere in moto; *business* mettere su; *~ to do sth, ~ doing sth* cominciare a fare qc; **starter** *of meal* antipasto *m*; *of car* motorino *m* d'avviamento; *in race* starter *m inv*; **starting point** punto *m* di partenza; **starting salary** stipendio *m* iniziale

startle ['stɑːtl] far trasalire; **startling** sorprendente

'**start-up** COM nuova azienda *f*

starvation [stɑː'veɪʃn] fame *f*; **starve** soffrire la fame; *I'm starving* F sto morendo di fame

state¹ [steɪt] **1** *n of car, house, part of country* stato *m*; **the States** gli Stati Uniti **2** *adj* di stato; *school* statale; *banquet etc* ufficiale

state² [steɪt] *v/t* dichiarare

'State Department Ministero *m* degli Esteri; **statement** *to police* deposizione *f*; *(announcement)* dichiarazione *f*; *(bank ~)* estratto *m* conto; **state of emergency** stato *m* d'emergenza; **state-of-the-art** allo stato dell'arte; **statesman** statista *m*

static (elec'tricity) ['stætɪk] elettricità *f* statica

station ['steɪʃn] **1** *n* stazione *f* **2** *v/t guard etc* disporre; **stationary** fermo

stationery ['steɪʃənərɪ] articoli *mpl* di cancelleria

'station wagon giardiniera *f*

statistical [stə'tɪstɪkl] statistico; **statistically** statisticamente; **statistician** esperto *m*, *-a f* di statistica; **statistics** *science* statistica *f*; *npl figures* statistiche *fpl*

statue ['stætjuː] statua *f*

status ['steɪtəs] posizione *f*; **status symbol** status symbol *m inv*

statute ['stætjuːt] statuto *m*

staunch [stɔːntʃ] leale

stay [steɪ] **1** *n* soggiorno *m* **2** *v/i in a place* stare; *in a condition* restare; **~ in a hotel** stare in albergo; **~ right there!** non ti muovere!

◆ **stay behind** rimanere

◆ **stay up** *(not go to bed)* rimanere alzato

steadily ['stedɪlɪ] *improve etc* costantemente; *look* fisso;

steady 1 *adj voice, hands* fermo; *job, boyfriend* fisso; *beat* regolare; *improvement, decline* costante **2** *adv:* **be going ~** fare coppia fissa; **~ on!** calma! **3** *v/t bookcase etc* rendere saldo

steak [steɪk] bistecca *f*, carne *f* (di manzo)

steal [stiːl] **1** *v/t* rubare **2** *v/i (be a thief)* rubare; **~ in / out** entrare / uscire furtivamente

stealthy ['stelθɪ] furtivo

steam [stiːm] **1** *n* vapore *m* **2** *v/t food* cuocere al vapore; **steamed up** *F angry* furibondo; **steamer** *for cooking* vaporiera *f*

steel [stiːl] **1** *n* acciaio *m* **2** *adj* d'acciaio; **steelworker** operaio *m* di acciaieria

steep¹ [stiːp] *adj hill etc* ripido; F *prices* alto

steep² [stiːp] *v/t (soak)* lasciare a bagno

steer¹ [stɪr] *n animal* manzo *m*

steer² [stɪə(r)] *v/t* manovrare; *person* guidare; *conversation* spostare; **steering** MOT sterzo *m*; **steering wheel** volante *m*

stem¹ [stem] *n of plant, glass* stelo *m*; *of word* radice *f*

stem² [stem] *v/t (block)* arginare

'stem cell cellula *f* staminale

stench [stentʃ] puzzo *m*

stencil ['stensɪl] **1** *n* stencil *m inv* **2** *v/t pattern* disegnare con lo stencil

step [step] **1** *n* (*pace*) passo *m*; (*stair*) gradino *m*; (*measure*) provvedimento *m*; ~ **by** ~ poco a poco **2** *v/i*: ~ **into** / **out of** salire in / scendere da

◆ **step down** *from post* ritirarsi

◆ **step up** (*increase*) aumentare

'stepbrother fratellastro *m*; **stepdaughter** figliastra *f*; **stepfather** patrigno *m*; **stepladder** scala *f* a libretto; **stepmother** matrigna *f*; **stepsister** sorellastra *f*; **stepson** figliastro *m*

stereo ['sterɪəʊ] (*sound system*) stereo *m inv*; **stereotype** stereotipo *m*

sterile ['sterail] sterile; **sterilize** sterilizzare

sterling ['stɜːlɪŋ] FIN sterlina *f*

stern¹ [stɜːn] *adj* severo

stern² [stɜːn] *n* NAUT poppa *f*

sternly ['stɜːnlɪ] severamente

steroids ['sterɔɪdz] anabolizzanti *mpl*

stethoscope ['steθəskəʊp] fonendoscopio *m*

stew [stjuː] spezzatino *m*

steward ['stjuːəd] *on plane, ship* steward *m inv*; *at demonstration, meeting* membro *m* del servizio d'ordine; **stewardess** *on plane, ship* hostess *f inv*

stick¹ [stɪk] *n wood* rametto *m*; (*walking* ~) bastone *m*; **out in the** ~**s** F a casa del diavolo F

stick² [stɪk] **1** *v/t with adhesive* attaccare; *needle, knife* conficcare; F (*put*) mettere **2** *v/i* (*jam*) bloccarsi; (*adhere*) attaccarsi

◆ **stick by** F *person* rimanere al fianco di

◆ **stick to** F (*keep to*) attenersi a; F (*follow*) seguire

◆ **stick up for** F difendere

sticker ['stɪkə(r)] adesivo *m*; **sticking plaster** cerotto *m*; **stick-in-the-mud** F abitudinario *m*, -a *f*; **sticky** appiccicoso; *label* adesivo

stiff [stɪf] **1** *adj brush, cardboard, leather* rigido; *muscle, body* anchilosato; *paste* sodo; *in manner* freddo; *drink, competition* forte; *fine* salato **2** *adv*: **be bored** ~ F essere annoiato a morte F; **stiffness** *of muscles* indoenzimento *m*; *of material* rigidità *f*; *of manner* freddezza *f*

stifle ['staɪfl] *also fig* soffocare; **stifling** soffocante

stigma ['stɪgmə] vergogna *f*

stilettos [stɪ'letəʊz] *npl* (*shoes*) scarpe *fpl* col tacco a spillo

still¹ [stɪl] **1** *adj* (*motionless*) immobile; *without wind* senza vento; *drink* non gas(s)ato **2** *adv*: **keep** / **stand** ~! stai fermo!

still² [stɪl] *adv* (*yet*) ancora; (*nevertheless*) comunque; **she ~ hasn't finished** non ha ancora finito; **~ more** ancora più

'stillborn nato morto; **still life** natura *f* morta

stilted ['stɪltɪd] poco naturale

stimulant ['stɪmjulənt] stimolante *m*; **stimulate** stimolare; **stimulating** stimolante; **stimulation** stimolazione *f*; **stimulus** (*incentive*) stimolo *m*

sting [stɪŋ] **1** *n from bee* puntura *f*; *from jellyfish* pizzico *m* **2** *v/t of bee* pungere; *of jellyfish* pizzicare **3** *v/i of eyes, scratch* bruciare; **stinging** *criticism* pungente

stingy ['stɪndʒɪ] F tirchio F

stink [stɪŋk] **1** *n* (*bad smell*) puzza *f*; F (*fuss*) putiferio *m* F; **kick up a ~** F fare un casino F **2** *v/i* (*smell bad*) puzzare; F (*be very bad*) fare schifo F

stipulate ['stɪpjuleɪt] stabilire; **stipulation** condizione *f*

stir [stɜː(r)] **1** *v/t* mescolare **2** *v/i of sleeping person* muoversi; **stirring** *music, speech* commovente

stitch [stɪtʃ] **1** *n in sewing* punto *m*; *in knitting* maglia *f*; **~es** MED punti *mpl* (di sutura); **be in ~es** *laughing* ridere a crepapelle **2** *v/t sew* cucire; **stitching** (*stitches*) cucitura *f*

stock [stɒk] **1** *n* (*reserves*) provvista *f*; COM *of store* stock *m inv*; *animals* bestiame *m*; FIN titoli *mpl*; *for soup etc* brodo *m*; **in ~** / **out of ~** disponibile / esaurito; **take ~** fare il punto **2** *v/t* COM vendere; **stockbroker** agente *m/f* di cambio; **stock exchange** borsa *f* valori; **stockholder** azionista *m/f*; **stockist** rivenditore *m*; **stock market** mercato *m* azionario; **stockpile 1** *n of food, weapons* scorta *f* **2** *v/t* fare scorta di

stocky ['stɒkɪ] tarchiato

stodgy ['stɒdʒɪ] *food* pesante

stoical ['stəʊɪkl] stoico; **stoicism** stoicismo *m*

stomach ['stʌmək] **1** *n* stomaco *m*; (*abdomen*) pancia *f* **2** *v/t* (*tolerate*) sopportare; **stomach-ache** mal *m* di stomaco

stone [stəʊn] pietra *f*; (*pebble*) sasso *m*; *in fruit* nocciolo *m*; **stoned** F *on drugs* fatto F; **stone-deaf** sordo (come una campana)

stool [stuːl] *seat* sgabello *m*

stoop¹ [stuːp] *v/i* (*bend down*) chinarsi; (*have back*) essere curvo

stoop² [stuːp] *n Am* (*porch*) porticato *m*

stop [stɒp] **1** *n for train, bus* fermata *f*; **put a ~ to** mettere fine a **2** *v/t* (*put an end to*) mettere fine a; (*prevent*) fermare; (*cease*) smettere; *per-*

son, car, bus fermare; *cheque* bloccare; ◆ **doing sth** smettere di fare qc **3** v/i (*come to a halt*) fermarsi; *of rain, noise* smettere

◆ **stop over** fare sosta

'**stopgap** *person* tappabuchi m/f inv; *thing* soluzione f temporanea; **stoplight** (*traffic light*) rosso m; (*brake light*) fanalino m d'arresto; **stopover** sosta f; *in air travel* scalo m intermedio; **stopper** tappo m; **stop sign** (segnale m di) stop m inv; **stopwatch** cronometro m

storage ['stɔːrɪdʒ]: **put sth in ~** mettere qc in magazzino; **store 1** n *large shop* negozio m; (*stock*) riserva f; (*storehouse*) deposito m **2** v/t tenere; COMPUT memorizzare; **storekeeper** Am negoziante m/f; **store window** Am vetrina f

storey ['stɔːrɪ] *of building* piano m

storm [stɔːm] tempesta f; **stormy** tempestoso

story¹ ['stɔːrɪ] (*tale*) racconto m; (*account*) storia f; (*newspaper article*) articolo m; F (*lie*) bugia f

story² ['stɔːrɪ] *of building* piano m

stout [staut] *person* robusto

stove [stəuv] *for cooking* cucina f; *for heating* stufa f

stow [stəu] riporre

◆ **stow away** imbarcarsi clandestinamente

'**stowaway** passeggero m, -a f clandestino, -a

straight [streɪt] **1** adj *line* retto; *hair, whisky* liscio; *back, knees* dritto; (*honest, direct*) onesto; (*tidy*) in ordine; (*conservative*) convenzionale; (*not homosexual*) etero; **keep a ~ face** non ridere **2** adv dritto; *think* con chiarezza; **go ~** F *of criminal* rigare dritto; **give it to me ~** F dimmi francamente; **~ ahead** avanti dritto; **carry ~ on** proseguire dritto; **~away, ~ off** immediatamente; **~ out** *say sth* chiaro e tondo; **straighten** raddrizzare; **straightforward** (*honest, direct*) franco; (*simple*) semplice

strain¹ [streɪn] **1** n *physical* sforzo m; *mental* tensione f **2** v/t (*injure*) affaticare; *finances*, gravare su

strain² [streɪn] v/t *vegetables* scolare; *oil, fat etc* filtrare

strained [streɪnd] *teso*; **strainer** *for vegetables etc* colino m

strait [streɪt] GEOG stretto m; **straitlaced** puritano

strand [strænd] piantare in asso F; **be ~ed** essere bloccato

strange [streɪndʒ] (*odd, curious*) strano; (*unknown, foreign*) sconosciuto; **strangely** (*oddly*) stranamente; **~ enough** strano ma vero;

stranger *person you don't know* sconosciuto *m*, -a *f*; **I'm a ~ here myself** non sono di queste parti

strangle ['stræŋgl] strangolare

strap [stræp] *of bag* tracolla *f*; *of bra, dress* bretellina *f*, spallina *f*; *of watch* cinturino *m*; *of shoe* listino *m*; **strapless** senza spalline

strategic [strə'tiːdʒɪk] strategico; **strategy** ['strætədʒi] strategia *f*

straw [strɔː] *of bag* tracolla *f*; *for drink* cannuccia *f*; **strawberry** fragola *f*

stray [streɪ] **1** *adj animal* randagio; *bullet* vagante **2** *n dog, cat* randagio *m* **3** *v/i of animal* smarrirsi; *of child* allontanarsi; *fig: of eyes, thoughts* vagare

streak [striːk] **1** *n of dirt, paint* striscia *f*; *in hair* mèche *f*; *fig: of nastiness etc* vena *f* **2** *v/i move quickly* sfrecciare

stream [striːm] **1** *n* ruscello *m*; *fig: of people, complaints* fiume *m*; **come on ~** *of plant* entrare in attività; *of oil* arrivare **2** *v/i* riversarsi; **streamline** *fig* snellire; **streamlined** *car, plane* aerodinamico; *organization* snellito

street [striːt] strada *f*; **in address** via *f*; **streetcar** *Am* tram *m inv*; **streetlight** lampione *m*; **street value** *of drugs* valore *m* di mercato; **streetwise** scafato F

strength [streŋθ] forza *f*; *(strong point)* punto *m* forte; **strengthen** **1** *v/t* rinforzare **2** *v/i* consolidarsi

strenuous ['strenjʊəs] faticoso; **strenuously** *deny* recisamente

stress [stres] **1** *n (emphasis)* accento *m*; *(tension)* stress *m inv* **2** *v/t syllable* accentare; *importance etc* sottolineare; **stressed out** stressato; **stressful** stressante

stretch [stretʃ] **1** *n of land, water* tratto *m*; **at a ~** *(non-stop)* di fila **2** *adj fabric* elasticizzato **3** *v/t material* tendere; *small income* far bastare; **~ the rules** F fare uno strappo (alla regola); **he ~ed out his hand** allungò la mano **4** *v/i to relax muscles* stirarsi; *to reach sth* allungarsi; *(spread)* estendersi; **stretcher** barella *f*

strict [strikt] *person* severo; *instructions* tassativo; **strictly**: **be brought up ~** ricevere un'educazione rigida; **it is ~ forbidden** è severamente proibito

stride [straɪd] **1** *n* falcata *f*; **take sth in one's ~** affrontare qc senza drammi; **make great ~s** *fig* far passi da gigante **2** *v/i* procedere a grandi passi; **he strode up to me** avanzò verso di me

strident ['straɪdnt] stridulo; *demands* veemente

strike [straɪk] **1** *n of workers* sciopero *m*; *of oil* scoperta *f*; **be on** ~ essere in sciopero **2** *v/i of workers* scioperare; *(attack)* aggredire; *of disaster* colpire; *of clock* suonare **3** *v/t (hit)* colpire; *match* accendere *(sfregando)*; *of idea, thought* venire in mente a; *oil* trovare; **she struck me as being ...** mi ha dato l'impressione di essere ...
♦ **strike out** *(delete)* depennare

strikebreaker crumiro *m*, -a *f*; **striker** *person on strike* scioperante *m/f*; *in football* bomber *m inv*, cannoniere *m*; **striking** *(marked)* marcato; *(eye-catching)* impressionante; *(attractive)* attraente; *colour* forte

string [strɪŋ] *(cord)* spago *m*; *of violin, tennis racket* corda *f*; **the** ~**s** MUS gli archi; **a** ~ **of** *(series)* una serie di; **stringed instrument** strumento *m* ad arco

stringent ['strɪndʒənt] rigoroso

strip [strɪp] **1** *n* striscia *f*; *(comic* ~*)* fumetto *m*; *of soccer player* divisa *f* **2** *v/t (remove)* staccare; *bed* disfare; *(undress)* spogliare; ~ **s.o. of sth** spogliare qu di qc **3** *v/i (undress)* spogliarsi; *of stripper* fare lo spogliarello; **strip club** locale *m* di spogliarelli

stripe [straɪp] striscia *f*; MIL gallone *m*; **striped** a strisce

stripper ['strɪpə(r)] spogliarellista *f*; **male** ~ spogliarellista *m*; **striptease** spogliarello *m*

strive [straɪv]: ~ **to do sth** sforzarsi di fare qc; ~ **for sth** lottare per (ottenere) qc

stroke [strəʊk] **1** *n* MED ictus *m inv*; *when painting* pennellata *f*; *style of swimming* stile *m* di nuoto; ~ **of luck** colpo di fortuna **2** *v/t* accarezzare

stroll [strəʊl] **1** *n* passeggiata *f*; **go for a** ~ fare una passeggiata **2** *v/i* fare due passi; **she** ~**ed back to the office** tornò in ufficio in tutta calma; **stroller** Am *for baby* passeggino *m*

strong [strɒŋ] forte; *structure* resistente; *candidate* valido; *taste, smell* intenso; *views, beliefs* fermo; *arguments* convincente; *objections* energico; ~ **support** largo consenso; **strongly** *believe, object* fermamente; *built* solidamente; **feel** ~ **about sth** avere molto a cuore qc; **strong-minded** risoluto; **strong point** (punto *m*) forte *m*; **strongroom** camera *f* blindata; **strong-willed** deciso

structural ['strʌktʃərəl] strutturale; **structure 1** *n something built* costruzione *f*; *of novel, society etc* struttura *f* **2** *v/t* strutturare

struggle ['strʌgl] **1** n (fight) colluttazione f; fig lotta f; (hard time) fatica f **2** v/i with a person lottare; (have a hard time) faticare; **~ to do sth** faticare a fare qc

strut [strʌt] camminare impettito

stub [stʌb] **1** n of cigarette mozzicone m; of cheque, ticket matrice f **2** v/t: **~ one's toe** urtare il dito del piede
♦ **stub out** spegnere

stubble ['stʌbl] on man's face barba f ispida

stubborn ['stʌbən] person testardo; defence, refusal ostinato

stubby ['stʌbɪ] tozzo

stuck [stʌk] F: **be~ on s.o.** essere cotto di qu F; **stuck-up** F presuntuoso

student ['stju:dnt] studente m, -essa f

studio ['stju:dɪəʊ] studio m; (recording **~**) sala f di registrazione

studious ['stju:dɪəs] studioso; **study 1** n studio m **2** v/t & v/i studiare

stuff [stʌf] **1** n roba f **2** v/t turkey farcire; **~ sth into sth** ficcare qc in qc; **stuffing** for turkey farcia f; in chair, teddy bear imbottitura f; **stuffy room** mal ventilato; person inquadrato

stumble ['stʌmbl] inciampare; **stumbling-block** fig scoglio m

stump [stʌmp] **1** n of tree ceppo m **2** v/t of question, questioner sconcertare

stun [stʌn] of blow stordire; of news sbalordire; **stunning** (amazing) sbalorditivo; (very beautiful) splendido

stunt [stʌnt] for publicity trovata f pubblicitaria; in film acrobazia f; **stuntman** in movie cascatore m

stupefy ['stju:pɪfaɪ] sbalordire

stupendous [stju:'pendəs] (marvellous) fantastico; mistake enorme

stupid ['stju:pɪd] stupido; **stupidity** stupidità f

sturdy ['stɜ:dɪ] robusto

stutter ['stʌtə(r)] balbettare

style [staɪl] stile m; (fashion) moda f; (fashionable elegance) classe f; (hair**~**) pettinatura f; **stylish** elegante; **stylist** (hair **~**) parrucchiere m, -a f

subcommittee ['sʌbkəmɪtɪ] sottocommissione f

subconscious [sʌb'kɒnʃəs] subconscio; **the ~ (mind)** il subconscio; **subconsciously** inconsciamente

subcontract [sʌbkən'trækt] subappaltare; **subcontractor** subappaltatore m, -trice f

subdivide [sʌbdɪ'vaɪd] suddividere

subdue [səb'dju:] sottomettere

subheading ['sʌbhediŋ] sottotitolo *m*

subhuman [sʌb'hjuːmən] subumano

subject 1 ['sʌbdʒikt] *n of monarch* suddito *m*, -a *f*; *(topic)* argomento *m*; EDU materia *f*; GRAM soggetto *m*; **change the ~** cambiare argomento **2** ['sʌbdʒikt] *adj*: **be ~ to** essere soggetto a; **~ to availability** nei limiti della disponibilità **3** [səb'dʒekt] *v/t* sottoporre; **subjective** soggettivo

sublet ['sʌblet] subaffittare

subma'chine gun mitra *m*

submarine ['sʌbməriːn] sottomarino *m*, sommergibile *m*

submerge [səb'mɜːdʒ] **1** *v/t* sommergere **2** *v/i of submarine* immergersi

submission [səb'mɪʃn] *(surrender)* sottomissione *f*; *request to committee etc* richiesta *f*; **submissive** sottomesso; **submit 1** *v/t plan, proposal* presentare **2** *v/i* sottomettersi

subordinate [sə'bɔːdɪnət] **1** *adj employee, position* subalterno **2** *n* subalterno *m*, -a *f*

subpoena [sə'piːnə] **1** *n* citazione *f* **2** *v/t person* citare in giudizio

◆ **subscribe to** [səb'skraɪb] *magazine etc* abbonarsi a; *theory* condividere

subscriber [səb'skraɪbə(r)] *to*

magazine abbonato *m*, -a *f*; **subscription** abbonamento *m*

subsequent ['sʌbsɪkwənt] successivo; **subsequently** successivamente

subside [səb'saɪd] *of waters, winds* calare; *of building* sprofondare; *of fears* calmarsi

subsidiary [səb'sɪdɪərɪ] filiale *f*

subsidize ['sʌbsɪdaɪz] sovvenzionare; **subsidy** sovvenzione *f*

substance ['sʌbstəns] sostanza *f*

substandard [sʌb'stændəd] scadente

substantial [səb'stænʃl] considerevole; *meal* sostanzioso; **substantially** *(considerably)* considerevolmente; *(in essence)* sostanzialmente

substantive [səb'stæntɪv] sostanziale

substitute ['sʌbstɪtjuːt] **1** *n for person* sostituto *m*, -a *f*; *for commodity* alternativa *f*; SP riserva *f* **2** *v/t*: **~ X for Y** sostituire Y con X **3** *v/i*: **~ for s.o.** sostituire qu; **substitution** *(act)* sostituzione *f*

subtitle ['sʌbtaɪtl] sottotitolo *m*

subtle ['sʌtl] sottile; *flavour* delicato

subtract [səb'trækt] sottrarre

suburb ['sʌbɜːb] sobborgo *m*; **the ~s** la periferia; **subur-**

ban di periferia

subversive [səb'vɜːsɪv] **1** *adj* sovversivo **2** *n* sovversivo *m*, -a *f*

subway ['sʌbweɪ] *Br* sottopassaggio *m*; *Am* metropolitana *f*

sub'zero: **~ temperatures** temperature sottozero

succeed [sək'siːd] **1** *v/i* avere successo; *to throne* succedere; **~ in doing sth** riuscire a fare qc **2** *v/t* (*come after*) succedere a; **success** successo *m*; **be a ~** avere successo; **successful** *person* affermato; *marriage, party* riuscito; **be ~** riuscire; **he's very ~** è arrivato; **successfully** con successo; **we ~ completed ...** siamo riusciti a portare a termine ...; **successive** successivo; **three ~ days** tre giorni di seguito; **successor** successore *m*

succinct [sək'sɪŋkt] succinto

succumb [sə'kʌm] (*give in*) cedere

such [sʌtʃ] **1** *adj* (*of that kind*) del genere; **~ a** (*so much of a*) un / una tale; **~ as** come; **he made ~ a fuss** ha fatto una tale scenata; **there is no ~ word as ...** la parola ... non esiste **2** *adv* così; **~ nice people** come così simpatica

suck [sʌk] **1** *v/t lollipop ecc* succhiare **2** *v/i*: **it ~s** P fa schifo P

◆ **suck up to** F leccare i pie-

di a F

sucker ['sʌkə(r)] F *person* pollo F; **suction** aspirazione *f*

sudden ['sʌdn] improvviso; **all of a ~** all'improvviso; **suddenly** improvvisamente

sue [suː] **1** *v/t* fare causa a **2** *v/i* fare causa

suede [sweɪd] pelle *f* scamosciata

suffer ['sʌfə(r)] **1** *v/i* (*be in pain*) soffrire; **be ~ing from** avere; **~ from** soffrire di **2** *v/t loss, setback* subire; **suffering** sofferenza *f*

sufficient [sə'fɪʃnt] sufficiente; **sufficiently** abbastanza

suffocate ['sʌfəkeɪt] soffocare; **suffocation** soffocamento *m*

sugar ['ʃʊɡə(r)] **1** *n* zucchero *m* **2** *v/t* zuccherare

suggest [sə'dʒest] proporre, suggerire; **suggestion** proposta *f*, suggerimento *m*

suicide ['suːɪsaɪd] suicidio *m*; **commit ~** suicidarsi; **suicide bomber** kamikaze *m inv*

suit [suːt] **1** *n for man* vestito *m*, completo *m*; *for woman* tailleur *m inv*; *in cards* seme *m* **2** *v/t of clothes, colour* stare bene a; **~ yourself!** F fai come ti pare!; **be ~ed for sth** essere fatto per qc; **suitable** adatto; **suitably** adeguatamente; **suitcase** valigia *f*

suite [swiːt] *of rooms* suite *f inv*; *of furniture* divano *m* e

poltrone *fpl* coordinati; MUS
suite *f inv*

sulk [sʌlk] fare il broncio;
sulky imbronciato

sullen ['sʌlən] crucciato

sultry ['sʌltrɪ] *climate* afoso;
sexually sensuale

sum [sʌm] somma *f*; *in arithmetic* addizione *f*

♦ **sum up 1** *v/t (summarize)*
riassumere; *(assess)* valutare
2 *v/i* LAW riepilogare

summarize ['sʌmǝraɪz] riassumere; **summary** riassunto
m

summer ['sʌmǝ(r)] estate *f*

summit ['sʌmɪt] *of mountain*
vetta *f*; POL summit *m inv*

summon ['sʌmǝn] convocare;
summons LAW citazione *f*

sun [sʌn] sole *m*; **in the ~** al
sole; **out of the ~** all'ombra;
sunbathe prendere il sole;
sunbed lettino *m* solare;
sunblock protezione *f* solare totale; **sunburn** scottatu-
ra *f*; **sunburnt** scottato;
Sunday domenica *f*; **sunglasses** occhiali *mpl* da sole; **sunny** *day* di sole; *spot*
soleggiato; *disposition* allegro; **it's ~** c'è il sole; **sunrise**
alba *f*; **sunset** tramonto *m*;
sunshade ombrellone *m*;
sunshine (luce *f* del) sole
m; **sunstroke** colpo *m* di sole; **suntan** abbronzatura *f*;
get a ~ abbronzarsi

super ['suːpǝ(r)] F fantastico

superb [suˈpɜːb] magnifico

superficial [suːpǝˈfɪʃl] superficiale

superfluous [suˈpɜːfluǝs] superfluo

super'human sovrumano

superintendent [suːpǝrɪn-
ˈtendǝnt] *Br of police* commissario *m*; *Am of apartment
block* custode *m/f*

superior [suːˈpɪǝrɪǝ(r)] **1** *adj*
(better) superiore **2** *n in organization* superiore *m*

superlative [suːˈpɜːlǝtɪv] **1**
adj (superb) eccellente **2** *n*
GRAM superlativo *m*

'supermarket supermarket
m inv, supermercato *m*

super'natural 1 *adj powers*
soprannaturale **2** *n*: **the ~** il
soprannaturale

'superpower POL superpo-
tenza *f*

supersonic [suːpǝˈsɒnɪk] su-
personico

superstition [suːpǝˈstɪʃn] superstizione *f*; **superstitious**
superstizioso

supervise ['suːpǝvaɪz] super-
visionare; **supervisor** *at
work* supervisore *m*

supper ['sʌpǝ(r)] cena *f*

supple ['sʌpl] *person, limbs*
snodato; *material* flessibile

supplement ['sʌplɪmǝnt]
supplemento *m*

supplier [sǝˈplaɪǝ(r)] COM fornitore *m*; **supply 1** *n* fornitura *f*; **~ and demand** doman-
da e offerta; **supplies 2** *v/t goods* fornire;

s.o. *with sth* fornire qc a qu
support [sə'pɔːt] **1** *n for structure* supporto *m*; *(backing)* sostegno *m* **2** *v/t structure*, *(back)* sostenere; *financially* mantenere; *football team* fare il tifo per; **supporter** sostenitore *m*, -trice *f*; *of football team* etc tifoso *m*, -a *f*; **supportive:** *be ~ towards s.o.* dare il proprio appoggio a qu

suppose [sə'pəʊz] *(imagine)* supporre; *it is up to ... (is meant to)* dovrebbe ... ...; *(is said to)* dicono che ...; *you are not ~d to ... (not allowed to)* non dovresti ...; **supposedly** presumibilmente

suppress [sə'pres] reprimere; **suppression** repressione *f*

supremacy [suː'preməsɪ] supremazia *f*; **supreme** supremo; **Supreme Court** Corte *f* Suprema

surcharge ['sɜːtʃɑːdʒ] *for travel* sovrapprezzo *m*; *for mail* soprattassa *f*

sure [ʃʊə(r)] **1** *adj* sicuro; *make ~ that ...* assicurarsi che ... **2** *adv* certamente; *~ enough* infatti; *~!* F certo!; **surely** certamente; *(gladly)* volentieri; *~ that's not right!* non può essere!; **surety** *for loan* cauzione *f*

surf [sɜːf] **1** *n on sea* spuma *f* **2** *v/t the Net* navigare in

surface ['sɜːfɪs] **1** *n* superficie

f; *on the ~ fig* superficialmente **2** *v/i from water* risalire in superficie; *(appear)* farsi vivo; **surface mail** posta *f* ordinaria

'**surfboard** tavola *f* da surf; **surfer** surfista *m/f*; **surfing** surf *m*; *go ~* fare surf

surge [sɜːdʒ] *in electric current* sovratensione *f* transitoria; *in demand* impennata *f*

surgeon ['sɜːdʒən] chirurgo *m*; **surgery** intervento *m* chirurgico; *place of work* ambulatorio *m*; *~ hours* orario *m* d'ambulatorio; **surgical** chirurgico; **surgically** chirurgicamente

surly ['sɜːlɪ] scontroso

surmount [sə'maʊnt] *difficulties* sormontare

surname ['sɜːneɪm] cognome *m*

surpass [sə'pɑːs] superare

surplus ['sɜːpləs] **1** *n surplus m inv* **2** *adj* eccedente

surprise [sə'praɪz] **1** *n* sorpresa *f* **2** *v/t* sorprendere; *be ~d* essere sorpreso; *look ~d* avere l'aria sorpresa; **surprising** sorprendente; **surprisingly** sorprendentemente

surrender [sə'rendə(r)] **1** *v/i of army* arrendersi **2** *v/t weapons etc* consegnare **3** *n* resa *f*

surrogate '**mother** ['sʌrəgət] madre *f* biologica

surround [sə'raʊnd] **1** *v/t* circondare **2** *n of picture etc* bordo *m*; **surrounding** circostante; **surroundings** dintorni *mpl*; *fig* ambiente *m*

survey 1 ['sɜːveɪ] *n of modern literature etc* quadro *m* generale; *of building* perizia *f*; *poll* indagine *f* **2** [sə'veɪ] *v/t* (*look at*) osservare; *building* periziare; **surveyor** perito *m*

survival [sə'vaɪvl] sopravvivenza *f*; **survive 1** *v/i* sopravvivere; *his two surviving daughters* le due figlie ancora in vita **2** *v/t* sopravvivere a; **survivor** superstite *m/f*; *he's a ~ fig* se la cava sempre

suspect 1 ['sʌspekt] *n* indiziato *m*, -a *f* **2** [sə'spekt] *v/t person* sospettare; (*suppose*) supporre; **suspected** *murderer* presunto; *cause, heart attack etc* sospetto

suspend [sə'spend] (*hang*), *from office* sospendere; **suspenders** [sə'spendəz] *fpl Br* giarrettiere *fpl*; *Am for pants* bretelle *fpl*

suspense [sə'spens] suspense *f*; **suspension** MOT, *from duty* sospensione *f*

suspicion [sə'spɪʃn] sospetto *m*; **suspicious** *causing suspicion* sospetto; *feeling suspicion* sospettoso; *be ~ of* sospettare di; **suspiciously** *behave* in modo sospetto; *examine* sospettosamente

sustain [sə'steɪn] sostenere; **sustainable** sostenibile

SUV [esjuː'viː] (= *sports utility vehicle*) Suv *m inv*, gip-pone *m*

swab [swɒb] tampone *m*

swallow[1] ['swɒləʊ] *v/t & v/i* inghiottire

swallow[2] ['swɒləʊ] *n bird* rondine *f*

swamp [swɒmp] **1** *n* palude *f* **2** *v/t*: *be ~ped with* essere sommerso da; **swampy** paludoso

swan [swɒn] cigno *m*

swap [swɒp] **1** *v/t*: *~ sth for sth* scambiare qc con qc **2** *v/i* fare scambio

swarm [swɔːm] **1** *n of bees* sciame *m* **2** *v/i*: *the town was ~ing with ...* la città brulicava di ...

swarthy ['swɔːðɪ] scuro

swat [swɒt] *fly* schiacciare

sway [sweɪ] **1** *n* (*power*) influenza *f* **2** *v/i* barcollare

swear [sweə(r)] **1** *v/i* (*use swearword*) imprecare; *~ at s.o.* dire parolacce a qu **2** *v/t* (*promise*) giurare; LAW, *on oath* giurare

◆ **swear in**: *the witness was sworn in* il testimone ha prestato giuramento

'swearword parolaccia *f*

sweat [swet] **1** *n* sudore *m* **2** *v/i* sudare; **sweat band** fascia *f* asciugasudore; **sweater** maglione *m*; **sweats** *Am* tuta *f* (da ginnastica); **sweatshirt** felpa *f*; **sweaty** *hands* sudato; *smell* di sudore

Swede [swiːd] svedese *m/f*; **Sweden** Svezia *f*; **Swedish**

1 *adj* svedese **2** *n* svedese *m*

sweep [swi:p] **1** *v/t floor, leaves* spazzare **2** *n* (*long curve*) curva *f*; **sweeping changes** radicale; **a ~ state-ment** una generalizzazione

sweet [swi:t] **1** *adj* dolce; F (*kind*) gentile; F (*cute*) carino **2** *n* caramella *f*; (*dessert*) dolce *m*; **sweet and sour** agrodolce; **sweetcorn** mais *m*; **sweeten** zuccherare; **sweet-heart** innamorato *m*, -a *f*

swell [swel] **1** *v/i of wound, limb* gonfiarsi **2** *n of the sea* mare *m* lungo; **swelling** MED gonfiore *m*

sweltering ['sweltərɪŋ] *heat* afoso, soffocante

swerve [swɜːv] *of driver, car* sterzare (bruscamente)

swift [swɪft] rapido

swim [swɪm] **1** *v/i* nuotare **2** *n* nuotata *f*; **go for a ~** andare a nuotare; **swimmer** nuotatore *m*, -trice *f*; **swimming** nuoto *m*; **swimming cos-tume** costume *m* da bagno; **swimming pool** piscina *f*; **swimsuit** *esp Am* costume *m* da bagno

swindle ['swɪndl] **1** *n* truffa *f* **2** *v/t* truffare; **a ~ s.o. out of sth** estorcere qc a qu (con l'inganno)

swing [swɪŋ] **1** *n of pendulum etc* oscillazione *f*; *for child* altalena *f*; **a ~ to the left** una svolta verso la sinistra **2** *v/t* far dondolare **3** *v/i* dondola-

re; (*turn*) girare; *of public opinion etc* indirizzarsi

Swiss [swɪs] **1** *adj* svizzero **2** *n person* svizzero *m*, -a *f*; **the ~** gli svizzeri

switch [swɪtʃ] **1** *n for light* interruttore *m*; (*change*) cambiamento *m* **2** *v/t* (*change*) cambiare **3** *v/i* (*change*) cambiare; **~ to** passare a

◆ **switch off** spegnere

◆ **switch on** accendere

Switzerland ['swɪtsələnd] Svizzera *f*

swivel ['swɪvl] girarsi

swollen ['swəʊlən] gonfio

sword [sɔːd] spada *f*; **sword-fish** pesce *m* spada *inv*

syllable ['sɪləbl] sillaba *f*

syllabus ['sɪləbəs] programma *m*

symbol ['sɪmbl] simbolo *m*; **symbolic** simbolico; **symbolism** simbolismo *m*; **symbolist** simbolista *m/f*; **symbolize** simboleggiare

symmetrical [sɪ'metrɪkl] simmetrico; **symmetry** simmetria *f*

sympathetic [sɪmpə'θetɪk] (*showing pity*) compassionevole; (*understanding*) comprensivo; **be ~ towards an idea** simpatizzare per un'idea

◆ **sympathize with** ['sɪmpə-θaɪz] *person, views* capire

sympathizer ['sɪmpəθaɪzə(r)] POL simpatizzante *m/f*; **sym-pathy** (*pity*) compassione *f*;

(*understanding*) comprensione *f*
symphony ['sɪmfənɪ] sinfonia *f*
symptom ['sɪmptəm] *also fig*
sintomo *m*; **symptomatic:
be ~ of** essere sintomatico di
synchronize ['sɪŋkrənaɪz]
sincronizzare
synonym ['sɪnənɪm] sinonimo *m*; **synonymous** sinonimo
synthesizer ['sɪnθəsaɪzə(r)]
MUS sintetizzatore *m*; **syn-**

thetic sintetico
syphilis ['sɪfɪlɪs] sifilide *f*
Syria ['sɪrɪə] Siria *f*; **Syrian 1**
adj siriano **2** *n* siriano *m*, -a
f
syringe [sɪ'rɪndʒ] siringa *f*
syrup ['sɪrəp] sciroppo *m*
system ['sɪstəm] *also computer* sistema *m*; (*orderliness*) ordine *m*; **systematic** sistema-
tico; **systematically** siste-
maticamente; **systems analyst** COMPUT analista *m*/*f* di
sistemi

T

table ['teɪbl] tavolo *m*; *of figures* tabella *f*, tavola *f*; **tablecloth** tovaglia *f*; **table lamp**
lampada *f* da tavolo; **table
of contents** indice *m*; **tablespoon** cucchiaio *m* da tavola
tablet ['tæblɪt] MED compressa *f*
'**table tennis** tennis *m* da tavolo, ping pong *m*
tabloid ['tæblɔɪd] *newspaper*
quotidiano *m* formato tabloid; *pej* quotidiano *m* scandalistico
taboo [tə'buː] tabù *m inv*
tacit ['tæsɪt] tacito
tack [tæk] **1** *n* (*nail*) chiodino
m **2** *v*/*t* (*sew*) imbastire **3** *v*/*i
of yacht* virare di bordo
tackle ['tækl] **1** *n* (*equipment*)
attrezzatura *f*; SP *in football*,

hockey contrasto *m*; *in rugby*
placcaggio *m* **2** *v*/*t in football,
hockey* contrastare; *in rugby*
placcare; *problem, intruder*
affrontare
tacky ['tækɪ] *paint* fresco; *glue*
appiccicoso; F (*cheap, poor
quality*) di cattivo gusto
tact [tækt] tatto *m*; **tactful**
pieno di tatto; **tactfully** con
grande tatto
tactical ['tæktɪkl] tattico; **tactics** tattica *f*
tactless ['tæktlɪs] privo di
tatto
tadpole ['tædpəʊl] girino *m*
tag [tæg] (*label*) etichetta *f*
tail [teɪl] coda *f*; **tailback** coda
f; **tail light** luce *f* posteriore
tailor ['teɪlə(r)] sarto *m*, -a *f*;
tailor-made *also fig* (fatto)
su misura

'tailpipe tubo *m* di scappamento

take [teɪk] prendere; (*transport*) portare; (*accompany*) accompagnare; (*accept: money, gift*) accettare; (*maths, French, photograph, exam, shower, stroll*) fare; (*endure*) sopportare; (*require*) richiedere; *how long does it ~?* quanto ci vuole?

◆ **take after** aver preso da

◆ **take away** *pain* far sparire; *object* togliere; MATH sottrarre; *take sth away from s.o.* togliere qc a qu; *to take away food* da asporto

◆ **take back** (*return: object*) riportare; (*receive back*) riprendere; *person* riaccompagnare; (*accept back: husband etc*) rimettersi insieme a; *sth said* ritirare; *that takes me back* mi riporta al passato

◆ **take down** *from shelf* tirare giù; *scaffolding* smontare; (*write down*) annotare

◆ **take in** (*take indoors*) portare dentro; (*give accommodation*) ospitare; (*make narrower*) stringere; (*deceive*) imbrogliare; (*include*) includere

◆ **take off 1** *v/t clothes, 10%* togliere; (*mimic*) imitare; *take a day off* prendere un giorno di ferie **2** *v/i of aeroplane* decollare; (*become popular*) far presa

◆ **take on** *job* intraprendere;

staff assumere

◆ **take out** *from bag, pocket* tirare fuori; *stain, appendix, tooth, word* togliere; *money from bank* prelevare; *to dinner etc* portar fuori; *insurance policy* stipulare; fare; *take it out on s.o.* prendersela con qu

◆ **take over 1** *v/t company etc* assumere il controllo di **2** *v/i of new management etc* assumere il controllo; (*do sth in s.o.'s place*) dare il cambio

◆ **take to** (*like*) prendere in simpatia; (*form habit of*) prendere l'abitudine di; *he immediately took to the new idea* la nuova idea gli è piaciuta subito

◆ **take up** *carpet etc* togliere; (*carry up*) portare sopra; *dress etc* accorciare; *judo, Spanish, new job* incominciare; *offer* accettare; *space, time* occupare; *I'll take you up on your offer* accetto la tua offerta

'takeoff *of airplane* decollo *m*; (*impersonation*) imitazione *f*; **takeover** COM rilevamento *m*; **takeover bid** offerta *f* pubblica di acquisto, OPA *f*; **takings** incassi *mpl*

tale [teɪl] storia *f*

talent ['tælənt] talento *m*; **talented** pieno di talento; **talent scout** talent scout *m/f inv*

talk [tɔːk] **1** *v/i* parlare **2** *v/t*

English etc parlare; *business,
politics* parlare di; **~ s.o. into
doing sth** convincere qu a
fare qc **3** (*conversation*)
conversazione *f*; (*lecture*)
conferenza *f*; **~s** (*negotiations*) trattative *fpl*
◆ **talk back** ribattere
talkative ['tɔːkətɪv] loquace;
talk show talk show *m inv*
tall [tɔːl] alto; **tall story** baggianata *f*
tally ['tælɪ] **1** *n* conto *m* **2** *v/i*
quadrare
tame [teɪm] *animal* addomesticato; *joke etc* blando
◆ **tamper with** ['tæmpə(r)]
manomettere
tampon ['tæmpɒn] tampone
m
tan [tæn] **1** *n from sun* abbronzatura *f*; *colour* marrone *m*
rossiccio **2** *v/i in sun* abbronzarsi **3** *v/t leather* conciare
tangent ['tændʒənt] MATH
tangente *f*
tangerine [tændʒə'riːn] tangerino *m*
tangible ['tændʒɪbl] tangibile
tangle ['tæŋgl] nodo *m*
tango ['tæŋgəʊ] tango *m*
tank [tæŋk] recipiente *m*; MOT
serbatoio *m*; MIL carro *m* armato; *for skin diver* bombola
f (d'ossigeno); **tanker** *ship*
nave *f* cisterna; *truck* autocisterna *f*
tanned [tænd] abbronzato
tantalizing ['tæntəlaɪzɪŋ] allettante; *smell* stuzzicante

tantamount ['tæntəmaʊnt]:
be ~ to essere equivalente a
tantrum ['tæntrəm] capricci
mpl; **throw a ~** fare (i) capricci
tap [tæp] **1** *n* rubinetto *m* **2** *v/t*
(*hit*) dare un colpetto a;
phone mettere sotto controllo; **tap dance** *n* tip tap *m*
tape [teɪp] **1** *n magnetic* nastro
m magnetico; *recorded* cassetta *f*; (*sticky*) nastro *m* adesivo; **on ~** registrato **2** *v/t conversation etc* registrare; **~ sth
to sth** attaccare qc a qc col
nastro adesivo; **tape deck**
registratore *m*; **tape drive**
COMPUT unità *f inv* di backup a nastro; **tape measure**
metro *m* a nastro
taper ['teɪpə(r)] assottigliarsi
◆ **tape recorder** registratore *m*
a cassette; **tape recording**
registrazione *f* su cassetta
tar [tɑː(r)] catrame *m*
tardy ['tɑːdɪ] *Am* tardivo; *arrival* in ritardo
target ['tɑːgɪt] **1** *n* bersaglio
m; *for sales etc* obiettivo *m*
2 *v/t market* rivolgersi a; **target audience** target *m inv* di
pubblico; **target date** data *f*
fissata; **target group** COM
gruppo *m* target; **target
market** mercato *m* target
tariff ['tærɪf] (*price*) tariffa *f*;
(*tax*) tassa *f*
tarmac ['tɑːmæk] *at airport* pista *f*
tarnish ['tɑːnɪʃ] *metal* ossida-

re; *reputation* macchiare
tarpaulin [ta:ˈpɔːlɪn] tela *f* cerata
tart [tɑːt] torta *f*
task [tɑːsk] compito *m*; **task force** task force *f inv*
taste [teɪst] **1** *n* gusto *m* **2** *v/t food* assaggiare; *(experience: freedom etc)* provare **3** *v/i: it ~s like ...* ha sapore di ...; *it ~s very nice* è molto buono; **tasteful** di gusto; **tastefully** con gusto; **tasteless** *food* insaporo; *remark, person* privo di gusto; **tasting** *of wine* degustazione *f*; **tasty** gustoso
tattered [ˈtætəd] malridotto
tattoo [təˈtuː] tatuaggio *m*
taunt [tɔːnt] **1** *n* scherno *m* **2** *v/t* schernire
Taurus [ˈtɔːrəs] ASTR Toro *m*
taut [tɔːt] teso
tax [tæks] **1** *n* tassa *f*; *before / after ~* al lordo / al netto di imposte **2** *v/t* tassare; **taxable income** reddito *m* imponibile; **taxation** tassazione *f*; **tax bracket** fascia *f* di reddito; **tax-deductible** deducibile dalle imposte; **tax disc** *for car* bollo *m* (di circolazione); **tax evasion** evasione *f* fiscale; **tax-free** esentasse *inv*; **tax haven** paradiso *m* fiscale
taxi [ˈtæksɪ] taxi *m inv*; **taxi driver** tassista *m/f*
taxing [ˈtæksɪŋ] estenuante
'taxi rank stazione *f* dei taxi

'taxpayer contribuente *m/f*;
tax return *form* dichiarazione *f* dei redditi; **tax year** anno *m* fiscale
TB [tiːˈbiː] (= **tuberculosis**) tbc *f* (= tubercolosi *f*)
tea [tiː] *drink* tè *m inv*; *meal* cena *f*; **teabag** bustina *f* di tè
teach [tiːtʃ] *subject* insegnare; *person* insegnare a; **~ s.o. to do sth** insegnare a qu a fare qc; **teacher** insegnante *m/f*; **teaching** *profession* insegnamento *m*
'tea-cup tazza *f* da tè
teak [tiːk] tek *m*
team [tiːm] *in sport* squadra *f*; *at work* équipe *f inv*; **team mate** compagno *m*, -a *f* di squadra; **team spirit** spirito *m* d'équipe; **teamster** *Am* camionista *m*; **teamwork** lavoro *m* d'équipe
teapot [ˈtiːpɒt] teiera *f*
tear[1] [ter] **1** *n in cloth etc* strappo *m* **2** *v/t paper, cloth* strappare; **be torn between two alternatives** essere combattuto tra due alternative **3** *v/i* *(run fast, drive fast)* sfrecciare

◆ **tear down** *poster* strappare; *building* buttar giù
◆ **tear out** *page* strappare; *hair* strapparsi
◆ **tear up** *paper* distruggere; *agreement* rompere
tear[2] [tɪr] *n in eye* lacrima *f*; **burst into ~s** scoppiare a piangere; **be in ~s** essere in

lacrime
tearful ['tɪrful] *look*, *voice*
piangente; **tear gas** gas *m* lacrimogeno
tease [tiːz] *person* prendere in
giro; *animal* stuzzicare
'**teaspoon** cucchiaino *m* da
caffè
technical ['teknɪkl] tecnico;
technically tecnicamente;
technician tecnico *m*; **technique** tecnica *f*
technological [teknə'lɒdʒɪkl]
tecnologico; **technology**
tecnologia *f*; **technophobia**
tecnofobia *f*
teddy bear ['tedɪbeə(r)] orsacchiotto *m*
tedious ['tiːdɪəs] noioso
tee [tiː] *in golf* tee *m inv*
teenage ['tiːneɪdʒ] *problems*
degli adolescenti; ~ **fashions** moda giovane; **teenager** adolescente *m/f*
teens [tiːnz] adolescenza *f*; **be in one's** ~ essere adolescente
teeny ['tiːnɪ] F piccolissimo
teeth [tiːθ] *pl* ☞ **tooth**
teethe [tiːð] mettere i denti;
teething problems difficoltà *fpl* iniziali
teetotal [tiː'təutl] *person* astemio; *party* senza alcolici
telecommunications [telɪkəmjuːnɪ'keɪʃnz] telecomunicazioni *fpl*
telegraph pole ['telɪɡrɑːpəul] palo *m* del telegrafo
telepathic [telɪ'pæθɪk] telepa-

tico; **telepathy** telepatia *f*
telephone ['telɪfəun] **1** *n* telefono *m* **2** *v/t person* telefonare a **3** *v/i* telefonare; **telephone book** guida *f* telefonica; **telephone booth** cabina *f* telefonica; **telephone call** telefonata *f*; **telephone conversation** conversazione *f* telefonica; **telephone directory** elenco *m* telefonico; **telephone number** numero *m* telefonico
telephoto lens [telɪfəutəu'lenz] teleobiettivo *m*
telesales ['telɪseɪlz] vendita *f* telefonica
telescope ['telɪskəup] telescopio *m*
televise ['telɪvaɪz] trasmettere in televisione
television ['telɪvɪʒn] *also set* televisione *f*; **on** ~ alla televisione; **television programme**, *Am* **television program** programma *m* televisivo; **television studio** studio *m* televisivo
tell [tel] **1** *v/t* dire; *story* raccontare; ~ **s.o. sth** dire qc a qu; ~ **s.o. to do sth** dire a qu di fare qc; **it's hard to** ~ è difficile a dirsi; **you never can** ~ non si può mai dire; ~ **X from Y** distinguere X da Y; **I can't** ~ **the difference between …** non vedo nessuna differenza tra … **2** *v/i* (*have effect*) farsi sentire; **time will** ~ il tempo lo dirà;

teller *in bank* cassiere *m*, -a *f*; **telling off** rimprovero *m*; **give s.o. a ~** rimproverare qu; **telltale 1** *adj signs* rivelatore **2** *n* spione *m*, spiona *f*

temp [temp] **1** *n employee* impiegato *m*, -a interinale **2** *v/i* fare lavori interinali

temper ['tempə(r)] : **have a terrible ~** (*bad ~*) essere irascibile; **be in a ~** essere arrabbiato; **keep one's ~** mantenere la calma; **lose one's ~** perdere le staffe

temperament ['temprəmənt] temperamento *m*; **temperamental** (*moody*) lunatico; *machine* imprevedibile

temperate ['tempərət] temperato

temperature ['temprətʃə(r)] temperatura *f*; (*fever*) febbre *f*

temple[1] ['templ] REL tempio *m*

temple[2] ['templ] ANAT tempia *f*

tempo ['tempəʊ] ritmo *m*; MUS tempo *m*

temporarily [tempə'reərɪlɪ] temporaneamente; **temporary** temporaneo, provvisorio

tempt [tempt] tentare; **temptation** tentazione *f*; **tempting** allettante; *meal* appetitoso

ten [ten] dieci

tenacious [tɪ'neɪʃəs] tenace; **tenacity** tenacità *f*

tenant ['tenənt] inquilino *m*, -a *f*, locatario *m*, -a *f*

tend[1] [tend] *v/t* (*look after*) prendersi cura di

tend[2] [tend] *v/i*: **~ to do sth** tendere a fare qc

tendency ['tendənsɪ] tendenza *f*

tender[1] ['tendə(r)] *adj* (*sore*) sensibile; (*affectionate*) tenero; *steak* tenero

tender[2] ['tendə(r)] *n* COM offerta *f* ufficiale

tenderness ['tendənɪs] (*soreness*) sensibilità *f*; *of kiss, steak* tenerezza *f*

tendon ['tendən] tendine *m*

tennis ['tenɪs] tennis *m*; **tennis ball** palla *f* da tennis; **tennis court** campo *m* da tennis; **tennis player** tennista *m/f*

tenor ['tenə(r)] MUS tenore *m*

tense[1] [tens] *adj* GRAM tempo *m*

tense[2] [tens] *voice, person* teso; *atmosphere* carico di tensione

tension ['tenʃn] tensione *f*

tent [tent] tenda *f*

tentative ['tentətɪv] esitante

tenterhooks ['tentəhʊks]: **be on ~** essere sulle spine

tenth [tenθ] decimo

tepid ['tepɪd] tiepido

term [tɜːm] periodo *m*; *of office* durata *f* in carica; EDU *three months* trimestre *m*; *two months* bimestre *m*; (*condition, word*) termine *m*; **be on good / bad ~s with s.o.** essere in buoni / cattivi rapporti con qu; **in the long / short ~** a lungo / breve termine; **come to ~s with sth** venire a patti con qc

terminal ['tɜ:mɪnl] **1** *n* at airport, for containers, COMPUT terminale *m*; for buses capolinea *m inv*; ELEC morsetto *m* **2** *adj illness* in fase terminale; **terminally:~ ill** malato (in fase) terminale; **terminate 1** *v/t contract, pregnancy* interrompere **2** *v/i* terminare; **termination** of *contract, pregnancy* interruzione *f*

terminology [tɜ:mɪ'nɒlədʒɪ] terminologia *f*

terminus ['tɜ:mɪnəs] for buses capolinea *m inv*; for trains stazione *f* di testa

terrace ['terəs] on hillside, at hotel terrazza *f*; of houses fila *f* di case a schiera

terracotta [terə'kɒtə] di terracotta

terrain [tə'reɪn] terreno *m*

terrestrial [tə'restrɪəl] **1** *n* terrestre *m/f* **2** *adj television* di terra

terrible ['terəbl] terribile; **terribly** *play* malissimo; *(very)* molto

terrific [tə'rɪfɪk] eccezionale; **~!** bene!; **terrifically** *(very)* eccezionalmente

terrify ['terɪfaɪ] terrificare; **terrifying** terrificante

territorial [terɪ'tɔ:rɪəl] territoriale; **territory** also fig territorio *m*

terror ['terə(r)] terrore *m*; **terrorism** terrorismo *m*; **terrorist** terrorista *m/f*; **terrorist attack** attentato *m* terroristico; **terrorize** terrorizzare

terse [tɜ:s] brusco

test [test] **1** *n* prova *f*, test *m inv*; for driving, medical esame *m*; **blood ~** analisi *f inv* del sangue **2** *v/t soup, bathwater* provare; *machine, theory* testare; *person, friendship* mettere alla prova

testament ['testəmənt]: **Old / New Testament** REL Vecchio / Nuovo Testamento

'test-drive: go for a ~ fare un giro di prova

testicle ['testɪkl] testicolo *m*

testify ['testɪfaɪ] LAW testimoniare

testimony ['testɪmənɪ] LAW testimonianza *f*

'test tube provetta *f*

testy ['testɪ] suscettibile

tetanus ['tetənəs] tetano *m*

text [tekst] **1** *n* testo *m*; *(message)* SMS *m inv*, messaggino *m* **2** *v/t* mandare un SMS a; **textbook** libro *m* di testo

textile ['tekstaɪl] tessuto *m*

'text-message SMS *m inv*, messaggino *m*

texture ['tekstʃə(r)] consistenza *f*

Thai [taɪ] **1** *adj* tailandese **2** *n*

person tailandese *m/f*; *language* tailandese *m*; **Thailand** Tailandia *f*

than [ðæn] che; *with numbers, pronouns, names* di; *older ~ me* più vecchio di me; *more French ~ Italian* più francese che italiana

thank [θæŋk] ringraziare; *~ you* grazie; *no ~* you no, grazie; **thankful** riconoscente; **thankfully** con riconoscenza; (*luckily*) fortunatamente; **thankless** ingrato; **thanks** ringraziamenti *mpl*; *~!* grazie!; *~ to* grazie a; **Thanksgiving** (Day) *in USA* giorno *m* del ringraziamento

that [ðæt] **1** *adj* quel; *with masculine nouns before s+consonant, gn, ps and z* quello; *~ one* quello **2** *pron* quello *m*, -a *f*; *what is ~?* cos'è?; *who is ~?* chi è?; *~'s mine* è mio; *~'s tea* quello è tè; *~'s very kind* è molto gentile **3** *relative pron* che; *the car ~ you saw* la macchina che hai visto; *the day ~ he was born* il giorno in cui è nato **4** *adv* (*so*) così; *~ expensive* così caro **5** *conj* che; *I think ~ ...* credo che ...

thaw [θɔː] *of snow* sciogliersi; *of frozen food* scongelare

the [ðiː] il *m*, la *f*; i *mpl*, le *fpl*; *with masculine nouns before s+consonant, gn, ps and z* lo *m*, gli *mpl*; *before vowel* l' *m/f*, gli *mpl*; *to ~ bathroom*

al bagno; *~ sooner ~ better* prima è, meglio è

theatre, *Am* **theater** ['θɪətə(r)] teatro *m*; MED sala *f* operatoria

theatrical [θɪˈætrɪkl] *also fig* teatrale

theft [θeft] furto *m*

their [ðeə(r)] il loro *m*, la loro *f*; i loro *mpl*, le loro *fpl*; (*his or her*) il suo *m*, la sua *f*, i suoi *mpl*, le sue *fpl*; **theirs** il loro *m*, la loro *f*; i loro *mpl*, le loro *fpl*; *it was an idea of ~* è stata una loro idea

them [ðem] *direct object* li *m*, le *f*; *referring to things* essi *m*, esse *f*; *indirect object* loro, gli; *after preposition* loro; *referring to things* essi *m*, esse *f*; (*him or her*) lo *m*, la *f*; *I know ~* li / le conosco; *I sold it to ~* gliel'ho venduto, l'ho venduto a loro

theme [θiːm] tema *m*; **theme park** parco *m* a tema

themselves [ðemˈselvz] si; *emphatic* loro stessi *mpl*, loro stesse *fpl*; *after prep* se stessi / se stesse; *they enjoyed ~* si sono divertiti

then [ðen] (*at that time, deducing*) allora; (*after that*) poi; *by ~* allora

theology [θɪˈɒlədʒɪ] teologia *f*

theoretical [θɪəˈretɪkl] teorico; **theoretically** teoricamente; **theory** teoria *f*

therapeutic [θerəˈpjuːtɪk] terapeutico; **therapist** terapista *m/f*, terapeuta *m/f*; **therapy** terapia *f*

there [ðeə(r)] lì, là; **over ~** là; **down ~** laggiù; **~ is ...** c'è; **~ are ...** ci sono; **is ~ ...?** c'è ...?; **are ~ ...?** ci sono ...?; **isn't ~?** non c'è ...?; **aren't ~?** non ci sono ...?; **~ you are** giving sth ecco qui; *finding sth ecco*; *completing sth* ecco fatto; **~ and back** andata e ritorno; **~ he is!** eccolo!; **~, ~!** *comforting* su, dai!; **thereabouts** giù di lì; **therefore** quindi, pertanto

thermometer [θə'mɒmɪtə(r)] termometro *m*

thermos flask ['θɜːməsflɑːsk] termos *m inv*

thermostat ['θɜːməstæt] termostato *m*

these [ðiːz] **1** *adj* questi **2** *pron* questi *m*, -e *f*

thesis ['θiːsɪs] tesi *f inv*

they [ðeɪ] ◇ loro; **~'re going to the theatre** vanno a teatro; **there ~ are** eccoli *mpl*, eccole *fpl* ◇ **if anyone looks at this, ~ will see that ...** se qualcuno lo guarda, vedrà che ...; **~ say that ...** si dice che ...; **~ are going to change the law** cambieranno la legge

thick [θɪk] spesso; *hair* folto; *fog, forest* fitto; *liquid* denso; F *(stupid)* ottuso; **thicken** *sauce* ispessire; **thick-skinned** *fig* insensibile

thief [θiːf] ladro *m*, -a *f*

thigh [θaɪ] coscia *f*

thin [θɪn] sottile; *person* magro; *hair* rado; *liquid* fluido

thing [θɪŋ] cosa *f*; **~s** *(belongings)* cose *fpl*; **it's a good ~ you told me** è un bene che tu me l'abbia detto

thingumajig ['θɪŋʌmədʒɪg] F coso *m*, cosa *f* F

think [θɪŋk] pensare; **I ~ so** penso *or* credo di sì; **I don't ~ so** non credo; **I'm ~ing about emigrating** sto pensando di emigrare

◆ **think over** riflettere su

◆ **think through** analizzare a fondo

◆ **think up** *plan* escogitare

'think tank comitato *m* di esperti

thin-skinned [θɪn'skɪnd] *fig* sensibile

third [θɜːd] **1** *adj* terzo **2** *n* terzo *m*; **thirdly** in terzo luogo; **third-party** terzi *mpl*; **third-party insurance** assicurazione *f* sulla responsabilità civile; **Third World** Terzo Mondo *m*

thirst [θɜːst] sete *f*; **thirsty** assetato; **be ~** avere sete

thirteen [θɜː'tiːn] tredici; **thirteenth** tredicesimo; **thirtieth** trentesimo; **thirty** trenta

this [ðɪs] **1** *adj* questo (qui) **2** *pron* questo *m*, -a *f*; **~ is easy** è facile; **~ is ...** *introducing s.o.* questo / questa è ... **3** *adv*: **~**

high alto così
thorn [θɔːn] spina *f*;**thorny** *also fig* spinoso
thorough ['θʌrə] *search, knowledge* approfondito; *person* scrupoloso; **thoroughbred** *horse* purosangue *inv*; **thoroughly** *search for* accuratamente; *know, understand, clean* completamente; *agree, spoil* completamente; *stupid, rude* extremamente
those [ðəuz] **1** *adj* quelli; *with masculine nouns before s+consonant, gn, ps and z* quegli **2** *pron* quelli *m*, -e *f*; *with masculine nouns before s+consonant, gn, ps and z* quegli
though [ðəu] **1** *conj* (*although*) benché (+*subj*); **as ~** come se **2** *adv* però
thought [θɔːt] pensiero *m*; **thoughtful** pensieroso; *reply* meditato; (*considerate*) gentile; **thoughtless** sconsiderato
thousand ['θauznd] mille; **~s of** migliaia di; **thousandth** millesimo
thrash [θræʃ] picchiare; *SP* battere
♦ **thrash out** *solution* mettere a punto
thrashing ['θræʃiŋ] botte *fpl*; *SP* batosta *f*
thread [θred] **1** *n* filo *m*; *of screw* filettatura *f* **2** *v/t needle* infilare il filo in; *beads* infila-

re; **threadbare** liso
threat [θret] minaccia *f*; **threaten** minacciare; **threatening** minaccioso; **~ letter** lettera *f* minatoria
three [θriː] tre; **three quarters** tre quarti *mpl*
threshold ['θreʃhəuld] *of house, new era* soglia *f*
thrifty ['θrɪftɪ] parsimonioso
thrill [θrɪl] **1** *n* emozione *f*; *physical feeling* brivido *m* **2** *v/t*: **be ~ed** essere emozionato; **thriller** giallo *m*; **thrilling** emozionante
thrive [θraɪv] *of plant* crescere rigoglioso; *of business* prosperare
throat [θrəut] gola *f*; **have a sore ~** avere mal di gola; **throat lozenge** pastiglia *f* per la gola
throb [θrɒb] pulsare; *of heart* battere; *of music* rimbombare
throne [θrəun] trono *m*
throttle ['θrɒtl] **1** *n on motorbike* manetta *f* di accelerazione; *on boat* leva *f* di accelerazione **2** *v/t* (*strangle*) strozzare
through [θruː] **1** *prep* (*across*) attraverso; (*during*) durante; (*by means of*) tramite; **go ~ the city** attraversare la città; **~ the winter** per tutto l'inverno; **arranged ~ him** organizzato tramite lui **2** *adv*: **wet ~** completamente bagnato **3** *adj*: **be ~ of couple** essersi la-

sciati; *have arrived: of news etc* essere arrivato; **I'm ~ with ...** (*finished with*) ho finito con ...; **I'm ~ with him** ho chiuso con lui; **throughout 1** *prep*: **~ the night** per tutta la notte **2** *adv* (*in all parts*) completamente

throw [θrəʊ] **1** *v/t* lanciare; *into bin etc* gettare; *of horse* disarcionare; (*disconcert*) sconcertare; *party* dare **2** *n* lancio *m*

◆ **throw away** buttare via, gettare

◆ **throw out** *old things* buttare via; *from bar, house etc* buttare fuori; *plan* scartare

◆ **throw up 1** *v/t ball* lanciare **2** *v/i* (*vomit*) vomitare

'throw-away *remark* buttato lì; (*disposable*) usa e getta *inv*; **throw-in** *n* rimessa *f*

thru [θruː] *Am* ☞ **through**

thrust [θrʌst] *v/t* (*push hard*) spingere; *knife* conficcare; **~ one's way through the crowd** farsi largo tra la folla

thud [θʌd] *n* tonfo *m*

thug [θʌɡ] *hooligan* teppista *m*; *tough guy* bullo *m*

thumb [θʌm] **1** *n* pollice *m* **2** *v/t*: **~ a lift** fare l'autostop; **thumbtack** *Am* puntina *f*

thunder ['θʌndə(r)] *n* tuono *m*; **thunderous** *applause* fragoroso; **thunderstorm** temporale *m*; **thunderstruck** allibito; **thundery** *weather* temporalesco

Thursday ['θɜːzdeɪ] giovedì *m inv*

thus [ðʌs] (*in this way*) così

thwart [θwɔːt] *person, plans* ostacolare

Tiber ['taɪbə(r)] Tevere *m*

tick [tɪk] **1** *n of clock* ticchettio *m*; *in text* segno *m* **2** *v/i of clock* ticchettare **3** *v/t with a ~* segnare

ticket ['tɪkɪt] biglietto *m*; *in cloakroom* scontrino *m*; **ticket machine** distributore *m* di biglietti; **ticket office** biglietteria *f*

ticking ['tɪkɪŋ] *noise* ticchettio *m*

tickle ['tɪkl] **1** *v/t person* fare il solletico a **2** *v/i of material* dare prurito; *of person* fare il solletico

tidal wave ['taɪdlweɪv] onda *f* di marea

tide [taɪd] marea *f*; **the ~ is in / out** c'è l'alta / la bassa marea

tidiness ['taɪdɪnɪs] ordine *m*; **tidy** ordinato

◆ **tidy up 1** *v/t room, shelves* mettere in ordine; **tidy o.s. up** darsi una sistemata **2** *v/i* mettere in ordine

tie [taɪ] **1** *n* (*necktie*) cravatta *f*; (*SP: even result*) pareggio *m*; **he doesn't have any ~s** non ha legami **2** *v/t knot, hands* legare **3** *v/i SP* pareggiare

◆ **tie down** *with rope* legare; (*restrict*) vincolare

◆ **tie up** *person, laces, hair* legare; *boat* ormeggiare; **I'm tied up tomorrow** sono impegnato domani

tier [tɪə(r)] *of hierarchy* livello *m*; *in stadium* anello *m*

tiger ['taɪgə(r)] tigre *f*

tight [taɪt] **1** *adj clothes* stretto; *security* rigido; *rope* teso; *not leaving much time* giusto; *schedule* serrato; F (*drunk*) sbronzo F **2** *adv*: **hold s.o. / sth ~** tenere qu / qc stretto; **shut sth ~** chiudere bene qc; **tighten** *screw* serrare; *belt* stringere; *rope* tendere; *security* intensificare; **tight-fisted** ☞ **tightly** ☞ **tight** *adv*; **tightrope** fune *f* (per funamboli); **tights** collant *mpl*

tile [taɪl] *on floor* mattonella *f*; *on wall* piastrella *f*; *on roof* tegola *f*

till[1] [tɪl] ☞ **until**

till[2] [tɪl] (*cash register*) cassa *f*

tilt [tɪlt] **1** *v/t* inclinare **2** *v/i* inclinarsi

timber ['tɪmbə(r)] legname *m*

time [taɪm] tempo *m*; *by the clock* ora *f*; (*occasion*) volta *f*; **for the ~** being al momento; **have a good ~!** divertiti!; **what's the ~?** che ora è?, che ore sono?; **the first ~** la prima volta; **take your ~** fai con calma; **for a ~** per un po'(di tempo); **at any ~** in qualsiasi momento; (**and**) **about ~!** era ora!;

two at a ~ due alla volta; **at the same ~** *speak, reply etc* contemporaneamente; (*however*) nel contempo; **in ~** in tempo; (*eventually*) col tempo; **on ~** in orario; **in no ~** in un attimo; **time bomb** bomba *f* a orologeria; **time difference** fuso *m* orario; **time-lag** scarto *m* di tempo; **time limit** limite *m* temporale; **timely** tempestivo; **time out** SP time-out *m inv*; **timer** cronometro *m*; *on oven* timer *m inv*; **time-saving** risparmio *m* di tempo; **timescale** *of project* cronologia *f*; **time share** (*house, apartment*) multiproprietà *f inv*; **time switch** interruttore *m* a tempo; **timetable** orario *m*; **timewarp** trasposizione *f* temporale; **time zone** zona *f* di fuso orario

timid ['tɪmɪd] timido

tin [tɪn] *metal* stagno *m*; *container* barattolo *m*; **tinfoil** carta *f* stagnola

tinge [tɪndʒ] sfumatura *f*

tingle ['tɪŋgl] pizzicare

tinkle ['tɪŋkl] *of bell* tintinnio *m*

'tin opener apriscatole *m inv*

tinsel ['tɪnsl] fili *mpl* d'argento

tint [tɪnt] **1** *n of colour* sfumatura *f*; *in hair* riflessante *m* **2** *v/t hair* fare dei riflessi a; **tinted** *glasses* fumé *inv*

tiny ['taɪnɪ] piccolissimo

tip¹ [tɪp] *n of stick, finger* punta *f; of cigarette* filtro *m*

tip² [tɪp] **1** *n advice* consiglio *m; money* mancia *f* **2** *v/t waiter etc* dare la mancia a

♦ **tip off** fare una soffiata a

'tip-off soffiata *f*

tipped [tɪpt] *cigarettes* col filtro

Tipp-Ex® ['tɪpeks] bianchetto *m*

tippy-toe ['tɪpɪtəʊ] *Am:* **on** ~ sulla punta dei piedi

tipsy ['tɪpsɪ] alticcio

'tip-toe: on ~ sulla punta dei piedi

tire¹ [taɪr] *n Am* gomma *f*, pneumatico *m*

tire² [taɪr] **1** *v/t* stancare **2** *v/i* stancarsi

tired [taɪəd] stanco; **be** ~ **of s.o. / sth** essere stanco di qu / sth; **tiredness** stanchezza *f*; **tireless** instancabile; **tiresome** *(annoying)* fastidioso; **tiring** stancante

tissue ['tɪʃuː] ANAT tessuto *m*; *(handkerchief)* fazzolettino *m* (di carta); **tissue paper** carta *f* velina

title ['taɪtl] titolo *m*; LAW diritto *m*; **titleholder** SP detentore *m*, -trice *f* del titolo

to [tuː] **1** *prep* a; ~ *Italy* in Italia; ~ *Rome* a Roma; *let's go* ~ *my place* andiamo a casa mia; ~ *the north of* … a nord di …; *give sth* ~ *s.o.* dare qc a qu; *from 10* ~ *15 people* tra 10 e 15 persone; *it's 5* ~ *11*

sono le undici meno cinque **2** *with verbs:* ~ *speak*, ~ *see* parlare, vedere; *learn* ~ *drive* imparare a guidare; *nice* ~ *eat* buono da mangiare; ~ *learn Italian in order to* per imparare l'italiano **3** *adv:* ~ *and fro* avanti e indietro

toast [təʊst] **1** *n* pane *m* tostato; *(drinking)* brindisi *m inv* **2** *v/t bread* tostare; *drinking* fare un brindisi a; **toaster** tostapane *m inv*

tobacco [tə'bækəʊ] tabacco *m*

today [tə'deɪ] oggi

toddler ['tɒdlə(r)] bambino *m*, -a *f* ai primi passi

to-'do F casino *m* F

toe [təʊ] dito *m* del piede; *of shoes, socks* punta *f*; **big** ~ alluce *m*; **toenail** unghia *f* del piede

toffee ['tɒfɪ] caramella *f* al mou

together [tə'geðə(r)] insieme

toilet ['tɔɪlɪt] gabinetto *m*; **go to the** ~ andare in bagno; **toilet paper** carta *f* igienica; **toiletries** prodotti *mpl* da toilette

token ['təʊkən] *(sign)* pegno *m*; *for gambling* gettone *m*; *(gift* ~) buono *m*

tolerable ['tɒlərəbl] *pain etc* tollerabile; *(quite good)* accettabile; **tolerance** tolleranza *f*; **tolerant** tollerante; **tolerate** tollerare

toll¹ [təʊl] v/i of bell suonare

toll² [təʊl] n (deaths) bilancio m delle vittime

toll³ [təʊl] n for bridge, road pedaggio m

'**toll booth** casello m; **toll-free number** Am TELEC numero m verde; **toll road** strada f a pedaggio

tomato [təˈmɑːtəʊ] pomodoro m; **tomato ketchup** ketchup m inv; **tomato sauce** for pasta etc salsa f or sugo m di pomodoro; (ketchup) ketchup m inv

tomb [tuːm] tomba f; **tombstone** lapide f

tomcat [ˈtɒmkæt] gatto m (maschio)

tomorrow [təˈmɒrəʊ] domani; **the day after ~** dopodomani; **~ morning** domattina, domani mattina

ton [tʌn] tonnellata f (Br 1016kg, Am 907kg)

tone [təʊn] of colour, musical instrument tonalità f inv; of conversation etc tono m; of neighbourhood livello m sociale; **~ of voice** tono di voce; **toner** toner m inv

tongue [tʌŋ] lingua f

tonic [ˈtɒnɪk] MED ricostituente m; **tonic (water)** acqua f tonica

tonight [təˈnaɪt] stanotte; (this evening) stasera

tonsillitis [tɒnsɪˈlaɪtɪs] tonsillite f

too [tuː] (also) anche; (excessively) troppo; **me ~** anch'io; **~ much rice** troppo riso; **~ many mistakes** troppi errori; **eat ~ much** mangiare troppo

tool [tuːl] attrezzo m; fig strumento m

tooth [tuːθ] (pl **teeth** [tiːθ]) dente m; **toothache** mal m di denti; **toothbrush** spazzolino m da denti; **toothpaste** dentifricio m; **toothpick** stuzzicadenti m inv

top [tɒp] 1 n of mountain, tree cima f, of wall, screen parte f alta; of page, list, street inizio m; (lid: of bottle etc, pen) tappo m; of the class, league testa f; (clothing) maglia f; (MOT: gear) marcia f più alta; **on ~ of** in cima a; **at the ~ of** list, tree, mountain in cima a; league in testa a; page, street all'inizio di; **get to the ~** of company etc arrivare in cima; **get to the ~** of mountain arrivare alla vetta; **be over the ~** (exaggerated) essere esagerato 2 adj branches più alto; floor ultimo; management di alto livello; official di alto rango; player migliore; speed, note massimo

topic [ˈtɒpɪk] argomento m; **topical** attuale

topless [ˈtɒplɪs] topless inv; **topmost** branches, floor più alto; **topping** on pizza guarnizione f

topple [ˈtɒpl] 1 v/i crollare 2

v/t government far cadere

top 'secret top secret *inv*

topsy-turvy [ˈtɒpsɪˈtɜːvɪ] sottosopra *inv*

torch [tɔːtʃ] pila *f*; *with flame* torcia *f*

torment 1 [ˈtɔːment] *n* tormento *m* **2** [tɔːˈment] *v/t* tormentare

tornado [tɔːˈneɪdəʊ] tornado *m*

torpedo [tɔːˈpiːdəʊ] **1** *n* siluro *m* **2** *v/t* silurare; *fig* far saltare

torrent [ˈtɒrənt] torrente *m*; *of lava* fiume *m*; *of abuse, words* valanga *f*; **torrential rain** torrenziale

tortoise [ˈtɔːtəs] tartaruga *f*

torture [ˈtɔːtʃə(r)] **1** *n* tortura *f* **2** *v/t* torturare

toss [tɒs] **1** *v/t ball* lanciare; *rider* disarcionare; *salad* mescolare; **~ a coin** fare testa o croce **2** *v/i*: **~ and turn** rigirarsi

total [ˈtəʊtl] **1** *n* totale *m* **2** *adj amount, disaster* totale; *stranger* perfetto; **totalitarian** totalitario; **totally** totalmente, completamente

totter [ˈtɒtə(r)] barcollare

touch [tʌtʃ] **1** *n* tocco *m*; *sense* tatto *m*; *in rugby* touche *f*; **lose one's ~** perdere la mano; **kick the ball into ~** calciare la palla fuoricampo; **lose ~ with s.o.** perdere i contatti con qu; **keep in ~ with s.o.** rimanere in contatto con qu; **be out of ~ with**

news non essere al corrente; *with people* non avere contatti **2** *v/t* toccare; *emotionally* commuovere **3** *v/i* toccare; *of two lines etc* toccarsi

◆ **touch down** *of plane* atterrare; SP fare meta

'touchdown *of plane* atterraggio *m*; *touching* commovente; **touchline** SP linea *f* laterale; **touch screen** schermo *m* tattile; **touchy** *person* suscettibile

tough [tʌf] *person* forte; *question, exam, meat, punishment* duro; *material* resistente

tour [tʊə(r)] **1** *n* giro *m*; *of tourist* giro *m* turistico; *of band* tournée *f inv* **2** *v/t area* girare **3** *v/i of tourist* andare in giro; *of band* andare in tournée; **tour guide** guida *f* turistica; **tourism** turismo *m*; **tourist** turista *m/f*; **tourist industry** industria *f* del turismo; **tourist (information) office** ufficio *m* informazioni turistiche

tournament [ˈtʊənəmənt] torneo *m*

'tour operator operatore *m* turistico

tow [təʊ] rimorchiare

◆ **tow away** *car* portare via col carro attrezzi

toward(s) [təˈrɔːd(z)] verso; **rude ~** maleducato nei confronti di; **work ~ (achieving) sth** lavorare per (raggiungere) qc

towel ['tauəl] asciugamano *m*

tower ['tauə(r)] torre *f*; **tower block** condominio *m* a torre

town [taun] città *f inv*; *opposed to city* cittadina *f*; **town centre**, *Am* **town center** centro *m*; **town council** consiglio *m* comunale; **town hall** municipio *m*

toxic ['tɒksɪk] tossico; **toxin** tossina *f*

toy [tɔɪ] giocattolo *m*

trace [treɪs] **1** *n of substance* traccia **2** *v/t (find)* rintracciare; *(draw)* tracciare

track [træk] *(path)* sentiero *m*; *on race course* pista *f*; *(race course)* circuito *m*; RAIL binario *m*; *on CD* brano *m*; **keep ~ of sth** tenersi al passo con qc

◆ **track down** rintracciare

'tracksuit tuta *f* (da ginnastica)

tractor ['træktə(r)] trattore *m*

trade [treɪd] **1** *n* commercio *m*; *(profession, craft)* mestiere *m* **2** *v/i (do business)* essere in attività; **~ in sth** commerciare in qc **3** *v/t (exchange)* scambiare (**for** con); **trade fair** fiera *f* campionaria; **trademark** marchio *m* registrato; **trader** commerciante *m/f*; **trade union** sindacato *m*

tradition [trə'dɪʃn] tradizione *f*; **traditional** tradizionale; **traditionally** tradizionalmente

traffic ['træfɪk] *on roads, in drugs* traffico *m*

◆ **traffic in** *drugs* trafficare

'traffic circle *Am* rotatoria *f*; **traffic cop** *F* vigile *m* (urbano); **traffic jam** ingorgo *m*; **traffic island** isola *f* spartitraffico; **traffic light(s)** semaforo *m*; **traffic police** polizia *f* stradale; **traffic sign** segnale *m* stradale; **traffic warden** ausiliario *m* (del traffico)

tragedy ['trædʒədɪ] tragedia *f*; **tragic** tragico

trail [treɪl] **1** *n (path)* sentiero *m*; *of person, animal* tracce *fpl*; *of blood* scia *f* **2** *v/t (follow)* seguire; *(drag)* trascinare; *caravan etc* trainare **3** *v/i (lag behind)* trascinarsi; **they're ~ing 3-1** stanno perdendo 3 a 1; **trailer** *pulled by vehicle* rimorchio *m*; *of film* trailer *m inv*; *(mobile home)* roulotte *f inv*

train[1] [treɪn] *n* treno *m*; **go by ~** andare in treno

train[2] [treɪn] **1** *v/t team, athlete* allenare; *employee* formare; *dog* addestrare **2** *v/i of team, athlete* allenarsi; *of teacher etc* fare il tirocinio

trainee [treɪ'niː] apprendista *m/f*; **trainer** SP allenatore *m*, -trice *f*; *of dog* addestratore *m*, -trice *f*; **~ shoes** scarpe *fpl* da ginnastica; **trainers** *shoes* scarpe *fpl* da ginnastica; **training** *of new staff* formazione f; SP allenamento m; **be in** ~ SP allenarsi; **be out of** ~ SP essere fuori allenamento

'train station stazione f ferroviaria

traitor ['treɪtə(r)] traditore m, -trice f

tram [træm] tram m inv

tramp [træmp] barbone m, -a f

♦ **trample on** calpestare

trampoline ['træmpəliːn] trampolino m

tranquil ['træŋkwɪl] tranquillo; **tranquillity**, Am **tranquility** tranquillità f; **tranquilizer**, Am **tranquillizer** tranquillante m

transaction [træn'zækʃn] transazione f

transatlantic [trænzət'læntɪk] transatlantico

transcript ['trænskrɪpt] trascrizione f

transfer 1 [træns'fɜː(r)] v/t trasferire; LAW cedere 2 [træns'fɜː(r)] v/i cambiare 3 ['trænsfɜː(r)] n trasferimento m; LAW cessione f; of money bonifico m bancario; **transferable** ticket trasferibile; **transfer fee** for football player prezzo m d'acquisto

transform [træns'fɔːm] trasformare; **transformation** trasformazione f; **transformer** ELEC trasformatore m

transfusion [træns'fjuːʒn] trasfusione f

transit ['trænzɪt]: **in** ~ in transito; **transition** transizione f; **transitional** di transizione; **transit lounge** at airport sala f passeggeri in transito; **transit passenger** passeggero m, -a f in transito

translate [træns'leɪt] tradurre; **translation** traduzione f; **translator** traduttore m, -trice f

transmission [trænz'mɪʃn] trasmissione f; **transmit** news, programme, disease trasmettere; **transmitter** RAD, TV trasmettitore m

transparency [træns'pærənsɪ] PHOT diapositiva f; **transparent** trasparente

transplant 1 [træns'plɑːnt] v/t MED trapiantare 2 ['trænsplɑːnt] n MED trapianto m

transport 1 [træn'spɔːt] v/t trasportare 2 ['trænspɔːt] n of trasporto m; means of transport mezzo m di trasporto; **public** ~ i trasporti pubblici; **transportation** trasporto m

transvestite [træns'vestaɪt] travestito m

trap [træp] 1 n trappola f; question tranello m 2 v/t intrappolare; **trappings** of power segni mpl esteriori

trash [træʃ] poor product robaccia *f*; *despicable person* fetente *m/f*; *Am* (*garbage*) spazzatura *f*; **trashcan** *Am* bidone *m* della spazzatura; **trashy** *goods, novel* scadente

trauma ['trɔːmə] trauma *m*; **traumatic** traumatico; **traumatize** traumatizzare

travel ['trævl] **1** *n* viaggiare *m*; *~s* viaggi *mpl* **2** *v/i* viaggiare; *I ~ to work by train* vado a lavorare in treno **3** *v/t miles* percorrere; **travel agency** agenzia *f* di viaggio; **travel agent** agente *m/f* di viaggio; **traveller**, *Am* **traveler** viaggiatore *m*, -trice *f*; **traveller's cheque**, *Am* **traveler's check** traveller's cheque *m inv*; **travel expenses** spese *fpl* di viaggio; **travel insurance** assicurazione *f* di viaggio

trawler ['trɔːlə(r)] pescherecci o *m*

tray [treɪ] *for food, photocopier* vassoio *m*; *to go in oven* teglia *f*

treacherous ['tretʃərəs] traditore; **treachery** tradimento *m*

tread [tred] **1** *n* passo *m*; *of staircase* gradino *m*; *of tyre* battistrada *m inv* **2** *v/i* camminare

treason ['triːzn] tradimento *m*

treasure ['treʒə(r)] **1** *n also person* tesoro *m* **2** *v/t gift etc* custodire gelosamente;

treasurer tesoriere *m*, -a *f*; **Treasury Department** *Am* tesoro *m*

treat [triːt] **1** *n* trattamento *m* speciale; *it's my ~* (*I'm paying*) offro io **2** *v/t* trattare; *illness* curare; *~ s.o. to sth* offrire qc a qu; **treatment** trattamento *m*; *of illness* cura *f*

treaty ['triːtɪ] trattato *m*

treble ['trebl] **1** *adv*: *~ the price* il triplo del prezzo **2** *v/i* triplicarsi

tree [triː] albero *m*

tremble ['trembl] tremare

tremendous [trɪ'mendəs] (*very good*) fantastico; (*enormous*) enorme; **tremendously** (*very*) incredibilmente; (*a lot*) moltissimo

tremor ['tremə(r)] *of earth* scossa *f*

trench [trentʃ] trincea *f*

trend [trend] tendenza *f*; **trendy** alla moda

trespass ['trespəs] invadere una proprietà privata; *no ~ing* divieto d'accesso; **trespasser** intruso *m*, -a *f*

trial ['traɪəl] LAW processo *m*; *of equipment* prova *f*; *on ~* LAW sotto processo; *stand ~ for sth* essere processato per qc; *have sth on ~ equipment* avere qc in prova; **trial period** periodo *m* di prova

triangle ['traɪæŋgl] triangolo *m*; **triangular** triangolare

tribe [traɪb] tribù *f inv*

tribunal [traɪ'bjuːnl] tribunale *m*

tributary ['trɪbjʊtərɪ] *of river* affluente *m*

trick [trɪk] **1** *n to deceive* stratagemma *m*; *(knack)* trucco *m*; **play a ~ on s.o.** fare uno scherzo a qu **2** *v/t* ingannare; **trickery** truffa *f*

trickle ['trɪkl] **1** *n* filo *m*; **a ~ of replies** poche risposte sporadiche **2** *v/i* gocciolare

tricky ['trɪkɪ] *(difficult)* complicato

trifle ['traɪfl] *n (triviality)* inezia *f*; *pudding* zuppa *f* inglese; **trifling** insignificante

trigger ['trɪgə(r)] *on gun* grilletto *m*

♦ **trigger off** scatenare

trim [trɪm] **1** *adj (neat)* ordinato; *figure* snello **2** *v/t hair, hedge* spuntare; *costs* tagliare; *(decorate: dress)* ornare **3** *n (light cut)* spuntata *f*; **in good ~** in buone condizioni

trinket ['trɪŋkɪt] ninnolo *m*

trio ['triːəʊ] MUS trio *m*

trip [trɪp] **1** *n (journey)* viaggio *m*, gita *f* **2** *v/i (stumble)* inciampare *(over* in*)* **3** *v/t (make fall)* fare inciampare

♦ **trip up 1** *v/t (make fall)* fare inciampare; *(cause to make a mistake)* confondere **2** *v/i (stumble)* inciampare; *(make a mistake)* sbagliarsi

triple ['trɪpl] ☞ **treble**

trite [traɪt] trito

triumph ['traɪʌmf] trionfo *m*

trivial ['trɪvɪəl] banale; **trivial-**

ity banalità *f inv*

trolley ['trɒlɪ] *in supermarket, at airport* carrello *m*

trombone [trɒm'bəʊn] trombone *m*

troops [truːps] truppe *fpl*

trophy ['trəʊfɪ] trofeo *m*

tropic ['trɒpɪk] tropico *m*; **tropical** tropicale; **tropics** tropici *mpl*

trot [trɒt] trottare

trouble ['trʌbl] **1** *n (difficulties)* problemi *mpl*; *(inconvenience)* fastidio *m*; *(disturbance)* disordini *mpl*; **the ~ with you is ...** il tuo problema è ...; **get into ~** mettersi nei guai **2** *v/t (worry)* preoccupare; *(bother, disturb)* disturbare; *of back, liver etc* dare dei fastidi a; **troublemaker** attaccabrighe *m/f inv*; **troubleshooting** mediazione *f*; *in software manual* ricerca *f* problemi e soluzioni; **troublesome** fastidioso

trousers ['traʊzəz] pantaloni *mpl*; **a pair of ~** un paio di pantaloni

trout [traʊt] trota *f*

truant ['truːənt]: **play ~** marinare la scuola

truce [truːs] tregua *f*

truck [trʌk] camion *m inv*; **truck driver** camionista *m*; **truck stop** *Am* posto *m* di ristoro per camionisti

trudge [trʌdʒ] **1** *v/i* arrancare; **~ around the shops** trascinarsi per i negozi **2** *n* cammi-

nata *f* stancante
true [truː] vero; **come ~** *of hopes, dream* realizzarsi; **truly** davvero; **Yours ~** distinti saluti
trumpet ['trʌmpɪt] tromba *f*
trunk [trʌŋk] *of tree, body* tronco *m*; *of elephant* proboscide *f*; *(large case)* baule *m*; MOT bagagliaio *m* inv
trust [trʌst] **1** *n* fiducia *f*, FIN fondo *m* fiduciario **2** *v/t* fidarsi di; **trusted** fidato; **trustee** amministratore *m*, -trice *f* fiduciario, -a; **trustful, trusting** fiducioso; **trustworthy** affidabile
truth [truːθ] verità *f* inv; **truthful** *account* veritiero; *person* sincero
try [traɪ] **1** *v/t* provare; LAW processare; *~ to do sth* provare a fare qc, cercare di fare qc **2** *v/i* provare, tentare; *you must ~ harder* devi provare con più impegno **3** *n* tentativo *m*; *in rugby* meta *f*; **trying** *(annoying)* difficile
T-shirt ['tiːʃɜːt] maglietta *f*
tub [tʌb] *(bath)* vasca *f* da bagno; *of liquid* tinozza *f*; *for yoghurt* barattolo *m*; **tubby** tozzo
tube [tjuːb] tubo *m*; *of toothpaste* tubetto *m*; **tubeless** *tyre* senza camera d'aria
Tuesday ['tjuːzdeɪ] martedì *m* inv
tuft [tʌft] ciuffo *m*
tug [tʌg] **1** *n* NAUT rimorchia-

tore *m* **2** *v/t (pull)* tirare
tuition [tjuˈɪʃn] lezioni *fpl*
tulip ['tjuːlɪp] tulipano *m*
tumble ['tʌmbl] ruzzolare; *of wall, prices* crollare; **tumbledown** in rovina, fatiscente; **tumbler** *for drink* bicchiere *m* (senza stelo); *in circus* acrobata *m/f*
tummy ['tʌmɪ] F pancia *f*; **tummy ache** mal *m* di pancia
tumour, *Am* **tumor** ['tuːmə(r)] tumore *m*
tumult ['tjuːmʌlt] tumulto *m*; **tumultuous** tumultuoso
tuna ['tjuːnə] tonno *m*
tune [tjuːn] **1** *n* motivo *m*; *in ~ instrument* accordata **2** *v/t instrument* accordare; *engine* mettere a punto
◆ **tune up 1** *v/i of orchestra* accordare gli strumenti **2** *v/t engine* mettere a punto
tuneful ['tjuːnfʊl] melodioso; **tuner** *(hi-fi)* sintonizzatore *m*, tuner *m* inv; **tune-up** *of engine* messa *f* a punto
tunnel ['tʌnl] galleria *f*, tunnel *m* inv
turbine ['tɜːbaɪn] turbina *f*
turbulence ['tɜːbjʊləns] *in air travel* turbolenza *f*; **turbulent** turbolento
turf [tɜːf] tappeto *m* erboso; *(piece)* zolla *f*
Turin [tjʊˈrɪn] Torino *f*
Turk [tɜːk] turco *m*, -a *f*; **Turkey** Turchia *f*
turkey ['tɜːkɪ] tacchino *m*

Turkish ['tɜːkɪʃ] **1** *adj* turco **2** *n language* turco *m*

turmoil ['tɜːmɔɪl] agitazione *f*

turn [tɜːn] **1** *n (rotation)* giro *m*; *in road* curva *f*; *in variety show* numero *m*; **take ∼s in doing sth** fare a turno a fare qc; **it's my ∼** è il mio turno, tocca a me; **do s.o. a good ∼** fare un favore a qu **2** *v/t wheel, corner* girare **3** *v/i of driver, car, wheel* girare; *(become)* diventare; **it has ∼ed cold** è diventato freddo; **he has ∼ed 40** ha compiuto 40 anni

◆ **turn around 1** *v/t object* girare; *company* dare una svolta positiva a; (COM *deal with*) eseguire; *order* evadere **2** *v/i of person* girarsi; *of driver* girare

◆ **turn away 1** *v/t (send away)* mandare via **2** *v/i (walk away)* andare via; *(look away)* girarsi dall'altra parte

◆ **turn back 1** *v/t edges, sheets* ripiegare **2** *v/i of walkers etc* tornare indietro; *in course of action* tirarsi indietro

◆ **turn down** *offer, invitation* rifiutare; *volume, heating* abbassare; *edge* ripiegare

◆ **turn in 1** *v/i (go to bed)* andare a letto **2** *v/t to police* denunciare

◆ **turn off 1** *v/t TV, engine* spegnere; *tap* chiudere; F *(sexually)* far passare la voglia a **2** *v/i of driver* svoltare

◆ **turn on 1** *v/t TV, engine* accendere; *tap* aprire; F *(sexually)* eccitare **2** *v/i of machine* accendersi

◆ **turn over 1** *v/i in bed* girarsi; *of vehicle* capottare **2** *v/t object, page* girare; FIN fatturare

◆ **turn up 1** *v/t collar, volume, heating* alzare **2** *v/i (arrive)* arrivare

turning ['tɜːnɪŋ] svolta *f*; **turning point** svolta *f* decisiva; **turnout** *of people* affluenza *f*; **turnover** FIN fatturato *m*; *of staff* ricambio *m*; **turnpike** *Am* strada *f* a pedaggio; **turn signal** *Am* MOT freccia *f*; **turn-up** *of trousers* risvolto *m*

turquoise ['tɜːkwɔɪz] turchese

turtle ['tɜːtl] tartaruga *f* marina; **turtleneck sweater** maglia *f* a lupetto

Tuscany ['tʌskənɪ] Toscana *f*

tusk [tʌsk] zanna *f*

tutor ['tjuːtə(r)] EDU *insegnante universitario che segue un piccolo gruppo di studenti*; **(private) ∼** insegnante *m/f* privato, -a

tuxedo [tʌk'siːdəʊ] *Am* smoking *m* inv

TV [tiː'viː] TV *f* inv; **on ∼** alla TV; **TV dinner** piatto *m* pronto; **TV guide** guida *f* dei programmi TV; **TV programme**, *Am* **TV program** programma *m* televisivo twang [twæŋ] **1** n in voice suono m nasale **2** v/t guitar string vibrare

tweezers ['twiːzəz] pinzette fpl

twelfth [twelfθ] dodicesimo; **twelve** dodici

twentieth ['twentiiθ] ventesimo; **twenty** venti; **twenty-four-seven** ventiquattr'ore su ventiquattro, sette giorni su sette

twice [twaɪs] due volte; **~ as much** il doppio; **~ as fast** veloce due volte tanto

twig [twɪg] ramoscello m

twilight ['twaɪlaɪt] crepuscolo m

twin [twɪn] gemello m; **twin beds** due lettini mpl

twinge [twɪndʒ] of pain fitta f

twinkle ['twɪŋkl] of stars, eyes scintillare

'twin room camera f a due letti; **twin town** città f inv gemellata

twirl [twɜːl] **1** v/t fare roteare **2** n of cream etc ricciolo m

twist [twɪst] **1** v/t attorcigliare; **~ one's ankle** prendere una storta **2** v/i of road snodarsi;

of river serpeggiare **3** n in rope attorcigliata f; in road curva f; in plot svolta f; **twisty** road contorto

twit [twɪt] F scemo m, -a f

twitch [twɪtʃ] **1** n nervous spasmo m **2** v/i (jerk) contrarsi

twitter ['twɪtə(r)] cinguettare

two [tuː] due; **the ~ of them** loro due

tycoon [taɪ'kuːn] magnate m

type [taɪp] **1** n (sort) tipo m **2** v/t & v/i (use a keyboard) battere (a macchina)

typhoon [taɪ'fuːn] tifone m

typhus ['taɪfəs] tifo m

typical ['tɪpɪkl] tipico; **that's ~ of you!** tipico!; **typically** tipicamente

typist ['taɪpɪst] dattilografo m, -a f

tyrannical [tɪ'rænɪkl] tirannico; **tyrannize** tiranneggiare; **tyranny** tirannia f; **tyrant** tiranno m, -a f

tyre [taɪr] gomma f, pneumatico m

Tyrol [tɪ'rɒl] Tirolo m; **Tyrolean** tirolese

Tyrrhenian Sea [taɪ'riːnɪən] mar m Tirreno

U

ugly ['ʌglɪ] brutto

UK [juː'keɪ] (= **United Kingdom**) Regno m Unito

ulcer ['ʌlsə(r)] ulcera f

ultimate ['ʌltɪmət] (best, de-

finitive) definitivo; (final) ultimo; (basic) fondamentale; **ultimately** (in the end) in definitiva

ultimatum [ʌltɪ'meɪtəm] ultimatum *m inv*

ultrasound [ˈʌltrəsaʊnd]
MED ecografia *f*

ultraviolet [ˌʌltrəˈvaɪələt] ultravioletto

umbrella [ʌmˈbrelə] ombrello *m*

umpire [ˈʌmpaɪə(r)] arbitro *m*

umpteenth [ˌʌmpˈtiːnθ] F ennesimo

UN [juːˈen] (= *United Nations*) ONU *f* (= Organizzazione *f* delle Nazioni Unite)

unable [ʌnˈeɪbl]: *be ~ to do sth* not know how to non saper fare qc; *not be in a position to* non poter fare qc

unacceptable [ʌnəkˈseptəbl] inaccettabile

unaccountable [ʌnəˈkaʊntəbl] inspiegabile

unanimous [juːˈnænɪməs] *verdict* unanime; **unanimously** all'unanimità

unapproachable [ʌnəˈprəʊtʃəbl] *person* inavvicinabile

unarmed [ʌnˈɑːmd] *person* disarmato; *~ combat* combattimento senz'armi

unassuming [ʌnəˈsjuːmɪŋ] senza pretese

unattached [ʌnəˈtætʃt] (*without a partner*) libero

unattended [ʌnəˈtendɪd] incustodito

unauthorized [ʌnˈɔːθəraɪzd] non autorizzato

unavoidable [ʌnəˈvɔɪdəbl]

inevitabile

unbalanced [ʌnˈbælənst] non equilibrato; PSYCH squilibrato

unbearable [ʌnˈbeərəbl] insopportabile

unbeatable [ʌnˈbiːtəbl] *team*, *quality* imbattibile

unbeaten [ʌnˈbiːtn] *team* imbattuto

unbelievable [ʌnbɪˈliːvəbl] incredibile

unbias(s)ed [ʌnˈbaɪəst] imparziale

unblock [ʌnˈblɒk] sbloccare

unbreakable [ʌnˈbreɪkəbl] *plates* infrangibile; *world record* imbattibile

unbutton [ʌnˈbʌtn] sbottonare

uncanny [ʌnˈkænɪ] *resemblance*, *skill* sorprendente; (*worrying: feeling*) inquietante

unceasing [ʌnˈsiːsɪŋ] incessante

uncertain [ʌnˈsɜːtn] incerto; *origins* dubbio; *be ~ about sth* non essere certo su qc; *uncertainty of the future* incertezza *f*; *there is still ~ about ...* ci sono ancora dubbi su ...

uncle [ˈʌŋkl] zio *m*

uncomfortable [ʌnˈkʌmftəbl] scomodo; *I feel ~ with him* mi sento a disagio con lui

uncommon [ʌnˈkɒmən] raro

uncompromising [ʌnˈkɒmprəmaizin] fermo; *in a negative way* intransigente

unconditional [ʌnkən'dɪʃnl] incondizionato

unconscious [ʌn'kɒnʃəs] MED svenuto; PSYCH inconscio; *knock s.o. ~* stordire qu con un colpo; *be ~ of sth (not aware)* non rendersi conto di qc

uncontrollable [ʌnkən'trəʊləbl] incontrollabile

unconventional [ʌnkən'venʃnl] poco convenzionale

uncooperative [ʌnkəʊ'ɒprətɪv] poco cooperativo

uncover [ʌn'kʌvə(r)] scoprire

undamaged [ʌn'dæmɪdʒd] intatto

undecided [ʌndɪ'saɪdɪd] *question* irrisolto; *be ~ about sth* essere indeciso su qc

undeniable [ʌndɪ'naɪəbl] innegabile

under ['ʌndə(r)] sotto; *(less than)* meno di; *it is ~ investigation* viene indagato

'undercarriage carrello *m* d'atterraggio

'undercover *agent* segreto

under'cut COM vendere a minor prezzo di

under'done *meat* al sangue; *(not cooked enough)* non cotto abbastanza

under'estimate, sottovalutare

under'fed malnutrito

under'go *treatment* sottoporsi a; *experiences* vivere

under'graduate studente *m*, -essa *f* universitario, -a

'underground 1 *adj passages etc* sotterraneo; POL clandestino **2** *adv work* sottoterra; *go ~* POL entrare in clandestinità **3** *n* RAIL metropolitana *f*

'undergrowth sottobosco *m*

under'hand *(devious)* subdolo

under'line *text* sottolineare

under'lying di fondo

under'mine *s.o.'s position* minare

underneath [ʌndə'ni:θ] sotto

'underpants mutande *fpl* da uomo

'underpass *for pedestrians* sottopassaggio *m*

underprivileged [ʌndə'prɪvɪlɪdʒd] svantaggiato

under'rate sottovalutare

'undershirt *Am* canottiera *f*

under'staffed [ʌndə'stɑ:ft] a corto di personale

under'stand capire; *I ~ that you …* mi risulta che tu …; **understandable** comprensibile; **understandably** comprensibilmente; **understanding 1** *adj person* comprensivo **2** *n* comprensione *f*; *(agreement)* intesa *f*

under'take *task* intraprendere; *~ to do sth* impegnarsi a fare qc; **undertaking** *(enterprise)* impresa *f*; *(promise)* promessa *f*

under'value sottovalutare

'**underwear** biancheria *f* intima

'**underworld** *criminal* malavita *f; in mythology* inferi *mpl*

under'**write** FIN sottoscrivere

undeserved [ʌndɪ'zɜːvd] immeritato

undesirable [ʌndɪ'zaɪərəbl] 1 *adj* indesiderabile 2 *n* persona *f* indesiderata

undisputed [ʌndɪ'spjuːtɪd] *champion* indiscusso

undo [ʌn'duː] *parcel* disfare; *shirt* sbottonare; *shoes* slacciare; *s.o.'s work* annullare

undoubtedly [ʌn'dautɪdlɪ] indubbiamente

undress [ʌn'dres] 1 *v/t* spogliare; **get ~ed** spogliarsi 2 *v/i* spogliarsi

undue [ʌn'djuː] (*excessive*) eccessivo; **unduly** (*excessively*) eccessivamente

unearth [ʌn'ɜːθ] *remains* portare alla luce; (*fig: find*) scovare

uneasy [ʌn'iːzɪ] *relationship*, *peace* precario; **feel ~ about** non sentirsela di

uneatable [ʌn'iːtəbl] immangiabile

uneconomic [ʌniːkə'nɒmɪk] poco redditizio

uneducated [ʌn'edjukeɪtɪd] senza istruzione

unemployed [ʌnɪm'plɔɪd] 1 *adj* disoccupato 2 *npl*: **the ~** i disoccupati; **unemployment** disoccupazione *f*; **~ benefit** sussidio *m* di disoc-

cupazione

unending [ʌn'endɪŋ] interminabile

unequal [ʌn'iːkwəl] disuguale

unerring [ʌn'erɪŋ] *judgement*, *instinct* infallibile

uneven [ʌn'iːvn] *quality* irregolare; *ground* accidentato

uneventful [ʌnɪ'ventful] *day*, *journey* tranquillo

unexpected [ʌnɪk'spektɪd] inatteso; **unexpectedly** inaspettatamente

unfair [ʌn'feə(r)] ingiusto

unfaithful [ʌn'feɪθful] *husband*, *wife* infedele; **be ~ to s.o.** essere infedele a qu

unfamiliar [ʌnfə'mɪljə(r)] sconosciuto; **be ~ with sth** non conoscere qc

unfasten [ʌn'fɑːsn] *belt* slacciare

unfavourable, *Am* **unfavorable** [ʌn'feɪvərəbl] *report*, *review* negativo; *weather conditions* sfavorevole

unfinished [ʌn'fɪnɪʃt] non terminato; **leave sth ~** non terminare qc

unfit [ʌn'fɪt] *adj physically* fuori forma; **be ~ to ... morally** non essere degno di ...; **~ to eat / drink** non commestibile / non potabile

unfold [ʌn'fəuld] 1 *v/t letter* spiegare; *arms* aprire 2 *v/i of story etc* svolgersi; *of view* spiegarsi

unforeseen [ʌnfɔː'siːn] imprevisto

unforgettable [ʌnfə'getəbl] indimenticabile

unforgivable [ʌnfə'gɪvəbl] imperdonabile

unfortunate [ʌn'fɔːtʃənət] *people* sfortunato; *event, choice of words* infelice; **that's ~ for you** è spiacevole per lei; **unfortunately** sfortunatamente

unfounded [ʌn'faʊndɪd] infondato

unfriendly [ʌn'frendlɪ] poco amichevole

ungrateful [ʌn'greɪtful] ingrato

unhappiness [ʌn'hæpɪnɪs] infelicità *f*; **unhappy** infelice; *customers etc* non soddisfatto (**with** di)

unharmed [ʌn'hɑːmd] illeso

unhealthy [ʌn'helθɪ] *person* malaticcio; *conditions* malsano; *food, atmosphere* poco sano; *economy* traballante

unheard-of [ʌn'hɜːdɒv] inaudito

unhygienic [ʌnhaɪ'dʒiːnɪk] non igienico

unification [juːnɪfɪ'keɪʃn] unificazione *f*

uniform ['juːnɪfɔːm] **1** *n* divisa *f*; MIL *also* uniforme *f* **2** *adj* uniforme

unify [juːnɪfaɪ] unificare

unilateral [juːnɪ'lætrəl] unilaterale

unimaginable [ʌnɪ'mædʒɪnəbl] inimmaginabile

unimaginative [ʌnɪ'mædʒɪnətɪv] senza fantasia

unimportant [ʌnɪm'pɔːtənt] senza importanza

uninhabitable [ʌnɪn'hæbɪtəbl] inabitabile; **uninhabited** *building* disabitato; *region* deserto

unintentional [ʌnɪn'tenʃnl] involontario; **unintentionally** involontariamente

uninteresting [ʌn'ɪntrəstɪŋ] poco interessante

uninterrupted [ʌnɪntə'rʌptɪd] ininterrotto

union ['juːnɪən] POL unione *f*; (*trade ~*) sindacato *m*

unique [juː'niːk] unico

unit ['juːnɪt] unità *f inv*; (*department*) reparto *m*

unit 'cost COM costo *m* unitario

unite [juː'naɪt] **1** *v/t* unire **2** *v/i* unirsi; **united** unito; **United Kingdom** Regno *m* Unito; **United Nations** Nazioni *fpl* Unite; **United States (of America)** Stati *mpl* Uniti (d'America); **unity** unità *f inv*

universal [juːnɪ'vɜːsl] universale; **universe** universo *m*

university [juːnɪ'vɜːsətɪ] università *f inv*

unjust [ʌn'dʒʌst] ingiusto

unkind [ʌn'kaɪnd] cattivo

unknown [ʌn'nəʊn] **1** *adj* sconosciuto **2** *n*: *a journey into the* **~** un viaggio nell'ignoto

unleaded [ʌn'ledɪd] senza

piombo
unless [ən'les] a meno che; ~ *he pays us tomorrow* a meno che non ci paghi domani; ~ *I am mistaken* se non mi sbaglio

unlikely [ʌn'laɪklɪ] improbabile

unlimited [ʌn'lɪmɪtɪd] illimitato

unload [ʌn'ləʊd] scaricare

unlock [ʌn'lɒk] aprire (con la chiave)

unluckily [ʌn'lʌkɪlɪ] sfortunatamente; **unlucky** *day, choice, person* sfortunato; *that was so ~ for you!* che sfortuna hai avuto!

unmanned [ʌn'mænd] *spacecraft* senza equipaggio

unmarried [ʌn'mærɪd] non sposato

unmistakable [ʌnmɪ'steɪkəbl] inconfondibile

unnatural [ʌn'nætʃrəl] non normale

unnecessary [ʌn'nesəsrɪ] non necessario; *comment, violence* gratuito

unnerving [ʌn'nɜːvɪŋ] inquietante

unobtainable [ʌnəb'teɪnəbl] *goods* introvabile; TELEC non ottenibile

unobtrusive [ʌnəb'truːsɪv] discreto

unoccupied [ʌn'ɒkjʊpaɪd] *building, house* vuoto; *post* vacante; *room* libero

unofficial [ʌnə'fɪʃl] non ufficiale; *announcement* ufficioso; **unofficially** non ufficialmente

unorthodox [ʌn'ɔːθədɒks] poco ortodosso

unpack [ʌn'pæk] **1** *v/t* disfare **2** *v/i* disfare le valige

unpaid [ʌn'peɪd] *work* non retribuito

unpleasant [ʌn'pleznt] *person, thing to say* antipatico; *smell, taste* sgradevole

unplug [ʌn'plʌg] *TV, computer* staccare (la spina di)

unpopular [ʌn'pɒpjʊlə(r)] *person* mal visto; *decision* impopolare

unprecedented [ʌn'presɪdentɪd] senza precedenti

unpredictable [ʌnprɪ'dɪktəbl] imprevedibile

unpretentious [ʌnprɪ'tenʃəs] senza pretese

unproductive [ʌnprə'dʌktɪv] *meeting* sterile; *soil* improduttivo

unprofessional [ʌnprə'feʃnl] *workmanship* poco professionale

unprofitable [ʌn'prɒfɪtəbl] non redditizio

unprovoked [ʌnprə'vəʊkt] *attack* non provocato

unqualified [ʌn'kwɒlɪfaɪd] *worker* non qualificato; *doctor, teacher* non abilitato

unquestionably [ʌn'kwestʃnəblɪ] indiscutibilmente; **unquestioning** *attitude* assoluto

unreadable [ʌnˈriːdəbl] *book* illeggibile

unrealistic [ʌnrɪəˈlɪstɪk] *person* poco realista; *expectations* poco realistico

unreasonable [ʌnˈriːznəbl] *person* irragionevole; *demand* eccessivo

unrelated [ʌnrɪˈleɪtɪd] *issues* senza (alcuna) attinenza; *people* non imparentato

unrelenting [ʌnrɪˈlentɪŋ] incessante

unreliable [ʌnrɪˈlaɪəbl] poco affidabile

unrest [ʌnˈrest] agitazione *f*

unrestrained [ʌnrɪˈstreɪnd] *emotions* incontrollato, sfrenato

unroll [ʌnˈrəʊl] srotolare

unruly [ʌnˈruːlɪ] indisciplinato

unsafe [ʌnˈseɪf] pericoloso; ~ *to drink* / *eat* non potabile / non commestibile; *it is* ~ *to …* è rischioso …

unsanitary [ʌnˈsænɪtrɪ] antigienico

unsatisfactory [ʌnsætɪsˈfæktrɪ] poco soddisfacente

unscathed [ʌnˈskeɪðd] (*not injured*) incolume; (*not damaged*) intatto

unscrew [ʌnˈskruː] svitare

unscrupulous [ʌnˈskruːpjələs] senza scrupoli

unselfish [ʌnˈselfɪʃ] *person* altruista; *act* altruistico

unsettled [ʌnˈsetld] *issue* irrisolto; *weather* instabile; *life-*style irrequieto; *bills* non pagato

unshaven [ʌnˈʃeɪvn] non rasato

unskilled [ʌnˈskɪld] non specializzato

unsophisticated [ʌnsəˈfɪstɪkeɪtɪd] *person, beliefs* semplice; *equipment* rudimentale

unstable [ʌnˈsteɪbl] instabile; *person* squilibrato

unsteady [ʌnˈstedɪ] *ladder* malsicuro; *be* ~ *on one's feet* non reggersi bene sulle gambe

unsuccessful [ʌnsəkˈsesful] *writer etc* di scarso successo; *candidate, party* sconfitto; *attempt* fallito; *he tried but was* ~ ha provato ma non ha avuto fortuna; *unsuccessfully* senza successo

unsuitable [ʌnˈsuːtəbl] *partner, clothing* inadatto; *thing to say* inappropriato

unswerving [ʌnˈswɜːvɪŋ] *loyalty* incrollabile

unthinkable [ʌnˈθɪŋkəbl] impensabile

untidy [ʌnˈtaɪdɪ] in disordine

untie [ʌnˈtaɪ] *knot* disfare; *laces* slacciare; *prisoner* slegare

until [ənˈtɪl] **1** *prep* fino a; *from Monday* ~ *Friday* da lunedì a venerdì; *not* ~ *Friday* non prima di venerdì **2** *conj* finché (non); *can you wait* ~ *I'm ready?* puoi aspettare che sia pronta?

untiring [ʌnˈtaɪrɪŋ] *efforts* instancabile

untold [ʌnˈtəʊld] *riches* incalcolabile; *suffering* indescrivibile; *story* inedito

untrue [ʌnˈtruː] falso

unused [ʌnˈjuːzd] mai usato

unusual [ʌnˈjuːʒʊəl] insolito; *it's ~ for them not to write* non è da loro non scrivere; *unusually* insolitamente

unveil [ʌnˈveɪl] *statue etc* scoprire

unwell [ʌnˈwel] *be / feel ~* stare / sentirsi male

unwilling [ʌnˈwɪlɪŋ] *be ~ to do* non essere disposto a fare; *unwillingly* malvolentieri

unwind [ʌnˈwaɪnd] **1** *v/t tape* svolgere **2** *v/i of tape* svolgersi; *of story* dipanarsi; *(relax)* rilassarsi

unwise [ʌnˈwaɪz] avventato, imprudente

unwrap [ʌnˈræp] aprire, scartare

unzip [ʌnˈzɪp] *dress etc* aprire (la chiusura lampo di); COMPUT espandere

up [ʌp] **1** *adv*: *~ in the sky / on the roof* in alto nel cielo / sul tetto; *~ here / there* quassù / lassù; *be ~ (out of bed)* essere in piedi; *of sun* essere sorto; *of temperature* essere aumentato; *(have expired)* essere scaduto; *what's ~?* F che c'è?; *~ to the year 1989* fino al 1989;

he came ~ to me mi si è avvicinato; *what are you ~ to these days?* cosa fai di bello?; *what are those kids ~ to?* cosa stanno combinando i bambini?; *be ~ to something (bad)* stare architettando qualcosa; *I don't feel ~ to it* non me la sento; *it's ~ to you* dipende da te; *it is ~ to them to solve it* their duty sta a loro risolverlo; *be ~ and about* after illness essersi ristabilito **2** *prep*: *further ~ the mountain* più in alto sulla montagna; *they ran ~ the street* corsero per strada; *we travelled ~ to Milan* siamo andati a Milano **3** *n*: *~s and downs* alti e bassi *mpl*

'upbringing educazione *f*

'upcoming *(forthcoming)* prossimo

up'date *file, records* aggiornare; *~ s.o. on sth* mettere qu al corrente di qc

up'grade *equipment etc* aggiornare; *memory* potenziare; *passenger* promuovere a una classe superiore; *product* migliorare

upheaval [ʌpˈhiːvl] *emotional* sconvolgimento *m*; *physical* scombussolamento *m*; *political, social* sconvolgimento *m*

uphill [ˈʌphɪl] **1** *adv*: *go / walk ~* salire 2 *adj climb* in salita; *struggle* arduo

up'hold *traditions, rights* sostenere; (*vindicate*) confermare

'**upkeep** manutenzione *f*

'**upload** COMPUT caricare, fare l'upload di

upon [ə'pɒn] *☞* **on**

upper ['ʌpə(r)] superiore; *deck, rooms* di sopra

upper 'class *adj accent* aristocratico; *family* dell'alta borghesia

'**upright 1** *adj citizen* onesto **2** *adv sit* (ben) dritto; **upright** (**piano**) pianoforte *m* verticale

'**uprising** insurrezione *f*

'**uproar** trambusto *m*; (*protest*) protesta *f*

'**upscale** *Am restaurant, hotel* elegante; *product* di qualità

up'set 1 *v/t drink, glass* rovesciare; (*make sad*) fare stare male; (*distress*) sconvolgere; (*annoy*) seccare **2** *adj* (*sad*) triste; (*distressed*) sconvolto; (*annoyed*) seccato; **be / get ~** prendersela (**about** per); **have an ~ stomach** avere l'intestino in disordine; **up'setting:** *it's so ~ (for me)* mi fa stare male, mi turba

upside 'down capovolto; *turn sth ~* capovolgere qc

up'stairs 1 *adv* di sopra **2** *adj room* al piano di sopra

'**upstream** a monte

up'tight F (*nervous*) nervoso; (*inhibited*) inibito

up-to-'date *information* aggiornato; *fashions* più attuale

'**up turn** *in economy* ripresa *f*

upward ['ʌpwəd] in su; *~ of 10,000* oltre 10.000

uranium [jʊ'reɪnɪəm] uranio *m*

urban ['ɜːbən] *areas, population* urbano; *redevelopment* urbanistico

urchin ['ɜːtʃɪn] monello *m*, -a *f*

urge [ɜːdʒ] **1** *n* (forte) desiderio *m* **2** *v/t: ~ s.o. to do sth* raccomandare (caldamente) a qu di fare qc; **urgency** urgenza *f*; *the ~ of the situation* la gravità della situazione; **urgent** urgente

urinate ['jʊərɪneɪt] orinare; **urine** urina *f*

US [juː'es] (= *United States*) USA *mpl*

us [ʌs] ci; *when two pronouns are used* ce; *after prep* noi; *don't leave ~* non ci lasciare, non lasciarci; *she gave them to ~* ce le ha date; *that's for ~* quello è per noi; *who's that? - it's ~* chi è? - siamo noi

USA [juːes'eɪ] (= *United States of America*) USA *mpl*

usage ['juːzɪdʒ] uso *m*

use 1 [juːz] *v/t tool, skills, knowledge* usare, utilizzare; *word, s.o.'s car* usare; *a lot of petrol* consumare; *pej: person* usare **2** [juːs] *n* uso *m*; *be*

of no ~ to s.o. non essere
d'aiuto a qu; **it's no ~ waiting** non serve a niente aspettare
◆ **use up** finire
used[1] [ju:zd] *adj car etc* usato
used[2] [ju:st]: **be ~ to** essere
abituato a; **get ~ to** abituarsi
a
used[3] [ju:st]: **I~ to know him**
lo conoscevo; **I~ to like him**
un tempo mi piaceva
useful ['ju:sfʊl] utile; *person*
di grande aiuto; **usefulness**
utilità *f*; **useless** *information, advice* inutile; F *person*
incapace; *machine* inservibi-
le; **feel ~** sentirsi inutile; **us-**

er *of product* utente *m/f*;
userfriendly di facile uso
usual ['ju:ʒʊəl] solito; **it's not
~ for this to happen** non
succede quasi mai; **as ~** come al solito; **usually** di solito
utensil [ju:'tensl] utensile *m*
utility [ju:'tɪlɪtɪ] (*usefulness*)
utilità *f*; **utility pole** *Am* palo
m del telegrafo; **utilize** utilizzare
utmost ['ʌtməʊst] **1** *adj* massimo **2** *n*: **do one's ~** fare
(tutto) il possibile
utter ['ʌtə(r)] **1** *adj* totale **2** *v/t
sound* emettere; *word* profe-
rire; **utterly** totalmente

V

vacancy ['veɪkənsɪ] *at work*
posto *m* vacante; *in hotel* camera *f* libera; **~ for a driver**
as advert autista cercasi; **"no
vacancies"** "completo"; **vacant** *building* vuoto; *room* libero; *look, expression* assente; *position* vacante; **va-
cantly** con sguardo assente;
vacate *room* lasciar libero; **be on
~** essere in vacanza
vaccinate ['væksɪneɪt] vaccinare; **vaccination** vaccinazione *f*; **vaccine** vaccino *m*
vacuum ['vækjʊəm] **1** *n also
fig* vuoto *m* **2** *v/t* floors passare l'aspirapolvere su

vagina [və'dʒaɪnə] vagina *f*
vague [veɪg] vago; **I'm still ~
about it** non ho ancora le
idee chiare al riguardo; **va-
guely** vagamente
vain [veɪn] **1** *adj person* vanitoso; *hope* vano **2** *n*: **in ~** invano
valiant ['vælɪənt] valoroso
valid ['vælɪd] valido; **validate**
with official stamp convalidare; *alibi* confermare; **validity**
of reason, argument validità *f*
valley ['vælɪ] valle *f*
valuable ['væljʊəbl] **1** *adj* prezioso **2** *n*: **~s** oggetti *mpl* di
valore; **valuation** valutazione *f*; **value 1** *n* valore *m* **2**

v/t friendship, freedom tenere a; **have an object ~d** far valutare un oggetto

valve [vælv] valvola *f*

van [væn] furgone *m*

vandal ['vændl] vandalo *m*; **vandalism** vandalismo *m*; **vandalize** vandalizzare

vanilla [və'nɪlə] **1** *n* vaniglia *f* **2** *adj* ice cream alla vaniglia; flavour di vaniglia

vanish ['vænɪʃ] sparire

vanity ['vænətɪ] of person vanità *f* inv

vapor ['veɪpə(r)] *Am* ☞ **vapour**, **vaporize** vaporizzare; **vapour** vapore *m*

variable ['veərɪəbl] **1** *adj* variabile *2 n* MATH, COMPUT variabile *f*; **variation** variazione *f*; **varied** range, diet vario; life movimentato; **variety** varietà *f* inv; (type) (different) diverso

varnish ['vɑːnɪʃ] **1** *n* for wood vernice *f*; (nail ~) smalto *m* **2** *v/t* wood verniciare; nails smaltare

vary ['veərɪ] variare

vase [vɑːz] vaso *m*

vast [vɑːst] vasto; improvement immenso; **vastly** immensamente

VAT [viːeɪ'tiː, væt] abbr (= **value added tax**) IVA *f* (= imposta *f* sul valore aggiunto)

Vatican ['vætɪkən]: **the ~** il Va-

ticano

vault[1] [vɔːlt] *n* in roof volta *f*; cellar cantina *f*; **~s of bank** caveau *m* inv

vault[2] [vɔːlt] **1** *n* SP volteggio *m* **2** *v/t* saltare

VCR [viːsiː'ɑː(r)] (= **video cassette recorder**) videoregistratore *m*

veal [viːl] (carne *f* di) vitello *m*

veer [vɪə(r)] of car sterzare; of wind, party cambiare direzione

vegan ['viːgən] food, person vegano

vegetable ['vedʒtəbl] verdura *f*; **vegetarian 1** *n* vegetariano *m*, -a *f* **2** *adj* vegetariano; **vegetation** vegetazione *f*

vehement ['viːəmənt] veemente

vehicle ['viːɪkl] veicolo *m*; for information etc mezzo *m*

veil [veɪl] velo *m*

vein [veɪn] ANAT vena *f*; **in this ~** fig su questo tono

Velcro® ['velkrəʊ] velcro *m*

velocity [vɪ'lɒsətɪ] velocità *f* inv

velvet ['velvɪt] velluto *m*

vendetta [ven'detə] vendetta *f*

vending machine ['vendɪŋ] distributore *m* automatico; **vendor** LAW venditore *m*, -trice *f*

veneer [və'nɪə(r)] impiallacciatura *f*; of politeness etc parvenza *f*

venerable ['venərəbl] venerabile; **veneration** venerazione f

venereal disease [vɪˈnɪərɪəl] malattia f venerea

Venetian [vəˈniːʃn] **1** adj veneziano **2** n veneziano m, -a f; **venetian blind** veneziana f; **Venice** Venezia f

venom [ˈvenəm] veleno m

ventilate [ˈventɪleɪt] ventilare; **ventilation** ventilazione f; **ventilator** ventilatore m; MED respiratore m

venture [ˈventʃə(r)] **1** n impresa f **2** v/i avventurarsi

venue [ˈvenjuː] for meeting, concert etc luogo m

veranda [vəˈrændə] veranda f

verb [vɜːb] verbo m; **verbal** (spoken) verbale; **verbally** verbalmente

verdict [ˈvɜːdɪkt] LAW verdetto m; (opinion, judgment) giudizio m

verge [vɜːdʒ] of road bordo m; **be on the ~ of** ... ruin, collapse essere sull'orlo di ...; **on the ~ of tears** sul punto di piangere

verification [verɪfɪˈkeɪʃn] verifica f; **verify** verificare

vermin [ˈvɜːmɪn] animali mpl nocivi

vermouth [ˈvɜːməθ] vermut m

versatile [ˈvɜːsətaɪl] versatile; **versatility** versatilità f

verse [vɜːs] poetry poesia f; part of poem, song strofa f

version [ˈvɜːʃn] versione f

versus [ˈvɜːsəs] contro

vertical [ˈvɜːtɪkl] verticale

vertigo [ˈvɜːtɪɡəʊ] vertigini fpl

very [ˈverɪ] **1** adv molto; **~ fast** molto veloce, velocissimo; **the ~ best** il meglio **2** adj: **at that ~ moment** in quel preciso momento; **that's the ~ thing I need** è proprio quello che mi serve

vessel [ˈvesl] NAUT natante m

vest [vest] Br undershirt canottiera f; Am gilè m inv

vestige [ˈvestɪdʒ] vestigio m; **not a ~ of truth** neanche un'ombra di verità

vet¹ [vet] n (veterinary surgeon) veterinario m, -a f

vet² [vet] v/t applicants etc passare al vaglio

vet³ [vet] n MIL reduce m/f

veteran [ˈvetərən] **1** n veterano m, -a f; MIL reduce m/f **2** adj veterano

veto [ˈviːtəʊ] **1** n veto m **2** v/t mettere il veto a

via [ˈvaɪə] attraverso

viable [ˈvaɪəbl] in grado di sopravvivere; alternative, plan fattibile

vibrate [vaɪˈbreɪt] vibrare; **vibration** vibrazione f

vicar [ˈvɪkə(r)] parroco m anglicano

vice¹ [vaɪs] vizio m

vice² [vaɪs] tool morsa f

vice 'president vice-presidente m

vice versa [vaɪsˈvɜːsə] vice-

versa
vicious ['vɪʃəs] *dog* feroce; *attack, criticism* brutale; **viciously** brutalmente
victim ['vɪktɪm] vittima *f*; **victimize** perseguitare
victorious [vɪk'tɔːrɪəs] *army* vittorioso; *team* vincente; **victory** vittoria *f*
video ['vɪdɪəʊ] **1** *n* video *m inv; tape* videocassetta *f;* (*VCR*) videoregistratore *m* **2** *v/t* registrare; **video camera** videocamera *f;* **video cassette** videocassetta *f;* **video conference** videoconferenza *f;* **video game** videogame *m inv;* **video recorder** videoregistratore *m;* **videotape** videocassetta *f*
vie [vaɪ] competere
Vietnam [vɪet'næm] Vietnam *m;* **Vietnamese 1** *adj* vietnamita **2** *n* vietnamita *m/f; language* vietnamita *m*
view [vjuː] **1** *n* veduta *f; of situation* parere *m;* **in** ~ **of** considerato; **be on** ~ *of paintings* essere esposto; **with a** ~ **to** con l'intenzione di **2** *v/t* vedere; *TV programme* guardare **3** *v/i* (*watch TV*) guardare la TV; **viewer** *TV* telespettatore *m,* -trice *f;* **viewpoint** punto *m* di vista
vigor ['vɪgə(r)] *Am* ☞ **vigour**
vigorous ['vɪgərəs] vigoroso; **vigorously** vigorosamente; **vigour** vigore *m*
village ['vɪlɪdʒ] paese *m;* vil-

lager abitante *m/f* (del paese)
villain ['vɪlən] cattivo *m,* -a *f; F criminal* delinquente *m/f*
vindicate ['vɪndɪkeɪt] (*prove correct*) confermare; (*prove innocent*) scagionare; **I feel ~d by the report** il resoconto mi dà ragione
vindictive [vɪn'dɪktɪv] vendicativo
vine [vaɪn] (*grape~*) vite *f; climber* rampicante *m*
vinegar ['vɪnɪgə(r)] aceto *m*
vineyard ['vɪnjɑːd] vigneto *m*
vintage ['vɪntɪdʒ] **1** *n of wine* annata *f* **2** *adj* (*classic*) d'annata
viola [vɪ'əʊlə] MUS viola *f*
violate ['vaɪəleɪt] violare; **violation** violazione *f; Am* (*traffic* ~) infrazione *f*
violence ['vaɪələns] violenza *f;* **violent** violento
violin [vaɪə'lɪn] violino *m;* **violinist** violinista *m/f*
VIP [viːaɪ'piː] (= *very important person*) VIP *m/f*
viral ['vaɪrəl] virale
virgin ['vɜːdʒɪn] vergine *m/f;* **virginity** verginità *f*
Virgo ['vɜːgəʊ] ASTR Vergine *f*
virile ['vɪraɪl] virile; **virility** virilità *f*
virtual ['vɜːtjʊəl] effettivo; COMPUT virtuale; **virtually** (*almost*) praticamente
virtue ['vɜːtjuː] virtù *f inv*
virtuoso [vɜːtʊ'əʊzəʊ] MUS virtuoso *m,* -a *f*

virtuous ['vɜ:tjʊəs] virtuoso

virus ['vaɪərəs] MED, COMPUT virus *m inv*

visa ['vi:zə] visto *m*

vise *Am* ☞ **vice²**

visibility [vɪzə'bɪlətɪ] visibilità *f*; **visible** visibile; *anger etc* evidente

vision ['vɪʒn] *(eyesight)* vista *f*; REL *etc* visione *f*

visit ['vɪzɪt] **1** *n* visita *f*; **pay s.o. a ~** fare una visita a qu **2** *v/t person* andare a trovare; *place, country, city, website* visitare; *doctor, dentist* andare da; **visitor** *(guest)* ospite *m*; *to museum etc* visitatore *m*, -trice *f*; *(tourist)* turista *m/f*

visor ['vaɪzə(r)] visiera *f*

visual ['vɪzjʊəl] *organs, memory* visivo; *arts* figurativo; **visualize** immaginare; *(foresee)* prevedere; **visually** visivamente

vital ['vaɪtl] *(essential)* essenziale; **vitality** vitalità *f*; **vitally: ~ important** di vitale importanza

vitamin ['vɪtəmɪn] vitamina *f*; **vitamin pill** (confetto *m* di) vitamina *f*

vivacious [vɪ'veɪʃəs] vivace; **vivacity** vivacità *f*

vivid ['vɪvɪd] vivido; **vividly** in modo vivido

V-neck ['vi:nek] maglione *m* con scollo a V

vocabulary [və'kæbjʊlərɪ] vocabolario *m*; *list of words* glossario *m*

vocal ['vəʊkl] *to do with the voice* vocale; *expressing opinions* eloquente; **become ~** cominciare a farsi sentire; **vocal group** MUS gruppo *m* vocale; **vocalist** MUS cantante *m/f*

vocation [və'keɪʃn] *(calling)* vocazione *f* **(for** a); *(profession)* professione *f*; **vocational** *guidance* professionale

vodka ['vɒdkə] vodka *f inv*

vogue [vəʊg] moda *f*; **be in ~** essere in voga

voice [vɔɪs] **1** *n* voce *f* **2** *v/t opinions* esprimere; **voice-activated** attivato dalla voce; **voice mail** segreteria *f* telefonica; *message* messagio *m* in segreteria

volatile ['vɒlətaɪl] *personality* volubile

volcano [vɒl'keɪnəʊ] vulcano *m*

volley ['vɒlɪ] *of shots* raffica *f*; *in tennis* volée *f inv*

volt [vəʊlt] volt *m inv*; **voltage** voltaggio *m*; **high ~** alta tensione *f*

volume ['vɒlju:m] volume *m*

voluntarily [vɒlən'teərɪlɪ] spontaneamente; **voluntary** volontario; **~ work** volontariato; **volunteer 1** *n* volontario *m*, -a *f* **2** *v/i* offrirsi volontario

vomit ['vɒmɪt] **1** *n* vomito *m* **2** *v/i* vomitare

voracious [vəˈreɪʃəs] vorace
vote [vəʊt] **1** n voto m; *right to vote* diritto m di voto **2** v/i POL votare (*for* a favore di, *against* contro); **voter** POL elettore m, -trice f; **voting** POL votazione f
◆ **vouch for** [vaʊtʃ] *truth* garantire; *person* garantire per

vow [vaʊ] **1** n voto m **2** v/t: ~ *to do* giurare di fare
vowel [vaʊl] vocale f
voyage [ˈvɔɪɪdʒ] viaggio m
vulgar [ˈvʌlɡə(r)] volgare
vulnerable [ˈvʌlnərəbl] vulnerabile
vulture [ˈvʌltʃə(r)] avvoltoio m

W

waddle [ˈwɒdl] camminare ondeggiando
wade [weɪd] guadare
wafer [ˈweɪfə(r)] *cookie* cialda f; REL ostia f
waffle [ˈwɒfl] (*to eat*) tipo di cialda
wag [wæɡ] *finger* scuotere; *the dog ~ged its tail* il cane scodinzolò
wages [ˈweɪdʒɪz] paga f
waggle [ˈwæɡl] far muovere
wail [weɪl] *of person* gemere; *of siren* ululare
waist [weɪst] vita f; **waistcoat** gilè m inv; **waistline** vita f
wait [weɪt] **1** n attesa f **2** v/i aspettare; *I can't ~ to ...* non vedo l'ora di ... **3** v/t *meal* ritardare
◆ **wait for** aspettare
◆ **wait on** (*serve*) servire
◆ **wait up** restare alzato ad aspettare
waiter [ˈweɪtə(r)] cameriere m; **waiting list** lista f d'attesa; **waiting room** sala f d'at-

tesa; **waitress** cameriera f
waive [weɪv] (*renounce*) rinunciare a; (*dispense with*) fare a meno di
wake [weɪk] **1** v/i: ~ (*up*) svegliarsi **2** v/t svegliare; **wake-up call** sveglia f (telefonica)
Wales [weɪlz] Galles m
walk [wɔːk] **1** n camminata f; *go for a ~* fare due passi **2** v/i camminare; *as opposed to driving* andare a piedi; (*hike*) passeggiare **3** v/t *dog* portare fuori; ~ *the streets* (*walk around*) girare in lungo e in largo
◆ **walk out** *of spouse etc, from theatre* andarsene; (*go on strike*) scendere in sciopero
◆ **walk out on** *spouse, family* abbandonare
walker [ˈwɔːkə(r)] (*hiker*) escursionista m/f; *for baby* girello m; *for old person* deambulatore m; *be a slow / fast ~* avere il passo lento / spedito; **walking** *as*

opposed to driving camminare *m*; (*hiking*) escursionismo *m*; **it's within ~ distance** ci si arriva a piedi; **Walkman®** walkman *m inv*; **walkout** *strike* sciopero *m* selvaggio; **walkover** (*easy win*) vittoria *f* facile

wall [wɔːl] *also fig* muro *m*; *internal* parete *f*; **~s** *of a city* mura *fpl*; **drive s.o. up the ~** F far diventare matto qu

wallet ['wɒlɪt] portafoglio *m*

'wallpaper 1 *n* tappezzeria *f*, carta *f* da parati **2** *v/t* tappezzare; **wall-to-wall carpet** moquette *f*

waltz [wɔːlts] valzer *m inv*

wan [wɒn] *face* pallido

wander ['wɒndə(r)] (*roam*) gironzolare; (*stray*) allontanarsi

wangle ['wæŋgl] F rimediare F

want [wɒnt] **1** *n*: **for ~** *of* per mancanza di **2** *v/t* volere; (*need*) avere bisogno di; **~ to do sth** volere fare qc; **she ~s you to go back** vuole che torni indietro **3** *v/i*: **~ for nothing** non mancare di niente; **wanted** *by police* ricercato

war [wɔː(r)] guerra *f*; *fig* lotta *f*

ward [wɔːd] *in hospital* corsia *f*; *child* minore *m* sotto tutela

◆ **ward off** *blow* parare; *attacker* respingere; *cold* combattere

warden ['wɔːdn] (*traffic ~*) vi-

gile *m* urbano; *of hostel* direttore *m*, -trice *f*; *of nature reserve* guardiano *m*, -a *f*; *of prison* agente *m/f* di custodia; *Am* direttore *m*, -trice *f*

'wardrobe *for clothes* armadio *m*; *clothes* guardaroba *m*

warehouse ['weəhaʊs] magazzino *m*

'warfare guerra *f*; **warhead** testata *f*

warily ['weərɪlɪ] con aria guardinga

warm [wɔːm] caldo; *welcome, smile* caloroso; **it's ~** *of weather* fa caldo

◆ **warm up 1** *v/t* scaldare **2** *v/i* scaldarsi; *of athlete etc* fare riscaldamento

warmly ['wɔːmlɪ] *dressed* con abiti pesanti; *welcome, smile* calorosamente; **warmth** calore *m*; *of welcome, smile* calorosità *f*; **warm-up** SP riscaldamento *m*

warn [wɔːn] avvertire; **warning** avvertimento *m*; **without ~** senza preavviso

warp [wɔːp] *of wood* deformarsi; **warped** *fig* contorto

'warplane aereo *m* militare

warrant ['wɒrənt] **1** *n* mandato *m* **2** *v/t* giustificare; **warranty** (*guarantee*) garanzia *f*

warrior ['wɒrɪə(r)] guerriero *m*, -a *f*

'warship nave *f* da guerra

wart [wɔːt] verruca *f*

wary ['weərɪ] guardingo; **be ~ of** diffidare di

wash [wɒʃ] **1** *n*: **have a ~** darsi una lavata **2** *v/t* lavare; **~ one's hair** lavarsi i capelli **3** *v/i* lavarsi

◆ **wash up** *Br* lavare i piatti; *Am* (*wash one's hands and face*) lavarsi

washable ['wɒʃəbl] lavabile; **washbasin**, **washbowl** lavandino *m*; **washcloth** *Am* guanto *m* di spugna; **washed out** sfinito; **washer** *for tap etc* guarnizione *f*; **washing** *washed clothes* bucato *m*; *clothes to be washed* biancheria *f* da lavare; **do the ~** fare il bucato; **washing machine** lavatrice *f*; **washing-up liquid** detersivo *m* per i piatti; **washroom** *Am* servizi *mpl*

wasp [wɒsp] vespa *f*

waste [weɪst] **1** *n* spreco *m*; *from industrial process* rifiuti *mpl*; **it's a ~ of time / money** è tempo sprecato / sono soldi sprecati **2** *adj material* di scarto **3** *v/t* sprecare; **waste disposal (unit)** tritarifiuti *m inv*; **wasteful** *person* sprecone; *methods* dispendioso; **wasteland** distesa *f* desolata; **wastepaper** cartaccia *f*; **wastepaper basket**, *Am* **waste basket** cestino *m* della cartaccia

watch [wɒtʃ] **1** *n* *timepiece* orologio *m*; MIL guardia *f*; **keep ~** stare all'erta **2** *v/t* guardare; (*spy on*) sorveglia-

re; (*look after*) tenere d'occhio **3** *v/i* guardare; **watchful** vigile

water ['wɔːtə(r)] **1** *n* acqua *f* **2** *v/t plant* annaffiare **3** *v/i of eyes* lacrimare; **my mouth is ~ing** ho l'acquolina in bocca; **watercolour**, *Am* **watercolor** acquerello *m*; **watered down** *fig* edulcorato; **waterfall** cascata *f*; **waterline** linea *f* di galleggiamento; **waterlogged** allagato; **watermelon** anguria *f*, cocomero *m*; **waterproof** impermeabile; **waterside**: **at the ~** sulla riva; **waterskiing** sci *m* nautico; **watertight** *compartment* stagno; *fig* inattaccabile; **waterway** corso *m* d'acqua navigabile; **watery** acquoso

watt [wɒt] watt *m inv*

wave¹ [weɪv] *n* *in sea* onda *f*

wave² [weɪv] **1** *n* *of hand* saluto *m* (con la mano) **2** *v/i with hand* salutare (con la mano) **3** *v/t flag etc* sventolare

'wavelength RAD lunghezza *f* d'onda; **be on the same ~** *fig* essere sulla stessa lunghezza d'onda

waver ['weɪvə(r)] vacillare

wavy ['weɪvɪ] ondulato

wax [wæks] *for furniture* cera *f*; *in ear* cerume *m*

way [weɪ] **1** *n* (*method, manner*) modo *m*; (*manner*) maniera *f*; (*route*) strada *f*; **this ~** (*like this*) così; (*in this direc-*

tion) da questa parte; **by the ~** (*incidentally*) a proposito; **in a ~** (*in certain respects*) in un certo senso; **be under ~** essere in corso; **give ~** MOT dare la precedenza; (*collapse*) crollare; **X has given ~ to Y** (*been replaced by*) Y ha preso il posto di X; **have one's** (*own*) **~** averla vinta; **lead the ~** *also fig* fare strada; **lose one's ~** smarrirsi; **be in the ~** (*be an obstruction*) essere d'intralcio; **it's on the ~ to the station** è sulla strada della stazione; **I was on my ~ to the station** stavo andando alla stazione; **no ~!** neanche per sogno!; **there's no ~ he can do it** è impossibile che ce la faccia **2** *adv* F (*much*): **it's ~ too soon** è veramente troppo presto; **they are ~ behind with their work** sono molto indietro con il lavoro; **way in** entrata *f*; **way of life** stile *m* di vita; **way out** uscita *f*, *fig: from situation* via *f* d'uscita

we [wiː] *noi*; **~'re the best** siamo i migliori

weak [wiːk] *debole*; *tea, coffee* leggero; **weaken 1** *v/t* indebolire **2** *v/i* indebolirsi; **weakness** debolezza *f*; **have a ~ for sth** (*liking*) avere un debole per qc

wealth [welθ] *ricchezza f*; **a ~ of** una grande abbondanza di; **wealthy** *ricco*

weapon ['wepən] *arma f*

wear [weə(r)] **1** *n*: **~** (*and tear*) usura *f* **2** *v/t* (*have on*) indossare; (*damage*) logorare **3** *v/i* (*wear out*) logorarsi; (*last*) durare

◆ **wear down** fiaccare
◆ **wear off** of effect svanire
◆ **wear out 1** *v/t* (*tire*) estenuare; *shoes* consumare **2** *v/i of shoes, carpet* consumarsi

wearily ['wɪərɪlɪ] *stancamente*; *weary stanco*

weather ['weðə(r)] **1** *n* tempo *m*; **be feeling under the ~** sentirsi poco bene **2** *v/t crisis* superare; **weather-beaten** segnato; **weather forecast** previsioni *fpl* del tempo; **weatherman** meteorologo *m*

weave [wiːv] **1** *v/t cloth* tessere; *basket* intrecciare **2** *v/i* (*move*) zigzagare

web [web] *of spider* ragnatela *f*; **the Web** COMPUT il web *m*; **web page** pagina *f* web; **web site** sito *m* web

wedding ['wedɪŋ] *matrimonio m*; **wedding anniversary** anniversario *m* di matrimonio; **wedding day** giorno *m* del matrimonio; **wedding dress** abito *m* or vestito *m* da sposa; **wedding ring** fede *f*

wedge [wedʒ] *to hold sth in place* zeppa *f*; *of cheese etc* fetta *f*

Wednesday ['wenzdeɪ] mercoledì *m inv*

weed [wiːd] **1** *n* erbaccia *f* **2** *v/t* diserbare; **weed-killer** diserbante *m*; **weedy** F mingherlino

week [wiːk] settimana *f*; *a ~ tomorrow* una settimana a domani; **weekday** giorno *m* feriale; **weekend** *m* settimana, weekend *m inv*; *on the ~* durante il fine settimana; **weekly 1** *adj* settimanale **2** *n magazine* settimanale *m* **3** *adv* settimanalmente

weep [wiːp] piangere

'wee-wee F pipì *f inv* F; *do a ~* fare la pipì

weigh [weɪ] pesare

♦ **weigh up** (*assess*) valutare

weight [weɪt] peso *m*; *put on / lose ~* ingrassare / dimagrire; **weightlessness** assenza *f* di peso; **weightlifter** pesista *m/f*; **weightlifting** sollevamento *m* pesi

weir [wɪə(r)] chiusa *f*

weird [wɪəd] strano; **weirdo** F pazzoide *m/f*

welcome ['welkəm] **1** *adj* benvenuto; *make s.o. ~* accogliere bene qu; *you're ~!* prego!; *you're ~ to try some* serviti pure **2** *n also fig* accoglienza *f* **3** *v/t guests etc* accogliere; *fig: decision etc* rallegrarsi di; *she ~s a challenge* apprezza le sfide

weld [weld] saldare

welfare ['welfeə(r)] bene *m*;

welfare check *Am* sussidio *m* di disoccupazione; **welfare state** stato *m* sociale; **welfare worker** assistente *m/f* sociale

well¹ [wel] *n for water, oil* pozzo *m*

well² [wel] **1** *adv* bene; *~ done!* bravo!; *as ~* (*too*) anche; *as ~ as in addition to* oltre a; *it's just as ~ you told me* hai fatto bene a dirmelo; *very ~ acknowledging order* benissimo; *reluctantly agreeing* va bene; *~, ~! surprise* bene, bene!; *~, ... uncertainty, thinking* beh ... **2** *adj: be ~* stare bene; *feel ~* sentirsi bene; *get ~ soon!* guarisci presto!

well-'balanced equilibrato; **well-behaved** educato; **well-being** benessere *m*; **well-done** *meat* ben cotto; **well-dressed** ben vestito; **well-earned** meritato; **well-heeled** F danaroso; **well-informed** ben informato; **well-known** famoso; **well-meaning** spinto da buone intenzioni

wellness benessere *m*, wellness *m*

well-off benestante; **well-timed** tempestivo

Welsh [welʃ] **1** *adj* gallese **2** *n language* gallese *m*; *the ~* i gallesi

west [west] **1** *n* ovest *m*, occidente *m*; *the West* POL l'Oc-

cidente **2** *adj* occidentale **3**
adv travel verso ovest; **~ of**
a ovest di; **westerly** occidentale; **western 1** *adj* occidentale; **Western** occidentale **2**
n (film) western *m inv*; **Westerner** occidentale *m/f*; **westernized** occidentalizzato; **West Indian 1** *adj* delle Indie Occidentali **2** *n* nativo
m delle Indie Occidentali; **West Indies: the ~** le Indie
Occidentali; **westward** verso ovest

wet [wet] bagnato; *(rainy)* piovoso; **~ paint** *as sign* vernice
fresca; **wet suit** *for diving*
muta *f*

whack [wæk] **1** *n* F *(blow)* colpo *m* **2** *v/t* F colpire;
whacked F stanco morto

whale [weɪl] balena *f*

wharf [wɔːf] *n* banchina *f*

what [wɒt] **1** *pron (che) cosa*;
~ is that? (che) cos'è?; **~ is
it?** *(what do you want)*
(che) cosa c'è?; **~?** cosa?;
it's not ~ I meant non è
ciò che volevo dire; **~ about
some dinner?** e se mangiassimo qualcosa?; **~ for?** *(why)*
perché? **2** *adj che inv, quale*;
~ colour is the car? di che
colore è la macchina? **3**
adv: **~ a brilliant idea!** che
bella idea!; whatever: **I'll
do ~ you want** farò (tutto)
quello che vuoi; **~ I do, it'll
be a probem** qualsiasi cosa
faccia, ci saranno problemi

~ people say qualunque cosa dica la gente; **~ gave you
that idea?** cosa mai te lo ha
fatto pensare?; **ok, ~** F va bene, come vuoi / volete

wheat [wiːt] grano *m*, frumento *m*

wheel [wiːl] ruota *f*; *(steering
~)* volante *m*

'wheelchair sedia *f* a rotelle;
wheel clamp ceppo *m* bloccaruote

wheeze [wiːz] ansimare

when [wen] quando; whenever *(each time)* ogni volta che;
regardless of when in qualunque momento

where [weə(r)] dove; **this is ~
I used to live** io abitavo qui;
whereabouts 1 *adv* dove **2**
npl: **know s.o.'s ~** sapere dove si trova qu; **whereas**
mentre; **wherever 1** *conj* dovunque; **~ you go** dovunque
tu vada **2** *adv*: dove; **~ can he
be?** dove sarà mai?

whet [wet] *appetite* stuzzicare

whether ['weðə(r)] se

which [wɪtʃ] **1** *adj quale*; **~ one
is yours?** qual è il tuo? **2**
pron interrogative quale; relative che; **the car ~ ...** la macchina che ...; **on / in ~**
su / in cui; **whichever 1** *adj*
qualunque **2** *pron* quello
che *m*, quella che *f*; **~ of
the methods** qualunque
metodo

whiff [wɪf]: **catch a ~ of** sentire

while [waɪl] **1** *conj* mentre; (*although*) benché (+ *subj*) **2** *n*: **a long ~ ago** molto tempo fa; **wait a long ~** aspettare molto *or* lungo; **for a ~** per un po'; **in a ~** fra poco

whim [wɪm] capriccio *m*

whimper ['wɪmpə(r)] gemere; *of animal* mugolare

whine [waɪn] *of dog* guaire; F (*complain*) piagnucolare

whip [wɪp] **1** *n* frusta *f* **2** *v/t* (*beat*) sbattere; *cream* montare; F (*defeat*) stracciare F

'whirlpool *in river* mulinello *m*; *for relaxation* vasca *f* per idromassaggio

whisk [wɪsk] **1** *n* frusta *f*; *mechanical* frullino *m* **2** *v/t eggs* frullare

whisky, *Am* **whiskey** ['wɪskɪ] whisky *m inv*

whisper ['wɪspə(r)] bisbigliare

whistle ['wɪsl] **1** *n sound* fischio *m*; *device* fischietto *m* **2** *v/i* fischiare **3** *v/t* fischiettare

white [waɪt] **1** *n* bianco *m*; *person* bianco *m*, -a *f* **2** *adj* bianco; *go ~* sbiancare (in viso); **white coffee** caffè *m inv* con latte *or* panna; **white-collar worker** impiegato *m*, -a *f*; **White House** Casa *f* Bianca; **white lie** bugia *f* innocente; **whitewash 1** *n* calce *f*; *fig* copertura *f* **2** *v/t* imbiancare (con calce); **white wine** vino *m* bianco

whittle ['wɪtl] *wood* intagliare
♦ **whittle down** ridurre

whizzkid ['wɪzkɪd] F mago *m*, -a *f* F

who [huː] *interrogative* chi; *relative* che; **the man ~ I was talking to** l'uomo con cui parlavo; **whoever** chiunque; (*interrogative*) chi mai; **~ can that be?** chi sarà mai?

whole [həʊl] **1** *adj* intero; **the ~ town** tutta la città; **two ~ hours / days** ben due ore / giorni; **it's a ~ lot easier** è molto più facile **2** *n* tutto *m*; **the ~ of the United States** tutti gli Stati Uniti; **on the ~** nel complesso; **whole-hearted** senza riserve; **wholemeal bread** pane *m* integrale; **wholesale** all'ingrosso; *fig* in massa; **wholesaler** grossista *m/f*; **wholesome** sano; **wholly** completamente

whom [huːm] *fml* chi; **to / for ~** a cui

whore [hɔː(r)] puttana *f*

whose [huːz] *interrogative* di chi; *relative* il / la cui; **~ is this?** di chi è questo?; **a man ~ wife ...** un uomo la cui moglie ...

why [waɪ] perché; **the reason ~** il motivo per cui

wicked ['wɪkɪd] (*evil*) malvagio; (*mischievous*) malizioso; P (*great*) grande

wicker ['wɪkə(r)] di vimini

wicket ['wɪkɪt] *Br* SP porta *f*;

Am in station, bank etc porta f

wide [waɪd] largo; *experience* vasto; *range* ampio; **be 12 metres ~** essere largo 12 metri; **widely** used, known largamente; **widen** 1 *v/t* allargare 2 *v/i* allargarsi; **wide-open** spalancato; **wide-ranging** di largo respiro; **widespread** diffuso

widow ['wɪdəʊ] vedova f; **widower** vedovo m

width [wɪdθ] larghezza f; *of fabric* altezza f

wield [wiːld] *weapon* brandire; *power* esercitare

wife [waɪf] moglie f

wig [wɪg] parrucca f

wiggle ['wɪgl] *loose screw* etc muovere; **~ one's hips** ancheggiare

wild [waɪld] **1** *adj animal, flowers* selvatico; *teenager, party* scatenato; *scheme* folle; *applause* fragoroso; **be ~ about ...** (*keen on*) andare pazzo per ...; **go ~** impazzire; (*become angry*) andare su tutte le furie **2** *n*: **the ~s** le zone sperdute

wilderness ['wɪldənɪs] deserto m; *fig: garden* etc giungla f

'wildlife fauna f

wilful ['wɪlfəl] *person* ostinato; *action* intenzionale

will¹ [wɪl] *n* LAW testamento m

will² [wɪl] *n* (*willpower*) volontà f inv

will³ [wɪl] *v/aux*: **I ~** *let you know tomorrow* ti farò sapere entro domani; **the car won't start** la macchina non parte; **~ you tell her that ...?** dille che ...; **~ you have some more tea?** vuoi dell'altro tè?; **~ you stop that!** smettila!

willful *Am* ☞ **wilful**

willing ['wɪlɪŋ] disponibile; **are you ~ to pay more?** sei disposto a pagare di più?; **willingly** volentieri; **willingness** disponibilità f; **willpower** forza f di volontà

willy-nilly [wɪlɪ'nɪlɪ] (*at random*) a casaccio

wilt [wɪlt] *of plant* appassire

wily ['waɪlɪ] astuto

wimp [wɪmp] F pappamolle m/f

win [wɪn] **1** *n* vittoria f **2** *v/t & v/i* vincere

wince [wɪns] fare una smorfia

wind¹ [wɪnd] *n* vento m; (*flatulence*) aria f

wind² [waɪnd] **1** *v/i of path, stream* snodarsi; *of plant* avvolgersi **2** *v/t* avvolgere

◆ **wind up** *v/t clock* caricare; *car window* tirar su; *speech* concludere; *affairs, company* chiudere **2** *v/i*: **wind up in hospital** finire in ospedale

'wind-bag F trombone m; **windfall** *fig* colpo m di fortuna

winding ['waɪndɪŋ] tortuoso

window ['wɪndəu] *also* COMPUT finestra *f; of shop* vetrina *f; of car, train* finestrino *m;* **in the ~** *of shop* in vetrina; **window box** fioriera *f;* **window seat** *on plane, train* posto *m* di finestrino; **window-shop: go ~ping** guardare le vetrine; **windowsill** davanzale *m;* **windscreen wiper** tergicristallo *m;* **windscreen,** *Am* **windshield** parabrezza *m inv;* **windsurfer** windsurfista *m/f;* **board** windsurf *m inv;* **windsurfing** windsurf *m;* **windy** ventoso; **it's getting ~** si sta alzando il vento

wine [waɪn] vino *m;* **wine glass** bicchiere *m* da vino; **wine merchant** *company* azienda *f* vinicola; *individual* vinaio *m,* -a *f;* **wine cellar** cantina *f;* **wine list** lista *f* dei vini; **winery** *Am* vigneto *m*

wing [wɪŋ] *also* SP ala *f; of car* parafango *m;* **wingspan** apertura *f* alare

wink [wɪŋk] *of person* strizzare gli occhi; **~ at s.o.** fare l'occhiolino a qu

winner ['wɪnə(r)] vincitore *m,* -trice *f;* **winning** vincente; **winning post** traguardo *m;* **winnings** vincita *fsg*

winter ['wɪntə(r)] inverno *m;* **winter sports** sport *m* invernali; **wintry** invernale

wipe [waɪp] *(dry)* asciugare;

(clean) pulire; *tape* cancellare; **wiper** MOT tergicristallo *m*

wire ['waɪə(r)] filo *m* di ferro; ELEC filo *m* elettrico; **wiring** ELEC impianto *m* elettrico; **wiry** *person* dal fisico asciutto

wisdom ['wɪzdəm] saggezza *f;* **wisdom tooth** dente *m* del giudizio

wise [waɪz] saggio; **wisecrack** F spiritosaggine *f;* **wisely** *act* saggiamente

wish [wɪʃ] **1** *n* desiderio *m;* **best ~es** *for birthday etc* tanti auguri; *as greetings* cordiali saluti **2** *v/t* volere; **~ s.o. well** fare tanti auguri a qu
♦ **wish for** desiderare

wisp [wɪsp] *of hair* ciocca *f; of smoke* filo *m*

wistful ['wɪstful] malinconico; **wistfully** malinconicamente

wit [wɪt] *(humour)* spirito *m; person* persona *f* di spirito; **be at one's ~s' end** non sapere più che fare; **keep one's ~s about one** non perdere la testa

witch [wɪtʃ] strega *f;* **witchhunt** *fig* caccia *f* alle streghe

with [wɪð] con; *(cause)* di; **shiver ~ fear** tremare di paura; **a girl ~ blue eyes** una ragazza dagli or con gli occhi azzurri; **I'm staying with my uncle** sto da mio zio; **are**

you ~ me? (*do you understand*) mi segui?; **~ no money** senza soldi

with'draw 1 v/t ritirare; *money from bank* prelevare **2** v/i ritirarsi; **withdrawal** ritiro *m*; *of money* prelievo *m*; **withdrawal symptoms** sindrome *f* da astinenza; **withdrawn** *person* chiuso

wither ['wɪðə(r)] seccare

with'hold *information* nascondere; *consent* rifiutare; *payment* trattenere

with'in (*inside*) dentro; *in expressions of time* nel giro di, entro; *in expressions of distance* a meno di

with'out senza; **~ you /** *him* senza (di) te / lui; **~ looking** senza guardare

with'stand resistere a

witness ['wɪtnɪs] **1** *n* testimone *m/f* **2** v/t essere testimone di; *signature* attestare l'autenticità di

witticism ['wɪtɪsɪzm] arguzia *f*; **witty** arguto

wobble ['wɒbl] *of person* vacillare; *of object* traballare; **wobbly** *person* vacillante; *object* traballante; *voice, hand* tremante

wolf [wʊlf] **1** *n animal* lupo *m* **2** v/t: **~** (**down**) divorare

woman ['wʊmən] donna *f*; **womanizer** donnaiolo *m*; **womanly** femminile

womb [wuːm] utero *m*

women [wɪmɪn] *pl* ☞ **woman**;

women's lib movimento *m* di liberazione della donna

wonder ['wʌndə(r)] **1** *n* (*amazement*), *of science etc* meraviglia *f*; **no ~!** non mi stupisce!; **it's a ~ that ...** è incredibile che ...; **I ~ if you could help** mi chiedevo se potessi aiutarmi; **wonderful** stupendo; **wonderfully** (*extremely*) estremamente

won't [wəʊnt] ☞ **will not**

wood [wʊd] legno *m*; *for fire* legna *f*; (*forest*) bosco *m*; **wooded** boscoso; **wooden** *made of wood* di legno; **woodpecker** picchio *m*; **woodwork** *parts made of wood* strutture *fpl* in legno; *activity* lavorazione *f* del legno

wool [wʊl] lana *f*; **woollen**, *Am* **woolen 1** *adj* di lana **2** *n* indumento *m* di lana

word [wɜːd] **1** *n* parola *f*; (*news*) notizie *fpl*; **have ~s** (*argue*) litigare; **have a ~ with s.o.** parlare con qu **2** v/t *article, letter* formulare; **word processor** word processor *m inv*

work [wɜːk] **1** *n* lavoro *m*; **out of ~** disoccupato **2** v/i *of person* lavorare; *study* studiare; *of machine*, (*succeed*) funzionare

◆ **work out 1** v/t *problem* capire; *solution* trovare **2** v/i *at gym* fare ginnastica; *of rela-*

tionship etc funzionare

workable ['wɜːkəbl] *solution* realizzabile; **workaholic** F stacanovista *m/f*; **workday** *hours of work* giornata *f* lavorativa; *not a holiday* giorno *m* feriale; **worker** lavoratore *m*, -trice *f*; **workforce** forza *f* lavoro; **work hours** orario *m* di lavoro; **working class** classe *f* operaia; **working-class** operaio; **working hours** ☞ **workhours**; **workload** carico *m* di lavoro; **workman** operaio *m*; **workmanlike** professionale; **workmanship** fattura *f*; **work of art** opera *f* d'arte; **workout** allenamento *m*; **work permit** permesso *m* di lavoro; **workshop** laboratorio *m*; *for mechanic* officina *f*; *(seminar)* workshop *m inv*

world [wɜːld] mondo *m*; **out of this ~** F fantastico; **world-class** di livello internazionale; **World Cup** mondiali *mpl* (di calcio); **world-famous** di fama mondiale; **worldly** *goods* materiale; *not spiritual* terreno; *power* temporale; *person* mondano; **world record** record *m inv* mondiale; **world war** guerra *f* mondiale; **worldwide 1** *adj* mondiale **2** *adv* a livello mondiale

worn-'out *shoes, carpet* logoro; *person* esausto

worried ['wʌrɪd] preoccupato; **worry 1** *n* preoccupazione *f* **2** *v/t* preoccupare; *(upset)* turbare **3** *v/i* preoccuparsi; **worrying** preoccupante

worse [wɜːs] **1** *adj* peggiore; *things will get ~* le cose peggioreranno **2** *adv* peggio; **worsen** peggiorare

worship ['wɜːʃɪp] **1** *n* culto *m* **2** *v/t* venerare; *fig* adorare

worst [wɜːst] **1** *adj* peggiore **2** *adv* peggio **3** *n*: *the ~* il peggio; *if the ~ comes to the ~* nel peggiore dei casi; **worst-case scenario**: *the ~* la peggiore delle ipotesi

worth [wɜːθ] **1** *adj*: *be ~* valere; *it's ~ reading* vale la pena leggerlo; *be ~ it* valerne la pena **2** *n* valore *m*; **worthwhile** *cause* lodevole; *be ~* *(worth the effort, worth doing)* valere la pena

worthy ['wɜːðɪ] degno; *cause* lodevole; *be ~ of (deserve)* meritare

would [wʊd]: *I ~ help if I could* ti aiuterei se potessi; *~ you like to go to the cinema?* vuoi andare al cinema?; *~ you tell her that ...?* le dica che ...; *~ you close the door?* le dispiace chiudere la porta?

wound [wuːnd] **1** *n* ferita *f* **2** *v/t* ferire

wow [waʊ] wow

wrap [ræp] *gift* incartare; *(wind, cover)* avvolgere;

wrapper incarto *m*; **wrapping** involucro *m*; **wrapping paper** carta *f* da regalo

wrath [rɒθ] ira *f*

wreath [ri:θ] corona *f*

wreck [rek] **1** *n* of ship relitto *m*; of car carcassa *f*; **be a nervous ~** sentirsi un rottame **2** *v/t* ship far naufragare; car demolire; plans, marriage distruggere; **wreckage** of car, plane rottami *mpl*; of marriage, career brandelli *mpl*; **wrecker** Am truck carro *m* attrezzi

wrench [rentʃ] **1** *n tool* chiave *f* inglese **2** *v/t* (*pull*) strappare

wrestle ['resl] fare la lotta; **wrestler** lottatore *m*, -trice *f*; **wrestling** lotta *f* libera

wriggle ['rɪgl] (*squirm*) dimenarsi; along the ground strisciare

wrinkle ['rɪŋkl] in skin ruga *f*, in clothes grinza *f*

wrist [rɪst] polso *m*; **wristwatch** orologio *m* da polso

write [raɪt] scrivere; cheque fare

◆ **write down** annotare, scrivere

◆ **write off** debt cancellare; car distruggere

writer ['raɪtə(r)] autore *m*, -trice *f*; professional scrittore *m*, -trice *f*; **write-up** F recensione *f*

writhe [raɪð] contorcersi

writing ['raɪtɪŋ] as career scrivere *m*; (*hand-writing*) scrittura *f*; (*words*) scritta *f*; (*script*) scritto *m*; **in ~** per iscritto; **writing paper** carta *f* da lettere

wrong [rɒŋ] **1** adj sbagliato; **be ~** of person sbagliare, avere torto; of answer, morally essere sbagliato; **get the ~ train** sbagliare treno; **what's ~?** cosa c'è?; **there is something ~ with the car** la macchina ha qualcosa che non va **2** adv in modo sbagliato; **go ~** of person sbagliare; of marriage, plan etc fallire **3** *n* immoral action torto *m*; immorality male *m*; **be in the ~** avere torto; **wrongful** illegale; **wrongly** erroneamente; **wrong number** numero *m* sbagliato

wry [raɪ] beffardo

X

xenophobia [zenəʊ'fəʊbɪə] xenofobia *f*

X-ray ['eksreɪ] **1** *n* radiografia *f* **2** *v/t* radiografare

Y

yacht [jɒt] *for pleasure* yacht *m inv*; *for racing* imbarcazione *f* da diporto; **yachting** navigazione *f* da diporto

Yank [jæŋk] F yankee *m inv*

yank [jæŋk] dare uno strattone a

yard¹ [jɑːd] *of prison, institution etc* cortile *m*; *for storage* deposito *m* all'aperto; *Am behind house* giardino *m*

yard² [jɑːd] *measurement* iarda *f*

'yardstick *fig* metro *m*

yarn [jɑːn] *(thread)* filato *m*; F *story* racconto *m*

yawn [jɔːn] **1** *n* sbadiglio *m* **2** *v/i* sbadigliare

year [jɪə(r)] anno *m*; **be six ~s old** avere sei anni; **yearly 1** *adj* annuale **2** *adv* annualmente; **twice ~** due volte (all')l'anno

yeast [jiːst] lievito *m*

yell [jel] **1** *n* urlo *m* **2** *v/t* & *v/i* urlare

yellow ['jeləʊ] giallo *m*; **yellow pages**® pagine *fpl* gialle

yelp [jelp] **1** *n* guaito *m* **2** *v/i* guaire

yes [jes] sì; **say ~** dire di sì; **yes-man** *pej* yes man *m inv*

yesterday ['jestədeɪ] ieri; **the day before ~** l'altro ieri

yet [jet] **1** *adv* finora; **the fast-**

est ~ il più veloce finora; **as ~ up to now** per ora; **have you finished ~?** (non) hai (ancora) finito?; **he hasn't arrived ~** non è ancora arrivato; **~ bigger** ancora più grande **2** *conj* eppure

yield [jiːld] **1** *n from fields etc* raccolto *m*; *from investment* rendita *f* **2** *v/t fruit, harvest* dare, produrre; *interest* fruttare **3** *v/i (give way)* cedere

yob [jɒb] P teppista *m/f*

yoga ['jəʊgə] yoga *m*

yoghurt ['jɒgət] yogurt *m inv*

yolk [jəʊk] tuorlo *m*

you [juː] ◇ *subject: familiar singular* tu; *familiar polite plural* voi; *polite singular* lei; **do ~ know him?** lo conosci / conosce / conoscete? ◇ *direct object: familiar singular* ti; *familiar polite plural* vi; *polite singular* la; **he knows ~** ti / vi / la conosce ◇ *indirect object: familiar singular* ti; *when two pronouns are used to: familiar polite plural* vi; *when two pronouns are used: polite singular* le; **did he talk to ~?** ti / vi / le ha parlato?; **I told ~** te / ve l'ho detto, glielo ho detto ◇ *after prep: familiar singular* te; *familiar polite plural* voi; *polite singular* lei;

this is for ~ questo è per te / voi / lei ◇ *impersonal*: ~ **have to pay** si deve pagare; *fruit is good for* ~ la frutta fa bene

young [jʌŋ] giovane; **youngster** ragazzo *m*, -a *f*

your [jɔː(r)], **yours** [jɔːz] *familiar singular* il tuo *m*, la tua *f*, i tuoi *mpl*, le tue *fpl*; *polite singular* il suo *m*, la sua *f*, i suoi *mpl*, le sue *fpl*; *familiar & polite plural* il vostro *m*, la vostra *f*, i vostri *mpl*, le vostre *fpl*; *your brother* tuo / suo / vostro fratello; *a friend of yours* un tuo / suo / vostro amico; *yours ... at end of letter* saluti ...; *yours sincerely* distinti saluti

your'self ti; *reflexive polite* si; *emphatic* tu stesso *m*, tu stessa *f*; *emphatic polite* lei stesso *m*, lei stessa *f*; *did you hurt* ~? ti sei / si è fatto male?

your'selves vi; *emphatic* voi stessi *mpl*; *emphatic* voi stesse *fpl*; *did you hurt* ~? vi siete fatti male?

youth [juːθ] gioventù *f*; (*young man*) ragazzo *m*; (*young people*) giovani *mpl*; **youth club** circolo *m* giovanile; **youthful** giovanile; *ideas* giovane

yo-yo ['jəʊjəʊ] yo-yo *m inv*; **yo-yo dieting** dieta *f* yo-yo

yuppie ['jʌpɪ] F yuppie *m/f inv*

Z

zap [zæp] F COMPUT (*delete*) cancellare; (*kill*) annientare; (*hit*) colpire; (*send*) mandare

zeal [ziːl] zelo *m*

zebra ['zebrə] zebra *f*; **zebra crossing** strisce *fpl* pedonali

zero ['zɪərəʊ] zero *m*

zest [zest] (*enthusiasm*) gusto *m*; (*peel*) scorza *f*

zigzag ['zɪgzæg] **1** *n* zigzag *m inv* **2** *v/i* zigzagare

zilch [zɪltʃ] F un bel niente

zip [zɪp] (*cerniera f*) lampo *f*

♦ **zip up** *dress, jacket* allacciare; COMPUT zippare

'zip code *Am* codice *m* di avviamento postale; **zipper** *Am* (cerniera *f*) lampo *f*

zit [zɪt] *Am* brufolo *m*

zone [zəʊn] zona *f*

zonked [zɒŋkt] P (*exhausted*) stanco morto

zoo [zuː] zoo *m*

zoology [zuː'ɒlədʒɪ] zoologia *f*

zoom lens [zuːm] zoom *m inv*

zucchini [zuː'kiːnɪ] *Am* zucchino *m*

Verbi irregolari inglesi

Si riportano le tre forme principali di ciascun verbo: infinito, passato, participio passato.

arise – arose – arisen

awake – awoke – awoken, awaked

be (am, is, are) – was (were) – been

bear – bore – borne

beat – beat – beaten

become – became – become

begin – began – begun

bend – bent – bent

bet – bet, betted – bet, betted

bid – bid – bid

bind – bound – bound

bite – bit – bitten

bleed – bled – bled

blow – blew – blown

break – broke – broken

breed – bred – bred

bring – brought – brought

broadcast – broadcast – broadcast

build – built – built

burn – burnt, burned – burnt, burned

burst – burst – burst

buy – bought – bought

cast – cast – cast

catch – caught – caught

choose – chose – chosen

cling – clung – clung

come – came – come

cost (v/i) – cost – cost

creep – crept – crept

cut – cut – cut

deal – dealt – dealt

dig – dug – dug

dive – dived, dove [dəʊv] (1) – dived

do – did – done

draw – drew – drawn

dream – dreamt, dreamed – dreamt, dreamed

drink – drank – drunk

drive – drove – driven

eat – ate – eaten

fall – fell – fallen

feed – fed – fed

feel – felt – felt

fight – fought – fought

find – found – found

flee - fled - fled
fling - flung - flung
fly - flew - flown
forbid - forbad(e) - forbidden
forecast - forecast(ed) - forecast(ed)
forget - forgot - forgotten
forgive - forgave - forgiven
freeze - froze - frozen
get - got - got, gotten (2)
give - gave - given
go - went - gone
grind - ground - ground
grow - grew - grown
hang - hung, hanged - hung, hanged (3)
have - had - had
hear - heard - heard
hide - hid - hidden
hit - hit - hit
hold - held - held
hurt - hurt - hurt
keep - kept - kept
kneel - knelt, kneeled - knelt, kneeled
know - knew - known
lay - laid - laid
lead - led - led

lean - leaned, leant - leaned, leant (4)
leap - leaped, leapt - leaped, leapt (4)
learn - learned, learnt - learned, learnt (4)
leave - left - left
lend - lent - lent
let - let - let
lie - lay - lain
light - lighted, lit - lighted, lit
lose - lost - lost
make - made - made
mean - meant - meant
meet - met - met
mow - mowed - mowed, mown
pay - paid - paid
plead - pleaded, pled - pleaded, pled (5)
prove - proved - proved, proven
put - put - put
quit - quit(ted) - quit(ted)
read - read [red] - read [red]
ride - rode - ridden
ring - rang - rung
rise - rose - risen
run - ran - run

saw - sawed - sawn, sawed

say - said - said

see - saw - seen

seek - sought - sought

sell - sold - sold

send - sent - sent

set - set - set

sew - sewed - sewed, sewn

shake - shook - shaken

shed - shed - shed

shine - shone - shone

shit - shit(ted), shat - shit(ted), shat

shoot - shot - shot

show - showed - shown

shrink - shrank - shrunk

shut - shut - shut

sing - sang - sung

sink - sank - sunk

sit - sat - sat

slay - slew - slain

sleep - slept - slept

slide - slid - slid

sling - slung - slung

slit - slit - slit

smell - smelt, smelled - smelt, smelled (4)

sow - sowed - sown, sowed

speak - spoke - spoken

speed - sped, speeded - sped, speeded

spell - spelt, spelled - spelt, spelled (4)

spend - spent - spent

spill - spilt, spilled - spilt, spilled (4)

spin - spun - spun

spit - spat - spat

split - split - split

spoil - spoiled, spoilt - spoiled, spoilt (4)

spread - spread - spread

spring - sprang, sprung - sprung

stand - stood - stood

steal - stole - stolen

stick - stuck - stuck

sting - stung - stung

stink - stunk, stank - stunk

stride - strode - stridden

strike - struck - struck

swear - swore - sworn

sweep - swept - swept

swell - swelled - swollen

swim - swam - swum

swing - swung - swung

take - took - taken

teach - taught - taught

tear - tore - torn

tell – told – told	**wake** – woke, waked – woken, waked
think – thought – thought	**wear** – wore – worn
thrive – throve – thriven, thrived (6)	**weave** – wove – woven (7)
throw – threw – thrown	**weep** – wept – wept
thrust – thrust – thrust	**win** – won – won
tread – trod – trodden	**wind** – wound – wound
	write – wrote – written

1) **dove** non si usa nell'inglese britannico
2) **gotten** non si usa nell'inglese britannico
3) **hung** per i quadri, ma **hanged** per gli omicidi
4) l'inglese parlato in America ha di solito la forma in **-ed**
5) **pled** si usa nell'inglese parlato in America e in Scozia
6) **thrived** è la forma più comune
7) ma **weaved** quando significa *zigzagare*

Numbers / Numerali

Cardinal Numbers / Numerali cardinali

  0 *zero* zero
  1 *one* uno
  2 *two* due
  3 *three* tre
  4 *four* quattro
  5 *five* cinque
  6 *six* sei
  7 *seven* sette
  8 *eight* otto
  9 *nine* nove
 10 *ten* dieci
 11 *eleven* undici
 12 *twelve* dodici
 13 *thirteen* tredici
 14 *fourteen* quattordici
 15 *fifteen* quindici
 16 *sixteen* sedici
 17 *seventeen* diciassette
 18 *eighteen* diciotto
 19 *nineteen* diciannove
 20 *twenty* venti
 21 *twenty-one* ventuno
 22 *twenty-two* ventidue
 23 *twenty-three* ventitrè
 28 *twenty-eight* ventotto
 29 *twenty-nine* ventinove
 30 *thirty* trenta

40	*forty* quaranta
50	*fifty* cinquanta
60	*sixty* sessanta
70	*seventy* settanta
80	*eighty* ottanta
100	*one/a hundred* cento
101	*one/a hundred and one* centouno
102	*one/a hundred and two* centodue
200	*two hundred* duecento
201	*two hundred and one* duecentouno
300	*three hundred* trecento
400	*four hundred* quattrocento
500	*five hundred* cinquecento
600	*six hundred* seicento
700	*seven hundred* settecento
800	*eight hundred* ottocento
900	*nine hundred* novecento
1,000	*one/a thousand* mille
1,001	*one/a thousand and one* milleuno/mille e uno
2,000	*two thousand* duemila
3,000	*three thousand* tremila
4,000	*four thousand* quattromila
5,000	*five thousand* cinquemila
10,000	*ten thousand* diecimila
100,000	*one/a hundred thousand* centomila
1,000,000	*one/a million* un milione
2,000,000	*two million* due milioni
1,000,000,000	*one/a billion* un miliardo

Note: i) 1,000,000 (in inglese) = 1.000.000 (in Italian)

ii) 1.25 (one point two five) = 1,25 (uno virgola venticinque)

Ordinal numbers / Numerali ordinali

1st	*first*	1°	il primo, la prima
2nd	*second*	2°	secondo
3rd	*third*	3°	terzo
4th	*fourth*	4°	quarto
5th	*fifth*	5°	quinto
6th	*sixth*	6°	sesto
7th	*seventh*	7°	settimo
8th	*eighth*	8°	ottavo
9th	*ninth*	9°	nono
10th	*tenth*	10°	decimo
11th	*eleventh*	11°	undicesimo
12th	*twelfth*	12°	dodicesimo
13th	*thirteenth*	13°	tredicesimo
14th	*fourteenth*	14°	quattordicesimo
15th	*fifteenth*	15°	quindicesimo
16th	*sixteenth*	16°	sedicesimo
17th	*seventeenth*	17°	diciassettesimo
18th	*eighteenth*	18°	diciottesimo
19th	*nineteenth*	19°	diciannovesimo
20th	*twentieth*	20°	ventesimo
21st	*twenty-first*	21°	ventunesimo
22nd	*twenty-second*	22°	ventiduesimo
30th	*thirtieth*	30°	trentesimo
40th	*fortieth*	40°	quarantesimo
50th	*fiftieth*	50°	cinquantesimo
60th	*sixtieth*	60°	sessantesimo

70th	*seventieth*	70°	settantesimo
80th	*eightieth*	80°	ottantesimo
90th	*ninetieth*	90°	novantesimo
100th	*hundredth*	100°	centesimo
101st	*hundred and first*	101°	centunesimo
103rd	*hundred and third*	103°	centotreesimo
200th	*two hundredth*	200°	duecentesimo
1000th	*thousandth*	1000°	millesimo
1001st	*thousand and first*	1001°	millesimo primo
2000th	*two thousandth*	2000°	duemillesimo
1,000,000th	*millionth*	1.000.000°	milionesimo

Note: Italian ordinal numbers are ordinary adjectives and consequently must agree:

her 13th granddaughter
la sua tredicesima nipote

Dates / Date

1996	nineteen ninety-six	*millenovecentonovantasei*
2005	two thousand and five	*duemilacinque*

the 10/11th of November,
Am **November 10/11 (ten/eleven)**
il dieci/undici novembre

the first of March, *Am* **March 1 (first)**
il primo marzo